BRITISH POLITICAL FACTS
1900–1975

BRITISH
POLITICAL FACTS
1900–1975

BY
DAVID BUTLER
AND
ANNE SLOMAN

FOURTH EDITION

First Edition 1963
Reprinted with corrections 1964
Second Edition (completely revised) 1968
Third Edition 1969
Fourth Edition (completely revised) 1975

Published by
THE MACMILLAN PRESS LTD
London and Basingstoke
Associated companies in New York
Dublin Melbourne Johannesburg and Madras

SBN 333 03360 4

Printed in Great Britain by
R. & R. CLARK LTD
Edinburgh

CONTENTS

IV. ELECTIONS

XII. THE ECONOMY

XIII. NATIONALISATION

XIV. LOCAL GOVERNMENT

XV. ROYALTY

INTRODUCTION TO THE FOURTH EDITION

THE toble of contents offers the simplest justification for this book — but inevitably it is a book that must justify itself in different ways to different readers. The scholar, the journalist, the politician and the club bore were all in the authors' minds at one point or another during its compilation. Some of those who look at this book will, we hope, be delighted to find in compact and reliable form data that might still have eluded them after searching through a dozen standard works of reference; others will at least discover from our pages where the information they seek may be found; a few, we fear, will be infuriated by our omissions and, despite all our efforts at checking, by our errors.

The idea of writing this book grew gradually in the mind of one of its authors as, in the course of his years as a student and a teacher at Nuffield College (which is devoted to research in contemporary subjects), he noticed the amount of time that he and others wasted in searching for seemingly obvious facts about twentieth-century Britain. If, therefore, any one reader has been especially in our minds, he is the graduate student writing a thesis on any domestic theme in the last seventy years. We hope he will find here not only an expeditious way of checking basic facts but also, if he finds time to browse through our lists and tables, a stimulating reminder of people and considerations that must have played a part, perhaps only as background, in the situations he is analysing.

But we are not concerned solely with academic needs. Experience of checking facts in newspaper offices and broadcasting studios, and the anecdotes of friends in Whitehall and Westminster have made plain to us how much elementary political data is annoyingly elusive. Many admirable works of reference exist but the right one is not always to hand; most of them, moreover, are compiled on an annual basis — which can be very frustrating for those who are trying to trace an office or a statistic over a number of years.

The compiler of any work of reference is limited by space and time. How much data shall be included? How far shall other works be duplicated? How many hours is it worth devoting to any particular entry? In this book we have had to exclude interesting information either because it would fill a disproportionate number of pages or because it could not be obtained without more labour than we thought justified. We have consoled ourselves for setting out data in abbreviated form by giving exact references to more exhaustive sources.

Indeed, since the compilation of reference books is, even more than other research, systematised plagiarism, perhaps the most valuable part of these pages lies in these citations. We have not attempted an exhaustive bibliography — except for a compilation of bibliographies and general reference books — but we have throughout tried to list all major authorities.

The title, *British Political Facts 1900–1975*, provides a reasonably close delimitation of the scope of this book. *British* indicates that we have been concerned with the domestic history of the United Kingdom. But it is not possible to set precise boundaries to the term 'domestic' and we have perhaps strayed beyond them by listing Colonies, Governors-General, and some Ambassadors.

Political is potentially ambiguous, but we have used it to stress that our interest is in the power of the state. We have tried to list the principal people who were involved in the government of Britain at any moment in this century; we have recorded election results — as providing the basis for political authority — and major legislation — as representing its use; we have assembled, in summary form, statistical data which show some of the social and economic background to all political action.

Facts indicates that we have tried to eschew political judgements as far as possible. Some value judgements may be implicit in our selection of material, but we believe that virtually everything here would be acceptable as non-controversial evidence in debates over the nature of twentieth-century British history. It is a waste of time to argue about verifiable questions of fact. But it is also a waste of time to assemble facts except as a basis for argument. Because in this book we have stuck rigidly to facts, it does not mean that we overrate them. Analysis of our past and present situation is far more important than mere fact-gathering. Unlike Martha we are fully aware which is the better part.

1900–1975 is a somewhat arbitrary period — but any historical period must be arbitrary. Our terminal date is simply as near to the present as publishing allows. Our opening date was a numerological accident — but it would be hard to find a better watershed without going back at least to 1885, which because of space, and still more because of the availability of data, was impracticable. We have endeavoured to treat every one of our seventy-odd years equally, providing as full and exact data about 1901 as about 1971. With some statistics this has proved impossible and some of our time-series are regrettably discontinuous. But in general it will be found that we have resisted the temptation to make a special favourite of the more recent past; it is not our fault that there were no Gallup polls before 1938 and that local election results cannot usefully be pursued very far back.

In compiling this book we have become very conscious of the strengths and weaknesses of other reference books — and particularly of the importance of pedantic accuracy and clear presentation. We have certainly not avoided all the pitfalls into which we have observed others falling; therefore, by way both of excuse and of warning, it may be worth describing a few of the difficulties we have faced.

The general problems of finding exact data on British politics were best exemplified in the gathering of complete lists of ministries over the last seventy years — the most time-consuming of all our operations. There are a number of publications which purport to list all ministerial appointments — the most useful of these are the two Parliamentary handbooks, *Dod* and *Vacher*. There is also the Stationery Office publication *H.M. Ministers and Heads of Public Departments* which has appeared four or five times a year since 1946. Lists of ministers are also printed in *Hansard* once a fortnight during sessions. But all these sources have the same disadvantage — no indication is given of the date when a minister was appointed or left office. A man may indeed be appointed and leave office between the publication of these lists, so that there is no record whatever of his elevation. *Keesing's Contemporary Archives* have since 1931 recorded most government appointments — but they depend solely on newspaper sources and are not altogether infallible. The *Indexes* to *The Times* are the best means of checking on ministerial changes, though here too there are problems. *Palmer's Index to the Times* which was not superseded by the *Official Index* until 1906 is far from satisfactory; under the heading 'Official Appointments' is the depressing injunction 'See every issue'. From 1906 the *Official Index* is much more thorough, although misprints and references to different editions of the paper do occur. Even *The Times*, moreover, has occasionally missed a minor government change. An additional complication lies in the range of possible days which might be considered the date of appointment: there is the announcement from Downing Street, the press report the following day, the official gazetting a week or more later, the exchange of seals and the kissing of hands. None of these may represent the precise date on which the new minister took over his duties, but wherever possible, we have used the date of *The Times* report, as being the earliest and most public announcement; however, when, as has happened more and more since 1960, a resignation or a reshuffle has been well publicised on the air on the previous evening, we have used the earlier date. Peerages sometimes cause further confusion, since weeks usually elapse before a newly elevated minister's title is announced. Care has also to be taken when a familiar minister disappears behind a new name — the fact that Mr Ivor Guest, Lord Ashby St Ledgers, and Viscount Wimborne were one and the same person is not immediately apparent. Another snag arises, particularly in wartime and in the late 1960s, when the titles and functions of ministries change kaleidoscopically.

In many other fields the sources of confusion were almost equally numerous. The search for reliable and consistent evidence about newspaper circulations, religious affiliations and trade disputes caused us particular trouble and we were surprised at the difficulties involved in compiling lists of all permanent secretaries of departments and assessing the size of the various grades of the civil service. But it would be tedious to quote all the gaps in existing works of reference which we have — with very varying success — tried to fill. We must, however, mention the complications which arise from the structure of the United Kingdom. The changes in Ireland in 1922 inevitably cause a break in all national statistical time-series and since then many tables have, perforce, to exclude Northern Ireland as well as Eire; but the administrative separation of Scotland causes almost as many difficulties. Statistics are compiled independently north and south of the Border, quite often on different bases. Sometimes this arises from the different legal or administrative systems — as with education; but in the case of population and vital statistics the Registrars-General seem ⸢unnecessarily perverse in presenting their census findings in differing forms.

This book was first compiled at the beginning of the 1960s. It has been checked, updated and modified through successive editions in response to the reactions of its readers. It is the people who have used the book most — academics, civil servants, librarians, journalists, party officials and officers of the Houses of Parliament — who have been its keenest and most constructive critics.

The preparation and revision of this book has indeed depended on a vast amount of help from many quarters, ranging from scholars and friends who have spent many hours assisting us to check on obscure details, to unidentified voices at the end of official telephones. We must thank above all Jennie Freeman, who in 1961 bore so much of the brunt of preparing the first edition, and after her the Warden, Fellows and Students of Nuffield College, who have made so many contributions over the years. But we owe a deep debt of gratitude to officials in Parliament, in Party Headquarters, in Government Departments and in newspaper offices, to many colleagues in the academic world, to complete strangers who have sent us corrections and suggestions, and to our publishers. We must also acknowledge what we owe to anonymous compilers of the many works of reference from which we have so freely drawn. We give here an incomplete list of those who have supplied information or emendations in the preparation of one or more of the successive editions of this book.

P. Addison	Miss S. J. Conwill	S. Gordon
R. K. Alderman	F. W. S. Craig	A. H. Halsey
R. F. Allen	J. A. Cross	M. Harrison
J. M. Austen	S. Cursley	A. J. Hastings
G. S. Bain	C. Dawson	S. C. Hawtrey
F. M. Barlow	N. Deakin	C. Hazlehurst
M. Beloff	A. Deyermond	J. Hemingway
H. B. Berrington	C. Dobson	R. J. Hetherington
N. Birnbaum	Mrs M. Dowley	A. E. Holmans
N. Blewett	G. Drewry	A. Hunt
G. D. M. Block	C. Driver	R. J. Jackson
J. M. Bowen	Miss D. Edmunds	D. Jeffcock
P. A. Bromhead	N. D. Ellis	R. Jenkins
R. Butt	Sir T. Evans	L. Keillor
P. Campbell	H. R. M. Farmer	B. Keith-Lucas
T. J. M. Cartwright	Sir E. Fellowes	A. S. King
A. N. Cass	A. Flanders	U. W. Kitzinger
J. Chesshire	A. Fox	A. L. Lamaison
Sir N. Chester	Lord Fraser of	F. Lawson
H. A. Clegg	Kilmorack	S. M. Lees
P. C. Collison	Yash Ghai	T. O. Lloyd

A. B. Lyons	J. Paxton	R. J. A. Skidelsky
K. MacDonald	H. Pelling	M. G. M. Sloman
Sir D. MacDougall	Dame M. Perham	M. Steed
A. MacIntyre	A. M. Potter	D. Stephen
R. McKibbin	D. Prysor-Jones	S. Symes
A. F. Madden	G. Pyatt	Mrs A. Taylor
G. Marshall	Miss A. Rhodes	A. J. P. Taylor
J. S. Milner	C. Raphael	Mrs I. Wagner
B. R. Mitchell	R. A. Rempel	R. Walford
Miss J. P. Morgan	P. G. Richards	N. D. Walker
J. Morland Craig	Mrs P. Ryan	W. Wallace
D. L. Munby	J. C. Sainty	A. H. Warren
R. Neuss	S. Sargent	Miss N. Watts
H. G. Nicholas	Miss K. Schott	Mrs J. Wigan
P. Oppenheimer	C. Seymour-Ure	P. M. Williams
J. Palmer	D. M. Shapiro	Mrs B. Williamson
C. Pannell	L. J. Sharpe	T. Wilson
M. Parker	Mrs A. Skeats	

While we could not have completed this book without these far-flung helpers (not to mention the encouragement and the understanding of our spouses and our children) we should stress our sole responsibility for its inevitable errors. Our readers are earnestly invited to let us know of any that they may detect.

DAVID BUTLER
ANNE SLOMAN

NUFFIELD COLLEGE, OXFORD
January 1975

I
MINISTRIES

THE following list contains all holders of paid and political ministerial offices since 1900. It leaves out some office-holders, since various offices in the Royal Household have during the past century ceased to be political appointments. The list also omits some politicians with governmental posts, since various other offices such as the Church Estates Commissioners are at times filled by M.P.s who are not regarded as part of the Ministry. Assistant Government Whips were unpaid until the 1964 Parliament and are not listed until then. Parliamentary Private Secretaries are also unlisted.

The problems of compiling this list are discussed on p. xvi. The dates are as far as possible the dates on which the announcement of the appointment appeared in *The Times*, except where is is plain that the news received wide publicity the previous day. Where more than one person holds the same title starting and finishing dates are given. In almost all other cases it may be assumed that the date of the new appointment represents the vacating of the office. **Ministers** in the cabinet are printed throughout this section in heavy type. MINISTERS outside the cabinet and Ministers of State are printed in capitals. Junior Ministers are in ordinary print. The seven leading offices are placed first in each Ministry; the remainder are arranged alphabetically, except the law offices and the political appointments to the Royal Household, which are placed at the end, together with the Treasury appointments which are held by Whips. In these tables (and throughout the book) titles are placed in brackets if acquired during the tenure of a particular office or on transfer to the next office. U-S. Under-Secretary; F.S. Financial Secretary; P.S. Parliamentary Secretary.

This section has been sub-divided chronologically at changes of Prime Minister, except when few other offices changed hands, as in 1902, 1923, 1937, 1955, and 1963; further subdivisions are made for the drastic reconstructions of 1915, 1931, and May 1945.

CONSERVATIVE GOVERNMENT, 1900–1905

	MINISTERS IN CABINET		JUNIOR MINISTERS ATTACHED
P.M.	**M of Salisbury (3rd)**		
		1900–11 Jul 02	
	A. Balfour	12 Jul 02–4 Dec 05	
1st Ld of[1] *Treasury*	**A. Balfour**	1900	
	(*office combined with P.M. when Balfour succeeded Salisbury*)		
Ld Pres.	**D of Devonshire**	1900	
	M of Londonderry	13 Oct 03	
Ld Chanc.	**E of Halsbury**	1900	
Privy S.	**Vt Cross**	1900	
	M of Salisbury (3rd) (P.M.)		
		1 Nov 00	
	A. Balfour (P.M.)	12 Jul 02	
	M of Salisbury (4th)	11 Oct 03	

[1] The only occasion in this century when 1st Ld of Treasury was not combined with P.M.

CONSERVATIVE GOVERNMENT, 1900–1905 (contd.)

MINISTERS IN CABINET			JUNIOR MINISTERS ATTACHED		
Exch.	**Sir M. Hicks Beach**	1900	*Treasury:*		
	C. Ritchie	8 Aug 02	*F.S.*	R. Hanbury	1900
	A. Chamberlain	6 Oct 03		A. Chamberlain	7 Nov 00
				W. Hayes Fisher	8 Aug 02
				A. Elliott	10 Apr 03
				V. Cavendish	9 Oct 03
For. O.	**M of Salisbury (3rd) (P.M.)**	1900	*U-S.*	St J. Brodrick	1900
	M of Lansdowne	1 Nov 00		Vt Cranborne[1] (4th M of Salisbury)	
					7 Nov 00
				Earl Percy[1]	9 Oct 03
Home O.	**Sir M. White Ridley**	1900	*U-S.*	J. Collings	1900
	C. Ritchie	1 Nov 00		T. Cochrane	8 Aug 02
	A. Akers-Douglas	8 Aug 02			
Admir.	**G. Goschen**	1900	*P. & F.S.:*		
	E of Selborne	1 Nov 00		Sir W. Macartney	1900
	Earl Cawdor	5 Mar 05		H. Arnold-Forster	7 Nov 00
				E. Pretyman	11 Oct 03
			Civil Ld:		
				A. Chamberlain	1900
				E. Pretyman	7 Nov 00
				A. Lee	11 Oct 03
Bd Ag. &	**W. Long**	1900			
Fish.	**R. Hanbury**	14 Nov 00			
	E of Onslow	19 May 03			
	A. Fellowes	12 Mar 05			
Col. O.	**J. Chamberlain**	1900	*U-S.*	E of Selborne	1900
	A. Lyttelton	6 Oct 03		E of Onslow	12 Nov 00
				D of Marlborough	23 Jul 03
Bd Educ.	**D of Devonshire**	1 Jan 00	*Sec.*	(*office not established*)	
	M of Londonderry	8 Aug 02		Sir W. Anson	8 Aug 02
				(*previously Vice-President of Committee of Council on Education—Sir J. Gorst 1900-8 Aug 02*)	
India O.	**Ld G. Hamilton**[1]	1900	*U-S.*	E of Onslow	1900
	St J. Brodrick	6 Oct 03		E of Hardwicke	12 Nov 00
				Earl Percy[1]	8 Aug 02
				E of Hardwicke	15 Oct 03
				M of Bath	19 Jan 05
Chief Sec. Ireland	(*office not in cabinet*)		*V. Pres. Dept. Agric. for Ireland:*		
	G. Wyndham	8 Aug 02		(Sir) H. Plunkett	1900
	W. Long	12 Mar 05			
Ld Chanc. Ireland	**Ld Ashbourne**	1900			
Ld Lieut. Ireland	**Earl Cadogan**	1900			
	(*E of Dudley 8 Aug 02 & office not in cabinet*)				
D. Lanc.	**Ld James of Hereford**	1900			
	(*Sir W. Walrond 8 Aug 02 & office not in cabinet*)				
Loc. Govt. Bd	**H. Chaplin**	1900	*P.S.*	T. Russell	1900
	W. Long	7 Nov 00		(Sir) J. Lawson	11 Nov 00
	G. Balfour	12 Mar 05		A. Jeffreys	27 Jun 05
Postm.-Gen.	(*office not in cabinet*)				
	M of Londonderry	7 Nov 00			
	A. Chamberlain	8 Aug 02			
	Ld Stanley[1]	6 Oct 03			
Scotland	**Ld Balfour of Burleigh**	1900			
	A. Murray	6 Oct 03			
	M of Linlithgow	2 Feb 05			

[1] Not a member of the House of Lords.

CONSERVATIVE GOVERNMENT, 1900–1905 *(contd.)*

MINISTERS IN CABINET			JUNIOR MINISTERS ATTACHED		
B.o.T.	C. Ritchie	1900	*P.S.*	E of Dudley	1900
	G. Balfour	7 Nov 00		A. Bonar Law	8 Aug 02
	M of Salisbury (4th)	12 Mar 05			
War O.	M of Lansdowne	1900	*F.S.*	J. Powell Williams	1900
	St J. Brodrick	1 Nov 00		Ld Stanley[1]	7 Nov 00
	H. Arnold-Forster	6 Oct 03		W. Bromley-Davenport	11 Oct 03
			P S.	G. Wyndham	1900
				Ld Raglan	12 Nov 00
				E of Hardwicke	8 Aug 02
				E of Donoughmore	15 Oct 03

1st *C. Works* A. Akers-Douglas   1900
(Ld Windsor 8 Aug 02 & office out of cabinet)

MINISTERS NOT IN CABINET

Chief Sec. Ireland	G. Balfour	1900		*(for Junior Ministers see above)*
	G. Wyndham	7 Nov 00		
	(8 Aug 02 office in cabinet)			
D. Lanc.	*(office in cabinet)*			
	Sir W. Walrond	8 Aug 02		
Paym.-Gen.	D of Marlborough	1900		
	Sir S. Crossley	11 Mar 02		
Postm.-Gen.	D of Norfolk	1900		
	M of Londonderry	2 Apr 00		
	(7 Nov 00 office in cabinet)			
1st *C. Works*	*(office in cabinet)*			
	Ld Windsor	8 Aug 02		

Law Officers:

			P.S. to Treasury:		
Att.-Gen.	Sir R. Webster	1900		Sir W. Walrond	1900
	Sir R. Finlay	7 May 00		Sir A. Acland Hood	8 Aug 02
Sol.-Gen.	Sir R. Finlay	1900	*Junior Lds of Treasury:*		
	Sir E. Carson	7 May 00		W. Hayes Fisher	1900–8 Aug 02
Ld Advoc.	A. Murray	1900		H. Anstruther	1900–11 Oct 03
	S. Dickson	18 Oct 03		Ld Stanley[1]	1900–7 Nov 00
Sol.-Gen Scotland	S. Dickson	1900		A. Fellowes	7 Nov 00–15 Mar 05
	D. Dundas	18 Oct 03		H. Forster	8 Aug 02–4 Dec 05
	E. Salvesen	30 Jan 05		Ld Balcarres[1]	11 Oct 03–4 Dec 05
	J. Clyde	16 Oct 05		Ld E. Talbot[1]	16 Jun 05–4 Dec 05
Att.-Gen. Ireland	J. Atkinson	1900			
Sol.-Gen. Ireland	D. Barton	1900			
	G. Wright	30 Jan 00			
	J. Campbell	8 Jul 03			

H.M. Household:

			Lds in Waiting		
Treas.	Vt Curzon[1] (Earl Howe)	1900		E of Clarendon	1900–30 Oct 00
	V. Cavendish	3 Dec 00		Ld Harris	1900–4 Dec 05
	M of Hamilton[1]	11 Oct 03		Ld Churchill (Vt)	1900–4 Dec 05
Comptr.	Vt Valentia[1]	1900		Ld Lawrence	1900–4 Dec 05
				E of Kintore	1900–4 Dec 05
V. Chamb.	A. Fellowes	1900		Ld Bagot	1900–2 Jul 1901
	Sir A. Acland Hood	3 Dec 00		E of Denbigh	1900–4 Dec 05
	Ld Wolverton	17 Nov 02		Earl Howe	30 Oct 00–1 Oct 03
Ld Chamb.	E of Hopetoun	1900		Ld Kenyon	4 Dec 00–4 Dec 05
	E of Clarendon	12 Nov 00		E of Erroll	19 Oct 03–4 Dec 05

Ld Steward E of Pembroke & Montgomery   1900

[1] Not a member of the House of Lords.

CONSERVATIVE GOVERNMENT, 1900–1905 (*contd.*)

MINISTERS NOT IN CABINET

Capt. Gents at Arms	LD BELPER	1900
Capt. Yeomen of Guard	EARL WALDEGRAVE	1900
Master of Horse	D OF PORTLAND	1900
Master of Buckhounds	E OF COVENTRY	1900
	LD CHESHAM	2 Nov 00

(*office abolished* 1901)

LIBERAL GOVERNMENT, 1905–1908

MINISTERS IN CABINET			JUNIOR MINISTERS ATTACHED		
P.M.	**Sir H. Campbell-Bannerman**	5 Dec 05–5 Apr 08			
Ld Pres.	**E of Crewe**	10 Dec 05			
Ld Chanc.	**Sir R. Reid** (*Ld Loreburn*)	10 Dec 05			
Privy S.	**M of Ripon**	10 Dec 05			
Exch.	**H. Asquith**	10 Dec 05	*Treasury:*		
			F.S.	R. McKenna	12 Dec 05
				W. Runciman	29 Jan 07
For. O.	**Sir E. Grey**	10 Dec 05	U-S.	Ld E. Fitzmaurice [1] (Ld)	18 Dec 05
Home O.	**H. Gladstone**	10 Dec 05	U-S.	H. Samuel	12 Dec 05
Admir.	**Ld Tweedmouth**	10 Dec 05	*P. & F.S.:*		
				E. Robertson	12 Dec 05
			Civil Ld:		
				G. Lambert	18 Dec 05
Bd Ag. & Fish.	**Earl Carrington**	10 Dec 05			
Col. O.	**E of Elgin**	10 Dec 05	U-S.	W. Churchill	12 Dec 05
Bd Educ.	**A. Birrell**	10 Dec 05	P.S.	T. Lough	18 Dec 05
	R. McKenna	23 Jan 07			
India O.	**J. Morley**	10 Dec 05	U-S.	J. Ellis	12 Dec 05
				C. Hobhouse	29 Jan 07
Chief Sec. Ireland	**J. Bryce**	10 Dec 05	*Vice-Pres. Dept. Agric. for Ireland:*		
	A. Birrell	23 Jan 07		Sir H. Plunkett	12 Dec 05
				T. Russell	21 May 07
D. Lanc.	**Sir H. Fowler**	10 Dec 05			
Loc. Govt. Bd.	**J. Burns**	10 Dec 05	P.S.	W. Runciman	18 Dec 05
				T. Macnamara	29 Jan 07
Postm.-Gen.	**S. Buxton**	10 Dec 05			
Scotland	**J. Sinclair**	10 Dec 05			
B.o.T.	**D. Lloyd George**	10 Dec 05	P.S.	H. Kearley	18 Dec 05
War O.	**R. Haldane**	10 Dec 05	P.S.	E of Portsmouth	12 Dec 05
			F.S.	T. Buchanan	14 Dec 05

1st C. Works   (*office not in cabinet*)
      L. Harcourt   27 Mar 07

MINISTERS NOT IN CABINET

Paym.-Gen.	R. CAUSTON	12 Dec 05
1st C. Works	L. HARCOURT	10 Dec 05

(27 *Mar* 07 *office in cabinet*)

[1] Not a member of the House of Lords.

LIBERAL GOVERNMENT, 1905–1908 (*contd.*)

MINISTERS NOT IN CABINET

Law Officers:

Att.-Gen.	SIR J. WALTON	12 Dec 05
	SIR W. ROBSON	28 Jan 08
Sol.-Gen.	SIR W. ROBSON	12 Dec 05
	SIR S. EVANS	28 Jan 08
Ld Advoc.	T. SHAW	12 Dec 05
Sol.-Gen. Scotland	A. URE	18 Dec 05
Att.-Gen. Ireland	R. CHERRY	20 Dec 05
Sol.-Gen. Ireland	R. BARRY	20 Dec 05

H.M. Household:

Treas.	SIR E. STRACHEY	18 Dec 05
Comptr.	MASTER OF ELIBANK	18 Dec 05
V. Chamb.	W. BEAUMONT (*Ld Allendale*)	18 Dec 05
	J. FULLER	27 Feb 07
Ld Chamb.	VT ALTHORP	18 Dec 05
Ld Steward	LD HAWKESBURY (*1st E of Liverpool*)	18 Dec 05
	EARL BEAUCHAMP	31 Jul 07
Master of Horse	E OF SEFTON	18 Dec 05
	E OF GRANARD	6 Sep 07
Capt. Gents at Arms	EARL BEAUCHAMP	18 Dec 05
	LD DENMAN	31 Jul 07
Capt. Yeomen of Guard	D OF MANCHESTER	18 Dec 05
	LD ALLENDALE	29 Apr 07

P.S. to Treasury:

G. Whiteley	12 Dec 05

Junior Lds of Treasury:

H. Lewis	18 Dec 05–5 Apr 08
J. Pease	18 Dec 05–5 Apr 08
F. Freeman-Thomas	21 Dec 05–2 Feb 06
C. Norton	21 Dec 05–5 Apr 08
J. Fuller	2 Feb 06–27 Feb 07
J. Whitley	27 Feb 07–5 Apr 08

Lds in Waiting:

Ld Denman	18 Dec 05–31 Jul 07
E of Granard	18 Dec 05–21 Aug 07
Ld Acton	18 Dec 05–5 Apr 08
Earl Granville	18 Dec 05–5 Apr 08
Ld Hamilton of Dalzell	18 Dec 05–5 Apr 08
Ld Colebrooke	20 Dec 05–5 Apr 08
Ld Herschell	31 Jul 07–5 Apr 08
Ld O'Hagan	1 Nov 07–5 Apr 08

LIBERAL GOVERNMENT, 1908–1915

MINISTERS IN CABINET

P.M.	**H. Asquith**	5 Apr 08–25 May 15
Ld Pres	**Ld Tweedmouth**	12 Apr 08
	Vt Wolverhampton	13 Oct 08
	Earl Beauchamp	16 Jun 10
	Vt Morley	3 Nov 10
	Earl Beauchamp	5 Aug 14
Ld Chanc.	**Ld Loreburn (Earl)**	12 Apr 08
	Vt Haldane	10 Jun 12
Privy S.	**M of Ripon**	12 Apr 08
	E of Crewe	9 Oct 08
	Earl Carrington	23 Oct 11
	M of Crewe	13 Feb 12
Exch.	**D. Lloyd George**	12 Apr 08
For. O.	**Sir E. Grey**	12 Apr 08

JUNIOR MINISTERS ATTACHED

Treasury:

F.S.	C. Hobhouse	12 Apr 08
	T. Wood	23 Oct 11
	C. Masterman	13 Feb 12
	E. Montagu	11 Feb 14
	F. Acland	3 Feb 15
U-S.	Ld Fitzmaurice	12 Apr 08
	T. Wood	19 Oct 01
	F. Acland	23 Oct 18
	N. Primrose	4 Feb 15

LIBERAL GOVERNMENT, 1908–1915 (contd.)

MINISTERS IN CABINET			JUNIOR MINISTERS ATTACHED		
Home O.	H. Gladstone	12 Apr 08	U-S.	H. Samuel	12 Apr 08
	W. Churchill	14 Feb 10		C. Masterman	7 Jul 09
	R. McKenna	23 Oct 11		E. Griffith	19 Feb 12
				C. Harmsworth	4 Feb 15
Admir.	R. McKenna	12 Apr 08	*P. & F.S.:*		
	W. Churchill	23 Oct 11		T. Macnamara	13 Apr 08
			Civil Ld:		
				G. Lambert	12 Apr 08
Bd Ag. & Fish.	Earl Carrington	12 Apr 08	P.S.	*(post not established)*	
				Sir E. Strachey	20 Dec 09
	W. Runciman	23 Oct 11		*(Ld Strachie)*	
	Ld Lucas	6 Aug 14		Ld Lucas	23 Oct 11
				Sir H. Verney	10 Aug 14
Att. Gen.	*(office not in cabinet)*				
	Sir R. Isaacs	4 Jun 12			
	Sir J. Simon	19 Oct 13			
Col. O.	E of Crewe	12 Apr 08	U-S.	J. Seely	12 Apr 08
	L. Harcourt	3 Nov 10		Ld Lucas	23 Mar 11
				Ld Emmott	23 Oct 11
				Ld Islington	10 Aug 14
Bd Educ.	W. Runciman	12 Apr 08	P.S.	T. Wood	13 Apr 08
	J. Pease	23 Oct 11		C. Trevelyan	19 Oct 08
				C. Addison	10 Aug 14
India O.	J. Morley (Vt)	12 Apr 08	U-S	T. Buchanan	12 Apr 08
	E of Crewe	3 Nov 10		Master of Elibank	25 Jun 09
	Vt Morley	7 Mar 11		E. Montagu	20 Feb 10
	E of Crewe (M)	25 May 11		C. Roberts	17 Feb 14
Chief Sec. Ireland	A. Birrell	12 Apr 08	*V. Pres. Dept. Agric. Ireland.*		
				T. Russell	12 Apr 08
D. Lanc.	Sir H. Fowler	12 Apr 08			
	(Vt Wolverhampton)				
	Ld Fitzmaurice	13 Oct 08			
	H. Samuel	25 Jun 09			
	J. Pease	14 Feb 10			
	C. Hobhouse	23 Oct 11			
	C. Masterman	11 Feb 14			
	E. Montagu	3 Feb 15			
Loc. Govt. Bd	J. Burns	12 Apr 08	P.S.	C. Masterman	12 Apr 08
	H. Samuel	11 Feb 14		H. Lewis	7 Jul 09
Postm.-Gen.	S. Buxton	12 Apr 08	Ass.	*(post not established)*	
	H. Samuel	14 Feb 10		Sir H. Norman	3 Jan 10
	C. Hobhouse	11 Feb 14		C. Norton	20 Feb 10
Scotland	J. Sinclair	12 Apr 08			
	(Ld Pentland)				
	T. Wood	13 Feb 12			
B.o.T.	W. Churchill	12 Apr 08	P.S.	(Sir) H. Kearley	12 Apr 08
	S. Buxton	14 Feb 10		H. Tennant	10 Jan 09
	J. Burns	11 Feb 14		J. Robertson	25 Oct 11
	W. Runciman	5 Aug 14			
War O.	R. Haldane (Vt)	12 Apr 08	F.S.	F. Acland	12 Apr 08
	J. Seely	12 Jun 12		C. Mallet	4 Mar 10
	H. Asquith (P.M.)	30 Mar 14		F. Acland	31 Jan 11
	Earl Kitchener	5 Aug 14		H. Tennant	25 Oct 11
				H. Baker	14 Jun 12
			U-S.	Ld Lucas	12 Apr 08
				J. Seely	23 Mar 11
				H. Tennant	14 Jun 21
1st C. Works	L. Harcourt	12 Apr 08			
	Earl Beauchamp	3 Nov 10			
	Ld Emmott	6 Aug 14			

LIBERAL GOVERNMENT, 1908–1915 (*contd.*)

MINISTERS NOT IN CABINET	JUNIOR MINISTERS ATTACHED

MINISTERS NOT IN CABINET

Paym.-Gen.	R. CAUSTON	12 Apr 08
	(Ld Southwark)	
	I. GUEST	23 Feb 10
	(Ld Ashby St Ledgers)	
	LD STRACHIE	23 May 12

Law Officers:

Att.-Gen.	SIR W. ROBSON	12 Apr 08
	SIR R. ISAACS	7 Oct 10
	(4 Jun 12 office in cabinet)	
Sol.-Gen.	SIR S. EVANS	12 Apr 08
	SIR R. ISAACS	6 Mar 10
	SIR J. SIMON	7 Oct 10
	SIR S. BUCKMASTER	19 Oct 13
Ld Advoc.	T. SHAW	12 Apr 08
	A. URE	14 Feb 09
	R. MUNRO	30 Oct 13
Sol.-Gen. Scotland	A. URE	12 Apr 08
	A. DEWAR	18 Feb 09
	W. HUNTER	18 Apr 10
	A. ANDERSON	3 Dec 11
	T. MORISON	30 Oct 13
Att.-Gen. Ireland	R. CHERRY	12 Apr 08
	R. BARRY	2 Dec 09
	C. O'CONNOR	26 Sep 11
	I. O'BRIEN	24 Jun 12
	T. MOLONY	10 Apr 13
	J. MORIARTY	20 Jun 13
	J. PIM	1 Jul 14
Sol.-Gen. Ireland	R. BARRY	12 Apr 08
	C. O'CONNOR	2 Dec 09
	I. O'BRIEN	19 Oct 11
	T. MOLONY	24 Jun 12
	J. MORIARTY	25 Apr 13
	J. PIM	20 Jun 13
	J. O'CONNOR	1 Jul 14

H.M. Household:

Treas.	SIR E. STRACHEY	12 Apr 08
	W. DUDLEY WARD	20 Dec 09
	F. GUEST	21 Feb 12
Comptr.	MASTER OF ELIBANK	12 Apr 08
	E OF LIVERPOOL (2nd)	12 Jul 09
	LD SAYE & SELE	1 Nov 12
V. Chamb.	(SIR) J. FULLER	12 Apr 08
	G. HOWARD	6 Feb 11
Ld Chamb.	VT ALTHORP	12 Apr 08
	(Earl Spencer)	
	LD SANDHURST	14 Feb 12
Ld Steward	EARL BEAUCHAMP	12 Apr 08
	E OF CHESTERFIELD	22 Jun 10
Master of Horse	E OF GRANARD	12 Apr 08
Capt. Gents at Arms	LD DENMAN	12 Apr 08
	LD COLEBROOKE	26 Jun 11
Capt. Yeomen of Guard	LD ALLENDALE (Vt)	12 Apr 08
	E OF CRAVEN	2 Oct 11

JUNIOR MINISTERS ATTACHED

P.S. to Treasury:

G. Whiteley	12 Apr 08
J. Pease	3 Jun 08
Master of Elibank	14 Feb 10
P. Illingworth	7 Aug 12
J. Gulland	24 Jan 15

Junior Lds of Treasury:

J. Pease	12 Apr 08–3 Jun 08
H. Lewis	12 Apr 08–7 Jul 09
C. Norton	12 Apr 08–20 Feb 10
J. Whitley	12 Apr 08–20 Feb 10
O. Partington	6 Jul 09–19 Jan 11
J. Gulland	7 Jul 09–24 Jan 15
W. Benn	20 Feb 10–25 May 15
E. Soares	20 Feb 10–16 Apr 11
P. Illingworth	28 Feb 10–7 Aug 12
W. Jones	19 Jan 11–25 May 15
F. Guest	16 Apr 11–21 Feb 12
Sir A. Haworth	23 Feb 12–16 Apr 12
H. Webb	16 Apr 12–25 May 15
C. Beck	3 Feb 15–25 May 15
W. Rea	3 Feb 15–25 May 15

Lds in Waiting:

Ld O'Hagan	12 Apr 08–15 Apr 10
Ld Hamilton of Dalzell	12 Apr 08–2 Oct 11
Ld Colebrooke	12 Apr 08–19 Jun 11
Ld Herschell	12 Apr 08–25 May 15
Ld Acton	12 Apr 08–25 May 15
Earl Granville	12 Apr 08–25 May 15
Ld Tweedmouth	15 Apr 10–4 Dec 11
Ld Willingdon	19 Jan 11–31 Jan 13
Vt Allendale	2 Oct 11–25 May 15
Ld Loch	4 Dec 11–1 May 14
Ld Ashby St Ledgers (Ld Wimborne)	31 Jan 13–8 Feb 15
Ld Stanmore	1 May 14–25 May 15
Ld Ranksborough	8 Feb 15–25 May 15

COALITION GOVERNMENT, 1915–1916

MINISTERS IN CABINET			JUNIOR MINISTERS ATTACHED
P.M.	**H. Asquith** (Lib)		
	25 May 15–5 Dec 16		
Ld Pres.	**M of Crewe** (Lib)	25 May 15	
Ld Chanc.	**Ld Buckmaster** (Lib)	25 May 15	
Privy S	**Earl Curzon** (C)	25 May 15	
Exch.	**R. McKenna** (Lib)	25 May 15	*Treasury:*
			F.S. E. Montagu (Lib) 26 May 15
			(*also D. Lanc., in cabinet from* 11 *Jan*16)
			T. Wood (Lib) 9 Jul 16
			(*also D. Lanc. in cabinet*)
For. O.	**Sir E. Grey** (Lib)	25 May 15	*U-S.* Ld R. Cecil[1] (C) 30 May 15
	(Vt)		(*also Blockade, in cabinet from* 23 *Feb* 16)
			Ass. Ld Newton (C) 18 Aug 16
Home O.	**Sir J. Simon** (Lib)	25 May 15	*U-S.* W. Brace (Lab) 30 May 15
	Sir H. Samuel (Lib)	10 Jan 16	
Admir.	**A. Balfour** (C)	25 May 15	*P. & F.S.:*
			T. Macnamara (Lib) 30 May 15
			Civil Ld:
			D of Devonshire (C) 9 Jun 15
			E of Lytton (C) 26 Jul 16
Bd Ag. &	**E of Selborne** (C)	25 May 15	*P.S.* F. Acland (Lib) 30 May 15
Fish.	**E of Crawford** (C)	11 Jul 16	
Att.-Gen.	**Sir E. Carson** (C)	25 May 15	
	Sir F. Smith (C)	3 Nov 15	
Blockade	**Ld R. Cecil**[1] (C)	23 Feb 16	
	(*also U-S. at F.O.*)		
Col. O.	**A. Bonar Law** (C)	25 May 15	*U-S.* A. Steel-Maitland (C) 30 May 15
Bd Educ.	**A. Henderson** (Lab)	25 May 15	*P.S.* H. Lewis (Lib) 30 May 15
	M of Crewe (Lib)	18 Aug 16	
Health &	**W. Long** (C)	25 May 15	*P.S.* W. Hayes Fisher (C) 30 May 15
Loc. Govt Bd			
India O.	**A. Chamberlain** (C)	25 May 15	*U-S.* Ld Islington (Lib) 30 May 15
Chief Sec.	**A. Birrell** (Lib)	25 May 15	*V. Pres. Dept. Agric. & Technical Instruction*
Ireland	**H. Duke** (C)	31 Jul 16	*Ireland:*
			T. Russell (Lib) 30 May 15
D. Lanc.	**W. Churchill** (Lib)	25 May 15	
	H. Samuel (Lib)	25 Nov 15	
	E. Montagu (Lib)	11 Jan 16	
	(*also F.S. at Treasury*)		
	T. Wood (Lib)	9 Jul 16	
	(*also F.S. at Treasury*)		
Munitions	**D. Lloyd George** (Lib)	25 May 15	*P.S.* C. Addison (Lib) 30 May 15–8 Dec 16
	E. Montagu (Lib)	9 Jul 16	A. Lee (C) 11 Nov 15[2]–9 Jul 16
Paym.-Gen.	(*office not in cabinet*)		
	A. Henderson (Lab)	18 Aug 16	
Min.	**M of Lansdowne** (C)	25 May 15	
without			
Portfolio			
Scotland	**T. Wood** (Lib)	25 May 15	
	H. Tennant (Lib)	9 Jul 16	
B.o.T.	**W. Runciman** (Lib)	25 May 15	*P.S.* E. Pretyman (C) 30 May 15
War O.	**Earl Kitchener**	25 May 15	*U-S.* H. Tennant (Lib) 30 May 15
	D. Lloyd George (Lib)	6 Jul 16	E of Derby (C) 6 Jul 16
			F.S. H. Forster (C) 30 May 15
1st C. Works	**L. Harcourt (Vt)** (Lib)	25 May 15	

[1] Not a member of the House of Lords.
[2] Date of first reply in Commons as *Parliamentary (Military) Secretary to the Munitions Department*.

COALITION GOVERNMENT, 1915–1916 (*contd.*)

MINISTERS NOT IN CABINET			JUNIOR MINISTERS ATTACHED		
Paym.-Gen.	LD NEWTON (C)	9 Jun 15			
	(*A. Henderson* 18 *Aug* 16 & *office in cabinet*)				
Postm.-Gen.	H. SAMUEL (Lib)	26 May 15	*Ass.*	H. Pike Pease (C)	30 May 15
	J. PEASE (Lib)	18 Jan 16			
Law Officers:			*P.S. to Treasury:*		
Att.-Gen.	(*office in cabinet*)			J. Gulland (Lib) 30 May 15–5 Dec 16	
Sol.-Gen.	SIR F. SMITH (C)	2 Jun 15		Ld E. Talbot [1] (C)	
	(SIR) G. CAVE (C)	8 Nov 15		30 May 15–5 Dec 16	
Ld Advoc.	R. MUNRO (Lib)	8 Jun 15	*Junior Lds of Treasury:*		
Sol.-Gen. Scotland	T. MORISON (Lib)	8 Jun 15		G. Howard (Lib) 27 May 15–5 Dec 16	
				G. Roberts (Lab)	
Att.-Gen. Ireland	J. GORDON (C)	8 Jun 15		27 May 15–5 Dec 16	
	J. CAMPBELL (C)	9 Apr 16		W. Bridgeman (C)	
Sol.-Gen. Ireland	J. O'CONNOR (Nat)	8 Jun 15		27 May 15–5 Dec 16	
				W. Rea (Lib) 27 May 15–5 Dec 16	
H.M. Household:			*Lds in Waiting:*		
Treas.	J. HOPE (C)	30 May 15		Ld Herschell (Lib) 9 Jun 15–5 Dec 16	
Comptr.	C. ROBERTS (Lib)	30 May 15		Vt Allendale (Lib) 9 Jun 15–5 Dec 16	
V. Chamb.	C. BECK (Lib)	30 May 15		Ld Stanmore (Lib) 9 Jun 15–5 Dec 16	
Ld Chamb.	LD SANDHURST (Lib)	9 Jun 15		Ld Ranksborough (Lib)	
Ld Steward	LD FARQUHAR (C)	9 Jun 15		9 Jun 15–5 Dec 16	
Master of Horse	E OF CHESTERFIELD (Lib)	9 Jun 15		Vt Valentia [1] (C) 9 Jun 15–5 Dec 16	
				Ld Hylton (C) 9 Jun 15–5 Dec 16	
Capt. Gents at Arms	LD COLEBROOKE (Lib)	9 Jun 15			
Capt. Yeomen of Guard	LD SUFFIELD (C)	9 Jun 15			

COALITION GOVERNMENT, 1916–1922

From 6 Dec 1916 to 31 Oct 1919 there was an inner war cabinet of 5–7 ministers. **D. Lloyd George, Earl Curzon,** and **A. Bonar Law** were members throughout; the other members were,

> **A. Henderson** (Lab) 10 Dec 16–12 Aug 17
> **Vt Milner** (C) 10 Dec 16–18 Apr 18
> **J. Smuts** [2] 22 Jun 17–10 Jan 19
> **G. Barnes** (Lab) 29 May 17–3 Aug 17, 13 Aug 17–10 Jan 19
> **A. Chamberlain** (C) 18 Apr 18–31 Oct 19
> **Sir E. Geddes** (C) 10 Jan 19–31 Oct 19

MINISTERS IN CABINET			JUNIOR MINISTERS ATTACHED	
P.M.	**D. Lloyd George** (Lib)	6 Dec 16–19 Oct 22		
Ld Pres.	**Earl Curzon** (C)	10 Dec 16		
	A. Balfour (C)	23 Oct 19		
Ld Chanc.	**Ld Finlay** (C)	10 Dec 16		
	Ld Birkenhead (Vt) (C)	10 Jan 19		
Privy S.	**E of Crawford** (C)	15 Dec 16		
	A. Bonar Law (C)	10 Jan 19		
	A. Chamberlain (C)	23 Mar 21		
Exch.	**A. Bonar Law** (C)	10 Dec 16	*Treasury:*	
	A. Chamberlain (C)	10 Jan 19	*F.S.* Sir H. Lever (Lib)	
	Sir R. Horne (C)	1 Apr 21	15 Dec 16–19 May 19	
			S. Baldwin (C) 18 Jun 17–1 Apr 21	
			E. Young (Lib) 1 Apr 21–19 Oct 22	

---

[1] Not a member of the House of Lords.
[2] Not a member of the House of Commons.

COALITION GOVERNMENT, 1916–1922 (contd.)

	MINISTERS IN CABINET		JUNIOR MINISTERS ATTACHED	
For. O.	**A. Balfour** (C)	10 Dec 16	U-S. Ld R. Cecil[1] (C)	10 Dec 16
	Earl Curzon (C)	23 Oct 19	C. Harmsworth (Lib)	10 Jan 19
	(Marquess)		Ass. U-S.:	
			Ld Newton (C)	10 Dec 16
			(post abolished 10 Jan 1919)	
Home O.	**Sir G. Cave (Vt)** (C)	10 Dec 16	U-S. W. Brace (Lab)	10 Dec 16
	E. Shortt (Lib)	10 Jan 19	Sir H. Greenwood (Lib)	10 Jan 19
			(Sir) J. Baird (C)	29 Apr 19
Admir.	**Sir E. Carson** (C)	10 Dec 16	P. & F.S.:	
	Sir E. Geddes (C)	17 Jul 17	T. Macnamara (Lib)	10 Dec 16
	W. Long (C)	10 Jan 19	Sir J. Craig (C)	2 Apr 20
	Ld Lee (C)	13 Feb 21	L. Amery (C)	1 Apr 21
			P.S. Addit.:	
			E of Lytton (C)	7 Feb 17
			(post abolished 27 Jan 1919)	
			Civil Ld:	
			E. Pretyman (C)	14 Dec 16
			E of Lytton (C)	27 Jan 19
			E of Onslow (C)	26 Oct 20
			B. Eyres-Monsell (C)	1 Apr 21
			2nd Civil Ld:	
			A. Pease (C)	10 Dec 16
			(post abolished 10 Jan 1919)	
Bd Ag. & Fish.	**R. Prothero** (C)	10 Dec 16	P.S. Sir R. Winfrey (Lib)	14 Dec 16
	(Ld Ernle)		D of Marlborough (C)	18 Feb 17
	Ld Lee (C)	15 Aug 19	Vt Goschen (C)	26 Mar 18
	(Min. 15 Aug 19)		Ld Clinton (C)	18 Jun 18
	Sir A. Griffith-Boscawen (C)		Sir A. Griffith-Boscawen (C)	
		13 Feb 21		10 Jan 19
			(& Dep. Min. Fisheries 18 Nov 19)	
			E of Onslow (C)	5 Apr 21
			E of Ancaster (C)	7 Apr 21
			(& Dep. Min. Fisheries 28 Oct 21)	
Att. Gen.	(office not in cabinet)			
	Sir G. Hewart (Lib)	7 Nov 21		
	(Sir E. Pollock (C) 6 Mar 22 & office not in cabinet)			
Col. O.	**W. Long** (C)	10 Dec 16	U-S. (Sir) A. Steel-Maitland (C)	10 Dec 16
	Vt Milner (C)	10 Jan 19	W. Hewins (C)	26 Sep 17
	W. Churchill (Lib)	13 Feb 21	L. Amery (C)	10 Jan 19
			E. Wood (C)	1 Apr 21
Bd Educ.	**H. Fisher** (Lib)	10 Dec 16	P.S. (Sir) H. Lewis (Lib)	10 Dec 16
Health	(Dept. under Loc. Govt Bd: see below)		P.S. (Loc. Govt Bd):	
			W. Hayes Fisher (C)	10 Dec 16
	C. Addison (Lib)	24 Jun 19	S. Walsh (Lab)	28 Jun 17
	Sir A. Mond (Lib)	1 Apr 21	W. Astor (Vt) (C)	27 Jan 19
			E of Onslow (C)	7 Apr 21
India O.	**A. Chamberlain** (C)	10 Dec 16	U-S. Ld Islington (Lib)	10 Dec 16
	E. Montagu (Lib)	17 Jul 17	Ld Sinha (Lib)	10 Jan 19
	Vt Peel (C)	19 Mar 22	E of Lytton (C)	22 Sep 20
			Earl Winterton[1] (C)	20 Mar 22
Chief Sec. Ireland	**(Sir) H. Duke** (C)	10 Dec 16	V. Pres. Dept. Agric. & Technical Instruction for Ireland:	
	E. Shortt (Lib)	5 May 18	(Sir) T. Russell (Lib)	10 Dec 16
	I. Macpherson (Lib)	10 Jan 19	H. Barrie (C)	15 Jan 19
	Sir H. Greenwood (Lib)	2 Apr 20		
Ld Lieut. Ireland	**Vt French** (E of Ypres)	6 May 18		
	(Not usually ministerial office. In cabinet only 28 Oct 19–2 Apr 21)			

Not a member of the House of Lords.

COALITION GOVERNMENT, 1916-1922 (contd.)

	MINISTERS IN CABINET		JUNIOR MINISTERS ATTACHED

Lab.
J. Hodge (Lab)   10 Dec 16
G. Roberts (Lab)   17 Aug 17
Sir R. Horne (C)   10 Jan 19
T. Macnamara (Lib)   19 Mar 20

P.S.   W. Bridgeman (C)   22 Dec 16
G. Wardle (Lab)   10 Jan 19
Sir A. Montague-Barlow (C)
   2 April 20

D. Lanc.
Sir F. Cawley (Lib)   10 Dec 16
Ld Beaverbrook (C)   10 Feb 18
(*& Min. of Propaganda/Information*)
Ld Downham (C)   4 Nov 18
(*E of Crawford (C) 10 Jan 19 &*
office not in cabinet)

Loc. Govt.
Bd
Ld Rhondda (Lib)   10 Dec 16
W. Hayes Fisher (C)   28 Jun 17
   (Ld Downham)
Sir A. Geddes (C)   4 Nov 18
C. Addison (Lib)   10 Jan 19
(*24 Jun 19 became Min. of Health:*
see above)

(*for Junior Ministers see above,*
under Health)

Munitions
(Supply)
C. Addison (Lib)   10 Dec 16
W. Churchill (Lib)   17 Jul 17
(*Ld Inverforth Min. of Supply 10*
Jan 19 & office not in cabinet)

P.S.   Sir L. Worthington-Evans (C)
   14 Dec 16-30 Jan 18
F. Kellaway (Lib)
   14 Dec 16-1 Apr 21
J. Seely (Lib)   18 Jul 18-10 Jan 19
J. Baird (C)   10 Jan 19-27 Jan 19
P. & F.S.:
Sir L. Worthington-Evans (C)
   30 Jan 18-13 May 18
J. Hope (C)   27 Jan 19-4 Apr 21

Min.
without
Portfolio
A. Henderson (Lab)
   10 Dec 16-12 Aug 17
Vt Milner (C) 10 Dec 16-18 Apr 18
Sir E. Carson (C)
   17 Jul 17-21 Jan 18
J. Smuts [1]   22 Jun 17-10 Jan 19
G. Barnes (Lab)
   13 Aug 17-27 Jan 20
A. Chamberlain (C)
   18 Apr 18-10 Jan 19
Sir E. Geddes (C)
   10 Jan 19-19 May 19
Sir L. Worthington-Evans (C)
   2 Apr 20-13 Feb 21
C. Addison (Lib) 1 Apr 21-14 Jul 21

Scotland
R. Munro (Lib)   10 Dec 16

P.S. Min. of Health for Scotland:
(Sir) J. Pratt (Lib)   8 Aug 19

B.o.T.
Sir A. Stanley (Lib)   10 Dec 16
Sir A. Geddes (C)   26 May 19
Sir R. Horne (C)   19 Mar 20
S. Baldwin (C)   1 Apr 21

P.S.   G. Roberts (Lab)   14 Dec 19
G. Wardle (Lab)   17 Aug 17
W. Bridgeman (C)   10 Jan 19
Sir P. Lloyd-Greame (C) 22 Aug 20
Sir W. Mitchell-Thomson (C)
   1 Apr 21
Sec. Dept. Overseas Trade:
Sir A. Steel-Maitland (C) 14 Sep 17
Sir H. Greenwood (Lib) 29 Apr 19
F. Kellaway (Lib)   2 Apr 20
Sir P. Lloyd-Greame (C) 1 Apr 21
   (*Director Overseas Trade Dept.*)
P.S. Mines Dept.:
W. Bridgeman (C)   22 Aug 20

[1] Not a member of the House of Commons.

COALITION GOVERNMENT, 1916–1922 (contd.)

MINISTERS IN CABINET			JUNIOR MINISTERS ATTACHED		
Transp.	*(office not established)*		*P.S.*	Sir R. Williams (Lib)	23 Sep 19
	Sir E. Geddes (C)	19 May 19		A. Neal (Lib)	28 Nov 19
	(Vt Peel 7 Nov 21 & office not in cabinet)				
	E of Crawford (C)	12 Apr 22			
War O.	**E of Derby** (C)	10 Dec 16	*U-S*	I. Macpherson (Lib)	14 Dec 11
	Vt Milner (C)	18 Apr 18		Vt Peel (C)	10 Jan 16
	(10 Jan 19 War O. & Air Min. combined)			Sir R. Sanders (C)	1 Apr 26
	W. Churchill (Lib)	10 Jan 19	*F.S.*	H. Forster (Ld) (C)	10 Dec 19
	(13 Feb 21 War O. only)			Sir A. Williamson (Lib)	18 Dec 19
	Sir L. Worthington-Evans (C)			G. Stanley (C)	1 Apr 21
		13 Feb 21	*P.S.*	Earl Stanhope (C)	14 Dec 16
1st C.Works	*(office not in cabinet)*			*(post abolished* 10 *Jan* 1919)	
	E of Crawford (C)	7 Apr 22			

MINISTERS NOT IN CABINET			JUNIOR MINISTERS ATTACHED		
Air	LD COWDRAY (Lib)	3 Jan 17	*P.S Air Council:*		
	LD ROTHERMERE (Lib)	26 Nov 17		J. Baird (C)	14 Dec 16
	LD WEIR (Lib)	26 Apr 18		*(post abolished* 10 *Jan* 19)	
	(War O. & Air Min. combined 10 Jan 19, see above)		*U-S*	J. Seely (Lib)	10 Jan 19
	W. CHURCHILL (Lib)	10 Jan 19		G. Tryon (C)	22 Dec 19
	F. GUEST (Lib)	1 Apr 21		M of Londonderry (C)	2 Apr 20
				Ld Gorell (Lib)	18 Jul 21
Blockade	LD R. CECIL [1] (C)	10 Dec 16	*P.S*	F. Leverton Harris	22 Dec 16
	(also U. S. at F.O.)			*(post abolished* 10 *Jan* 19)	
	SIR L. WORTHINGTON-EVANS (C)				
		18 Jul 18			
	(office abolished 10 *Jan* 1919)				
Food Control	VT DEVONPORT (Lib)	10 Dec 16	*P.S.*	(Sir) C. Bathurst (C)	12 Dec 16
	LD RHONDDA (Vt) (Lib)	19 Jun 17		J. Clynes (Lab)	2 Jul 17
	J. CLYNES (Lab)	9 Jul 18		W. Astor (C)	18 Jul 18
	G. ROBERTS (Lab)	10 Jan 19		C. McCurdy (Lib)	27 Jan 19
	C. MCCURDY (Lib)	19 Mar 20		Sir W. Mitchell-Thomson (C)	
	(office abolished 31 *Mar* 21)				19 Apr 20
Ld Chanc. Ireland	SIR I. O'BRIEN (Lib)	10 Dec 16			
	SIR J. CAMPBELL (C)	4 Jun 18			
	SIR J. ROSS (C)	27 Jun 21			
D. Lanc.	*(office of cabinet rank see above)*				
	E OF CRAWFORD (C)	10 Jan 19			
	VT PEEL (C)	1 Apr 21			
	SIR W. SUTHERLAND (Lib)	7 Apr 22			
Nat. S.	N. CHAMBERLAIN	19 Aug 16	*P.S.*	Vt Peel (C) 15 Apr 18–19 Dec 19	
	SIR A. GEDDES (C)	17 Aug 17		S. Walsh (Lab) 17 Mar 17–28 Jun 17	
	(office held joint with B of Trade Jan-Aug 19 *and then abolished)*			C. Beck (Lib) 28 Jun 17–19 Dec 19	
				(post abolished 19 *Dec* 19)	
Paym.-Gen.	SIR J. COMPTON-RICKETT (Lib)				
		15 Dec 16			
	SIR T. WALTERS (Lib)	26 Oct 19			
Pensions	G. BARNES (Lab)	10 Dec 16	*P.S.*	Sir A. Griffith-Boscawen (C)	
	J. HODGE (Lab)	17 Aug 17			22 Dec 16
	SIR L. WORTHINGTON-EVANS (C)			Sir J. Craig (C)	10 Jan 19
		10 Jan 19		G. Tryon (C)	2 Apr 20
	I. MACPHERSON (Lib)	2 Apr 20			
Postm.-Gen.	A. ILLINGWORTH (Lib)	10 Dec 16	*Ass.*	H. Pike Pease (C)	10 Dec 16
	F. KELLAWAY (Lib)	1 Apr 21			
Reconstruction	C. ADDISON (Lib)	17 Jul 17		*(for Junior Ministers see above, under National Service & Reconstruction)*	
	(office abolished 10 *Jan* 1919)				

[1] Not a member of the House of Lords.

COALITION GOVERNMENT, 1916–1922 (contd.)

MINISTERS NOT IN CABINET	JUNIOR MINISTERS ATTACHED

Shipping   SIR J. MACLAY (LD) (Lib) 10 Dec 16   *P.S.*   Sir L. Chiozza Money (Lib) 22 Dec 16
         (*office abolished* 31 *Mar* 21)   L. Wilson (C)   10 Jan 19

Supply   LD INVERFORTH (C)   10 Jan 19   (*for Junior Ministers see above*)
         (*office abolished* 21 *Mar* 21)

Transp.   (*office in cabinet* 19 *May* 19–
                7 *Nov* 21)
       VT PEEL (C)   7 Nov 21
         (E *of Crawford* 12 *Apr* 22 &
             office in cabinet)

1st C. Works   SIR A. MOND (Lib)   10 Dec 16
         E OF CRAWFORD (C)   1 Apr 21
         (*office in cabinet* 7 *Apr* 22)

Law Officers:

Att.-Gen.   SIR F. SMITH (C)   10 Dec 16   *P.S. to Treasury:*
         (*Ld Birkenhead*)   Ld E. Talbot [1] (C) 14 Dec 16–1 Apr 21
         SIR G. HEWART (Lib)   10 Jan 19   N. Primrose (Lib)
         (*office in cabinet* 7 *Nov* 21)   14 Dec 16–2 Mar 17
         SIR E. POLLOCK (C)   6 Mar 22   F. Guest (Lib)   2 Mar 17–1 Apr 21
                                           C. McCurdy (Lib)
Sol.-Gen.   SIR G. HEWART (Lib)   10 Dec 16   1 Apr 21–19 Oct 22
         SIR E. POLLOCK (C)   10 Jan 19   L. Wilson (C)   1 Apr 21–19 Oct 22
         (SIR) L. SCOTT (C)   6 Mar 22   *Junior Lds of Treasury:*

Ld Advoc.   J. CLYDE (C)   10 Dec 16   J. Hope (C)   14 Dec 16–27 Jan 19
         T. MORISON (Lib)   25 Mar 20   J. Pratt (Lib)   14 Dec 16–8 Aug 19
         C. MURRAY (C)   5 Mar 22   S. Baldwin (C)   29 Jan 17–21 Jun 17
                                        J. Parker (Lab)   29 Jan 17–19 Oct 22
Sol.-Gen.   T. MORISON (Lib)   10 Dec 16   J. Towyn Jones (Lib)
Scotland   C. MURRAY (C)   25 Mar 20   29 Jan 17–4 Jul 22
         A. BRIGGS CONSTABLE (C)   (Sir) R. Sanders (C)
                    16 Mar 22   5 Feb 19–1 Apr 21
         W. WATSON (C)   24 Jul 22   Sir G. Collins (Lib)
Att.-Gen.   J. CAMPBELL (C)   20 Dec 16   8 Aug 19–10 Feb 20
Ireland   J. O'CONNOR (Nat)   8 Jan 17   Sir W. Sutherland (Lib)
         A. SAMUELS (C)   7 Apr 18   15 Feb 20–7 Apr 22
         D. HENRY (C)   6 Jul 19   Sir J. Gilmour (C)
         T. BROWN (C)   5 Aug 21   1 Apr 21–19 Oct 22
         (*post vacant from* 16 *Nov* 21)   T. Lewis (Lib)   4 Jul 22–19 Oct 22

Sol.-Gen.   J. CHAMBERS (C)   19 Mar 17
Ireland   A. SAMUELS (C)   12 Sep 17
         J. POWELL (C)   7 Apr 18
         D. HENRY (C)   27 Nov 18
         D. WILSON (C)   6 Jul 19
         T. BROWN (C)   12 Jun 21
         (*post vacant from* 5 *Aug* 21)

H.M. Household:

Treas.   (SIR) J. CRAIG (C)   14 Dec 16   *Lds in Waiting:*
         R. SANDERS (C)   10 Jan 19   Ld Herschell (Lib)
         B. EYRES-MONSELL (C)   5 Feb 19   14 Dec 16–11 Feb 19
         G. GIBBS (C)   1 Apr 21   Ld Stanmore (Lib)
                                         14 Dec 16–19 Oct 22
Comptr.   SIR E. CORNWALL (Lib) 14 Dec 16   Ld Ranksborough (Lib)
         G. STANLEY (C)   28 Feb 19   14 Dec 16–4 Apr 21
         H. BARNSTON (C)   7 Apr 21   Vt Valentia [1] (C) 14 Dec 16–19 Oct 22
V. Chamb.   C. BECK (Lib)   14 Dec 16   Ld Hylton (C) 14 Dec 16–18 May 18
         W. DUDLEY WARD (Lib)   9 Dec 17   Ld Kenyon (C) 14 Dec 16–11 Sep 18
                                         Ld Somerleyton (C)
Ld Chamb.   LD SANDHURST (Vt) (Lib) 14 Dec 16   18 May 18–19 Oct 22
         D OF ATHOLL (C)   20 Nov 21   E of Jersey (C) 11 Jan 19–17 Aug 19
                                         E of Bradford (C)
Ld Steward   LD FARQUHAR (Vt) (C) 14 Dec 16   11 Feb 19–19 Oct 22
Master of   E OF CHESTERFIELD (Lib) 14 Dec 16   E of Onslow (C) 17 Aug 19–12 Nov 20
Horse   E of Lucan (C) 12 Nov 20–19 Oct 22
Capt. Gents   LD COLEBROOKE (Lib)   14 Dec 16   E of Clarendon (C)
at Arms   7 Apr 21–19 Oct 22

---

[1] Not a member of the House of Lords. Viscount Valentia became a U.K. Peer (Ld Annesley) in 1917.

CONSERVATIVE GOVERNMENT, 1922–1924 *(contd.)*

MINISTERS NOT IN CABINET		JUNIOR MINISTERS ATTACHED
H.M. Household:		
Capt.	Ld Suffield (C)	14 Dec 16
Yeomen of	Ld Hylton (C)	21 May 18
Guard		

CONSERVATIVE GOVERNMENT, 1922–1924

MINISTERS IN CABINET			JUNIOR MINISTERS ATTACHED		
P.M.	**A. Bonar Law**				
	23 Oct 22–20 May 23				
	S. Baldwin 22 May 23–22 Jan 24				
Ld Pres.	**M of Salisbury**	24 Oct 22			
Ld Chanc.	**Vt Cave**	24 Oct 22			
Privy S.	*(office vacant)*				
	Ld R. Cecil [1]	25 May 23			
Exch.	**S. Baldwin**	24 Oct 22	*Treasury:*		
	(*& P.M. from 22 May* 23)		*F.S.* J. Hills		6 Nov 22
	N. Chamberlain	27 Aug 23	A. Boyd-Carpenter		12 Mar 23
F.S. to	*(office not in cabinet)*		(*Sir W. Joynson-Hicks* 25 May 23 *&*		
Treasury	**Sir W. Joynson-Hicks** 25 May 23		*seat in cabinet*)		
	(*W. Guinness* 5 Oct 23 *& office*		W. Guinness		5 Oct 23
	not in cabinet)				
For. O.	**Marquess Curzon**	24 Oct 22	*U-S.* R. McNeill		31 Oct 22
Home O.	**W. Bridgeman**	24 Oct 22	*U-S.* G. Stanley		31 Oct 22
			G. Locker-Lampson		12 Mar 23
Admir.	**L. Amery**	24 Oct 22	*P. & F.S.:*		
			B. Eyres-Monsell		31 Oct 22
			A. Boyd-Carpenter		25 May 23
			Civil Ld:		
			M of Linlithgow		31 Oct 22
Ag. & Fish.	**Sir R. Sanders**	24 Oct 22	*P.S. Ag. & Deputy Min. Fisheries:*		
			E of Ancaster		31 Oct 22
Air	*(office not in cabinet)*		*U-S.* D of Sutherland		31 Oct 22
	Sir S. Hoare	25 May 23			
Col. O.	**D of Devonshire**	24 Oct 22	*U-S.* W. Ormsby-Gore		31 Oct 22
Bd Educ.	**E. Wood**	24 Oct 22	*P.S.* Ld E. Percy [1]		21 Mar 23
			E of Onslow		25 May 23
Health	**Sir A. Griffith-Boscawen**		*P.S.* E of Onslow		31 Oct 22
		24 Oct 22	Ld E. Percy [1]		25 May 23
	N. Chamberlain	7 Mar 23			
	Sir W. Joynson-Hicks 27 Aug 23				
India O.	**Vt Peel**	24 Oct 22	*U-S.* Earl Winterton [1]		31 Oct 22
Lab.	**Sir A. Montague-Barlow**		*P.S.* A. Boyd-Carpenter		6 Nov 22
		31 Oct 22	H. Betterton		12 Mar 23
D. Lanc.	**M of Salisbury**	24 Oct 22			
	(*J. Davidson & office not in*				
	cabinet 25 May 23)				
Postm.-Gen.	*(office not in cabinet)*				
	Sir L. Worthington-Evans				
		28 May 23			
Scotland	**Vt Novar**	24 Oct 22	*P.S. Min. of Health for Scotland:*		
			J. Kidd		31 Oct 22
			W. Elliot		15 Jan 23

[1] Not a member of the House of Lords.

COALITION GOVERNMENT, 1916–1922 (contd.)

MINISTERS IN CABINET		JUNIOR MINISTERS ATTACHED	

B.o.T.   **Sir P. Lloyd-Greame**   24 Oct 22

P.S.   Vt Wolmer [1]   31 Oct 22
Sec. Overseas Trade Dept.:
    Sir W. Joynson-Hicks
       31 Oct 22–12 Mar 23
    A. Buckley   12 Mar 23–18 Nov 23
P.S. Mines Dept.:
    G. Lane-Fox   6 Nov 22

War O.   **E of Derby**   24 Oct 22

U-S.   W. Guinness   31 Oct 22
    W. Ashley   8 Oct 23
F.S.   S. Jackson   31 Oct 22
    R. Gwynne   15 Mar 23

MINISTERS NOT IN CABINET		JUNIOR MINISTERS ATTACHED	

Air   Sir S. Hoare   31 Oct 22
    (*office in cabinet 25 May 23*)

(*for Junior Ministers see above*)

D. Lanc.   (*office in cabinet*)
    J. Davidson   25 May 23

Paym.-Gen.   (*office vacant*)
    N. Chamberlain   5 Feb 23
    Sir W. Joynson-Hicks   15 Mar 23
    A. Boyd-Carpenter   25 May 23

Pensions   G. Tryon   31 Oct 22

P.S.   C. Craig   13 Feb 23

Postm.-Gen.   N. Chamberlain   31 Oct 22
    Sir W. Joynson-Hicks   7 Mar 23
    (*Sir L. Worthington-Evans & office
      in cabinet 28 May 23*)

Transp.   Sir J. Baird   31 Oct 22

P.S. Office of Works & Min. of Transp.:
    W. Ashley   31 Oct 22
    J. Moore-Brabazon   8 Oct 23
    (*to Min. Transp. only*)

1st C. Works   Sir J. Baird   31 Oct 22

Law Officers:

P.S. to Treasury:
    L. Wilson   31 Oct 22
    B. Eyres-Monsell   25 Jul 23

Att.-Gen.   Sir D. Hogg   24 Oct 22
Sol.-Gen.   Sir T. Inskip   31 Oct 22
Ld Advoc.   W. Watson   24 Oct 22
Sol.-Gen.   D. Fleming   6 Nov 22
Scotland   F. Thomson   5 Apr 23

Junior Lds of Treasury:
    D. King   31 Oct 22–22 Jan 24
    A. Buckley   31 Oct 22–12 Mar 23
    G. Hennessy   11 Dec 22–22 Jan 24
    F. Thomson   7 Feb 23–25 May 23
    W. Cope   20 Mar 23–22 Jan 24
    P. Ford   25 May 23–20 Dec 23

H.M. Household:

Lds in Waiting:
    Vt Valentia   20 Nov 22–22 Jan 24
    Ld Somerleyton
       20 Nov 22–22 Jan 24

Treas.   G. Gibbs   6 Nov 22
Comptr.   H. Barnston   31 Oct 22
V. Chamb.   D. Hacking   20 Nov 22

    E of Bradford   20 Nov 22–22 Jan 24
    E of Lucan   20 Nov 22–22 Jan 24
    E of Malmesbury

Ld Chamb.   E of Cromer   20 Nov 22
Ld Steward   E of Shaftesbury   20 Nov 22
Master of Horse   M of Bath   20 Nov 22

       20 Nov 22–22 Jan 24
    E of Albemarle   20 Nov 22–22 Jan 24

Capt. Gents at Arms   E of Clarendon   20 Nov 22

Capt. Yeomen of Guard   Ld Hylton   20 Nov 22

[1] Not a member of the House of Lords.

LABOUR GOVERNMENT, 1924

MINISTERS IN CABINET			JUNIOR MINISTERS ATTACHED		
P.M.	**J. R. MacDonald**				
	22 Jan 24–3 Nov 24				
Ld Pres.	**Ld Parmoor**	22 Jan 24			
Ld Chanc.	**Vt Haldane**	22 Jan 24			
Privy S.	**J. Clynes**	22 Jan 24			
Exch.	**P. Snowden**	22 Jan 24	*Treasury:*		
			F.S. W. Graham	23 Jan 24	
For. O.	**J. R. MacDonald (P.M.)**	22 Jan 24	*U-S.* A. Ponsonby	23 Jan 24	
Home O.	**A. Henderson**	22 Jan 24	*U-S.* R. Davies	23 Jan 24	
Admir.	**Vt Chelmsford**	22 Jan 24	*P. & F.S.:*		
			C. Ammon	23 Jan 24	
			Civil Ld:		
			F. Hodges	24 Jan 24	
Ag. & Fish	**N. Buxton**	22 Jan 24	*P.S.* W. Smith	23 Jan 24	
Air	**Ld Thomson**	22 Jan 24	*U-S.* W. Leach	23 Jan 24	
Col. O.	**J. Thomas**	22 Jan 24	*U-S.* Ld Arnold	23 Jan 24	
Bd Educ.	**C. Trevelyan**	22 Jan 24	*P.S.* M. Jones	23 Jan 24	
Health	**J. Wheatley**	22 Jan 24	*P.S.* A. Greenwood	23 Jan 24	
India O.	**Ld Olivier**	22 Jan 24	*U-S.* R. Richards	23 Jan 24	
Lab.	**T. Shaw**	22 Jan 24	*P.S.* Miss M. Bondfield	23 Jan 24	
D. Lanc.	**J. Wedgwood**	22 Jan 24			
Postm.-Gen.	**V. Hartshorn**	22 Jan 24			
Scotland	**W. Adamson**	22 Jan 24	*U-S. Health for Scotland:*		
			J. Stewart	23 Jan 24	
B.o.T.	**S. Webb**	22 Jan 24	*P.S.* A. Alexander	23 Jan 24	
			P.S. Overseas Trade Dept.:		
			W. Lunn	23 Jan 24	
			P.S. Mines Dept.:		
			E. Shinwell	23 Jan 24	
War O.	**S. Walsh**	22 Jan 24	*U-S.* C. Attlee	23 Jan 24	
			F.S. J. Lawson	23 Jan 24	
1st C. Works	**F. Jowett**	22 Jan 24			

MINISTERS NOT IN CABINET			JUNIOR MINISTERS ATTACHED		
Paym.-Gen.	H. GOSLING	6 May 24			
Pensions	F. ROBERTS	23 Jan 24	*P.S.* J. Muir	28 Jan 24	
Transp.	H. GOSLING	24 Jan 24	*P.S.* (vacant)		
Law Officers:			*P.S. to Treasury:*		
Att.-Gen.	SIR P. HASTINGS	23 Jan 24	B. Spoor	23 Jan 24	
Sol.-Gen.	SIR H. SLESSER	23 Jan 24	*Junior Lds of Treasury:*		
Ld Advoc.	H. MACMILLAN [1]	8 Feb 24	F. Hall	2 Feb 24	
Sol.-Gen.	J. FENTON [1]	18 Feb 24	T. Kennedy	2 Feb 24	
Scotland			J. Robertson	2 Feb 24	
			G. Warne	24 Feb 24	
H.M. Household:			*Lds in Waiting:*		
Treas.	T. GRIFFITHS	2 Feb 24	Earl De La Warr	8 Feb 24	
Comptr.	J. PARKINSON	2 Feb 24	Ld Muir-Mackenzie	8 Feb 24	
V. Chamb.	J. DAVISON	2 Feb 24			

[1] Non-political appointments. Not members of the House of Commons.

CONSERVATIVE GOVERNMENT, 1924–1929

MINISTERS IN CABINET		JUNIOR MINISTERS ATTACHED	
P.M.	**S. Baldwin** 4 Nov 24–4 Jun 29		
Ld Pres.	**Marquess Curzon** 6 Nov 24		
	E of Balfour 27 Apr 25		
Ld Chanc.	**Vt Cave** 6 Nov 24		
	Ld Hailsham (Vt) 28 Mar 28		
Privy S.	**M of Salisbury** 6 Nov 24		
Exch.	**W. Churchill** 6 Nov 24	*Treasury:*	
		F.S. W. Guinness	11 Nov 24
		R. McNeill	5 Nov 25
		(*Ld Cushendun*)	
		A. Samuel	1 Nov 27
For. O.	**(Sir) A. Chamberlain** 6 Nov 24	*U–S.* R. McNeill	11 Nov 24
		G. Locker-Lampson	7 Dec 25
Home O.	**Sir W. Joynson-Hicks** 6 Nov 24	*U–S.* G. Locker-Lampson	11 Nov 24
		D. Hacking	8 Dec 25
		Sir V. Henderson	9 Nov 27
Admir.	**W. Bridgeman** 6 Nov 24	*P. & F.S.:*	
		J. Davidson	11 Nov 24
		C. Headlam	16 Dec 26
		Civil Ld:	
		Earl Stanhope	11 Nov 24
Ag. & Fish.	**E. Wood** 6 Nov 24	*P.S. Ag. & Deputy Min. of Fisheries:*	
	W. Guinness 4 Nov 25	Ld Bledisloe	11 Nov 24
		E of Stradbroke	5 Feb 28
Air	**Sir S. Hoare** 6 Nov 24	*U–S.* Sir P. Sassoon	11 Nov 24
Att.-Gen.	**Sir D. Hogg** (*Ld Hailsham*) 6 Nov 24		
	(*28 Mar 28 Sir T. Inskip & office*		
	not in cabinet)		
Col. O.	**L. Amery** 6 Nov 24	*U–S.* W. Ormsby-Gore	12 Nov 24
Dom. O.	**L. Amery** 11 Jun 25	*U–S.* E of Clarendon	5 Aug 25
		Ld Lovat	5 May 27
		E of Plymouth	1 Jan 29
Bd Educ.	**Ld E. Percy**[1] 6 Nov 24	*P.S.* Duchess of Atholl	11 Nov 24
Health	**N. Chamberlain** 6 Nov 24	*P.S.* Sir K. Wood	11 Nov 24
India O.	**E of Birkenhead** 6 Nov 24	*U–S.* Earl Winterton[1]	11 Nov 24
	Vt Peel 18 Oct 28		
Lab.	**Sir A. Steel-Maitland** 6 Nov 24	*P.S.* H. Betterton	11 Nov 24
D. Lanc.	**Vt Cecil** 10 Nov 24		
	Ld Cushendun 19 Oct 27		
Scot. O.	**Sir J. Gilmour** 6 Nov 24	*U–S.* W. Elliot	26 Jul 26
	(*became Sec. of State for Scotland*	*P.S. Health for Scotland:*	
	15 Jul 26)	W. Elliot	11 Nov 24
		(*post abolished 26 Jul 26*)	
B.o.T.	**Sir P. Lloyd-Greame** 6 Nov 24	*P.S.* Sir B. Chadwick	11 Nov 24
	(*changed name to Sir P. Cunliffe-*	H. Williams	13 Jan 28
	Lister 27 Nov 24)	*P.S. Overseas Trade Dept.:*	
		A. Samuel	11 Nov 24
		D. Hacking	9 Nov 27
		P.S. Mines Dept.:	
		G. Lane-Fox	11 Nov 24
		D. King	13 Jan 28
War O.	**Sir L. Worthington-Evans**	*U–S.* E of Onslow	11 Nov 24
	6 Nov 24	D of Sutherland	2 Dec 28
		F.S. D. King	11 Nov 24
		A. Duff Cooper	13 Jan 28
1st C. Works	**Vt Peel** 10 Nov 24		
	M of Londonderry 18 Oct 28		

---

[1] Not a member of the House of Lords.

CONSERVATIVE GOVERNMENT, 1924–1929 (contd.)

MINISTERS NOT IN CABINET			JUNIOR MINISTERS ATTACHED		
Paym.-Gen.	*(office vacant)*				
	D of Sutherland	28 Jun 25			
	E of Onslow	2 Dec 28			
Pensions	G. Tryon	11 Nov 24	*P.S.*	G. Stanley	11 Nov 24
Postm.-Gen.	Sir W. Mitchell-Thomson		*Ass.*	Vt Wolmer [1]	11 Nov 24
		11 Nov 24			
Transp.	W. Ashley	11 Nov 24	*P.S.*	J. Moore-Brabazon	11 Nov 24
				(post vacant from 14 Jan 27)	
Law Officers:			*P.S. to Treasury:*		
Att.-Gen.	*(office in cabinet)*			B. Eyres-Monsell	7 Nov 24
	Sir T. Inskip	28 Mar 28	*Junior Lds of Treasury:*		
Sol.-Gen.	Sir T. Inskip	11 Nov 24		G. Hennessy	13 Nov 24–10 Dec 25
	Sir F. Merriman	28 Mar 28		Ld Stanley [1]	13 Nov 24–9 Nov 27
Ld Advoc.	W. Watson	11 Nov 24		F. Thomson	13 Nov 24–14 Jan 28
	A. MacRobert	23 Apr 29		(Sir) W. Cope	13 Nov 24–14 Jan 28
Sol.-Gen.	D. Fleming	11 Nov 24		Vt Curzon [1]	13 Nov 24–15 Jan 28
Scotland	A. MacRobert	30 Dec 25		D. Margesson	28 Aug 26–4 Jun 29
	W. Normand	23 Apr 29		G. Bowyer	28 Dec 27–4 Jun 29
				F. Penny	13 Jan 28–4 Jun 29
				M of Titchfield [1]	13 Jan 28–4 Jun 29
				E. Wallace	1 Jan 29–4 Jun 29
H.M. Household:			*Lds in Waiting:*		
Treas.	G. Gibbs	13 Nov 24		Vt Gage	1 Dec 24–4 Jun 29
	Sir G. Hennessy	13 Jan 28		Ld Somers	1 Dec 24–23 Mar 26
Comptr.	Sir H. Barnston	13 Nov 24		E of Lucan	1 Dec 24–1 Jan 29
	Sir W. Cope	13 Jan 28		E of Airlie	1 Apr 26–4 Jun 29
V. Chamb.	D. Hacking	13 Nov 24		Ld Templemore	1 Jan 29–4 Jun 29
	(Sir) G. Hennessy	10 Dec 25			
	(Sir) F. Thomson	13 Jan 28			
Capt. Gents at Arms	E of Clarendon	1 Dec 24			
	E of Plymouth	26 Jun 25			
	E of Lucan	1 Jan 29			
Capt. Yeomen of Guard	Ld Desborough	1 Dec 24			

LABOUR GOVERNMENT, 1929–1931

MINISTERS IN CABINET			JUNIOR MINISTERS ATTACHED		
P.M.	J. R. MacDonald				
	5 Jun 29–24 Aug 31				
Ld Pres.	Ld Parmoor	7 Jun 29			
Ld Chanc.	Ld Sankey	7 Jun 29			
Privy S.	J. Thomas	7 Jun 29			
	V. Hartshorn	5 Jun 30			
	T. Johnston	24 Mar 31			
Exch.	P. Snowden	7 Jun 29	*Treasury:*		
			F.S.	F. Pethick-Lawrence	11 Jun 29
For. O.	A. Henderson	7 Jun 29	*U-S.*	H. Dalton	11 Jun 29
Home O.	J. Clynes	7 Jun 29	*U-S.*	A. Short	11 Jun 29
Admir.	A. Alexander	7 Jun 29	*P. & F.S.:*		
				C. Ammon	11 Jun 29
			Civil Ld:		
				G. Hall	11 Jun 29
Ag. & Fish.	N. Buxton	7 Jun 29	*P.S.*	C. Addison	11 Jun 29
	C. Addison	5 Jun 30		Earl De La Warr	5 Jun 30

[1] Not a member of the House of Lords.

LABOUR GOVERNMENT, 1929–1931 (*contd.*)

	MINISTERS IN CABINET			JUNIOR MINISTERS ATTACHED	
Air	**Ld Thomson**	7 Jun 29	*U.-S.*	F. Montague	11 Jun 29
	Ld Amulree	14 Oct 30			
Col. O.	**Ld Passfield**	7 Jun 29	*U.-S.*	W. Lunn	11 Jun 29
				D. Shiels	1 Dec 29
Dom. O.	**Ld Passfield**	7 Jun 29	*U.-S.*	A. Ponsonby	11 Jun 29
	J. Thomas	5 Jun 30		W. Lunn	1 Dec 29
Bd Educ.	**Sir C. Trevelyan**	7 Jun 29	*P.S.*	M. Jones	11 Jun 29
	H. Lees-Smith	2 Mar 31			
Health	**A. Greenwood**	7 Jun 29	*P.S.*	Miss S. Lawrence	11 Jun 29
India O.	**W. Benn**	7 Jun 29	*U.-S.*	D. Shiels	11 Jun 29
				Earl Russell	1 Dec 29
				Ld Snell	13 Mar 31
Lab.	**Miss M. Bondfield**	7 Jun 29	*P.S.*	J. Lawson	11 Jun 29
Scot. O.	**W. Adamson**	7 Jun 29	*U.-S.*	T. Johnston	7 Jun 29
				J. Westwood	25 Mar 31
B.o.T.	**W. Graham**	7 Jun 29	*P.S.*	W. Smith	11 Jun 29
				P.S. Overseas Trade Dept.:	
				G. Gillett	7 Jul 29
				P.S. Mines Dept.:	
				B. Turner	1 Jun 29
				E. Shinwell	5 Jun 30
Transp.	(*office not in cabinet*)		*P.S.*	Earl Russell	11 Jun 29
	H. Morrison	19 Mar 31		A. Ponsonby (Ld)	1 Dec 29
				J. Parkinson	1 Mar 31
War O.	**T. Shaw**	7 Jun 29	*U.-S.*	Earl De La Warr	11 Jun 29
				Ld Marley	5 Jun 30
			F.S.	E. Shinwell	11 Jun 29
				W. Sanders	5 Jun 30
1st C. Works	**G. Lansbury**	7 Jun 29			

	MINISTERS NOT IN CABINET			JUNIOR MINISTERS ATTACHED	
D. Lanc.	Sir O. Mosley	7 Jun 29			
	C. Attlee	23 May 30			
	Ld Ponsonby	13 Mar 31			
Paym.-Gen.	Ld Arnold	7 Jun 29			
Pensions	F. Roberts	7 Jun 29	*P.S.*	(*post vacant*)	
Postm.-Gen.	H. Lees-Smith	7 Jun 29	*Ass.*	S. Viant	7 Jul 29
	C. Attlee	2 Mar 31			
Transp.	H. Morrison	7 Jun 29		(*for Junior Ministers see above*)	
	(*office in cabinet* 19 Mar 31)				

Law Officers:

P.S. to Treasury:
T. Kennedy — 14 Jun 29

				Junior Lds of Treasury:	
Att.-Gen.	Sir W. Jowitt	7 Jun 29		J. Parkinson	11 Jun 29–13 Mar 31
Sol.-Gen.	Sir J. Melville	7 Jun 29		C. Edwards	11 Jun 29–24 Aug 31
	Sir S. Cripps	22 Oct 30		A. Barnes	11 Jun 29–23 Oct 30
Ld Advoc.	C. Aitchison	17 Jun 29		W. Whiteley	27 Jun 29–24 Aug 31
Sol.-Gen.	J. Watson	17 Jun 29		W. Paling	27 Jun 29–24 Aug 31
Scotland				E. Thurtle	23 Oct 30–24 Aug 31
				H. Charleton	13 Mar 31–24 Aug 31

H.M. Household:

Lds in Waiting:
Earl De La Warr

Treas.	B. Smith	24 Jun 29

18 Jul 29–24 Aug 31

LABOUR GOVERNMENT, 1929–1931 (*contd.*)

MINISTERS NOT IN CABINET			JUNIOR MINISTERS ATTACHED	
H.M. Household:			Ld Muir-Mackenzie	
Comptr.	T. HENDERSON	24 Jun 29		18 Jul 29–22 May 30
V. Chamb.	J. HAYES	24 Jun 29	Ld Marley	17 Jan 30–24 Aug 31

NATIONAL GOVERNMENT, 1931–1935

MINISTERS IN CABINET			JUNIOR MINISTERS ATTACHED		
P.M.	**J. R. MacDonald** (N. Lab) 24 Aug 31–7 Jun 35				
Ld Pres.	**S. Baldwin** (C)	25 Aug 31			
Ld Chanc.	**Ld Sankey (Vt)** (N. Lab)	25 Aug 31			
Privy S.	(*office not in cabinet*)				
	Vt Snowden (N. Lab)	5 Nov 31			
	S. Baldwin (C)	29 Sep 32			
	(*31 Dec 33 A. Eden & office not in cabinet*)				
Exch.	**P. Snowden (Vt)** (N. Lab)		*Treasury:*		
		25 Aug 31	*F.S.*	W. Elliot (C)	3 Sep 31
	N. Chamberlain (C)	5 Nov 31		L. Hore-Belisha (L. Nat)	29 Sep 32
				A. Duff Cooper (C)	29 Jun 34
For. O.	**M of Reading** (Lib)	25 Aug 31	*U-S.*	A. Eden (C)	3 Sep 31
	Sir J. Simon (L. Nat)	5 Nov 31		Earl Stanhope (C)	18 Jan 34
Home O.	**Sir H. Samuel** (Lib)	25 Aug 31	*U-S.*	O. Stanley (C)	3 Sep 31
	Sir J. Gilmour (C)	28 Sep 32		D. Hacking (C)	22 Feb 33
				H. Crookshank (C)	29 Jun 34
Admir.	(*office not in cabinet*)		*P. & F.S.:*		
	Sir B. Eyres-Monsell (C)			Earl Stanhope (C)	3 Sep 31
		5 Nov 31		Ld Stanley[1] (C)	10 Nov 31
			Civil Ld:	(*vacant*)	
				E. Wallace (C)	10 Nov 31
Ag. & Fish.	(*office not in cabinet*)		*P.S.*	(*vacant*)	
	Sir J. Gilmour (C)	5 Nov 31		Earl De La Warr (N. Lab)	10 Nov 31
	W. Elliot (C)	28 Sep 32			
Air	(*office not in cabinet*)		*U-S.*	Sir P. Sassoon (C)	3 Sep 31
	M of Londonderry (C)	5 Nov 31			
Col. O.	**J. Thomas** (N. Lab)	25 Aug 31	*U-S.*	Sir R. Hamilton (Lib)	3 Sep 31
	Sir P. Cunliffe-Lister (C)			E of Plymouth (C)	29 Sep 32
		5 Nov 31			
Dom. O.	**J. Thomas** (N. Lab)	25 Aug 31	*U-S.*	M. MacDonald (N. Lab)	3 Sep 31
Bd Educ.	(*office not in cabinet*)		*P.S.*	Sir K. Wood (C)	3 Sep 31
	Sir D. Maclean (Lib)	5 Nov 31		H. Ramsbotham (C)	10 Nov 31
	Ld Irwin (*Vt Halifax*) (C)				
		15 Jun 32			
Health	**N. Chamberlain** (C)	25 Aug 31	*P.S.*	E. Simon (Lib)	22 Sep 31
	Sir E. Young (C)	5 Nov 31		E. Brown (L. Nat.)	10 Nov 31
				G. Shakespeare (L. Nat)	30 Sep 32
India O.	**Sir S. Hoare** (C)	25 Aug 31	*U-S.*	(*vacant*)	
				M of Lothian (Lib)	10 Nov 31
				R. Butler (C)	29 Sep 32
Lab.	(*office not in cabinet*)		*P.S.*	M. Gray (Lib)	3 Sep 31
	Sir H. Betterton (C)	5 Nov 31		R. Hudson (C)	10 Nov 31
	O. Stanley (C)	29 Jun 34			
Postm.-Gen.	(*office not in cabinet*)		*Ass.*	G. White (Lib)	3 Sep 31
	Sir K. Wood (C)	20 Dec 33		Sir E. Bennett (N. Lab)	21 Oct 32
Scot. O.	(*office not in cabinet*)		*U-S.*	N. Skelton (C)	3 Sep 31
	Sir A. Sinclair (Lib)	5 Nov 31			
	Sir G. Collins (L. Nat)	28 Sep 32			

[1] Not a member of the House of Lords.

NATIONAL GOVERNMENT, 1931–1935 (*contd.*)

MINISTERS IN CABINET		JUNIOR MINISTERS ATTACHED	
B.o.T.	**Sir P. Cunliffe-Lister** (C) 25 Aug 31	*P.S.*	G. Lloyd-George (Lib) 3 Sep 31
	W. Runciman (Ld) (L. Nat.) 5 Nov 31		L. Hore-Belisha (L. Nat) 10 Nov 31
			L. Burgin (L. Nat) 29 Sep 32
		P.S. Overseas Trade Dept.:	
			Sir E. Young (C) 3 Sep 31
			J. Colville (C) 10 Nov 31
		P.S. Mines Dept.:	
			I. Foot (Lib) 3 Sep 31
			E. Brown (L. Nat) 30 Sep 32
War O.	(*office not in cabinet*)	*U-S.*	(*vacant*)
	Vt Hailsham (C) 5 Nov 31		Earl Stanhope (C) 10 Nov 31
			Ld Strathcona & Mount Royal (C) 24 Jan 34
		F.S.	A. Duff Cooper (C) 3 Sep 31
			D. Hacking (C) 29 Jun 34
1st C. Works	(*office not in cabinet*)		
	W. Ormsby-Gore (C) 5 Nov 31		

MINISTERS NOT IN CABINET		JUNIOR MINISTERS ATTACHED	
Admir.	Sir A. Chamberlain (C) 25 Aug 31 (*5 Nov 31 Sir B. Eyres-Monsell & office in cabinet*)		(*for Junior Ministers see above*)
Ag. & Fish.	Sir J. Gilmour (C) 25 Aug 31 (*5 Nov 31 office in cabinet*)		(*for Junior Ministers see above*)
Air	Ld Amulree (N. Lab) 25 Aug 31 (*5 Nov 31 M of Londonderry & office in cabinet*)		(*for Junior Ministers see above*)
Bd Educ.	Sir D. Maclean (Lib) 25 Aug 31 (*5 Nov 31 office in cabinet*)		(*for Junior Ministers see above*)
Lab.	Sir H. Betterton (C) 25 Aug 31 (*5 Nov 31 office in cabinet*)		(*for Junior Ministers see above*)
D. Lanc.	M of Lothian (Lib) 25 Aug 31 (Sir) J. Davidson (C) 10 Nov 31		
Paym.-Gen.	Sir T. Walters (Lib) 4 Sep 31 Ld Rochester (N. Lab) 23 Nov 31		
Pensions	G. Tryon (C) 3 Sep 31	*P.S.*	(*vacant*) C. Headlam (C) 10 Nov 31 (*vacant from 29 Sep 32*)
Postm.-Gen.	W. Ormsby-Gore (C) 3 Sep 31 Sir K. Wood (C) 10 Nov 31 (*20 Dec 33 office in cabinet*)		(*for Junior Ministers see above*)
Privy S.	Earl Peel (C) 3 Sep 31 (*5 Nov 31 Vt Snowden & office in cabinet*) A. Eden (C) 31 Dec 33		
Scot. O.	Sir A. Sinclair (Lib) 25 Aug 31 (*5 Nov 31 office in cabinet*)		(*for Junior Ministers see above*)
Transp.	J. Pybus (L. Nat) 3 Sep 31 O. Stanley (C) 22 Feb 33 L. Hore-Belisha (L. Nat) 29 Jun 34	*P.S.*	(Sir) G. Gillett (N. Lab) 4 Sep 31 E of Plymouth (C) 25 Nov 31 C. Headlam (C) 29 Sep 32 (*5 Jul 34 vacant*) A. Hudson (C) 12 Apr 35
War O.	M of Crewe (Lib) 26 Aug 31 (*5 Nov 31 Vt Hailsham & office in cabinet*)		(*for Junior Ministers see above*)
1st C. Works	M of Londonderry (C) 25 Aug 31 (*5 Nov 31 W. Ormsby-Gore & office in cabinet*)		
Law Officers:		*P.S. to Treasury:*	
Att.-Gen.	Sir W. Jowitt (N. Lab) 3 Sep 31 Sir T. Inskip (C) 26 Jan 32		Sir B. Eyres-Monsell (C) 3 Sep 31 D. Margesson (C) 10 Nov 31

NATIONAL GOVERNMENT, 1931–1935 (contd.)

MINISTERS NOT IN CABINET			JUNIOR MINISTERS ATTACHED	

Sol.-Gen. SIR T. INSKIP (C) — 3 Sep 31
SIR F. MERRIMAN (C) — 26 Jan 32
SIR D. SOMERVELL (C) — 29 Sep 33
Ld Advoc. C. AITCHISON (N. Lab) — 3 Sep 31
W. NORMAND (C) — 2 Oct 33
D. JAMIESON (C) — 28 Mar 35
Sol.-Gen. J. WATSON (N. Lab) — 4 Sep 31
Scotland W. NORMAND (C) — 10 Nov 31
D. JAMIESON (C) — 2 Oct 33
T. COOPER (C) — 15 May 35

Junior Lds of Treasury:
D. Margesson (C) — 26 Aug 31–10 Nov 31
Sir F. Penny (C) 3 Sep 31–12 Nov 31
A. Glassey (Lib) 14 Sep 31–12 Nov 31
M of Titchfield [1] (C) — 3 Sep 31–12 Nov 31
E. Wallace (C) 3 Sep 31–12 Nov 31
(Sir) W. Womersley (C) — 12 Nov 31–7 Jun 35
Sir V. Warrender (C) — 12 Nov 31–30 Sep 32
G. Shakespeare (L. Nat) — 12 Nov 31–30 Sep 32
A. Hudson (C) 12 Nov 31–12 Apr 35
Sir L. Ward (C) 12 Nov 31–1 May 35
G. Davies (C) 11 Oct 32–7 Jun 35
J. Blindell (L. Nat) — 30 Sep 32–7 Jun 35
J. Stuart (C) 1 May 35–7 Jun 35
A. Southby (C) 23 Apr 35–7 Jun 35

H.M. Household:
Treas. SIR G. HENNESSY (C) — 3 Sep 31
SIR F. THOMSON (C) — 12 Nov 31
SIR F. PENNY (C) — 1 May 35
Comptr. G. OWEN (Lib) — 14 Sep 31
W. REA (Lib) — 12 Nov 31
SIR F. PENNY (C) — 30 Sep 32
SIR V. WARRENDER (C) — 1 May 35
V. Chamb. SIR F. THOMSON (C) — 3 Sep 31
SIR F. PENNY (C) — 12 Nov 31
SIR V. WARRENDER (C) — 30 Sep 32
SIR L. WARD (C) — 1 May 35
Capt. Gents at Arms E OF LUCAN (C) — 12 Nov 31
Capt. Yeomen of Guard LD STRATHCONA & MOUNT ROYAL (C) — 12 Nov 31
LD TEMPLEMORE (C) — 24 Jan 34

Lds in Waiting:
Ld Templemore (C) — 12 Nov 31–24 Jan 34
Vt Gage (C) 12 Nov 31–7 Jun 35
Vt Allendale (Lib) — 12 Nov 31–28 Sep 32
E of Munster (C) 24 Jan 34–7 Jun
E of Feversham (C) — 35
24 Jan 34–7 Jun 35

NATIONAL GOVERNMENT, 1935–1940

MINISTERS IN CABINET

P.M. **S. Baldwin** 7 Jun 35–28 May 37
[2] N. Chamberlain 28 May 37–10 May 40

Ld Pres. **J. R. MacDonald** 7 Jun 35
Vt Halifax 28 May 37
Vt Hailsham 9 Mar 38
Vt Runciman 31 Oct 38
Earl Stanhope 3 Sep 39

Ld Chanc. **Vt Hailsham** 7 Jun 35
Ld Maugham 9 Mar 38
Vt Caldecote 3 Sep 39

Privy S. **M of Londonderry** 7 Jun 35
Vt Halifax 22 Nov 35
Earl De La Warr 28 May 37
Sir J. Anderson 31 Oct 38
[2] Sir S. Hoare 3 Sep 39
Sir K. Wood 3 Apr 40

[1] Not a member of the House of Lords.
[2] Denotes member of the War Cabinet. Following the British declaration of war against Germany on 3 Sep 39, all members of the cabinet formally surrendered their portfolios to the P.M.; in the evening of the same day the formation of a war cabinet was announced.

NATIONAL GOVERNMENT, 1935–1940 (contd.)

MINISTERS IN CABINET			JUNIOR MINISTERS ATTACHED		
Exch.	**N. Chamberlain**	7 Jun 35	*Treasury:*		
	[2] Sir J. Simon	28 May 37	*F.S.*	A. Duff Cooper	18 Jun 35
				W. Morrison	22 Nov 35
				J. Colville	29 Oct 36
				E. Wallace	16 May 38
				H. Crookshank	21 Apr 39
For. O.	**Sir S. Hoare**	7 Jun 35	*U-S.*	Earl Stanhope	18 Jun 35–16 Jun 36
	A. Eden	22 Dec 35		Vt Cranborne [1]	6 Aug 35–20 Feb 38
	[2] Vt Halifax	21 Feb 38		*(for League of Nations Affairs)*	
				E of Plymouth	30 Jul 36–May 39
				R. Butler	25 Feb 38–10 May 40
Home O.	**Sir J. Simon**	7 Jun 35	*U-S.*	E. Wallace	18 Jun 35
	Sir S. Hoare	28 May 37		G. Lloyd	28 Nov 35
	Sir J. Anderson	3 Sep 39		O. Peake	21 Apr 39
			P.S. Min. Home Security:		
				A. Lennox-Boyd	6 Sep 39
				W. Mabane	24 Oct 39
Admir.	**Sir B. Eyres-Monsell**	7 Jun 35	*P. & F.S.:*		
	(Vt Monsell)			Sir V. Warrender	18 Jun 35
	Sir S. Hoare	5 Jun 36		Ld Stanley [1]	28 Nov 35
	A. Duff Cooper	28 May 37		G. Shakespeare	28 May 37
	Earl Stanhope	27 Oct 38		Sir V. Warrender	3 Apr 40
	[2] W. Churchill	3 Sep 39	*Civil Ld:*		
				K. Lindsay	18 Jun 35
				J. Llewellin	28 May 37
				A. Hudson	14 Jul 39
Ag. & Fish.	**W. Elliot**	7 Jun 35	*P.S.*	Earl De La Warr	18 Jun 35
	W. Morrison	29 Oct 36		H. Ramsbotham	28 Nov 35
	Sir R. Dorman-Smith	29 Jan 39		E of Feversham	30 Jul 36
				Ld Denham	19 Sep 39
Air	**Sir P. Cunliffe-Lister**		*U-S.*	Sir P. Sassoon	18 Jun 35
	(Vt Swinton)	7 Jun 35		A. Muirhead	28 May 37
	[2] Sir K. Wood	16 May 38		H. Balfour	16 May 38
	Sir S. Hoare	3 Apr 40			
Col. O.	**M. MacDonald**	7 Jun 35	*U-S.*	E of Plymouth	18 Jun 35
	J. Thomas	22 Nov 35		Earl De La Warr	30 Jul 36
	W. Ormsby-Gore	28 May 36		M of Dufferin & Ava	28 May 37
	M. MacDonald	16 May 38			
Min. for Co-ordina-tion of Defence	*(office not established)*				
	Sir T. Inskip	13 Mar 36			
	[2] Ld Chatfield	29 Jan 39			
	(office abolished 3 Apr 40)				
Dom. O.	**J. Thomas**	7 Jun 35	*U-S.*	Ld Stanley [1]	18 Jun 35
	M. MacDonald	22 Nov 35		D. Hacking	28 Nov 35
	Ld Stanley [1]	16 May 38		M of Hartington [1]	4 Mar 36
	M. MacDonald	31 Oct 38		*(D of Devonshire)*	
	Sir T. Inskip	29 Jan 39			
	(Vt Caldecote)				
	A. Eden	3 Sep 39			
Bd Educ.	**O. Stanley**	7 Jun 35	*P.S.*	H. Ramsbotham	18 Jun 35
	Earl Stanhope	28 May 37		Earl De La Warr	28 Nov 35
	Earl De La Warr	27 Oct 38		G. Shakespeare	30 Jul 36
	H. Ramsbotham	3 Apr 40		K. Lindsay	28 May 37
Food	*(combined with D. Lanc. 4 Sep 39)*		*P.S.*	A. Lennox-Boyd	11 Oct 39
	Ld Woolton	3 Apr 40			
Health	**Sir K. Wood**	7 Jun 35	*P.S.*	G. Shakespeare	18 Jun 35
	W. Elliot	16 May 38		R. Hudson	30 Jul 36
				R. Bernays	28 May 37
				Miss F. Horsbrugh	14 Jul 39

[1] Not a member of the House of Lords.
[2] Denotes member of the War Cabinet. Following the British declaration of war against Germany on 3 Sep 39, all members of the cabinet formally surrendered their portfolios to the P.M.; in the evening of the same day the formation of a war cabinet was announced.

NATIONAL GOVERNMENT, 1935–1940 (contd.)

	MINISTERS IN CABINET			JUNIOR MINISTERS ATTACHED	
India O. (& Burma O. 1937–)	M of Zetland	7 Jun 35	U-S.	R. Butler	18 Jun 35
				Ld Stanley [1]	28 May 37
				A. Muirhead	16 May 38
				Sir H. O'Neill	11 Sep 39
Information	(office not established)		P.S.	Sir E. Grigg	19 Sep 39
	Ld Macmillan	4 Sep 39		(office vacant 3 Apr 40)	
	Sir J. Reith	5 Jan 40			
Lab.	E. Brown	7 Jun 35	P.S.	A. Muirhead	18 Jun 35
	(3 Sep 39 Lab. & Nat S.)			R. Butler	28 May 37
				A. Lennox-Boyd	25 Feb 38
				R. Assheton	6 Sep 39
D. Lanc.	(office not in cabinet)				
	Earl Winterton [1]	11 Mar 38			
	W. Morrison	29 Jan 39			
	(4 Sep 39–3 Apr 40 combined with Min. of Food)				
	G. Tryon	3 Apr 40			
Min. without Portfolio for League of Nations Affairs	A. Eden	7 Jun 35–22 Dec 35			
Min. without Portfolio	Ld E. Percy [1]	7 Jun 35–31 Mar 36			
	L. Burgin	21 Apr 39–14 Jul 39			
	[2] Ld Hankey	3 Sep 39–10 May 40			
Scot. O.	Sir G. Collins	7 Jun 35	U-S.	N. Skelton	18 Jun 35
	W. Elliot	29 Oct 36		J. Colville	28 Nov 35
	J. Colville	16 May 38		H. Wedderburn	29 Oct 36
				J. McEwen	6 Sep 39
Shipping	(office not established)		P.S.	Sir A. Salter	13 Nov 39
	Sir J. Gilmour	13 Oct 39			
	R. Hudson	3 Apr 40			
Supply	(office not established)		P.S.	J. Llewellin	14 Jul 39
	L. Burgin	14 Jul 39			
B.o.T.	Ld Runciman (Vt)	7 Jun 35	P.S.	L. Burgin	18 Jun 35
	O. Stanley	28 May 37		E. Wallace	28 May 37
	Sir A. Duncan	5 Jan 40		R. Cross	16 May 38
				G. Lloyd-George	6 Sep 39
			P.S. Overseas Trade Dept.:		
				J. Colville	18 Jun 35
				E. Wallace	28 Nov 35
				R. Hudson	28 May 37
				G. Shakespeare	3 Apr 40
			P.S. Mines Dept.:		
				H. Crookshank	18 Jun 35
				G. Lloyd	21 Apr 39
Transp.	(office not in cabinet)		P.S.	A. Hudson	18 Jun 35
	L. Hore-Belisha	29 Oct 36		R. Bernays	14 Jul 39
	L. Burgin	28 May 37			
	E. Wallace	21 Apr 39			
War O.	Vt Halifax	7 Jun 35	U-S.	Ld Strathcona & Mount Royal	
	A. Duff Cooper	22 Nov 35			18 Jun 35
	[2] L. Hore-Belisha	28 May 37		E of Munster	29 Jan 39
	O. Stanley	5 Jan 40		Vt Cobham	19 Sep 39
			F.S.	D. Hacking	18 Jun 35
				Sir V. Warrender	28 Nov 35
				Sir E. Grigg	3 Apr 40

[1] Not a member of the House of Lords.
[2] Denotes member of the War Cabinet. Following the British declaration of war against Germany on 3 Sep 39, all members of the cabinet formally surrendered their portfolios to the P.M.; in the evening of the same day the formation of a war cabinet was announced.

NATIONAL GOVERNMENT, 1935–1940 *(contd.)*

MINISTERS IN CABINET		JUNIOR MINISTERS ATTACHED

1st *C. Works* **W. Ormsby-Gore**   7 Jun 35
                    Earl Stanhope   16 Jun 36
                    (28 *May* 37 *Sir P. Sassoon &*
                    office out of cabinet)

MINISTERS NOT IN CABINET

Econ. Warfare	R. CROSS	3 Sep 39		
D. Lanc.	SIR J. DAVIDSON	18 Jun 35		
	EARL WINTERTON [1]	28 May 37		
	(*office in cabinet* 11 *Mar* 38)			
Paym.-Gen.	LD ROCHESTER	18 Jun 35		
	LD HUTCHISON	6 Dec 35		
	E OF MUNSTER	2 Jun 38		
	EARL WINTERTON [1]	29 Jan 39		
	(*office vacant from Nov* 39)			
Pensions	R. HUDSON	18 Jun 35		
	H. RAMSBOTHAM	30 Jul 36		
	SIR W. WOMERSLEY	7 Jun 39		
Postm.-Gen.	G. TRYON	7 Jun 35	*Ass.*	Sir E. Bennett 18 Jun 35
	W. MORRISON	3 Apr 40		Sir W. Womersley 6 Dec 35
				W. Mabane 7 Jun 39
				C. Waterhouse 24 Oct 39
Transp.	L. HORE-BELISHA	18 Jun 35		
	(*office in cabinet* 29 *Oct* 36)			
1st *C. Works*	(*office in cabinet*)			
	SIR P. SASSOON	28 May 37		
	H. RAMSBOTHAM	7 Jun 39		
	EARL DE LA WARR	3 Apr 40		

Law Officers:

Att.-Gen.	SIR T. INSKIP	18 Jun 35	
	SIR D. SOMERVELL	18 Mar 36	
Sol.-Gen.	SIR D. SOMERVELL	18 Jun 35	
	SIR T. O'CONNOR	19 Mar 36	
Ld Advoc.	D. JAMIESON	18 Jun 35	
	T. COOPER	25 Oct 35	
Sol.-Gen. Scotland	T. COOPER	18 Jun 35	
	A. RUSSELL	29 Nov 35	
	J. REID	25 Jun 36	

P.S. to Treasury:
D. Margesson   18 Jun 35
Junior Lds of Treasury:
J. Stuart   18 Jun 35–10 May 40
(Sir) A Southby
                    18 Jun 35–28 May 37
Sir W. Womersley
                    18 Jun 35–6 Dec 35
G. Davies   18 Jun 35–6 Dec 35
(Sir) J. Blindell
                    18 Jun 35–28 May 37
A. Hope   6 Dec 35–28 May 37
(Sir) H. Morris-Jones
                    6 Dec 35–28 May 37
C. Kerr   28 May 37–4 Apr 39
T. Dugdale   28 May 37–12 Feb 40
C. Waterhouse
                    28 May 37–18 Oct 37
R. Cross   28 May 37–18 Oct 37
P. Munro   18 Oct 37–10 May 40
R. Grimston   18 Oct 37–18 May 38
S. Furness   20 May 38–10 May 40
Sir J. Edmondson
                    4 Apr 39–13 Nov 39
P. Buchan-Hepburn
                    13 Nov 39–10 May 40
W. Boulton   12 Feb 40–10 May 40

[1] Not a member of the House of Lords.

NATIONAL GOVERNMENT, 1935–1940 (contd.)

MINISTERS NOT IN CABINET			JUNIOR MINISTERS ATTACHED	
H.M. Household:			*Lds in Waiting:*	
Treas.	SIR F. PENNY	18 Jun 35	Vt Gage	18 Jun 35–11 Apr 39
	SIR L. WARD	28 May 37	E of Munster	18 Jun 35–2 Jun 38
	A. HOPE	18 Oct 37	E of Feversham	18 Jun 35–30 Jul 36
	C. WATERHOUSE	4 Apr 39	M of Dufferin & Ava	
	R. GRIMSTON	12 Nov 39		29 Oct 36–28 May 37
Comptr.	SIR G. BOWYER	21 Jun 35	E of Erne	29 Oct 36–25 Jul 39
	SIR L. WARD	6 Dec 35	Earl Fortescue	
	SIR G. DAVIES	28 May 37		26 Aug 37–10 May 40
	C. WATERHOUSE	18 Oct 37	E of Birkenhead	
	C. KERR	4 Apr 39		12 Jul 38–10 May 40
V. Chamb.	SIR L. WARD	18 Jun 35	Vt Bridport	11 Apr 39–10 May 40
	(SIR) G. DAVIES	6 Dec 35	Ld Ebury	25 Jul 39–10 May 40
	A. HOPE	28 May 37		
	R. CROSS	18 Oct 37		
	R. GRIMSTON	18 May 38		
	SIR J. EDMONDSON	12 Nov 39		
Capt. Gents at Arms	E OF LUCAN	18 Jun 35		
Capt. Yeomen of Guard	LD TEMPLEMORE	18 Jun 35		

COALITION GOVERNMENT, 1940–1945

MINISTERS IN WAR CABINET			JUNIOR MINISTERS ATTACHED	
P.M.	**W. Churchill** (C)			
		10 May 40–23 May 45		
Ld Pres.	**N. Chamberlain** (C)	11 May 40		
	Sir J. Anderson (Nat)	3 Oct 40		
	C. Attlee (Lab)	24 Sep 43		
Ld Chanc.	(*office not in war cabinet*)			
Privy S.	**C. Attlee** (Lab)	11 May 40		
	Sir S. Cripps (Lab)	19 Feb 42		
	(*Vt Cranborne 22 Nov 42 & office not in war cabinet*)			
Exch.	(*office not in war cabinet*)		*Treasury:*	
	Sir K. Wood (C)	3 Oct 40	*F.S.* H. Crookshank (C)	15 May 40
	(*19 Feb 42 office not in war cabinet*)		R. Assheton (C)	7 Feb 43
	Sir J. Anderson (Nat)	24 Sep 43	O. Peake (C)	29 Oct 44
For. O.	**Vt Halifax** (C)	11 May 40	*Min. of State:*	
	A. Eden (C)	22 Dec 40	R. LAW (C)	24 Sep 43
Min. of State	**Ld Beaverbrook** (C)	1 May 41	*U–S.* R. Butler (C)	15 May 40
	O. Lyttelton (C)	29 Jun 41	R. Law (C)	20 Jul 41
	(*became Min. of Production*) 12 Mar 42 & remained in war cabinet)		G. Hall (Lab)	25 Sep 43
Home O. & Home Security	(*office not in war cabinet*)		*U–S.* O. Peake (C)	15 May 40
	H. Morrison (Lab)	22 Nov 42	E of Munster (C)	31 Oct 44
			P.S. Home Security:	
			W. Mabane (L. Nat)	
				15 May 40–3 Jun 42
			Miss E. Wilkinson (Lab)	
				8 Oct 40–23 May 45
Aircraft Production	(*office not in war cabinet*)		(*for Junior Ministers see below*)	
	Ld Beaverbrook (C)	2 Aug 40		
	(*J. Moore-Brabazon* 1 May 41 & office not in war cabinet*)			
Def.	**W. Churchill (P.M.)** (C)			
		10 May 40		

COALITION GOVERNMENT, 1940–1945 (*contd.*)

MINISTERS IN WAR CABINET		JUNIOR MINISTERS ATTACHED

Dom. O. (*office not in war cabinet*)
C. Attlee (Lab) 19 Feb 42
(*Vt Cranborne 24 Sep 43 & office not in war cabinet*)

(*for Junior Ministers see below*)

Lab. & (*office not in war cabinet*)
Nat. S. **E. Bevin** (Lab) 3 Oct 40

P.S. R. Assheton (C) 15 May 40–4 Feb 42
G. Tomlinson (Lab)
8 Feb 41–23 May 45
M. McCorquodale (C)
4 Feb 42–23 May 45

Min. resident in **O. Lyttelton** (C) 19 Feb 42
Mid. East **R. Casey**[1] 19 Mar 42
(*office not in war cabinet 23 Dec 43*)

Deputy Min. of State:
Ld Moyne (C) 27 Aug 42–28 Jan 44

Min. without Portfolio **A. Greenwood** (Lab)
11 May 40–22 Feb 42
(*Sir W. Jowitt appointed 30 Dec 42 not in war cabinet*)

Reconstruction (*office not established*)
Ld Woolton (C) 11 Nov 43

Supply (*office not in war cabinet*)
Ld Beaverbrook (C) 29 Jun 41
(*Sir A. Duncan & office not in war cabinet 4 Feb 42*)

(*for Junior Ministers see below*)

(War) Production (*office not established*)
Ld Beaverbrook (C) 4 Feb 42
(*office vacant 19 Feb 42*)
O. Lyttelton (C) 12 Mar 42
(*Minister of Production*)

P.S. G. Garro-Jones (Lab) 10 Sep 42

MINISTERS NOT IN WAR CABINET		JUNIOR MINISTERS ATTACHED

Admir. A. ALEXANDER (Lab) 11 May 40

P. & F.S.:
Sir V. Warrender (C) 17 May 40
(*Ld Bruntisfield*)
Civil Ld:
A. Hudson (C) 15 May 40
R. Pilkington (C) 4 Mar 42
F.S. G. Hall (Lab) 4 Feb 42
J. Thomas (C) 25 Sep 43

Ag. & Fish. R. HUDSON (C) 14 May 40

P.S. Ld Moyne (C) 15 May 40–8 Feb 41
T. Williams (Lab)
15 May 40–23 May 45
D of Norfolk (C)
8 Feb 41–23 May 45

Air SIR A. SINCLAIR (Lib) 11 May 40

P.S. H. Balfour (C) 15 May 40–21 Nov 44
Ld Sherwood (Lib)
20 Jul 41–23 May 45
R. Brabner (C) 21 Nov 44–27 Mar 45
Q. Hogg (C) 12 Apr 45–23 May 45

Aircraft Production LD BEAVERBROOK (C) 14 May 40
(*office in war cabinet 2 Aug 40*)
J. MOORE-BRABAZON (C) 1 May 41
J. LLEWELLIN (C) 22 Feb 42
SIR S. CRIPPS (Lab) 22 Nov 42

P.S. J. Llewellin (C) 15 May 40
F. Montague (Lab) 1 May 41
B. Smith (Lab) 4 Mar 42
A. Lennox-Boyd (C) 11 Nov 43

Civil Av. (*office not established*)
VT SWINTON (C) 8 Oct 44

P.S. R. Perkins (C) 22 Mar 45

Col. O. LD LLOYD (C) 12 May 40
LD MOYNE (C) 8 Feb 41
VT CRANBORNE (C) 22 Feb 42
O. STANLEY (C) 22 Nov 42

U-S. G. Hall (Lab) 15 May 40
H. Macmillan (C) 4 Feb 42
D of Devonshire (C) 1 Jan 43

---

[1] Not a member of the House of Commons.

COALITION GOVERNMENT, 1940–1945 (contd.)

MINISTERS NOT IN WAR CABINET			JUNIOR MINISTERS ATTACHED		
Dom. O.	Vt Caldecote (C)	14 May 40	U-S.	G. Shakespeare (L. Nat)	15 May 40
	Vt Cranborne [1] (C)	3 Oct 40		P. Emrys-Evans (C)	4 Mar 42
	(C. Attlee 19 Feb 42 & office in war cabinet)				
	Vt Cranborne (C)	24 Sep 43			
Economic Warfare	H. Dalton (Lab)	15 May 40	P.S.	D. Foot (Lib)	17 May 40
	Vt Wolmer [1]	22 Feb 42			
	(E of Selborne)				
Bd Educ.	H. Ramsbotham (C)	14 May 40	P.S.	C. Ede (Lab)	15 May 40
	R. Butler (C)	20 Jul 41			
	(3 Aug 44 becomes Min. of Educ.)				
Exch.	Sir K. Wood (C)	12 May 40		(for Financial Secretary to Treasury see above)	
	(3 Oct 40 office in war cabinet, 19 Feb 42 out of war cabinet again)				
	(24 Sep 43 Sir J. Anderson & office in war cabinet)				
Food	Ld Woolton (C)	13 May 40	P.S.	R. Boothby (C)	15 May 40
	J. Llewellin (C)	11 Nov 43		G. Lloyd-George (Ind. L)	22 Oct 40
				W. Mabane (L. Nat)	3 Jun 42
Fuel, Light & Power	(office not established)		P.S.	G. Lloyd (C) 3 Jun 42–23 May 45	
	G. Lloyd-George (Ind L.)			T. Smith (Lab) 3 Jun 42–23 May 45	
		3 Jun 42			
Health	M. MacDonald (N. Lab)	13 May 40	P.S.	Miss F. Horsbrugh (C)	15 May 40
	E. Brown (L. Nat)	8 Feb 41			
	H. Willink (C)	11 Nov 43			
Home O. & Home Security	Sir J. Anderson (Nat)	12 May 40		(for Junior Ministers see above)	
	H. Morrison (Lab)	3 Oct 40			
	(22 Nov 42 office in war cabinet)				
India & Burma O.	L. Amery (C)	13 May 40	P.S.	D of Devonshire (C)	17 May 40
				E of Munster (C)	1 Jan 43
				E of Listowel (Lab)	31 Oct 44
Information	A. Duff Cooper (C)	12 May 40	P.S.	H. Nicolson (N. Lab)	17 May 40
	(attended war cabinet from 28 May 40)			E. Thurtle (Lab)	20 Jul 41
	B. Bracken (C)	20 Jul 41			
Lab. & Nat. S.	E. Bevin (Lab)	13 May 40		(for Junior Ministers see above)	
	(office in war cabinet 3 Oct 40)				
D. Lanc.	Ld Hankey (Ind)	14 May 40			
	A. Duff Cooper (C)	20 Jul 41			
	E. Brown (L. Nat)	11 Nov 43			
Ld Chanc.	Vt Simon (L. Nat)	12 May 40			
Min. resident at Allied H.Q. in N.W. Africa	H. Macmillan (C)	30 Dec 42			
Min. resident in Washington for Supply	J. Llewellin (C)	22 Nov 42			
	B. Smith (Lab)	11 Nov 43			
Min. resident in W. Africa	Vt Swinton (C)	8 Jun 42			
	H. Balfour (C)	21 Nov 44			
Min. of State in Mid. East	(office in war cabinet)			(for Junior Ministers see above)	
	Ld Moyne (C)	28 Jan 44			
	Sir E. Grigg (C)	21 Nov 44			

[1] Not a member of the House of Lords. Viscount Wolmer was moved to the House of Lords by writ of acceleration in October 1940. The same was done for Viscount Cranborne in January 1941.

COALITION GOVERNMENT, 1940–1945 (contd.)

MINISTERS NOT IN WAR CABINET	JUNIOR MINISTERS ATTACHED

Paym.-Gen. Vt CRANBORNE [1] (C)   15 May 40
  (*office vacant* 3 Oct 40)
  Ld HANKEY (Ind)   20 Jul 41
  Sir W. JOWITT (Lab)   4 Mar 42
  Ld CHERWELL (C)   30 Dec 42

Pensions Sir W. WOMERSLEY (C) 15 May 40
  P.S. Miss E. Wilkinson (Lab) 17 May 40
    Ld Tryon (C)   8 Oct 40
    W. Paling (Lab)   8 Feb 41

Min.   (*in war cabinet*
without   11 *May* 40–22 *Feb* 42)
Portfolio Sir W. JOWITT (Lab)
              30 Dec 42–8 Oct 44

Postm.-Gen. W. MORRISON (C)   15 May 40
  H. CROOKSHANK (C)   30 Dec 42
  Ass. C. Waterhouse (C)   17 May 40
    A. Chapman (C)   1 Mar 41
    R. Grimston (C)   4 Mar 42

Privy S.   (*office in war cabinet*)
  Vt CRANBORNE (C)   22 Nov 42
  Ld BEAVERBROOK (C)   24 Sep 43

Scot. O. E. BROWN (L. Nat)   14 May 40
  T. JOHNSTON (Lab)   8 Feb 41
  P.S. J. Westwood (Lab)
                17 May 40–23 May 45
    H. Wedderburn (C)
                8 Feb 41–4 Mar 42
    A. Chapman (C) 4 Mar 42–23 May 45

Shipping R. CROSS (C)   14 May 40
  (1 *May* 41 *combined with Min. of*
  Transport, as Min. of War Transport
  see below)
  P.S. Sir A. Salter (Ind) 15 May 40

Soc. Insur.   (*office not established*)
  Sir W. JOWITT (Lab)   8 Oct 44
  (*renamed National Insurance*
  17 *Nov* 44)
  P.S. C. Peat (C)   22 Mar 45

Supply H. MORRISON (Lab)   12 May 40
  Sir A. DUNCAN (C)   3 Oct 40
  (*Ld Beaverbrook* 29 *Jun* 41 &
  office in war cabinet)
  Sir A. DUNCAN (C)   4 Feb 42
  P.S. H. Macmillan (C)
                15 May 40–4 Feb 42
    Ld Portal (C)   4 Sep 40–4 Mar 42
    R. Assheton (C) 4 Feb 42–30 Dec 42
    C. Peat (C)   4 Mar 42–22 Mar 45
    D. Sandys (C) 30 Dec 42–21 Nov 44
    J. Wilmot (Lab)
                21 Nov 44–23 May 45
    J. de Rothschild (Lib)
                22 Mar 45–23 May 45

T. & C.   (*office not established*)
Planning W. MORRISON (C)   30 Dec 42
  (*Minister designate until* 5 *Feb* 43)
  P.S. H. Strauss (C)   30 Dec 42
    A. Jenkins (Lab)   22 Mar 45

B.o.T. Sir A. DUNCAN (C)   12 May 40
  O. LYTTELTON (C)   3 Oct 40
  Sir A. DUNCAN (C)   29 Jun 41
  J. LLEWELLIN (C)   4 Feb 42
  H. DALTON (Lab)   22 Feb 42
  P.S. G. Lloyd-George (Ind L.) 15 May 40
        (& *P.S. Food* 22 Oct 40)
    C. Waterhouse (C)   8 Feb 41
  Sec. Bd Overseas Trade:
    H. Johnstone (Lib)   15 May 40
    S. Summers (C)   22 Mar 45
  Mines Dept.:
    D. Grenfell (Lab)   15 May 40
  Sec. Petrol Dept.:
    G. Lloyd (C)   15 May 40–3 Jun 42
    (3 *Jun* 42 *combined in Min. of Fuel,*
        Light & Power)

Transp. Sir J. REITH (Nat)   14 May 40
  J. MOORE-BRABAZON (C)   3 Oct 40
  (1 *May* 41 *became Min. of War*
  Transport, see below)
  (*for Junior Ministers see below, under*
        War Transport)

---

[1] Not a member of the House of Lords.

COALITION GOVERNMENT, 1940–1945 *(contd.)*

MINISTERS NOT IN WAR CABINET			JUNIOR MINISTERS ATTACHED		
War O.	A. EDEN (C)	11 May 40	*U-S.*	Sir H. Page Croft (C)	
	D. MARGESSON (C)	22 Dec 40		*(Ld Croft)* 17 May 40–23 May 45	
	SIR J. GRIGG (Nat)	22 Feb 42		Sir E. Grigg (C)	
				17 May 40–4 Mar 42	
				A. Henderson (Lab)	
				4 Mar 42–30 Dec 42	
			F.S.	R. Law (C)	17 May 40
				D. Sandys (C)	20 Jul 41
				A. Henderson (Lab)	7 Feb 43
War	LD LEATHERS (C)	1 May 41	*P.S.*	F. Montague (Lab)	
Transp.				18 May 40–1 May 41	
				(renamed War Transport 1 May 41)	
				J. Llewellin (C) 1 May 41–4 Feb 42	
				Sir A. Salter (Ind)	
				29 Jun 41–4 Feb 42	
				P. Noel-Baker (Lab)	
				4 Feb 42–23 May 45	
1st.C.Works	LD TRYON (C)	18 May 40	*P.S.*	G. Hicks (Lab) 19 Nov 40–23 May 45	
	SIR J. REITH (LD) (Nat)	3 Oct 40		H. Strauss (C) 4 Mar 42–30 Dec 42	
	(Min. of Works & Buildings &				
	1st C. Works 3 Oct 40)				
	LD PORTAL (C)	22 Feb 42			
	(Min. of Works and Planning 11 Feb				
	42. Min. of Works Feb 43)				
	D. SANDYS (C)	21 Nov 44			
Law Officers:			*P.S. to Treasury:*		
Att.-Gen.	SIR D. SOMERVELL (C)	15 May 40		D. Margesson (C)	
Sol.-Gen.	SIR W. JOWITT (Lab)	15 May 40		17 May 40–22 Dec 40	
	SIR D. MAXWELL FYFE (C)	4 Mar 42		Sir C. Edwards (Lab)	
Ld Advoc.	T. COOPER (C)	15 May 40		17 May 40–12 Mar 42	
	J. REID (C)	5 Jun 41		J. Stuart (C) 14 Jan 41–23 May 45	
Sol.-Gen.	J. REID (C)	15 May 40		W. Whiteley (Lab)	
Scotland	(SIR) D. MURRAY (C)	5 Jun 41		12 Mar 42–23 May 45	
			Junior Lds of Treasury:		
				S. Furness (L. Nat)	
				12 May 40–18 May 40	
				J. Stuart (C) 12 May 40–14 Jan 41	
				P. Munro (C) 12 May 40–13 Mar 42	
				P. Buchan-Hepburn (C)	
				12 May 40–26 Jun 40	
				W. Boulton (C) 12 May 40–13 Mar 42	
				W. Paling (Lab) 18 May 40–8 Feb 41	
				J. Thomas (C) 26 Jun 40–25 Sep 43	
				T. Dugdale (C) 8 Feb 41–23 Feb 42	
				W. Adamson (Lab)	
				1 Mar 41–2 Oct 44	
				A. Young (C) 23 Feb 42–3 Jul 44	
				J. McEwen (C) 13 Mar 42–6 Dec 44	
				L. Pym (C) 13 Mar 42–23 May 45	
				A. Beechman (L. Nat)	
				25 Sep 43–23 May 45	
				C. Drewe (C) 3 Jul 44–23 May 45	
				W. John (Lab) 2 Oct 44–23 May 45	
				P. Buchan-Hepburn (C)	
				6 Dec 44–23 May 45	
H.M. Household:			*Lds in Waiting:*		
Treas.	R. GRIMSTON (C)	17 May 40		Earl Fortescue (C)	
	SIR J. EDMONDSON (C)	12 Mar 42		31 May 40–22 Mar 45	
Comptr.	W. WHITELEY (Lab)	17 May 40		Vt Clifden (Lib) 31 May 40–23 May 45	
	W. JOHN (Lab)	12 Mar 42		Ld Alness (L. Nat)	
	G. MATHERS (Lab)	2 Oct 44		31 May 40–23 May 45	
				M of Normanby (C)	
				22 Mar 45–23 May 45	

COALITION GOVERNMENT, 1940–1945 (*contd.*)

MINISTERS NOT IN WAR CABINET	JUNIOR MINISTERS ATTACHED

V. Chamb.   Sir J. Edmondson (C)   17 May 40
           W. Boulton (C)   12 Mar 42
           A. Young (C)   13 Jul 44

Capt. Gents   Ld Snell (Lab)
at Arms   31 May 40–21 Apr 44
           Earl Fortescue (C)   22 Mar 45

Capt.   Ld Templemore (C)   31 May 40
Yeomen of
Guard

CARETAKER GOVERNMENT, 1945

MINISTERS IN CABINET	JUNIOR MINISTERS ATTACHED

P.M.   **W. Churchill** 23 May 45–26 Jul 45

Ld Pres.   **Ld Woolton**   25 May 45

Ld Chanc.   (*office not in cabinet*)

Privy S.   **Ld Beaverbrook**   25 May 45

Exch.   **Sir J. Anderson**   25 May 45   *Treasury:*
                                        F.S.   O. Peake   26 May 45

For. O.   **A. Eden**   25 May 45   *Min. of State:*
                                        W. Mabane   25 May 45
                                  U-S.   Ld Dunglass [1]   26 May 45
                                        Ld Lovat   26 May 45

Home O.   **Sir D. Somervell**   25 May 45   *U-S.*   E of Munster   26 May 45

Admir.   **B. Bracken**   25 May 45   *P. & F.S.:*
                                        Ld Bruntisfield   26 May 45
                                  Civil Ld:
                                        R. Pilkington   26 May 45
                                    F.S.   J. Thomas   26 May 45

Ag. & Fish.   **R. Hudson**   25 May 45   *P.S.*   D of Norfolk   26 May 45
                                        D. Scott   26 May 45

Air   **H. Macmillan**   25 May 45   *U-S.*   Q. Hogg   26 May 45
                                        Earl Beatty   26 May 45

Col. O.   **O. Stanley**   25 May 45   *U-S.*   D of Devonshire   26 May 45

Def.   **W. Churchill (P.M.)**   25 May 45

Dom. O.   **Vt Cranborne**   25 May 45   *U-S.*   P. Emrys-Evans   26 May 45

India &   **L. Amery**   25 May 45   *P.S.*   E of Scarbrough   26 May 45
Burma O.

Lab. &   **R. Butler**   25 May 45   *P.S.*   M. McCorquodale   26 May 45
Nat. S.

Production   **O. Lyttelton**   25 May 45   *P.S.*   J. Maclay   28 May 45
             (*& Pres. B.o.T.*)

Scot. O.   **E of Rosebery**   25 May 45   *P.S.*   A. Chapman   26 May 45
                                        T. Galbraith   26 May 45

B.o.T.   **O. Lyttelton**   25 May 45   *P.S.*   C. Waterhouse   26 May 45
         (*& Min. of Production*)   *Sec. Bd Overseas Trade:*
                                        S. Summers   26 May 45

War O.   **Sir J. Grigg**   25 May 45   *U-S.*   Ld Croft   26 May 45
                                       F.S.   M. Petherick   26 May 45

MINISTERS NOT IN CABINET	JUNIOR MINISTERS ATTACHED

Aircraft   E. Brown   25 May 45   *P.S.*   A. Lennox-Boyd   26 May 45
Production

---

[1] Not a member of the House of Lords.

CARETAKER GOVERNMENT, 1945 (*contd.*)

MINISTERS NOT IN CABINET			JUNIOR MINISTERS ATTACHED		
Civil Av.	Vt Swinton	25 May 45	*P.S.*	R. Perkins	26 May 45
Educ.	R. Law	25 May 45	*P.S.*	Mrs T. Cazalet-Keir	26 May 45
Food	J. Llewellin	25 May 45	*P.S.*	Miss F. Horsbrugh	26 May 45
Fuel & P.	G. Lloyd-George	25 May 45	*P.S.*	Sir A. Hudson	26 May 45
Health	H. Willink	25 May 45	*P.S.*	H. Kerr	26 May 45
Information	G. Lloyd	25 May 45			
D. Lanc.	Sir A. Salter	25 May 45			
Ld Chanc.	Vt Simon	25 May 45			
Min. resident in Mid. East	Sir E. Grigg	25 May 45			
Min. resident in W. Africa	H. Balfour	25 May 45			
Nat. Ins.	L. Hore-Belisha	25 May 45	*P.S.*	C. Peat	26 May 45
Paym.-Gen.	Ld Cherwell	25 May 45			
Pensions	Sir W. Womersley	25 May 45	*P.S.*	W. Sidney (Ld De L'Isle)	26 May 45
Postm.-Gen.	H. Crookshank	25 May 45	*Ass.*	W. Anstruther-Gray	26 May 45
Supply	Sir A. Duncan	25 May 45	*P.S.*	R. Grimston	26 May 45
T. & C. Planning	W. Morrison	25 May 45	*P.S.*	R. Tree	26 May 45
War Transp.	Ld Leathers	25 May 45	*P.S.*	P. Thorneycroft	26 May 45
Works	D. Sandys	25 May 45	*P.S.*	R. Manningham-Buller	26 May 45
Law Officers:			*P.S. to Treasury:*		
Att.-Gen.	Sir D. Maxwell Fyfe	25 May 45		J. Stuart	26 May 45
Sol.-Gen.	Sir W. Monckton [1]	25 May 45	*Junior Lds of Treasury:*		
Ld Advoc.	J. Reid	25 May 45		A. Beechman	28 May 45
Sol.-Gen. Scotland	Sir D. Murray	25 May 45		C. Drewe	25 May 45
				P. Buchan-Hepburn	25 May 45
				R. Cary	28 May 45
H.M. Household:				C. Mott-Radclyffe	28 May 45
Treas.	Sir J. Edmondson	28 May 45	*Lds in Waiting:*		
Comptr.	L. Pym	28 May 45		Ld Alness	28 May 45
V. Chamb.	A. Young	28 May 45		M of Normanby	28 May 45
Capt. Gents at Arms	Earl Fortescue	28 May 45		D of Northumberland	28 May 45
Capt. Yeomen of Guard	Ld Templemore	28 May 45			

LABOUR GOVERNMENT, 1945–1951

MINISTERS IN CABINET			JUNIOR MINISTERS ATTACHED
P.M.	**C. Attlee**	26 Jul 45–26 Oct 51	
Ld Pres.	**H. Morrison**	27 Jul 45	
	Vt Addison	9 Mar 51	
Ld Chanc.	**Ld Jowitt**	27 Jul 45	

[1] Not a member of the House of Commons

LABOUR GOVERNMENT, 1945–1951 (*contd.*)

MINISTERS IN CABINET		JUNIOR MINISTERS ATTACHED	
Privy S.	A. Greenwood 27 Jul 45 Ld Inman 17 Apr 47 Vt Addison 7 Oct 47 E. Bevin 9 Mar 51 R. Stokes 26 Apr 51 (*also Min. of Materials from* 6 *Jul* 51)		
Exch.	H. Dalton 27 Jul 45 Sir S. Cripps 13 Nov 47 H. Gaitskell 19 Oct 50	*Min. Econ. Affairs:* H. GAITSKELL	28 Feb 50–19 Oct 50
Min. Econ. Affairs	(*office not established*) Sir S. Cripps 29 Sep 47 (*office combined with Exch* 13 *Nov* 47)	*Treasury:* F.S. W. Hall D. Jay *Econ. S.:* D. Jay (*post vacant* 28 *Feb* 50) J. Edwards	4 Aug 45 2 Mar 50 5 Dec 47 19 Oct 50
For. O.	E. Bevin 27 Jul 45 H. Morrison 9 Mar 51	*Min. of State:* P. NOEL-BAKER H. McNEIL K. YOUNGER U-S. H. McNeil C. Mayhew Ld Henderson E. Davies	3 Aug 45 4 Oct 46 28 Feb 50 4 Aug 45–4 Oct 46 4 Oct 46–2 Mar 50 7 Jun 48–26 Oct 51 2 Mar 50–26 Oct 51
Home O.	C. Ede 3 Aug 45	U-S. G. Oliver K. Younger G. de Freitas (*for Junior Ministers see below*)	4 Aug 45 7 Oct 47 2 Mar 50
Admir.	A. Alexander 3 Aug 45 (*office not in cabinet* 4 *Oct* 46)		
Ag. & Fish.	T. Williams 3 Aug 45	P.S. E of Huntingdon 4 Aug 45–22 Nov 50 P. Collick 5 Sep 45–7 Oct 47 G. Brown 7 Oct 47–26 Apr 51 E of Listowel 22 Nov 50–26 Oct 51 A. Champion 26 Apr 51–26 Oct 51 (*for Junior Ministers see below*)	
Air	Vt Stansgate 3 Aug 45 (*office not in cabinet* 4 *Oct* 46)		
Civil Av.	(*office not in cabinet*) Ld Pakenham 31 May 48 (*office not in cabinet* 28 *Feb* 50)	P.S. I. Thomas G. Lindgren F. Beswick	10 Aug 45 4 Oct 46 2 Mar 50
Col. O.	G. Hall 3 Aug 45 A. Creech Jones 4 Oct 46 J. Griffiths 28 Feb 50	Min. E OF LISTOWEL J. DUGDALE U-S. A. Creech Jones I. Thomas D. Rees-Williams T. Cook	4 Jan 48 28 Feb 50 4 Aug 45 4 Oct 46 7 Oct 47 2 Mar 50
C.R.O.	(*office not established*) Vt Addison 7 Jul 47 P. Noel-Baker 7 Oct 47 P. Gordon Walker 28 Feb 50	Min. A. HENDERSON (*office in cabinet* 7 *Oct* 47) U-S. P. Gordon Walker Ld Holden D. Rees-Williams (*Ld Ogmore*) E of Lucan	14 Aug 47 7 Oct 47 2 Mar 50 4 Jul 50 1 Jun 51
Def.	C. Attlee (P.M.) 27 Jul 45 A. Alexander (Vt) 20 Dec 46 E. Shinwell 28 Feb 50		
Dom. O.	Vt Addison 3 Aug 45 (*became C.R.O.* 7 *Jul* 47 *see above*)	U-S. J. Parker A. Bottomley	4 Aug 45 10 May 46
Educ.	Miss E. Wilkinson 3 Aug 45 G. Tomlinson 10 Feb 47	P.S. A. Jenkins D. Hardman	4 Aug 45 30 Oct 45

LABOUR GOVERNMENT, 1945–1951 *(contd.)*

MINISTERS IN CABINET			JUNIOR MINISTERS ATTACHED		
Fuel & P.	**E. Shinwell**	3 Aug 45		*(for Junior Ministers see below)*	
	(H. Gaitskell 7 Oct 47 & office				
	not in cabinet)				
Health	**A. Bevan**	3 Aug 45	*P.S.*	C. Key	4 Aug 45
	(H. Marquand 17 Jan 51 & office			J. Edwards	12 Feb 47
	not in cabinet)			A. Blenkinsop	1 Feb 49
India O. &	**Ld Pethick-Lawrence**	3 Aug 45	*U-S.*	A. Henderson	4 Aug 45
Burma O.	**E of Listowel**	17 Apr 47			
	(4 Jan 48 offices abolished)				
Lab. &	**G. Isaacs**	3 Aug 45	*P.S.*	N. Edwards	4 Aug 45
Nat. S.	**A. Bevan**	17 Jan 51		F. Lee	2 Mar 50
	A. Robens	24 Apr 51			
D. Lanc.	*(office not in cabinet)*				
	H. Dalton	31 May 48			
	Vt Alexander	28 Feb 50			
Paym.-Gen.	*(office vacant)*				
	A. Greenwood	9 Jul 46			
	(H. Marquand 5 Mar 47 & office				
	not in cabinet)				
	Vt Addison	2 Jul 48			
	(Ld Macdonald 1 Apr 49 & office				
	not in cabinet)				
Min.	**A. Alexander** 4 Oct 46–20 Dec 46				
without	**A. Greenwood**				
Portfolio	17 Apr 47–29 Sep 47				
Scot. O.	**J. Westwood**	3 Aug 45	*U-S.*	G. Buchanan	4 Aug 45–7 Oct 47
	A. Woodburn	7 Oct 47		T. Fraser	4 Aug 45–26 Oct 51
	H. McNeil	28 Feb 50		J. Robertson	7 Oct 47–2 Mar 50
				Miss M. Herbison	
					2 Mar 50–26 Oct 51
T. & C.	*(office not in cabinet)*		*P.S.*	F. Marshall	10 Aug 45
Planning	**H. Dalton**	28 Feb 50		E. King	7 Oct 47
	(recast as Local Government &			G. Lindgren	2 Mar 50
	Planning 31 Jan 51)				
B.o.T.	**Sir S. Cripps**	27 Jul 45	*P.S.*	E. Smith	4 Aug 45
	H. Wilson	29 Sep 47		J. Belcher	12 Jan 46
	Sir H. Shawcross	24 Apr 51		J. Edwards	1 Feb 49
				H. Rhodes	2 Mar 50
			Sec. Overseas Trade Dept.:		
				H. Marquand	4 Aug 45
				H. Wilson	5 Mar 47
				A. Bottomley	7 Oct 47
War O.	**J. Lawson**	3 Aug 45		*(for Junior Ministers see below)*	
	(office not in cabinet 4 Oct 46)				

MINISTERS NOT IN CABINET			JUNIOR MINISTERS ATTACHED		
Admir.	*(office in cabinet)*		*P. & F.S.:*		
	Vt HALL	4 Oct 46		J. Dugdale	4 Aug 45
	Ld PAKENHAM	24 May 51		J. Callaghan	2 Mar 50
			Civil Ld:		
				W. Edwards	4 Aug 45
Air	*(office in cabinet)*		*U-S.*	J. Strachey	4 Aug 45
	P. NOEL-BAKER	4 Oct 46		G. de Freitas	27 May 46
	A. HENDERSON	7 Oct 47		A. Crawley	2 Mar 50
Civil Av.	Ld WINSTER	4 Aug 45		*(for Junior Ministers see above)*	
	Ld NATHAN	4 Oct 46			
	(Ld Pakenham 31 May 48 & office				
	in cabinet)				
	Ld PAKENHAM	28 Feb 50			
	Ld OGMORE	1 Jun 51			

LABOUR GOVERNMENT, 1945–1951 *(contd.)*

MINISTERS NOT IN CABINET			JUNIOR MINISTERS ATTACHED		
Food	Sir B. Smith	3 Aug 45	*P.S.*	Edith Summerskill	4 Aug 45
	J. Strachey	27 May 46		S. Evans	2 Mar 50
	M. Webb	28 Feb 50		F. Willey	18 Apr 50
Fuel & P.	*(office in cabinet)*		*P.S.*	W. Foster	4 Aug 45
	H. Gaitskell	7 Oct 47		H. Gaitskell	10 May 46
	P. Noel-Baker	28 Feb 50		A. Robens	7 Oct 47
				H. Neal	26 Apr 51
Health	*(office in cabinet)*			*(for Junior Ministers see above)*	
	H. Marquand	17 Jan 51			
Information	E. Williams	4 Aug 45			
	(office wound up 31 Mar 46)				
D. Lanc.	J. Hynd	4 Aug 45			
	Ld Pakenham	17 Apr 47			
	(H. Dalton 31 May 48 & office				
	in cabinet)				
Nat. Ins.	J. Griffiths	4 Aug 45	*P.S.*	G. Lindgren	4 Aug 45
	Edith Summerskill	28 Feb 50		T. Steele	4 Oct 46
				H. Taylor	2 Mar 50
Paym.-Gen.	*(office in cabinet)*				
	H. Marquand	5 Mar 47			
	(Vt Addison 2 Jul 48 & office				
	in cabinet)				
	Ld Macdonald of Gwaenysgor				
		1 Apr 49			
Pensions	W. Paling	3 Aug 45	*P.S.*	Mrs J. Adamson	4 Aug 45
	J. Hynd	17 Apr 47		A. Blenkinsop	10 May 46
	G. Buchanan	7 Oct 47		C. Simmons	1 Feb 49
	H. Marquand	2 Jul 48			
	G. Isaacs	17 Jan 51			
Postm.-Gen.	E of Listowel	4 Aug 45	*Ass.*	W. Burke	10 Aug 45
	W. Paling	17 Apr 47		C. Hobson	7 Oct 47
	N. Edwards	28 Feb 50			
Supply	J. Wilmot	3 Aug 45	*P.S.*	W. Leonard ⎫	
	G. Strauss	7 Oct 47		A. Woodburn ⎭	4 Aug 45
				J. Freeman ⎫	
				J. Jones ⎭	7 Oct 47
				J. Freeman	2 Mar 50
				M. Stewart	2 May 51
T. & C.	L. Silkin	4 Aug 45		*(for Junior Ministers see above)*	
Planning	*(H. Dalton 28 Feb 50 & office*				
	in cabinet)				
Transp.	A. Barnes	3 Aug 45	*P.S.*	G. Strauss	4 Aug 45
				J. Callaghan	7 Oct 47
				Ld Lucas of Chilworth	2 Mar 50
War O.	*(office in cabinet)*		*U.-S.*	Ld Nathan	4 Aug 45
	F. Bellenger	4 Oct 46		Ld Pakenham	4 Oct 46–17 Apr 47
	E. Shinwell	7 Oct 47	*F.S.*	F. Bellenger	4 Aug 45
	J. Strachey	28 Feb 50		J. Freeman	4 Oct 46–17 Apr 47
			U. &	J. Freeman	17 Apr 47
			F.S.	M. Stewart	7 Oct 47
				W. Wyatt	2 May 51
Works	G. Tomlinson	4 Aug 45	*P.S.*	H. Wilson	4 Aug 45
	C. Key	10 Feb 47		E. Durbin	5 Mar 47
	R. Stokes	28 Feb 50		Ld Morrison	26 Sep 48
	G. Brown	26 Apr 51			
Law Officers:			*P.S. to Treasury:*		
Att.-Gen.	Sir H. Shawcross	4 Aug 45		W. Whiteley	3 Aug 45
	Sir F. Soskice	24 Apr 51	*Junior Lds of Treasury:*		
				R. Taylor	4 Aug 45–26 Oct 51
Sol.-Gen.	Sir F. Soskice	4 Aug 45		J. Henderson	4 Aug 45–1 Jan 50
	Sir L. Ungoed-Thomas	24 Apr 51		M. Stewart	10 Aug 45–30 Mar 46

LABOUR GOVERNMENT, 1945–1951 (contd.)

MINISTERS NOT IN CABINET

Law Officers:

Ld Advoc.	G. Thomson	10 Aug 45
	J. Wheatley	7 Oct 47
Sol.-Gen.	D. Blades	10 Sep 45 [1]
Scotland	J. Wheatley	19 Mar 47
	D. Johnston	24 Oct 47

H.M. Household:

Treas.	G. Mathers	4 Aug 45
	A. Pearson	30 Mar 46
Comptr.	A. Pearson	4 Aug 45
	M. Stewart	30 Mar 46
	F. Collindridge	9 Dec 46
V. Chamb.	J. Snow	10 Aug 45
	M. Stewart	9 Dec 46
	E. Popplewell	16 Oct 47
Capt. Gents at Arms	Ld Ammon	4 Aug 45
	Ld Shepherd	18 Oct 49
Capt. Yeomen of Guard	Ld Walkden	4 Aug 45
	Ld Shepherd	6 Jul 49
	Ld Lucas of Chilworth	18 Oct 49
	E of Lucan	5 Mar 50
	Ld Archibald	8 Jun 51

JUNIOR MINISTERS ATTACHED

A. Blenkinsop	10 Aug 45–10 May 46
F. Collindridge	10 Aug 45–9 Dec 46
C. Simmons	30 Mar 46–1 Feb 49
W. Hannan	10 May 46–26 Oct 51
J. Snow	9 Dec 46–3 Mar 50
R. Adams	1 Feb 49–23 Apr 50
W. Wilkins	1 Jan 50–26 Oct 51
H. Bowden	3 Mar 50–26 Oct 51
C. Royle	23 Apr 50–26 Oct 51

Lds in Waiting:

Ld Westwood	10 Sep 45–17 Jan 47
Ld Pakenham	14 Oct 45–4 Oct 46
Ld Henderson	21 Oct 45–7 Jun 48
Ld Chorley	11 Oct 46–31 Mar 50
Ld Morrison	17 Jan 47–26 Sep 48
Ld Lucas of Chilworth	9 Jul 48–18 Oct 49
Ld Shepherd	14 Oct 48–6 Jul 49
Ld Kershaw	6 Jul 49–26 Oct 51
Ld Darwen	18 Oct 49–26 Dec 50
Ld Burden	31 Mar 50–26 Oct 51
Ld Haden-Guest	13 Feb 51–26 Oct 51

CONSERVATIVE GOVERNMENT, 1951–1957

MINISTERS IN CABINET

P.M.	(Sir) W. Churchill	26 Oct 51–5 Apr 55
	Sir A. Eden	6 Apr 55–9 Jan 57
Ld. Pres.	Ld Woolton	28 Oct 51
	M of Salisbury	24 Nov 52
Ld Chanc.	Ld Simonds	30 Oct 51
	Vt Kilmuir	18 Oct 54
Privy S.	M of Salisbury	28 Oct 51
	H. Crookshank	7 May 52
	R. Butler	20 Dec 55
Exch.	R. Butler	28 Oct 51
	H. Macmillan	20 Dec 55
For. O.	(Sir) A. Eden	28 Oct 51
	H. Macmillan	7 Apr 55
	S. Lloyd	20 Dec 55

JUNIOR MINISTERS ATTACHED

Min. Econ. Affs.

Sir A. Salter	31 Oct 51
(24 Nov 52 office abolished)	

Treasury:

F.S.	J. Boyd-Carpenter	31 Oct 51
	H. Brooke	28 July 54
Econ. S.:	R. Maudling	24 Nov 52
	Sir E. Boyle	7 Apr 55
	D. Walker-Smith	11 Nov 56

Min. of State

S. Lloyd	30 Oct 51–18 Oct 54
M of Reading	11 Nov 53–9 Jan 57
A. Nutting	18 Oct 54–3 Nov 56
A. Noble	9 Nov 56–9 Jan 57

U-S.	M of Reading	31 Oct 51–11 Nov 53
	A. Nutting	31 Oct 51–18 Oct 54
	A. Dodds-Parker	11 Nov 53–9 Jan 57
	R. Turton	18 Oct 54–20 Dec 55

---

[1] Non-political appointments.

CONSERVATIVE GOVERNMENT, 1951–1957 (contd.)

MINISTERS IN CABINET			JUNIOR MINISTERS ATTACHED		
				Ld J. Hope	18 Oct 54–9 Dec 56
				D. Ormsby-Gore	9 Nov 56–9 Jan 57
Home O. &	**Sir D. Maxwell Fyfe**	28 Oct 51	*U-S.*	D. Llewellyn	5 Nov 51–14 Oct 52
Welsh Affs.	**(Vt Kilmuir)**			Sir H. Lucas-Tooth	
	G. Lloyd-George	18 Oct 54			3 Feb 52–20 Dec 55
				Ld Lloyd	24 Nov 52–18 Oct 54
				Ld Mancroft	18 Oct 54–9 Jan 57
Ag. & Fish.	*(office not in cabinet)*			W. Deedes	20 Dec 55–9 Jan 57
	Sir T. Dugdale	3 Sept 53	*P.S.*	Ld Carrington	5 Nov 51–18 Oct 54
	D. Heathcoat Amory	28 Jul 54		R. Nugent	5 Nov 51–9 Jan 57
	(18 Oct 54 Min. of Ag. & Fish.)			Earl St Aldwyn	18 Oct 54–9 Jan 57
	combined with Min. of Food)			H. Nicholls	7 Apr 55–9 Jan 57
Col. O.	**O. Lyttelton**	28 Oct 51	*Min.*	A. LENNOX-BOYD	2 Nov 51
	A. Lennox-Boyd	28 Jul 54		H. HOPKINSON	7 May 52
				J. HARE	20 Dec 55
				J. MACLAY	18 Oct 56
			U-S.	E of Munster	5 Nov 51
				Ld Lloyd	18 Nov 54
C.R.O.	**Ld Ismay**	28 Oct 51	*U-S.*	J. Foster	3 Nov 51
	M of Salisbury	12 Mar 52		A. Dodds-Parker	18 Oct 54
	Vt Swinton	24 Nov 52		A. Noble	20 Dec 55
	E of Home	7 Apr 55		Ld J. Hope[1]	9 Nov 56
Co-ordina-	**Ld Leathers**	30 Oct 51			
tion of	*(3 Sep 53 office abolished)*				
Transport,					
Fuel & Power					
Def.	**W. Churchill (P.M.)**	28 Oct 51	*P.S.*	N. Birch	28 Feb 52
	Earl Alexander	1 Mar 52		Ld Carrington	18 Oct 54
	H. Macmillan	18 Oct 54		E of Gosford	26 May 56
	S. Lloyd	7 Apr 55			
	Sir W. Monckton	20 Dec 55			
	A. Head	18 Oct 56			
Educ.	*(office not in cabinet)*		*P.S.*	K. Pickthorn	5 Nov 51
	Miss F. Horsbrugh	3 Sep 53		D. Vosper	18 Oct 54
	Sir D. Eccles	18 Oct 54			
Food	*(office not in cabinet)*				
	G. Lloyd-George	3 Sep 53	*P.S.*	C. Hill	31 Oct 51
	D. Heathcoat Amory	18 Oct 54			
	(& combined with Min. of				
	Ag. & Fish.)				
Health	**H. Crookshank**	30 Oct 51	*P.S.*	Miss P. Hornsby-Smith	3 Nov 51
	(7 May 52 office not in cabinet)				
Housing &	**H. Macmillan**	30 Oct 51	*P.S.*	E. Marples	3 Nov 51
Loc. Govt.	**D. Sandys**	18 Oct 54		W. Deedes	18 Oct 54
				E. Powell	20 Dec. 55
Lab. &	**Sir W. Monckton**	28 Oct 51	*P.S.*	Sir P. Bennett	31 Oct 51
Nat. S.	**I. Macleod**	20 Dec 55		H. Watkinson	28 May 52
				R. Carr	20 Dec 55
D. Lanc.	*(office not in cabinet)*				
	Ld Woolton (Vt)	24 Nov 52			
	(3 Sep 53–15 Jul 54 also				
	Min. of Materials)				
	E of Selkirk	20 Dec 55			
Paym.-Gen.	**Ld Cherwell**	30 Oct 51			
	(11 Nov 53 E of Selkirk &				
	office not in cabinet)				
	Sir W. Monckton	18 Oct 56			
Pensions &	*(office not in cabinet)*			*(for Junior Ministers see below)*	
Nat. Ins.	**O. Peake**	18 Oct 54			
	(20 Dec 55 J. Boyd-Carpenter &				
	office not in cabinet)				

[1] Not a member of the House of Lords.

CONSERVATIVE GOVERNMENT, 1951–1957 *(contd.)*

MINISTERS IN CABINET		JUNIOR MINISTERS ATTACHED	
Scot. O.	**J. Stuart** 30 Oct 51	*Min.*	E OF HOME 2 Nov 51
			T. GALBRAITH 7 Apr 55
			(Ld Strathclyde)
		U.-S.	T. Galbraith 2 Nov 51–5 Apr 55
			W. Snadden 2 Nov 51–13 Jun 55
			J. Henderson Stewart
			4 Feb 52–9 Jan 57
			N. Macpherson 13 Jun 55–9 Jan 57
B.o.T	**P. Thorneycroft** 30 Oct 51	*Min.*	D. HEATHCOAT AMORY 3 Sep 53
			T. Low 28 Jul 54
		P.S.	H. Strauss 3 Nov 51
			D. Kaberry 7 Apr 55
			D. Walker-Smith 19 Oct 55
			F. Erroll 11 Nov 56
		Sec. Overseas Trade:	
			H. Hopkinson 3 Nov 51
			H. Mackeson 28 May 52
			(3 Sep 53 office abolished, Min.
Works	*(office not in cabinet)*		*of State established)*
	P. Buchan-Hepburn 20 Dec 55	*(for Junior Ministers see below)*	

MINISTERS NOT IN CABINET		JUNIOR MINISTERS ATTACHED	
Admir.	J. THOMAS 31 Oct 51	*P. & F.S.:*	
	(Vt Cilcennin)		A. Noble 5 Nov 51
	VT HAILSHAM 2 Sep 56		G. Ward 20 Dec 55
		Civil Ld:	
			S. Wingfield Digby 5 Nov 51
Ag. & Fish.	SIR T. DUGDALE 31 Oct 51	*(for Junior Ministers see above)*	
	(3 Sep 53 office in cabinet)		
Air	LD DE L'ISLE AND DUDLEY	*U.-S.*	N. Birch 3 Nov 51
	31 Oct 51		G. Ward 29 Feb 52
	N. BIRCH 20 Dec 55		C. Soames 20 Dec 55
Educ.	MISS F. HORSBURGH 2 Nov 51	*(for Junior Ministers see above)*	
	(3 Sep 53 office in cabinet)		
Food	G. LLOYD-GEORGE 31 Oct 51	*(for Junior Ministers see above)*	
	(3 Sep 53 office in cabinet)		
Fuel & P.	G. LLOYD 31 Oct 51	*P.S.*	L. Joynson-Hicks 5 Nov 51
	A. JONES 20 Dec 55		D. Renton 20 Dec 55
Health	*(office in cabinet)*	*(for Junior Ministers see above)*	
	I. MACLEOD 7 May 52		
	R. TURTON 20 Dec 55		
D. Lanc.	VT SWINTON 31 Oct 51–24 Nov 52		
	(also Min. of Materials, 24 Nov 52,		
	Ld Woolton became D. Lanc. &		
	office in cabinet)		
Materials	VT SWINTON 31 Oct 51–24 Nov 52		
	(also D. Lanc.)		
	SIR A. SALTER 24 Nov 52–1 Sep 53		
	(1 Sep 53–15 Jul 54 Ld Woolton		
	combined Materials with D. Lanc.		
	in cabinet. 15 Jul 54 Min. of		
	Materials wound up)		
Min.	E OF MUNSTER 18 Oct 54–9 Jan 57		
Without			
Portfolio			
Nat. Ins.	O. PEAKE 31 Oct 51	*P.S.*	R. Turton 5 Nov 51–3 Sep 53
	(3 Sep 53 combined with Min. of		
	Pensions, see below)		
Paym.-Gen.	*(office in cabinet)*		
	E OF SELKIRK 11 Nov 53		
	(20 Dec 55 office vacant, Sir W.		
	Monckton 18 Oct 56 & office in		
	cabinet)		

CONSERVATIVE GOVERNMENT, 1951–1957 (*contd.*)

MINISTERS NOT IN CABINET			JUNIOR MINISTERS ATTACHED		
Pensions	D. HEATHCOAT AMORY	5 Nov 51	*P.S.*	J. Smyth	5 Nov 51–20 Dec 55
(& Nat.	(1 *Sep 53 combined Min. of*			R. Turton	3 Sep 53–18 Oct 54
Ins.)	*Pensions & National Insurance*)			E. Marples	18 Oct 54–20 Dec 55
	O. PEAKE	3 Sep 53		Miss E. Pitt	20 Dec 55–9 Jan 57
	(18 *Oct 54 office in cabinet*)			R. Wood	20 Dec 55–9 Jan 57
	J. BOYD-CARPENTER	20 Dec 55			
Postm.-Gen.	EARL DE LA WARR	5 Nov 51	*Ass.*	D. Gammans	5 Nov 51
	C. HILL	7 Apr 55		C. Alport	20 Dec 55
Power	(*see Fuel & Power above*)				
Supply	D. SANDYS	31 Oct 51	*P.S.*	T. Low	3 Nov 51
	S. LLOYD	18 Oct 54		Sir E. Boyle	28 Jul 54
	R. MAUDLING	7 Apr 55		F. Erroll	7 Apr 55
				I. Harvey	11 Nov 56
Transp. (&	J. MACLAY	31 Oct 51			
Civil Av.)	A. LENNOX-BOYD	7 May 52	*P.S.*	J. Gurney Braithwaite	
	(*Ministries of Transport & Civil*				5 Nov 51–1 Nov 53
	Aviation merged 1 *Oct* 53)			R. Maudling	18 Apr 52–24 Nov 52
	J. BOYD-CARPENTER	28 Jul 54		J. Profumo	24 Nov 52–5 Apr 55
	H. WATKINSON	20 Dec 55		H. Molson	11 Nov 53–5 Apr 55
War O.	A. HEAD	31 Oct 51	*U-S. & F.S.*		
	J. HARE	18 Oct 56		J. Hutchison	5 Nov 51
				F. Maclean	18 Oct 54
Works	(SIR) D ECCLES	1 Nov 51	*P.S.*	H. Molson	3 Nov 51
	N. BIRCH	18 Oct 54		J. Bevins	11 Nov 53
	(20 *Dec* 55 *P. Buchan-Hepburn*				
	& *office in cabinet*)				

Law Officers:
Att.-Gen.	SIR L. HEALD	3 Nov 51	*P.S. to Treasury:*		
	SIR R. MANNINGHAM-BULLER			P. Buchan-Hepburn	30 Oct 51
		18 Oct 54		E. Heath	30 Dec 55
Sol.-Gen.	SIR R. MANNINGHAM-BULLER		*Junior Lds of Treasury:*		
		3 Nov 51		H. Mackeson	7 Nov 51–28 May 52
	SIR H. HYLTON-FOSTER	18 Oct 54		(Sir) H. Butcher	7 Nov 51–3 Jul 53
Ld Advoc.	J. CLYDE	2 Nov 51		E. Heath	7 Nov 51–20 Dec 55
	W. MILLIGAN	30 Dec 54		T. Galbraith	7 Nov 51–4 Jun 54
Sol.-Gen.	W. MILLIGAN	3 Nov 51		D. Vosper	7 Nov 51–18 Oct 54
Scotland	W. GRANT	10 Jan 55		H. Oakshott	28 May 52–13 June 55
				M. Redmayne	3 Jul 53–14 Jun 55
				R. Thompson	28 Jul 54–8 Apr 56
				G. Wills	26 Oct 54–9 Jan 57
				P. Legh	13 Jun 55–9 Jan 57
				E. Wakefield	24 Jan 56–9 Jan 57
				H. Harrison	8 Apr 56–9 Jan 57

H.M. Household:
Treas.	(SIR) C. DREWE	7 Nov 51	*Lds in Waiting:*		
	T. GALBRAITH	13 Jun 55		E of Birkenhead	5 Nov 51–28 Jan 55
Comptr.	R. CONANT	7 Nov 51		E of Selkirk	5 Nov 51–11 Nov 53
	T. GALBRAITH	7 Jun 54		Ld Lloyd	7 Nov 51–24 Nov 52
	H. OAKSHOTT	13 Jun 55		Ld Mancroft	15 Dec 52–18 Oct 54
				Ld Hawke	11 Nov 53–9 Jan 57
				Ld Fairfax	18 Oct 54–9 Jan 57
V. Chamb.	H. STUDHOLME	7 Nov 51		Ld Chesham	28 Jan 55–9 Jan 57
	R. THOMPSON	8 Apr 56			
Capt. Gents	EARL FORTESCUE	5 Nov 51			
at Arms					
Capt.	E OF ONSLOW	5 Nov 51			
Yeomen of					
Guard					

CONSERVATIVE GOVERNMENT, 1957–1964

MINISTERS IN CABINET		JUNIOR MINISTERS ATTACHED	

P.M.	**H. Macmillan** 10 Jan 57–13 Oct 63	
	Sir A. Douglas-Home	
	(*formerly E of Home*)	
	18 Oct 63–16 Oct 64	

First Sec.	**R. Butler**	13 Jul 62	
of State	(*office wound up* 18 Oct 63)		
Ld Pres.	**M of Salisbury**	13 Jan 57	
	E of Home	29 Mar 57	
	Vt Hailsham	17 Sep 57	
	E of Home	14 Oct 59	
	Vt Hailsham (*Q. Hogg*)	27 Jul 60	
	(*also Min. for Science*)		
Ld. Chanc.	**Vt Kilmuir**	14 Jan 57	
	Ld Dilhorne	13 Jul 62	
Privy S.	**R. Butler**	13 Jan 57	
	(*also Home Sec.*)		
	Vt Hailsham	14 Oct 59	
	(*also Min. for Science*)		
	E. Heath	27 Jul 60	
	S. Lloyd	20 Oct 63	

Exch.	**P. Thorneycroft**	13 Jan 57	*Treasury:*		
	D. Heathcoat Amory	6 Jan 58	*F.S.*	E. Powell	16 Jan 57
	S. Lloyd	27 Jul 60		J. Simon	6 Jan 58
	R. Maudling	13 Jul 62		Sir E. Boyle	22 Oct 59
	(*see also Paymaster-General*)			A. Barber	16 Jul 62
				A. Green	23 Oct 63
			Econ. S.:		
				N. Birch	16 Jan 57
				(*vacant 6 Jan 58*)	
				F. Erroll	23 Oct 58
				A. Barber	22 Oct 59
				E. du Cann	16 Jul 62
				M. Macmillan	21 Oct 63
For. O.	**S. Lloyd**	14 Jan 57	*Min. of State:*		
	E of Home	27 Jul 60		A. NOBLE	16 Jan 57–16 Jan 59
	R. Butler	20 Oct 63		D. ORMSBY-GORE	
					16 Jan 57–27 Jun 61
				J. PROFUMO	16 Jan 59–27 Jul 60
				J. GODBER	27 Jun 61–27 Jun 63
				E OF DUNDEE	9 Oct 61–16 Oct 64
				P. THOMAS	27 Jun 63–16 Oct 64
			U-S.	E of Gosford	18 Jan 57–23 Oct 58
				I. Harvey	18 Jan 57–24 Nov 58
				J. Profumo	28 Nov 58–16 Jan 59
				M of Lansdowne	
					23 Oct 58–20 Apr 62
				R. Allan	16 Jan 59–7 Oct 60
				J. Godber	28 Oct 60–27 Jun 61
				P. Thomas	27 Jun 61–27 Jun 63
				(*post left vacant*)	
				P. Smithers	16 Jul 62–29 Jan 64
				R. Mathew	30 Jan 64–16 Oct 64

CONSERVATIVE GOVERNMENT, 1957–1964 (contd.)

MINISTERS IN CABINET		JUNIOR MINISTERS ATTACHED	
Home O.	R. Butler　13 Jan 57 H. Brooke　13 Jul 62	Min. Home Affs.: 　D. VOSPER 　D. RENTON 　EARL JELLICOE 　LD DERWENT	 28 Oct 60 27 Jan 61 17 Jul 62 21 Oct 63
		U-S.　P. Hornsby-Smith 　　　18 Jan 57–22 Oct 59 　J. Simon　18 Jan 57–6 Jan 58 　D. Renton　17 Jan 58–27 Jun 61 　D. Vosper　22 Oct 59–28 Oct 60 　Ld Bathurst　8 Feb 61–16 Jul 62 　C. Fletcher-Cooke 　　　27 Jun 61–27 Feb 63 　C. Woodhouse　16 Jul 62–16 Oct 64 　Miss M. Pike　1 Mar 63–16 Oct 66	
Ag. Fish. & Food	D. Heathcoat Amory　14 Jan 57 J. Hare　6 Jan 58 C. Soames　27 Jul 60	P.S.　Earl St Aldwyn 18 Jan 57–27 Jun 58 　J. Godber　18 Jan 57–28 Oct 60 　Earl Waldegrave 27 Jan 58–16 Jul 62 　W. Vane　28 Oct 60–16 Jul 62 　Ld St. Oswald　16 Jul 62–16 Oct 64 　J. Scott-Hopkins 　　　16 Jul 62–16 Oct 64	
Aviation	(see Transp. & Civil Av.) D. Sandys　14 Oct 59 P. Thorneycroft　27 Jul 60 J. Amery　16 Jul 62	(for Junior Ministers see below 　Transp. & Civil Aviation) P.S.　G. Rippon 　C. Woodhouse 　B. de Ferranti 　N. Marten	 22 Oct 59 9 Oct 61 16 Jul 62 3 Dec 62
Col. O.	A. Lennox-Boyd　14 Jan 57 I. Macleod　14 Oct 59 R. Maudling　9 Oct 61 (joint minister with C.R.O. 13 Jul 62) D. Sandys　13 Jul 62	Min.　E OF PERTH　16 Jan 57 　M OF LANSDOWNE　20 Apr 62 　　(joint with C.R.O. 21 Oct 63) U-S.　J. Profumo　18 Jan 57 　J. Amery　28 Nov 58 　H. Fraser　28 Oct 60 　N. Fisher　16 Jul 62–16 Oct 64 　R. Hornby　24 Oct 63–16 Oct 64 　　(joint with C.R.O. 21 Oct 63)	
C.R.O.	E of Home　14 Jan 57 D. Sandys　27 Jul 60 (joint minister with Col. O 13 Jul 62)	Min.　C. ALPORT　22 Oct 59–8 Feb 61 　D OF DEVONSHIRE 　　　6 Sep 62–16 Oct 64 　　(joint with Col. O. 21 Oct 63) U-S.　C. Alport　18 Jan 57 　R. Thompson　22 Oct 59 　D of Devonshire 　　　28 Oct 60–6 Sep 62 　B. Braine　8 Feb 61–16 Jul 62 　J. Tilney　16 Jul 62–16 Oct 64 　　(joint with Col. O. 21 Oct 63)	
Defence	D. Sandys　13 Jan 57 H. Watkinson　14 Oct 59 P. Thorneycroft　13 Jul 62	P.S.　Ld Mancroft　18 Jan 57 　　(11 Jun 57 office vacant) 　　(reorganisation 1 Apr 64) 　Ministers of State: Air　H. FRASER　1 Apr 64 Army　J. RAMSDEN　1 Apr 64 Navy　EARL JELLICOE　1 Apr 64 U-S.　J. Ridsdale　1 Apr 64 Air U-S.　P. Kirk　1 Apr 64 Army U-S.　J. Hay　1 Apr 64 Navy	
Educ.	Vt Hailsham　13 Jan 57 G. Lloyd　17 Sep 57	P.S.　Sir E. Boyle　18 Jan 57 　K. Thompson　22 Oct 59	

CONSERVATIVE GOVERNMENT, 1957–1964 (contd.)

MINISTERS IN CABINET		JUNIOR MINISTERS ATTACHED	
	Sir D. Eccles	14 Oct 59	C. Chataway	16 Jul 62
	Sir E. Boyle	13 Jul 62	(reorganisation 1 Apr 64)
	(Educ. & Science 1 Apr 64)		Ministers of State:
	Q. Hogg	1 Apr 64	(Sir E. Boyle, and seat in cabinet)
	(formerly Vt Hailsham)			1 Apr 64

MINISTERS IN CABINET / **JUNIOR MINISTERS ATTACHED**

Sir D. Eccles — 14 Oct 59
Sir E. Boyle — 13 Jul 62
(Educ. & Science 1 Apr 64)
Q. Hogg — 1 Apr 64
(formerly Vt Hailsham)

C. Chataway — 16 Jul 62
(reorganisation 1 Apr 64)
Ministers of State:
(Sir E. Boyle, and seat in cabinet) — 1 Apr 64

Min. of State Educ. Sir E. Boyle — 1 Apr 64

P.S. Ld NEWTON — 11 Mar 64
Ld Bessborough — 1 Apr 64
C. Chataway — 1 Apr 64

Health (office not in cabinet)
E. Powell — 13 Jul 62
A. Barber — 20 Oct 63

(for Junior Ministers see below)

Housing, Loc. Govt. & Welsh Affs.
H. Brooke — 13 Jan 57
C. Hill — 9 Oct 61
Sir K. Joseph — 13 Jul 62

Min. Ld BRECON — 12 Dec 57
P.S. J. Bevins — 18 Jun 57
Sir K. Joseph — 22 Oct 59–9 Oct 61
Earl Jellicoe — 27 Jun 61–16 Jul 62
G. Rippon — 9 Oct 61–16 Jul 62
F. Corfield — 16 Jul 62–16 Oct 64
Ld Hastings — 3 Dec 62–16 Oct 64

Lab. & Nat. S.
I. Macleod — 14 Jan 57
E. Heath — 14 Oct 59
(12 Nov 59—Min. of Labour)
J. Hare — 27 Jul 60
J. Godber — 20 Oct 63

P.S. R Carr — 19 Jan 57
R. Wood — 14 Apr 58
P. Thomas — 22 Oct 59
A. Green — 27 Jun 61
W. Whitelaw — 16 Jul 62

D. Lanc.
C. Hill — 13 Jan 57
I. Macleod — 9 Oct 61
Ld Blakenham (J. Hare) 20 Oct 63

Paym.-Gen. (office not in cabinet)
R. Maudling — 17 Sep 57
Ld Mills — 14 Oct 59
(after 9 Oct 61 Chief Sec. to Treasury & Paymaster-General)
H. Brooke — 9 Oct 61
J. Boyd-Carpenter — 13 Jul 62

Min. without Portfolio (office not in cabinet)
Ld Mills — 9 Oct 61–14 Jul 62
W. Deedes — 13 Jul 62–16 Oct 64
Ld Carrington — 20 Oct 63–16 Oct 64

Power
Ld Mills — 13 Jan 57
(14 Oct 59 R. Wood & office not in cabinet)
F. Erroll — 20 Oct 63

P.S. D. Renton — 18 Jan 57
Sir I. Horobin — 17 Jan 58
J. George — 22 Oct 59
J. Peyton — 25 Jun 62

Science
Vt Hailsham — 14 Oct 59
(1 Apr 64 Educ. & Science)

P.S. D. Freeth — 8 Feb 61
Ld Bessborough — 24 Oct 63
(1 Apr 64, Educ. & Science)

Scot. O.
J. Maclay — 13 Jan 57
M. Noble — 13 Jul 62

Min. Ld STRATHCLYDE — 17 Jan 57
Ld FORBES — 23 Oct 58
J. BROWNE — 22 Oct 59
(Ld Craigton)
U-S. J. Browne — 18 Jan 57–22 Oct 59
N. Macpherson — 19 Jan 57–28 Oct 60
Ld J. Hope — 18 Jan 57–22 Oct 59
T. Galbraith — 22 Oct 59–8 Nov 62
G. Leburn — 22 Oct 59–15 Aug 63
R. Brooman-White — 28 Oct 60–12 Dec 63
Lady Tweedsmuir — 3 Dec 62–16 Oct 64
J. Stodart — 19 Aug 63–16 Oct 64
G. Campbell — 12 Dec 63–16 Oct 64

CONSERVATIVE GOVERNMENT, 1957–1964 *(contd.)*

MINISTERS IN CABINET				JUNIOR MINISTERS ATTACHED		

B.o.T. **Sir D. Eccles** 13 Jan 57
R. Maudling 14 Oct 59
F. Erroll 9 Oct 61
E. Heath 20 Oct 63
(also Sec. of State for Industry,
Trade & Regional Development)

Min. D. WALKER-SMITH 16 Jan 57
J. VAUGHAN-MORGAN 17 Sep 57
F. ERROLL 22 Oct 59
SIR K. JOSEPH 9 Oct 61
A. GREEN 16 Jul 62–23 Oct 63
LD DERWENT 6 Sep 62–23 Oct 63
LD DRUMALBYN 23 Oct 63–16 Oct 64
(formerly N. Macpherson)
E. DU CANN 21 Oct 63–16 Oct 64

P.S. J. Rodgers 24 Oct 58
N. Macpherson 28 Oct 60
D. Price 17 Jul 62

Transp. & **H. Watkinson** 13 Jan 57
Civil Av. *(14 Oct 59 Min of Transp. only)*
E. Marples 14 Oct 59
(see above, Min. of Aviation)

P.S. R. Nugent 18 Jan 57–22 Oct 59
A. Neave 18 Jan 57–16 Jan 59
J. Hay 16 Jan 59–3 May 63
Ld Chesham 22 Oct 59–16 Oct 64
J. Hughes-Hallett
26 April 61–16 Oct 64
T. Galbraith 3 May 63–16 Oct 64
(for Junior Ministers see below)

Works *(office not in cabinet)*
G. Rippon 20 Oct 63
(Min. of Public Building & Works)

MINISTERS NOT IN CABINET				JUNIOR MINISTERS ATTACHED		

Admir. E OF SELKIRK 16 Jan 57
LD CARRINGTON 16 Oct 59
EARL JELLICOE 22 Oct 63
(1 Apr 64, reorganised
under Min. of Defence)

P. & C. Soames 18 Jan 57
F.S. R. Allan 17 Jan 58
C. Orr Ewing 16 Jan 59
(16 Oct 59 office vacant)

Civil Ld:
T. Galbraith 18 Jan 57
C. Orr Ewing 16 Oct 59
J. Hay 3 May 63

Air G. WARD 16 Jan 57
J. AMERY 28 Oct 60
H. FRASER 16 Jul 62
(1 Apr 64, reorganised
under Min of Defence)

U-S. C. Orr Ewing 18 Jan 57
A. Neave 16 Jan 59
W. Taylor 16 Oct 59
J. Ridsdale 16 Jul 62

Health D. VOSPER 16 Jan 57
D. WALKER-SMITH 17 Sep 57
E. POWELL 27 Jul 60
(13 Jul 62 E. Powell & office
in cabinet)

P.S. J. Vaughan-Morgan 18 Jan 57
R. Thompson 17 Sep 57
Miss E. Pitt 22 Oct 59
B. Braine 16 Jul 62–16 Oct 64
Ld Newton 6 Sep 62–11 Mar 64
M of Lothian 24 Mar 64–16 Oct 64

Paym.-Gen. R. MAUDLING 16 Jan 57
(17 Sep 57 office in cabinet)

Pensions & J. BOYD-CARPENTER 16 Jan 57
Nat. Ins. N. MACPHERSON 16 Jul 62
R. WOOD 21 Oct 63

P.S. Miss E. Pitt 19 Jan 57–22 Oct 59
R. Wood 19 Jan 57–14 Apr 58
W. Vane 14 Apr 58–28 Oct 60
Miss P. Hornsby-Smith
22 Oct 59–31 Aug 61
B. Braine 28 Oct 60–8 Feb 61
R. Sharples 8 Feb 61–16 Jul 62
Mrs M. Thatcher
9 Oct 61–16 Oct 64
S. Maydon 16 Jul 62–16 Oct 64

Min. E OF MUNSTER 16 Jan 57–11 Jun 57
without LD MANCROFT 11 Jun 57
Portfolio E OF DUNDEE 23 Oct 58
(9 Oct 61 Ld Mills & office in cabinet)

CONSERVATIVE GOVERNMENT, 1957–1964 (contd.)

MINISTERS NOT IN CABINET		JUNIOR MINISTERS ATTACHED	
Postm.-Gen.	E. MARPLES 16 Jan 57 R. BEVINS 22 Oct 59	*Ass.*	K. Thompson 18 Jan 57 Miss M. Pike 22 Oct 59 R. Mawby 1 Mar 63
Power	*(office in cabinet)* R. WOOD 14 Oct 59 (20 Oct 63, F. Erroll & office in cabinet)		*(for Junior Ministers see above)*
Supply	A. JONES 16 Jan 57 *(office wound up 22 Oct 59)*	*P.S.*	W. Taylor 18 Jan 57 *(office wound up 22 Oct 59)*
Technical *Cooperation*	*(office not established)* D. VOSPER 27 Jun 61 R. CARR 9 May 63		
War O.	J. HARE Jan 57 C. SOAMES 6 Jan 58 J. PROFUMO 27 Jul 60 J. GODBER 27 Jun 63 J. RAMSDEN 21 Oct 63 *(1 Apr 64, reorganised under Min. of Defence)*	*U-S. & F.S.:*	J. Amery 18 Jan 57 H. Fraser 28 Nov 58 J. Ramsden 28 Oct 60 P. Kirk 24 Oct 63
Works	H. MOLSON 16 Jan 57 LD J. HOPE 22 Oct 59 *(16 Jul 62, Min. of Public Building & Works)* G. RIPPON 16 Jul 62 *(20 Oct 63, G. Rippon & office in cabinet)*	*P.S.*	H. Nicholls 18 Jan 57 R. Thompson 28 Oct 60 R. Sharples 16 Jul 62

Law officers:

Att.-Gen. SIR R. MANNINGHAM-BULLER 17 Jan 57
SIR J. HOBSON 16 Jul 62

Sol.-Gen. SIR H. HYLTON-FOSTER 17 Jan 57
SIR J. SIMON 22 Oct 59
SIR J. HOBSON 8 Feb 62
SIR P. RAWLINSON 19 Jul 62

Ld. Advoc.
W. MILLIGAN 17 Jan 57
W. GRANT 5 Apr 60
I. SHEARER 12 Oct 62

Sol.-Gen. W. GRANT 17 Jan 57
Scotland D. ANDERSON 11 May 60
N. WYLIE 27 Apr 64

P.S. to Treasury:
E. Heath 17 Jan 57
M. Redmayne 14 Oct 59

Junior Lds of Treasury:
M. Redmayne 21 Jan 57–14 Oct 59
P. Legh 21 Jan 57–17 Sep 57
E. Wakefield 21 Jan 57–23 Oct 58
H. Harrison 21 Jan 57–16 Jan 59
A. Barber 9 Apr 57–19 Feb 58
R. Brooman-White 28 Oct 57–21 Jan 60
P. Bryan 19 Feb 58–9 Feb 61
M. Hughes-Young 23 Oct 58–6 Mar 62
G. Finlay 16 Jan 59–28 Oct 60
D. Gibson-Watt 22 Oct 59–29 Nov 61
R. Chichester-Clark 21 Jun 60–29 Nov 61
J. Hill 28 Oct 60–16 Oct 64
W. Whitelaw 6 Mar 61–16 Jul 62
J. Peel 29 Nov 61–16 Oct 64
M. Noble 29 Nov 61–13 Jul 62
F. Pearson 6 Mar 62–19 Oct 63
G. Campbell 6 Sep 62–12 Dec 63
M. Hamilton 6 Sep 62–16 Oct 64
M. McLaren 21 Nov 63–16 Oct 64
I. MacArthur 12 Dec 63–16 Oct 64

H.M. Household:
Treas. H. OAKSHOTT 19 Jan 57
P. LEGH (*Ld Newton*) 16 Jan 59
E. WAKEFIELD 21 Jun 60
M. HUGHES-YOUNG 6 Sep 62

Lds in Waiting:
Ld Hawke 21 Jan 57–11 Jun 57
Ld Fairfax 21 Jan 57–21 Jun 57
Ld Chesham 21 Jan 57–22 Oct 59
M of Lansdowne 11 Jun 57–23 Oct 58

CONSERVATIVE GOVERNMENT, 1957–1964 (contd.)

MINISTERS NOT IN CABINET			JUNIOR MINISTERS ATTACHED	
Comptr.	(SIR) G. WILLS	19 Jan 57	E of Gosford	23 Oct 58–22 Oct 59
	E. WAKEFIELD	23 Oct 58	Earl Bathurst	17 Sep 57–8 Feb 61
	H. HARRISON	16 Jan 59	Ld St Oswald	22 Oct 59–16 Jul 62
	R. CHICHESTER-CLARK	29 Nov 61	Earl Jellicoe	8 Feb 61–27 Jun 61
			Ld Denham	27 Jun 61–16 Oct 64
V. Chamb.	R. THOMPSON	21 Jan 57	M of Lothian	6 Sep 62–23 Mar 64
	P. LEGH	17 Sep 57	Ld Hastings	6 Mar 61–3 Dec 62
	E. WAKEFIELD	16 Jan 59	Earl Ferrers	3 Dec 62–10 Oct 64
	R. BROOMAN-WHITE	21 Jun 60		
	G. FINLAY	28 Oct 60		
Capt. Gents	EARL FORTESCUE	21 Jan 57		
at Arms	EARL ST ALDWYN	27 Jun 58		
Capt.	E OF ONSLOW	21 Jan 57		
Yeomen of	LD NEWTON	28 Oct 60		
Guard	VT GOSCHEN	6 Sep 62		

LABOUR GOVERNMENT, 1964–1970

MINISTERS IN CABINET			JUNIOR MINISTERS ATTACHED	
P.M.	**H. Wilson**	16 Oct 64–19 Jun 70		
First Sec. of	**G. Brown**	16 Oct 64		
State	**M. Stewart**	11 Aug 66–18 Mar 68		
	(office linked to Min. of Econ.			
	Affairs 16 Oct 64–29 Aug 67)			
	Mrs B. Castle	6 Apr 68		
	(office linked to Min. of Employment)			
Ld Pres.	**H. Bowden**	16 Oct 64		
	R. Crossman	11 Aug 66		
	F. Peart	18 Oct 68		
Ld Chanc.	**Ld Gardiner**	16 Oct 64		
Privy S.	**E of Longford**	18 Oct 64		
	Sir F. Soskice	23 Dec 65		
	E of Longford	6 Apr 66		
	Ld Shackleton	16 Jan 68		
	F. Peart	6 Apr 68		
	Ld Shackleton	18 Oct 68		
Exch.	**J. Callaghan**	16 Oct 64	*Treasury: Chief Sec.*	
	R. Jenkins	30 Nov 67	J. Diamond	20 Oct 64
Treasury: Chief Sec. (office not in cabinet)			*(1 Nov 68 office in cabinet)*	
	J. Diamond	1 Nov 68	*Min of State.*	
			D. TAVERNE	6 Apr 68
			W. RODGERS	13 Oct 69
			F.S. N. MacDermot	21 Oct 64
			H. Lever	29 Aug 67
			D. TAVERNE	13 Oct 69
			Econ. A. Crosland	19 Oct 64
			S. (de facto Min. of State, Econ. Affs.	
			Office abolished 22 Dec 64)	
Econ. Affs.	**G. Brown**	16 Oct 64	*Min. of State*	
	M. Stewart	11 Aug 66	A. CROSLAND	20 Oct 64
	P. Shore	29 Aug 67	*(until 22 Dec 64 nominally Econ.*	
	(office abolished 6 Oct 69)		*Sec. to Treas.)*	
			A. ALBU	27 Jan 65–7 Jan 67
			T. URWIN	6 Apr 68
			U-S. M. Foley	21 Oct 64–7 Jan 67
			W. Rodgers	21 Oct 64–7 Jan 67
			H. Lever	7 Jan 67–29 Aug 67
			P. Shore	7 Jan 67–29 Aug 67
			A. Williams	29 Aug 67–6 Oct 69
			E. Dell	29 Aug 67–6 Oct 69

LABOUR GOVERNMENT, 1964-1970 (*contd.*)

MINISTERS IN CABINET	JUNIOR MINISTERS ATTACHED

For. O.   P. Gordon Walker   16 Oct 64
(*& Comm.*   M. Stewart   22 Jan 65
O.)   G. Brown   11 Aug 66
  M. Stewart   16 Mar 68
  (*merged with Comm. O.* 17 *Oct* 68)

Min. of State
  LD CARADON   16 Oct 64–19 Jun 70
  G. THOMSON   19 Oct 64–6 Apr 66
    7 Jan 67–29 Aug 67
  W. PADLEY   19 Oct 64–7 Jan 67
  LD CHALFONT   23 Oct 64–19 Jun 70
  MRS E. WHITE   11 Apr 66–7 Jan 67
  F. MULLEY   7 Jan 67–6 Oct 69
  G. ROBERTS   29 Aug 67–13 Oct 69
  LD SHEPHERD   17 Oct 68–19 Jun 70
U-S.   Ld Walston   20 Oct 64–7 Jan 67
  W. Rodgers   7 Jan 67–3 Jul 68
  M. Foley   3 Jul 68–19 Jun 70
  W. Whitlock   26 Jul 67–13 Oct 69
  E. Luard   13 Oct 69–19 Jun 70

Home O.   Sir F. Soskice   18 Oct 64
  R. Jenkins   23 Dec 65
  J. Callaghan   30 Nov 67

Min. of State
  MISS A. BACON   19 Oct 64
  LD STONHAM   29 Aug 67
  MRS S. WILLIAMS   13 Oct 69
U-S.   Ld Stonham   20 Oct 64–29 Aug 67
  G. Thomas   20 Oct 64–6 Apr 66
  M. Foley   25 Jan 66–7 Jan 67
  D. Taverne   6 Apr 66–6 Apr 68
  D. Ennals   7 Jan 67–1 Nov 68
  E. Morgan   6 Apr 68–19 Jun 70
  M. Rees   1 Nov 68–19 Jun 70

Ag. Fish.   F. Peart   18 Oct 64
& Food   C. Hughes   6 Apr 68
Col. O.   A. Greenwood   18 Oct 64
  E of Longford   23 Dec 65
  F. Lee   6 Apr 66
  (*came under Dept of Common-*
  wealth Affs. 1 *Jul* 66. *Office*
  abolished 7 *Jan* 67)

P.S.   J. Mackie   20 Oct 64
  J. Hoy   21 Oct 64
U-S.   Mrs E. White   20 Oct 64–11 Apr 66
  Ld Taylor   20 Oct 64–11 Oct 65
  Ld Beswick   11 Oct 65–1 Jul 66
  (*Ld Taylor & Ld Beswick were*
  also U-S. at C.R.O.)
  J. Stonehouse   6 Apr 66–7 Jan 67

C.R.O.   A. Bottomley   18 Oct 64
  (*re-named Commonwealth*
  Affairs 1 *Aug* 66)
  H. Bowden   11 Aug 66
  G. Thomson   29 Aug 67
  (*merged with For. O.* 17 *Oct* 68)

Min.   C. HUGHES   19 Oct 64–6 Apr 66
of   MRS J. HART   6 Apr 66–26 Jul 67
State   G. THOMAS   7 Jan 67–6 Apr 68
  LD SHEPHERD   26 Jul 67
U-S.   Ld Taylor   20 Oct 64
  Ld Beswick   11 Oct 65
  (*held jointly with U-S. at Col. O.*
  until 1 *Jul* 66)
  W. Whitlock   26 Jul 67

Def.   D. Healey   16 Oct 64

Min.   F. MULLEY   19 Oct 64
Army   G. REYNOLDS   24 Dec 65
& Dep.   (*no Dep. Sec. of State after*
Sec. of   24 Dec 65. *Office abolished*
State   7 *Jan* 67)
U-S.   G. Reynolds   20 Oct 64
for   M. Rees   24 Dec 65
Army   D. Ennals   6 Apr 66
  J. Boyden   7 Jan 67
  I. Richard   13 Oct 69
Min.   C. MAYHEW   19 Oct 64
for   J. MALLALIEU   19 Feb 66
Navy   (*office abolished* 7 *Jan* 67)
U-S.   J. Mallalieu   21 Oct 64
for   Ld Winterbottom   6 Apr 66
Navy   M. Foley   7 Jan 67
  D. Owen   3 Jul 68
Min.   LD SHACKLETON   19 Oct 64
for Air Force (*office abolished* 7 *Jan* 67)
U-S.   B. Millan   20 Oct 64
for Air   M. Rees   6 Apr 66
Force   Ld Winterbottom   1 Nov 68

MINISTERS IN CABINET			JUNIOR MINISTERS ATTACHED		
			Min.	G. REYNOLDS	7 Jan 67
			of Defence for Administration		
				R. HATTERSLEY	15 Jul 69
			Min.	R. MASON	7 Jan 67
			of Defence for Equipment		
				J. MORRIS	6 Apr 68
Educ. &	M. Stewart	18 Oct 64	Min.	LD BOWDEN	19 Oct 64–11 Oct 65
Science	A. Crosland	22 Jan 65	*of*	R. PRENTICE	20 Oct 64–6 Apr 66
	P. Gordon Walker	29 Aug 67	*State*	E. REDHEAD	11 Oct 65–7 Jan 67
	E. Short	6 Apr 68		G. ROBERTS	6 Apr 66–29 Aug 67
				Mrs S. WILLIAMS	7 Jan 67–13 Oct 69
				MISS J. LEE	17 Feb 67–19 Jun 70
				MISS A. BACON	29 Aug 67–19 Jun 70
				G. FOWLER	13 Oct 69–19 Jun 70
			U-S.	J. Boyden	20 Oct 64–24 Feb 65
				D. Howell	20 Oct 64–13 Oct 69
				Miss J. Lee	24 Feb 65–17 Feb 67
				Miss J. Lestor	13 Oct 69–19 Jun 70
Emp. &	Mrs B. Castle	6 Apr 68	*Min.*	E. DELL	13 Oct 69
Productivity			*of State*		
			U-S.	E. Fernyhough	6 Apr 68–13 Oct 69
				R. Hattersley	6 Apr 68–15 Jul 69
				H. Walker	6 Apr 68–19 Jun 70
Health &	R. Crossman	1 Nov 68	*Min.*	S. SWINGLER	1 Nov 68–19 Feb 69
Soc. Sec.			*of*	D. ENNALS	1 Nov 68–19 Jun 70
			State	LADY SEROTA	25 Feb 69–19 Jun 70
			U-S.	N. Pentland	1 Nov 68–13 Oct 69
				C. Loughlin	1 Nov 68–20 Nov 68
				J. Snow	1 Nov 68–13 Oct 69
				B. O'Malley	13 Oct 69–19 Jun 70
				J. Dunwoody	13 Oct 69–19 Jun 70
Housing &	R. Crossman	18 Oct 64	*Min.*	F. WILLEY	17 Feb 67
Local Govt.	A. Greenwood	11 Aug 66	*of*	N. MACDERMOT	29 Aug 67–28 Sep 68
	(*office out of cabinet* 6 Oct 69)		*State*		
			Min.	K. ROBINSON	1 Nov 68
			for planning and Land		
				(*office abolished* 6 Oct 69)	
			P.S.	R. Mellish	18 Oct 64–29 Aug 67
				J. MacColl	20 Oct 64–13 Oct 69
				Ld Kennet	6 Apr 66–13 Oct 69
				A. Skeffington	17 Feb 67–13 Oct 69
Labour	R. Gunter	18 Oct 64	*P.S.*	R. Marsh	20 Oct 64–11 Oct 65
	(6 *Apr* 68 *reorganised as Min. of*			E. Thornton	21 Oct 64–6 Apr 66
	Employment & Productivity)			Mrs S. Williams	6 Apr 66–7 Jan 67
				E. Fernyhough	7 Jan 67–6 Apr 68
				R. Hattersley	7 Jan 67–6 Apr 68
D. Lanc.	D. Houghton	18 Oct 64			
	(*G. Thomson* 6 *Apr* 66 & *office*				
	not in cabinet)				
	G. Thomson	6 Oct 69			
Local Govt.	(*office created* 6 Oct 69)		*Min.*	T. URWIN	6 Oct 69
& Regional	A. Crosland	6 Oct 69	*of State*		
Planning					
Overseas	Mrs B. Castle	18 Oct 64	*P.S.*	A. Oram	21 Oct 64
Develop-	A. Greenwood	23 Dec 65			
ment	A. Bottomley	11 Aug 66			
	(*R. Prentice* 29 *Aug* 67 & *office*				
	not in cabinet)				
Paym.-Gen.	(*office not in cabinet*)				
	Ld Shackleton	6 Apr 68			
	Mrs J. Hart	1 Nov 68			
	H. Lever	6 Oct 69			

LABOUR GOVERNMENT, 1964–1970 (contd.)

MINISTERS IN CABINET			JUNIOR MINISTERS ATTACHED		
Min. with-	D. Houghton	6 Apr 66			
out Portfolio	P. Gordon Walker	7 Jan 67			
	(office vacant 29 *Aug* 67)				
	G. Thomson	17 Oct 68			
	P. Shore	6 Oct 69			
Power	F. Lee	18 Oct 64	*P.S.*	J. Morris	21 Oct 64
	R. Marsh	6 Apr 66		Ld Lindgren	10 Jan 66
	R. Gunter	6 Apr 68		J. Bray	6 Apr 66
	R. Mason	1 Jul 68		R. Freeson	7 Jan 67
	(office abolished 6 *Oct* 69)				
Scot.O.	W. Ross	18 Oct 64	*Min.*	G. WILLIS	20 Oct 64–7 Jan 67
			of		
			State	D. MABON	7 Jan 67–19 Jun 70
				LD HUGHES	13 Oct 69–19 Jun 70
			U-S.	Ld Hughes	21 Oct 64–13 Oct 69
				Mrs J. Hart	20 Oct 64–6 Apr 66
				D. Mabon	21 Oct 64–7 Jan 67
				B. Millan	6 Apr 66–19 Jun 70
				N. Buchan	7 Jan 67–19 Jun 70
Tech.	F. Cousins	18 Oct 64	*Min. of State*		
	A. Wedgwood Benn	4 Jul 66		J. STONEHOUSE	15 Feb 67–1 Jul 68
				J. MALLALIEU	1 Jul 68–6 Oct 69
				R. PRENTICE	6 Oct 69–10 Oct 69
				LD DELACOURT-SMITH	
					13 Oct 69–19 Jun 70
				E. VARLEY	13 Oct 69–19 Jun 70
			P.S.	Ld Snow	19 Oct 64–6 Apr 66
				R. Marsh	11 Oct 65–6 Apr 66
				P. Shore	6 Apr 66–7 Jan 67
				E. Dell	6 Apr 66–29 Aug 67
				J. Bray	7 Jan 67–24 Sep 69
				G. Fowler	29 Aug 67–13 Oct 69
				A. Williams	6 Oct 69–19 Jun 70
				N. Carmichael	13 Oct 69–19 Jun 70
				E. Davies	13 Oct 69–19 Jun 70
B. of T.	D. Jay	18 Oct 64	*Min.*	G. DARLING	20 Oct 64–6 Apr 68
	A. Crosland	29 Aug 67	*of*	E. REDHEAD	20 Oct 64–11 Oct 65
	R. Mason	6 Oct 69	*State*	R. MASON	20 Oct 64–7 Jan 67
				LD BROWN	11 Oct 65–19 Jun 70
				J. MALLALIEU	7 Jan 67–1 Jul 68
				E. DELL	6 Apr 68–13 Oct 69
				W. RODGERS	1 Jul 68–13 Oct 69
				G. ROBERTS	13 Oct 69–19 Jun 70
			P.S.	Ld Rhodes	20 Oct 64
				Ld Walston	7 Jan 67
				Mrs G. Dunwoody	29 Aug 67
Transport	T. Fraser	18 Oct 64	*Min.*	S. SWINGLER	29 Aug 67–1 Nov 68
	Mrs B. Castle	23 Dec 65	*of State*		
	R. Marsh	6 Apr 68	*P.S.*	Ld Lindgren	20 Oct 64–10 Jan 66
	(F. Mulley 6 *Oct* 69 *& office not*			S. Swingler	20 Oct 64–29 Aug 67
	in cabinet)			J. Morris	10 Jan 66–6 Apr 68
				N. Carmichael	29 Aug 67–13 Oct 69
				R. C. Brown	6 Apr 68–19 Jun 70
				A. Murray	13 Oct 69–19 Jun 70
Wales	J. Griffiths	18 Oct 64	*Min.*	G. ROBERTS	20 Oct 64
	C. Hughes	6 Apr 66	*of*	G. THOMAS	6 Apr 66
	G. Thomas	6 Apr 68	*State*	MRS E. WHITE	7 Jan 67
			U-S.	H. Finch	21 Oct 64
				I. Davies	6 Apr 66
				E. Rowlands	13 Oct 69
	MINISTERS NOT IN CABINET				
Aviation	R. JENKINS	18 Oct 64	*P.S.*	J. Stonehouse	20 Oct 64
	F. MULLEY	23 Dec 65		J. Snow	6 Apr 66
	J. STONEHOUSE	7 Jan 67			
	(office abolished 15 *Feb* 67)				

LABOUR GOVERNMENT, 1964–1970 (*contd.*)

MINISTERS NOT IN CABINET			JUNIOR MINISTERS ATTACHED		
D. Lanc.	*(office in cabinet)*				
	G. THOMSON	6 Apr 66			
	F. LEE	7 Jan 67			
	(G. Thomson 6 Oct 69 & office in cabinet)				
Health	K. ROBINSON	18 Oct 64	*P.S.*	Sir B. Stross	20 Oct 64
	(office abolished 1 Nov 68)			C. Loughlin	24 Feb 65
				J. Snow	7 Jan 67
			Min.	D. HOWELL	13 Oct 69
Housing &	*(office in cabinet)*		*of State*		
Local Govt.	A. GREENWOOD	6 Oct 69	*P.S.*	A. Skeffington	13 Oct 69–19 Jun 70
	R. MELLISH	31 May 70		Ld Kennet	13 Oct 69–19 Jun 70
				R. Freeson	13 Oct 69–19 Jun 70
Land &	F. WILLEY	18 Oct 64	*P.S.*	Ld Mitchison	20 Oct 64–6 Apr 66
Nat. Res.	*(office wound up 17 Feb 67)*			A. Skeffington	21 Oct 64–17 Feb 67
Overseas	*(office in cabinet)*				
Dev.	R. Prentice	29 Aug 67	*P.S.*	A. Oram	29 Aug 67
	Mrs J. Hart	6 Oct 69		B. Whitaker	13 Oct 69
Paym.-Gen.	G. WIGG	19 Oct 64–12 Nov 67			
	(office vacant 12 Nov 67)				
	(Ld Shackleton 6 Apr 68 & office in cabinet)				
Pensions &	MISS M. HERBISON	18 Oct 64	*P.S.*	H. Davies	20 Oct 64–7 Jan 67
Nat. Ins.	*(6 Aug 66 became Min. of Social Security)*			N. Pentland	21 Oct 64–6 Aug 66
Min.	SIR E. FLETCHER 19 Oct 64–6 Apr 66				
without	LD CHAMPION	21 Oct 64–7 Jan 67			
Portfolio	LD SHACKLETON 7 Jan 67–16 Jan 68				
Postm.-Gen.	A. WEDGWOOD BENN	19 Oct 64	*Ass.*	J. Slater	20 Oct 64
	E. SHORT	4 Jul 66			
	R. MASON	6 Apr 68			
	J. STONEHOUSE	1 Jul 68			
	(1 Oct 69 Post Office became a Public Corporation)				
Posts &	J. STONEHOUSE	1 Oct 69	*P.S.*	N. Pentland	13 Oct 69
Telecommunications					
Public	C. PANNELL	19 Oct 64	*P.S.*	Miss J. Lee	20 Oct 64
Building	R. PRENTICE	6 Apr 66		J. Boyden	24 Feb 65
& Works	R. MELLISH	29 Aug 67		Ld Winterbottom	7 Jan 67
	J. SILKIN	30 Apr 69		C. Loughlin	20 Nov 68
Social	MISS M. HERBISON	6 Aug 66	*P.S.*	H. Davies	6 Nov 66–7 Jan 67
Security	MRS J. HART	26 Jul 67		N. Pentland	6 Aug 66–1 Nov 68
	(office abolished 1 Nov 68, see Health & Social Security)			C. Loughlin	7 Jan 67–1 Nov 68
Transport	*(office in cabinet)*			*(for Junior Ministers see above)*	
	F. MULLEY	6 Oct 69			
Law Officers:				*P.S. to Treasury:*	
Att.-Gen.	SIR E. JONES	18 Oct 64		E. Short	18 Oct 64
				J. Silkin	4 Jul 66
Sol.-Gen.	SIR D. FOOT	18 Oct 64		R. MELLISH	30 Apr 69
	SIR A. IRVINE	24 Aug 67		*(office vacant 31 May 70)*	
Ld Advoc.	G. STOTT[1]	20 Oct 64			
	H. S. WILSON (LD)[1]	26 Oct 67		*Junior Lds. of Treasury*	
Sol.-Gen.	J. LEECHMAN[1]	20 Oct 64		G. Rogers	21 Oct 64–11 Jan 66
Scotland	H. S. WILSON[1]	11 Oct 65		G. Lawson	21 Oct 64–1 Apr 67
	E. STEWART[1]	26 Oct 67		J. McCann	21 Oct 64–11 Apr 66
					29 Jul 67–13 Oct 69
				I. Davies	21 Oct 64–6 Apr 66
				Mrs H. Slater	21 Oct 64–6 Apr 66
				J. Silkin	11 Jan 66–11 Apr 66
				A. Fitch	16 Apr 66–13 Oct 69
				J. Harper	16 Apr 66–19 Jun 70
				W. Whitlock	11 Apr 66–7 Jul 66
					1 Apr 67–28 Jul 67

[1] Not a member of the House of Commons.

LABOUR GOVERNMENT, 1964–70 (contd.)

MINISTERS NOT IN CABINET	JUNIOR MINISTERS ATTACHED	
	W. Howie	16 Apr 66–1 Apr 67
	H. Gourlay	7 Jul 66–29 Oct 68
	B. O'Malley	1 Apr 67–13 Oct 69
	W. Harrison	29 Oct 68–19 Jun 70
	N. McBride	13 Oct 69–19 Jun 70
	E. Perry	13 Oct 69–19 Jun 70
	E. Armstrong	13 Oct 69–19 Jun 70
	Asst. Govt. Whips:	
	A. Fitch	22 Oct 64 [1]–16 Apr 66
	H. Gourlay	22 Oct 64 [1]–7 Jul 66
	J. Harper	22 Oct 64 [1]–16 Apr 66
	W. Howie	22 Oct 64 [1]–16 Apr 66
	B. O'Malley	22 Oct 64 [1]–1 Apr 67
	J. Silkin	22 Oct 64 [1]–11 Jan 66
	C. Morris	25 Jan 66–29 Jul 67
	E. Bishop	16 Apr 66–1 Apr 67
	R. W. Brown	16 Apr 66–20 Jan 67
	W. Harrison	16 Apr 66–28 Oct 68
	N. McBride	16 Apr 66–13 Oct 69
	I. Evans	7 Jul 66–6 Feb 68
	E. Armstrong	20 Jan 67–13 Oct 69
	H. Walker	1 Apr 67–5 Mar 68
	E. Varley	29 Jul 67–30 Nov 68
	E. Perry	6 Feb 68–13 Oct 69
	J. Concannon	11 Apr 68–19 Jun 70
	M. Miller	29 Oct 68–13 Oct 69
	T. Boston	13 Oct 69–19 Jun 70
	J. Hamilton	13 Oct 69–19 Jun 70
	R. Dobson	13 Oct 69–19 Jun 70
	W. Hamling	13 Oct 69–19 Jun 70

	H.M. Household:		*Lds in Waiting:*	
Treas.	S. IRVING	21 Oct 64	Ld Hobson	21 Oct 64–17 Feb 66
	J. SILKIN	11 Apr 66	Ld Beswick	28 Dec 64–11 Oct 65
	C. GREY	7 July 66	Ld Sorensen	28 Dec 64–20 Apr 68
	C. MORRIS	13 Oct 69	Lady Phillips	10 Dec 65–19 Jun 70
Comptr.	C. GREY	21 Oct 64	Ld Hilton	6 Apr 66–19 Jun 70
	W. WHITLOCK	7 Jul 66	Lady Serota	23 Apr 68–25 Feb 69
			Lady Llewelyn-Davies	
	W. HOWIE	1 Apr 67		13 Oct 69–19 Jun 70
	J. McCANN	29 Jul 67		
	I. EVANS	6 Feb 68		
	A. FITCH	13 Oct 69		
V. Chamb.	W. WHITLOCK	21 Oct 64		
	J. McCANN	11 Apr 66		
	C. MORRIS	29 Jul 67		
Capt. Gents at Arms	LD SHEPHERD	21 Oct 64		
	LD BESWICK	29 Jul 67		
Capt. Yeomen of Guard	LD BOWLES			

CONSERVATIVE GOVERNMENT, 1970–74

	MINISTERS IN CABINET		JUNIOR MINISTERS ATTACHED	
P.M.	E. Heath	19 Jun 70–4 Mar 74	*P.S. Civil Service Dept.*	
			D. Howell[2]	23 Jun 70
			K. Baker	7 Apr 72
			G. Johnson-Smith	5 Nov 72
Ld Pres.	W. Whitelaw	20 Jun 70		
	R. Carr	7 Apr 72		
	J. Prior	5 Nov 72		

[1] The appointment of Assistant Government Whips as paid Ministers of the Crown dates technically from 12 Nov 64.
[2] Also Junior Ld of Treasury 23 Jun 70–6 Jan 71, P.S. Dept. of Employment 5 Jan 71–24 Jan 72.

CONSERVATIVE GOVERNMENT 1970–74 *(contd.)*

MINISTERS IN CABINET		JUNIOR MINISTERS ATTACHED
Ld Chanc.	**Q. Hogg (Ld Hailsham)** 20 Jun 70	
Privy S.	**Earl Jellicoe** 20 Jun 70 **Ld Windlesham** 5 Jun 73	
Exch.	**I. Macleod** 20 Jun 70 **A. Barber** 25 Jul 70 *Treasury: Chief Sec. (office not in cabinet)* **T. Boardman** 8 Jan 74	*Treasury: Chief Sec.* M. MACMILLAN 23 Jun 70 P. JENKIN 7 Apr 72 *(office in Cabinet 8 Jan 74)* *Min. of State* T. HIGGINS 23 Jun 70 J. NOTT 7 Apr 72 *F.S.* P. JENKIN 23 Jun 70 T. HIGGINS 7 Apr 72
For.O.	**Sir A. Douglas-Home** 20 Jun 70	*Min. of State* J. GODBER 23 Jun 70–5 Nov 72 LADY TWEEDSMUIR 7 Apr 72–4 Mar 74 J. AMERY 5 Nov 72–4 Mar 74 LD BALNIEL 5 Nov 72–4 Mar 74 *U-S.* M. of Lothian 24 Jun 70–7 Apr 73 A. Royle 24 Jun 70–8 Jan 74 A. Kershaw 15 Oct 70–5 Jun 73 P. Blaker 8 Jan 74–4 Mar 74 *Min. for Overseas Development* R. WOOD[1] 15 Oct 70
Home O.	**R. Maudling** 20 Jun 70 **R. Carr** 18 Jul 72	*Min. of State* R. SHARPLES 23 Jun 70–7 Apr 72 LD WINDLESHAM 23 Jun 70–26 Apr 72 M. CARLISLE 7 Apr 72–4 Mar 74 VT COLVILLE 26 Apr 72–4 Mar 74 *U-S.* M. Carlisle 24 Jun 70 D. Lane 7 Apr 72
Ag. Fish & *Food*	**J. Prior** 20 Jun 70 **J. Godber** 5 Nov 72	*Min. of State* A. STODART 7 Apr 72 *P.S.* A. Stodart 24 Jun 70 P. Mills 7 Apr 72 Mrs. P. Fenner 5 Nov 72 Earl Ferrers 8 Jan 74
Defence	**Ld Carrington** 20 Jun 70 **I. Gilmour** 8 Jan 74	*Min. of State* LD BALNIEL 23 Jun 70 I. GILMOUR 5 Nov 72 G. YOUNGER 8 Jan 74 *Min. of State for Procurement* I. GILMOUR 7 Apr 71 *(office abolished 5 Nov 72)* *U-S. for Navy* P. Kirk 24 Jun 70 A. Buck 5 Nov 72 *U-S. for Air Force* Ld Lambton 24 Jun 70 A. Kershaw 5 Jun 73 Ld Strathcona & Mount Royal 8 Jan 74 *U-S. for Army* I. Gilmour 24 Jun 70 G. Johnson-Smith 7 Apr 71 P. Blaker 5 Nov 72 D. Smith 8 Jan 74

The Ministry of Overseas Development formally came under the F.O. 12 Nov 70.

CONSERVATIVE GOVERNMENT, 1970–74 (contd.)

MINISTERS IN CABINET		JUNIOR MINISTERS ATTACHED	

Educ. & Mrs M. Thatcher 20 Jun 70
Science

Min. of State
N. St. John-Stevas 2 Dec 73
U-S. Ld Belstead 24 Jun 70–5 Jun 73
W. Van Straubenzee
  24 Jun 70–5 Nov 72
N. St. John-Stevas
  5 Nov 72–2 Dec 73
Ld Sandford 5 Jun 73–4 Mar 74
T. Raison 2 Dec 73–4 Mar 74

Employment R. Carr 20 Jun 70
(& Produc- M. Macmillan 7 Apr 72
tivity till W. Whitelaw 2 Dec 73
12 Nov 70)

Min. of State
P. Bryan 23 Jun 70
R. Chichester-Clark 7 Apr 72
U-S. D. Smith 24 Jun 70–8 Jan 74
D. Howell 5 Jan 71–26 Mar 72
N. Scott 8 Jan 74–4 Mar 74

Energy Ld Carrington (SofS) 8 Jan 74
P. Jenkin (Min) 8 Jan 74

Min. of State
D. Howell 8 Jan 74
U-S. P. Emery 8 Jan 74

Environment P. Walker 15 Oct 70
G. Rippon 5 Nov 72

Min. for Local Govt. & Development
G. Page 15 Oct 70
Min. for Housing & Construction
J. Amery 15 Oct 70
P. Channon 5 Nov 72
Min. for Transport Industries
J. Peyton 15 Oct 70
U-S. E. Griffiths 15 Oct 70–4 Mar 74
P. Channon 15 Oct 70–26 Mar 72
M. Heseltine 15 Oct 70–7 Apr 72
Ld Sandford 15 Oct 70–5 Jun 73
K. Speed 7 Apr 72–4 Mar 74
R. Eyre 7 Apr 72–4 Mar 74
Lady Young 5 Jun 73–4 Mar 74
H. Rossi 8 Jan 74–4 Mar 74

Health & Sir K. Joseph 20 Jun 70
Social
Security

Min. of State
Ld Aberdare 23 Jun 70–8 Jan 74
P.S. P. Dean 24 Jun 70–4 Mar 74
M. Alison 24 Jun 70–4 Mar 74

Housing & P. Walker 20 Jun 70–15 Oct 70[1]
Local Govt.

(15 Oct 70 office reorganised under
Environment)

Min. of State
G. Page 23 Jun 70–15 Oct 70
P.S. P. Channon 24 Jun 70–15 Oct 70
E. Griffiths 24 Jun 70–15 Oct 70
Ld Sandford 24 Jun 70–15 Oct 70

D. Lanc. A. Barber 20 Jun 70
(with special G. Rippon 28 Jul 70
responsi- J. Davies 5 Nov 72
bility for
Europe)

Northern W. Whitelaw 24 Apr 72
Ireland F. Pym 2 Dec 73

Min. of State
P. Channon 26 Mar 72–5 Nov 72
Ld Windlesham
  26 Mar 72–5 Jun 73
W. Van Straubenzee
  5 Nov 72–4 Mar 74
D. Howell 5 Nov 72–8 Jan 74
U-S. D. Howell 26 Mar 72–5 Nov 72
P. Mills 5 Nov 72–4 Mar 74
Ld Belstead 5 Jun 73–4 Mar 74

Paymaster- (office not in cabinet)
General M. Macmillan 2 Dec 73
Scot. O. G. Campbell 20 Jun 70

Min. of State:
Lady Tweedsmuir 23 Jun 70
Ld Polwarth 7 Apr 72

Formally the changes took effect on 12 Nov 70.

CONSERVATIVE GOVERNMENT, 1970–74 (*contd.*)

MINISTERS IN CABINET			JUNIOR MINISTERS ATTACHED		
			U-S. A. Buchanan-Smith		24 Jun 70–4 Mar 74
			G. Younger		24 Jun 70–8 Jan 74
			P.S. E. Taylor		24 Jun 70–28 Jul 71
			H. Monro		28 Jul 71–4 Mar 74
			E. Taylor		8 Jan 74–4 Mar 74
Tech.	**G. Rippon**	20 Jun 70	*Min. of State:*		
	J. Davies	28 Jul 70–15 Oct 70	Sir J. Eden	23 Jun 70–15 Oct 70	
	(15 Oct 70 office reorganised under Trade and Industry)		E. of Bessborough		24 Jun 70–15 Oct 70
			P.S. D. Price	24 Jun 70–15 Oct 70	
			N. Ridley	24 Jun 70–15 Oct 70	
B.ofT.	**M. Noble**	20 Jun 70–15 Oct 70	*Min. of State:*		
			F. Corfield	24 Jun 70–15 Oct 70	
			P.S. A. Grant	24 Jun 70–15 Oct 70	
Trade and	**J. Davies**	15 Oct 70	*Min. for Trade:*		
Industry	**P. Walker**	5 Nov 72	M. Noble		15 Oct 70
Trade and	**Sir G. Howe**	5 Nov 72	(Sir G. Howe & in cabinet 5 Nov 72)		
Consumer			U-S. A. Grant		15 Oct 70
Affairs			E. of Limerick		7 Apr 72
			Min. of Industry:		
			Sir J. Eden		15 Oct 70
			T. Boardman	7 Apr 72–8 Jan 74	
			U-S. N. Ridley		15 Oct 70
			P. Emery	7 Apr 72–8 Jan 74	
			Min. for Aerospace:		
			F. Corfield		1 May 71
			M. Heseltine		7 Apr 72
			U-S. D. Price		1 May 71
			C. Onslow		7 Apr 72
			Min. for Industrial Development:		
			C. Chataway		7 Apr 72
			U-S. A. Grant		7 Apr 72
			Min. of State:		
Wales	**P. Thomas**	20 Jun 70	D. Gibson-Watt		23 Jun 80

MINISTERS NOT IN CABINET

Aviation	F. Corfield	15 Oct 70[2]	P.S. D. Price		15 Oct 70–1 May 71
Supply	(abolished 1 May 71 and responsibilities transferred to Procurement Executive, Min. of Defence)				
Overseas	R. Wood	23 Jun 70–15 Oct 70[1]			
Development	(15 Oct 70[1] came under Foreign Office)				
Paym.-Gen.	Ld Eccles	23 Jun 70			
	(M. Macmillan & office in cabinet 2 Dec 73)				
Min. without Portfolio	Ld Drumalbyn	15 Oct 70			
	Ld Aberdare	8 Jan 74			
Posts & Tel.	C. Chataway	24 Jun 70			
	Sir J. Eden	7 Apr 72			
Public Buildings & Works	J. Amery	23 Jun 70–15 Oct 70	P.S. A. Kershaw		24 Jun 70–15 Oct 70[1]
	(15 Oct 70[1] office reorganised as Housing and Construction under Dept. of Environment)				
Transport	J. Peyton	23 Jun 70–15 Oct 70[1]	P.S. M. Heseltine		24 Jun 70–15 Oct 70[1]

MINISTERS IN CABINET

Law Officers:			*P.S. to Treasury:*		
Att.-Gen.	Sir P. Rawlinson	23 Jun 70	F. Pym		20 Jan 70
Sol.-Gen.	Sir G. Howe	23 Jun 70	H. Atkins		2 Dec 73
	Sir M. Havers	5 Nov 72			

[1] Formally the changes took effect on 12 Nov 70.
[2] Formally the changes took effect on 20 Oct 70.

CONSERVATIVE GOVERNMENT, 1970–74 (*contd.*)

MINISTERS IN CABINET			JUNIOR MINISTERS ATTACHED	

MINISTERS IN CABINET

Ld Advoc.	N. WYLIE	23 Jun 70
Sol.-Gen.	D. BRAND[1]	23 Jun 70
Scotland	I. STEWART[1]	5 Nov 72

JUNIOR MINISTERS ATTACHED

Junior Lds of Treasury

R. Eyre	24 Jun 70–23 Sep 70
D. Howell[2]	24 Jan 70–6 Jan 71
H. Monro	24 Jun 70–28 Jul 71
B. Weatherill	24 Jun 70–17 Oct 71
W. Clegg	24 Jun 70–7 Apr 72
V. Goodhew	21 Oct 70–9 Oct 73
P. Hawkins	5 Jan 71–
T. Fortescue	8 Nov 71–21 Sep 73
K. Speed	8 Nov 71–7 Apr 72
H. Rossi	7 Apr 72–
O. Murton	7 Apr 72–30 Oct 73
M. Jopling	30 Oct 73–4 Mar 74
H. Gray	30 Oct 73–4 Mar 74
J. Thomas	30 Oct 73–4 Mar 74
M. Fox	2 Dec 73–4 Mar 74
K. Clarke	8 Jan 74–4 Mar 74

Asst. Govt. Whips:

V. Goodhew	29 Jun 70–21 Oct 70
P. Hawkins	29 Jun 70–5 Jan 71
T. Fortescue	29 Jun 70–7 Nov 71
K. Speed	29 Jun 70–7 Nov 71
H. Rossi	21 Oct 70–7 Apr 72
H. Gray	8 Nov 71–30 Oct 73
J. Thomas	8 Nov 71–30 Oct 73
M. Jopling	8 Nov 71–30 Oct 73
O. Murton	8 Nov 71–7 Apr 72
M. Fox	13 Apr 72–2 Dec 73
K. Clarke	13 Apr 72–8 Jan 74
D. Walder	30 Oct 73–4 Mar 74
A. Hall-Davis	30 Oct 73–4 Mar 74
R. Hicks	30 Oct 73–4 Mar 74
A. Butler	8 Jan 74–4 Mar 74
C. Parkinson	8 Jan 74–4 Mar 74

H.M. Household:

Treas.	H. ATKINS	24 Jun 70
	B. WEATHERILL	2 Dec 73
Comptr.	R. ELLIOTT	24 Jun 70
	R. EYRE	24 Sep 70
	B. WEATHERILL	7 Apr 72
	W. CLEGG	2 Dec 73
V. Chamb.	J. MORE	24 Jun 70
	B. WEATHERILL	17 Oct 71
	W. CLEGG	7 Apr 72
	P. HAWKINS	2 Dec 73
Capt. Gents at Arms	E of ST ALDWYN	24 Jun 70
Capt. Yeomen of Guard	LD GOSCHEN	24 Jun 70
	LD DENHAM	20 Nov 71

Lds in Waiting:

Ld Mowbray	29 Jun 70–4 Mar 74
Ld Denham	24 Jun 70–20 Nov 71
Ld Bethell	24 Jun 70–5 Jan 71
Earl Ferrers	5 Jan 71–8 Jan 74
M of Lothian	7 Apr 72–27 Jul 73
E of Gowrie	7 Apr 72–4 Mar 74
Lady Young	21 Apr 72–5 Jun 73
Ld Strathcona & Mount Royal	27 Jun 73–8 Jan 74
Ld Sandys	8 Jan 74–4 Mar 74
Earl Cowley	8 Jan 74–4 Mar 74
Earl Alexander of Tunis	8 Jan 74–4 Mar 74

[1] Not a member of the House of Commons.
[2] See footnote [2] on page 50.

LABOUR GOVERNMENT, 1974–

MINISTERS IN CABINET			JUNIOR MINISTERS ATTACHED	
P.M.	**H. Wilson**	4 Mar 74	*Civil Service Dept. Min. of State:*	
			R. SHELDON	7 Mar 74
			C. MORRIS	18 Oct 74
			U-S. J. Grant	7 Mar 74–18 Oct 74
Ld Pres.	**E. Short**	5 Mar 74	*Privy Council Office, Min. of State:*	
			G. FOWLER	18 Oct 74
			U-S. W. Price	18 Oct 74
Ld Chanc.	**Ld Elwyn-Jones**	5 Mar 74		
Privy S.	**Ld Shepherd**	7 Mar 74		
Exch.	**D. Healey**	5 Mar 74	*Paym. Gen.*	
			E. DELL	7 Mar 74
			Chief Sec.	
			J. BARNETT	7 Mar 74
P.S. to	*(office not in Cabinet)*		*F.S.* J. GILBERT	7 Mar 74
Treasury	**R. Mellish**	26 Jul 74	*Min. of State:*	
			R. SHELDON	18 Oct 74
For. O.	**J. Callaghan**	5 Mar 74	*Min. of State:*	
			D. ENNALS	7 Mar 74–
			R. HATTERSLEY	7 Mar 74–
			U-S. Ld GORONWY-	
			ROBERTS	8 Mar 74–
			Miss J. Lestor	8 Mar 74–
			(see also Overseas Development)	
Home O.	**R. Jenkins**	5 Mar 74	*Min. of State:*	
			Ld HARRIS	8 Mar 74–
			A. LYON	8 Mar 74–
			U-S. Dr. S. Summerskill	8 Mar 74
Ag., Fish. and Food	**F. Peart**	5 Mar 74	*Min. of State:*	
			N. BUCHAN	8 Mar 74
			E. BISHOP	18 Oct 74
			U-S. R. Moyle	11 Mar 74
			E. Bishop	28 Jul 74
			G. Strang	18 Oct 74
Defence	**R. Mason**	5 Mar 74	*Min. of State:*	
			W. RODGERS	8 Mar 74
			U-S. for Navy	
			F. Judd	8 Mar 74
			U-S. for Army	
			Ld Brayley	8 Mar 74
			R. C. Brown	18 Oct 74
			U-S. for Air Force:	
			B. John	8 Mar 74
Educ. & Science	**R. Prentice**	5 Mar 74	*Min. of State:*	
			G. FOWLER	8 Mar 74
			Ld CROWTHER-HUNT	18 Oct 74
			U-S. E. Armstrong	7 Mar 74–
			H. Jenkins	8 Mar 74–
Employment	**M. Foot**	5 Mar 74	*Min. of State:*	
			A. BOOTH	8 Mar 74
			U-S. J. Fraser	8 Mar 74–
			H. Walker	11 Mar 74–
Energy	**E. Varley**	5 Mar 74	*Min. of State:*	
			Ld BALOGH	7 Mar 74
			U-S. G. Strang	7 Mar 74–18 Oct 74
			A. Eadie	7 Mar 74–
			J. Smith	18 Oct 74–

LABOUR GOVERNMENT, 1974– *(contd.)*

MINISTERS IN CABINET			JUNIOR MINISTERS ATTACHED		
Environ- *ment*	**A. Crosland**	5 Mar 74	*Min. for Transport:* F. MULLEY		7 Mar 74
			Min. for Planning & Local Govt. J. SILKIN		7 Mar 74
Planning & *Local Govt.* *(in Dept. of* *Environment)*	(office not in Cabinet) **J. Silkin**	18 Oct 74	(office in Cabinet 18 Oct 74)		
			Min. for Housing & Construction: R. FREESON		7 Mar 74
			Min. of State (Urban Affs.): C. MORRIS		7 Mar 74
			(post abolished 18 Oct 74)		
			Min. of State (Sport & Recreation) D. HOWELL		7 Mar 74
			U-S. N. Carmichael	8 Mar 74–	
			G. Kaufman	8 Mar 74–	
			G. Oakes	8 Mar 74–	
			Baroness Birk	18 Oct 74–	
Health & *Social* *Security*	**Mrs B. Castle**	5 Mar 74	*Min. of State:* B. O'MALLEY	8 Mar 74–	
			D. OWEN	26 Jul 74–	
			U-S. (Health): D. Owen	8 Mar 74–26 Jul 74	
			U-S. (Social Security): R. C. Brown	8 Mar 74–18 Oct 74	
			A. Jones	18 Oct 74–	
			U-S. (Disabled): A. Morris	11 Mar 74–	
Industry	**A. Wedgwood Benn** (also 7 Mar–29 Mar 74 *Min. for* *Posts and Telecommunications*)	5 Mar 74	*Min. of State:* E. HEFFER	7 Mar 74–9 Apr 75	
			LD BESWICK	11 Mar 74–	
			U-S. G. MacKenzie	7 Mar 74–	
			M. Meacher	7 Mar 74–	
D. Lanc.	**H. Lever**	5 Mar 74			
Northern *Ireland*	**M. Rees**	5 Mar 74	*Min. of State:* S. ORME	7 Mar 74–	
			R. MOYLE	27 Jun 74–	
			U-S. Ld Donaldson	11 Mar 74–	
			J. Concannon	27 Jun 74–	
Prices & *Consumer* *Protection*	**Mrs S. Williams**	5 Mar 74	*Min. of State:* A. WILLIAMS		8 Mar 74
			U-S. R. MacLennan		11 Mar 74
Scot. O.	**W. Ross**	5 Mar 74	*Min. of State:* B. MILLAN	8 Mar 74–	
			LD HUGHES	8 Mar 74–	
			U-S. R. Hughes	11 Mar 74–	
			H. Brown	28 Jun 74–	
			H. Ewing	26 Jul 74–	
Trade	**P. Shore**	5 Mar 74	*U-S.* E. Deakins	8 Mar 74–	
			S. Clinton Davis	8 Mar 74–	
Wales	**J. Morris**	5 Mar 74	*U-S.* E. Rowlands	7 Mar 74–	
			B. Jones	7 Mar 74–	

MINISTRIES
(for addenda)

LABOUR GOVERNMENT, 1974- *(contd.)*

MINISTERS IN CABINET			JUNIOR MINISTERS ATTACHED		
Overseas Development[1]	MRS J. HART	7 Mar 74	*U-S.*	W. Price	11 Mar 74
				J. Grant	18 Oct 74
Law Officers:					
Att.-Gen.	S. SILKIN	7 Mar 74	*U-S.*	A. Davidson	26 Jul 74
Sol.-Gen.	P. ARCHER	7 Mar 74			
Ld Advoc.	R. KING MURRAY	8 Mar 74			
Sol-Gen. for Scotland	J. McCLUSKEY[2]	14 Mar 74			

P.S. to Treasury:
R. MELLISH   5 Mar 74
(office in Cabinet 26 Jul 74)
Junior Lds of Treasury:

D. Coleman	8 Mar 74–
J. Dunn	8 Mar 74–
J. Golding	8 Mar 74–18 Oct 74
J. Pendry	8 Mar 74–
J. Hamilton	8 Mar 74–28 Jun 74
M. Cocks	28 Jun 74–
J. Dormand	18 Oct 74–

Asst. Govt. Whips:

M. Cocks	8 Mar 74–24 Jun 74
T. Cox	8 Mar 74–
E. Perry	8 Mar 74–24 Oct 74
J. Dormand	14 Mar 74–18 Oct 74
L. Pavitt	14 Mar 74–
W. Johnson	22 Jun 74–23 Jan 75
Miss B. Boothroyd	24 Oct 74–
J. Ellis	24 Oct 74–
Miss M. Jackson	27 Jan 75–

H.M. Household:			*Lds in Waiting:*	
Treas.	W. HARRISON	7 Mar 74	Ld Jacques	14 Mar 74–
Comptr.	J. HARPER	8 Mar 74	Ld Garnsworthy	14 Mar 74–4 Sep 74
V. Chamb.	J. CONCANNON	8 Mar 74	Baroness Birk	14 Mar 74–18 Oct 74
	J. HAMILTON	28 Jan 74	Ld Wells-Pestell	14 Mar 74–
Capt. Gents at Arms	BARONESS LLEWELYN-DAVIES	11 Mar 74	Ld Winterbottom	29 Oct 74–
Capt. Yeomen of the Guard	LD STRABOLGI	11 Mar 74	Ld Lovell-Davis	29 Oct 74–
			Ld Melchett	29 Oct 74–

---

[1] Formally under Foreign Office until 27 Jun 74.
[2] Not a member of the House of Commons.

MINISTRIES
(for addenda)

Ministerial Salaries

	Prime Minister	Lord Chancellor	Secretaries of State	Other Dept. Ministers[1]
1831	£5,000	£10,000	£5,000	£2,000
1937	£10,000	£10,000	£5,000	£5,000
1964	£14,000	£14,500	£8,500	£8,500
1972	£20,000	£20,000	£13,000	£9,500

There have been many anomalies, e.g. the Secretary of State for Scotland only received £2,000 up to 1937 but the Minister of Health received £5,000 from 1919 onwards. After 1937 most Ministers who were in the Cabinet received £5,000. After 1972 virtually all the Ministers who were members of the Cabinet received £13,000. Rates have varied for specific jobs. The last column represents the most common salary immediately after the rates were changed.

Ministerial Offices, 1900–

This list includes all specifically named ministerial offices held by Ministers or Ministers of State, apart from appointments in the Royal Household or after 1945 Ministers of State without a functional title. It does not include offices held by junior ministers.

Admiralty. First Lord of the Admiralty, 1900–64

Aerospace. Minister, 1971–74

Agriculture. President of the Board of Agriculture, 1900–3; President of the Board of Agriculture and Fisheries, 1903–19; Minister of Agriculture and Fisheries, 1919–1955; Minister of Agriculture, Fisheries and Food, 1955– (see *Food*)

Air. President of the Air Board, 1917; President of the Air Council, 1917–1918; Secretary of State, 1918–64

Aircraft Production. Minister, 1940–1946

Attorney-General, 1900–

Attorney-General for Ireland, 1900–22

Aviation. Minister, 1959–67 (see *Civil Aviation*)

Aviation Supply. Minister, 1970–71

Blockade. Minister, 1916–19

Burma. Secretary of State for India and Burma, 1937–47

Civil Aviation. Minister, 1944–53; Minister of Transport and Civil Aviation, 1953–59; Minister of Aviation, 1959–67

Civil Service. Minister for the, 1968–

Colonies. Secretary of State, 1900–67

Commonwealth. Secretary of State for Dominions 1925–47; Secretary of State for Commonwealth Relations 1947–66; Secretary of State for Commonwealth Affairs 1966–68

Co-ordination of Defence. Minister, 1936–40

Co-ordination of Transport, Fuel and Power. Secretary of State, 1951–53

Defence. Minister, 1940–64[1]; Secretary of State 1964–

Defence Procurement. Minister of State, 1971–2

Defence for Administration. Minister of, 1967–70

Defence for Equipment. Minister of, 1967–70

Dominions. Secretary of State, 1925–47

Duchy of Lancaster. Chancellor, 1900–

Economic Affairs. Minister, Sep–Nov 1947, Feb–Oct 1950; Secretary of State 1964–69

Economic Warfare. Minister, 1939–45

Education. President of the Board of Education, 1900–44; Minister of Education, 1944–64; Secretary of State for Education and Science 1964–

Employment and Productivity. Secretary of State, 1968–70

Employment. Secretary of State, 1970–

Energy. Secretary of State, 1974–

Environment. Secretary of State, 1970–

First Secretary of State, 1962–63, 1964–1970

Foreign Affairs. Secretary of State, 1900–1968

Foreign and Commonwealth Affairs. Secretary of State, 1968–

Food. Minister, 1916–21, and 1939–55 (see *Agriculture*)

Fuel and Power. Minister, 1944–57; Minister of Power, 1957–

Fuel, Light and Power. Minister, 1942–4 (see *Fuel and Power*)

Health. Minister, 1919–68; Minister of State, 1968–70

Health and Social Security. See *Social Services*)

Home Affairs. Secretary of State, 1900–

Home Security. Minister, 1939–45

Housing and Local Government. Minister of Town and Country Planning, 1943–51; Minister of Local Government and Planning, 1951; Minister of Housing and Local Government, 1951–70 (see *Local Government*)

Housing and Construction. Minister, 1970–

India. Secretary of State for India, 1900–37; Secretary of State for India and Burma, 1937–47

Industrial Development. Minister, 1972–

Industry. Minister, 1970–74; Secretary of State, 1974–

Information. Minister, Mar–Nov 1918 and 1939–46

Ireland. Chief Secretary to the Lord Lieutenant of Ireland, 1900–22 (*Irish Office wound up 1924*).

Labour. Minister of Labour, 1916–39; Minister of Labour and National Service, 1939–59; Minister of Labour, 1959–68

Land and Natural Resources. Minister, 1964–67

Local Government. President of the Local Government Board, 1900–19 (see *Housing and Local Government*)

Local Government and Development. Minister, 1970–74

Local Government and Planning. Minister, 1951 (see *Housing and Local Government*), *Secretary of State,*

[1] From 1940 to 1946 the office was held by the Prime Minister. A permanent department for Defence was not established until 1946.

1969–70 (see *Planning and Local Government*)

Lord Advocate, 1900–

Lord Chancellor, 1900–

Lord Chancellor of Ireland, 1900–22

Lord President of the Council, 1900–

Lord Privy Seal, 1900–

Materials. Minister, 1951–54

Mines. Secretary for Mines Department, 1920–42

Munitions. Minister, 1915–19 (see *Supply*)

National Insurance. Minister, 1944–53; Minister of Pensions and National Insurance, 1953–66

National Service. Minister, 1917–19; Minister of Labour and National Service, 1939–59

Northern Ireland. Secretary of State, 1972–

Overseas Development. Minister, 1964–

Overseas Trade. Secretary for Overseas Trade, 1917–53

Paymaster-General, 1900–

Pensions. Minister of Pensions, 1916–1953; Minister of Pensions and National Insurance, 1953–66

Petroleum. Secretary for Petroleum Department, 1940–42

Planning and Local Government. Minister for Planning and Local Government, 1974–

Portfolio. Minister without portfolio, 1915–21, 1935–36, 1939–42, 1942–1944, 1946, 1947, 1954–68, 1968–

Post Office. Postmaster-General, 1900–1969

Posts and Telecommunications. Minister, 1969–74

Power. Minister, 1957–69 (see *Fuel and Power*)

Prices and Consumer Protection. Secretary of State, 1974–

Prime Minister, 1900–

Privy Council Office. Minister of State, 1974–

Production. Minister, 1942–45

Public Building and Works. Minister, 1962–70 (See *Housing and Construction*)

Reconstruction. Minister, 1917–19 and 1944–45

Science. Minister, 1959–64

Scotland. Secretary, 1900–26; Secretary of State, 1926–

Shipping. Minister, 1916–21 and 1939–1941 (see *War Transport*)

Social Insurance. Minister, Oct–Nov 1944 (see *National Insurance*)

Social Security. Minister, 1966–68

Social Services. Secretary of State, 1968–

Solicitor-General, 1900–

Solicitor-General for Ireland, 1900–22

Solicitor-General for Scotland, 1900–

State. Minister of, 1941–2; First Secretary of, 1962–3, 1964–70.

Sport and Recreation. Minister of State, 1974–

Supply. Minister, 1919–21 and 1939–59

Technology. Minister, 1964–70

Town and Country Planning. Minister of Town and Country Planning, 1943–51 (see *Local Government and Planning*)

Trade. President of the Board of Trade, 1900–70; Secretary of State for Trade and Industry, 1970–4; Secretary of State for Trade, 1974–, *also* Minister for Trade, 1970–2; Minister for Trade and Consumer Affairs, 1972–4.

Transport. Minister of Transport, 1919–41; Minister of War Transport, 1941–45; Minister of Transport, 1945–53; Minister of Transport and Civil Aviation, 1953–59; Minister of Transport, 1959–70; Minister for Transport Industries, 1970–4; Minister for Transport, 1974

Treasury. Chancellor of the Exchequer, 1900–

Urban Affairs. Minister of State, 1974

Wales. Minister for Welsh Affairs, 1954–64; Secretary of State for Wales, 1964–

War. Secretary of State, 1900–64

War Transport. Minister, 1941–45 (see *Shipping* and *Transport*)

Works. First Commissioner of Works, 1900–40; Minister of Works and Buildings, 1940–42; Minister of Works and Planning, 1942–43; Minister of Works, 1943–62, Minister of Public Building and Works, 1962–70

SOURCE.—For a full table of changes within the central administration between 1914–56 see *The Organisation of British Central Government, 1914–1956*, by D. N. Chester and F. M. G. Willson (1957), especially Appendix C, pp. 385–420.

Holders of Ministerial Offices

Prime Minister

1900	M of Salisbury (3rd)
12 Jul 02	A. Balfour
5 Dec 05	Sir H. Campbell-Bannerman
5 Apr 08	H. Asquith
6 Dec 16	D. Lloyd George
23 Oct 22	A. Bonar Law
22 May 23	S. Baldwin
22 Jan 24	J. R. MacDonald
4 Nov 24	S. Baldwin
5 Jun 29	J. R. MacDonald
7 Jun 35	S. Baldwin
28 May 37	N. Chamberlain
10 May 40	W. Churchill
26 Jul 45	C. Attlee
26 Oct 51	(Sir) W. Churchill
6 Apr 55	Sir A. Eden
10 Jan 57	H. Macmillan
18 Oct 63	Sir A. Douglas-Home
16 Oct 64	H. Wilson
19 Jun 70	E. Heath
4 Mar 74	H. Wilson

Lord President of the Council

1900	D of Devonshire
13 Oct 03	M of Londonderry
10 Dec 05	E of Crewe

12 Apr 08 Ld Tweedmouth
13 Oct 08 Vt Wolverhampton
16 Jun 10 Earl Beauchamp
3 Nov 10 Vt Morley
5 Aug 14 Earl Beauchamp
25 May 15 M of Crewe
10 Dec 16 Earl Curzon
23 Oct 19 A. Balfour
24 Oct 22 M of Salisbury (4th)
22 Jan 24 Ld Parmoor
6 Nov 24 Marquess Curzon
27 Apr 25 E of Balfour
7 Jun 29 Ld Parmoor
25 Aug 31 S. Baldwin
7 Jun 35 J. R. MacDonald
28 May 37 Vt Halifax
9 Mar 38 Vt Hailsham (1st)
31 Oct 38 Vt Runciman
3 Sep 39 Earl Stanhope
11 May 40 N. Chamberlain
3 Oct 40 Sir J. Anderson
24 Sep 43 C. Attlee
25 May 45 Ld Woolton
27 Jul 45 H. Morrison
9 Mar 51 Vt Addison
28 Oct 51 Ld Woolton
24 Nov 52 M of Salisbury (5th)
29 Mar 57 E of Home
17 Sep 57 Vt Hailsham (2nd)
14 Oct 59 E of Home
27 Jul 60 Vt Hailsham (2nd) (Q. Hogg)
16 Oct 64 H. Bowden
11 Aug 66 R. Crossman
18 Oct 68 F. Peart
20 Jun 70 W. Whitelaw
7 Apr 72 R. Carr
5 Nov 72 J. Prior
5 Mar 74 E. Short

Lord Chancellor

1900 E of Halsbury
10 Dec 05 Ld Loreburn (E)
10 Jun 12 Vt Haldane
25 May 15 Ld Buckmaster
10 Dec 16 Ld Finlay
10 Jan 19 Ld Birkenhead (Vt)
24 Oct 22 Vt Cave
22 Jan 24 Vt Haldane
6 Nov 24 Vt Cave
28 Mar 28 Ld Hailsham (Vt)
7 Jun 29 Ld Sankey (Vt)
7 Jun 35 Vt Hailsham
9 Mar 38 Ld Maugham (Vt)
3 Sep 39 Vt Caldecote
12 May 40 Vt Simon
27 Jul 45 Ld Jowitt
30 Oct 51 Ld Simonds
18 Oct 54 Vt Kilmuir
13 Jul 62 Ld Dilhorne
16 Oct 64 Ld Gardiner
20 Jun 70 Ld Hailsham
5 Mar 74 Ld Elwyn-Jones

Lord Privy Seal

1900 Vt Cross
1 Nov 00 M of Salisbury (3rd)
12 Jul 02 A. Balfour
11 Oct 03 M of Salisbury (4th)
10 Dec 05 M of Ripon
9 Oct 08 E of Crewe
23 Oct 11 Earl Carrington
13 Feb 12 M of Crewe
25 May 15 Earl Curzon
15 Dec 16 E of Crawford
10 Jan 19 A. Bonar Law
23 Mar 21 A. Chamberlain
24 Oct 22 (office vacant)
25 May 23 Ld R. Cecil
22 Jan 24 J. Clynes
6 Nov 24 M of Salisbury (4th)
7 Jun 29 J. Thomas
5 Jun 30 V. Hartshorn
24 Mar 31 T. Johnston
3 Sep 31 Earl Peel
5 Nov 31 Vt Snowden
29 Sep 32 S. Baldwin
31 Dec 33 A. Eden
7 Jun 35 M of Londonderry
22 Nov 35 Vt Halifax
28 May 37 Earl De La Warr
31 Oct 38 Sir J. Anderson
3 Sep 39 Sir S. Hoare
3 Apr 40 Sir K. Wood
11 May 40 C. Attlee
19 Feb 42 Sir S. Cripps
22 Nov 42 Vt Cranborne (5th M of Salisbury)
24 Sep 43 Ld Beaverbrook
27 Jul 45 A. Greenwood
17 Apr 47 Ld Inman
7 Oct 47 Vt Addison
9 Mar 51 E. Bevin
26 Apr 51 R. Stokes
28 Oct 51 M of Salisbury (5th)
7 May 52 H. Crookshank
20 Dec 55 R. Butler
14 Oct 59 Vt Hailsham
27 Jul 60 E. Heath
20 Oct 63 S. Lloyd
18 Oct 64 E of Longford
23 Dec 65 Sir F. Soskice
6 Apr 66 E of Longford
16 Jan 68 Ld Shackleton
6 Apr 68 F. Peart
18 Oct 68 Ld Shackleton
20 Jun 70 Earl Jellicoe
5 Jun 73 Ld Windlesham
7 Mar 74 Ld Shepherd

Secretary of State for Economic Affairs

16 Oct 64 G. Brown
11 Aug 66 M. Stewart
29 Aug 67 P. Shore
(office abolished 8 Oct 69)

Chancellor of the Exchequer

1900 Sir M. Hicks-Beach
8 Aug 02 C. Ritchie
6 Oct 03 A. Chamberlain
10 Dec 05 H. Asquith
12 Apr 08 D. Lloyd George
25 May 15 R. McKenna
10 Dec 16 A. Bonar Law
10 Jan 19 A. Chamberlain
1 Apr 21 Sir R. Horne
24 Oct 22 S. Baldwin
27 Aug 23 N. Chamberlain
22 Jan 24 P. Snowden
6 Nov 24 W. Churchill
7 Jun 29 P. Snowden
5 Nov 31 N. Chamberlain
28 May 37 Sir J. Simon
12 May 40 Sir K. Wood
24 Sep 43 Sir J. Anderson
27 Jul 45 H. Dalton
13 Nov 47 Sir S. Cripps
19 Oct 50 H. Gaitskell
28 Oct 51 R. Butler
20 Dec 55 H. Macmillan
13 Jan 57 P. Thorneycroft
6 Jan 58 D. Heathcoat Amory
27 Jul 60 S. Lloyd
13 Jul 62 R. Maudling
16 Oct 64 J. Callaghan
30 Nov 67 R. Jenkins
20 Jun 70 I. Macleod
25 Jul 70 A. Barber
5 Mar 74 D. Healey

Secretary of State for Foreign Affairs

1900 M of Salisbury (3rd)
1 Nov 00 M of Lansdowne
10 Dec 05 Sir E. Grey (Vt)
10 Dec 16 A. Balfour
23 Oct 19 Earl Curzon (M)
22 Jan 24 J. R. MacDonald
6 Nov 24 (Sir) A. Chamberlain
7 Jun 29 A. Henderson
25 Aug 31 M of Reading
5 Nov 31 Sir J. Simon
7 Jun 35 Sir S. Hoare
22 Dec 35 A. Eden
21 Feb 38 Vt Halifax
22 Dec 40 A. Eden
27 Jul 45 E. Bevin
9 Mar 51 H. Morrison
28 Oct 51 (Sir) A. Eden
7 Apr 55 H. Macmillan
20 Dec 55 S. Lloyd
27 Jul 60 E of Home
20 Oct 63 R. Butler
16 Oct 64 P. Gordon Walker
22 Jan 65 M. Stewart
11 Aug 66 G. Brown
16 Mar 68 M. Stewart

(Secretary of State for Foreign and Commonwealth Affairs)

17 Oct 68 M. Stewart
20 Jun 70 Sir A. Douglas-Home
5 Mar 74 J. Callaghan

Secretary of State for the Home Department

1900 Sir M. White- Ridley
1 Nov 00 C. Ritchie
8 Aug 02 A. Akers-Douglas
10 Dec 05 H. Gladstone
14 Feb 10 W. Churchill
23 Oct 11 R. McKenna
25 May 15 Sir J. Simon
10 Jan 16 Sir H. Samuel
10 Dec 16 Sir G. Cave (Vt)
10 Jan 19 E. Shortt
24 Oct 22 W. Bridgeman
22 Jan 24 A. Henderson
6 Nov 24 Sir W. Joynson-Hicks
7 Jun 29 J. Clynes
25 Aug 31 Sir H. Samuel
28 Sep 32 Sir J. Gilmour
7 Jun 35 Sir J. Simon
28 May 37 Sir S. Hoare
3 Sep 39 Sir J. Anderson
3 Oct 40 H. Morrison
25 May 45 Sir D. Somervell
3 Aug 45 C. Ede
28 Oct 51 Sir D. Maxwell-Fyfe
18 Oct 54 G. Lloyd-George
13 Jan 57 R. Butler
13 Jul 62 H. Brooke
18 Oct 64 Sir F. Soskice
23 Dec 65 R. Jenkins
30 Nov 67 J. Callaghan
20 Jun 70 R. Maudling
19 Jul 72 R. Carr
5 Mar 74 R. Jenkins

First Lord of the Admiralty

1900 G. Goschen
1 Nov 00 E of Selborne
5 Mar 05 Earl Cawdor
10 Dec 05 Ld Tweedmouth
12 Apr 08 R. McKenna
23 Oct 11 W. Churchill
25 May 15 A. Balfour
10 Dec 16 Sir E. Carson
17 Jul 17 Sir E. Geddes
10 Jan 19 W. Long
13 Feb 21 Ld Lee
24 Oct 22 L. Amery
22 Jan 24 Vt Chelmsford
6 Nov 24 W. Bridgeman
7 Jun 29 A. Alexander
25 Aug 31 Sir A. Chamberlain
5 Nov 31 Sir B. Eyres-Monsell (Vt Monsell)

5 Jun 36 Sir S. Hoare
28 May 37 A. Duff Cooper
27 Oct 38 Earl Stanhope
3 Sep 39 W. Churchill
11 May 40 A. Alexander
25 May 45 B. Bracken
3 Aug 45 A. Alexander
4 Oct 46 Vt Hall
24 May 51 Ld Pakenham
31 Oct 51 J. Thomas (Vt Cilcennin)
2 Sep 56 Vt Hailsham
16 Jan 57 E of Selkirk
16 Oct 59 Ld Carrington
22 Oct 63 Earl Jellicoe
(*office abolished* 1 *Apr* 64)

Minister for Aerospace

1 May 71 F. Corfield
7 Apr 72 M. Heseltine
(*office abolished* 5 *Mar* 74)

President of the Board of Agriculture and Fisheries

1900 W. Long
14 Nov 00 R. Hanbury
19 May 03 E of Onslow
12 Mar 05 A. Fellowes
10 Dec 05 Earl Carrington
23 Oct 11 W. Runciman
6 Aug 14 Ld Lucas
25 May 15 E of Selborne
11 Jul 16 E of Crawford
10 Dec 16 R. Prothero (Ld Ernle)

(Minister of Agriculture and Fisheries)

(*and Food, since* 18 *Oct* 54)

15 Aug 19 Ld Lee
13 Feb 21 Sir A. Griffith-Boscawen
24 Oct 22 Sir R. Sanders
22 Jan 24 N. Buxton
6 Nov 24 E. Wood
4 Nov 25 W. Guinness
7 Jun 29 N. Buxton
5 Jun 30 C. Addison
25 Aug 31 Sir J. Gilmour
28 Sep 32 W. Elliot
29 Oct 36 W. Morrison
29 Jan 39 Sir R. Dorman-Smith
14 May 40 R. Hudson
3 Aug 45 T. Williams
31 Oct 51 Sir T. Dugdale
28 Jul 54 D. Heathcoat Amory
6 Jan 58 J. Hare
27 Jul 60 C. Soames
18 Oct 64 F. Peart
6 Apr 68 C. Hughes
20 Jun 70 J. Prior
5 Nov 72 J. Godber
5 Mar 74 F. Peart

President of the Air Board

3 Jan 17 Ld Cowdray

President of the Air Council

26 Nov 17 Ld Rothermere
26 Apr 18 Ld Weir

Secretary of State for Air

10 Jan 19 W. Churchill
1 Apr 21 F. Guest
31 Oct 22 Sir S. Hoare
22 Jan 24 Ld Thomson
6 Nov 24 Sir S. Hoare
7 Jun 29 Ld Thomson
14 Oct 30 Ld Amulree
5 Nov 31 M of Londonderry
7 Jun 35 Sir P. Cunliffe-Lister (Vt Swinton)
16 May 38 Sir K. Wood
3 Apr 40 Sir S. Hoare
11 May 40 Sir A. Sinclair
25 May 45 H. Macmillan
3 Aug 45 Vt Stansgate
4 Oct 46 P. Noel-Baker
7 Oct 47 A. Henderson
31 Oct 51 Ld De L'Isle
20 Dec 55 N. Birch
16 Jan 57 G. Ward
28 Oct 60 J. Amery
16 Jul 62 H. Fraser
(*office abolished* 1 *Apr* 64)

Minister of Aircraft Production

14 May 40 Ld Beaverbrook
1 May 41 J. Moore-Brabazon
22 Feb 42 J. Llewellin
22 Nov 42 Sir S. Cripps
25 May 45 E. Brown
(*office abolished* 26 *Jul* 45)

Attorney-General

1900 Sir R. Webster
7 May 00 Sir R. Finlay
12 Dec 05 Sir J. Walton
28 Jan 08 Sir W. Robson
7 Oct 10 Sir R. Isaacs
19 Oct 13 Sir J. Simon
25 May 15 Sir E. Carson
3 Nov 15 Sir F. Smith
10 Jan 19 Sir G. Hewart
6 Mar 22 Sir E. Pollock
24 Oct 22 Sir D. Hogg
23 Jan 24 Sir P. Hastings
6 Nov 24 Sir D. Hogg
28 Mar 28 Sir T. Inskip
7 Jun 29 Sir W. Jowitt
26 Jan 32 Sir T. Inskip
18 Mar 36 Sir D. Somervell
25 May 45 Sir D. Maxwell Fyfe
4 Aug 45 Sir H Shawcross.

24 Apr 51	Sir F. Soskice
3 Nov 51	Sir L. Heald
18 Oct 54	Sir R. Manning-ham-Buller
16 Jul 62	Sir J. Hobson
1 Oct 64	Sir E. Jones
23 Jun 70	Sir P. Rawlinson
7 Mar 74	S. Silkin

Minister of Blockade

10 Dec 16	Ld R. Cecil
18 Jul 18	Sir L. Worthington-Evans

(*office abolished* 10 *Jan* 19)

Minister of Civil Aviation

8 Oct 44	Vt Swinton
4 Aug 45	Ld Winster
4 Oct 46	Ld Nathan
31 May 48	Ld Pakenham
1 Jun 51	Ld Ogmore
31 Oct 51	J. Maclay
7 May 52	A. Lennox-Boyd

(Minister of Transport and Civil Aviation)

1 Oct 53	A. Lennox-Boyd
28 Jul 54	J. Boyd-Carpenter
20 Dec 55	H. Watkinson

(Minister of Aviation)

14 Oct 59	D. Sandys
27 July 60	P. Thorneycroft
16 Jul 62	J. Amery
18 Oct 64	R. Jenkins
23 Dec 65	F. Mulley
7 Jan 67	J. Stonehouse

(*office absorbed into Ministry of Technology* 15 *Feb* 67)

Minister of Aviation Supply

15 Oct 70	F. Corfield

(*office absorbed into Ministry of Defence* 1 *May* 72)

Minister for the Civil Service

1 Nov 68	H. Wilson
19 Jun 70	E. Heath
4 Mar 74	H. Wilson

Secretary of State for the Colonies

1900	J. Chamberlain
6 Oct 03	A. Lyttelton
10 Dec 05	E of Elgin
12 Apr 08	E of Crewe
3 Nov 10	L. Harcourt
25 May 15	A. Bonar Law
10 Dec 16	W. Long
10 Jan 19	Vt Milner

13 Feb 21	W. Churchill
24 Oct 22	D of Devonshire
22 Jan 24	J. Thomas
6 Nov 24	L. Amery
7 Jun 29	Ld Passfield
25 Aug 31	J. Thomas
5 Nov 31	Sir P. Cunliffe-Lister
7 June 35	M. MacDonald
22 Nov 35	J. Thomas
28 May 36	W. Ormsby-Gore
16 May 38	M. MacDonald
12 May 40	Ld Lloyd
8 Feb 41	Ld Moyne
22 Feb 42	Vt Cranborne
22 Nov 42	O. Stanley
3 Aug 45	G. Hall
4 Oct 46	A. Creech Jones
28 Feb 50	J. Griffiths
28 Oct 51	O. Lyttelton
28 Jul 54	A. Lennox-Boyd
14 Oct 59	I. Macleod
9 Oct 61	R. Maudling
13 Jul 62	D. Sandys
18 Oct 64	A. Greenwood
23 Dec 65	E of Longford
6 Apr 66	F. Lee

(*office came under Commonwealth Affairs* 1 *Jul* 66 *and abolished* 6 *Jan* 67)

Minister for Co-ordination of Defence

13 Mar 36	Sir T. Inskip
29 Jan 39	Ld Chatfield

(Minister of Defence)

10 May 40	W. Churchill
27 Jul 45	C. Attlee
20 Dec 46	A. Alexander
28 Feb 50	E. Shinwell
28 Oct 51	W. Churchill
1 Mar 52	Earl Alexander
18 Oct 54	H. Macmillan
7 Apr 55	S. Lloyd
20 Dec 55	Sir W. Monckton
18 Oct 56	A. Head
13 Jan 57	D. Sandys
14 Oct 59	H. Watkinson
13 Jul 62	P. Thorneycroft

(Secretary of State)

16 Oct 64	D. Healey
8 Jan 74	I. Gilmour
5 May 74	R. Mason
20 Jun 70	Ld Carrington
5 Mar 74	R. Mason

Minister for Defence Procurement

7 Apr 71	I. Gilmour

(*office abolished* 5 *Nov* 72)

Minister of Defence for Administration

7 Jun 67	G. Reynolds
15 Jul 69	R. Hattersley

(*office abolished* 19 *Jun* 70)

Minister of Defence for Equipment

7 Jan 67	R. Mason
6 Apr 68	J. Morris

Secretary of State for Dominion Affairs

11 Jun 25	L. Amery
7 Jun 29	Ld Passfield
5 Jun 30	J. Thomas
22 Nov 35	M. MacDonald
16 May 38	Ld Stanley
31 Oct 38	M. MacDonald
29 Jan 39	Sir T. Inskip (Vt Caldecote)
3 Sep 39	A. Eden
14 May 40	Vt Caldecote
3 Oct 40	Vt Cranborne
19 Feb 42	C. Attlee
24 Sep 43	Vt Cranborne
3 Aug 45	Vt Addison

(Secretary of State for Commonwealth Relations)

7 Jul 47	Vt Addison
7 Oct 47	P. Noel-Baker
28 Feb 50	P. Gordon Walker
28 Oct 51	Ld Ismay
12 Mar 52	M of Salisbury
24 Nov 52	Vt Swinton
7 Apr 55	E of Home
27 Jul 60	D. Sandys
18 Oct 64	A. Bottomley

(Secretary of State for Commonwealth Affairs)

1 Aug 66	A. Bottomley
11 Aug 66	H. Bowden
29 Aug 67	G. Thomson

(17 *Oct* 68 *office merged with Foreign Office*)

Minister of Economic Warfare

3 Sep 39	R. Cross
15 May 40	H. Dalton
22 Feb 42	Vt Wolmer (E of Selborne)

(*office wound up* 23 *May* 45)

President of the Board of Education

1 Jan 00	D of Devonshire
8 Aug 02	M of Londonderry
10 Dec 05	A. Birrell

23 Jan 07 R. McKenna
12 Apr 08 W. Runciman
23 Oct 11 J. Pease
25 May 15 A. Henderson
18 Aug 16 M of Crewe
10 Dec 16 H. Fisher
24 Oct 22 E. Wood
22 Jan 24 C. Trevelyan
6 Nov 24 Ld E. Percy
7 Jun 29 Sir C. Trevelyan
2 Mar 31 H. Lees-Smith
25 Aug 31 Sir D. Maclean
15 Jun 32 Ld Irwin (Vt
          Halifax)
7 Jun 35 O. Stanley
28 May 37 Earl Stanhope
27 Oct 38 Earl De La Warr
3 Apr 40 H. Ramsbotham
20 Jul 41 R. Butler

(Minister of Education)

3 Aug 44 R. Butler
25 May 45 R. Law
3 Aug 45 Miss E. Wilkin-
          son
10 Feb 47 G. Tomlinson
2 Nov 51 Miss F. Hors-
          brugh
18 Oct 54 Sir D. Eccles
13 Jan 57 Vt Hailsham
          (2nd)
17 Sep 57 G. Lloyd
14 Oct 59 Sir D. Eccles
13 Jul 62 Sir E. Boyle

(Secretary of State for Education and Science)

1 Apr 64 Q. Hogg
18 Oct 64 M. Stewart
22 Jan 65 A. Crosland
29 Aug 67 P. Gordon
          Walker
6 Apr 68 E. Short
20 Jun 70 Mrs M. Thatcher
5 Mar 74 R. Prentice

Secretary of State for Employment and Productivity

6 Apr 68 Mrs B. Castle
20 Jun 70 R. Carr

(Secretary of State for Employment)

12 Nov 70 R. Carr
7 Apr 72 M. Macmillan
2 Dec 73 W. Whitelaw
5 Mar 74 M. Foot

Secretary of State for Energy

8 Jan 74 Ld Carrington
5 Mar 74 E. Varley

Secretary of State for the Environment

15 Oct 70 P. Walker
5 Nov 72 G. Rippon
5 Mar 74 A. Crosland

Minister of Food Control

10 Dec 16 Vt Devonport
19 Jun 17 Ld Rhondda (Vt)
9 Jul 18 J. Clynes
10 Jan 19 G. Roberts
19 Mar 20 C. McCurdy
(office abolished 31 Mar 21)

Minister of Food

4 Sep 39 W. Morrison
3 Apr 40 Ld Woolton
11 Nov 43 J. Llewellin
3 Aug 45 Sir B. Smith
27 May 46 J. Strachey
28 Feb 50 M. Webb
31 Oct 51 G. Lloyd-George
18 Oct 54 D. Heathcoat
          Amory
(and combined with Minister of Agriculture and Fisheries)

Minister of Fuel, Light and Power

3 Jun 42 G. Lloyd-George

(Minister of Fuel and Power)

25 May 45 G. Lloyd-George
3 Aug 45 E. Shinwell
7 Oct 47 H. Gaitskell
28 Feb 50 P. Noel-Baker
31 Oct 51 G. Lloyd
20 Dec 55 A. Jones

(Minister of Power)

13 Jan 57 Ld Mills
14 Oct 59 R. Wood
20 Oct 63 F. Erroll
18 Oct 64 F. Lee
6 Apr 66 R. Marsh
6 Apr 68 R. Gunter
6 Jul 68 R. Mason
(office absorbed into Ministry of Technology 6 Oct 69)

Minister of Health
(See below, under Local Government)

Minister of Housing
(See below, under Local Government)

Secretary of State for India (and Burma 1937-48)

1900 Ld G. Hamilton

6 Oct 03 St J. Brodrick
10 Dec 05 J. Morley (Vt)
3 Nov 10 E of Crewe
7 Mar 11 Vt Morley
25 May 11 E of Crewe (M)
25 May 15 A. Chamberlain
17 Jul 17 E. Montagu
19 Mar 22 Vt Peel
22 Jan 24 Ld Olivier
6 Nov 24 E of Birkenhead
18 Oct 28 Vt Peel
7 Jun 29 W. Benn
25 Aug 31 Sir S. Hoare
7 Jun 35 M of Zetland
13 May 40 L. Amery
3 Aug 45 Ld Pethick-
          Lawrence
17 Apr 47 E of Listowel
(4 Jan 1948 India & Burma
         Offices wound up)

Minister for Industrial Development

7 Apr 72 C. Chataway
(office abolished 5 Mar 74)

Minister for Industry

15 Oct 70 Sir J. Eden
7 Apr 72 T. Boardman
(office abolished 8 Jan 74)

Secretary of State for Industry

5 Mar 74 A. Wedgwood
         Benn

Minister of Information

10 Feb 18 Ld Beaverbrook
4 Nov 18 Ld Downham
(office abolished 10 Jan 19)
4 Sep 39 Ld Macmillan
5 Jan 40 Sir J. Reith
12 May 40 A. Duff Cooper
20 Jul 41 B. Bracken
25 May 45 G. Lloyd
4 Aug 45 E. Williams
(office abolished 31 Mar 46)

Chief Secretary for Ireland

1900 G. Balfour
7 Nov 00 G. Wyndham
12 Mar 05 W. Long
10 Dec 05 J. Bryce
23 Jan 07 A. Birrell
31 Jul 16 (Sir) H. Duke
5 May 18 E. Shortt
10 Jan 19 I. Macpherson
2 Apr 20 Sir H. Green-
         wood
(post vacant 19 Oct 22, office
       abolished 6 Dec 22)

Lord Chancellor of Ireland

1900 Ld Ashbourne
12 Dec 05 Sir S. Walker
26 Sep 11 R. Barry
10 Apr 13 (Sir) I. O'Brien
4 Jun 18 Sir J. Campbell
27 Jun 21 Sir J. Ross
(ceased to be executive office 27 Jun 21)

Lord Lieutenant of Ireland

(See p. 351. *Office in Cabinet only Jun 95-8 Aug 02 and 28 Oct 19-2 Apr 21*)

Attorney-General for Ireland

1900 J. Atkinson
20 Dec 05 R. Cherry
2 Dec 09 R. Barry
26 Sep 11 C. O'Connor
24 Jun 12 I. O'Brien
10 Apr 13 T. Molony
20 Jun 13 J. Moriarty
1 Jul 14 J. Pim
8 Jun 15 J. Gordon
9 Apr 16 J. Campbell
8 Jan 17 J. O'Connor
7 Apr 18 A. Samuels
6 Jul 19 D. Henry
5 Aug 21 T. Brown
(post vacant from 16 Nov 21)

Solicitor-General for Ireland

1900 D. Barton
30 Jan 00 G. Wright
8 Jan 03 J. Campbell
20 Dec 05 R. Barry
2 Dec 09 C. O'Connor
19 Oct 11 I. O'Brien
24 Jun 12 T. Molony
25 Apr 13 J. Moriarty
20 Jun 13 J. Pim
1 Jul 14 J. O'Connor
19 Mar 17 J. Chambers
12 Sep 17 A. Samuels
7 Apr 18 J. Powell
27 Nov 18 D. Henry
6 Jul 19 D. Wilson
2 Jun 21 T. Brown
(post vacant from 5 Aug 21)

Minister of Labour

10 Dec 16 J. Hodge
17 Aug 17 G. Roberts
10 Jan 19 Sir R. Horne
19 Mar 20 T. Macnamara
31 Oct 22 Sir A. Montague-Barlow
22 Jan 24 T. Shaw
6 Nov 24 Sir A. Steel-Maitland

7 Jun 29 Miss M. Bondfield
25 Aug 31 Sir H. Betterton
29 Jun 34 O. Stanley
7 Jun 35 E. Brown

(Minister of Labour and National Service)

3 Sep 39 E. Brown
13 May 40 E. Bevin
25 May 45 R. Butler
3 Aug 45 G. Isaacs
17 Jan 51 A. Bevan
24 Apr 51 A. Robens
28 Oct 51 Sir W. Monckton
20 Dec 55 I. Macleod
14 Oct 59 E. Heath

(Minister of Labour)

12 Nov 59 E. Heath
27 Jul 60 J. Hare
20 Oct 63 J. Godber
18 Oct 64 R. Gunter
(*6 Apr 68 office reorganised as Ministry of Employment and Productivity*)

Chancellor of the Duchy of Lancaster

1900 Ld James
8 Aug 02 Sir W. Walrond
10 Dec 05 Sir H. Fowler (Vt Wolverhampton)
13 Oct 08 Ld Fitzmaurice
25 Jun 09 H. Samuel
14 Feb 10 J. Pease
23 Oct 11 C. Hobhouse
11 Feb 14 C. Masterman
3 Feb 15 E. Montagu
25 May 15 W. Churchill
25 Nov 15 H. Samuel
11 Jan 16 E. Montagu
9 Jul 16 T. McKinnon Wood
10 Dec 16 Sir F. Cawley
10 Feb 18 Ld Beaverbrook
4 Nov 18 Ld Downham
10 Jan 19 E of Crawford
1 Apr 21 Vt Peel
7 Apr 22 Sir W. Sutherland
24 Oct 22 M of Salisbury
25 May 23 J. Davidson
22 Jan 24 J. Wedgwood
10 Nov 24 Vt Cecil
19 Oct 27 Ld Cushendun
7 Jun 29 Sir O. Mosley
23 May 30 C. Attlee
13 May 31 Ld Ponsonby
25 Aug 31 M of Lothian
10 Nov 31 (Sir) J. Davidson
28 May 37 Earl Winterton
29 Jan 39 W. Morrison
3 Apr 40 G. Tryon
14 May 40 Ld Hankey
20 Jul 41 A. Duff Cooper

11 Nov 43 E. Brown
25 May 45 Sir A. Salter
4 Aug 45 J. Hynd
27 Apr 47 Ld Pakenham
11 May 48 H. Dalton
38 Feb 50 Vt Alexander
31 Oct 51 Vt Swinton
24 Nov 52 Ld Woolton
20 Dec 55 E of Selkirk
13 Jan 57 C. Hill
9 Oct 61 I. Macleod
20 Oct 63 Ld Blakenham
18 Oct 64 D. Houghton
6 Apr 66 G. Thomson
7 Jan 67 F. Lee
20 Jun 70 A. Barber
28 Jul 70 G. Rippon
5 Nov 72 J. Davies
5 Mar 74 H. Lever

President of the Local Government Board

1900 H. Chaplin
7 Nov 00 W. Long
12 Mar 05 G. Balfour
10 Dec 05 J. Burns
11 Feb 14 H. Samuel
25 May 15 W. Long
10 Dec 16 Ld Rhondda
28 Jun 17 W. Hayes Fisher
4 Nov 18 Sir A. Geddes
10 Jan 19 C. Addison
(*24 Jun 19 the Local Government Board became the Ministry of Health*)

Minister of Health

24 Jun 19 C. Addison
1 Apr 21 Sir A. Mond
24 Oct 22 Sir A. Griffith Boscawen
7 Mar 23 N. Chamberlain
27 Aug 23 Sir W. Joynson-Hicks
22 Jan 24 J. Wheatley
6 Nov 24 N. Chamberlain
7 Jun 29 A. Greenwood
25 Aug 31 N. Chamberlain
5 Nov 31 Sir E. Young
7 Jun 35 Sir K. Wood
16 May 38 W. Elliot
13 May 40 M. MacDonald
8 Feb 41 E. Brown
11 Nov 43 H. Willink
3 Aug 45 A. Bevan
17 Jan 51 H. Marquand
30 Oct 51 H. Crookshank
7 May 52 I. Macleod
20 Dec 55 R. Turton
16 Jan 57 D. Vosper
17 Sep 57 D. Walker-Smith
27 Jul 60 E. Powell
20 Oct 63 A. Barber
18 Oct 64 K. Robinson
(*1 Nov 68 combined with Ministry of Social Security. See Social Services*)

Minister of Land and Natural Resources
17 Oct 64 F. Willey
(17 Feb 67 office wound up)

(Minister for Planning and Land)
1 Nov 68 K. Robinson
(6 Oct 69 office wound up)

Minister of Local Government and Planning
31 Jan 51 H. Dalton

(Minister of Housing and Local Government)
30 Oct 51 H. Macmillan
18 Oct 54 D. Sandys
13 Jan 57 H. Brooke
9 Oct 61 C. Hill
13 Jul 62 Sir K. Joseph
18 Oct 64 R. Crossman
11 Aug 66 A. Greenwood
31 May 70 R. Mellish
20 Jun 70 P. Walker
(15 Oct 70 reorganised as Local Government and Development under Dept. of Environment)

Minister of Local Government and Development
15 Oct 70 G. Page

(Minister for Planning and Local Government)
7 Mar 74 J. Silkin

Minister of Housing and Construction
15 Oct 70 J. Amery
5 Nov 72 P. Channon
7 Mar 74 R. Freeson

Minister of Materials
6 Jul 51 R. Stokes
31 Oct 51 Vt Swinton
24 Nov 52 Sir A. Salter
1 Sep 53 Ld Woolton
(15 Jul 54 office wound up)

Minister of Munitions
25 May 15 D. Lloyd George
9 Jul 16 E. Montagu
10 Dec 16 C. Addison
17 Jul 17 W. Churchill
10 Jan 19 Ld Inverforth
(and Minister designate for Ministry of Supply. Office abolished 21 Mar 21)

Secretary of State for Northern Ireland
24 Apr 72 W. Whitelaw
2 Dec 73 F. Pym
5 Mar 74 M. Rees

Minister of Overseas Development
18 Oct 64 Mrs B. Castle
23 Dec 65 A. Greenwood
11 Aug 66 A. Bottomley
29 Aug 67 R. Prentice
6 Oct 69 Mrs J. Hart
23 Jun 70 R. Wood
7 Mar 74 Mrs J. Hart

Paymaster-General
1900 D of Marlborough
11 Mar 02 Sir S. Crossley
12 Dec 05 R. Causton (Ld Southwark)
23 Feb 10 I. Guest (Ld Ashby St Ledgers)
23 May 12 Ld Strachie
9 Jun 15 Ld Newton
18 Aug 16 A. Henderson
15 Dec 16 Sir J. Compton-Rickett
26 Oct 19 Sir T. Walters
24 Oct 22 (office vacant)
5 Feb 23 N. Chamberlain
15 Mar 23 Sir W. Joynson-Hicks
25 May 23 A. Boyd-Carpenter
6 May 24 H. Gosling
6 Nov 24 (office vacant)
28 Jul 25 D of Sutherland
2 Dec 28 E of Onslow
7 Jun 29 Ld Arnold
4 Sep 31 Sir T. Walters
23 Nov 31 Ld Rochester
6 Dec 35 Ld Hutchison
2 Jun 38 E of Munster
29 Jan 39 Earl Winterton
Nov 39 (office vacant)
15 May 40 Vt Cranborne
3 Oct 40 (office vacant)
20 Jul 41 Ld Hankey
4 Mar 42 Sir W. Jowitt
30 Dec 42 Ld Cherwell
3 Aug 45 (office vacant)
9 Jul 46 A. Greenwood
5 Mar 47 H. Marquand
2 Jul 48 Vt Addison
1 Apr 49 Ld Macdonald
30 Oct 51 Ld Cherwell
11 Nov 53 E of Selkirk
20 Dec 55 (office vacant)
18 Oct 56 Sir W. Monckton
16 Jan 57 R. Maudling
14 Oct 59 Ld Mills
9 Oct 61 H. Brooke
13 Jul 62 J. Boyd-Carpenter
19 Oct 64 G. Wigg
12 Nov 67 (office vacant)
6 Apr 68 Ld Shackleton

1 Nov 68 Mrs J. Hart
6 Oct 69 H. Lever
23 Jun 70 Ld Eccles
2 Dec 73 M. Macmillan
7 Mar 74 E. Dell

Minister of Pensions
10 Dec 16 G. Barnes
17 Aug 17 J. Hodge
10 Jan 19 Sir L. Worthington-Evans
2 Apr 20 I. Macpherson
31 Oct 22 G. Tryon
23 Jan 24 F. Roberts
11 Nov 24 G. Tryon
7 Jun 29 F. Roberts
3 Sep 31 G. Tryon
18 Jun 35 R. Hudson
30 Jul 36 H. Ramsbotham
7 Jun 39 Sir W. Womersley
3 Aug 45 W. Paling
17 Apr 47 J. Hynd
7 Oct 47 G. Buchanan
2 Jul 48 H. Marquand
17 Jan 51 G. Isaacs
5 Nov 51 D. Heathcoat Amory

(Minister of Pensions and National Insurance)
3 Sep 53 O. Peake
20 Dec 55 J. Boyd-Carpenter
16 Jul 62 N. Macpherson
21 Oct 63 R. Wood
18 Oct 64 Miss M. Herbison
(6 Aug 66 recast as Social Security)

Minister of Social Insurance
8 Oct 44 Sir W. Jowitt

(Minister of National Insurance)
17 Nov 44 Sir W. Jowitt
25 May 45 L. Hore-Belisha
4 Aug 45 J. Griffiths
28 Feb 50 Edith Summerskill
31 Oct 51 O. Peake
(3 Sep 53 combined with Ministry of Pensions)

Minister without Portfolio
25 May 15–5 Dec 16
    M of Lansdowne
10 Dec 16–12 Aug 17
    A. Henderson
10 Dec 16–18 Apr 18
    Vt Milner
17 Jul 17–21 Jan 18
    Sir E. Carson

29 May 17–27 Jan 20
  G. Barnes
22 Jun 17–10 Jan 19
  J. Smuts
18 Apr 18–10 Jan 19
  A. Chamberlain
10 Jan 19–19 May 19
  Sir E. Geddes
2 Apr 20–13 Feb 21
  Sir L. Worthington-Evans
1 Apr 21–14 Jul 21
  C. Addison
7 Jun 35–22 Dec 35
  A. Eden
7 Jun 35–31 Mar 36
  Ld E. Percy
21 Apr 39–14 Jul 39
  L. Burgin
3 Sep 39–10 May 40
  Ld Hankey
11 May 40–22 Feb 42
  A. Greenwood
30 Dec 42–8 Oct 44
  Sir W. Jowitt
4 Oct 46–20 Dec 46
  A. Alexander
17 Apr 47–29 Sep 47
  A. Greenwood
18 Oct 54–11 Jun 57
  E of Munster
11 Jun 57–23 Oct 58
  Ld Mancroft
23 Oct 58–9 Oct 61
  E of Dundee
9 Oct 61–14 Jul 62
  Ld Mills
13 Jul 62–16 Oct 64
  W. Deedes
20 Oct 63–16 Oct 64
  Ld Carrington
19 Oct 64–6 Apr 66
  E. Fletcher
21 Oct 64–7 Jan 67
  Ld Champion
7 Jan 66–29 Aug 67
  P. Gordon Walker
7 Jan 66–16 Jan 68
  Ld Shackleton
6 Apr 66–7 Jan 67
  D. Houghton
17 Oct 68–6 Oct 69
  G. Thomson
6 Oct 69–19 Jun 70
  P. Shore
15 Oct 70–8 Jan 74
  Ld Drumalbyn
8 Jan 74–4 Mar 74
  Ld Aberdare

Secretary of State for Prices and Consumer Protection

5 Mar 74 Mrs S. Williams

Postmaster-General

1900 D of Norfolk
2 Apr 00 M of London-
      derry

8 Aug 02 A. Chamberlain
6 Oct 03 Ld Stanley
10 Dec 05 S. Buxton
14 Feb 10 H. Samuel
11 Feb 14 C. Hobhouse
26 May 15 H. Samuel
18 Jan 16 J. Pease
10 Dec 16 A. Illingworth
1 Apr 21 F. Kellaway
31 Oct 22 N. Chamberlain
7 Mar 23 Sir W. Joynson-
      Hicks
28 May 23 Sir L. Worthing-
      ton-Evans
22 Jan 24 V. Hartshorn
11 Nov 24 Sir W. Mitchell-
      Thomson
Jun 29 H. Lees-Smith
Mar 31 C. Attlee
3 Sep 31 W. Ormsby-Gore
10 Nov 31 Sir K. Wood
7 Jun 35 G. Tryon
3 Apr 40 W. Morrison
30 Dec 42 H. Crookshank
4 Aug 45 E of Listowel
17 Apr 47 W. Paling
28 Feb 50 N. Edwards
5 Nov 51 Earl De La Warr
7 Apr 55 C. Hill
16 Jan 57 E. Marples
22 Oct 59 J. Bevins
19 Oct 64 A. Wedgwood
      Benn
4 Jul 66 E. Short
6 Apr 68 R. Mason
1 Jul 68 J. Stonehouse
(*Post Office became a Public Corporation* 1 Oct 69)

(Minister for Posts and Telecommunications)

1 Oct 69 J. Stonehouse
24 Jun 70 C. Chataway
7 Apr 72 Sir J. Eden
9 Mar 74 A. Wedgwood
      Benn
(29 *Mar* 74 *office wound up*)

Minister of Public Building and Works

16 Jul 62 G. Rippon
18 Oct 64 C. Pannell
6 Apr 66 R. Prentice
29 Aug 67 R. Mellish
30 Apr 69 J. Silkin
23 Jun 70 J. Amery
(15 *Oct* 70 *reorganised as Housing and Construction under Dept of Environment. See Local Government*)

Minister Resident in Middle East

19 Feb 42 O. Lyttelton
19 Mar 42 R. Casey

(Minister of State in Middle East)

28 Jan 44 Ld Moyne
21 Nov 44 Sir E. Grigg
(*office abolished* 27 *Jul* 45)

Minister Resident at Allied H.Q. in N.W. Africa

30 Dec 42 H. Macmillan
(*office abolished* 23 *May* 45)

Minister Resident in W. Africa

8 Jun 42 Vt Swinton
21 Nov 44 H. Balfour
(*office abolished* 27 *Jul* 45)

Minister Resident in Washington for Supply

22 Nov 42 J. Llewellin
11 Nov 43 B. Smith
(*office abolished* 23 *May* 45)

Minister of Reconstruction

17 Jul 17–10 Jan 19
  C. Addison
11 Nov 43–23 May 45
  Ld Woolton

Minister for Science

14 Oct 59 Vt Hailsham
(1 *Apr* 64 *combined with Dept. of Education*)

Secretary for Scotland

1900 Ld Balfour
6 Oct 03 A. Murray
2 Feb 05 M of Linlithgow
10 Dec 05 J. Sinclair (Ld
      Pentland)
13 Feb 12 T. Wood
9 Jul 16 H. Tennant
10 Dec 16 R. Munro
24 Oct 22 Vt Novar
22 Jan 24 W. Adamson
6 Nov 24 Sir J. Gilmour

(Secretary of State for Scotland)

15 Jul 26 Sir J. Gilmour
7 Jun 29 W. Adamson
25 Aug 31 Sir A. Sinclair
28 Sep 32 Sir G. Collins
29 Oct 36 W. Elliot
16 May 38 J. Colville
14 May 40 E. Brown
8 Feb 41 T. Johnston
25 May 45 Ld Rosebery
3 Aug 45 J. Westwood
7 Oct 47 A. Woodburn
28 Feb 50 H. McNeil

30 Oct 51 J. Stuart
13 Jan 57 J. Maclay
13 Jul 62 M. Noble
18 Oct 64 W. Ross
19 Jun 70 G. Campbell
5 Mar 74 W. Ross

Lord Advocate
1900 A. Murray
18 Oct 03 S. Dickson
12 Dec 05 T. Shaw
14 Feb 09 A. Ure
30 Oct 13 R. Munro
10 Dec 16 J. Clyde
25 Mar 20 T. Morison
5 Mar 22 C. Murray
6 Nov 22 D. Fleming
5 Apr 23 F. Thomson
8 Feb 24 H. Macmillan
11 Nov 24 W. Watson
23 Apr 29 A. MacRobert
17 Jun 29 C. Aitchison
2 Oct 33 W. Normand
28 Mar 35 D. Jamieson
25 Oct 35 T. Cooper
5 Jun 41 J. Reid
10 Aug 45 G. Thomson
7 Oct 47 J. Wheatley
2 Nov 51 J. Clyde
30 Dec 54 W. Milligan
5 Apr 60 W. Grant
27 Apr 64 I. Shearer
20 Oct 64 G. Stott
23 Jun 70 N. Wylie
8 Mar 74 R. King Murray

Solicitor-General for Scotland
1900 S. Dickson
18 Oct 03 D. Dundas
30 Jan 05 E. Salvesen
16 Oct 05 J. Clyde
18 Dec 05 A. Ure
18 Feb 08 A. Dewar
18 Apr 10 W. Hunter
3 Dec 11 A. Anderson
30 Oct 13 T. Morison
25 Mar 20 C. Murray
16 Mar 22 A. Briggs Constable
24 Jul 22 W. Watson
18 Feb 24 J. Fenton
11 Nov 24 D. Fleming
30 Dec 25 A. MacRobert
23 Apr 29 W. Normand
17 Jun 29 J. Watson
10 Nov 31 W. Normand
2 Oct 33 D. Jamieson
15 May 35 T. Cooper
29 Nov 35 A. Russell
25 Jun 36 J. Reid
5 Jun 41 (Sir) D. Murray
10 Sep 45 D. Blades
19 Mar 47 J. Wheatley
24 Oct 47 D. Johnston
3 Nov 51 W. Milligan

10 Jan 55 W. Grant
11 May 60 D. Anderson
27 Apr 64 N. Wylie
20 Oct 64 J. Leechman
11 Oct 65 H. S. Wilson
23 Jun 70 D. Brand
5 Nov 72 I. Stewart
14 Mar 74 J. McCluskey

Minister of Shipping
10 Dec 16 Sir J. Maclay (Ld)
(*office abolished 31 Mar 21*)
13 Oct 39 Sir J. Gilmour
3 Apr 40 R. Hudson
14 May 40 R. Cross
(*1 May 41 combined with Ministry of Transport to form Ministry of War Transport*)

Minister of Social Security
6 Aug 66 Miss M. Herbison
26 Jul 67 Mrs J. Hart

(Secretary of State for Social Services)
17 Oct 68 R. Crossman
20 Jun 70 Sir K. Joseph
5 Mar 74 Mrs B. Castle

Solicitor-General
1900 Sir R. Finlay
7 May 00 Sir E. Carson
12 Dec 05 Sir W. Robson
28 Jan 08 Sir S. Evans
6 Mar 10 Sir R. Issaacs
7 Oct 10 Sir J. Simon
19 Oct 13 Sir S. Buckmaster
2 Jun 15 Sir F. Smith
18 Jan 16 Sir G. Cave
10 Dec 16 Sir G. Hewart
10 Jan 19 Sir E. Pollock
6 Mar 22 Sir L. Scott
31 Oct 22 Sir T. Inskip
23 Jan 24 Sir H. Slesser
11 Nov 24 Sir T. Inskip
28 Mar 28 Sir F. Merriman
7 Jun 29 Sir J. Melville
22 Oct 30 Sir S. Cripps
3 Sep 31 Sir T. Inskip
26 Jan 32 Sir F. Merriman
29 Sep 33 Sir D. Somervell
19 Mar 36 Sir J. O'Connor
15 May 40 Sir W. Jowitt
4 Mar 42 Sir D. Maxwell-Fyfe
25 May 45 Sir W. Monckton
4 Aug 45 Sir F. Soskice
24 Apr 51 Sir L. Ungoed-Thomas
3 Nov 51 Sir R. Manningham-Buller
18 Oct 54 Sir H. Hylton Foster

22 Oct 59 Sir J. Simon
8 Feb 62 Sir J. Hobson
19 Jul 62 Sir P. Rawlinson
18 Oct 64 Sir D. Foot
24 Aug 67 Sir A. Irvine
23 Jun 70 Sir G. Howe
5 Nov 72 Sir M. Havers
7 Mar 74 P. Archer

Minister of State
1 May 41 Ld Beaverbrook
29 Jun 41 O. Lyttelton
(*office abolished 12 Mar 42*)

First Secretary of State
13 Jul 62 R. Butler
18 Oct 63 *office vacant*
16 Oct 64 G. Brown
11 Aug 66 M. Stewart
6 Apr 68 Mrs B. Castle
19 Jun 70 *office vacant*

Minister of Supply
14 Jul 39 L. Burgin
12 May 40 H. Morrison
3 Oct 40 Sir A. Duncan
29 Jun 41 Ld Beaverbrook
4 Feb 42 Sir A. Duncan
3 Aug 45 J. Wilmot
7 Oct 47 G. Strauss
31 Oct 51 D. Sandys
18 Oct 54 S. Lloyd
7 Apr 55 R. Maudling
16 Jan 57 A. Jones
(*office wound up 22 Oct 59*)

Ministry of Technology
18 Oct 64 F. Cousins
4 Jul 66 A. Wedgwood Benn
20 Jun 70 G. Rippon
28 Jul 70 J. Davies
(*15 Oct 70 office reorganised under Trade and Industry*)

Minister of Town and Country Planning
30 Dec 42 W. Morrison
4 Aug 45 L. Silkin
28 Feb 50 H. Dalton
(*recast as Local Government and Planning 31 Jan 51*)

President of the Board of Trade
1900 C. Ritchie
7 Nov 00 G. Balfour
12 Mar 05 M of Salisbury
10 Dec 05 D. Lloyd George
12 Apr 08 W. Churchill
14 Feb 10 S. Buxton
11 Feb 14 J. Burns
5 Aug 14 W. Runciman

10 Dec 16	Sir A. Stanley
26 May 19	Sir A. Geddes
19 Mar 20	Sir R. Horne
1 Apr 21	S. Baldwin
24 Oct 22	Sir P. Lloyd-Greame
22 Jan 24	S. Webb
6 Nov 24	Sir P. Lloyd-Greame (changed name to Cunliffe-Lister 27 Nov 24)
7 Jun 29	W. Graham
25 Aug 31	Sir P. Cunliffe-Lister
5 Nov 31	W. Runciman (Ld)
28 May 37	O. Stanley
5 Jan 40	Sir A. Duncan
3 Oct 40	O. Lyttelton
29 Jun 41	Sir A. Duncan
4 Feb 42	J. Llewellin
22 Feb 42	H. Dalton
25 May 45	O. Lyttelton
27 Jul 45	Sir S. Cripps
29 Sep 47	H. Wilson
24 Apr 51	Sir H. Shawcross
30 Oct 51	P. Thorneycroft
13 Jan 57	Sir D. Eccles
14 Oct 59	R. Maudling
9 Oct 61	F. Erroll
20 Oct 63	E. Heath
18 Oct 64	D. Jay
29 Aug 67	A. Crosland
20 Oct 63	E. Heath
18 Oct 64	D. Jay
29 Aug 67	A. Crosland
6 Oct 69	R. Mason
20 Jun 70	M. Noble

(Secretary of State for Trade and Industry)

15 Oct 70	J. Davies
5 Nov 72	P. Walker

(Secretary of State for Trade)

5 Mar 74	P. Shore

(see also Industry)

Minister for Trade

15 Oct 70	M. Noble

(Minister for Trade and Consumer Affairs)

5 Nov 72	Sir G. Howe

(office abolished 5 Mar 74)

Minister of Transport

19 May 19	Sir E. Geddes
7 Nov 21	Vt Peel
12 Apr 22	E of Crawford
31 Oct 22	Sir J. Baird
24 Jan 24	H. Gosling
11 Nov 24	W. Ashley
7 Jun 29	H. Morrison
3 Sep 31	J. Pybus
22 Feb 33	O. Stanley
29 Jun 34	L. Hore-Belisha
28 May 37	L. Burgin
21 Apr 39	E. Wallace
14 May 40	Sir J. Reith
3 Oct 40	J. Moore-Brabazon

(Minister of War Transport)

1 May 41	Ld Leathers

(Minister of Transport)

3 Aug 45	A. Barnes
31 Oct 51	J. Maclay
7 May 52	A. Lennox-Boyd

(Minister of Transport and Civil Aviation)

1 Oct 53	A. Lennox-Boyd
28 Jul 54	J. Boyd-Carpenter
20 Dec 55	H. Watkinson

(Minister of Transport)

14 Oct 59	E. Marples
Oct 64	T. Fraser
23 Dec 65	Mrs B. Castle
6 Apr 68	R. Marsh
6 Oct 69	R. Mason
23 Jun 70	J. Peyton

(Minister for Transport Industries)

15 Oct 70	J. Peyton

(Minister for Transport)

7 Mar 74	F. Mulley

Secretary of State for War

1900	M of Lansdowne
1 Nov 00	St J. Brodrick
6 Oct 03	H. Arnold-Forster
10 Dec 05	R. Haldane (Vt)
12 Jun 12	J. Seely
30 Mar 14	H. Asquith
5 Aug 14	Earl Kitchener
6 Jul 16	D. Lloyd George
10 Dec 16	E of Derby
18 Apr 18	Vt Milner
10 Jan 19	W. Churchill
13 Feb 21	Sir L. Worthington-Evans
24 Oct 22	E of Derby
22 Jan 24	S. Walsh
6 Nov 24	Sir L. Worthington-Evans
7 Jun 29	T. Shaw
26 Aug 31	M of Crewe

5 Nov 31	Vt Hailsham
7 Jun 35	Vt Halifax
22 Nov 35	A. Duff Cooper
28 May 37	L. Hore-Belisha
5 Jan 40	O. Stanley
11 May 40	A. Eden
22 Dec 40	D. Margesson
22 Feb 42	Sir J. Grigg
3 Aug 45	J. Lawson
4 Oct 46	F. Bellenger
7 Oct 47	E. Shinwell
28 Feb 50	J. Strachey
31 Oct 51	A. Head
18 Oct 56	J. Hare
6 Jan 58	C. Soames
27 Jul 60	J. Profumo
27 Jun 63	J. Godber
21 Oct 63	J. Ramsden

(office abolished 1 Apr 64)

Minister of State for Welsh Affairs

28 Oct 51	Sir D. Maxwell Fyfe
18 Oct 54	G. Lloyd-George
13 Jan 57	H. Brooke
13 Jul 62	Sir K. Joseph

(Secretary of State for Wales)

18 Oct 64	J. Griffiths
6 Apr 66	C. Hughes
6 Apr 68	G. Thomas
20 Jun 70	P. Thomas
5 Mar 74	J. Morris

First Commissioner of Works

1900	A. Akers-Douglas
8 Aug 02	Ld Windsor
10 Dec 05	L. Harcourt
3 Nov 10	Earl Beauchamp
6 Aug 14	Ld Emmott
25 May 15	L. Harcourt (Vt)
10 Dec 16	Sir A. Mond
1 Apr 21	E of Crawford
31 Oct 22	Sir J. Baird
22 Jan 24	F. Jowett
10 Nov 24	Vt Peel
18 Oct 28	M of Londonderry
7 Jun 29	G. Lansbury
25 Aug 31	M of Londonderry
5 Nov 31	W. Ormsby-Gore
16 Jun 36	Earl Stanhope
28 May 37	Sir P. Sassoon
7 Jun 39	H. Ramsbotham
3 Apr 40	Earl De La Warr
18 May 40	Ld Tryon
3 Oct 40	Sir J. Reith (Ld)

(Minister of Works & Buildings and First Commissioner of Works)

23 Oct 40	Ld Reith

(Minister of Works and Planning)

11 Feb 42	Ld Reith
21 Feb 42	Ld Portal

(Minister of Works)

Feb 43	Ld Portal
21 Nov 44	D. Sandys
4 Aug 45	G. Tomlinson
10 Feb 47	C. Key

28 Feb 50	R. Stokes
26 Apr 51	G. Brown
18 Nov 51	(Sir) D. Eccles
1 Oct 54	N. Birch
20 Dec 55	P. Buchan-Hepburn
16 Jan 57	H. Molson
22 Oct 59	Ld J. Hope

(16 *Jul* 62 *recast as Public Building and Works*)

Leaders of the House of Commons

1900	A. Balfour
5 Dec 05	Sir H. Campbell-Bannerman
5 Apr 08	H. Asquith
10 Dec 16	A. Bonar Law
23 Mar 21	A. Chamberlain
23 Oct 22	A. Bonar Law
22 May 23	S. Baldwin
22 Jan 24	J. R. MacDonald
4 Nov 24	S. Baldwin
5 Jun 29	J. R. MacDonald
7 Jun 35	S. Baldwin
28 May 37	N. Chamberlain
11 May 40	C. Attlee [1]
19 Feb 42	Sir S. Cripps
22 Nov 42	A. Eden
27 Jul 45	H. Morrison
9 Mar 51	C. Ede
30 Oct 51	H. Crookshank
7 Apr 55	R. Butler
9 Oct 61	I. Macleod
20 Oct 63	S. Lloyd
16 Oct 64	H. Bowden
11 Aug 66	R. Crossman
6 Apr 68	F. Peart
20 Jun 70	W. Whitelaw
7 Apr 72	R. Carr
5 Nov 72	J. Prior
5 Mar 74	E. Short

Leaders of the House of Lords

1900	3rd M of Salisbury
12 Jul 02	D of Devonshire
13 Oct 03	M of Lansdowne
10 Dec 05	M of Ripon
14 Apr 08	E of Crewe (M) [2]
10 Dec 16	Earl Curzon (M)
22 Jan 24	Vt Haldane
6 Nov 24	Marquess Curzon
27 Apr 25	4th M of Salisbury
7 Jun 29	Ld Parmoor
25 Aug 31	M of Reading
5 Nov 31	1st Vt Hailsham

7 Jun 35	M of Londonderry
22 Nov 35	Vt Halifax
27 Oct 38	Earl Stanhope
14 May 40	Vt Caldecote
3 Oct 40	Vt Halifax
22 Dec 40	Ld Lloyd
8 Feb 41	Ld Moyne
21 Feb 42	Vt Cranborne (5th M of Salisbury)
3 Aug 45	Vt Addison
28 Oct 51	5th M of Salisbury
29 Mar 57	E of Home
27 Jul 60	2nd Vt Hailsham
20 Oct 63	Ld Carrington
18 Oct 64	E of Longford
16 Jan 68	Ld Shackleton
20 Jun 70	Earl Jellicoe
5 Jun 73	Ld Windlesham
7 Mar 74	Ld Shepherd

Government Chief Whip

(Parliamentary Secretary to the Treasury)

1900	Sir W. Walrond
8 Aug 02	Sir A. Acland Hood
12 Dec 05	G. Whiteley
3 Jun 08	J. Pease
14 Feb 10	Master of Elibank
7 Aug 12	P. Illingworth
24 Jan 15	J. Gulland
30 May 15	J. Gulland
−5 Dec 16	Ld E. Talbot
14 Dec 16	Ld E. Talbot
−2 Mar 17	N. Primrose
2 Mar 17	Ld E. Talbot
−1 Apr 21	F. Guest
1 Apr 21–	C. McCurdy
19 Oct 22	L. Wilson
31 Oct 22	L. Wilson
25 Jul 23	B. Eyres-Monsell
23 Jun 24	B. Spoor
7 Nov 24	B. Eyres-Monsell
14 Jun 29	T. Kennedy
3 Sep 31	Sir B. Eyres-Monsell
10 Nov 31	D. Margesson
17 May 40	D. Margesson
−14 Jan 41	Sir C. Edwards

---

[1] Although Mr Attlee fulfilled the role of Leader of the House of Commons during this period, he was technically only Deputy Leader.

[2] During the critical summer of 1911 Vt Morley was temporarily Leader of the House of Lords in place of the M of Crewe.

14 Jan 41–	Sir C. Edwards
12 Mar 42	J. Stuart
12 Mar 42–	J. Stuart
23 May 45	W. Whiteley
26 May 45	J. Stuart
3 Aug 45	W. Whiteley
30 Oct 51	P. Buchan-Hepburn
30 Dec 55	E. Heath
14 Oct 59	M. Redmayne
18 Oct 64	E. Short
4 Jul 66	J. Silkin
30 Apr 69	R. Mellish
20 Jun 70	F. Pym
2 Dec 73	H. Atkins
5 Mar 74	R. Mellish

Government Chief Whip in the House of Lords

(*usually Captain of the Gentlemen at Arms — see footnotes for exceptions*)

1900	Earl Waldegrave[1]
18 Dec 05	Earl Beauchamp
31 Jul 07	Ld Denman
26 Jun 11	Ld Colebrooke
20 Nov 22	E of Clarendon
22 Jan 24	Ld Muir-Mackenzie[2]
1 Dec 24	E of Clarendon
26 Jun 25	E of Plymouth
1 Jan 29	E of Lucan
18 Jul 29	Ld Muir-Mackenzie[2]
22 May 30	Earl de la Warr[2]
12 Nov 31	E of Lucan
31 May 40	Ld Templemore[1]
22 Mar 45	Earl Fortescue
4 Aug 45	Ld Ammon
18 Oct 49	1st Ld Shepherd
5 Nov 51	Earl Fortescue
27 Jun 68	Earl St Aldwyn
21 Oct 64	2nd Ld Shepherd
29 Jul 67	Ld Beswick
24 Jun 70	Earl St Aldwyn
11 Mar 74	Lady Llewelyn-Davies

[1] Captain of the Yeoman of the Guard.
[2] A Lord in Waiting.

Size of Cabinets and Governments

	1900	1910	1917	1920	1930	1940	1950	1960	1970	1974	1975
Cabinet Ministers	19	19	5	19	19	9	18	19	21	21	23
Non-Cabinet Ministers	10	7	33	15	9	25	20	20	33	30	31
Junior Ministers[a]	31	36	47	47	30	40	43	43	48	48	49
Number of M.P.s in paid Government Posts	33	43	60	58	50	58	68	65	85	79	86
Number of Peers in paid Government Posts	27	19	25	22	12	19	13	18	17	20	17
Total paid Government Posts	60	62	85	81	58	74	81	82	102	99	103
Parliamentary Private Secretaries in Commons	9	16	12	13	26	25	27	36	30	33	32
Total number of M.P.s involved in Government	42	59	72	71	76	83	95	101	115	112	118

[a] Including the political appointments of the Royal Household. In 1901 the Master of the Buckhounds ceased to be a political appointment. Since 1905 the Paymaster-General has been a non-Cabinet or Cabinet Ministerial post. Since 1924 the offices of Lord Chamberlain, Lord Steward, and Master of the House have been non-political. In 1930 the Captain Gentleman at Arms and Captain Yeoman of the Guard were non-political appointments. There have always been some non-political Lords in Waiting.

SOURCES.—Members of the Government from *Hansard*, the first volume of each year. P.P.S.s from *Whitaker's Almanack* (the figures for 1900–40 are only approximate), and from *H.M. Ministers and Heads of Public Departments, 1946–67* (H.M.S.O.).

Social and Educational Composition of British Cabinets 1895-1974[1]

Date	Party	P.M.	Cabinet Size	Aristo-crats	Middle Class	Working Class	Public school		University educat	
							All	Eton	All	Oxbridg
Aug. 1895	Con.	Salisbury	19	8	11	—	16	7	15	14
Jul. 1902	Con.	Balfour	19	9	10	—	16	9	14	13
Dec. 1905	Lib.	Campbell-Bannerman	19	7	11	1	11	3	14	12
Jul. 1914	Lib.	Asquith	19	6	12	1	11	3	15	13
Jan. 1919	Coal.	Lloyd George	21	3	17	1	12	2	13	8
Nov. 1922	Con.	Bonar Law	16	8	8	—	14	8	13	13
Jan. 1924	Lab.	MacDonald	19	3	5	11	8	—	6	6
Nov. 1924	Con.	Baldwin	21	9	12	—	21	7	16	16
Jan. 1929	Lab.	MacDonald	18	2	4	12	5	—	6	3
May 1931	Nat.	MacDonald	20	8	10	2	13	6	11	10
Jun. 1935	Con.	Baldwin	22	9	11	2	14	9	11	10
May 1937	Con.	Chamberlain	21	8	13	—	17	8	16	13
May 1945	Con.	Churchill	16	6	9	1	14	7	11	9
Aug. 1945	Lab.	Attlee	20	—	8	12	5	2	10	5
Oct. 1951	Con.	Churchill	16	5	11	—	14	7	11	9
Apr. 1955	Con.	Eden	18	5	13	—	18	10	16	14
Jan. 1957	Con.	Macmillan	18	4	14	—	17	8	16	15
Oct. 1963	Con.	Home	24	5	19	—	21	11	17	17
Oct. 1964	Lab.	Wilson	23	1	14	8	8	1	13	11
Jun. 1970	Con.	Heath	18	4	14	—	15	4	15	15
Mar. 1974	Lab.	Wilson	21	1	16	4	7	—	16	11
Average 21 Cabinets			19½	5	11½	3	13	5	13	11
12 Con. Cabinets			19	7	12	—	16½	7½	14	13
5 Lab. Cabinets			20	1	9½	9½	7	½	10	5
2 Lib. Cabinets			19	6	11½	1	11	3	14½	12½

[1] This table is largely based on W. L. Guttsman, *The British Political Elite* (1963). Aristocrats are those who had an their grandparents the holder of a hereditary title. Working class are those whose fathers appear to have had a manual o pation when they were growing up. Schools are classified as Public Schools if members of the Headmasters' Conference

Durability of Prime Ministers 1900-1974

	Length of Service as P.M.		Separate Times in Office	Age on First becoming P.M. (Years)	H. of Commons Service at First Premiership (Years)	Time in H. of Commons after Last Premiership (Years)
	Years	Months				
M of Salisbury	13	9	3	55	15[1]	0
H. Asquith	8	8	1	55	22	4
(Sir) W. Churchill	8	8	2	65	38	9
S. Baldwin	6	10	3	56	15	0
J. R. MacDonald	6	9	2	58	14	2
H. Macmillan	6	9	1	62	29	1
C. Attlee	6	2	1	62	23	4
D. Lloyd George	5	10	1	53	26	22
H. Wilson	5	8[3]	2	48	19	..
E. Heath	3	8	1	53	20	..
A. Balfour	3	5	1	53	28	17
N. Chamberlain	2	11	1	68	19	½
Sir H. Campbell-Bannerman	2	4	1	69	37	0
Sir A. Eden	1	9	1	57	32	0
Sir A. Douglas-Home	1	0	1	60	15[2]	10
A. Bonar Law	0	7	1	63	22	0

[1] Plus 19 years in House of Lords.   [2] Plus 13 years in House of Lords.   [3] Length of first Premiership 1964-70.

Ministerial Resignations

Resignations from ministerial office are not easy to classify. A retirement on the ground of ill-health may always conceal a protest or a dismissal. However, there are some cases where ministers have unquestionably left office because they were not willing to continue to accept collective responsibility for some part of Government policy and some cases where the individual actions of ministers have been thought impolitic or unworthy. The following list does not include resignations made necessary because of private scandals, except when the resignation became the subject of public comment.

16 Sep 03	J. Chamberlain (*Imperial preference*)
4–15 Sep 03	C. Ritchie, Ld Balfour of Burleigh, Ld G. Hamilton, D of Devonshire, A. Elliott (*Free Trade*)
6 Mar 05	G. Wyndham (*Ireland*)
30 Mar 14	J. Seely (*Curragh mutiny*)
2 Aug 14	Vt Morley, J. Burns (*Entry into war*)
5 Aug 14	C. Trevelyan (*Entry into war*)
19 Oct 15	Sir E. Carson (*Conduct of War in the Balkans*)
31 Dec 15	Sir J. Simon (*Compulsory National Service*)
3 May 16	A. Birrell (*Irish rebellion*)
25 Jun 16	E of Selborne (*Irish Policy*)
12 Jul 17	A. Chamberlain (*Campaign in Mesopotamia*)
8 Aug 17	N. Chamberlain (*Ministry of National Service*)
17 Nov 17	Ld Cowdray (*Conduct of the Air Ministry*)
21 Jan 18	Sir E. Carson (*Ireland*)
25 Apr 18	Ld Rothermere (*Air Force*)
22 Nov 18	Ld R. Cecil (*Welsh disestablishment*)
12 Nov 19	J. Seely (*Role of Air Ministry*)
14 Jul 21	C. Addison (*Housing*)
9 Mar 22	E. Montagu (*Turkey*)
18 Nov 23	A. Buckley (*Abandonment of Free Trade*)
28 Aug 27	Vt Cecil (*Disarmament*)
19 May 30	Sir O. Mosley (*Unemployment*)
2 Mar 31	Sir C. Trevelyan (*Education*)
9 Oct 31	G. Lloyd-George, G. Owen (*Decision to hold a General Election*)
28 Sep 32	Sir H. Samuel, Sir A. Sinclair, Vt Snowden, M of Lothian, I. Foot, Sir R. Hamilton, G. White, W. Rea, Vt Allendale (*Free Trade*)
18 Dec 35	Sir S. Hoare (*Laval Pact*)
22 May 36	J. Thomas (*Budget leak*)
20 Feb 38	A. Eden, Vt Cranborne (*Negotiations with Mussolini*)
12–16 May 38	Earl Winterton ⎱ (*Criticism of Air strength*) Vt Swinton ⎰
16 May 38	Ld Harlech (*Partition of Palestine*)
1 Oct 38	A. Duff Cooper (*Munich*)
21 Jan 41	R. Boothby (*Blocked Czechoslovakian assets*)
1 Mar 45	H. Strauss (*Treatment of Poles by Yalta Conference*)
26 May 46	Sir B. Smith (*Overwork and criticism*)
13 Nov 47	H. Dalton (*Budget leak*)
3 Feb 49	J. Belcher (*Lynskey tribunal*)
16 Apr 50	S. Evans (*Agricultural subsidies*)
23–24 Apr 51	A. Bevan, H. Wilson, J. Freeman (*Budget proposals*)
20 Jul 54	Sir T. Dugdale (*Crichel Down*)

31 Oct 56   A. Nutting (*Suez*)
5 Nov 56   Sir E. Boyle (*Suez*)
29 Mar 57   M of Salisbury (*Release of Archbishop Makarios*)
6 Jan 58   P. Thorneycroft, E. Powell, N. Birch (*Economic policy*)
24 Nov 58   I. Harvey (*Private scandal*)
8 Nov 62   T. Galbraith (*Security: Exonerated and given new office 5 May 63*)
5 Jun 63   J. Profumo (*Lying to the House of Commons*)
19 Feb 66   C. Mayhew (*Defence estimates*)
3 Jul 66   F. Cousins (*Incomes policy*)
26 Jul 67   Miss M. Herbison (*Social Services policy*)
16 Jan 68   E of Longford (*Postponement of raising School Leaving Age*)
16 Mar 68   G. Brown (*Conduct of Government business*)
1 Jul 68   R. Gunter (*General dissatisfaction*)
24 Sep 69   J. Bray (*Permission to publish*)
28 Jul 71   E. Taylor (*Entry into the E.E.C.*)
17 Oct 71   J. More (*Entry into the E.E.C.*)
18 Jul 72   R. Maudling (*Poulson Inquiry*)
22 May 73   Ld Lambton (*Private scandal*)
23 May 73   Earl Jellicoe (*Private scandal*)
25 Sep 74   Ld Brayley (*Inquiry into former business interests*)
17 Oct 74   N. Buchan (*Agriculture Department policy*)
9 Apr 75   E. Heffer (*speaking against E.E.C. membership in House of Commons*)[1]

SOURCES.—R. C. K. Ensor, *England 1870–1914*, (1936); C. L. Mowat, *Britain Between the Wars* (1955); *The Annual Register, 1900–1973*; *Keesing's Archives, 1931–1973*; S. E. Finer, 'The Individual Responsibility of Ministers', *Public Administration*, Winter 1956, pp. 377–96; P. J. Madgwick, 'Resignations', *Parliamentary Affairs*, Winter 1966, pp. 59–76; R. K. Alderman and J. A. Cross, *Tactics of Resignation* (1968).

Parliamentary Private Secretaries to Prime Ministers

1900–02	E. Cecil	1929–31	{ L. MacNeil Weir { R. Morrison	1955	R. Carr
1906–08	H. Carr-Gomm			1955–58	R. Allan
1908–10	G. Howard	1931–32	{ R. Glyn { F. Markham	1958–59	A. Barber
1910–15	C. Lyell			1959–63	S. Cunningham
1915–16	Sir J. Barran	1932–35	{ (Sir) R. Glyn { J. Worthington	1963–64	F. Pearson
1916–17	D. Davies			1964–66	{ P. Shore
1918	W. Astor	1935	G. Lloyd	1964–67	{ E. Fernyhough
1918–20	(Sir) W. Sutherland	1935–37	T. Dugdale	1967–68	H. Davies
1920–22	Sir P. Sassoon	1937–40	Ld Dunglass	1968–69	{ H. Davies
1922–23	J. Davidson	1940–41	B. Bracken		{ E. Varley
1923–24	S. Herbert	1941–45	G. Harvie-Watt	1969–70	H. Davies
1924	L. MacNeil Weir	1945–46	G. de Freitas	1970–74	T. Kitson
1924–27	S. Herbert	1946–51	A. Moyle	1974–75	W. Hamling
1927–29	C. Rhys	1952–55	C. Soames	1975	K. Marks

Biographical Notes

Prime Ministers, Chancellors of the Exchequer, and Foreign Secretaries.[2]

Anderson, John (Sir). 1st Vt Waverley (1952)
     b. 1882. *Educ.* George Watson's Coll., Edin.; Edinburgh and Leipzig Univs. Entered Col. O., 1905. Sec. to Min. of Shipping, 1917–19. K.C.B., 1919. Addit. Sec. to Loc. Govt. Bd., 1919. 2nd Sec. to Min. of Health, 1919. Ch. of Bd. of Inland Revenue, 1919–22. Joint U.-S. to Ld. Lieut. of Ireland, 1920–22. P.U.-S. Home O., 1922–32. Gov. of Bengal, 1932–37. M.P. (Nat.) for Scottish Univs., 1938–50. Ld. Privy S., 1938–39. Home Sec. and Min. of Home Security, 1939–40. Ld. Pres. of Council, 1940–43. Chanc. of Exch., 1943–45. d. 1958.

[1] Technically a dismissal, not a resignation.
[2] Virtually all the most eminent politicians of this century held one of these three offices. But common sense being more important than consistency, we have added biographies of the three most outstanding exceptions — Joseph Chamberlain, Aneurin Bevan and Margaret Thatcher.

Asquith, Herbert Henry. 1st E of Oxford and Asquith (1925)
b. 1852. *Educ.* City of London School; Oxford. Barrister, 1876, practised
M.P. (Lib.) for E. Fife, 1886–1918. M.P. for Paisley, 1920–24. Home Sec.,
1892–95. Chanc. of Exch., 1905–8. P.M. and Leader of Lib. party, 1908–
1916. Sec. for War, 1914. Formed Coalition Govt., 1915. Resigned as P.M.,
became Leader of Opposition, 1916. Resigned Leadership of Lib. party, 1926.
d. 1928.

Attlee, Clement Richard. 1st Earl Attlee (1955)
b. 1883. *Educ.* Haileybury; Oxford. Barrister, 1906; practised, 1906–9.
Lecturer at L.S.E., 1913–23. M.P. (Lab.) for Limehouse, Stepney, 1922–50.
M.P. for W. Walthamstow, 1950–55. P.P.S. to J. R. MacDonald, 1922–24.
U.-S. for War, 1924. Chanc. of D. of Lanc., 1930–31. Postm.-Gen., 1931.
Dep. Leader of Lab. party in Commons, 1931–35. Leader of Lab. party,
1935–55. Leader of Opposition, 1935–40. Ld. Privy S., 1940–42. Sec. for
Dominions, 1942–43. Ld. Pres. of Council, 1943–45. Dep. P.M., 1942–45.
P.M., 1945–51. Min. of Def., 1945–46. Leader of Opposition, 1951–
1955. d. 1967.

Baldwin, Stanley. 1st Earl Baldwin of Bewdley (1937)
b. 1867. *Educ.* Harrow; Cambridge. Family business. M.P. (Con.) for
Bewdley div. of Worcs., 1908–37. Joint F.S. to Treas., 1917–21; Pres. of Bd.
of Trade, 1921–22; Chanc. of Exch., 1922–23. Leader of Con. party, 1923–37.
P.M., 1923–24 and 1924–29. Leader of Opposition, 1924, 1929–31. Ld. Pres. of
Council, 1931–35. Ld. Privy S., 1932–33. P.M., 1935–37. d. 1947.

Balfour, Arthur James. 1st Earl of Balfour (1922)
b. 1848. *Educ.* Eton; Cambridge. M.P. (Con.) for Hertford, 1874–85. M.P.
for E. Manchester, 1885–1906. M.P. for City of London, 1906–22. P.P.S. to
Ld. Salisbury, 1878–80. Pres. of Loc. Govt. Bd., 1885. Sec. for Scotland, 1886.
(Member of Cabinet, Nov 1886.) Ch. Sec. for Ireland, 1887–91. Leader
of Commons and 1st Ld. of Treas., 1891–92 and 1895–1902. P.M.,
1902–5. Leader of Con. party, 1902–11. Member of Committee of Imperial
Defence, 1914. Attended war cabinet meetings, 1914–15. 1st Ld. of Admir.,
1915–16. For. Sec., 1916–19. Ld. Pres. of Council, 1919–22 and 1925–29.
d. 1930.

Barber, Anthony Perrinott Lysberg. Ld Barber (Life Peer 1974)
b. 1920. *Educ.* Retford G.S.; Oxford. Barrister, 1948. M.P. (Con.) for Don-
caster, 1951–64. M.P. for Altrincham and Sale, 1965–74. Con. Whip, 1955–58;
P.P.S. to P.M., 1958–59. Econ. S. to Treasury, 1959–62. F.S., 1962–63. Min.
of Health, 1963–64. Ld Privy Seal, 1970. Chancellor of Exchequer, 1970–74.

Bevan, Aneurin
b. 1897. *Educ.* Elem.; Central Labour College. Miner. M.P. (Lab.) for Ebbw
Vale, 1929–60. Deputy Leader of Lab. party, 1959–60. Min. of Health, 1945–51.
Min. of Lab. and Nat. Service, 1951. Resigned, 1951. Treasurer of Lab. party,
1956–60. d. 1960.

Bevin, Ernest
b. 1881. *Educ.* Elem. National Organiser of Dockers' Union, 1910–21. Gen.
Sec. of T. & G.W.U., 1921–40. Member of General Council of T.U.C., 1925–40.
M.P. (Lab.) for C. Wandsworth, 1940–50. M.P. for E. Woolwich, 1950–51.
Min. of Lab. and Nat. Service, 1940–45. For. Sec., 1945–51. Ld. Privy S.,
Mar–Apr 1951. d. 1951.

Bonar Law, Andrew
b. 1858. *Educ.* Canada and Glasgow H.S. Family business. M.P. (Con.) for
Blackfriars, Glasgow, 1900–6. M.P. for Dulwich, 1906–10. M.P. for Bootle,
1911–18. M.P. for C. Glasgow, 1918–23. P.S. to Bd. of Trade, 1902–5. Leader
of Con. party in Commons, 1911–21. Col. Sec., 1915–16. Chanc. of Exch.,
1916–18. Ld. Privy S. and Leader of Commons, 1919–21. Resigned, 1921.
P.M. and Leader of Con. party, 1922–23. Resigned, 1923. d. 1923.

Brown, George Alfred. Life Peer (1970) Ld George-Brown.
b. 1914. *Educ.* Secondary. M.P. (Lab.) for Belper 1945–70. P.P.S. to Min.

of Lab. and Nat. Service, 1945–47, and to C. of Exchequer, 1947. Joint Parliamentary Secretary, Min. of Ag. and Fish., 1947–51. Min. of Works, Apr–Oct 1951. First Sec. of State and Sec. of State for Econ. Affairs, 1964–66. For. Sec. 1966–68. Resigned, 1968. Deputy Leader of the Labour Party, 1960–70.

Butler, Richard Austen. Life Peer (1965) Ld Butler of Saffron Walden.
b. 1902. *Educ.* Marlborough; Cambridge. M.P. (Con.) for Saffron Walden, 1929–65. U.-S. India O., 1932–37. P.S. Min. of Lab., 1937–38. U.-S. For. O., 1938–41. Pres. Bd. of Educ., 1941–44. Min. of Educ., 1944–45. Min. of Lab., 1945. Chanc. of Exch., 1951–55. Leader of Commons, 1955–61. Ld. Privy S., 1955–59. Hom. Sec., 1957–62. First Sec. of State and Min. in charge of C. African O., 1962–63. For. Sec., 1963–64. Ch. of Con. party organisation 1959–61. Master of Trinity College, Cambridge, 1965–.

Callaghan, (Leonard) James
b. 1912. *Educ.* Elem. and Portsmouth Northern Secondary Schools. M.P. (Lab.) for S. Cardiff, 1945–50. M.P. for S.E. Cardiff since 1950. P.S. Min. of Transport, 1947–50. P.S. and F.S. Admiralty, 1950–51. Chanc. of the Exch., 1964–67. Home Sec., 1967–70. For. Sec., 1974–.

Campbell-Bannerman, Henry (Sir)
b. 1836. *Educ.* Glasgow H.S. ; Glasgow Univ. and Cambridge. Family business. M.P. (Lib.) for Stirling Burghs, 1868–1908. F.S. to War O., 1871–74 and 1880–82. Sec. to Admir., 1882–84. Ch. Sec. for Ireland (without seat in cabinet), 1884–85. Sec. for War, 1886 and 1892–95. G.C.B., 1895. Leader of Lib. party in Commons, 1899–1908. P.M., 1905–8. Resigned, 1908. d. 1908.

Chamberlain, (Arthur) Neville
b. 1869. *Educ.* Rugby; Mason Science College, Birmingham. Birmingham and business career. Ld. Mayor of Birmingham, 1915–16. Dir.-Gen. of Nat. Service, 1916–17. M.P. (Con.) for Ladywood, Birmingham, 1918–29. M.P. for Edgbaston, Birmingham, 1929–40. Postm.-Gen., 1922–23. Paym.-Gen., 1923. Min. of Health, 1923. Chanc. of Exch., 1923–24. Min. of Health, 1924–29 and 1931. Ch. of Con. party organisation, 1930–31. Chanc. of Exch., 1931–37. P.M. and Leader of Con. party, 1937–40. Ld. Pres. of Council, 1940. Resigned, 1940. d. 1940.

Chamberlain, Joseph
b. 1836. *Educ.* University College School. Family business. Mayor of Birmingham, 1873–75. M.P. (Lib.) for Birmingham, 1876–85. M.P. for Birmingham W., 1885–86. M.P. (Lib. U.) for Birmingham W., 1886–1914. Pres. of Bd. of Trade, 1880–85. Pres. of Loc. Govt. Bd., 1886. Col. Sec., 1895–1903. d. 1914.

Chamberlain, (Joseph) Austen (Sir)
b. 1863. *Educ.* Rugby; Cambridge. M.P. (Con.) for E. Worcs., 1892–1914. M.P. for W. Birmingham, 1914–37. Lib. U. Whip, 1892. Civil Ld. of Admir., 1895–1900. F.S. to Treas., 1900–2. Postm.-Gen., 1902–3. Chanc. of Exch., 1903–5. Sec. for India, 1915–17. Resigned, 1917. Min. without Portfolio in war cabinet, 1918–19. Chanc. of Exch., 1919–21. Ld. Privy S. and Leader of Con. party in Commons, 1921–22. For. Sec., 1924–29. K.G., 1925. 1st Ld. of Admir., 1931. d. 1937.

Churchill, Winston Leonard Spencer (Sir)
b. 1874. *Educ.* Harrow; Sandhurst. Army, 1895–1900. M.P. (Con.) for Oldham, 1900–04. M.P. (Lib.) for Oldham 1904–06. M.P. (Lib) for N.W. Manchester, 1906–08. M.P. (Lib.) for Dundee, 1908–22. M.P. (Const.) for Epping, 1924–29. M.P. (Con.) for Epping, 1929–45; M.P. (Con.) for Woodford, 1945–64. U.-S. for Col. O., 1906–08. Pres. of Bd. of Trade, 1908–10. Home Sec., 1910–11. 1st Ld. of Admiralty, 1911–15. Chanc. of D. of Lanc., 1915. Min. of Munitions, 1917–19. Sec. for War and Air, 1919–21. Sec. for Air and Col., 1921. Col. Sec., 1921–22. Chanc. of Exch., 1924–29. 1st Ld. of Admir., 1939–40. Min. of Def., and P.M., 1940–45. Leader of Con. Party, 1940–55. Leader of Opposition, 1945–51. Min. of Def., 1951–52. P.M., 1951–55. K.G., 1953. d. 1965.

Cripps, (Richard) Stafford (Sir)
b. 1889. *Educ.* Winchester; London. Barrister, 1913. M.P. (Lab.) for E. Bristol, 1931–50. M.P. for S.E. Bristol, 1950. Kt., 1930. Sol. Gen., 1930–31.

Brit. Amb. to U.S.S.R., 1940–42. Ld. Privy S. and Leader of Commons, 1942. Min. of Aircraft Prod., 1942–45. Pres. of Bd. of Trade, 1945–47. Min. for Econ. Affairs, 1947. Chanc. of Exch., 1947–50. d. 1952.

Curzon, George Nathaniel. Ld Curzon (1898), 1st Earl (1911), 1st Marquess Curzon of Kedleston (1921)
b. 1859. *Educ.* Eton and Oxford. M.P. (Con.) for Southport, 1886–98. U.-S. India O., 1891–92. U.-S. For. O., 1895–98. Viceroy of India, 1899–1905. Entered H. of Lords as Irish Representative Peer, 1908. Ld. Privy Seal, 1915–16. Pres. of Air Bd., 1916. Ld. Pres. of Council, 1916–19. Member of war cabinet, Leader of Lords, 1916–24. For. Sec., 1919–24. Ld. Pres. of Council, 1924–25. Leader of Cons. party, Lords, 1916–25. d. 1925.

Dalton, (Edward) Hugh John Neale. (Life Peer, 1960). Ld Dalton.
b. 1887. *Educ.* Eton; Cambridge, L.S.E. Barrister, 1914. Univ. Lecturer, London, 1919–36. M.P. (Lab.) for Camberwell, 1924–29. M.P. Bishop Auckland, 1929–31 and 1935–59. U.-S. For. O., 1929–31. Min. of Econ. Warfare, 1940–42. Pres. of Bd. of Trade, 1942–45. Chanc. of Exch., 1945–47. Chanc. of D. of Lanc., 1948–50. Min. of Town and Country Planning, 1950–51. Min. of Loc. Govt. and Planning, 1951. d. 1962.

Douglas-Home, Sir Alec (Alexander Frederick). Ld Dunglass (1918–51) 14th E of Home (1951–63). Ld Home of the Hirsel (Life Peer 1974).
b. 1903. *Educ.* Eton; Oxford. M.P. (Con.) for S. Lanark, 1931–45. M.P. for Lanark, 1950–51. M.P. for Kinross and W. Perthshire, 1963–74. P.P.S. to N. Chamberlain, 1937–40. Joint U.-S. For. O., 1945. (Succ. to E. 1951) Min. of State Scottish O., 1951–55. Sec. Commonwealth Relations 1955–60. Dep. Leader of Lords, 1956–57. Ld. Pres. of Council, 1957 and 1959–60. Leader of Lords, 1957–60. For. Sec. 1960–63. P.M. 1963–64 (Renounced peerage 1963) Leader of Cons. Party, 1963–65. For. Sec., 1970–4.

Eden, (Robert) Anthony (Sir). 1st E of Avon (1961)
b. 1897. *Educ.* Eton; Oxford. M.P. (Con.) for Warwick and Leamington, 1923–57. P.P.S. to Sir A. Chamberlain (For. Sec.), 1926–29. U.-S. For. O., 1931–33. Ld. Privy S., 1934–35. Min. without Portfolio for League of Nations Affairs, 1935. For. Sec., 1935–38. Resigned, 1938. Sec. for Dominions, 1939–40. Sec. for War, 1940. For. Sec., 1940–45. Leader of Commons, 1942–45. Dep. Leader of Opposition, 1945–51. For. Sec., 1951–55. K.G., 1954. P.M. and Leader of Con. party, 1955–57.

Gaitskell, Hugh Todd Naylor
b. 1906. *Educ.* Winchester; Oxford. M.P. (Lab.) for S. Leeds 1945–63. Princ. Private Sec. to Min. of Econ. Warfare, 1940–42. Princ. Asst. Sec. Bd. of Trade, 1942–45. P.S. Min. of Fuel and Power, 1946–47. Min. of Fuel and Power, 1947–50. Min. of State for Econ. Affairs, 1950. Chanc. of Exch., 1950–51. Leader of Lab. party, 1955–63. d. 1963.

Gordon Walker, Patrick Christian. (Life Peer 1974). Ld Gordon-Walker.
b. 1907. *Educ.* Wellington; Oxford. University Teacher. M.P. (Lab.) for Smethwick, 1945–64. M.P. (Lab.) Leyton 1966–74 P.P.S. to H. Morrison, 1946. Parl. U.-S., Commonwealth Relations O., 1947–50. Sec. of State for Commonwealth Relations, 1950–51. For. Sec., 1964–65. Min. without Portfolio, 1967. Sec. for Educ. and Science, 1967–68.

Grey, Edward, (Sir) 1st Vt Grey of Fallodon (1916)
b. 1862. *Educ.* Winchester; Oxford. Succ. to Btcy., 1882. M.P. (Lib.) for Berwick-on-Tweed, 1885–1916. U.-S. For. O., 1892–95. For. Sec., 1905–16. (For. Sec. in Lords, 1916). Leader of Liberal party, Lords 1923–24. d. 1933.

Halifax, 3rd Vt (1934), Edward Frederick Lindley Wood. 1st Ld Irwin (1925), 1st E of (1944)
b. 1881. *Educ.* Eton; Oxford. M.P. (Con.) for Ripon, 1910–25. U.-S. Col. O., 1921–22. Pres. of Bd. of Educ., 1922–24. Min. of Agric., 1924–25. Viceroy of India, 1926–31. Pres. of Bd. of Educ., 1932–35. Sec. for War, 1935. Ld. Privy S., 1935–37. Leader of Lords, 1935–38. Ld. Pres. of Council, 1937–38. For. Sec., 1938–40. Leader of Lords, 1940. Brit. Amb. to U.S.A., 1941–46. d. 1959.

Healey, Denis Winston

    b. 1917. *Educ.* Bradford G.S.; Oxford. M.P. (Lab.) for Leeds South-East, 1952–55. M.P. for Leeds East 1955–. Sec. for Defence 1964–70. Chanc. of Exch., 1974–.

Heath, Edward Richard George

    b. 1916. *Educ.* Chatham House School, Ramsgate; Oxford. M.P. (Con.) for Bexley 1950–74. M.P. for Sidcup 1974–. Con. Whip, 1951–55. Chief Whip, 1955–59. Min. of Labour, 1959–60. Lord Privy Seal, 1960–63. Sec. for Trade & Industry, 1963–64. Leader of the Con. Party, 1965–75. P.M. 1970–74. Leader of the Opposition, 1974–75.

Heathcoat Amory, Derick. 1st Vt Amory (1960)

    b. 1899. *Educ.* Eton; Oxford. M.P. (Con.) for Tiverton, 1945–60. Min. of Pensions, 1951–53. Min. of State for Bd. of Trade, 1953–54. Min. of Ag., Fish. and Food, 1954–58. Chanc. of Exch., 1958–60. High Commissioner for the U.K. in Canada, 1961–63.

Henderson, Arthur

    b. 1863. *Educ.* Elem. M.P. (Lab.) for Barnard Castle, 1903–18. M.P. for Widnes, 1919–22. M.P. for Newcastle E., 1923. M.P. for Burnley, 1924–31. M.P. for Clay Cross, 1933–35. Sec. of Lab party, 1911–34. Treasurer of Lab. party, 1930–35. Leader of Lab. party in Commons, 1908–10 and 1914–17. Chief Whip, 1914. Pres. Bd. of Educ., 1915–16. Paym.-Gen., 1916. Min. without portfolio and member of war cabinet, 1916–17. Resigned from cabinet, 1917. Chief Lab. party Whip, 1920–24 and 1925–27. Home Sec., 1924. For. Sec., 1929–31. Leader of Lab. Opposition, 1931–32. d. 1935.

Hicks Beach, Michael Edward (Sir). 1st Vt St Aldwyn (1906), 1st Earl (1915)

    b. 1837. *Educ.* Eton; Oxford. Succ. to Btcy., 1854. M.P. (Con.) for E. Gloucs., 1864–85. M.P. for W. Bristol, 1885–1906. Sec. of Poor Law Bd., 1868. U.-S. Home O., 1868. Ch. Sec. for Ireland, 1874–78. (Seat in cabinet, 1876.) Sec. for Col., 1878–80. Chanc. of Exch. and Leader of Commons, 1885–86. Leader of Opposition in Commons, 1886. Ch. Sec. for Ireland, 1886–87. Resigned 1887, but remained in cabinet without portfolio. Pres. of Bd. of Trade, 1888–92. Chanc. of Exch., 1895–1902. Resigned 1902. d. 1916.

Hoare, Samuel John Gurney (Sir). 1st Vt Templewood (1944)

    b. 1880. *Educ.* Harrow; Oxford. M.P. (Con.) for Chelsea, 1910–44. Succ. to Btcy., 1915. Sec. for Air, 1922–24 and 1924–29. Sec. for India, 1931–35. For. Sec., 1935. 1st Ld. of Admir., 1936–37. Home Sec., 1937–39. Ld. Privy S., 1939–40. Sec. for Air, 1940. Brit. Amb. to Spain, 1940–44. d. 1959.

Horne, Robert Stevenson (Sir). 1st Vt Horne of Slamannan (1937)

    b. 1871. *Educ.* George Watson's Coll., Edin.; Glasgow Univ. Member of Faculty of Advocates, 1896. K.B.E., 1918. M.P. (Con.) for Hillhead, Glasgow, 1918–37. Min. of Lab., 1919–20. Pres. of Bd. of Trade, 1920–21. Chanc. of Exch., 1921–22. d. 1940.

Jenkins, Roy Harris

    b. 1920. *Educ.* Abersychan G.S.; Oxford. Army, 1939–45. M.P. (Lab.) for Central Southwark, 1948–50. M.P. (Lab.) for Stechford, Birmingham, since 1950. P.P.S. Commonwealth Relations O., 1949–50. Min. of Aviation, 1964–5. Home Sec., 1965–67. Chanc. of Exch., 1967–70. Deputy Leader of Lab. party, 1970–1972. Home Sec., 1974–.

Lansdowne, 5th M of (1866). Henry Charles Keith Petty-Fitzmaurice, Vt Clanmaurice (1845–63), E of Kerry (1863–66)

    b. 1845. *Educ.* Eton; Oxford. Succ. to M. 1866. Junior Ld. of Treas. (Lib.), 1869–72. U.-S. for War, 1872–74. U.-S. India O., 1880. Resigned and opposed Lib. Govt. in Lords, 1880. Gov.-Gen. of Canada, 1883–88. Viceroy of India, 1888–94. Sec. for War (Con.), 1895–1900. For. Sec., 1900–5. Leader of Con. party in Lords, 1903–16. Min. without portfolio, member of war cabinet, 1915–16. Left Con. party, 1917. d. 1927.

Lloyd, (John) Selwyn Brooke

    b. 1904. *Educ.* Fettes; Cambridge. Barrister, 1930. M.P. (Con.) for Wirral since 1945. Min. of State For. O., 1951–54. Min. of Supply, 1954–55. Min.

of Def., 1955. For. Sec., 1955–60. Chanc. of Exch., 1960–62. Lord Privy Seal and Leader of the House of Commons, 1963–64. Speaker of the House of Commons, 1971–.

Lloyd George, David. 1st Earl Lloyd George of Dwyfor (1945)
b. 1863. *Educ.* Church School. Solicitor, 1884. M.P. (Lib.) for Caernarvon Boroughs, 1890–1945 (Ind. L., 1931–35). Pres. of Bd. of Trade, 1905–8. Chanc. of Exch., 1908–15. Min. of Munitions, 1915–16. Sec. for War, 1916. Resigned, 1916. P.M., 1916–22. Leader of Lib. party, 1926–31. d. 1945.

MacDonald, James Ramsay
b. 1866. *Educ.* Drainie School. M.P. (Lab.) for Leicester, 1906–18. M.P. for Aberavon, Glamorganshire, 1922–29. M.P. for Seaham, 1929–35. (Nat. Lab., 1931–37.) M.P. for Scottish Univs., 1936–37. Sec. of L.R.C. and Lab. party, 1900–12. Treas. of Lab. party, 1912–35. Chairman of I.L.P., 1906–9. Ch. of Lab. party, 1911–14. Resigned Chairmanship, 1914. Ch. of P.L.P. and Leader of official Opposition, 1922. Leader of Lab. party, 1922–31. P.M. and For. Sec., 1924. P.M., 1929–31. P.M. of National Govt., 1931–35. Ld. Pres. of Council, 1935–37. d. 1937.

McKenna, Reginald
b. 1863. *Educ.* St. Malo, Ebersdorf and King's Coll. School; Cambridge. Barrister, 1887. M.P. (Lib.) for N. Monmouthshire, 1895–1918. F.S. to Treas., 1905–7. Pres. Bd. of Educ., 1907–8. 1st Ld. of Admir., 1908–11. Home Sec., 1911–15. Chanc. of Exch., 1915–16. Ch. of Midland Bank, 1919–43. d. 1943.

Macleod, Iain Norman
b. 1913. *Educ.* Fettes; Cambridge. Journalist. M.P. (Con.) for Enfield West, 1950–70. Min. of Health, 1952–55. Min. of Labour, 1955–59. Sec. of State for Colonies, 1959–61. Chanc. of D. of Lanc. and Leader of House of Commons, 1961–63. Ch. of Con. Party Organisation, 1961–63. Editor of *Spectator*, 1963–65. Chanc. of Exch., 1970. d. 1970.

Macmillan, (Maurice) Harold
b. 1894. *Educ.* Eton; Oxford. M.P. (Con.) for Stockton-on-Tees, 1924–29 and 1931–45. M.P. (Con.) for Bromley, 1945–64. P.S. Min. of Supply, 1940–42. U.-S. Col. O., 1942. Min. resident at Allied H.Q. in N.W. Africa, 1942–45. Sec. for Air, 1945. Min. of Housing and Loc. Govt., 1951–54. Min. of Def., 1954–55. For. Sec., 1955, Chanc. of Exch., 1955–57. P.M. and Leader of Con. party, 1957–63.

Maudling, Reginald
b. 1917. *Educ.* Merchant Taylors'; Oxford. Barrister 1940. M.P. (Con.) for Barnet, 1950–74. M.P. for Chipping Barnet, 1974–. P.S. Min. of Civil Aviation, 1952. Econ. Sec. to Treasury, 1953–55. Min. of Supply, 1955–57. Paym.-Gen., 1957–59. Pres. Bd. of Trade, 1959–61. Sec. of State for Colonies, 1961–62. Chanc. of Exch., 1962–64. Deputy Leader of Con. Party, 1965–72. Home Sec., 1970–72. Resigned, 1972.

Morrison, Herbert Stanley. Life Peer (1959), Ld Morrison of Lambeth
b. 1888. *Educ.* Elem. Member of L.C.C., 1922–45. Leader of Council, 1934–40. M.P. (Lab.) for S. Hackney, 1923–24, 1929–31, 1935–45. M.P. for E. Lewisham, 1945–50. M.P. for S. Lewisham, 1950–59. Min. of Transport, 1929–31. Min. of Supply, 1940. Home Sec. and Min. of Home Security, 1940–45. Member of war cabinet, 1942–45. Dep. P.M., 1945–51. Ld. Pres. of Council and Leader of Commons, 1945–51. For. Sec., 1951. Dep. Leader of Opposition, 1951–55. d. 1965.

Reading, 1st M of (1926). Rufus Daniel Isaacs (Sir), 1st Ld (1914), 1st Vt (1916)
1st E of (1917)
b. 1860. *Educ.* Brussels, Anglo-Jewish Acad., London, University College Sch. Family Business. Barrister, 1887. M.P. (Lib.) for Reading, 1904–13. Kt., 1910. Sol. Gen., 1910. Att. Gen., 1910–13 (seat in cabinet, 1912). Ld. Chief Justice, 1913–21. Brit. Amb. to U.S.A., 1918–19. Viceroy of India 1921–26. For. Sec., 1931. Leader of Lords 1931; Leader of Liberal Party, Lords 1930–35. d. 1935.

Ritchie, Charles Thomson. 1st Ld Ritchie of Dundee (1905)
  b. 1838. *Educ.* City of London School. M.P. (Con.) for Tower Hamlets, 1874–85. M.P. for St. George's in the East, 1885–92. M.P. for Croydon, 1895–1903. F.S. to Admir., 1885–86. Pres. of Loc. Govt. Bd., 1886–92. Pres. of Bd. of Trade, 1895–1900. Home Sec., 1900–2. Chanc. of Exch., 1902–3. Resigned, 1903. d. 1906.

Salisbury, 3rd M of (1868). Robert Arthur Talbot Gascoyne-Cecil, Vt Cranborne (1865–68)
  b. 1830. *Educ.* Eton; Oxford. M.P. (Con.) for Stamford, 1853–68. Sec. for India, 1866. Resigned, 1867. Succ. to M. 1868. Sec. for India, 1874–76. For. Sec., 1878–80. Leader of Opposition in Lords, 1881–85. Leader of the Con. party, 1885–1902. P.M. and For. Sec., 1885–86. P.M. 1886. P.M. and For. Sec., 1887–92 and 1895–1900. P.M. and Ld. Privy S., 1900–2. d. 1903.

Simon, John Allsebrook (Sir). 1st Vt Simon (1940)
  b. 1873. *Educ.* Fettes; Oxford. Barrister, 1899. M.P. (Lib.) for Walthamstow. 1906–18. M.P. for Spen Valley, 1922–31. M.P. (L. Nat.) for Spen Valley, 1931–40. Kt., 1910. Sol. Gen., 1910–13. Att. Gen. (with seat in cabinet), 1913–15. Home Sec., 1915–16. For. Sec., 1931–35. Leader of L. Nat. party, 1931–40. Home Sec. and Dep. Leader of Commons, 1935–37. Chanc. of Exch., 1937–40. Ld. Chanc., 1940–45. d. 1954.

Snowden, Philip. 1st Vt Snowden (1931)
  b. 1864. *Educ.* Bd. School. M.P. (Lab.) for Blackburn, 1906–18. M.P. for Colne Valley, 1922–31. Ch. of ILP 1903–6 and 1917–20. Chanc. of Exch., 1924, 1929–31, and 1931. Ld. Privy S., 1931–32. Resigned, 1932. d. 1937.

Stewart, (Robert Maitland) Michael
  b. 1906. *Educ.* Christ's Hospital; Oxford. Teacher. M.P. (Lab.) Fulham East, 1945–55 and for Fulham since 1955. Vice-Chamberlain, H.M. Household, 1946. Comptroller, H.M. Household, 1946–47. U.-S. for War 1947–51. P.S. Min. of Supply, 1951. Min. for Educ. and Science, 1964–65. For. Sec., 1965–66. Sec. of State for Econ. Affairs, 1966–67. First Sec. of State, 1966–68. For. (and Commonwealth) Sec., 1968–70.

Thatcher, Mrs Margaret Hilda (nee Roberts)
  b. 1925. *Educ.* Grantham High School; Oxford. Research Chemist. Barrister. M.P. (Con.) for Finchley, 1959–. P.S. to Min. of Pensions and Nat. Insurance, 1961–64. Sec. of State for Education and Science, 1970–74. Leader of the Conservative Party, 1975–.

Thorneycroft, (George Edward) Peter. Life Peer (1967), Ld Thorneycroft of Dunston
  b. 1909. *Educ.* Eton; Woolwich. Barrister, 1935. M.P. (Con.) for Stafford, 1938–45. M.P. (Con.) for Monmouth 1945–1966. P.S. Min. of War Transport, 1945. Pres. of Bd. of Trade, 1951–57. Chanc. of Exch., 1957–58. Resigned, 1958. Min. of Aviation, 1960–62. Min. of Defence 1962–64. Sec. of State for Defence 1964.

Wilson, (James) Harold
  b. 1916. *Educ.* Wirral G.S.; Oxford. University teacher. Director of Economics and Statistics, Min. of Fuel and Power, 1943–44. M.P. (Lab.) for Ormskirk, 1945–50, and for Huyton (Lab.) since 1950. P.S. Min. of Works, 1945–47. Sec. for Overseas Trade, 1947. Pres. Bd. of Trade, 1947–51. Resigned 1951. Leader, Lab. Party, 1963–. P.M., 1964–70. Leader of the Opposition, 1970–4. P.M. 1974–.

Wood, (Howard) Kingsley (Sir)
  b. 1881. *Educ.* Central Foundation Boys' School. Solicitor, 1903. Kt., 1918. M.P. (Con.) for W. Woolwich, 1918–43. P.P.S. to Min. of Health, 1919–22. P.S. Min. of Health, 1924–29. P.S. Bd. of Educ., 1931. Postm.-Gen., 1931–35 (seat in cabinet, 1933). Min. of Health, 1935–38. Sec. for Air, 1938–40. Ld. Privy S., 1940. Chanc. of Exch., 1940–43. d. 1943.

Sources.—*Dictionary of National Biography, 1900–1960; Who Was Who, 1900–1970; Who's Who*

Index of Ministers

This index covers every reference to a Minister given in the Tables of Ministries, pp. 1-58.
It does not cover the supplementary information on Ministers and Ministries, pp. 60–82.

The educational information is necessarily incomplete. It is not always possible to trace the name or status of an elementary or secondary school. When several schools are recorded, the last is normally named here. All schools that are unstarred are 'public schools' or, more precisely, were in the 1960s members of the Headmasters' Conference. RNC Dartmouth is also unstarred. By courtesy, we have listed the Royal Military College (Sandhurst) and the Royal Military Academy (Woolwich) in the University column. In this index promotion from a knighthood to a higher order of chivalry or to a baronetcy is not recorded.

† denotes a Privy Councillor.

When an individual appears more than once on a page, the number is indicated. Double entries are given when an individual held office under different names, and where a title was acquired after office had been held.

Name	Born	School	Univ.	Died	Page references
†Abercorn, 3rd D of (1913) J. A. E. Hamilton, M of Hamilton (1885)	1869	Eton	..	1953	3
†Aberdare, 4th Ld (1957). M. G. L. Bruce	1919	Winchester	Oxford	..	52, 53
†Acland, Sir F. D. (14th Bt 1926)	1874	Rugby	Oxford	1939	5², 6², 8
†Acland Hood, Sir A. F. (4th Bt (1892), 1st Ld St Audries (1911)	1853	Eton	Oxford	1917	3²
Acton, 2nd Ld (1902). R. M. Dalberg-Acton	1870	Privately	Oxford	1924	5, 7
Adams, (H.) R.	1912	Emanuel	London	..	35
Adamson, Mrs J. L.	1882	Elementary	..	1962	3
†Adamson, W.	1863	Elementary	..	1936	16, 19
Adamson, W. M.	1881	Elementary	..	1945	30
†Addison, 1st Vt (1945). C. Addison	1869	Trinity Coll., Harrogate*	London	1951	6, 8, 10, 11³, 12, 18², 32, 33³, 34, 35
†Ailwyn, 1st Ld (1921). Sir A. E. Fellowes (K.C.V.O. 1911)	1855	Eton	Cambridge	1924	2, 3²
Airlie, 12th E of (1900). D. L. G. W. Ogilvy	1893	Eton	..	1968	18
Aitchison, Ld (Scot. judge 1933). C. M. Aitchison	1882	Falkirk H.S.*	Edinburgh	1941	19, 22
†Akers-Douglas, A., 1st Vt Chilston (1911)	1851	Eton	Oxford	1926	2, 3
Albemarle, 8th E of (1884). A. A. C. Keppel	1858	Eton	..	1942	15
Albu, A. H.	1903	Tonbridge	London	..	45
†Aldington, 1st Ld (1962). Sir T. A. R. W. Low (K.C.M.G. 1957)	1914	Winchester	Oxford	..	38, 39
Alexander, 1st E (1952). H. R. L. G. Alexander, 1st Vt (1946)	1891	Harrow	Sandhurst	1969	37
Alexander, 2nd E (1969). S. W. D. Alexander, Ld Rideau (1952)	1935	Harrow	..	..	54
†Alexander of Hillsborough, 1st E (1963). A. V. Alexander, 1st Vt (1950)	1885	Elementary	..	1965	16, 18, 27, 33², 34²
Alison, M. J. H.	1926	Eton	Oxford	..	
Allan, of Kilmahew, Ld (Life Peer 1973). R. A. Allan	1914	Harrow	Cambridge	..	40, 43
†Allendale, 1st Vt (1911). W. C. B. Beaumont, 2nd Ld Allendale (1907)	1860	Eton	Cambridge	1923	5², 7², 9
Allendale, 2nd Vt (1923). W. H. C. Beaumont	1890	Eton	Cambridge	1956	22
†Alness, 1st Ld (1934). R. Munro	1868	Aberdeen G.S.*	Edinburgh	1955	7, 9, 11, 30, 32

Name	Born	School	Univ.	Died	Page references
†Alport, Ld (Life Peer 1961). C. J. Alport	1912	Haileybury	Cambridge	..	39, 41[2]
†Althorp, 1st Vt (1905). C. R. Spencer, Vt Althorp (1857). 6th Earl of Spencer (1910)	1857	Harrow	Cambridge	1922	5, 7
†Altrincham, 1st Ld (1945). Sir E. W. M. Grigg (K.C.V.O. 1920)	1879	Winchester	Oxford	1955	24[2], 28, 30, 32
†Alverstone, 1st Vt (1913). Sir R. E. Webster (G.C.M.G. 1893). 1st Ld Alverstone (1900)	1842	King's Coll. Sch. & Charter-house	Cambridge	1915	3
†Amery, J.	1919	Eton	Oxford	..	41[2], 43, 44, 51, 52, 53
†Amery, L. S.	1873	Harrow	Oxford	1955	10[2], 14, 17[2], 28, 31
†Ammon, 1st Ld (1944). C. G. Ammon	1875	Elementary	..	1960	16, 18, 36
†Amory, 1st Vt (1960). D. Heathcoat Amory	1899	Eton	Oxford	..	37[2], 38, 39, 40
Amulree, 1st Ld (1929). Sir W. W. Mackenzie (K.B.E. 1918)	1860	Perth Academy*	Edinburgh & London	1942	19, 21
Amwell, 1st Ld (1947). F. Montague	1876	Elementary	..	1966	19, 27, 30
†Ancaster, 2nd E (1910). G. H. D. Willoughby	1867	Eton	Cambridge	1951	10, 14
Anderson, Ld (Scot. judge 1913). A. M. Anderson	1862	Dundee H.S.*	Edinburgh	1936	7
Anderson, D. C.	1916	Trinity Coll. Glenalmond	Oxford & Edinburgh	..	44
†Anderson, Sir J. (K.C.B. 1919). 1st Vt Waverley (1952)	1882	George Watson's Coll., Edin.	Edinburgh & Leipzig	1958	22, 23, 26[2], 28[2], 31
Anson, Sir W. (3rd Bt 1873)	1843	Eton	Oxford	1914	2
Anstruther, H. T.	1860	Eton	Edinburgh	1926	3
†Anstruther-Gray, Sir W. J. (1st Bt 1956) Ld Kilmany (Life Peer 1966)	1905	Eton	Oxford	..	32
Archibald, 1st Ld (1949). G. Archibald	1898	Allan Glen's H.S. Glasg.*	..	1975	36
Archer, P. K.	1926	Wednesbury Boys' H.S.*	London	..	58
Armstrong, E.	1915	Wolsingham G.S.*	..	..	50[2], 55
Arnold, 1st Ld (1924). S. Arnold	1878	Manchester G.S.	..	1945	16, 19
†Arnold-Foster, H. O.	1855	Rugby	Oxford	1909	2, 3
†Ashbourne, 1st Ld (1885). E. Gibson	1837		Dublin	1913	2
†Ashby St Ledgers, 1st Ld (1910). I. C. Guest, 2nd Ld Wimborne (1914), 1st Vt Wimborne (1918)	1873	Eton	Cambridge	1939	7[2]
†Ashfield, 1st Ld (1920). Sir A. H. Stanley (Kt 1914)	1874	American Schs.	..	1948	11
†Ashley, W. W. 1st Ld Mount Temple (1932)	1867	Harrow	Oxford	1939	15[2], 18
†Asquith, H. H. 1st E of Oxford & Asquith (1925)	1852	City of London	Oxford	1928	4, 5, 6, 8
†Assheton, R. 1st Ld Clitheroe (1955)	1901	Eton	Oxford	..	24, 26, 27, 29
Astor, 2nd Vt (1919). W. Astor	1879	Eton	Oxford	1952	10, 12
†Atholl, 8th D of (1917). J. G. Stewart-Murray, M of Tullibardine (1871)	1871	Eton	..	1942	13
Atholl, Duchess of, K. M.	1874	Wimbledon H.S.	..	1960	17
†Atkins, H.E.	1922	Wellington	..	..	53, 54
†Atkinson, Ld (Ld of Appeal 1905). J. Atkinson	1844	Royal Belfast Academical Institution*	Queen's Coll., Gal-way	1932	3

Name	Born	School	Univ.	Died	Page references
†Freeman-Thomas, F. 1st Ld Willingdon (1910), 1st Vt (1924), 1st E of (1931), 1st M of (1936)	1866	Eton	Cambridge	1941	5, 7
Freeson, R.	1926	Elementary	..	..	48, 49, 56
Freeth, D.	1924	Sherborne	Oxford	..	42
†French, Sir J. D. P. (K.C.B. 1900). 1st Vt French of Ypres (1915), 1st E of Ypres (1921)	1852	H.M.S. Britannia*	..	1925	10
Fuller, Sir J. M. F. (1st Bt 1910)	1864	Winchester	Oxford	1915	5,[2] 7
Furness, S. N.	1902	Charterhouse	Oxford	1974	25, 30
Gage, 6th Vt (1912). H. R. Gage	1895	Eton	Oxford	..	18, 22, 26
†Gainford, 1st Ld (1917). J. A. Pease	1860	Tottenham*	Cambridge	1943	5, 6[2], 7[2], 9
†Gaitskell, H. T. N.	1906	Winchester	Oxford	1963	32[2], 34, 35[2]
†Galbraith, T. D. 1st Ld Strathclyde (1955)	1891	Glasgow Acad., R.N.C. Osborne & Dartmouth	..	..	31, 38[3], 39[3], 42
Galbraith, T. G. D.	1917	Wellington	Oxford	..	42, 43[2]
Gammans, Sir (L.) D. (1st Bt 1955)	1895	Portsmouth G.S.	London	1957	39, 42
†Gardiner, Ld (Life Peer 1964). G. A. Gardiner	1900	Harrow	Oxford	..	45
Garnsworthy, Ld (Life Peer 1967). C. J. Garnsworthy	1906	Wellington	..	1974	58
Garro-Jones, G. M. 1st Ld Trefgarne (1947). *Surname changed to Trefgarne in 1954*	1894	Caterham	..	1960	27
†Geddes, 1st Ld (1942). Sir A. C. Geddes (K.C.B. 1917)	1879	George Watson's Coll., Edin.	Edinburgh	1954	11[3], 12
†Geddes, Sir E. C. (Kt 1916)	1875	Merchiston Castle Sch.	..	1937	9, 10, 12[2]
†Geoffrey-Lloyd, Ld (Life Peer 1974). G. Lloyd	1902	Harrow	Cambridge	..	23, 24, 28, 29, 32, 37[2], 38
George, Sir J. C. (K.B.E. 1963)	1901	Ballingry, Fife*	..	..	42
†George-Brown, Ld (Life Peer 1970). G. A. Brown	1914	Secondary	..	..	33, 35, 45[2], 46
†Gibbs, G. A. 1st Ld Wraxall (1928)	1873	Eton	Oxford	1931	13, 15, 18
†Gibson-Watt, Sir (J.) D. (Kt 1974)	1918	Eton	Cambridge	..	44, 53
Gilbert, J. W.	1927	Merchant Taylors Sch.	Oxford & New York	..	55
Gillett, Sir G. M. (Kt 1931)	1870	Secondary	..	1939	19, 21
†Gilmour, Sir J. (2nd Bt 1920)	1876	Trinity Coll. Glenalmond	Edinburgh & Cambridge	1940	13, 17, 20[2], 21, 24
†Gilmour, I. H. J. L.	1926	Eton	Oxford	..	51[4]
†Gladstone, 1st Vt (1910) H. J. Gladstone	1854	Eton	Oxford	1930	4, 6
Glassey, A. E.	1887	Penistone G.S.*	..	1971	22
Glenavy, 1st Ld (1921). Sir J. H. M. Campbell (1st Bt 1916)	1851	Kingstown*	Dublin	1931	3, 9, 12, 13
†Glendevon, 1st Ld (1964). Ld J. A. Hope	1912	Eton	Oxford	..	37[2], 42, 44
†Glenkinglass, Ld (Life Peer 1974). M. A. C. Noble	1913	Eton	Oxford	..	42, 44, 53[2]
†Godber, J. B.	1914	Bedford	..	..	40[2], 41, 42, 44, 51[2]
Golding, J.	1931	Chester G.S.*	London & Keele	..	58
Goodhew, V. H.	1919	King's Coll. Sch.	..	..	54[2]
Gordon, J.	1849	Royal Acad. Institution	Queen's Coll., Belfast	1922	9
†Gordon Walker, Ld (Life Peer 1974). P. C. Gordon Walker	1907	Wellington	Oxford	..	33[2], 46, 47, 48

Name	Born	School	Univ.	Died	Page references
†Kilmuir, 1st E (1962). D. P. Maxwell Fyfe, 1st Vt Kilmuir (1954)	1900	George Watson's Coll., Edin.	Oxford	1967	30, 32, 36, 37, 40
King, E. M.	1907	Cheltenham	Cambridge	..	34
King, (H.) D.	1877	Training ship	..	1930	15, 17[2]
†Kintore 10th E of (1880). A. H. T. Keith-Falconer	1852	Eton	Cambridge	1930	3
Kirk, P. M.	1928	Marlborough	Oxford	..	41, 44, 51
†Kitchener of Khartoum, 1st E (1914) H. H. Kitchener, 1st Ld (1898), 1st Vt (1902)	1850	France	Woolwich	1916	6, 8
†Lambert, 1st Vt (1945). G. Lambert	1866	Privately	..	1958	4, 6
Lambton, Vt (1941–69). A. C. F. Lambton (6th Earl of Durham, disclaimed 1970)	1922	Harrow	..	..	51
Lane, D. W. S. S.	1922	Eton	Cambridge	..	51
†Lane-Fox, G. R. 1st Ld Bingley (1933)	1870	Eton	Oxford	1947	15, 17
†Lansbury, G.	1859	Elementary	..	1940	19
†Lansdowne, 5th M of (1866). H. C. K. Petty-Fitzmaurice, Vt Clanmaurice (1845). E of Kerry (1863)	1845	Eton	Oxford	1927	2, 3, 8
†Lansdowne, 8th M of (1944). G. J. C. M. N. Petty-Fitzmaurice	1912	Eton	Oxford	..	40, 41, 43, 44
†Law, A. Bonar	1858	Glasgow H.S.*	..	1923	3, 8, 9[3], 14
†Law, R. K. 1st Ld Coleraine (1954)	1901	Shrewsbury	Oxford	..	26[2], 30, 32
Lawrence, 2nd Ld (1879). J. H. Lawrence	1846	Wellington	Cambridge	1913	3
Lawrence, Miss (A.) S.	1871	Privately	Cambridge	1947	19
†Lawson, 1st Ld (1950). J. J. Lawson	1881	Elementary	..	1965	16, 19, 34
Lawson, G. M.	1906	Elementary	..	..	49
Lawson, Sir J. G. (1st Bt (1905)	1856	Harrow	Oxford	1919	2
Leach, W.	1870	Bradford G.S.	..	1949	16
†Leathers, 1st Vt (1954). F. J. Leathers, 1st Ld (1941)	1883	Elementary	..	1965	30, 32, 37
Leburn, (W.) G.	1913	Strathallan*	..	1963	42
†Lee of Fareham, 1st Vt (1922). Sir A. Lee (K.C.B. 1916). 1st Ld (1918)	1868	Cheltenham	Woolwich	1947	2, 8, 10[2]
†Lee of Newton, Ld (Life Peer 1974). F. Lee	1906	Langworthy Rd.*	..	..	34, 46, 48, 49
†Lee of Asheridge, Lady (Life Peer 1970). Miss J. Lee (Mrs A. Bevan)	1904	Benton*	Edinburgh	..	47[2], 49
Leechman, J.	1906	Glasgow H.S.*	Glasgow	..	49
†Lees-Smith, H. B.	1878	Aldenham	..	1941	19[2]
Legh, P. R. 4th Ld Newton (1960)	1915	Eton	Oxford	..	39, 42, 43, 44[2], 45[3]
†Lennox-Boyd, A. T. 1st Vt Boyd (1960)	1904	Sherborne	Oxford	..	23, 24, 27, 31, 37[2], 39, 41
Leonard, W.	1887	Elementary	..	..	35
Lestor, Miss J.	1931	William Morris S.S.*	London	..	47, 55
Lever, Sir (S.) H. (K.C.B. 1917)	1869	Merchant Taylors' Sch., Crosby	..	1947	9
†Lever, H.	1914	Manchester G.S.	..	..	45[2], 56
†Lewis, Sir (J.) H. (G.B.E. 1922)	1858	Secondary	McGill & Oxford	1933	5, 6, 7, 8, 10
Lewis, T. A.	1881	Denbigh G.S.*	Cardiff	1923	13
Limerick, 6th E of (1967). P. E. Pery	1930	Eton	Oxford	..	53

Name	Born	School	Univ.	Died	Page references
†Rothermere, 1st Vt (1919). Sir H. S. Harmsworth (1st Bt 1910), 1st Ld Rothermere (1914)	1868	Secondary	..	1940	12
Rothschild, J. A. de	1878	Lycée Louis le Grand*	Cambridge	1957	29
Rowlands, E.	1940	Wirral G.S.*	London	..	48, 56
†Rowley, Ld (Life Peer 1966). A. Henderson	1893	Queen's Coll., Taunton*	Cambridge	1968	30^2 33, 34^2
Royle, Ld (Life Peer 1964). C. Royle	1896	Stockport G.S.*	..	..	36
Royle, Sir A. H. F. (KCMG 1947)	1927	Harrow	Sandhurst	..	51
†Runciman, of Doxford 1st Vt (1937). W. Runciman, 2nd Ld Runciman (1933)	1870	S. Shields H.S.* & Privately	Cambridge	1949	4^2, 6^3, 8, 21, 22, 24
Runcorn, Ld (Life Peer 1964). D. F. Vosper	1916	Marlborough	Cambridge	1968	37, 39, 41^2, 43, 44
†Rushcliffe, 1st Ld (1935). Sir H. B. Betterton (1st Bt 1929)	1872	Rugby	Oxford	1949	14, 17, 20, 21
Russell, 2nd E (1878). J. F. S. Russell	1865	Winchester	Oxford	1931	19^2
Russell, Ld (Scot. judge 1936). A. Russell	1884	Glasgow Acad.	Glasgow	1970	25
Russell, Sir T. W. (1st Bt 1917)	1841	Madras Acad., Fife*	..	1920	2, 4, 6, 8, 10
†St Aldwyn, 1st E (1915). M. E. Hicks Beach, 1st Vt St Aldwyn (1906)	1837	Eton	Oxford	1916	2
†St Aldwyn, 2nd E (1915). M. J. Hicks Beach	1912	Eton	Oxford	..	37, 41, 45, 54
†St Audries, 1st Ld (1911). Sir A. F. Acland Hood (4th Bt 1892)	1853	Eton	Oxford	1917	3^2
St. Helens, 1st Ld (1964). M. H. C. Hughes-Young	1912	Harrow	Sandhurst	..	44^2
St John-Stevas, N. A. F.	1929	Ratcliffe*	Cambridge & Oxford	..	52^2
St Oswald, 4th Ld (1957). R. D. G. Winn	1916	Stowe	Bonn & Freiburg	..	41, 45
†Salisbury, 3rd M of (1868). R. A. T. Gascoyne-Cecil, Vt Cranborne (1865)	1830	Eton	Oxford	1903	1^2, 2
†Salisbury, 4th M of (1903). J. E. H. Gascoyne-Cecil, Vt Cranborne (1868)	1861	Eton	Oxford	1947	1, 2, 3, 14^2, 17
†Salisbury, 5th M of (1947). R. A. J. Gascoyne-Cecil, Vt Cranborne (1903)	1893	Eton	Oxford	1972	23, 26, 27, 28^2, 29^2 31, 36^2, 37, 40
†Salter, 1st Ld (1953). Sir (J.) A. Salter (K.C.B. 1922)	1881	Oxford H.S.*	Oxford	..	24, 29, 30, 32, 36, 38
†Salvesen, Ld (Scot. judge 1905). E. Salvesen	1857	Collegiate Sch., Edin.*	Edinburgh	1942	3
†Samuel, 1st Vt (1937). Sir H. L. Samuel (G.B.E. 1920)	1870	University Coll. Sch.	Oxford	1963	4, 6^4, 8^2, 9, 20
Samuel, Sir A. M. (1st Bt 1932). 1st Ld Mancroft (1937)	1872	Norwich G.S.*	..	1942	17^2
Samuels, A. W.	1852	Royal Sch., Dungannon *	Dublin	1925	13^2
†Sanders, Sir R. A. (1st Bt 1920). 1st Ld Bayford (1929)	1867	Harrow	Oxford	1940	12, 13^2, 14
Sanders, W. S.	1871	Elementary	Berlin	1941	19
Sandford, 1st Ld (1945). Sir A. J. Edmondson (Kt 1934)	1887	University Coll. Sch.	..	1959	25, 26, 30, 31, 32

II
PARTIES

Conservative Party

Party Leaders

1900	M of Salisbury	9 Oct 40	(Sir) W. Churchill
14 Jul 02	A. Balfour	21 Apr 55	Sir A. Eden
13 Nov 11	A. Bonar Law [1]	22 Jan 57	H. Macmillan
21 Mar 21	A. Chamberlain [1]	11 Nov 63	Sir A. Douglas-Home
23 Oct 22	A. Bonar Law [1]	2 Aug 65	E. Heath [3]
28 May 23	S. Baldwin	11 Feb 75	Mrs. M. Thatcher [4]
31 May 37	N. Chamberlain [2]		

Deputy Leaders

4 Aug 65–18 Jul 72	R. Maudling
12 Feb 75–	W. Whitelaw

Leaders in the House of Lords

1900	3rd M of Salisbury	1941	Ld Lloyd
1902	D of Devonshire	1941	Ld Moyne
1903	M of Lansdowne	1942	Vt Cranborne
1916	Earl Curzon (M)		(5th M of Salisbury)
1925	4th M of Salisbury	1957	E of Home
1930	1st Vt Hailsham	1960	2nd Vt Hailsham
1935	M of Londonderry	1963	Ld Carrington
1935	Vt Halifax	1970	Earl Jellicoe
1938	Earl Stanhope	1973	Ld Windlesham
1940	Vt Caldecote	1974	Ld Carrington
1940	Vt Halifax		

Principal Office-holders

Chairmen of the Party Organisation

Jun 11–Dec 16	A. Steel-Maitland
Dec 16–Mar 23	Sir G. Younger
Mar 23–Nov 26	S. Jackson
Nov 26–May 30	J. Davidson
Jun 30–Apr 31	N. Chamberlain
Apr 31–Mar 36	Ld Stonehaven
Mar 36–Mar 42	(Sir) D. Hacking
Mar 42–Sep 44	T. Dugdale
Oct 44–Jul 46	R. Assheton
Oct 46–Jul 55	Ld Woolton (Vt)
Jul 55–Sep 57	O. Poole
Sep 57–Oct 59	Vt Hailsham
Oct 59–Oct 61	R. Butler
Oct 61–Apr 63	I. Macleod
Apr 63–Oct 63	I. Macleod } Ld Poole }

Oct 63–Jan 65	Vt Blakenham
Jan 65–Sep 67	E. du Cann
Sep 67–Jul 70	A. Barber
Jul 70–Apr 72	P. Thomas
Apr 72–Jun 74	Ld Carrington
Jun 74–Feb 75	W. Whitelaw
Feb 75–	Ld Thorneycroft

Deputy Chairmen

May 24–Jan 26	M of Linlithgow
Sep 57–Oct 59	O. Poole (Ld)
Oct 59–Oct 63	Sir T. Low
	(Ld Aldington)
Oct 64–	Sir M. (Ld) Fraser
Apr 72–Jun 74	J. Prior
Feb 75–	W. Clark
Feb 75–	A. Maude

[1] A. Bonar Law, 1911–21, and A. Chamberlain, 1921–22, were Leaders of the Conservative Party in the House of Commons. Formerly, when the party was in opposition, there were separate Leaders in the Commons and the Lords; and the present title 'Leader of the Conservative and Unionist Party' did not officially exist. It was first conferred, in Oct 1922, on A. Bonar Law when he was selected for his second term of office.
[2] N. Chamberlain remained Leader of the Conservative party until 4 Oct 40, though he was succeeded as Prime Minister by W. Churchill on 10 May 40, and resigned from the Government on 30 Sep 40.
[3] In 1965 E. Heath was the first Conservative leader to be elected by a ballot of M.P.s. He received 150 votes to 133 for R. Maudling and 15 for E. Powell. Although the new rules required a larger majority, Mr Maudling instantly withdrew in favour of Mr. Heath.
[4] In a first ballot on 4 Feb 75 Mrs Thatcher won 130 votes to 119 for E. Heath and 16 for H. Fraser. In a second ballot Mrs Thatcher won 146 votes; W. Whitelaw 79; J. Prior 19; Sir G. Howe 19; J. Peyton 11.

Principal Agents

Mar 1885–Jul 03	R. Middleton
Jul 03–Nov 05	L. Wells
Nov 05–Dec 06	A. Haig
Dec 06–Jan 12	P. Hughes
May 12–Jun 15	J. Boraston
Jun 15–Apr 20	(Sir) J. Boraston
	& W. Jenkins
Apr 20–Dec 20	W. Jenkins
Dec 20–Mar 23	Sir M. Fraser
Mar 23–Feb 24	Sir R. Hall
Mar 24–Jan 27	(Sir) H. Blain
Jan 27–Feb 28	Sir L. Maclachlan
Feb 28–Feb 31	R. Topping

General Directors

Feb 31–Sep 45	(Sir) R. Topping
Oct 45–Aug 57	(Sir) S. Pierssené
Aug 57–Jun 66	(Sir) W. Urton
(office abolished Jun 66)	

Director-General

Apr 74–Feb 75	M. Wolff

Director of Organisation

Jun 66–	(Sir) R. Webster

Treasurers

1919–23	Earl Farquhar
1923–29	Vt Younger
1930–31	Sir S. Hoare
Jul 31–Nov 33	Ld Ebbisham
Nov 33–Jun 38	Vt Greenwood
Jun 38–Feb 47	Vt Marchwood
Feb 47–Apr 60	C. Holland-Martin
Feb 48–Mar 52	Ld De L'Isle [1]
Mar 52–Oct 55	O. Poole
Oct 55–Jan 62	Sir H. Studholme
Oct 60–Nov 65	R. Allan
Jan 62–Aug 66	R. Stanley
Nov 65–	Ld Chelmer
Aug 66–Apr 74	Sir T. Brinton
Apr 74–	Sir A. Silverstone (Ld Ashdown)
Apr 74–Feb 75	W. Clark

Conservative Research Department 1929

Director		Chairman	
1930–39	(Sir) J. Ball	1929	N. Chamberlain
1939–45	vacant	1940	Sir K. Wood
1945–51	D. Clarke (joint from 48)	1943	Sir J. Ball (Acting Hon. Chairman)
1948–50	H. Hopkinson (joint)		
1948–59	P. Cohen (joint)	1945	R. Butler
1951–64	(Sir) M. Fraser (joint to 59)	1964	(post vacant)
1964–70	B. Sewill	1970	Sir M. (Ld) Fraser
1970–74	J. Douglas	1974	I. Gilmour
1974–	C. Patten	1975	A. Maude

SOURCES.—Annual Conference Reports of the National Union of Conservative and Unionist Associations, and information from the Conservative Research Department.

Chief Whips in the House of Commons

1900	Sir W. Walrond
1902	Sir A. Acland Hood
1911	Ld Balcarres
1912	Ld E. Talbot
1921	L. Wilson
1923	(Sir) B. Eyres-Monsell
1931	D. Margesson
1941	J. Stuart
1948	P. Buchan-Hepburn
1955	E. Heath
1959	M. Redmayne
1964	W. Whitelaw
1970	F. Pym
1973	H. Atkins

Chief Whips in the House of Lords

1900	Earl Waldegrave
1911	D of Devonshire
1916	Ld Hylton
1922	E of Clarendon
1925	E of Plymouth
1929	E of Lucan (5th)
1940	Ld Templemore
1945	Earl Fortescue
1958	Earl St Aldwyn

SOURCE.—Dod's Parliamentary Companion, 1900– . For a full list of whips see F. M. G. Willson 'Some Career Patterns in British Politics: Whips in the House of Commons 1906–66', Parliamentary Affairs, 25 (Winter 1970–1) pp. 33–42.

[1] Since February 1948 the office of Treasurer has been held jointly.

Chairmen of 1922 Committee [1]

Jan 23–Nov 32	(Sir) G. Rentoul	Aug 45–Nov 51	Sir A. Gridley
Dec 32–Dec 35	W. Morrison	Nov 51–Nov 55	D. Walker-Smith
Dec 35–Jul 39	Sir H. O'Neill	Nov 55–Nov 64	J. Morrison
Sep 39–Nov 39	Sir A. Somerville	Nov 64–Mar 66	Sir W. Anstruther-Gray
Dec 39–Dec 40	W. Spens	May 66–Jul 70	Sir A. Harvey
Dec 40–Dec 44	A. Erskine Hill	Jul 70–Nov 72	Sir H. Legge-Bourke
Dec 44–Jun 45	J. McEwen	Nov 72–	E. du Cann

SOURCE.—*The Times Index, 1923–70*, information from the 1922 Committee, R. T. McKenzie, *British Political Parties* (1955), pp. 57–61, P. Goodhart, *The 1922* (1973) and Conservative Research Department.

Conservative Shadow Cabinets

Little has been published about the Conservative arrangements when in opposition. The situation appears to have been as follows:—

1906–14   After the 1906 defeat Conservative ex-ministers met regularly in what was known as a 'Shadow' Cabinet. Only after 1910 was new blood brought in, e.g. F. E. Smith and Sir A. Steel-Maitland.

1924   S. Baldwin summoned a formal Shadow Cabinet of all ex-ministers which met weekly during the Session and which had a secretariat.

1929–31   There was a Consultative Committee which met regularly and was serviced by the Research Department.

1945–51   The Chief Whip sent out notices to a regular Shadow Cabinet meeting, formally known as the Consultative Committee. Names were added but never subtracted and W. Churchill allowed the numbers to grow to about 24. No formal minutes were kept. The following seem to have attended regularly.

W. Churchill
———

Sir J. Anderson	A. Eden	O. Stanley
R. Assheton	W. Elliot	J. Stuart
B. Bracken	R. Law	H. Willink
P. Buchan-Hepburn	O. Lyttelton	Vt Woolton
R. Butler	H. Macmillan	
Ld Cherwell	D. Maxwell Fyfe	
H. Crookshank	W. Morrison	
	M of Salisbury	

(H. Hopkinson acted as secretary 1945–50, D. Clark 1950–1)

1964   A Leaders' Consultative Committee has met regularly when the party has been in opposition and formal minutes have been kept.

1964–70

Sir A. Douglas-Home (1964–5)	Ld Dilhorne (1964–6)	M. Noble (1964–9)
E. Heath (1965–7)	Sir A. Douglas-Home (1965–70)	Miss M. Pike (1966–7)
	E. du Cann (1965–7)	E. Powell (1964–8)
Lord Balniel (1967–70)	J. Godber	M. Redmayne (1964–6)
A. Barber (1966–70)	Ld Harlech (1966–7)	G. Rippon (1966–70)
Ld Blakenham (1964–5)	E. Heath (1964–5)	D. Sandys (1964–6)
J. Boyd-Carpenter (1964–6)	Q. Hogg	C. Soames (1964–6)
	Earl Jellicoe (1967–70)	Mrs M. Thatcher (1967–70)
Sir E. Boyle (1964–9)	Sir K. Joseph	
R. A. Butler (1964–5)	S. Lloyd (1964–6)	P. Thorneycroft (1964–6)
G. Campbell (1969–70)	I. Macleod	P. Walker (1966–70)
R. Carr (1967–70)	E. Marples (1964–6)	(W. Whitelaw) (1966–70)
Ld Carrington	R. Maudling	Sir M. Fraser (Secretary)

[1] Or the Conservative (Private) Members' Committee. This is an organisation of the entire backbench membership of the Conservative Party in the Commons. It acts as a sounding-board of Conservative opinion in the House, but is not authorised to formulate policy.

1974–
E. Heath (–1975)
Mrs. M. Thatcher
          (1975–)

H. Atkins
A. Barber (1974)
A. Buchanan-Smith
R. Carr (–1975)
Ld Carrington
P. Channon (–1975)
Sir A. Douglas-Home
          (–1974)
N. Edwards (1975–)

N. Fowler (1975–)
I. Gilmour
Ld Hailsham
Sir G. Howe
P. Jenkin
M. Jopling (1975–)
Sir K. Joseph
M. Macmillan (–1974)
R. Maudling (1975–)
A. Neave (1975–)
M. S. Oppenheim (1975–)
J. Peyton
J. Prior
F. Pym (1975–)
T. Raison

G. Rippon (–1975)
N. St. John Stevas
N. Scott (–1975)
Mrs. M. Thatcher (–1975)
P. Thomas (–1975)
W. van Straubenzee
          (–1974)
P. Walker (–1975)
W. Whitelaw
Ld Windlesham (–1974)

Sir M. (Ld) Fraser
          (Secretary)

SOURCES.—R. M. Punnett, *Front Bench Opposition* (1973); D. Turner, *The Shadow Cabinet in British Politics* (1969).

Party Membership

The Conservative Party has seldom published figures of its total membership. Membership is a loose term, usually associated with the payment of an annual subscription, but exact records are not always kept locally, let alone nationally. In 1953 it was claimed that the party had reached an all-time record membership of 2,805,832, but this was a temporary peak. One estimate for 1969–70 suggests that the party's membership in Great Britain was then $1\frac{1}{4}$ to $1\frac{1}{2}$ million. Membership of the Young Conservatives fell from a peak of 157,000 in 1949 to 80,000 in 1959 and to 50,000 in 1968.

SOURCE.—See *The British General Election of 1970* (1971), pp. 278–9, 287.

Party Finance

The Conservative Party did not publish its expenditure until 1968.[1] In 1912 Sir A. Steel-Maitland, the Party Chairman, put the party's annual income centrally at £80,000 and suggested that the extra expenses of a general election, centrally, were £80,000 to £120,000. In 1929 J. Davidson, then Chairman, put the cost of a general election at £300,000.

The Conservative Party reported its central expenses in the 1970 election as £618,000; for the February 1974 election the figure was £280,000 (unlike 1970 this figure is for the 3-week campaign only). It has been estimated that

[1] The routine central expenditure annually reported since 1968 was:

1967–68	£1,071,000
1968–69	£1,054,000
1969–70	£1,052,000
1970–71	£1,668,000
1971–72	£1,249,000
1972–73	£1,481,000
1973–74	£2,134,000

in 1966–67 the total expenditure of all Conservative constituency associations was about £1¾ million.

SOURCES.—N. Blewett, *The Peers, the Parties and the People: The General Elections of 1910* (1972) p. 291; R. Rhodes James, *Memoirs of a Conservative* (1969); M. Harrison, in R. Rose and A. Heidenheimer (eds.), *Comparative Political Finance* (1963); R. Rose, *Influencing Voters* (1967) pp. 260–8; M. Pinto-Duschinsky, *The British General Election of 1970* (1971), pp. 282–3, and 'Central Office and "Power" in the Conservative Party', *Political Studies*, **20** (Mar 1972) pp. 1–16.

National Union of Conservative and Unionist Associations — Annual Conferences,[1] 1900–

Date	Place	President	Chairman
19 Dec 00	London	M of Zetland	Ld Windsor
26–27 Nov 01	Wolverhampton	Ld Llangattock	Sir A. Hickman
14–15 Oct 02	Manchester	E of Dartmouth	Sir C. Cave
1–2 Oct 03	Sheffield	E of Derby	F. Lowe
28–29 Oct 04	Southampton	D of Norfolk	H. Bowles
14–15 Nov 05	Newcastle upon Tyne	Ld Montagu of Beaulieu	Sir W. Plummer
27 Jul 06	London	D of Northumberland	H. Imbert-Terry
14–15 Nov 07	Birmingham	"	D of Rutland
19–20 Nov 08	Cardiff	E of Plymouth	Sir R. Hodge
17–18 Nov 09	Manchester	E Cawdor	Sir T. Wrightson
17 Nov 10	Nottingham	E of Derby	H. Chaplin
16–17 Nov 11	Leeds	D of Portland	Ld Kenyon
14–15 Nov 12	London	Ld Faber	Sir W. Crump
12–14 Nov 13	Norwich	Ld Farquhar	A. Salvidge
1914–16	*No conference held*	Sir A. Fellowes	Sir H. Samuel
1917	London	"	"
1918–19	*No conference held*	"	J. Williams
10–11 Jun 20	Birmingham	"	Sir A. Benn
17–18 Nov 21	Liverpool	A. Chamberlain	Sir A. Leith
15–16 Dec 22	London	E of Derby	Sir H. Nield
25–26 Oct 23	Plymouth	Ld Mildmay of Flete	E of Selborne
2–3 Oct 24	Newcastle upon Tyne	D of Northumberland	Sir P. Woodhouse
8–9 Oct 25	Brighton	G. Loder	Dame C. Bridgeman
7–8 Oct 26	Scarborough	G. Lane-Fox	
6–7 Oct 27	Cardiff	Vt Tredegar	Sir R. Sanders
27–28 Sep 28	Great Yarmouth	Ld Queenborough	J. Gretton
21–22 Nov 29	London	Ld Faringdon	G. Rowlands
1 Jul 30	London	N. Chamberlain	Countess of Iveagh
1931	*No conference held*	"	G. Herbert
6–7 Oct 32	Blackpool	Ld Stanley	Earl Howe
5–6 Oct 33	Birmingham	E of Plymouth	Sir G. Ellis
4–5 Oct 34	Bristol	Ld Bayford	Miss R. Evans
3–4 Oct 35	Bournemouth	G. Herbert	Sir W. Cope
1–2 Oct 36	Margate	Ld Ebbisham	Sir L. Brassey
7–8 Oct 37	Scarborough	Ld Bingley	Mrs C. Fyfe
1938	*No conference held*	M of Londonderry	Sir E. Ramsden
1939	"		N. Colman
1940	"	Ld Queenborough	Lady Hillingdon
1941	"		Sir C. Headlam
1942	"	M of Salisbury	R. Catterall
20–21 May 43	London	"	
1944	*No conference held*		Mrs L. Whitehead
14–15 Mar 45	London	Ld Courthope	R. Butler
3–5 Oct 46	Blackpool	O. Stanley	R. Proby
2–4 Oct 47	Brighton	H. Macmillan	Mrs Hornyold-Strickland
7–9 Oct 48	Llandudno	G. Summers	Sir H. Williams
12–14 Oct 49	London	Vt Swinton	D. Graham
12–14 Oct 50	Blackpool	Sir D. Maxwell Fyfe	A. Nutting
1951	*No conference held*	Ld Ramsden	Mrs L. Sayers

[1] 1900–12, National Union of Conservative and Constitutional Associations, 1912–17 National Unionist Association of Conservative and Liberal-Unionist Associations, 1917–24 National Unionist Association, 1924– National Union of Conservative and Unionist Associations.

Date	Place	President	Chairman
9–11 Oct 52	Scarborough	Sir T. Dugdale	C. Waterhouse
8–10 Oct 53	Margate	M of Salisbury	Mrs J. Warde
7–9 Oct 54	Blackpool	A. Eden	Sir G. Llewellyn
6–8 Oct 55	Bournemouth	Mrs L. Sayers	Mrs E. Emmet
11–13 Oct 56	Llandudno	R. Butler	Sir E. Edwards
10–12 Oct 57	Brighton	E of Woolton	Mrs W. Elliot
8–11 Oct 58	Blackpool	Sir R. Proby	Sir S. Bell
1959	No conference held	H. Brooke	E. Brown
12–15 Oct 60	Scarborough	,,	,,
11–14 Oct 61	Brighton	Vt Hailsham	Sir D. Glover
10–13 Oct 62	Llandudno	Sir G. Llewellyn	Sir J. Howard
8–11 Oct 63	Blackpool	E of Home	Mrs T. Shepherd
64	No conference held	Vtess Davidson	Sir M. Bemrose
12–15 Oct 65	Brighton	Vtess Davidson	Sir M. Bemrose
13–16 Oct 66	Blackpool	S. Lloyd	Sir D. Mason
18–21 Oct 67	Brighton	Ld Chelmer	Mrs A. Doughty
9–12 Oct 68	Blackpool	R. Maudling	Sir T. Constantine
8–11 Oct 69	Brighton	Lady Brooke	D. Crossman
7–10 Oct 70	Blackpool	I. Macleod	Sir E. Leather
13–16 Oct 71	Brighton	W. Whitelaw	Miss U. Lister
11–14 Oct 72	Blackpool	Dame M. Shepherd	W. Harris
10–13 Oct 73	Blackpool	A. Barber	Mrs R. Smith
74	No conference held	P. Thomas	Sir A. Graesser

SOURCES.—*National Union Gleanings 1900–12, Gleanings and Memoranda 1912–33, Politics in Review 1934–39*, all published by the National Union of Conservative Associations; *National Union of Conservative and Unionist Associations, Annual Conference Reports, 1958–*; for Conservative Party Manifestos and major recent reports, pamphlets, etc., see G. D. M. Block, *A Source Book of Conservatism* (1964). See also I. Bulmer-Thomas, *The Growth of the British Party System* (1965).

Labour Party

Party Leaders and Deputy Leaders

Chairman of the Parliamentary Party

1906	J. K. Hardie
1908	A. Henderson
1910	G. Barnes
1911	J. R. MacDonald
1914	A. Henderson
1917	W. Adamson
1921	J. Clynes

Chairman and Leader of the Parliamentary Party

1922	J. R. MacDonald [1]
1931	A. Henderson [2]
1932	G. Lansbury
1935	C. Attlee[1]
1955	H. Gaitskell
1963	H. Wilson

Vice Chairman

1906	D. Shackleton
1908	G. Barnes
1910	J. Clynes
1911	W. Brace
1912	J. Parker
1914	A. Gill
1915	J. Hodge
1916	G. Wardle } *Acting Chairmen*
1918	J. Clynes
1921	J. Thomas S. Walsh } *joint*

Deputy Leader

1922	S. Walsh J. Wedgwood } *joint*
1923	J. Clynes
1931	C. Attlee
1935	A. Greenwood
1945	H. Morrison
1955	J. Griffiths
1959	A. Bevan
1960	G. Brown
1970	R. Jenkins
1972	E. Short

[1] When the Labour Party was in power in 1924, 1929–31, 1940–45, 1945–51, and 1964–70, a Liaison Committee was set up. The Chairmen of these committees are listed on p. 106.
[2] A. Henderson lost his seat in the 1931 election. The acting leader of the Parliamentary Labour Party in 1931 was G. Lansbury.

Since 1922 the Labour Party, when in opposition, has elected its Leader and Deputy Leader at the beginning of each session. Most elections have been uncontested, but there have been these exceptions. (The figures in brackets show the result of the first ballot. The date is for the final ballot.)

	Leader				Deputy Leader		
Nov 22	J. R. MacDonald		61				
	J. Clynes		56	2 Feb 55	J. Griffiths		141
					A. Bevan		111
3 Dec 35	C. Attlee	(58)	88				
	H. Morrison	(44)	48	10 Nov 60	G. Brown	(118)	146
	A. Greenwood	(33)			F. Lee	(73)	83
					J. Callaghan	(55)	
14 Dec 55	H. Gaitskell		157	2 Nov 61	G. Brown		169
	A. Bevan		70		Mrs B. Castle		56
	H. Morrison		40				
				8 Nov 62	G. Brown		133
3 Nov 60	H. Gaitskell		166		H. Wilson		103
	H. Wilson		81				
				8 Jul 70	R. Jenkins		133
2 Nov 61	H. Gaitskell		171		M. Foot		67
	A. Greenwood		59		F. Peart		48
14 Feb 63	H. Wilson	(115)	144	Dec 71	R. Jenkins	(140)	142
	G. Brown	(88)	103		M. Foot	(96)	135
	J. Callaghan	(41)			A. Wedgwood Benn	(46)	
				Apr 72	E. Short	(111)	145
					M. Foot	(89)	116
					A. Crosland	(61)	

SOURCES.—*Labour Party Annual Conference Reports, Labour Year Books*; H. Pelling, *A Short History of the Labour Party* (1961; 2nd ed. 1965), p. 130.

Leaders in the House of Lords

1924	Vt Haldane	1952	Earl Jowitt
1928	Ld Parmoor	1955	Vt (Earl) Alexander of
1931	Ld Ponsonby		Hillsborough
1935	Ld Snell	1964	E of Longford
1940	Ld (Vt) Addison	1968	Ld Shackleton
		1974	Ld Shepherd

Chief Whips in the House of Commons

1906	D. Shackleton	1916	J. Parker	1931	(Sir) C. Edwards
1906	A. Henderson	1919	W. Tyson Wilson	1942	W. Whiteley
1907	G. Roberts	1920	A. Henderson	1955	H. Bowden
1914	A. Henderson	1924	B. Spoor	1964	E. Short
1914	F. Goldstone	1925	A. Henderson	1966	J. Silkin
1916	G. Roberts	1927	T. Kennedy	1969	R. Mellish

SOURCE.—For a full list of Whips see F. M. G. Willson, 'Some Career Patterns in British Politics Whips on the House of Commons 1906–66', *Parliamentary Affairs*, 24 (Winter 1970–1) pp. 33–42.

Chief Whips in the House of Lords

1924	Ld Muir-Mackenzie	1945	Ld Ammon
1924	E De La Warr	1949	Ld Shepherd (1st)
1930	Ld Marley	1954	E of Lucan (6th)
1937	Ld Strabolgi	1964	Ld Shepherd (2nd)
1941	E of Listowel	1967	Ld Beswick
1944	Ld Southwood	1973	Lady Llewelyn-Davies

SOURCES.—*Dod's Parliamentary Companion, 1900–*, *Labour Party Annual Conference Reports*.

Labour Representation Committee—Executive Officers

	Chairman		Treasurer
1900	F. Rogers	1902	F. Rogers
1902	R. Bell	1903	A. Gee
1904	D. Shackleton	1904	A. Henderson

	Secretary
1900	J. R. MacDonald

Labour Party — National Executive Committee

Chairman		Treasurer	
(listed as chairman of		1906	A. Henderson
annual conferences at end		1912	J. R. MacDonald
of term of office see p. 134)		1929	A. Henderson
		1936	G. Lathan
Secretary		1943	A. Greenwood
1906	J. R. MacDonald	1954	H. Gaitskell
1912	A. Henderson	1956	A. Bevan
1935	J. Middleton	1960	H. Nicholas
1944	M. Phillips	1964	D. Davies (*acting*)
1962	A. Williams	1965	D. Davies
1968	Sir H. Nicholas	1967	J. Callaghan
1972	R. Hayward		

National Agent		Research Secretary[1]	
1908	A. Peters	1942	M. Phillips
1919	E. Wake	1945	M. Young
1929	G. Shepherd	1950	W. Fienburgh
1946	R. Windle	1952	D. Ginsburg
1951	A. Williams	1960	P. Shore
1962	Miss S. Baker	1965	T. Pitt
1969	R. Hayward	1974	G. Bish
1972	R. Underhill		

SOURCES.—*Labour Representation Committee Annual Conference Reports, 1900–5,* and *Labour Party Annual Conference Reports, 1906– .*

Parliamentary Labour Party — Parliamentary Committee

This committee was originally known as the Executive Committee of the Parliamentary Labour Party. Its name was changed in 1951 to avoid confusion with the N.E.C. The committee was first elected in 1923 to take the place of the Policy Committee of the P.L.P. It consists of twelve Commons' members, elected at the opening of every session of Parliament by members of the P.L.P. with seats in the House of Commons. There are six *ex officio* members: the Leader and Deputy Leader of the Party, the Chief Whip in the House of Commons, the Leader of the Labour Peers, the Chief Whip of the Labour Peers and their elected representative. The elected Commons' members of the Parliamentary Committee sit on the Front Bench with the Party's Leader, Deputy Leader, Chief Whip and the Assistant Whips. Ex-Labour Ministers have the right, by custom of the House, to sit on the Front Bench, but usually prefer a place on the Back Benches. The officers and the elected twelve are joined on the Front Benches by a number of other members who have been allotted the responsibility of looking after particular subjects. After 1955 it became the practice of the Leader of the P.L.P. to invite members to take charge of particular subjects, and these members included some who are not members of the Parliamentary Committee. In 1924 and 1929 when the Labour Party was in office a Consultative Committee of twelve was appointed representative of both Front and Back Benches. During the war-time coalition the P.L.P. elected an Administrative Committee of twelve, with Peers' representation, all of whom were non-Ministers.

[1] From 1922 to 1942 A. Greenwood acted as Secretary to the Research Department which was established in 1922 (at first as a Joint Research and Information Department).

When the Labour Party was in office from 1945 to 1951, and in 1964 to 1970, the P.L.P. set up a small Liaison Committee of three elected Back Bench M.P.s, the Leader of the House, the Government Chief Whip, and an elected Back Bench Labour Peer. Until 1964 the Leader acted as Chairman at P.L.P. meetings when the party was in Opposition. Since 1970 the P.L.P. has elected a separate chairman.

Parliamentary Labour Party — Executive Committee

The figures denote the order of successful candidates in the ballot.

1923–29

	Feb 1923	Dec 1924	Dec 1925	Dec 1926	Dec 1927	1928
W. Adamson	9	..	11	11	8	There is no record of an Executive Committee election in 1928
H. Dalton	..	..	12	3	7	
R. Davies	12	..	..	..	..	
W. Graham	..	8	2	2	3	
A. Henderson	..	10	..	12	2	
T. Johnston	3	..	..	4	4	
F. Jowett	6	..	..	..	..	
G. Lansbury	2	1	10	9	10	
H. Lees-Smith	..	11	4	6	6	
J. Maxton	..	6	..	..	..	
E. Morel	5	..	..	..	..	
F. Roberts	..	12	..	..	..	
T. Shaw	11	..	7	..	12	
E. Shinwell	7	..	..	..	..	
R. Smillie	..	2	5	7	..	
P. Snowden	1	3	1	1	1	
J. Thomas	4	4	3	5	5	
C. Trevelyan	..	7	6	8	11	
S. Walsh	..	..	8	..	..	
S. Webb	10	..	9	10	9	
J. Wedgwood	..	9	..	..	..	
J. Wheatley	8	5	..	..	..	

1931–35

	Nov 1931	Nov 1932	Nov 1933	Nov 1934
Sir S. Cripps	1	1	2	1
D. Grenfell	2	2	1	2
G. Hicks	4	3	3	5
M. Jones	7	7	4	6
W. Lunn	5	4	6	4
N. Maclean	6	6	7	7
T. Williams	3	5	5	3

1935–40

	Nov 1935	Nov 1936	Nov 1937	Nov 1938	Nov 1939
A. Alexander	6	5	2	2	1
W. Wedgwood Benn	..	..	7	5	2
J. Clynes	1	6	..	..	..
H. Dalton	2	3	5	3	10
D. Grenfell	5	4	4	4	4
G. Hall	..	..	..	..	7
T. Johnston	3	2	3	6	..
M. Jones	10	8	11	12	..
J. Lawson	..	..	..	..	12
H. Lees-Smith	9	11	8	8	5
W. Lunn	11	..	..	..	..
N. Maclean	12	..	..	..	..
H. Morrison	4	1	1	1	8
P. Noel-Baker	..	10	12	10	11
F. Pethick-Lawrence	8	9	9	9	6
D. Pritt	..	12	..	..	..
E. Shinwell	..	..	10	11	9
T. Williams	7	7	6	7	3

Parliamentary Labour Party (Parliamentary Committee)
(number indicates position in ballot)

1951–63

	Nov 1951	Nov 1952	Nov 1953	Nov 1954	Jun 1955	Nov 1956	Nov 1957	Nov 1958	Nov 1959	Nov 1960	Nov 1961	Nov 1962	Nov 1963
A. Bevan	..	12	9 [a]	..	7	3	3	1	..	..	..	..	..
A. Bottomley	..	..	..	..	..	..	12	9	..	..	..	..	..
G. Brown	..	..	..	..	8	10	9	..	8	..	..	..	..
J. Callaghan	7	6	4	10	3	5	5	5	2	1	7	1	2
R. Crossman	..	..	..	..	..	..	..	..	13 [d]	..	..	..	..
H. Dalton	8	5	5	4	..	..	..	..	..	..	..	..	..
J. Chuter Ede	5	2	6	9	..	..	..	..	..	..	..	..	..
T. Fraser	..	..	..	..	14 [c]	12	8	12	7	6	9	5	6
H. Gaitskell	3	3	2	1 [b]	2 [c]	..	..	..	..	..	..	..	..
P. Gordon Walker	..	..	..	..	..	..	11	6	9	8	11	6	5
A. Greenwood	12	..	..	..	10	6	7	8	6 [d]	..	..	..	..
J. Griffiths	1	1	1	1 [b]	1 [c]	..	..	..	..	..	..	..	..
R. Gunter	..	..	..	..	..	..	..	..	..	7	6	10	8
W. Glenvil Hall	2	9	12	11	..	..	..	..	..	..	..	..	..
D. Healey	..	..	..	..	..	..	..	..	12	5	4	9	7
D. Houghton	..	..	..	..	..	..	..	..	..	10	3	4	3
D. Jay	..	..	..	..	..	..	..	..	..	..	..	..	11
F. Lee	..	..	..	..	..	..	..	..	5	12	12	12	10
G. Mitchison	..	..	..	..	12	4	2	3	10	3	8	7	12
P. Noel-Baker	9	8	10	8	9	8	10	10	..	..	..	..	..
A. Robens	4	4	7	6	4	2	6	7	4	..	..	..	..
E. Shinwell	11	11	11	7	..	..	..	..	..	..	..	..	..
Sir F. Soskice	..	7	3	3	..	7	4	4	3	2	2	2	4
M. Stewart	..	..	..	..	..	..	..	..	..	4	5	8	1
R. Stokes	6	..	..	..	11	..	..	..	..	..	..	..	..
E. Summerskill	10	10	8	5	6	9	..	11	..	..	..	..	..
F. Willey	..	..	..	..	..	..	..	..	11	11	10	11	9
H. Wilson	..	..	13 [a]	12	5	1	1	2	1	9	1	3	..
K. Younger	..	..	..	..	13 [c]	11	..	..	..	..	..	..	..

[a] A. Bevan resigned from the Parliamentary Committee on 14 Apr 54, H. Wilson, who was 13th in order of votes obtained, took his place on the Committee on 28 Apr 54.
[b] H. Gaitskell and J. Griffiths both obtained 170 votes and tied for first place.
[c] H. Gaitskell and J. Griffiths were elected Leader and Deputy Leader of the Parliamentary Labour Party on 14 Dec 55 and 2 Feb 56, K. Younger and T. Fraser as runners-up filled the vacant places on the Parliamentary Committee.
[d] A. Greenwood resigned from the Parliamentary Committee on 13 Oct 60. R. Crossman, who was 13th in order of votes obtained, took his place on the Committee for a few weeks until the 1960–61 sessional elections in November.

1970–73

	Nov 1970	Nov 1971	Nov 1972	Nov 1973
A. Benn	5	10	11	8
J. Callaghan	1	4	5	1
Mrs B. Castle	12	15[a]	..	..
A. Crosland	3	8	3	4
M. Foot	6	2	4	2
D. Healey	2	12	6	7
D. Houghton	4	..	..	
R. Jenkins	..	..	..	5
H. Lever	8	7[a]	9	8
F. Peart	10	6	8	..
R. Prentice	..	13[a]	1	3
M. Rees	..	..	10	10
W. Ross	..	5	7	12
P. Shore	..	11	12[b]	11
E. Short	9	1	..	..
J. Silkin	..	14[a]	(12[b])	(13)
G. Thomson	11	9[a]	..	..
Mrs S. Williams	7	3	1	6

[a] H. Lever and G. Thomson resigned on 10 Apr 1972. They were replaced by R. Prentice and J. Silkin, who had 13th and 14th place respectively in the original ballot. When E. Short became Deputy Leader, Mrs B. Castle beat E. Heffer 111–89, to take his place on the Committee on 3 May 1972.
[b] J. Silkin, who tied with P. Shore for 12th place, withdrew, making a second ballot unnecessary

Chairmen of Parliamentary Committee when Labour has been in power

1924 *Parliamentary Executive Committee*
    1924 R. Smillie

1929–31 *Consultative Committee*
    1929 H. Snell
    1930 J. Barr

1940–45 *Administrative Committee*
    1940 H. Lees-Smith (*acting*) [1]
    1941 H. Lees-Smith (*acting*) [1]
    1942 F. Pethick-Lawrence (*acting*) [1]
    1942 A. Greenwood (*acting*) [1]
    1943 A. Greenwood (*acting*) [1]
    1944 A. Greenwood (*acting*) [1]

1945–51 *Liaison Committee*
    1945 N. Maclean
    1946 M. Webb
    1947 M. Webb
    1948 M. Webb
    1949 M. Webb
    1950 W. Glenvil Hall

1964–70 *Liaison Committee*
    1964 E. Shinwell
    1967 D. Houghton

Chairmen of Parliamentary Labour Party, 1970

    1970 D. Houghton   1974 C. Hughes
    1974 I. Mikardo

SOURCES.—1923–29, *Daily Herald* and *Directory for National Council of Labour, TUC General Council, Labour Party and the Parliamentary Labour Party* (published annually by the Labour Party); 1931–, *Labour Party Annual Conference Reports*; *The Times*; and *Labour Party Directory*.

Labour Representation Committee — Annual Conferences, 1900–1905

Date	Place	Chairman
27–28 Feb 00	London	W. Steadman
1 Feb 01	Manchester	J. Hodge
20–22 Feb 02	Birmingham	W. Davis
19–21 Feb 03	Newcastle upon Tyne	J. Bell
4–5 Feb 04	Bradford	J. Hodge
26–29 Jan 05	Liverpool	A. Henderson

Labour Party — Annual Conferences, 1906–

Date	Place	Chairman
15–17 Feb 06	London	A. Henderson
24–26 Jan 07	Belfast	J. Stephenson

[1] During C. Attlee's membership of the war-time Coalition, the Labour Party appointed an Acting Chairman each session.

Date	Place	Chairman
20–22 Jan 08	Hull	W. Hudson
27–29 Jan 09	Portsmouth	J. Clynes
9–11 Feb 10	Newport	J. Keir Hardie
1–3 Feb 11	Leicester	W. Robinson
24–26 Jan 12	Birmingham	B. Turner
29–31 Jan 13	London	G. Roberts
27–30 Jan 14	Glasgow	T. Fox
1915	*No conference held*	
26–28 Jan 16	Bristol	W. Anderson
23–26 Jan 17 [1]	Manchester	G. Wardle
23–25 Jan 18	Nottingham	W. Purdy
26–28 Jun 18	London	W. Purdy
25–27 Jun 19	Southport	J. McGurk
22–25 Jun 20	Scarborough	W. Hutchinson
21–24 Jun 21	Brighton	A. Cameron
27–30 Jun 22	Edinburgh	F. Jowett
26–29 Jun 23	London	S. Webb
7–10 Oct 24	London	J. Ramsay MacDonald
29 Sep–2 Oct 25	Liverpool	C. Cramp
11–15 Oct 26	Margate	R. Williams
3–7 Oct 27	Blackpool	F. Roberts
1–5 Oct 28	Birmingham	G. Lansbury
30 Sep–4 Oct 29	Brighton	H. Morrison
6–10 Oct 30	Llandudno	Susan Lawrence
5–8 Oct 31	Scarborough	S. Hirst
3–7 Oct 32	Leicester	G. Lathan
2–6 Oct 33	Hastings	J. Compton
1–5 Oct 34	Southport	W. Smith
30 Sep–4 Oct 35	Brighton	W. Robinson
5–9 Oct 36	Edinburgh	Jennie Adamson
4–8 Oct 37	Bournemouth	H. Dalton
1938	*No conference held*	
29 May–2 Jun 39	Southport	G. Dallas
13–16 May 40	Bournemouth	Barbara Gould
2–4 Jun 41	London	J. Walker
25–28 May 42	London	W. Green
14–18 Jun 43	London	A. Dobbs
11–15 Dec 44	London	G. Ridley
21–25 May 45	Blackpool	Ellen Wilkinson
10–14 Jun 46	Bournemouth	H. Laski
26–30 May 47	Margate	P. Noel-Baker
17–21 May 48	Scarborough	E. Shinwell
6–10 Jun 49	Blackpool	J. Griffiths
2–6 Oct 50	Margate	S. Watson
1–3 Oct 51	Scarborough	Alice Bacon
29 Sep–3 Oct 52	Morecambe	H. Earnshaw
28 Sep–2 Oct 53	Margate	A. Greenwood
27 Sep–1 Oct 54	Scarborough	W. Burke
10–14 Oct 55	Margate	Edith Summerskill
1–5 Oct 56	Blackpool	E. Gooch
30 Sep–4 Oct 57	Brighton	Margaret Herbison
29 Sep–3 Oct 58	Scarborough	T. Driberg
28–29 Nov 59	Blackpool	Barbara Castle
3–7 Oct 60	Scarborough	G. Brinham
2–6 Oct 61	Blackpool	R. Crossman
2–5 Oct 62	Brighton	H. Wilson
30 Sep–4 Oct 63	Scarborough	D. Davies
12–13 Dec 64	Brighton	A. Greenwood
27 Sep–1 Oct 65	Blackpool	R. Gunter
3–7 Oct 66	Brighton	W. Padley
2–6 Oct 67	Scarborough	J. Boyd
30 Sep–4 Oct 68	Blackpool	Jennie Lee
29 Sep–3 Oct 69	Brighton	Eirene White
28 Sep–2 Oct 70	Blackpool	A. Skeffington
4–8 Oct 71	Brighton	I. Mikardo
2–6 Oct 72	Blackpool	A. Benn
1–5 Oct 73	Blackpool	W. Simpson
27–30 Nov 74	London	J. Callaghan

[1] Adjourned for one month. Resumed 26 Feb 18 in London.

SOURCES.—*1900–5 Reports of the Labour Representation Committee Annual Conferences, Labour Party Annual Conference Reports 1906–.*

Labour Party — Membership Statistics

Year	No. Constit. & Central Parties	Total Indiv. Members ('000s)	T.U.s		Soc. & Co-op. Socs.		Total Membership ('000s)
			No.	Members ('000s)	No.	Members ('000s)	
1900–01	7	..	41	353	3	23	376
1901–02	21	..	65	455	2	14	469
1902–03	49	..	127	847	2	14	861
1903–04	76	..	165	956	2	14	970
1904–05	73	..	158	855	2	15	900
1905–06	73	..	158	904	2	17	921
1906–07	83	..	176	975	2	21	998
1907	92	..	181	1,050	2	22	1,072
1908	133	..	176	1,127	2	27	1,159
1909	155	..	172	1,451	2	31	1,486
1910	148	..	151	1,394	2	31	1,431
1911	149	..	141	1,502	2	31	1,539
1912	146	..	130	1,858	2	31	1,895
1913	158	..	a	a	2	33	a
1914	179	..	101	1,572	2	33	1,612
1915	177	..	111	2,054	2	33	2,093
1916	199	..	119	2,171	3	42	2,220
1917	239	..	123	2,415	3	47	2,465
1918	389	b	131	2,960	4	53	3,013
1919	418	..	126	3,464	7	47	3,511
1920	492	..	122	4,318	5	42	4,360
1921	456	..	116	3,974	5	37	4,010
1922	482	..	102	3,279	5	32	3,311
1923	503	..	106	3,120	6	36	3,156
1924	529	..	108	3,158	7	36	3,194
1925	549	..	106	3,338	8	36	3,374
1926	551	..	104	3,352	8	36	3,388
1927	532	..	97	3,239	6	55c	3,294
1928	535	215	91	2,025d	7	52	2,292d
1929	578	228	91	2,044	6	59	2,331
1930	607	277	89	2,011	7	58	2,347
1931	608	297	80	2,024	7	37	2,358
1932	608	372	75	1,960	9	40	2,372
1933	612	366	75	1,899	9	40	2,305
1934	614	381	72	1,858	8	40	2,278
1935	614	419	72	1,913	9	45	2,378
1936	614	431	73	1,969	9	45	2,444
1937	614	447	70	2,037	8	43	2,528
1938	614	429	70	2,158	9	43	2,630
1939	614	409	72	2,214	6	40	2,663
1940	614	304	73	2,227	6	40	2,571
1941	585	227	68	2,231	6	28	2,485
1942	581	219	69	2,206	6	29	2,454
1943	586	236	69	2,237	6	30	2,503
1944	598	266	68	2,375	6	32	2,673
1945	649	487	69	2,510	6	41	3,039
1946	649	645	70	2,635d	6	42	3,322d
1947	649	608	73	4,386	6	46	5,040
1948	656	629	80	4,751	6	42	5,422
1949	660	730	80	4,946	5	41	5,717
1950	661	908	83	4,972	5	40	5,920

a Owing to the operation of the Osborne Judgement it was made impossible to compile membership statistics for 1913.

b Individual membership statistics were not compiled 1918–27.

c The Royal Arsenal Co-operative Society, through its Political Purposes Committee, continued its affiliation with the Labour Party; its membership is included in the 1927–60 totals.

d From 1928 to 1946 inclusive, trade unionist members of the Labour Party had to 'contract in' to payment to party political funds.

Labour Party — Membership Statistics

Year	No. Constit. & Central Parties	Total Indiv. Members ('000s)	T.U.s		Soc. & Co-op. Socs.		Total Member-ship ('000s)
			No.	Members ('000s)	No.	Members ('000s)	
1951	667	876	82	4,937	5	35	5,849
1952	667	1,015	84	5,072	5	21	6,108
1953	667	1,005	84	5,057	5	34	6,096
1954	667	934	84	5,530	5	35	6,498
1955	667	843	87	5,606	5	35	6,484
1956	667	845	88	5,658	5	34	6,537
1957	667	913	87	5,644	5	26	6,583
1958	667	889	87	5,628	5	26	6,542
1959	667	848	87	5,564	5	25	6,437
1960	667	790	86	5,513	5	25	6,328
1961	667	751	86	5,550	5	25	6,326
1962	667	767	86	5,503	5	25	6,296
1963	667	830	83	5,507	6	21	6,358
1964	667	830	83	5,502	6	21	6,353
1965	659	817	79	5,602	6	21	6,440
1966	658	776	79	5,539	6	21	6,336
1967	657	734	75	5,540	6	21	6,295
1968	656	701	68	5,364	6	21	6,087
1969	656	681	68	5,462	6	22	6,164
1970	656	680	67	5,519	6	24	6,223
1971	659	700	67	5,559	6	25	6,284
1972	659	703	62	5,425	9	40	6,169
1973	659	665	62	5,425	9	40	6,131

SOURCE.—*Labour Party Annual Conference Reports.*

The Labour Party — Organisation and Constitutions

The Labour Representation Committee was formed on 27 Feb 1900 to promote a distinct Labour group in Parliament, representing the affiliated trade unions and socialist societies. After the General Election of 1906 the L.R.C. group of M.P.s decided to assume the title of 'Labour Party' and elected their first officers and whips. Policy was determined by the Labour Party through the annual conference and its executive authority, the National Executive Committee. There was no official party leader, but an annually elected chairman of the parliamentary party. There were scarcely any official Labour Party constituency organisations (except for those provided by local trades councils, groups of miners' lodges, and local branches of the I.L.P.). In 1914 there were only two constituency associations with individual members, Woolwich and Barnard Castle, which Will Crooks and Arthur Henderson had built up on their own.

The Reorganisation of the Labour Party, 1918

The reorganisation of the Labour Party was projected by Arthur Henderson in collaboration with Sidney Webb. Their main aims were to provide local Labour Parties in every constituency or group of constituencies. These local Labour Parties were to be based fundamentally on individual subscribing membership, though representation was provided for trades councils, trade union branches, and socialist societies. The members of the N.E.C. were to be elected by the annual conference as a whole (though eleven were to be elected from candidates nominated by the trade unions and socialist societies as a single group, five were to represent the local Labour Parties, and four were to be women). The scheme also involved an increase in affiliation fees.

The original plan was amended, so that the N.E.C. was increased to a membership of 23 (adding two to the number specified for affiliated organisations). It was agreed that the election programme should be produced by the N.E.C. and P.L.P. jointly — subject to the aims of the Party and the decisions of the annual conferences. The object of the pre-war Party had been to 'organise and maintain in Parliament and in the country a political Labour Party'. In 1918 this was changed to a new formula: 'to secure for the producers by hand and by brain the full fruits of their industry, and the most equitable distribution thereof that may be possible, upon the basis of the common ownership of the means of production and the best obtainable system of popular administration and control of each industry and service'.[1]

Modifications since 1918

The 1918 constitution was modified in 1937 in favour of the local constituency Labour Parties, which had repeatedly demanded a greater share in the control of party affairs. Representation of the constituency parties on the N.E.C. was increased from five to seven. The seven were to be elected by the vote of the constituency delegates alone. The twelve trade union representatives and one representative of the socialist societies were to be elected separately by their respective conference delegations. The five women members may be nominated by any affiliated organisation and are elected by a vote of the whole party conference. The Leader (since 1929) and the Deputy Leader (since 1953) are *ex officio* members of the N.E.C. The Treasurer of the Party may be nominated by any affiliated organisation, and is elected by the vote of the whole party conference. In 1972 a Young Socialist elected by the National Conference of Labour Party Young Socialists was added to the N.E.C.

SOURCES.—H. Pelling, *The Origins of the Labour Party, 1880–1900* (1954); F. Bealey and H. Pelling, *Labour and Politics, 1900–1906* (1958); P. Poirier, *The Advent of the Labour Party* (1958); G. D. H. Cole, *British Working-Class Politics, 1832–1914* (1941); G. D. H. Cole, *A History of the Labour Party from 1914* (1948); R. T. McKenzie, *British Political Parties* (1955). Since 1918 complete lists of Labour Party publications have been given in the Labour Party Annual Conference Reports. See also I. Bulmer-Thomas, *The Growth of the British Party System* (1965).

Sponsored M.P.s

The table on p. 138 summarises information on sponsored Labour M.P.s.

M.P.s are also sponsored by organisations which are not members of the Trades Union Congress. The two major instances of this are the National Union of Teachers and the National Farmers' Union.

National Union of Teachers

The N.U.T. sponsored and assisted parliamentary candidates from 1895

[1] The 1914 and 1918 Labour Party constitutions are set out and compared in G. D. H. Cole, *A History of the Labour Party from 1914* (1948), pp. 71–81.

Trades Union-sponsored M.P.s, 1918–1974 (Labour)

No figures for Trades Union-sponsored M.P.s are available before 1918. Unions are here listed under their 1974 titles. M.P.s sponsored by Unions which subsequently amalgamated with other Unions and adopted other titles are listed under their present titles.

Trade Unions	1918	1922	1923	1924	1929	1931	1935	1945	1950	1951	1955	1959	1964	1966	1970	Feb 1974	Oct 1974
Nat. U. of Mineworkers (Miners' Federation of G.B., 1918–45)	25	41	43	40	42	26	32	34	37	36	34	31	28	26	20	18	18
Transport and General Workers' U.	3	7	10	10	13	1	7	17	16	14	14	14	21	25	19	23	22
Nat. U. of Railwaymen	1	3	4	3	8	..	5	12	10	9	8	5	6	7	5	6	6
Transport Salaried Staffs Ass. (Railway Clerks' Ass., 1918–50)	..	..	..	..	7	..	6	9	7	7	5	5	7	6	4	3	3
Nat. U. of General and Municipal Workers	4	5	5	4	6	2	6	10	6	6	4	4	9	11	12	13	13
Ass. Society of Woodworkers	1	1	3	2	6	1	..	3	3	3	2	1	..	..	..	2	3
U. of Shop, Distributive and Allied Workers	..	1	4	4	4	1	6	8	8	9	9	9	10	8	7	6	5
British Iron, Steel and Kindred Trades Ass	..	2	1	3	4	1	1	2	2	2	2	2	1	1	2	2	1
United Textile Factory Workers' Ass.	4	3	3	2	4	..	..	3	2	1	1	1	..	1	..	..	..
Amalgamated Engineering U. (Amalgamated U. of Engineering Workers 1920–70)	1	7	4	4	3	2	3	4	8	8	6	8	18	18	16	22	21
Nat. U. of Boot and Shoe Operatives	1	2	1	..	2	..	..	4	1	1	..	..	..	..	..	..	..
Ass. Society of Locomotive Engineers and Firemen	..	..	..	1	1	1	1	2	2	2	2	3	1	1	..	..	..
United Society of Boilermakers, etc.	1	1	2	2	1	1	1	..	2	2	1	..	1	..	..	..	..
U. of Post Office Workers	..	2	3	2	..	..	..	..	1	2	1	2	2	3	1	2	2
Nat. U. of Agricultural Workers	..	..	1	1	..	..	..	..	1	1	1	2	1	1	..	..	..
Electrical Trades U.	..	..	..	..	..	..	..	..	1	1	..	..	1	1	3	3	3
Ass. of Scientific, Technical and Managerial Staffs (A.S.S.E.T. 1951–68)	..	..	..	..	..	..	..	..	..	..	..	..	..	..	2	6	10
Clerical and Administrative Workers U. (APEX)	..	..	..	..	..	..	..	..	1	1	2	2	3	4	3	6	6
Others	8	11	18	11	13	..	8	9	5	5	4	3	10	18	17	15	13
Total T.U. M.P.s	49	86	102	88	114	35	78	120	111	108	95	92	120	127	112	127	126
Co-operative Party M.P.s	1	4	6	5	9	1	9	23	18	16	18	16	20	18	17	16	16
Total unsponsored M.P.s	7	52	83	58	164	10	67	250	186	171	164	150	177	218	158	143	177
Total Labour M.P.s	57	142	191	151	287	46	154	393	315	295	277	258	317	363	287	301	319

to 1974. The number of sponsored candidates varied, but a strict parity between the parties was always attempted.

N.U.T. adopted and supported M.P.s, 1900–1974

Election	Total	Con.	Lab.	Lib.
1900	3	I	..	2
1906	2	..	..	2
1910 (Jan)	I	..	..	I
1910 (Dec)	2	..	I	I
1918	I	I	..	..
1922	3	I	2	..
1923	3	..	3	..
1924	4	I	3	..
1929	5	..	5	..
1931	3	I	2	..
1935	5	I	4	..
1945	2	..	2	..
1950	4	..	4	..
1951	4	..	4	..
1955	6	2	4	..
1959	6	2	4	..
1964	5	I	4	..
1966	4	I	3	..
1970	5	2	3	..
1974 (Feb)	5	I	4	..

SOURCE.—Information received from the National Union of Teachers. J. D. Stewart, *British Pressure Groups* (1958).

National Farmers' Union

In 1909 the N.F.U. set up a Parliamentary Fund with the object of sending two sponsored M.P.s to Parliament from each side of the House. Although sometimes 'independent on agricultural questions' all N.F.U. M.P.s have been Conservatives. Since 1945 the N.F.U. has not sponsored any candidates and has adopted a position of strict neutrality between the political parties.

N.F.U.-sponsored M.P.s, 1922–1935

Election	No. of M.P.s
1922	4
1923	3
1924	2
1929	No candidates
1931	No candidates
1935	2

SOURCES.—*National Farmers' Union Yearbooks, 1900–60*; P. Self and H. Storing, *The State and the Farmer* (1962), pp. 42–7, 204; J. D. Stewart, *British Pressure Groups* (1958), pp. 173–4.

Liberal Party

Party Leaders[1]

1900	Sir H. Campbell-Banner-man	4 Nov 31	Sir H. Samuel[4]
		26 Nov 35	Sir A. Sinclair
30 Apr 08	H. Asquith (E of Oxford and Asquith)[2]	2 Aug 45	C. Davies
		5 Nov 56	J. Grimond
14 Oct 26	D. Lloyd George[3]	18 Jan 67	J. Thorpe

Deputy Leaders

1929–31	H. Samuel
1949–51	Lady M. Lloyd George
1962–64	D. Wade

Leaders in the House of Lords

1900	Earl of Kimberley	1931	M of Reading
1902	Earl Spencer	1936	M of Crewe
1905	M of Ripon	1944	Vt Samuel
1908	E (M) of Crewe	1955	Ld Rea
1923	Vt Grey	1967	Ld Byers
1924	Earl Beauchamp		

National Liberal Federation, 1900–1936

Chairman of Committee

1900	(Sir) E. Evans	1910	F. Wright
1918	Sir G. Lunn	1923	Sir R. Hudson
1920	A. Brampton	1927	Sir F. Layland-Barratt
1931	R. Muir	1934	P. Heffer
1933	R. Walker		
1934	M. Gray		

Treasurer

1901	W. Hart
1903	J. Massie
1907	R. Bird

Secretary

1893	(Sir) R. Hudson
1922	F. Barter
1925	H. Oldman
1930	H. Oldman & W. Davies
1931	W. Davies

Liberal Party Organisation, 1936–

Head

1936	W. Davies (*Secretary*)
1952	H. Harris (*General Director*)
1960	D. Robinson (*Directing Secretary*)
1961	P. Kemmis (*Secretary*)
1965	T. Beaumont (*Head of Liberal Party Organisation*)
1966	P. Chitnis (*Head of Liberal Party Organisation*)
1970	E. Wheeler (*Head of Liberal Party Organisation*)[5]

Chairman of Executive Committee

1936	M. Gray
1946	P. Fothergill
1949	Ld Moynihan
1950	F. Byers
1952	P. Fothergill
1954	G. Acland
1957	D. Abel
1959	L. Behrens
1961	D. Banks
1963	B. Wigoder
1965	G. Evans
1968–69[6]	J. Baker

[1] All were Liberal 'Leaders in the House of Commons'. Sir H. Campbell-Bannerman from 1899 to 1908 and H. Asquith 1908 to 1926 were the only 'Leaders of the Liberal Party' from 1900 to 1960.

[2] After H. Asquith's defeat at the 1918 General Election, Sir D. Maclean was elected leader of the Parliamentary Party but relinquished this post on H. Asquith's return to the Commons in Mar 1920.

[3] D. Lloyd George was Chairman of the Parliamentary Liberal Party from Dec 1924. He assumed the leadership of the Party after Asquith's death.

[4] At the General Election in 1931 there were three Liberal groups in the House of Commons. Sir H. Samuel led the main group of Liberal M.P.s. D. Lloyd George led a small family group of Independent Liberals, and Sir J. Simon (Ld) led what was to become in 1932 the Liberal National Group (see *Minor Parties*). On 25 Nov 35 D. Lloyd George and the other Independent Liberals rejoined the Liberal Party in the House of Commons.

[5] P. Chitnis resigned in 1969. From Oct 69 to Nov 70 E. Wheeler was Director of Organisation. From Dec 69 to Jun 70 Mrs D. Gorsky was General Election Campaign Editor.

[6] In 1969 the post of Chairman of the Executive Committee was combined with the Chairmanship of the party.

Chairman

1966	Ld Byers
1967	T. Beaumont (Ld)
1968	Ld Henley
1969	D. Banks
1970	R. Wainwright
1972	C. Carr
1973	K. Vaus

Treasurer [1]

1937–50	Sir A. McFadyean	1955–59	P. Fothergill
1937–41	P. Heffer	1959–62	Miss H. Harvey
1941–47	Ld Rea	1959–60	P. Lort-Phillips
1942–47	H. Worsley	1961–62	J. McLaughlin
1947–53	Ld Moynihan	1962–65	R. Gardner-Thorpe
1950–58	W. Grey	1962–66	Sir A. Murray
1950–52	Vt Wimborne	1963–65	T. Beaumont
1953–62	Sir A. Suenson-Taylor	1966–67	J. Thorpe
	(Ld Grantchester)	1967–68	L. Smith
		1968–69	J. Pardoe
		1969–72	Sir F. Medlicott
		1972–	P. Watkins

SOURCES.—*Liberal Magazine 1900–1950*; *Liberal Year Book 1900–1939*; *Dod's Parliamentary Companion 1950–*. Annual Reports of the Liberal Party 1956–.

Chief Whips in House of Commons

1900	H. Gladstone	1931	G. Owen		*Coalition Liberal*
1905	G. Whiteley	1932	W. Rea	1916	N. Primrose
1908	J. Pease	1935	Sir P. Harris	1917	F. Guest
1910	Master of Elibank	1945	T. Horabin	1921	C. McCurdy
1912	P. Illingworth	1946	F. Byers	1922	E. Hilton Young
1915	J. Gulland	1950	J. Grimond		
1919	G. Thorne	1956	D. Wade		
1923	V. Phillipps	1962	A. Holt		
1924	Sir G. Collins	1963	E. Lubbock		
1926	Sir R. Hutchinson	1970	D. Steel		
1930	Sir A. Sinclair				

Chief Whips in House of Lords

1896	Ld Ribblesdale		1944	Vt Mersey	
1907	Ld Denman		1949	M of Willingdon	
1911–22	Ld Colebrooke		1950	Ld Moynihan	
1919	Ld Denman (*Ind. Lib.*)		1950	Ld Rea	
1924	Ld Stanmore		1955	Ld Amulree	

SOURCE.—*Dod's Parliamentary Companion 1900–*.

National Liberal Federation — Annual Conferences, 1900–1935

Date	Place	President
27–28 Mar 00	Nottingham	R. Spence Watson
14–15 May 01	Bradford	,,
13–14 May 02	Bristol	A. Birrell
14–15 May 03	Scarborough	,,
12–13 May 04	Manchester	,,
18–19 May 05	Newcastle upon Tyne	,,
23–24 May 06	Liverpool	A. Acland
6–7 Jun 07	Plymouth	,,
18–19 Jun 08	Birmingham	Sir W. Angus
1–2 Jul 09	Southport	,,
25 Nov 10	Hull	,,
23–24 Nov 11	Bath	Sir J. Brunner
21–22 Nov 12	Nottingham	,,
26–27 Nov 13	Leeds	,,

[1] Until 1965 the post of Treasurer was held jointly by two or three officers.

Date	Place	President
1914–1918	*No conference held*	
27–28 Nov 19	Birmingham	Sir G. Lunn
25–26 Nov 20	Bradford	J. Robertson
24–25 Nov 21	Newcastle upon Tyne	,,
17–18 May 22	Blackpool	,,
30 May–1 Jun 23	Buxton	Sir D. Maclean
22–23 May 24	Brighton	,,
14–15 May 25	Scarborough	,,
17–18 Jun 26	Weston-super-Mare	J. Spender
26–27 May 27	Margate	Sir C. Hobhouse
11–12 Oct 28	Great Yarmouth	,,
3–4 Oct 29	Nottingham	,,
16–17 Oct 30	Torquay	A. Brampton
14–15 May 31	Buxton	,,
28–29 Apr 32	Clacton-on-Sea	,,
18–19 May 33	Scarborough	R. Muir
2–5 May 34	Bournemouth	,,
23–25 May 35	Blackpool	,,

Liberal Party — Annual Assemblies, 1936–

18–19 Jun 36	London	Ld Meston
27–31 May 37	Buxton	,,
19–20 May 38	Bath	,,
11–12 May 39	Scarborough	,,
1940	*No assembly held*	
18–19 Jul 41	London	,,
4–5 Sep 42	London	,,
15–17 Jul 43	London	,,
1944	*No assembly held*	
1– 3 Feb 45	London	Lady V. Bonham-Carter
9–11 May 46	London	,,
24–26 Apr 47	Bournemouth	I. Foot
22–24 Apr 48	Blackpool	E. Dodds
24–26 Mar 49	Hastings	Sir A. MacFadyean
27–28 Jan 50	London	,,
29–30 Sep 50	Scarborough	P. Fothergill
1951	*No assembly held*	
15–17 May 52	Hastings	R. Walker
9–11 Apr 53	Ilfracombe	L. Robson
22–24 Apr 54	Buxton	H. Graham White
14–16 Apr 55	Llandudno	Ld Rea
27–29 Sep 56	Folkestone	L. Behrens (*acting*)
19–21 Sep 57	Southport	,,
18–21 Sep 58	Torquay	N. Micklem
1959	*No assembly held*	Sir A. Comyns Carr
29 Sep–1 Oct 60	Eastbourne	Sir A. Murray
21–23 Sep 61	Edinburgh	Sir A. Murray
19–22 Sep 62	Llandudno	E. Malindine
10–14 Sep 63	Brighton	Sir F. Brunner
4– 5 Sep 64	London	Ld Ogmore
22–25 Sep 65	Scarborough	R. Fulford
21–24 Sep 66	Brighton	Miss N. Seear
20–23 Sep 67	Blackpool	Ld Henley
18–21 Sep 68	Edinburgh	D. Banks
17–20 Sep 69	Brighton	Ld Beaumont
23–26 Sep 70	Eastbourne	Mrs S. Robson
15–18 Sep 71	Scarborough	S. Terrell
19–23 Sep 72	Margate	T. Jones
18–22 Sep 73	Southport	Ld Lloyd of Kilgerran
17–21 Sep 74	Brighton	A. Holt

SOURCES.—*Liberal Year Book 1902–1939*; *The Liberal Magazine 1900–1950*; *National Liberal Federation, Annual Reports 1900–1936*; *Keesing's Archives 1939–*.
The Liberal Publication Department published miscellaneous collections of *Pamphlets and Leaflets*, 1908–30. The *Liberal Magazine* was published from 1893 until 1950. J. S. Rasmussen, *The Liberal Party, A Study of Retrenchment and Revival* (1965); Alan Watkins, *The Liberal Dilemma* (1966); Trevor Wilson, *The Downfall of the Liberal Party 1914–1935* (1966). See also I. Bulmer-Thomas, *The Growth of the British Party System* (1965).

Minor Parties

Common Wealth

This party was founded in 1942 by Sir Richard Acland (Liberal M.P. for Barnstaple) during the war-time electoral truce. Its immediate aim was to contest all by-elections where a 'reactionary' candidate was in the field, and was not opposed by a Labour or other 'progressive' candidate. Seats were won at Eddisbury (J. Loverseed, 1943), Skipton (H. Lawson, 1944), and Chelmsford (E. Millington, 1945). In 1943 membership of Common Wealth was proscribed by the Labour Party. In the 1945 General Election Common Wealth put up twenty-three candidates but were only successful in Chelmsford, where no Labour candidate stood: the victor there, E. Millington, joined the Labour Party. Sir R. Acland joined the Labour Party as soon as the 1945 results were known. Common Wealth survived as an organisation but contested no further parliamentary elections.

Communist Party

The Communist Party of Great Britain was founded in July 1920. In its early years it sought to affiliate to the Labour Party but was rebuffed. In 1922 J. T. W. Newbold (Motherwell) was elected to Parliament; S. Saklatvala (N. Battersea) was also elected in 1922 as a Labour M.P. (although a member of the Communist Party). After defeat in 1923, he was elected again in 1924 as a Communist. Since 1924 the Labour Party has ruled that no member of the Communist Party could be an individual member of the Labour Party and in 1935, 1943, and 1946 the Labour Party turned down further Communist requests for affiliation. In 1935 and again in 1945 W. Gallacher was elected as a Communist for W. Fife; and in 1945 P. Piratin was elected for the Mile End division of Stepney.

Secretaries of the Communist Party: 1920–29 A. Inkpin, 1929–56 H. Pollitt, 1956– J. Gollan.

Communist Candidates

1922	. 5	1931	. 26	1951	. 10	1966	. 57
1923	. 8	1935	. 2	1955	. 17	1970	. 58
1924	. 8	1945	. 21	1959	. 18	1974 Feb	44
1929	. 25	1950	. 100	1964	. 36	1974 Oct	29

SOURCE.—H. Pelling, *The British Communist Party* (1958).

Co-operative Party

In 1917 the Co-operative Congress agreed to organise as a political party. In the 1918 General Election one Co-operative M.P. was elected; he joined with the Labour Party in the House of Commons. Labour and Co-operative candidates never opposed each other at elections but it was not till 1926 that a formal understanding was reached and Co-operative Parties were made eligible for affiliation to divisional Labour Parties. In 1938 the Co-operative Party adopted a written constitution and in 1941 its representatives were invited to attend meetings of the National Council of Labour on equal terms with the Labour Party and the T.U.C. In 1946, the 1926 agreement with the Labour Party was replaced; Co-operative candidates were to run formally as Co-operative and Labour Candidates,[1] and after the General Election of 1959 it was agreed that the number of Co-operative candidates should be limited to 30.[2]

In 1951 the Co-operative Party adopted a new constitution to prevent its members from joining organisations proscribed by the Labour Party.

Co-operative M.P.s and Candidates

1918	. 1 (10)	1945	. 23 (33)	1970	. 17 (27)
1922	. 4 (11)	1950	. 18 (33)	1974 Feb	16 (25)
1923	. 6 (10)	1951	. 16 (37)	1974 Oct	16 (22)
1924	. 5 (10)	1955	. 18 (38)		
1929	. 9 (12)	1959	. 16 (30)		
1931	. 1 (18)	1964	. 19 (27)		
1935	. 9 (21)	1966	. 18 (24)		

SOURCES.—J. Bailey, *The British Co-operative Movement* (1955), *Reports of the Annual Co-operative Congress 1900–* , *The People's Year Book 1932.*

Independent Labour Party

The Independent Labour Party, formed in 1893, was one of the founding bodies of the Labour Representation Committee in 1900. The I.L.P. was affiliated to the Labour Party but it held its own conferences, sponsored its own parliamentary candidates, and maintained its own policies, even after the 1918 revision of the Labour Party constitution. Differences with the Labour Party grew in the late 1920's and the 37 I.L.P. Members among the 288 Labour M.P.s elected in 1929 provided some of the second Labour Government's strongest critics. At the 1930 conference of the I.L.P., it was agreed that I.L.P. members should vote against the Labour Government when its actions conflicted with I.L.P. policy. The I.L.P. was disaffiliated by the 1932 Labour Party Conference. In 1935 17 I.L.P. candidates stood, all against Labour candidates, and four (all in Glasgow) were successful. In 1945 three of the five I.L.P. candidates won but, after the death of the party's leader, James Maxton in 1946, the I.L.P. M.P.s one by one rejoined the Labour Party. In the elections of 1950 and 1951 there were three I.L.P. candidates and in 1955 and 1959 two candidates. All lost their deposits. There were no candidates in 1964, 1966, 1970 or 1974.

M.P.s (since 1931)

1932–46	J. Maxton	1932–33	R. Wallhead
1932–47	J. McGovern	1935–47	C. Stephen
1932–39	G. Buchanan	1946–47	J. Carmichael
1932–33	D. Kirkwood		

SOURCE.—R. E. Dowse, *Left in the Centre* (1966).

Irish Nationalist Party up to 1922

From the days of Parnell until the First World War between 80 and 86 Irish Nationalists sat in the House of Commons — at times divided by internal frictions but with a safe control of more than three-quarters of the seats in Ireland. Divisions over support for the war and the Easter Rebellion broke the party's hold and in 1918 only 7 of its 58 candidates were elected, (while Sinn Fein candidates won 73 seats). T. P. O'Connor, from 1885 the solitary Irish Nationalist Member representing an English constituency,

L.P. Annual Report, 1946, pp. 229-31.   [2] L.P. Annual Report, 1960, p. 24.

continued to be returned unopposed for the Scotland Division of Liverpool until his death in 1929.

Chairmen of the Irish Parliamentary Party

1900   J. Redmond   1917   J. Dillon

SOURCE.—F. S. L. Lyons, *The Irish Parliamentary Party 1890–1910* (1951).

Irish Parties since 1922

Since 1922 candidates under the label 'Irish Nationalist' have fought only two or three of the Northern Ireland seats, but from 1922 to 1924 they held one of the two Fermanagh and Tyrone Seats (the other was held by Sinn Fein) and from 1929 to 1955 they held both.   T. P. O'Connor continued to represent the Scotland division of Liverpool until 1929 and one or two Liverpool seats were fought by Nationalists.

Sinn Fein reappeared as a political force in 1955 and 1959, contesting all 12 Northern Ireland seats.   In 1955 Sinn Fein candidates won Mid-Ulster and Fermanagh and South Tyrone but they were disqualified as felons.

From 1943 to 1950, from 1951 to 1955 and from 1966 onwards Belfast West was held by candidates using the label 'Eire Labour', 'Republican Labour', and then 'Social Democratic and Labour'.   The S.D.L.P. founded in 1970 became the main party representing the Republican or Nationalist aspirations of the Roman Catholic minority.

Nationalist M.P.s

1922–29	T. P. O'Connor	1929–34	J. Devlin
1922–24	T. Harbison	1934–35	J. Stewart
1922–24		1935–50	P. Cunningham
1931–35	(S.F.) C. Healy	1935–51	A. Mulvey
1950–55		1951–55	M. O'Neill

Sinn Fein M.P.s

| 1955–55 | P. Clarke | 1955–56 | T. Mitchell |

Eire Labour M.P.

1943–50 ⎱ J. Beattie
1951–55 ⎰

Republican Labour M.P.

1966–70   G. Fitt

S.D.L.P. M.P.

1970–   G. Fitt

Independent Unity

1969–74 Feb	Bernadette Devlin (Mrs B. McAliskey)
1970–74 Feb	F. McManus
1974 Oct–	F. Maguire

After 1969 increasing fissures developed in the Ulster Unionist Party which had dominated Northern Ireland's representation at Westminster.   In 1970 I. Paisley standing as a Protestant Unionist defeated the Official Unionist Candidates in North Antrim.   In 1971 he formed the Democratic Unionist Party.   In 1970 W. Craig formed the Vanguard Movement and in January 1974 the Unionists split further.   In the February 1974 election, 11 of the 12 Ulster seats were won by candidates standing under the banner of a new

United Ulster Unionist Council in opposition to those Unionists who supported Mr Faulkner's Executive Council and the Sunningdale proposals for a Council of Ireland. Of the 11, 8 were members of the Unionist party under H. West, 2 carried the Vanguard label and I. Paisley was successful as a Democratic Unionist. In October 1974 H. West who had acted as Unionist Leader was the only one of the 11 to be defeated. J. Molyneaux succeeded him as leader.

The non-Sectarian Alliance Party, founded in 1970, was joined by S. Mills, a Unionist M.P., in 1972. He did not stand in Feb 1974, when 2 of their 3 candidates lost their deposits. In October 1974 they put up 5 candidates and 4 saved their deposits.

Liberal National Party (National Liberal Party since 1948)

In October 1931 23 Liberal Members broke with the party and formed the Liberal National Group. The subsequent electoral history of the Liberal National Party falls into three periods: at the 1931 General Election some of the Liberal National candidates were opposed by Conservatives but none of them were by Liberals. After 1931, a Conservative only once opposed a Liberal National (Scottish Universities 1946) but they were not opposed by Liberals (except in Denbigh 1935 and St. Ives 1937) until 1945. Of 41 candidates in 1931, 35 were returned as Members of Parliament and when the 'Samuelite' Liberals left the government over the Ottawa Agreements in 1932, the 'Simonite' Liberal Nationals remained. In 1935 33 of 44 candidates were returned, and in 1945 13 of 51 candidates. E. Brown, however, who had succeeded Sir J. Simon as leader on 4 December 1940 was defeated. In May 1947 the Woolton-Teviot agreement was signed, which urged the combination of Conservative and Liberal National Constituency Associations, and in 1948 the party was renamed the National Liberal Party. After the 1966 General Election only two M.P.s styled themselves Conservative and National Liberal. Two other members of the Group were elected as Conservatives by Joint Associations. In 1966 these four M.P.s relinquished the room assigned to them in the House of Commons to the Liberal Party. The Group became an integral part of the Conservative Party.

Chairmen of the Parliamentary Party		Chief Whips	
1931	Sir J. Simon	1931	A. Glassey
1940	E. Brown	1931	G. Shakespeare
1945	(Sir) J. Henderson-Stewart	1932	(Sir) J. Blindell
1946	Sir S. Holmes	1937	C. Kerr
1947	J. Maclay	1940	H. Holdsworth
1956	(Sir) J. Duncan	1945–66	(Sir) H. Butcher
1959	Sir J. Henderson-Stewart		
1961–4	Sir C. Thornton Kemsley		

SOURCES.—Information from the National Liberal Party, and *Dod's Parliamentary Companion, 1931–66.*

Liberal Unionist Party

The Liberal Unionist Party was based upon those Liberals who, under J. Chamberlain and the M of Hartington, broke with the party over Irish Home Rule in 1886. After they accepted office in Ld Salisbury's 1895 government, they became increasingly fused with the Conservative Party and, although they had preserved a separate organisation with separate funds, the final merger in 1912 was to some extent a recognition of a *fait accompli*. The President between 1886 and 1904 was M of Hartington (D of Devonshire) and between 1904 and 1912 J. Chamberlain. The Organising Secretary between 1895 and 1912 was J. Boraston.

Liberal Unionist M.P.s

| 1900 | . | 68 | . | Jan 1910 | . | 31 |
| 1906 | . | 23 | . | Dec 1910 | . | 35 |

National Party

A small group of dissident Conservatives led by H. Page Croft, formed this party in September 1917, with a programme described by one historian as of 'xenophobic imperialism'. Most of its members drifted back to the Conservative fold and fought under the Conservative label in 1918: only Sir H. Page Croft and Sir R. Cooper survived the election (when they made a special point of attacking the sale of honours) and in 1921 it was decided not to maintain a separate parliamentary party.

SOURCES. Ld Croft, *My Life of Strife* (1948). M. Foot, 'Henry Page Croft, Baron Croft', *Dictionary of National Biography 1941–50*.

National Democratic Party

The National Democratic Party was formed in 1918 to unite support amongst the Labour Movement for the Lloyd George Government. The N.D.P. had its origins in the dispute within the Labour Movement during the war and its greatest strength in the jingoist trade unions — the Liverpool Dockers, the Musicians' Union, some of the Textile Workers, and parts of the Miners Federation. It was also, in part, the successor to the projected anti-socialist Trade Union Labour Party and included among its members the Labour Ministers who refused to resign from the Government in 1918. G. Barnes, Labour member of the War Cabinet, was its accepted leader. In the 1918 Election the Party put up 28 candidates, all for working-class constituencies, and returned 15 to Parliament. Before the 1922 Election the surviving N.D.P. M.P.s joined the National Liberal Party, but only one (G. Roberts) was re-elected. The Party ceased to exist in 1923.

SOURCES.—G. D. H. Cole, *A History of the British Labour Party from 1914* (1945); G. N. Barnes *From Workshop to War Cabinet* (1924); *Labour Party Annual Conference Reports*, 1916–18; *Trades Union Congress Reports*, 1916–18.

National Labour Party

The party was formed in 1931 from the small group of Labour M.P.s who supported the National Government under Ramsay MacDonald. In the 1931 General Election 13 of its 20 candidates were elected. In 1935 8 of its 20 candidates were elected. The party wound itself up just before the 1945 election and in 1945 of the 7 surviving National Labour members 3 retired, 2 stood unsuccessfully as National candidates, and 2 as Independents (one, K. Lindsay, stood successfully — but in a new constituency, English Universities).

New Party, British Union of Fascists, Union Movement

Sir Oswald Mosley (Conservative, then Independent M.P. 1918–24, Labour M.P. 1926–31) resigned from the Labour Government in May 1930 after his *Memorandum* for dealing with unemployment had been rejected by the Cabinet. In October 1930 a resolution calling upon the National Executive to consider the Memorandum was narrowly defeated at the Labour Party Conference. On 6 December 1930 the *Mosley Manifesto* summarising the main proposals in the Memorandum was published, signed by 17 Labour M.P.s. Six of the 17 signatories of the Manifesto resigned from the Labour Party to form the New Party in February 1931 (Sir Oswald and Lady Cynthia Mosley, O. Baldwin, W. J. Brown, R. Forgan, and J. Strachey), but Baldwin and Brown remained members for only one day and Strachey resigned in June. The New Party received two further recruits before the 1931 General Election, W. E. D. Allen (Conservative) and R. Dudgeon (Liberal). In the Election the New Party contested 24 seats but failed to win a single one, the New Party M.P.s all losing their seats, and, apart from Sir Oswald Mosley, their deposits.

In 1932 the New Party was renamed the British Union of Fascists after Mosley had been to Italy to study the 'modern movements'. The Director of Organisation and Deputy Leader was R. Forgan. In the 1935 General Election, the B.U.F. put up no candidates and, with the slogan 'Fascism next Time', advised their supporters not to vote. The B.U.F. fought a number of by-elections in 1939 and 1940, before it was proscribed by the Government on 30 May 1940.

In 1948, Sir Oswald Mosley formed the Union Movement. Its first Parliamentary contest was in the 1959 General Election, when he fought North Kensington, losing his deposit. The Union Movement fought two by-elections in the 1959 Parliament and in the 1966 General Election Sir Oswald Mosley and 3 other candidates stood; they gained on average 3·7% of the vote.

SOURCE.—C. Cross, *The Fascists in Britain* (1961), R. Skidelsky, *Oswald Mosley* (1975)

The National Front

The National Front was formed by a merger of the League of Empire Loyalists and the British National Party in 1966. The Greater Britain Movement joined in 1967. The leader of the League of Empire Loyalists, A. K. Chesterton, became Policy Director of the National Front; Andrew Fontaine, President of the British National Party, became Executive Director. In 1970 A. K. Chesterton was succeeded by John O'Brien, who was succeeded in 1972 by John Tyndall (previously leader of the Greater Britain Movement) and in 1974 by J. Read.

National Front Candidates

	No.	Av. % vote	Highest Vote
1970	10	3·6	5·6
1974 Feb	54	3·3	7·8
1974 Oct	90	3·1	9·5

Plaid Cymru (Welsh Nationalist Party)

The party was founded in 1925 and has fought elections consistently since then, but without any success at the parliamentary level until a by-election victory in Carmarthen in 1966. The seat was lost in 1970 but in the February 1974 election, two seats, Caernarvon and Merioneth were won and in October 1974 Carmarthen was recaptured.

Welsh Nationalist Candidates

						Seats	% of Welsh Vote
1929	. 1	1951	. 4	1970	. 36	–	11·5
1931	. 2	1955	. 11	1974 Feb	. 36	2	10·7
1935	. 1	1959	. 20	1974 Oct	. 36	3	10·0
1945	. 8	1964	. 23				
1950	. 7	1966	. 20				

Plaid Cymru M.P.s

1966–70	G. Evans	1974 Feb– D. Wigley	1974 Feb– D. Thomas
1974 Oct–			

Scottish National Party

The party was formed in 1928 as the National Party of Scotland. In 1933 it merged with a body called the Scottish Party (founded 1930) and the name was then changed to the Scottish National Party. Its first success was in the Motherwell by-election of April 1945; but the victor, R. D. McIntyre, was defeated in the General Election three months later. In 1967 a seat was won in the Hamilton by-election but lost in 1970. In 1970, however, a Scottish Nationalist won Western Isles. In November 1973 the Govan, Glasgow, seat was won in a by-election but lost four months later. In the General Elections the Scottish Nationalists made great advances in votes and seats.

Scottish National Party Candidates

						% of Scottish Vote	Seats
1929	. 2	1951	. 1	1970	. 65	11·4	1
1931	. 3	1955	. 2	1974 Feb	. 70	21·9	7
1935	. 6	1959	. 5	1974 Oct	. 71	30·0	11
1945	. 8	1964	. 15				
1950	. 4	1966	. 23				

Scottish National Party M.P.s

1945–45	R. McIntyre	1974 Feb– D. Henderson	1974 Oct– Mrs M. Bain
1967–70	Mrs W. Ewing	1974 Feb– I. MacCormick	1974 Oct– G. Crawford
1974 Feb–		1974 Feb– G. Reid	1974 Oct– G. Thompson
1970–	D. Stewart	1974 Feb– H. Watt	1974 Oct– A. Welsh
1973–74	Mrs M. Macdonald	1974 Feb– G. Wilson	

Independent M.P.s

The number of Independent M.P.s has been small and, even among those few elected without the label of one of the parties already listed, a substantial proportion were in fact elected with the tacit support of a major party or in default of its candidate. M.P.s elected as Independents fall into six broad categories.

Independents in University Seats

J. Butler	1922	Miss E. Rathbone	1929	Sir A. Salter	1937
G. Davies	1923		1931		1945
(Sir) E. Graham-Little	1924		1935	T. Harvey	1937
	1929		1945	A. Hill	1940
	1931	(Sir) A. Herbert	1935	K. Lindsay	1945
	1935		1945	Sir J. Boyd Orr	1945
	1945			W. Harris	1945

Independents emerging from war-time situations

N. Billing	1917	W. Kendall	1941	W. Brown	1942
	1918		1945		1945
H. Bottomley	1918	G. Reakes	1942	C. White	1944
R. Barker	1918	T. Driberg	1942		

Dissident Conservatives

T. Sloan	1902	J. Erskine	1921	E. Taylor	1930
	1906		1922	D. Lipson	1937
E. Mitchell	1903	H. Becker	1922		1945 [1]
C. Palmer	1920	G. Hall Caine	1922	Sir C. Headlam	1940
Sir C. Townshend	1920	O. Mosley	1922	J. McKie	1945
Sir T. Polson	1921		1923 [1]	J. Little	1945
		Sir R. Newman	1929	Sir D. Robertson	1959

Dissident Liberal

Sir J. Austin	1900	A. Hopkinson	1922
J. Wason	1902		1923
G. Roberts	1922		1924 [1]
			1931 [1]
			1935 [1]
		Sir T. Robinson	1929

Dissident Labour

C. Stanton	1915	D. Taverne	1972
Sir O. Thomas	1922		1974 Feb
D. Pritt	1945	E. Milne	1974 Feb
S. Davies	1970		

Supported by the Left

E. Scrymgeour	1922	E. Scrymgeour	1929
	1923	V. Bartlett	1938
	1924		1945 [1]

[1] These later candidacies might be put into a different category.

Minor Parties — Representation in the House of Commons

	Total	Ir. Nat.	S.N.P.	P.C.	Ind. Un.	Comm.	I.L.P.	Ind. Con.	Ind. Lab.	Other
1900	82	82	..	..	..	..	..	..	..	..
1906	83	83	..	..	..	..	..	..	..	..
1910J	82	84	..	..	..	..	..	..	..	..
1910D	84	84	..	..	..	..	..	..	..	..
1918	83	80ᵃ	..	..	..	..	..	..	..	3
1922	12	3	..	..	..	1	..	4	1	3
1923	7	3	..	..	..	..	..	..	..	4
1924	5	1	..	..	..	1	..	..	..	3
1929	8	3	..	..	..	..	..	1	..	4
1931	5	2	..	..	..	..	..	..	..	3
1935	9	2	..	..	..	1	4	..	..	2
1945	22	3	..	..	1	2	3	4	1	8
1950	3	2	..	..	..	..	..	..	..	1
1951	3	3	..	..	..	..	..	..	..	..
1955	2	2	..	..	..	..	..	..	..	..
1959	1	..	..	..	..	..	..	1	..	..
1964	..	..	..	..	..	..	..	..	..	..
1966	1	1	..	..	..	..	..	..	..	..
1970	6	3	1	..	1	..	..	..	1	..
1974F	24	1	7	2	11	..	..	..	2	1
1974O	26	2	11	3	10	..	..	..	..	..

ᵃ There were 73 Sinn Fein candidates elected in Ireland who never took their seats. There were also 9 Nationalists elected.
ᵇ This 'other' candidate was the Speaker.

SOURCES.—*The Constitutional Year Book, 1919*; D. E. Butler, *The Electoral System in Britain since 1918* (1963); G. Thayer, *The British Political Fringe* (1965); F. W. S. Craig, *British Parliamentary Election Statistics, 1918-70* (1970).

III

PARLIAMENT

House of Commons

Speaker of the House of Commons

1895	W. Gully (Vt Selby)	Lib.
20 Jun 05	J. Lowther (Vt Ullswater)	Con.
28 Apr 21	J. Whitley	Co. Lib.
21 Jun 28	E. Fitzroy [1]	Con.
9 Mar 43	D. Clifton Brown (Vt Ruffside)	Con.
1 Nov 51	W. Morrison (Vt Dunrossil)	Con.
21 Oct 59	Sir H. Hylton-Foster [1]	Con.
26 Oct 65	Dr. H. King (Ld Maybray-King)	Lab.
12 Jan 71	S. Lloyd	Con.

Chairman of Ways and Means Committee

1900	J. Lowther	Con.
1905	G. Lawson	Con.
1906	A. Emmott	Lib.
1911	J. Whitley	Lib.
1921	J. Hope	Con.
1924	R. Young	Lab.
1929	R. Young	Lab.
1931	Sir D. Herbert	Con.
1943	D. Clifton Brown	Con.
1943	J. Milner	Lab.
1945	C. Williams	Con.
1945	J. Milner	Lab.
1951	Sir C. MacAndrew	Con.
1959	Sir G. Touche	Con.
1962	Sir W. Anstruther-Gray	Con.
1964	Dr. H. King	Lab.
1965	Sir S. Storey	Con.
1966	Sir E. Fletcher	Lab.
1968	S. Irving	Lab.
1970	Sir R. Grant-Ferris	Con.
1974	G. Thomas	Lab.

Deputy Chairman of Ways and Means Committee
(office created 1902)

1902	A. Jeffreys	Con.
1905	L. Hardy	Con.
1906	J. Caldwell	Lib.
1910	J. Whitley	Lib.
1911	D. Maclean	Lib.
1919	Sir E. Cornwall	Lib.
1922	E. Fitzroy	Con.
1924	C. Entwistle	Lib.
1928	D. Herbert	Con.
1929	H. Dunnico	Lab.
1931	R. Bourne [1]	Con.
1938	D. Clifton Brown	Con.
1943	J. Milner	Lab.
1943	C. Williams	Con.
1945	Sir C. MacAndrew	Con.
1945	H. Beaumont [1]	Lab.
1948	F. Bowles	Lab.
1950	Sir C. MacAndrew	Con.
1951	Sir R. Hopkin Morris [1]	Lib.
1956	Sir G. Touche	Con.
1959	Sir W. Anstruther-Gray	Con.
1962	Sir R. Grimston	Con.
1964	Sir S. Storey	Con.
1965	R. Bowen	Lib.
1966	S. Irving	Lab.
1968	H. Gourlay	Lab.
1970	Miss B. Harvie Anderson	Con.
1973	E. Mallalieu	Lab.
1974	O. Murton	Con.

Second Deputy Chairman of Ways and Means
(office created 1971)

1971	E. Mallalieu	Lab.
1973	O. Murton	Con.
1974	*(office vacant)*	
1974	Sir M. Galpern	Lab.

[1] Died in office.

153

Officers of the House of Commons

	Clerk		Librarian
1900	(Sir) A. Milman	1887	R. Walpole
1902	Sir C. Ilbert	1908	A. Smyth
1921	(Sir) T. Webster	1937	V. Kitto
1930	(Sir) H. Dawkins	1946	H. Saunders
1937	(Sir) G. Campion	1950	S. Gordon
1948	(Sir) F. Metcalfe	1968	D. Holland
1954	(Sir) E. Fellowes		
1962	(Sir) B. Cocks		
1974	(Sir) D. Lidderdale		

Parliamentary Sessions

In 1900 sessions of Parliament lasted from February to July or August. Occasionally Parliament sat through the summer. In 1930 both Houses agreed that they should adjourn between July and October, and that the session should last from September or October to the September or October of the following year. During the adjournments the Speaker or the Lord Chancellor has the power to give notice of an earlier meeting of Parliament if it is in the national interest.

Parliamentary Hours of Sitting

In 1902 the House of Commons met from 2 until 11.30 p.m., but this was altered in 1906 to 2.45 until 11.30, to allow more time for lunch. During the 1939–45 war the time for rising in the evening was changed to 10.30 p.m. Since 1945 the normal hours for sitting have been 2.30 until 10.30 p.m. on every weekday except Friday although the House usually sits later than this. From 1900 to 1939 the House met on Fridays from 12 a.m. to 5.30 p.m. Since 1939 the House meets on Fridays at 11 a.m. and normally adjourns for the weekend at 4.30 p.m. In 1967 as an experiment, the House also met from 10 a.m. to 1 p.m. on Mondays and Wednesdays but these morning sittings were discontinued in October 1967.

Government and Private Members' Time

Until 1939 Government business had precedence at every sitting of the House of Commons except certain Wednesdays and Fridays and Tuesday evenings after 8.15 p.m. until Easter. This generally gave Private Members about 8 Wednesdays and 13 Fridays on which they had precedence. This was always subject to the possibility that the House, or Government, might direct that the time was needed for Government business. Between 1914 and 1918 and between 1939 and 1948 Private Members' time was abolished completely. When Private Members' time was restored, the Government retained precedence on all days except for 20 Fridays. In the nine sessions 1950–51 to 1958–59 an average of ten days was allotted to Private Members' bills and 9 days to Private Members' motions. In 1960 four extra half-days (two Mondays and two Wednesdays) were allotted for consideration of Private Members' motions in addition to the twenty Fridays. From 1967 to 1970 sixteen of the twenty Fridays were given to Bills and four to motions. Since 1970–72 the number of Fridays for Bills has been between eight and ten.

SOURCES.—Sir I. Jennings, *Parliament* (2nd ed., 1957), pp. 95–9, 121–2; Sir T. Erskine May, *Parliamentary Practice* (18th ed.); Sir G. Campion, *An Introduction to the Procedure of the House of Commons* (1950); *Report of the Select Committee on the Hours of Meeting and Rising of the House*, H.C. 126 of 1930; 'The Times of Sittings of the House', *Report by Select Committee on Procedure*, Aug 1966, H.C. 153 of 1966–67.

Main Occupations of Members of Parliament 1918– (percentages)

	Conservative				Labour			
	1918–35 Average	1945	1950	1951	1918–35 Average	1945	1950	1951
Employers and Managers	32	32½	30½	32½	4	9½	9½	9
Rank and File workers	4	3	3	4½	72	41	43	45
Professional workers	52	61	62	57½	24	48½	46½	45½
Unpaid domestic workers	—	½	—	—	—	1	1	—
Unoccupied	12	3	4½	5½	—	—	—	—
	100	100	100	100	100	100	100	100

	Conservative								Labour							
	1951	1955	1959	1964	1966	1970	Feb 1974	Oct 1974	1951	1955	1959	1964	1966	1970	Feb 1974	Oct 1974
Professional	41	46	46	48	46	45	44	46	35	36	38	41	43	40	46	49
Business	37	30	30	26	29	30	32	33	9	12	10	11	9	10	9	8
Misc.	22	24	23	25	23	24	23	20	19	17	17	16	18	16	15	15
Workers	—	—	1	1	1	1	1	1	37	35	35	32	30	26	30	28
	100	100	100	100	100	100	100	100	100	100	100	100	100	100	100	100

Education of Conservative and Labour M.P.s 1906–1974 (percentages)

	Conservatives		Labour	
	Public School	University Educated	Public School	University Educated
1906	67	57	0	0
1910 Jan	74	58	0	0
1910 Dec	76	59	0	0
1918	81	49	3	5
1922	78	48	9	15
1923	79	50	8	14
1924	78	53	7	14
1929	79	54	12	19
1931	77	55	8	17
1935	81	57	10	19
1945	85	58	23	32
1950	85	62	22	41
1951	75	65	23	41
1955	76	64	22	40
1959	72	60	18	39
1964	75	63	18	46
1966	80	67	18	51
1970	74	64	17	53
1974 Feb	74	68	17	56
1974 Oct	75	69	18	57

SOURCE.—Data for 1906 and 1910 are based on J. A. Thomas, *The House of Commons 1906–1911* (1958). From 1918 to 1950 J. F. S. Ross provides the data on university education in *Elections and Electors* (1955) and on public school education for Conservatives. The figures for Labour public schoolboys up to 1935 have been calculated afresh for this table. All figures from 1951 onwards are taken from the Nuffield studies.

House of Commons Business

Sessions		Allocation of Parliamentary Time			Parliamentary Bills		Questions to Ministers		
Parliament Met	Parliament Prorogued	Total Days on which House sat	Average length of Day	Private Members' Days[a]	Total Bills Introduced	Total Bills Receiving Royal Assent	Daily Average Starred[b] Questions	Daily Average Unstarred Questions	Sessional Total of all Questions
3 Dec 00	15 Dec 00	11	5h 38m	3	..	..	..	..	314
23 Jan 01	17 Aug 01[c]	121	9h 5m	14	303	127	69	..	6,448[e]
16 Jan 02	18 Dec 02	181	8h 51m	17	300	121	..	..	7,168
17 Feb 03	14 Aug 03	115	9h 8m	14	311	311	28	18	4,536
2 Feb 04	15 Aug 04	124	9h 19m	13	308	121	38	18	5,933
14 Feb 05	11 Aug 05	114	9h 12m	12	309	86	47	19	6,244
Date of Dissolution 8 Jan 06. Duration of Parliament 5 yrs, 2 mths, 7 days.									
13 Feb 06	21 Dec 06	156	8h 32m	16	346	121	70	22	11,865
12 Feb 07	28 Aug 07	131	8h 28m	13	294	116	72	21	10,147
29 Jan 08	21 Dec 08	171	7h 39m	18	364	129	75	21	13,811
16 Feb 09	3 Dec 09	179	8h 38m	14	325	110	62	19	12,251
Date of Dissolution 10 Jan 10. Duration of Parliament 3 yrs, 10 mths, 28 days.									
15 Feb 10	28 Nov 10	103	6h 36m	9	289	101	81	24	8,201
Date of Dissolution 28 Nov 10. Duration of Parliament 9 mths, 3 days									
31 Jan 11	16 Dec 11	172	7h 49m	11	373	134	87	21	15,439
14 Feb 12	7 Mar 13	206	8h 1m	14	343	101	97	19	19,913
10 Mar 13	15 Aug 13	102	7h 55m	10	315	108	88	18	8,936
10 Feb 14	18 Sep 14	130	7h 14m	16	391	168	55	16	7,705
11 Nov 14	27 Jan 16	155	6h 40m	..	162	152	72	16	12,976
15 Feb 16	22 Dec 16	127	7h 11m	..	112	105	108	20	15,743
7 Feb 17	6 Feb 18	181	7h 21m	..	102	91	92	16	19,146
12 Feb 18	21 Nov 18	119	7h 16m	..	99	86	89	15	12,025
Date of Dissolution 25 Nov 18. Duration of Parliament 7 yrs, 9 mths, 25 days.									
4 Feb 19	23 Dec 19	163	7h 16m	16	203	152	126	27	20,523
10 Feb 20	23 Dec 20	167	8h 20m	17½	215	138	110	22	18,652
15 Feb 21	10 Nov 21	141	8h 0m	11¾	202	125	} 101[d]	} 19[d]	} 14,133[d]
14 Dec 21	19 Dec 21	4	6h 5m	..	..	..			
7 Feb 22	4 Aug 22	113	8h 3m	11	196	105	..[e]	..[e]	..[e]
Date of Dissolution 26 Oct 22. Duration of Parliament 3 yrs, 9 mths, 5 days.									
20 Nov 22	15 Dec 22	20	7h 54m	..	10	10	103[e]	18[e]	12,860[e]
13 Feb 23	16 Nov 23	114	8h 34m	17¼	181	78	107	21	12,370
Date of Dissolution 16 Nov 23. Duration of Parliament 11 mths, 27 days.									
8 Jan 24	9 Oct 24	129	7h 50m	21½	248	79	101	25	13,092
Date of Dissolution 9 Oct 24. Duration of Parliament 9 mths, 1 day.									
2 Dec 24	22 Dec 25	148	8h 17m	22½	247	145	91	23	14,035
2 Feb 26	15 Dec 26	151	7h 55m	21	180	105	71	17	10,713
8 Feb 27	22 Dec 27	144	7h 53m	19¾	195	91	74	14	10,536
7 Feb 28	3 Aug 28	115	7h 34m	24½	168	79	67	13	7,559
6 Nov 28	10 May 29	100	7h 0m	..	115	64	68	17	7,074
Date of Dissolution 10 May 29. Duration of Parliament 4 yrs, 7 mths, 2 days.									
25 Jun 29	1 Aug 30	189	7h 57m	31	237	132	93	24	18,327
28 Oct 30	7 Oct 31	187	7h 47m	21¼	212	106	78	15	14,373
Date of Dissolution 8 Oct 31. Duration of Parliament 2 years, 4 mths, 28 days.									

House of Commons Business

Sessions		Allocation of Parliamentary Time			Parliamentary Bills		Questions to Ministers		
Parliament Met	Parliament Prorogued	Total Days on which House sat	Average length of Day	Private Members' Days[a]	Total Bills Introduced	Total Bills Receiving Royal Assent	Daily Average Starred Questions[b]	Daily Average Unstarred Questions	Sessional Total of all Questions
3 Nov 31	17 Nov 32	155	7h 32m	1	125	103	69	10	9,667
22 Nov 32	17 Nov 33	143	7h 33m	26½	147	92	58	8	7,559
21 Nov 33	16 Nov 34	156	7h 49m	22¼	173	111	58	9	8,768
20 Nov 34	25 Oct 35	151	7h 36m	..	116	98	59	9	8,449

Date of Dissolution 25 Oct 35. Duration of Parliament 3 yrs, 11 mths, 21 days.

26 Nov 35	30 Oct 36	137	7h 55m	19½	149	111	82	13	10,215
3 Nov 36	22 Oct 37	157	7h 47m	24	170	126	79	11	11,769
26 Oct 37	4 Nov 38	168	7h 42m	26¼	179	113	85	14	13,787
8 Nov 38	23 Nov 39	200	7h 34m	14	227	171	92	17	18,460
28 Nov 39	20 Nov 40	127	6h 53m	..	80	73	84	27	13,536
21 Nov 40	11 Nov 41	113	5h 50m	..	55	54	77	23	10,825
12 Nov 41	10 Nov 42	116	6h 23m	..	46	46	80	23	11,592
11 Nov 42	23 Nov 43	122	7h 1m	..	59	58	83	22	11,911
24 Nov 43	28 Nov 44	153	7h 14m	..	55	52	77	17	11,498
29 Nov 44	15 Jun 45	95	6h 51m	..	57	48	91	18	7,856

Date of Dissolution 15 Jun 45. Duration of Parliament 9 yrs, 5 mths, 20 days.

1 Aug 45	6 Nov 46	212	7h 45m	..	106	104	128	30	27,313
12 Nov 46	20 Oct 47	164	8h 38m	..	73	71	108	22	17,310
21 Oct 47	13 Sep 48	171	8h 13m	..	92	89	97	21	16,303
14 Sep 48	25 Oct 48	10	7h 2m	..	..	..	132	41	853
26 Oct 48	16 Dec 49	208	7h 48m	10½	146	125	86	18	17,334

Date of Dissolution 3 Feb 50. Duration of Parliament 4 yrs, 4 mths, 15 days.

1 Mar 50	26 Oct 50	105	7h 50m	5	58	57	105	19	9,861
31 Oct 50	4 Oct 51	153	8h 20m	19	107	81	108	18	15,720

Date of Dissolution 5 Oct 51. Duration of Parliament 1 yr, 6 mths, 4 days.

31 Oct 51	30 Oct 52	157	8h 48m	18½	113	88	99	17	14,192
4 Nov 52	29 Oct 53	162	8h 12m	20	78	62	91	16	13,878
3 Nov 53	25 Nov 54	187	8h 11m	19	113	95	89	15	15,990
30 Nov 54	6 May 55	84	7h 58m	10	72	33	90	17	7,262

Date of Dissolution 6 May 55. Duration of Parliament 3 yrs, 6 mths, 6 days.

7 Jun 55	5 Nov 56	219	7h 57m	25½	126	101	86	16	18,285
6 Nov 56	1 Nov 57	159	7h 40m	20	93	75	90	20	14,259
5 Nov 57	23 Oct 58	156	7h 54m	20	112	89	84	18	12,734
28 Oct 58	18 Sep 59	159	7h 48m	20	113	89	89	21	14,518

Date of Dissolution 18 Sep 59. Duration of Parliament 4 yrs, 3 mths, 11 days.

20 Oct 59	27 Oct 60	160	8h 2m	22	103	80	81	21	13,471
1 Nov 60	24 Oct 61	168	8h 30m	22	117	79	73	22	13,778
31 Oct 61	25 Oct 62	160	8h 23m	22	108	75	65	23	12,226
30 Oct 62	24 Oct 63	162	8h 15m	22	105	72	67	31	13,948
12 Nov 63	31 Jul 64	155	8h 14m	22	155	102	66	37	14,291

Date of Dissolution 25 Sep 64. Duration of Parliament 5 yrs, 7 days.

a 'Notional' days on which Private Members' business had precedence. The idea of parliamentary 'days' must be treated with [cau]tion since actual days vary in length. In recent years Private Members' days have usually been Fridays and only 5 hours long [whe]reas Government 'days' are usually at least 6½ hours long and are frequently extended by suspension of the ten o'clock rule [and] by the practice of taking the affirmative and negative resolutions after ten o'clock.
b Including oral questions receiving a written reply.
c Although the session of 1901 was not due to begin until 14 Feb, Parliament sat for three days between 23 and 25 Jan to discuss [bus]iness arising out of the death of Queen Victoria.
d For both sessions in 1921.
e For both sessions in 1922.

House of Commons Business

Sessions		Allocation of Parliamentary Time			Parliamentary Bills		Questions to Ministers		
Parliament Met	Parliament Prorogued	Total Days on which House sat	Average length of Day	Private Members' Days[a]	Total Bills Introduced	Total Bills Receiving Royal Assent	Daily Average Starred Questions[b]	Daily Average Unstarred Questions	Sessional Total of all Questions
27 Oct 64	10 Mar 66	177	9h 0m	22	158	94	74	46	19,148
9 Nov 65	8 Nov 65	65	8h 15m	22	74	21	67	56	7,978

Date of Dissolution 10 Mar 66.   Duration of Parliament 1 yr, 5 mths, 13 days.

18 Apr 66	27 Oct 67	246	9h 50m	25	210	127	69	69	33,965
31 Oct 67	25 Oct 68	176	9h 2m	22	142	76	64	77	24,910
30 Oct 68	22 Oct 69	164	9h 26m	24	158	73	81	78	2,3464
28 Oct 69	29 May 70	122	8h 16m	24	152	60	81	78	17,461

Date of Dissolution 29 May 70.   Duration of Parliament 4 yrs, 1 mth, 11 days.

29 Jun 70	28 Oct 71	206	8h 16m	24	164	110	83	99	33,946
2 Nov 71	26 Oct 72	180	9h 17m	24	149	84	77	97	28,594
31 Oct 72	25 Oct 73	164	8h 53m	24	153	83	47	109	35,731
30 Oct 73	8 Feb 74	60	8h 21m	6½	77	17	41	104	8,690

Date of Dissolution 8 Feb 1974.   Duration of Parliament 3 yrs, 7 mths, 10 days.

6 Mar 74	20 Sep 74	87	8h 28m	10½	86	50	48	133	15,738

Date of Dissolution 20 Sep 1974.   Duration of Parliament 6 mths, 12 days.

22 Oct 74									

[a] 'Notional' days on which Private Members' business had precedence.   The idea of parliamentary 'days' must be treated w caution since actual days vary in length.   Private Members' days are usually Fridays and only 5 hours long whereas Governm 'days' are usually at least 6½ hours long and are frequently extended by suspension of the ten o'clock rule and by the practice taking the affirmative and negative resolutions after ten o'clock.   [b] Including oral questions receiving a written reply.

SOURCES.—Information from the 'Black Book', a compilation of Parliamentary statistics at the House of Commons, and *Sessional Returns of the House of Commons*. Questions to Ministers taken from D. N. Chester and N. Bowring, *Questions in Parlian* (1962), pp. 87-8, and 316; and information from the Journal Office, House of Commons.

Fathers of the House of Commons[a]

Name	Member of Parliament until	Length of service as M.P.		Length of service as Father	
		y.	m.	y.	m.
W. Bramston Beach	August 1901	44	4	2	4
Sir M. Hicks Beach	January 1906	41	6	4	5
G. Finch	May 1907	39	6	1	4
Sir H. Campbell-Bannerman	April 1908	39	6		11
Sir J. Kennaway	January 1910	39	9	1	9
T. Burt	December 1918	44	10	8	11
T. P. O'Connor	November 1929	49	7	10	11
D. Lloyd George	December 1944	54	8	15	1
Earl Winterton	October 1951	46	11	6	10
Sir H. O'Neill	October 1952	37	8	1	0
D. Grenfell	September 1959	37	2	6	11
Sir W. Churchill	September 1964	62	0[b]	5	0
R. Butler	January 1965	35	8		4
(Sir) R. Turton	February 1974	44	8	9	1
G. Strauss	(elected October 1934[c])				

[a] The only M.P.s in this century other than those listed here to serve continuously for over 40 years were Sir W. Hart Dyke (1865–1905), J. Talbot (1865–1908), and (Sir) A. Chamberlain (1892–1937).
[b] By tradition the title of Father of the House is conferred on the member who has the longest *continuous* service in the House in point of time.   Churchill's service was broken in 1908 and again in 1922-4. His length of continuous service was therefore exactly 40 years.
[c] G. Strauss also served as an M.P. from May 1929 to October 1931.

SOURCE.—J. F. S. Ross, *Elections and Electors* (1955), p. 470.

Regnal Years

Until 1962 the dates of Acts of Parliament were recorded in terms of the regnal years during the session in which they were passed. Regnal years date from the accession of the sovereign. Thus the act listed as *11 & 12 Geo. VI, c. 65* was passed in the parliamentary session during the eleventh and twelfth regnal year of George VI (1948). The parliamentary session of 1948–49 covered three regnal years, and its acts appear under the style *12, 13 & 14 Geo. VI*. Since 1963 Acts of Parliament have been recorded by the calendar year and the chapter number, e.g. *Finance Act 1963, c. 25.*

Sovereign	Regnal Year	Date
Victoria	63	20 Jun 1899–19 Jun 1900
	64	20 Jun 1900–22 Jan 01
Edward VII	1	22 Jan 01–21 Jan 02
	10	22 Jan 10–6 May 10
George V	1	6 May 10–5 May 11
	26	6 May 35–20 Jan 36
Edward VIII	1	20 Jan 36–11 Dec 36
George VI	1	11 Dec 36–10 Dec 37
	16	11 Dec 51–6 Feb 52
Elizabeth II	1	6 Feb 52–5 Feb 53
	10	6 Feb 61–5 Feb 62

SOURCES.—Regnal years from 1154–1945 are listed in *Handbook of Dates*, ed. C. R. Cheney (1945), pp. 18–21; *Where to Look for Your Law* (1965).

Select Committees

Select Committees have been appointed for many purposes and have a long history in both Houses.

In the Commons Select Committees have long been used in connection with public expenditure, parliamentary procedure, legislation, and for *ad hoc* enquiries, sometimes of a quasi-judicial character. In the nineteenth century and up to 1914 Select Committees were also used for a wide range of specific enquiries, many of which would now be undertaken by a Government Inquiry or even a Royal Commission. Between the wars Select Committees were also used to examine Empire matters. Select Committees may be set up for a session or part of a session to consider a specific matter e.g. the Select Committee on Patent Medicines in 1914, or the Select Committee on Tax-Credit in 1972–1973. Others are set up more regularly by custom.[1]

The Public Accounts Committee has existed continuously since 1862. An Estimates Committee now subsumed in the Expenditure Committee, has been set up in one form or another most sessions since 1912. Although the Nationalised Industries Committee has existed since 1956 other 'specialist Committees' to consider either a subject area e.g. Race Relations and Immigration or a Department e.g. Education and Science have been appointed every session.

[1] Since 1968–69 Select Committee returns showing Select Committees, membership, attendances, etc., have been printed by H.M.S.O.

Powers: In their order of reference, and under Standing Orders, Commons Select Committees have had powers of varying extent given to them by the House.

Except for Select Committees on Bills or procedure committees both Sessional Committees and specialist committees are now usually given powers to send for persons, papers and records (although only the House can compel the appearance of persons and the production of papers), to sit at times when the House is adjourned, to meet outside the Palace of Westminster ('to adjourn from place to place'), to report from time to time ('to report to the House and publish as many reports as they wish'), to appoint sub-committees from among their own members, and to appoint expert advisers.

Duration: Some Select Committees are more permanent than others. All share a degree of impermanence in that their membership needs to be re-appointed every session. In March 1974 for the first time the membership of a Select Committee (the Expenditure Committee) was appointed for the duration of a Parliament.

In November 1974 the Select Committees set up under Standing Orders, together with Specialist Committees, were constituted for the full life of the Parliament.

Among the Committees described below, the only Select Committees appointed by Standing Order are the Committee of Public Accounts and the Expenditure Committee. The remainder required their terms of reference, powers and composition to be renewed on motions brought before the House every session. Technically, and sometimes in fact, each session's Committee is a new Committee, although it may have identical terms of reference, powers and compositions to its predecessor.

Chairmen: Apart from the Public Accounts Committee, the Committee on Statutory Instrument, the Committee on the Parliamentary Commissioner and latterly the Select Committee on European Secondary Legislation, the Chairmen of the Select Committees are usually of the Government Party. This does not, however, necessarily apply to sub-committees.

Chairmen's Liaison Committee: In recent sessions the practice has grown up for Chairmen of Select Committees to meet in an informal Committee from time to time to discuss subjects of commons interest such as the allocation of funds available for overseas visits. The Committee is not a Select Committee of the House.

Committee of Selection, 1840–

Chairmen (since 1945)

1945	T. Smith	1964	C. Kenyon
1947	G. Mathers	1969	G. Rogers
1951	Sir G. Touche	1970	H. Gurden
1956	Sir R. Conant	1974	F. Willey
1960	Sir P. Agnew		

Although the task of the Committee of Selection has for many years been predominately the selection of Members to serve on Standing Committees on Bills, the Committee was originally set up to appoint Committees on Private Bills and is still appointed under Private Business S.O. 109. It has 11 Members.

The Committee of Selection nominates:

Public Business

(1) Members of Standing Committees;
(2) Some or all members of Select Committees on hybrid Bills (if the House orders);
(3) The Commons members of Joint Committees on hybrid Bills (if the House orders);
(4) The two members whom Mr Speaker is to consult, if practicable, before giving his certificate to a money bill.

Private Business

(1) The panel of members to serve on committees on unopposed bills;
(2) Committees on unopposed bills;
(3) Members of committees on opposed bills;
(4) Eight members to serve on the Standing Orders Committee under S.O. 103;
(5) The panel of members to act as commissioners under the Private Legislation Procedure (Scotland) Act 1936;
(6) Commons Members on Joint Committees on special procedure petitions.

Terms of Reference: The Committee would appear to interpret its instructions in S.O. 62 to have 'regard ... to the composition of the House' by choosing Standing Committees as far as possible in direct ratio to the size of the parties in the House, except that since the 1930s the Liberal Party has usually been given a higher representation than its size would merit on this basis — a Liberal member being appointed to all Committees of 45 members and above. In the three Parliaments since the war in which the size of the Government majority has been small the Committee of Selection has usually selected Members so as to give the Government a majority of one. In the 1974 Parliament, with a minority Government, no party had a majority on any standing Committee. The Committee tends to appoint those Members who spoke on the second reading of the Bill. In recent times of heavy legislation and expanding parliamentary activity it would appear that the position of the whips to offer advice as to which members are anxious, willing, or available to serve on a particular Committee has been strengthened. Although no Government whip is appointed to the Committee a senior opposition whip was always appointed until 1974.

SOURCES.—The History of the Committee is given in Erskine May, *Parliamentary Practice* (18th ed. pp. 906–7. Details of responsibilities of Standing Committees pp. 672–3.

Committee on Public Accounts, 1862–

Chairmen

1896	A. O'Connor	1919	F. Acland
1901	Sir A. Hayter	1921	A. Williams
1906	V. Cavendish	1923	F. Jowett
1908	(Sir) R. Williams	1924	W. Guinness

1924	W. Graham	1950	C. Waterhouse
1929	A. Samuel	1951	J. Edwards
1931	M. Jones	1952	(Sir) G. Benson
1938	F. Pethick-Lawrence	1959	H. Wilson
1941	W. Elliot	1962	D. Houghton
1943	Sir A. Powna	1964	J. Boyd-Carpenter
1945	O. Peake	1970	H. Lever
1948	R. Assheton	1974	E. du Cann
1950	Sir R. Cross		

The Committee is made up of no more than 15 members, including the Chairman, and meets on about 30 days each session. The Chairman is usually a member of the Opposition.

Usual Terms of Reference: 'for the examination of the accounts showing the appropriation of the sums granted by parliament to meet the public expenditure', 'and of such other accounts laid before parliament as the committee may think fit' (*added 15 Nov 34*). 'The Committee shall have power to send for persons, papers and records, and to report from time to time' (*added 14 Nov 33*). The Committee is aided in its work by the Comptroller and Auditor-General whose staff audit the accounts of government departments. These audits and the Comptroller's subsequent report to the House of Commons provided the basic materials for the Committee's enquiries.

SOURCES.—*Reports of the Select Committee on Public Accounts*; *Select Committee Returns, 1900–* ; L. A. Abraham and S. C. Hawtrey, *A Parliamentary Dictionary* (1956); B. Chubb, *The Control of Public Expenditure* (1952).

Estimates Committee, 1912–1970
Chairmen

1912	Sir F. Banbury	1935	Sir I. Salmon
1914	(*suspended*)	1939	(*see National Expenditure*
1917	(*see National Expenditure*		*Committee*)
	Committee)	1945	B. Kirby
1920	Sir F. Banbury	1950	A. Anderson
1924	Sir J. Marriott	1951	Sir R. Glyn
1926	(Sir) V. Henderson	1953	C. Waterhouse
1927	A. Bennett	1957	R. Turton
1929	H. Charleton	1961	Sir G. Nicholson
1930	H. Romeril	1964	W. Hamilton
1931	Sir V. Henderson		

The Committee originally consisted of 15 members. In 1921 this was increased to 24, and in 1924 to 28. From 1948 to 1960 it had 36 members and from 1960 to 1970 43 members. The Chairman was usually a Government supporter.

Terms of Reference: 'to examine and report upon such of the Estimates presented to the Committee as may seem fit to the Committee' (*7 Apr 12 original terms*), 'and to suggest the form in which the estimates shall be presented for examination, and to report what if any economies consistent with the policy implied in those estimates may be effected therein' (*added in 1921*). Until 1939 the Estimates Committee seldom appointed sub-committees, although power to do so had been given in 1924; since 1945, however, following the example set by the Select Committee on National Expenditure, it has invariably done so. In 1956 the wording of the terms of reference was rearranged but the substance remained unchanged.

In 1960 the terms were altered to read : 'to examine such of the estimates presented to this House as may seem fit to the committee and report how, if at all, the policy implied in those estimates may be carried out more economically and, if the committee think fit, to consider the principal variations between the estimates and those relating to the previous financial year, and the form in which the estimates are presented to the House'. The committee had power to send for persons, papers, and records, and sit notwithstanding any adjournment of the House, to adjourn from place to place, and to report from time to time: to appoint sub-committees and to refer to such sub-committees any of the matters referred to the committee [each sub-committee has the same powers of sending for persons, etc., sitting and adjourning as the main committee], and to report from time to time the minutes of evidence taken before sub-committees and reported by them to the committee. In Sessions 1965 and 1966 the House gave the Estimates Committee the power 'to appoint persons with technical or scientific knowledge for the purpose of particular enquiries, either to supply information which is not readily available or to elucidate matters of complexity within the Committee's order of reference'. From 1965–70 the practice was to appoint sub-committees specialising in particular fields. The Select Committee was replaced by the Expenditure Committee in 1970.

SOURCE.—N. Johnson, *Parliament and Administration: The Estimates Committee, 1945–65* (1966).

Committee on National Expenditure, 1917–1920 and 1939–1945
Chairmen

1917   H. Samuel   1939–45   Sir J. Wardlaw-Milne
1919–20   Sir F. Banbury

No Estimates were presented to Parliament during the two wars, and the Committee on Estimates lapsed. A Committee on National Expenditure was established each year. It consisted of 26 members 1917–20, and 32 members 1939–45. It met about 13 days a session between 1917–20, and about 19 days a session between 1939–45.

1939–45 Terms of Reference: 'to examine the current expenditure defrayed out of moneys provided by Parliament for the Defence Services, for Civil Defence, and for other services directly connected with the war, and to report what, if any, economies, consistent with the execution of the policy decided by the Government, may be effected therein'.

SOURCES.—*Reports of the Select Committee on Estimates; Select Committee Returns, 1900–   ;* Sir I. Jennings, *Parliament* (2nd ed., 1957), pp. 303–16; E. Taylor, *The House of Commons at Work* (7th ed., 1967).

Expenditure Committee, 1970–
Chairmen

1970   E. du Cann   1974   J. Boyden
1973   Sir H. D'Avigdor-Goldsmid

The Committee consists of 49 Members with a quorum of 9.

Terms of Reference: 'to consider how, if at all, the policies implied in the figures of expenditure and in the estimates may be carried out more economically, and to examine the form of the papers and of the estimates presented to this House'.

Nationalised Industries Committee, 1956–

Chairmen

1956	Sir P. Spens	1970	Sir H. D'Avigdor-Goldsmid
1957	Sir T. Low	1972	(Sir) J. Hall
1961	Sir R. Nugent	1974	R. Kerr
1964	E. Popplewell		
1966	I. Mikardo		

The Committee is appointed on a sessional basis; it had 13 members (1956–66), 18 members (1966–70), 14 members (1970–). The Chairman has always been a Government supporter.

Terms of Reference: 'to examine the reports and accounts of the nationalised industries established by statute, whose controlling boards are wholly appointed by Ministers of the Crown and whose annual receipts are not wholly or mainly derived from moneys provided by Parliament or advanced by the Exchequer'. In the 1965–66 and 1966–67 Sessions the Committee's terms of reference were amended to enable them to inquire into the Post Office. From 1968–69 the Committee's terms of reference were extended to include the Independent Television Authority and Cable and Wireless Ltd, the Horserace Totalisator Board and certain activities of the Bank of England.

SOURCES.—*Reports of the Select Committee on Nationalised Industries (Reports and Accounts), 1957– ; Select Committee Returns, 1957–   ; D. Coombes, The Member of Parliament and the Administration, the Case of the Select Committee on Nationalised Industries (1966).*

Committee on Agriculture, 1966–1969

Chairman 1966–69　　T. Watkins

Terms of Reference: 'To consider the activities in England and Wales of the Ministry of Agriculture, Fisheries and Food.' The Committee had power to send for persons, papers, and records, to sit notwithstanding any adjournment of the House, to adjourn from place to place, and to admit strangers during the examination of witnesses unless they otherwise order. The Committee ceased to exist in Feb. 1969.

Committee on Science and Technology, 1966–

Chairmen

1966	A. Palmer	1974	A. Palmer
1970	A. Neave		

Terms of Reference: 'To consider Science and Technology.' The Committee has power to send for persons, papers.

Committee on Education and Science, 1968–1970

Chairman 1968–70　　F. Willey

Terms of Reference: 'To consider the activities of the Department of Education and Science and the Scottish Education Department.' The Committee ceased to exist in 1970.

Race Relations and Immigration, 1968–

Chairmen

1968	A. Bottomley	1974	F. Willey
1970	W. Deedes		

The Committee has 12 Members, and a quorum of 4.

Terms of Reference: 'To review policies, but not individual cases, in relation to: (*a*) the operation of the Race Relations Act 1968 with particular reference to the work of the Race Relations Board and the Community Relations Commission, and (*b*) the admission into the United Kingdom of Commonwealth citizens and foreign nationals for settlement.'

Overseas Aid, 1968–1971; Overseas Development, 1973–

Chairmen

1968	Miss M. Herbison	1973	Sir B. Braine
1970–71	B. Braine	1974	Sir G. de Freitas

The first Committee had between 10 and 18 Members, with a quorum of between 4 and 9.   After 1973 it had 9 Members.

Terms of Reference: 'to consider the activities of the Ministry of Overseas Development'.   The Committee ceased to exist in 1971.   It was re-established under a new title in 1973, 'to consider United Kingdom assistance for Overseas Development'.

Scottish Affairs, 1969–1972

Chairmen

1969	T. Steele
1970	Sir J. Gilmour
1971	J. Brewis

The Committee had 16 Members and a quorum of 8.

Terms of Reference: 'to consider Scottish Affairs'.

European Secondary Legislation, 1974–

Chairman

1974   J. Davies

The Committee is appointed on a sessional basis.   In 1974 it had 16 members and the Chairman was drawn from the Opposition.

Terms of Reference.   To consider draft proposals of EEC secondary legislation and to 'report their opinion as to whether such proposals or other documents raise questions of legal and political importance' . . . 'and to what extent they may affect the law of the United Kingdom'.   The Committee has powers to send for persons, papers and records, to sit during the Adjournment, and to adjourn from place to place.

Procedure, 1961–

Chairmen

1961	I. Macleod	1966	D. Chapman
1963	S. Lloyd	1970	Sir R. Turton
1964	A. Irvine	1974	S. Irving
1965	A. Blenkinsop		

The Committee has 10 Members and a quorum of 4.

It was long the practice of the House to set up Committees from time to time to make recommendations on its procedure.   But since 1961 a Select Committee on Procedure has been appointed every Session to report on matters which the House refers to it.   It has powers to send for persons, papers and records and to report from time to time.   It lapsed between Feb 74 and Nov 74.

House of Commons Services Committee, 1965–

Chairmen

1965	H. Bowden	1972	R. Carr
1966	R. Crossman	1972	J. Prior
1968	F. Peart	1974	A. Bottomley
1970	W. Whitelaw		

Terms of Reference: 'To advise Mr Speaker on the control of the accommodation and services in that part of the Palace of Westminster and its precincts occupied by or on behalf of the House of Commons and to report thereon to this House.' This Committee was set up as a result of a recommendation of the Select Committee on the Palace of Westminster of Sessions 1964–65 whose main task had been to consider the arrangements to be made by the Commons following the transfer on 26 Apr 1965 of control of the Palace from the Lord Great Chamberlain on behalf of the Crown to the two Houses.

The Committee consists of 16 members appointed by the House. It has power to send for persons, papers, and records, to sit notwithstanding the adjournment of the House, to report from time to time, and to appoint Sub-Committees, each of which consists of three members. Each Sub-Committee has similar powers to the main Committee (except of course power to nominate Sub-Committees). The Committee usually appoints three main Sub-Committees: the Accommodation and Administration Sub-Committee, the Catering Sub-Committee and the Library Sub-Committee. The Catering Sub-Committee replaced the 'Select Committee on Kitchen and Refreshment Rooms' appointed every session since the late nineteenth century.

Until 1974 the Leader of the House was always appointed Chairman of the Committee.

Select Committee of Privileges, c. 1630–

The Select Committee of Privileges only meets when prima facie breaches of privileges are referred to it by the House. Unlike other committees it includes senior members from both the Front Benches. It is ordered to be appointed by long-standing tradition on the first day of every session. Until 1940 it was chaired by the Prime Minister. From 1940 to 1945 C. Attlee, as Deputy Prime Minister, took the chair. Since 1945 the Chairman has usually but not always been the Leader of the House.

Chairmen

1940	C. Attlee	1965	H. Bowden
1945	H. Morrison	1967	R. Crossman
1946	A. Greenwood	1968	F. Peart
1947	H. Morrison	1971	W. Whitelaw
1948	C. Ede	1972	R. Carr
1952	H. Crookshank	1973	J. Prior
1956	R. Butler	1974	G. Strauss
1964	S. Lloyd		

The following include all Reports of the Select Committee of Privileges and a few from *Ad Hoc* Committees.

1902	Imprisonment of a Member: C. O'Kelly.
1902	Imprisonment of a Member: P. McHugh.
1909	D of Norfolk: alleged interference in an election.
1911	E of Aberdeen and E of Roden: alleged interference in an election.

1924   *Daily Herald*: reflection on the impartiality of the Chairman of Committees.

1926   *Daily Mail*: allegations of corrupt motives against M.P.s.

1929–30   E. Sandham: allegations of drunkenness and acceptance of bribes against M.P.s.

1932–33   H. Bowles and E. Huntsman: reflections on a Private Bill Committee's impartiality.

1933–34   Sir S. Hoare and E of Derby: alleged improper pressure on witnesses to a Committee.

1937–38   D. Sandys: summons to Military court of Inquiry.

1937–38   Official Secrets Acts.

1938–39   Official Secrets Acts.

1939–40   Detention of A. Ramsay under 18B of Defence of the Realm Act.

1939–40   Conduct of R. Boothby.

1940–41   Conduct of R. Boothby.

1940–41   *Observer* publication of Secret Session debate.

1940–41   Grampian electricity supply bill: Highland Development League circular to M.P.s alleging irregularities in bill procedure.

1941–42   Disclosure of Secret Session proceedings by J. McGovern.

1942–43   H. Metcalf and J. Reid: payment of expense cheque to M.P. to attend prosecution by Board of Trade.

1943–44   N.U.D.A.W.: withdrawal of Trade Union financial support from W. Robinson on ground of refusal to resign seat.

1944–45   G. Reakes and D. Henderson. Offer to make donation to constituency association in return for M.P.s help.

1945–46   Writ of Summons served on officer of House within precincts.

1945–46   Disclosure in conversation of Secret Session information by E. Granville.

1945–46   Posters threatening publication of names of M.P.s voting for bread rationing.

1946–47   Assault on P. Piratin in precincts of the House.

1946–47   Action by Civil Service Clerical Association calculated to influence W. Brown.

1946–47   G. Schofield and S. Dobson (Editor and Political Correspondent of *Evening News*): refusal to reveal source of information to Committee.

1946–47   Article by G. Allighan alleging disclosure to newspapers of information from party meetings.

1946–47   Disclosure of party meeting information by E. Walkden in return for payment.

1947–48   H. Dalton: Budget disclosure.

1947–48   The Chairman of Ways and Means (J. Milner): personal explanation that he acted professionally as a solicitor against a Member.

1947–48   Broadcast and interview in *Daily Mail* by C. Brogan alleging that Secret Session information would be given to Russia.

1948–49   Alleged misrepresentation by *Daily Worker* of Member's speech (A. Blackburn).

1950   J. MacManaway: election of a Member, being a clergyman of the
            Church of Ireland.

1951   Abuse of members not related to transactions in House (S. Silver-
            man, I. Mikardo).   Comment on B.B.C. 'Any Questions' pro-
            gramme on matter referred to Committee.

1951   Report in *Sutton Coldfield News* of speech by Lady Mellor criticis-
            ing ruling by the Chair.

1951   Obstruction of J. Lewis by the police.

1952–53   Amendment of the law relating to the disability of some clergy
            from sitting and voting in the House of Commons.

1953   Article by Mrs P. Ford in *Sunday Express* (Mrs Braddock).

1953   *Daily Worker* article (M.P.s vote money into their own pockets).

1955   Action by Bishop against chaplain after communication with M.P.

1956   *Sunday Graphic* advocates telephone campaign against A. Lewis.

1956   *Sunday Express* article on M.P.s' petrol rationing allowances.

1956   *Evening News* cartoon on petrol rationing.

1956–57   G. Strauss: threat of libel action by the London Electricity Board,
            following letter from the Member to the Paymaster General.

1957   Comment on B.B.C. 'Any Questions' programme on matter
            referred to Committee: report of speech in *Romford Recorder*
            on petrol rationing.

1957–58   Order in Council directing that the Report of the Judicial
            Committee on a Question of Law concerning the Parliamentary
            Privilege Act 1770, be communicated to the House of
            Commons.

1957–58   G. Strauss: recommendations of the Committee arising out of
            the case involving the London Electricity Board.

1958–59   Report of an Inquiry into the methods adopted by the London
            Electricity Board for the disposal of scrap cable.

1959–60   C. Pannell: allegation of threat in a letter from C. Jordan.

1960–61   A. Wedgwood Benn: petition for redress of grievances regarding
            the disqualification of peers.

1963–64   Q. Hogg: complaint by G. Wigg concerning a speech at the Town
            Hall, Chatham, on 19 Mar 64.

1964–65   P. Duffy: complaint concerning speech at Saddleworth on 12
            Feb 65 alleging drunkenness among Conservative Members.

1964–65   F. Allaun: complaint concerning letter addressed to Members
            and advocating racial and anti-semitic views.

1964–65   The Chancellor of the Exchequer: complaint by Sir R. Cary
            concerning passages of speech reported in the *Daily Telegraph*
            5 Jul 65, on Members' business interests.

1966–67   G. Fitt: complaint concerning allegations of treachery in *Prot-
            estant Telegraph*.

1967–68   E. Hooson: complaint concerning allegations of treachery in inter-
            view published in *Town* magazine.

1967–68   W. Hannan: complaint concerning letter in the *Scotsman* by
            Mrs W. Ewing, M.P., reflecting on the conduct of members.

1967–68   A. Palmer: complaint concerning article about biological warfare published in the *Observer* from information allegedly supplied by T. Dalyell, M.P.

1968–69   Mrs R. Short: report in *Wolverhampton Press* and *Star* of a speech by Alderman Peter Farmer imputing partial conduct to a Member.

1968–69   Sir D. Glover: certain events attending to a visit of a Sub-Committee of the Select Committee on Education and Science to the University of Essex.

1968–69   R. Maxwell: article published in the *Sunday Times* reflecting on the conduct of a Member as Chairman of the Catering Sub-Committee of the Select Committee on House of Commons Services and as a member of that Committee.

1969–70   J. Mackintosh: matter reported in *The Times* which disclosed a breach of privilege.

1970–71   D. Steel: report in the *Sun* of alleged attempt by a trade union to influence actions of certain Members. (Report made in following Session.)

1970–71   A. Lewis: assault upon a servant of the House.

1970–71   W. Hamilton: publication by the *Daily Mail* of an article purporting to give an account of proceedings in a Select Committee not yet reported to the House. (Report made in following Session.)

1970–71   On a Motion moved by the Leader of the House. Rights of Members detained in prison.

1971–72   On a Motion moved by a member of the Government. Matter of the style and title of the Member for Berwick upon Tweed.

1972–73   R. Carter: serving of writ within the precincts of the House of Commons.

1974   A. Wedgwood Benn: alleged intimidation by Aims of Industry.

1974   J. Ashton: allegations about Members' financial interests.

Statutory Instruments, 1947 (Statutory Rules and Orders, 1944–47)
(since 1972 a Joint Committee of both Houses)

Chairmen

1944	Sir C. MacAndrew	1964	G. Page
1950	G. Nicholson	1970	A. Booth
1951	E. Fletcher	1974	G. Page

The Committee has had between 7 and 11 members, meeting fortnightly on about 16 days each session. The Chairman has always been an opposition member.

Terms of Reference: The original terms of 21 Jun 44 have been considerably enlarged by additional powers conferred in subsequent years.

In 1972 the procedure for considering Statutory Instruments was changed. The vast majority of instruments are now considered by a Joint Committee of Members of both Houses. However, the Statutory Instruments Committee still exists to consider instruments on which proceedings are subject to proceedings in the House of Commons only.

The Joint Committee has power to consider every instrument which is laid before each House of Parliament and upon which proceedings may be or might have been taken in either House of Parliament in pursuance of an Act of Parliament. It also has power to draw the attention of the House of Commons to other Statutory Instruments on any of the following grounds: (i) that they involve public money; (ii) that they are immune from challenge in the courts; (iii) that they have effect retrospectively; (iv) that there seems to have been an unjustifiable delay in publication of the S.I. or in laying it before Parliament; (v) that there seems to have been an unjustifiable delay in sending notification to the Speaker; (vi) that it appears to make unusual or unexpected use of the powers conferred by the Statute under which it is made; (vii) if elucidation is considered necessary; (viii) that the drafting appears to be defective.

The Committee has powers to sit when it wishes, to report from time to time, to call for witnesses and to appoint sub-committees. It is obliged to give any government department an opportunity to explain an S.I. or other document before drawing it to the attention of the House.

Since 1890 the Statutory Rules and Orders, and since 1948 the S.I.s, have been published in annual volumes. The average total of Orders made between 1894 and 1900 was just over 1,000.

The distinction between 'General' and 'Local' follows that adopted between public Acts and local and personal Acts of Parliament. The documents registered as Statutory Instruments do *not* include rules of an executive character, or rules made by other bodies, e.g. local authorities, unless confirmed by a government department. Statutory Instruments also include some rules made by statutory authorities which are not government departments, e.g. the Law Society, General Dental Council, Rule Committee of Church Assembly.

Statutory Instruments

Year	Annual Total	General	Local
1900	995	174	821
1910	1,368	218	1,150
1920	2,475	916	1,559
1929	1,262	391	871
1940	2,222	1,626	596
1950	2,144	1,211	933
1960	2,495	733	1,762
1970	2,044	1,040	1,004

The figures for the earlier years were given by Sir C. Carr in evidence before the *Committee on Ministers' Powers: Minutes of Evidence, II*, p. 205; the *Select Committee on Procedure* (H.C. 189 of 1945–46, p. 243); and the *Select Committee on Delegated Legislation* (H.C. 3010 of 1953, p. 2). The figures for 1950 are based on J. E. Kersell, *Parliamentary Supervision of Delegated Legislation* (1960). The figures for 1960 and 1970 are from the Statutory Publications Office.

Sources.—*Select Committee Returns, 1944–*; *Select Committee on Statutory Instruments (Rules and Orders, 1944–47)*; Sir I. Jennings, *Parliament* (2nd ed. 1957), pp. 489–516 (quotes Sir C. Carr's figures); Ld Hewart, *The New Despotism* (1929); G. W. Keeton, *The Passing of Parliament* (1952); S. C. Hawtry and H. M. Barclay, *A Parliamentary Dictionary* (1970) and information from the Committee Office of the House of Commons; C. K. Allen, *Law and Orders* (3rd ed. 1965); Statutory Publications Office; H. C. Deb. 728, c. 1564; Select Committee on Statutory Instruments, *Special Report for the Session 1966–67* (No. 266).

Committee on Public Petitions, 1842–74

Chairmen (since 1945)

1945	S. Viant	1966	D. Griffiths
1951	C. Lancaster	1970	J. Jennings
1964	G. Pargiter		

The Committee was appointed during most sessions since April 1842. It had 10 members, and a quorum of 3. It had power to send for persons, papers and records. It was abolished in 1974.

Terms of Reference: To clarify and prepare abstracts of Petitions 'in such form and manner as shall appear to them best suited to convey to the House all requisite information respecting their contents'. 'All Petitions presented to the House, with the exception of such as are deposited in the Private Bill Office' are referred to the Committee. The Committee was required in its reports to state the number of signatures to each Petition. It had no power to consider the merits of the petitions.

Committee on Parliamentary Commission for Administration, 1967–

Chairmen

1967	Sir H. Munro-Lucas-Tooth	1974	C. Fletcher-Cooke
1970	M. Stewart		

The Committee has 10 members, and a quorum of 4.

Terms of Reference: 'To examine the reports laid before this House by the Parliamentary Commissioner for Administration and Matters in Connection therewith.' The Committee has power to send for persons and papers.

Parliamentary Commissioner for Administration (Ombudsman)

The Parliamentary Commissioner for Administration is appointed by Letters Patent under the provisions of the Parliamentary Commissioner Act, 1967, which came into force on 1 Apr 67.

His function is to investigate complaints referred to him by Members of the House of Commons from members of the public who claim to have sustained injustice in consequence of maladministration in connection with actions taken by or on behalf of Government Departments. (Other public bodies such as the nationalised industries and local government are outside his jurisdiction.)[1] Under the Act the Commissioner is required to report the results of each investigation to the Member who referred the complaint to him and also to make an annual report to each House of Parliament on the performance of his functions. In addition he may make other reports to Parliament with respect to those functions if he thinks fit; and he may make a special report to Parliament if he considers that injustice caused to the complainant by maladministration has not been or will not be remedied.

The Commissioner may be removed from office only upon an Address from both Houses of Parliament.

Parliamentary Commissioners

1 Apr 67	Sir E. Compton
1 Apr 71	Sir A. Marre

[1] Under the National Health Service (Scotland) Act, 1972, and the National Health Service Reorganisation Act, 1973, provision was made for the appointment of Health Service Commissioners for Scotland, England and Wales. Sir A. Marre was appointed to these three posts with effect from 1 Oct 73, in addition to his post as Parliamentary Commissioner for Administration.

Ombudsman Cases

	No. of cases completed during the year	Member informed case outside jurisdiction	Member informed case is discontinued	Investigation completed and result reported to Member
1967[1]	849	561	100	188
1968	1,181	727	80	374
1969	790	445	43	302
1970	651	362	30	259
1971	516	295	39	182
1972	596	318	17	261
1973	536	285	12	239

[1] From 1 Apr.

SOURCES.—H.M.S.O., *The Parliamentary Commissioner for Administration* (Cmnd. 2767). H.M.S.O., *Annual Reports of the Parliamentary Commissioner for Administration*; F. A. Stacey, *The British Ombudsman* (1971).

Payment of M.P.s

1912   M.P.s receive first salary; £400 per year paid to all members not receiving salaries as Ministers or officers of the House.

1913   £100 of M.P.s' salaries made tax-exempt in respect of parliamentary expenses. This remained in force until 1954.

1924   M.P.s allowed free rail travel between London and their constituencies.

1931   Salary cut to £360 as an economy measure.

1934   Salary restored to £380 and then to £400.

1937   Salary increased to £600.

1946   Salary increased to £1,000 and salaries of £500 authorised for M.P.s who, as Ministers or Leaders of the Opposition, had an official salary of less than £5,000. Free travel was granted between M.P.s' homes and Westminster as well as to their constituencies.

1953   A sessional allowance of £2 per day introduced for every day (except Friday) on which the House sat: this was payable to all M.P.s including Ministers.

1957   The sessional allowance (usually amounting to about £280 p.a.), was replaced by an annual £750 to cover parliamentary expenses. The whole £1,750 drawn by ordinary M.P.s was subject to tax but M.P.s could claim as tax free any expenses up to £1,750 incurred in respect of parliamentary duties.

1964   Salary increased to £3,250 per year, following Lawrence Committee Report.

1965   Members' Pensions Act. First comprehensive pensions scheme introduced for M.P.s and dependants. Members contribute £150 per year and the Exchequer an amount equal to the aggregate of the Members' contributions. Members receive pensions from the age of 65 or on ceasing to be an M.P. if later, provided they have served for 10 years or more. The pension of £600 per year for 10 years' service increases to £900 after 15 years' service and by £24 for each further year thereafter.

1969   Secretarial allowance of up to £500 introduced. Members to have free telephone calls within the U.K.

1972 M.P.s' pay increased to £4,500 following Boyle Committee recommendations. Secretarial allowance increased to up to £1,000. An allowance of up to £750 for additional cost of living away from main residence and London members to receive a London supplement of £175 p.a. Travel allowances extended and a terminal grant equivalent to 3 months' salary established for M.P.s who lose their seats at a General Election.

Parliamentary and Other Pensions Act. Existing pensions scheme revised. Minimum qualifying period reduced from 10 years to 4. M.P.s' benefits based on 1/60th of final salary for each year of reckonable service. Contributions to be 5% of salary. Early retirement option available from 60 onwards on an actuarially reduced pension.

1974 Secretarial allowance increased to up to £1,750 and allowance for living away from main residence increased to £1,050. London supplement increased to £228 p.a.

SOURCES.—H.C. 255 of 1920, *Report of the Select Committee on Members' Expenses*; Cmd. 5624, 1937–38, *Report of the Departmental Committee on an M.P.s' Pension Scheme*; H.C. 93 of 1945–46, *Report of the Select Committee on Members' Expenses*; H.C. 72 of 1954, *Report of the Select Committee on Members' Expenses, etc.*; *Ministerial Salaries Act, 1957*; *Report of the Committee on the Remuneration of Ministers and Members of Parliament* (Lawrence) Cmnd. 2516; *Ministerial Salaries and Members' Pensions Act* (1965); *Second Interim Report of the Committee on Top Salaries* (Cmnd. 5372/1972); Fees Office, House of Commons.

Seats Forfeited

These members left or were expelled from the House before or after their conviction and imprisonment on criminal charges.

2 Mar 03	A. Lynch	Nat.	Galway
1 Aug 22	H. Bottomley	Ind.	Hackney South
31 Jul 41	Sir P. Latham	Con.	Scarborough & Whitby
16 Dec 54	P. Baker	Con.	S. Norfolk

These members forfeited their seats as a result of being adjudged bankrupt.

Sep 03	P. McHugh	Nat.	N. Leitrim (re-elected)
15 Jul 09	N. Murphy	Nat.	S. Kilkenny
1 Oct 28	C. Homan	Con.	Ashton under Lyne

In addition, H. Bottomley resigned his seat 16 May 12 after filing his bankruptcy petition.

These members forfeited their seats when it transpired that they held a government contract. All but one were re-elected in the ensuing by election.

2 Feb 04	A. Gibbs	City of London (re-elected)
2 Feb 04	V. Gibbs	St Albans (defeated)
21 Apr 12	Sir S. Samuel	Whitechapel (re-elected)
10 Feb 25	W. Preston	Walsall (re-elected)

In Nov 1924, J. Astor (Dover) forfeited his seat for inadvertently voting before taking the oath. He was re-elected unopposed in the ensuing by-election.

These members gave up their seats when under censure for some aspect of their parliamentary conduct.

26 Feb 31	T. Mardy Jones	Lab.	Pontypridd (*abuse of travel voucher*)

11 Jun	36	J. Thomas	Nat. Lab.	Derby (*Budget leak*)
11 Jun	36	Sir A. Butt	Con.	Balham & Tooting (*Budget leak*)
30 Oct	47	G. Allighan	Lab.	Gravesend (*expelled by a vote of 187–75 for breach of privilege*)
3 Feb	49	J. Belcher	Lab.	Sowerby (*following Lynskey Tribunal*)
5 Jun	63	J. Profumo	Con.	Stratford-on-Avon (*lying to the House*)

A. Ramsay, Con. Peebles and Southern, remained an M.P. from 1940 to 1945 although, being detained under Regulation 18B of the Defence of the Realm Act until Dec 1944, he was unable to sit from May 40 to Dec 44.

Various other members have resigned their seats while under the shadow of some minor private or public scandal but in almost every case it seems that they could well have remained as members had they chosen to do so.

House of Lords

Lord Chairmen of Committees

(*Deputy Speaker of the House of Lords. The Lord Chancellor (see p. 63) acts as Speaker.*)

1889	E of Morley	1944	Ld Stanmore
1905	4th E of Onslow	1946	E of Drogheda
1911	E of Donoughmore	1957	Ld Merthyr
1931	5th E of Onslow	1965	E of Listowel

Officers of the House of Lords

Clerk of the Parliaments		*Librarian*	
1885	(Sir) H. Graham	1897	A. Strong
1917	Sir A. Thring	1904	E. Gosse
1930	Sir E. Alderson	1914	A. Butler
1934	(Sir) H. Badeley	1922	C. Clay
1949	(Sir) R. Overbury	1956	C. Dobson
1953	(Sir) F. Lascelles		
1959	(Sir) V. Goodman		
1963	(Sir) D. Stephens		
1974	P. Henderson		

SOURCES.—*Dod's Parliamentary Companion*; *Whitaker's Almanack*; *Hansard*.

Composition of the House of Lords
(including minors)

Year	Dukes[a]	Mar-quesses	Earls	Vis-counts	Barons	Life Peers[b]	Law Lords[c]	Repres. Scot-land[d]	Repres. Ireland[d]	Archbps. and Bishops	Total
1901	26	22	123	32	314	..	4	16	28	26	591
1910	25	23	124	42	334	..	4	16	28	26	622
1920	26	29	130	64	393	..	6	16	27	26	716
1930	24	26	134	73	428	..	7	16	18	26	753
1939	24	28	139	84	456	..	7	16	13	26	785
1950	23	30	137	95	503	..	11	16	6	26	847
1960	25	26	132	111	531	31	8	16	1	26	908
1970	29	28	163	110	530	163	11	..	..	26	1,057
1974	29	28	161	109	502	237	14	..	..	26	1,107

[a] Including Royal Dukes.
[b] Created by the Life Peers Act, 1958.
[c] Lords of Appeal in Ordinary.
[d] Scottish and Irish peers sitting by virtue of UK title are listed under the letter. In 1963 all Scottish peers became entitled to sit and are listed under their senior title.

SOURCES.—*Constitutional Year Books*, 1900–39; *Dod's Parliamentary Companion*, 1940– .

In 1974, of the 1,107 members of the House of Lords, 767 were peers by succession, 63 were hereditary peers of the first creation, 251 were life peers, and 26 were bishops. Of the hereditary peers 18 were women; of the life peers 33 were women.

Creation of Peerages

Administration[a]		New Hereditary Creations[a]	Life Peers Law	Life Peers Other	Advanced in Rank	Total	Duration of Ministry (Yrs.)	Average Annual Creations[b]
Salisbury	1895–02	42	2	..	n.a.	44	7	6
Balfour	1902–05	17	1	..	5	23	$3\frac{1}{2}$	7
Campbell-Bannerman	1905–08	20	1	..	..	21	$2\frac{1}{3}$	9
Asquith	1908–15	61	6	..	13	80	7	11
Asquith	1915–16	17	..	..	2	19	$1\frac{1}{2}$	13
Lloyd George	1916–22	90	1	..	25	116	$5\frac{3}{4}$	20
Bonar Law	1922–23	3	..	..	..	3	$\frac{1}{2}$	6
Baldwin	1923–24	7	1	..	1	9	$\frac{2}{3}$	14
MacDonald	1924	4	..	..	1	5	$\frac{3}{4}$	7
Baldwin	1924–29	37	5	..	10	52	$4\frac{1}{2}$	12
MacDonald	1929–31	18	2	..	..	20	$2\frac{1}{4}$	9
MacDonald	1931–35	43	1	..	6	50	$3\frac{3}{4}$	13
Baldwin	1935–37	27	2	..	5	34	2	17
Chamberlain	1937–40	18	2	..	4	24	3	8
Churchill	1940–45	60	2	..	9	71	$5\frac{1}{4}$	14
Attlee	1945–51	75	11	..	8	94	$6\frac{1}{4}$	15
Churchill	1951–55	31	2	..	6	39	$3\frac{1}{2}$	11
Eden	1955–57	19	..	..	3	22	$1\frac{3}{4}$	13
Macmillan	1957–63	42	9	47	6	14	6	7
Douglas-Home	1963–64	14	1	16	1	32	1	32
Wilson	1964–70	6	2	152	1	161	$5\frac{3}{4}$	38
Heath	1970–74	..	4	30	..	34	$3\frac{1}{2}$	10

[a] These figures can be misleading as dissolution honours created by an outgoing ministry fall, in fact, into the following ministry. E.g., of H. Wilson's new creations 6 were those of Sir A. Douglas-Home.
[b] New Creations only.

Party Strengths in the House of Lords 1900–38

Year	Con.	Lib. U.	Lib.	Lab.	Irish Nat.	Not stated (inc. Bishops)	Minors	Total
1 Dec 00	354	111	69	..	1	39	15	589
31 Mar 16	360	107	93	..	1	51	11	623
10 Feb 20	491	..	130	1	1	67	26	716
31 Dec 30	489	..	79	17	..	140	27	753
31 Oct 38	519	23	55	13	..	141	24	785

SOURCE.—*Constitutional Year Book.*

Since 1945 *Vacher's Parliamentary Companion*, which has always been more sparing in giving party labels, suggests that in 1945 there were 400 Conservatives, 63 Liberals and 16 Labour among the 769 adult peers. For Aug 1955 the figures were Conservative 507, Liberal 42 and Labour 55 (out of 855). The most reliable recent information on party membership comes from the 1968 White Paper on House of Lords Reform.

Attendance at the House of Lords

by those who were members on 1 Aug 68 for the period 31 Oct 67 to 1 Aug 68

Party	Peers who attended more than 33⅓% ('working House')			Peers who attended more than 5% but less than 33⅓%			Peers who attended up to 5%			Peers who did not attend[a]			Totals		
	C	S	Total	C	S	Total	C	S	Total	C	S	Total	C	S	Total
Labour	81	14	95	8	5	13	4	1	5	2	1	3	95	21	116
Conservative	38	87	125	24	86	110	9	70	79	6	31	37	77	274	351
Liberal	8	11	19	2	6	8	2	8	10	1	3	4	13	28	41
Peers not in receipt of a party whip	26	26	52	61	24	85	22	56	78	32	307	339	141	413	554
Total	153	138	291	95	121	216	37	135	172	41	342	383	326	736	1,062

C= Created peers.   S = Peers by succession.   Attendance at committees of the House (other than the Apellate Committee) has been taken into account.
[a] Including 192 peers with leave of absence; 81 peers without writs of summons.

SOURCES.—*House of Lords Reform* (Cmnd. 3799/1968).

Party Organisation in the House of Lords

Since the early 1920s there has been an Association of Independent Unionist Peers, meeting weekly, much on the lines of the 1922 Committee. From 1945 to 1974 Liberal peers held their weekly meetings jointly with Liberal M.P.s. Labour peers are entitled to attend the meetings of the Parliamentary Labour Party, but since the 1930s they have also had their own weekly meetings.

House of Lords Sittings

Since 1945 the number and length of sitting days has increased, and the number of Peers attending the House each day has also continued to grow. About 200 Peers have applied each Session for leave of absence since the scheme was introduced in 1958 but, as an applicant may subsequently change his mind, the records are of little practical value.

Year	Number of Sittings	Sitting time to nearest ¼ hour	Membership	Average daily attendance	Leave of absence
1905	83	..	594	75	..
1910	85	..	623	..	..
1920	111	..	716	..	..
1930	104	..	758	109	..
1948–49	139	..	843	105	..
1955–56	136	3½	876	104	..
1961–62	115	4¼	644	143	214
1967–68	139	5¾	778	225	200
1970–71	141	6½	805	265	190

House of Lords Business

Proceedings in the Lords are not strictly comparable to those of the Commons (starred questions, for example, are limited to four a day with unlimited supplementaries) and it is less usual for the House to divide. However, the records (not available before 1953) show that after about 1960 business has become heavier (and divisions more frequent) partly as a result of a deliberate effort to introduce more government legislation into the Lords as first House.

Year	Starred Qs.	Q. Written Answer	Public Bills introduced in House of Lords	Divisions
1953–54	165* put up to 3 a day	..	7	32
1954–55	53	..	5	7
1955–56	203	..	5	26
1956–57	209	..	3	32
1957–58	184	..	3	19
1958–59	244* put up to 4 a day	..	6	26
1959–60	264	..	11	16
1960–61	290	..	9	48
1961–62	275	72	8	47
1962–63	297	84	11	158
1963–64	340	77	14	25
1964–65	370	73	5	34
1965–66	161	33	7	16
1966–67	660	96	18	85
1967–68	437	92	14	72
1968–69	363	92	9	47
1969–70	287	108	12	18
1970–71	511	283	13	196
1971–72	494	315	15	171
1972–73	460	281	32	73
1973–74	139	92	44	19

Main landmarks in the Reform of the House of Lords, 1900–

In 1900 the legislative powers of the two Houses were in theory equal, with the exception that the privileges of the House of Commons in relation to financial measures should be initiated in that House.

1908 *Rosebery Committee's Report.* The House approved the following principal recommendations:

(1) That a strong and efficient second Chamber was necessary for the balance of Parliament;

(2) That this objective should be achieved by the reform and reconstitution of the House of Lords;

(3) That, as a necessary preliminary to reform, it should be accepted that the possession of a peerage should no longer of itself entail the right to sit and vote in the House.

No action was taken to implement these recommendations.

1911 *Parliament Act.* Provided that—

(1) Bills certified by the Speaker of the House of Commons as Money Bills were to receive the Royal Assent one month after being sent to the House of Lords, even without the consent of the latter House; and

(2) any other Public Bill (except one for extending the life of a Parliament) passed by the House of Commons in three successive Sessions and rejected by the House of Lords was nevertheless to

receive the Royal Assent, provided that 2 years had elapsed between the second reading in the first session and the third reading in the third session of the House of Commons.

1918 *Bryce Report.* Recommended that the differences between the 2 Houses should be settled by some means of joint consultation. Proposed that the House should consist of two elements. (i) 246 members elected by members of the House of Commons arranged in geographical areas and voting by Proportional Representation with a single transferable vote. (ii) 80 peers to be elected for a period of 12 years by a joint Committee of both Houses of Parliament on which all parties should be represented. No action was taken to implement this Report.

1946 *Travelling Expenses.* Agreed that regular attenders at the House of Lords should be reimbursed for their travelling expenses. In practice made to apply to peers attending at least one-third of the sittings of the House.

1948 *Agreed Statement of Party Leaders.* A statement of nine principles agreed to but not acted upon. The most important of these were:
 (1) The second Chamber should be complementary to and not a rival to the lower House, and
 (2) The revised constitution of the House of Lords should be such as to secure as far as practicable that a permanent majority was not assured for any one political party.

1948 *Criminal Justice Act.* Privileges of Peers in Criminal Proceedings abolished.

1949 *Parliament Act.* Reduced the delaying powers of the House to two sessions and one year.

1956 *Swinton Committee Report.* Recommended provision of official Leave of Absence. This was put into effect in 1958. There are normally about 200 members of the House who have Leave of Absence at any one time.

1957 *Expenses.* Provision made for Peers to claim a maximum of three guineas a day for expenses incurred in attendance at the House. This was in addition to travelling expenses and claims were not subject to any minimum number of attendances.

1958 *Life Peerages Act.* Provided for the creation by the Sovereign, on the advice of the Prime Minister, of Life Peers and Peeresses. Women were thus for the first time enabled to become Members of the House of Lords. One of the objectives of this Act was to provide more balance of parliamentary representation in the House of Lords. This is achieved by the convention enabling recommendations for Life Peerages made by Opposition party leaders to be conveyed to the Queen through the agency of the Prime Minister.

1963 *Peerage Act.* Provided for—
 (1) the option for Peers to disclaim within one year (one month in the case of Members of the House of Commons) their peerages

for life without such a disclaimer affecting the subsequent devolution of the peerage; [1]

(2) the abolition of elections for Scottish Representative Peers and
the admission of all Scottish Peers to membership of the House;

(3) the removal from Irish Peers of certain disabilities relating to
their voting and candidature at parliamentary elections;

(4) the admission of all female holders of hereditary peerages to
membership of the House of Lords.

1964 *Expenses.* Provision made for increasing the maximum expenses to
which Peers were entitled from three guineas to four-and-a-half
guineas per day (increased to £6 10s. in 1969 and to £8.50 in 1972).

1967–9 The Government announced their intention of introducing legislation to reform the House of Lords and an all-party committee was
established. Formal discussions were broken off after the Lords'
rejection of the Southern Rhodesia Sanctions order in Jun 1968 and
the Government introduced their own Parliament (No. 2) Bill dealing
with both powers and composition. Though the Peers themselves
approved of the proposals, the Government bowed to backbench
pressure in the Commons and the Bill was dropped in Apr 1970.

[1] These peers have in fact disclaimed their titles.

1963	Vt Stansgate (A. Wedgwood Benn)
	Ld Altrincham (J. Grigg)
	E of Home (Sir A. Douglas-Home) — re-ennobled 1974
	Vt Hailsham (Q. Hogg) — re-ennobled 1970
1964	Ld Southampton (E. Fitzroy)
	Ld Monkswell (W. Collier)
	Ld Beaverbrook (Sir M. Aitken)
	E of Sandwich (V. Montagu)
1966	Ld Fraser of Allander (Sir H. Fraser)
1970	E of Durham (A. Lambton)
1971	Ld Reith (C. Reith)
1973	Ld Silkin (A. Silkin)

SOURCES.—1908 (H.L. 234), *Select Committee Report on the House of Lords*; Cd. 9038/1918, *The Reform of the Second Chamber* (Conference: Vt Bryce); Cmd. 7380/1948, *Report of the Inter Party Conference on the Parliament Bill*; H.M.S.O. (24 Jan 56), *Report of the Select Committee on the Power of the House in Relation to the Attendance of its Members*; Cmnd. 3779/1968, *House of Lords Reform*; P. A. Bromhead, *The House of Lords and Contemporary Politics, 1911–1957* (1958); Sir I. Jennings, *Parliament* (2nd ed., 1957); *10th Report of House of Lords Select Committee on Procedure* (Aug 1971); *The House of Lords and the Labour Government, 1964–70*, J. P. Morgan (1975).

IV

ELECTIONS

General Election Statistics

IT is impossible to present election statistics in any finally authoritative way. British law makes no acknowledgement of the existence of political parties, and in most general elections the precise allegiance of at least a few of the candidates is in doubt. This, far more than arithmetic error, explains the discrepancies between the figures provided in various works of reference.

Such discrepancies, however, are seldom on a serious scale (except, perhaps, for 1918). Election figures suffer much more from being inherently confusing than from being inaccurately reported. The complications that arise from unopposed returns, from plural voting, from two-member seats, and, above all, from variations in the number of candidates put up by each party are the really serious hazards in psephological interpretation.

In the figures which follow an attempt is made to allow for these factors by a column which shows the average vote won by each opposed candidate (with the vote in two-member seats halved, and with University seats excluded). This still gives a distorted picture, especially when, as in 1900 or 1931, there were many unopposed candidates or when, as in 1929, 1931, or 1950 there was a sharp change in the number of Liberals standing; in 1918 the situation was so complicated that any such statistics are omitted, as they are likely to confuse more than to clarify; for other elections they should be regarded as corrective supplements to the cruder percentages in the previous column rather than as substitutes for them.

The turn-out percentages are modified to allow for the distorting effect of the two-member seats which existed up to 1950.

To simplify classification, some arbitrary decisions have been made. Before 1918 candidates have been classified as Conservative, Liberal, or Irish Nationalist, even if their designation had a prefix such as Tariff Reform or Independent, but only officially sponsored candidates are classed as Labour. From 1918 onwards candidates not officially recognised by their party have been classified with 'Others' (except that in 1935 Ind. Lib. are placed with Lib.). Liberal Unionists have been listed as Conservatives throughout. Liberal National, National Labour, and National candidates are listed with Conservatives except in 1931.

	Total Votes	M.P.s Elected	Candidates	Unopposed Returns	% Share of Total Vote	Average % Vote per Opposed Candidate
1900. 28 Sep–24 Oct						
Conservative	1,797,444	402	579	163	51·1	52·5
Liberal	1,568,141	184	406	22	44·6	48·2
Labour	63,304	2	15	..	1·8	26·6
Irish Nationalist	90,076	82	100	58	2·5	80·0
Others	544	..	2	..	0·0	2·2
Elec. 6,730,935 Turnout 74·6%	3,519,509	670	1,102	243	100·0	..
1906. 12 Jan–7 Feb						
Conservative	2,451,454	157	574	13	43·6	44·1
Liberal	2,757,883	400	539	27	49·0	52·6
Labour	329,748	30	51	..	5·9	39·9
Irish Nationalist	35,031	83	87	74	0·6	63·1
Others	52,387	..	22	..	0·9	18·8
Elec. 7,264,608 Turnout 82·6%	5,626,503	670	1,273	114	100·0	..
1910. 14 Jan–9 Feb						
Conservative	3,127,887	273	600	19	46·9	47·5
Liberal	2,880,581	275	516	1	43·2	49·2
Labour	505,657	40	78	..	7·6	38·4
Irish Nationalist	124,586	82	104	55	1·9	77·7
Others	28,693	..	17	..	0·4	15·4
Elec. 7,694,741 Turnout 86·6%	6,667,404	670	1,315	75	100·0	..
1910. 2–19 Dec						
Conservative	2,420,566	272	550	72	46·3	47·9
Liberal	2,295,888	272	467	35	43·9	49·5
Labour	371,772	42	56	3	7·1	42·8
Irish Nationalist	131,375	84	106	53	2·5	81·9
Others	8,768	..	11	..	0·2	9·1
Elec. 7,709,981 Turnout 81·1%	5,228,369	670	1,190	163	100·0	..
1918. Sat., 14 Dec [1]						
Coalition Unionist	3,504,198	335	374	42	32·6	
Coalition Liberal	1,455,640	133	158	27	13·5	
Coalition Labour	161,521	10	18	..	1·5	
(Coalition)	(5,121,359)	(478)	(550)	(69)	(47·6)	
Conservative	370,375	23	37	..	3·4	
Irish Unionist	292,722	25	38	..	2·7	
Liberal	1,298,808	28	253	..	12·1	
Labour	2,385,472	63	388	12	22·2	
Irish Nationalist	238,477	7	60	1	2·2	
Sinn Fein	486,867	73	102	25	4·5	
Others	572,503	10	197	..	5·3	
Elec. 21,392,322 Turnout 58·9%	10,766,583	707	1,625	107	100·0	

[1] Result announced 28 Dec 1918.

General Election Results, 1922–1931

	Total Votes	M.P.s Elected	Candidates	Unopposed Returns	% Share of Total Vote	Average % Vote per Opposed Candidate
1922. Wed., 15 Nov						
Conservative	5,500,382	345	483	42	38·2	48·6
National Liberal	1,673,240	62	162	5	11·6	39·3
Liberal	2,516,287	54	328	5	17·5	30·9
Labour	4,241,383	142	411	4	29·5	40·0
Others	462,340	12	59	1	3·2	28·3
Elec. 21,127,663	14,393,632	615	1,443	57	100·0	··
Turnout 71·3%						
1923. Thu., 6 Dec						
Conservative	5,538,824	258	540	35	38·1	42·6
Liberal	4,311,147	159	453	11	29·6	37·8
Labour	4,438,508	191	422	3	30·5	41·0
Others	260,042	7	31	1	1·8	27·6
Elec. 21,281,232	14,548,521	615	1,446	50	100·0	··
Turnout 70·8%						
1924. Wed., 29 Oct						
Conservative	8,039,598	419	552	16	48·3	51·9
Liberal	2,928,747	40	340	6	17·6	30·9
Labour	5,489,077	151	512	9	33·0	38·2
Communist	55,346	1	8	··	0·3	25·0
Others	126,511	4	16	1	0·8	29·1
Elec. 21,731,320	16,639,279	615	1,428	32	100·0	··
Turnout 76·6%						
1929. Thu., 30 May						
Conservative	8,656,473	260	590	4	38·2	39·4
Liberal	5,308,510	59	513	··	23·4	27·7
Labour	8,389,512	288	571	··	37·1	39·3
Communist	50,614	··	25	··	0·3	5·3
Others	243,266	8	31	3	1·0	21·2
Elec. 28,850,870	22,648,375	615	1,730	7	100·0	··
Turnout 76·1%						
1931. Tue., 27 Oct						
Conservative	11,978,745	473	523	56	55·2⎫	62·9
National Labour	341,370	13	20	··	1·6⎪	
Liberal National	809,302	35	41	··	3·7⎭	
Liberal	1,403,102	33	112	5	6·5	28·8
(National Government)	(14,532,519)	(554)	(696)	(61)	(67·0)	··
Independent Liberal	106,106	4	7	··	0·5	35·8
Labour	6,649,630	52	515	6	30·6	33·0
Communist	74,824	··	26	··	0·3	7·5
New Party	36,377	··	24	··	0·2	3·9
Others	256,917	5	24	··	1·2	21·9
Elec. 29,960,071	21,656,373	615	1,292	67	100·0	··
Turnout 76·3%						

	Total Votes	M.P.s Elected	Candidates	Unopposed Returns	% Share of Total Vote	Average % Vote per Opposed Candidate
1935. Thu., 14 Nov						
Conservative	11,810,158	432	585	26	53·7	54·8
Liberal	1,422,116	21	161	..	6·4	23·9
Labour	8,325,491	154	552	13	37·9	40·3
Independent Labour Party	139,577	4	17	..	0·7	22·2
Communist	27,117	1	2	..	0·1	38·0
Others	272,595	4	31	1	1·2	21·3
Elec. 31,379,050 Turnout 71·2%	21,997,054	615	1,348	40	100·0	..
1945. Thu., 5 Jul [1]						
Conservative	9,988,306	213	624	1	39·8	40·1
Liberal	2,248,226	12	306	..	9·0	18·6
Labour	11,995,152	393	604	2	47·8	50·4
Communist	102,780	2	21	..	0·4	12·7
Common Wealth	110,634	1	23	..	0·4	12·6
Others	640,880	19	104	..	2·0	15·4
Elec. 33,240,391 Turnout 72·7%	25,085,978	640	1,682	3	100·0	..
1950. Thu., 23 Feb						
Conservative	12,502,567	298	620	2	43·5	43·7
Liberal	2,621,548	9	475	..	9·1	11·8
Labour	13,266,592	315	617	..	46·1	46·7
Communist	91,746	..	100	..	0·3	2·0
Others	290,218	3	56	..	1·0	12·6
Elec. 33,269,770 Turnout 84·0%	28,772,671	625	1,868	2	100·0	..
1951. Thu., 25 Oct						
Conservative	13,717,538	321	617	4	48·0	48·6
Liberal	730,556	6	109	..	2·5	14·7
Labour	13,948,605	295	617	..	48·8	49·2
Communist	21,640	..	10	..	0·1	4·4
Others	177,329	3	23	..	0·6	16·8
Elec. 34,645,573 Turnout 82·5%	28,595,668	625	1,376	4	100·0	..
1955. Thu., 26 May						
Conservative	13,286,569	344	623	..	49·7	50·2
Liberal	722,405	6	110	..	2·7	15·1
Labour	12,404,970	277	620	..	46·4	47·3
Communist	33,144	..	17	..	0·1	4·2
Others	313,410	3	39	..	1·1	20·8
Elec. 34,858,263 Turnout 76·7%	26,760,498	630	1,409	..	100·0	..

[1] Result announced 26 July 1945

General Election Results, 1959–1970

	Total Votes	M.P.s Elected	Candi- dates	Unopposed Returns	% Share of Total Vote	Average % Vote per Opposed Candidate
1959. Thu., 8 Oct						
Conservative	13,749,830	365	625	..	49·4	49·6
Liberal	1,638,571	6	216	..	5·9	16·9
Labour	12,215,538	258	621	..	43·8	44·5
Communist	30,897	..	18	..	0·1	4·1
Plaid Cymru	77,571	..	20	..	0·3	9·0
Scottish Nat. P.	21,738	..	5	..	0·1	11·4
Others	124,64	1	31	..	0·4	11·0
Elec. 35,397,080	27,859,241	630	1,536	..	100·0	..
Turnout 78·8%						
1964. Thu., 15 Oct						
Conservative	12,001,396	304	630	..	43·4	43·4
Liberal	3,092,878	9	365	..	11·2	18·5
Labour	12,205,814	317	628	..	44·1	44·1
Communist	45,932	..	36	..	0·2	3·4
Plaid Cymru	69,507	..	23	..	0·3	8·4
Scottish Nat. P.	64,044	..	15	..	0·2	10·7
Others	168,422	..	60	..	0·6	6·4
Elec. 35,892,572	27,655,374	630	1,757	..	100·0	..
Turnout 77·1%						
1966. Thu., 31 Mar						
Conservative	11,418,433	253	629	..	41·9	41·8
Liberal	2,327,533	12	311	..	8·5	16·1
Labour	13,064,951	363	621	..	47·9	48·7
Communist	62,112	..	57	..	0·2	3·0
Plaid Cymru	61,071	..	20	..	0·2	8·7
Scottish Nat. P.	128,474	..	20	..	0·2	14·1
Others	170,569	2	31	..	0·6	8·6
Elec. 35,964,684	27,263,606	630	1,707	..	100·0	..
Turnout 75·8%						
1970. Thu., 18 Jun						
Conservative	13,145,123	330	628	..	46·4	46·5
Liberal	2,117,035	6	332	..	7·5	13·5
Labour	12,179,341	287	624	..	43·0	43·5
Communist	37,970	..	58	..	0·1	1·1
Plaid Cymru	175,016	..	36	..	0·6	11·5
Scottish Nat. P.	306,802	1	65	..	1·1	12·2
Others	383,511	6	94	..	1·4	9·1
Elec. 39,342,013	28,344,798	630	1,837	..	100·0	..
Turnout 72·0%						

General Election Results, 1974–

	Total Votes	M.P.s Elected	Candi-dates	Unopposed Returns	% Share of Total Vote	Average % Vote per Opposed Candidate
1974. Thu., 28 Feb						
Conservative	11,868,906	297	623	..	37·9	38·8
Liberal	6,063,470	14	517	..	19·3	23·6
Labour	11,639,243	301	623	..	37·1	38·0
Communist	32,741	..	44	..	0·1	1·7
Plaid Cymru	171,364	2	36	..	0·6	10·7
Scottish Nat. P.	632,032	7	70	..	2·0	21·9
National Front	76,865	..	54	..	0·3	3·2
Others (G.B.)	131,059	2	120	..	0·4	2·2
Others (N.I.)[1]	717,986	12	48	..	2·3	25·0
Elec. 39,798,899 Turnout 78·7%	31,333,226	635	2,135	..	100·0	..
1974. Thu., 10 Oct						
Conservative	10,464,817	277	623	..	35·8	36·7
Liberal	5,346,754	13	619	..	18·3	18·9
Labour	11,457,079	319	623	..	39·2	40·2
Communist	17,426	..	29	..	0·1	1·5
Plaid Cymru	166,321	3	36	..	0·6	10·8
Scottish Nat. P.	839,617	11	71	..	2·9	30·4
National Front	113,843	..	90	..	0·4	2·9
Others (G.B.)	81,227	..	118	..	0·3	1·5
Others (N.I.)[1]	702,094	12	43	..	2·4	27·9
Elec. 40,072,971 Turnout 72·8%	29,189,178	635	2,252	..	100·0	..

[1] For the 1974 elections, no candidates in Northern Ireland are included in the major party totals although it might be argued that some independent Unionists should be classed with the Conservatives and that Northern Ireland Labour candidates should be classed with Labour.

General Election Results by Regions

	1900	1906	Jan 1910	Dec 1910	1918ᵃ	1922	1923	1924	1929	1931
County of London										
Conservative	51	19	33	30	Coal.	43	29	39	24	53
Liberal	8	38	25	26	53	9	11	3	2	4
Labour	..	2	1	3	Op.	9	22	19	36	5
Others	..	..	..	..	9	1	..	1	..	..
Rest of S. England										
Conservative	123	45	107	103	Coal.	130	89	150	111	156
Liberal	32	107	46	49	149	23	48	5	18	4
Labour	..	3	2	2	Op.	9	27	10	35	5
Others	..	..	..	1	16	3	1	..	1	..
Midlands										
Conservative	60	27	49	50	Coal.	53	45	64	35	80
Liberal	27	59	31	30	67	17	17	2	5	3
Labour	1	2	8	8	Op.	17	25	21	47	4
Others	..	..	..	..	20	..	..	..	..	..
Northern England										
Conservative	98	31	45	50	Coal.	82	57	101	51	146
Liberal	55	102	86	82	121	27	48	9	10	9
Labour	..	20	22	21	Op.	60	64	59	108	15
Others	1	1	1	1	50	2	2	2	2	1
Wales										
Conservative	6	..	2	3	Coal.	6	4	9	1	11
Liberal	27	33	27	26	20	10	12	10	9	8
Labour	1	1	5	5	Op.	18	19	16	25	16
Others	..	..	..	..	15	1	..	..	..	..
Scotland										
Conservative	36	10	9	9	Coal.	13	14	36	20	57
Liberal	34	58	59	58	54	27	22	8	13	7
Labour	..	2	2	3	Op.	29	34	26	37	7
Others	..	..	..	..	17	2	1	1	1	..
Ireland										
Conservative	19	16	19	17	Coal.	10	10	12	10	10
Liberal	1	3	1	1	1	..	..	..	..	..
Labour	..	..	..	..	Op.	..	..	..	..	..
Others	81	82	81	83	100	2	2	..	2	2
Universities										
Conservative	9	9	9	9	Coal.	8	9	8	8	8
Liberal	..	..	..	..	13	3	2	3	2	2
Labour	..	..	..	..	Op.	..	..	..	..	..
Others	..	..	..	..	2	1	1	1	2	2
Totals										
Conservative	402	157	273	272	Coal.	345	258	419	260	521
Liberal	184	400	275	272	478	116	159	40	59	37
Labour	2	30	40	42	Op.	142	191	151	288	52
Others	82	83	83	84	229	12	7	5	8	5
Total seats	670	670	670	670	707	615	615	615	615	615

ᵃ In 1918 all Coalition and all non-Coalition candidates are listed together. In fact a substantial number of the 48 Conservatives who were elected without the Coupon worked with the Government. Virtually no Coupons were issued to Irish candidates but 23 of the 101 non-University seats in Ireland went to Unionists.

The heavy vertical lines indicate redistributions of seats.
Northern England includes Cheshire, Lancashire, Yorkshire, and all counties to their north.
Midlands includes Hereford, Worcs., Warwickshire, Northants, Lincs., Notts., Leics., Staffs., Salop Derbyshire.
Southern England includes the rest of England , except for the County of London.

General Election Results by Regions

	1935	1945	1950	1951	1955	1959	1964	1966	1970	Feb 1974	Oct 1974
County of London											
Conservative	39	12	12	14	15	18	10	6	9	6	6
Liberal	1	..	..	..	..	..	..	..	..	..	..
Labour	22	48	31	29	27	24	32	36	33	29	..
Others	..	2	..	..	..	..	..	..	..	..	29
Rest of S. England											
Conservative	147	88	144	153	163	171	157	134	169	172	163
Liberal	3	3	1	..	..	1	3	4	2	5	5
Labour	15	91	54	46	42	34	46	67	34	42	51
Others	..	3	..	..	1	..	..	1	1	..	..
Midlands											
Conservative	67	24	35	35	39	49	42	35	51	43	40
Liberal	1	..	..	..	..	..	..	..	..	..	..
Labour	19	64	59	59	57	47	54	61	45	54	58
Others	..	2	..	..	..	..	..	..	..	1	..
Northern England											
Conservative	106	43	61	69	75	77	53	44	63	47	44
Liberal	5	2	1	2	2	2	..	2	..	4	3
Labour	60	128	107	99	90	88	114	121	104	112	117
Others	..	..	..	..	..	..	..	..	..	1	..
Wales											
Conservative	11	4	4	6	6	7	6	3	7	8	8
Liberal	6	6	5	3	3	2	2	1	1	2	2
Labour	18	25	27	27	27	27	28	32	27	24	23
Others	..	..	..	..	..	..	..	..	1	2	3
Scotland											
Conservative	43	29	32	35	36	31	23	20	23	21	16
Liberal	3	..	2	1	1	1	4	5	3	3	3
Labour	20	27	37	35	34	38	43	46	44	40	41
Others	5	5	..	..	..	1	..	..	1	7	11
Ireland											
Conservative	10	9	10	9	10	12	12	11	8	..	..
Liberal	..	..	..	..	..	..	..	..	..	..	..
Labour	..	..	..	..	..	..	..	..	..	..	..
Others	2	3	2	3	2	..	..	1	4	12	12
Universities											
Conservative	9	4	..	..	..	..	..	..	..	..	..
Liberal	1	1	..	..	..	..	..	..	..	..	..
Labour	..	..	..	..	..	..	..	..	..	..	..
Others	2	7	..	..	..	..	..	..	..	..	..
Totals											
Conservative	432	213	298	321	344	365	304	253	330	297	277
Liberal	20	12	9	6	6	6	9	12	6	14	13
Labour	154	397	315	295	277	258	317	363	287	301	319
Others	9	22	3	3	3	1	..	2	7	23	26
Total seats	615	640	625	625	630	630	630	630	630	635	635

The heavy vertical lines indicate redistributions of seats.
Northern England includes Cheshire, Lancashire, Yorkshire, and all counties to their north.
Midlands includes Hereford, Worcs., Warwickshire, Northants, Lincs., Notts., Leics., Staffs., S p, Derby-shire.
Southern England includes the rest of England, except for the County of London.

Party Changes between Elections

The party composition of the House of Commons changes continuously partly owing to Members changing their allegiance and partly owing to by-election results. The following table shows the net change due to both causes during the life of each Parliament. (Seats vacant at dissolution are included under the last incumbent's party.)

		Con.	Lib.	Lab.	Others
1895–1900	Dissolution	399	189	..	82
1900–05	Election	402	184	2	82
	Dissolution	369	215	4	82
1906–09	Election	157	400	30	83
	Dissolution	168	373	46	83
1910	Election	273	275	40	82
	Dissolution	274	274	40	82
1910–18	Election	272	271	42	85
	Dissolution	281	260	39	90
1918–22 [a]	Election	383	161	73	90
	Dissolution	378	155	87	87
1922–23	Election	345	116	142	12
	Dissolution	344	117	144	10
1923–24	Election	258	159	191	7
	Dissolution	259	158	193	5
1924–29	Election	419	40	151	5
	Dissolution	400	46	162	7
1929–31	Election	260	59	288	8
	Dissolution	263	57	281 [b]	14
1931–35	Election	521	37	52	5
	Dissolution	512	34	59	10
1935–45	Election	432	20	154	9
	Dissolution	398	18	166	33
1945–50	Election	213	12	393	22
	Dissolution	218	10	391	21
1950–51	Election	298	9	315	3
	Dissolution	298	9	314	4
1951–55	Election	321	6	295	3
	Dissolution	322	6	294	3
1955–59	Election	344	6	277	3
	Dissolution	340	6	281	3
1959–64	Election	365	6	258	1
	Dissolution	360	7	262	2
1964–66	Election	304	9	317	..
	Dissolution	304	10	316	..
1966	Election	253	12	363	2
	Dissolution	264	13	346	7

[a] In this form the 1918–22 figures are highly misleading. This amplification may help:

	Co. U.	Con.	Co. Lib.	Lib.	Co. Lab.	Lab.	O.
Election . .	335	48	133	28	10	63	90
Dissolution . .	313	65	120	35	11	76	87

[b] This figure includes 15 National Labour M.P.s.

Party Changes between Elections (*contd.*)

		Con.	Lib.	Lab.	Others
1970	Election	330	6	287	7
	Dissolution	323	11	287	9
1974 Feb	Election	297	14	301	23
	Dissolution	297	15	300	23
1974 Oct	Election	277	13	319	26

M.P.s' Changes of Allegiance

The difficulties in compiling an exact and comprehensive list of all floor-crossings, Whip withdrawals, Whip resignations, and Whip restorations are enormous. The list which follows is probably fairly complete as far as floor crossings go (except for 1918–22) but it certainly omits a number of Members who relinquished the Whip for a time. It also omits cases of M.P.s who stood without official party support in their constituencies but who remained in good standing with the Whips and some cases of M.P.s taking the Whip immediately before a General Election (as happened with several Members in 1918 and a few in 1945) or immediately after a General Election (as happened with the Lloyd George Group in 1935). No attempt has been made to record shifts between the various factions of Irish Nationalism. Throughout this list the test, in so far as it can be applied, is whether the M.P. was officially in receipt of the weekly documentary Whip.

Parliament of 1900–05

			from	to	
Nov 02	J. Wason	Orkney & Shetland	L.U.	Ind.	Won by-el Nov 02 took Lib. Whip by 05
Apr 03	J. W. Wilson	N. Worcs.	L.U.	Lib.	
Apr 03	Sir M. Foster	London Univ.	L.U.	Lib.	
Jan 04	W. Churchill	Oldham	Con.	Ind.	Con. Whip restored after 2 weeks; Lib. Whip taken Apr 04
Jan 04	Sir J. Dickson-Poynder	Chippenham	Con.	Ind.	
Feb 04	T. Russell	S. Tyrone	L.U.	Lib.	
Feb 04	J. Wilson	Falkirk Burghs	L.U.	Lib.	
Mar 04	J. Seely	I. of Wight	Con.	Ind.	Won by-el Apr 04 unop.; took Lib. Whip May 04
Apr 04	I. Guest	Plymouth	Con.	Lib.	
Aug 04	E. Hain	St Ives	L.U.	Lib.	
Aug 04	G. Kemp	Heywood	L.U.	Lib.	
Jul 04	J. Jameson	W. Clare	I. Nat.	Con.	
Nov 04	R. Rigg	Appleby	Lib.	Ind.	Resigned seat Dec 04
Mar 05	E. Mitchell	N. Fermanagh	Ind.C.	Lib.	
Mar 05	J. Wood	E. Down	L.U.	Lib.	
Mar 05	E. Hatch	Gorton	Con.	Ind.	
Mar 05	Sir E. Reed	Cardiff D.	Lib.	L.U.	

Parliament of 1906–09

			from	to	
Feb. 06	J. W. Taylor	Chester-le-Street	Lib.	Lab.	
Feb 06	A. Taylor	E. Toxteth	Con.	Lib.	
Feb 07	R. Hunt	Ludlow	Con.	—	Whip withdrawn. Whip restored Mar 07.
Nov 07	L. Renton	Gainsborough	Lib.	Con.	
Aug 08	A. Corbett	Tradeston	L.U.	Ind.	
Mar 09	T. Kincaid Smith	Stratford-on-Avon	Lib.	Ind.	Lost by-el May 09
May 09	A. Cross	Camlachie	L.U.	Lib.	
Oct 09	C. Bellairs	King's Lynn	Lib.	L.U.	

				from	to	

Parliament of 1910

Nov 10	Sir J. Rees	Montgomery D.	Lib.	L.U.

Parliament of 1911–18

Jan	14	D. Mason	Coventry	Lib.	Ind.	
Feb	14	B. Kenyon	Chesterfield	Lab.	Lib.	Introduced as new M.P. by Lab. but resigned Whip after 2 weeks
Apr	14	W. Johnson	Nuneaton	Lab.	Lib.	Lab. Whip withdrawn
Apr	15	J. Hancock	Mid-Derbyshire	Lab.	Lib.	Lab. Whip withdrawn
Sep	17	H. Page Croft	Christchurch	Con.	Nat.P.	
Sep	17	Sir R. Cooper	Walsall	Con.	Nat.P.	
Jul	18	E. John	E. Denbigh	Lib.	Lab.	
Jul	18	J. Martin	St. Pancras E.	Lib.	Lab.	

In Nov 18 a number of Liberals became Independent or Labour and some Labour members accepted the label Coalition Labour or Coalition National Democratic Party shortly before the dissolution of Parliament.

Parliament of 1919-22

Throughout this parliament the confusion of party labels and the movements within and between the Coalition and non-Coalition wings of each party make it impossible to attempt any comprehensive listing of all switches. The following changes were, however, more clear cut.

Apr	19	J. Wedgwood	Newcastle-under-Lyme	Co.Lib.	Lab.	Lab. Whip granted May 19
Oct	19	E. Hallas	Duddeston	Co. N.D.P.	Lab.	
Nov	19	C. Malone	Leyton E.	Co.Lib.	Ind.	Joined Communist party Jul 20
Oct	20	O. Mosley	Harrow	Co.Con.	Ind.	
Oct	20	Sir O. Thomas	Anglesey	Lab.	Ind.	
Feb	22	A. Hopkinson	Mossley	Co.Lib.	Ind.	

Parliament of 1922-23

Jul	23	A. Evans	Leicester E.	N.Lib.	Con.
Oct	23	G. Roberts	Norwich	Ind.	Con.

Parliament of 1923-24

Feb	24	G. Davies	Welsh Univ.	Ind.	Lab.
May	24	O. Mosley	Harrow	Ind.	Lab.

Parliament of 1924-29 [1]

Jan	26	Sir A. Mond	Carmarthen	Lib.	Con.	Made peer Jun 28
Feb	26	E. Hilton Young	Norwich	Lib.	Ind.	Took Con. Whip May 26
Oct	26	J. Kenworthy	Hull C.	Lib.	Lab.	Won by-el Nov 26
Nov	26	D. Davies	Montgomery	Lib.	Ind.	
Feb	27	G. Spencer	Broxtowe	Lab.	Ind.	Expelled from party
Feb	27	W. Benn	Leith	Lib	Ind.	Resigned seat Feb 27
Feb	27	L. Haden Guest	Southwark N.	Lab.	Ind.	Lost by-el Mar 27
Oct	27	Sir R. Newman	Exeter	Con.	Ind.	
Jul	28	Sir B. Peto	Barnstaple	Con.	—	Whip withdrawn; restored Nov 28

[1] The 7 members, all former Liberal M.P.s, elected under the label 'Constitutional' never acted as a group. Two, W. Churchill and Sir H. Greenwood took the Conservative whip from the start and one, A. Moreing, later. Three reverted during the Parliament to their former Liberalism, J. Edwards, A. England, and J. Ward. One, Sir T. Robinson, became an Independent.

Parliament of 1929-31

Jun	29	Sir W. Jowitt	Preston	Lib.	Lab.	Won by-el Jun 29
Feb	31	Sir O. Mosley	Smethwick	Lab.	N.P.	
Feb	31	Lady C. Mosley	Stoke	Lab.	N.P.	
Feb	31	R. Forgan	W. Renfrew	Lab.	N.P.	
Feb	31	W. Allen	Belfast W.	Con.	N.P.	
Feb	31	C. R. Dudgeon	Galloway	Lib.	N.P.	
Feb	31	J. Strachey	Aston	Lab.	N.P.	Became Ind. Jun 31

			from	to	
Feb 31	O. Baldwin	Dudley	Lab.	Ind.	
Feb 31	W. Brown	Wolverhampton W.	Lab.	Ind.	
Mar 31	Sir W. Wayland	Canterbury	Con.	—	Whip withdrawn; restored Apr 31
Jun 31	E. Brown	Leith	Lib.	Ind.⎫	
Jun 31	Sir R. Hutchison	Montrose	Lib.	Ind.⎬ Became L.Nat. Oct 31	
Jun 31	Sir J. Simon	Spen Valley	Lib.	Ind.⎭	

In Oct 31 23 Liberal Members broke with the party to form the Liberal National Group. A further 6 Liberals, most notably the Lloyd George family, became Independent Liberals. 15 Labour members under R. MacDonald formed the National Labour Group.

Parliament of 1931-35

			from	to	
Nov 31	G. Buchanan	Gorbals	Lab.	ILP.	
Nov 31	J. McGovern	Shettleston	Lab.	ILP.	
Nov 31	J. Maxton	Bridgeton	Lab.	ILP.	
Nov 31	D. Kirkwood	Dumbarton	Lab.	ILP.	Returned to Lab. Aug 33
Nov 31	R. Wallhead	Merthyr	Lab.	ILP.	Returned to Lab. Sep 33
Dec 32	A. Curry	Bishop Auckland	L.Nat.	Lib.	
Dec 32	F. Llewellyn Jones	Flint	L.Nat.	Lib.	
Feb 33	H. Nathan	Bethnal Green N.E.	Ind.L.	Ind.	Took Lab. Whip Jun 34
Jun 34	J. Hunter	Dumfries	Lib.	L.Nat.	
Jun 34	J. Lockwood	Shipley	Con.	Ind.	
May 35	F. Astbury	Salford W.	Con.	Ind.⎫	
May 35	L. Thorp	Nelson & Colne	Con.	Ind.⎬	
May 35	A. Todd	Berwick-on-Tweed	Con.	Ind.⎭	
May 35	Duchess of Atholl	Kinross E. & Perth	Con.	Ind.	Whip restored Sep 35
May 35	Sir J. Nall	Hulme	Con.	Ind.	Whip restored Nov 35
Early 35	G. Morrison	Scottish Univ.	Lib.	L.Nat.	

Parliament of 1935-45

			from	to	
Jun 36	H. Macmillan	Stockton-on-Tees	Con.	Ind.	Whip restored Jul 37
Sep 36	R. Bernays	Bristol N.	Lib.	L.Nat.	
Apr 38	Duchess of Atholl	Kinross & W. Perth	Con.	Ind.	Lost by-el Dec 38
Oct 38	H. Holdsworth	Bradford S.	Lib.	L.Nat.	
Nov 38	A. Hopkinson	Mossley	Nat.	Ind.	
Jan 39	Sir S. Cripps	Bristol E.	Lab.	—	Expelled from party; Whip restored Feb 45
Mar 39	A. Bevan	Ebbw Vale	Lab.	—	Expelled from party; Whip restored Dec 39
Mar 39	G. Strauss	Lambeth N.	Lab.	—	Expelled from party; Whip restored Feb 40
May 39	G. Buchanan	Gorbals	ILP.	Lab.	
Dec 39	C. Davies	Montgomery	L.Nat.	Ind.	Took Lib. Whip Aug 42
Mar 40	D. Pritt	Hammersmith N.	Lab.	—	Expelled from party
May 40	A. Ramsay	Peebles & S.	Con.	Ind.	Detained until Dec 44
Feb 42	E. Granville	Eye	L.Nat.	Ind.	Took Lib. Whip Apr 45
Feb 42	Sir M. Macdonald	Inverness	L.Nat.	Ind.	Whip restored by 45
Feb 42	L. Hore-Belisha	Devonport	L.Nat.	Ind.	
Feb 42	S. King-Hall	Ormskirk	N.Lab.	Ind.	
Feb 42	Sir H. Morris-Jones	Denbigh	L.Nat.	Ind.	Whip restored May 43
Feb 42	K. Lindsay	Kilmarnock	N.Lab.	Ind.	
May 42	C. Cunningham-Reid	St Marylebone	Con.	—	Whip withdrawn
Sep 42	Sir R. Acland	Barnstaple	Lib.	C.W.	
Mar 43	A. Maclaren	Burslem	Lab.	Ind.	
Nov 44	J. Loverseed	Eddisbury	C.W.	Ind.	Took Lab. Whip May 45
Jan 45	T. Driberg	Maldon	Ind.	Lab.	
May 45	D. Little	Down	U.U.	Ind.	
May 45	C. White	W. Derbyshire	Ind.	Lab.	

Parliament of 1945-50

			from	to	
Apr 46	E. Millington	Chelmsford	C.W.	Lab.	
Oct 46	T. Horabin	N. Cornwall	Lib.	Ind.	Took Lab. Whip Nov 47
Mar 47	J. McGovern	Shettleston	ILP.	Lab.	

			from	to	
Jul 47	C. Stephen	Camlachie	ILP.	Ind.	Took Lab. Whip Oct 47
Oct 47	J. Carmichael	Bridgeton	ILP.	Ind.	Took Lab. Whip Nov 47
Nov 47	E. Walkden	Doncaster	Lab.	Ind.	
Mar 48	J. McKie	Galloway	Ind.Con.	Con.	
Apr 48	J. Platts-Mills	Finsbury	Lab.	—	Expelled from party
May 48	A. Edwards	Middlesbrough	Lab.	—	Expelled from party, took Con. Whip Aug 49
Oct 48	I. Bulmer-Thomas	Keighley	Lab.	Ind.	Took Con. Whip Jan 49
Nov 48	E. Gander Dower	Caithness & Sutherland	Con.	Ind.	
May 49	L. Solley	Thurrock	Lab.	—	Expelled from party
May 49	K. Zilliacus	Gateshead	Lab.	—	Expelled from party
Jul 49	L. Hutchinson	Rusholme	Lab.	—	Expelled from party

Parliament 1950-51

Aug 50	R. Blackburn	Northfield	Lab.	Ind.	

Parliament of 1951-55

Jun 54	Sir J. Mellor	Sutton Coldfield	Con.	Ind.	Whip restored Jul 54
Jul 54	H. Legge-Bourke	Isle of Ely	Con.	Ind.	Whip restored Oct 54
Nov 54	G. Craddock	Bradford S.	Lab.	—	
Nov 54	S. Davies	Merthyr	Lab.	—	
Nov 54	E. Fernyhough	Jarrow	Lab.	—	Whip withdrawn; restored Feb 55
Nov 54	E. Hughes	S. Ayrshire	Lab.	—	
Nov 54	S. Silverman	Nelson & Colne	Lab.	—	
Nov 54	V. Yates	Ladywood	Lab.	—	
Nov 54	J. McGovern	Shettleston	Lab.	—	Whip withdrawn; restored Mar 55
Mar 55	A. Bevan	Ebbw Vale	Lab.	—	Whip withdrawn; restored Apr 55
Mar 55	Sir R. Acland	Gravesend	Lab.	Ind.	Resigned seat to fight by-el; expelled from party

Parliament of 1955-59

Nov 56	C. Banks	Pudsey	Con.	Ind.	Whip restored Dec 58
May 57	P. Maitland	Lanark	Con.	Ind.	Whip restored Dec 57
May 57	Sir V. Raikes	Garston	Con.	Ind.	Resigned seat Oct 57
May 57	A. Maude	Ealing S.	Con.	Ind.	Resigned seat Apr 58
May 57	J. Biggs-Davison	Chigwell	Con.	Ind.	
May 57	A. Fell	Yarmouth	Con.	Ind.	
May 57	Vt Hinchingbrooke	S. Dorset	Con.	Ind.	Whip restored Jul 58
May 57	L. Turner	Oxford	Con.	Ind.	
May 57	P. Williams	Sunderland S.	Con.	Ind.	
Nov 57	Sir F. Medlicott	C. Norfolk	Con.	Ind.	Whip restored Nov 58
Jan 59	Sir D. Robertson	Caithness & Sutherland	Con.	Ind.	

Parliament of 1959-64

Mar 61	A. Brown	Tottenham	Lab.	Ind.	Took Con. Whip May 62
Mar 61	W. Baxter	W. Stirlingshire	Lab.	—	
Mar 61	S. Davies	Merthyr	Lab.	—	
Mar 61	M. Foot	Ebbw Vale	Lab.	—	Whip withdrawn; restored May 63
Mar 61	E. Hughes	S. Ayrshire	Lab.	—	
Mar 61	S. Silverman	Nelson & Colne	Lab.	—	
Mar 61	K. Zilliacus	Gorton	Lab.	—	Whip suspended; party membership restored Jan 62
Oct 61	Sir W. Duthie	Banff	Con.	Ind.	Whip restored Nov 63
Jan 64	D. Johnson	Carlisle	Con.	Ind.	

Parliament of 1964-66   [None]

Parliament of 1966-

				from	to	
Jul	66	G. Hirst	Shipley	Con.	Ind.	
Dec	66	R. Paget	Northampton	Lab.	Ind.	Whip restored Jun 67
Jan	68	D. Donnelly	Pembroke	Lab.	Ind.	Expelled from party Mar 68
Feb	68	24 M.P.s		Lab.	—	Whip suspended for one month

Parliament of 1970-74

				from	to	
Aug	66	G. Fitt	Belfast W.	Rep.Lab.SDLP.		Expelled by Rep. Lab.
Oct	71	I. Paisley	N. Antrim	Prot.U.	Dem.U.	
Oct	72	D. Taverne	Lincoln	Lab.	Dem.Lab.	Won by-el Mar 73
Dec	72	S. Mills	Belfast N.	U.U.	Con.	Joined Alliance Party Apr 73

Parliament of 1974

Jul	74	C. Mayhew	Woolwich W.	Lab.	Lib.	

SOURCE.—For details of changes of allegiance in 1945-66 see R. J. Jackson, *Whips and Rebels* (1968).

In addition to the floor crossings recorded above there are the following instances of ex-M.P.s, after an interval out of parliament, returning to the House under a designation basically different from the ones under which they had previously sat.

(Sir) R. Acland	Lib. 35–42 C.W. 42–45 Lab. 47–55
C. Addison	Lib. 10–22 Lab. 29–31, 34–35
P. Alden	Lib. 06–18 Lab. 23–24
W. Allen	Lib. 92–00 Nat. 31–35
C. Bellairs	Lib. 06–10 Con, 15–31
(Sir) A. Bennett	Lib. 22–23 Con. 24–30
(Sir) E. Bennett	Lib. 06–10 Lab. 29–31 N. Lab. 31–45
H. Bottomley	Lib. 06–12 Ind. 18–22
T. Bowles	Con. 92–05 Lib. 10–10
J. Bright	L.U. 89–95 Lib. 06–10
W. Brown	Lab. 29–31 Ind. 42–50
C. Buxton	Lib. 10–10 Lab 22–23, 29–31
N. Buxton	Lib. 05–06, 10–18 Lab. 22–24, 29–30
(Sir) W. Churchill	Con. 00–04 Lib. 04–22 Con. 24–64
(Sir) H. Cowan	Lib. 06–22 Con. 24–29
A. Crawley	Lab. 45–51 Con. 62–67
R. Denman	Lib. 10–18 Lab. 29–31 N. Lab. 31–45
(Sir) C. Entwhistle	Lib. 18–24 Con. 31–45
R. Fletcher	Lib. 23–24 Lab. 35–42
(Sir) D. Foot	Lib. 31–45 Lab. 57–70
G. Garro-Jones	Lib. 24–29 Lab. 35–47
W. Grenfell	Lib. 80–82, 85–86, 92–93 Con 00–05
Sir E. Grigg	Lib. 22–25 Con. 33–45
C. Guest	Lib. 10–18, 22–23 Con. 37–45
F. Guest	Lib. 10–22, 23–29 Con. 31–37
O. Guest	Co.Lib. 18–22 Con. 35–45
T. Harvey	Lib. 10–18, 23–24 Ind. 37–45
E. Hemmerde	Lib. 06–10, 12–18 Lab. 22–24
(Sir) B. Janner	Lib. 31–35 Lab. 45–70
E. King	Lab. 45–50 Con. 64–
H. Lawson	Lib. 85–92, 93–95 L.U. 05–06, 10–16
H. Lees-Smith	Lib. 10–18 Lab. 22–31, 35–42
G. Lloyd-George	Lib. 22–24, 29–50 Con. 51–56
(Lady) M. Lloyd-George	Lib. 29–51 Lab. 57–66
E. Mallalieu	Lib. 31–35 Lab. 48–74
C. Malone	Co.Lib. 18–19 Ind. then Comm. 19–22 Lab. 28–31
(Sir) F. Markham	Lab. 29–31 N. Lab. 35–45 Con.51–64
H. Mond	Lib. 23–24 Con. 29–30
(Sir) O. Philipps	Lib. 06–10 Con. 16–22

A. Ponsonby   Lib. 08–18 Lab. 22–30
S. Saklatvala   Lab. 22–23, Comm. 24–29
Sir A. Salter   Ind. 37–50 Con. 52–54
J. Seddon   Lab. 06–10, Co.N.D.P. 18–22
(Sir) E. Spears   Lib. 22–24 Con. 31–45
G. Spero   Lib. 23–24 Lab. 29–31
C. Stephen   Lab. 22–31 I.L.P. 37–47 Lab. 47–48
(Sir) C. Trevelyan   Lib. 99–18 Lab. 22–31
J. (Havelock) Wilson   Lib. 92–00 Lab. 06–10 Co.N.D.P. 18–22

By-elections

	Total [a] By-elections	Changes	Con. +	Con. −	Lib. +	Lib. −	Lab. +	Lab. −	Others +	Others −
1900–05	113	30	2	26	20	4	5	..	5	..
1906–09	101	20	12	..	..	18	5	..	3	2
1910	20	..	..	..	..	..	..	..	..	..
1911–18	245	31	16	4	4	16	2	4	10	8
1918–22	108	27	4	13	5 [b]	11 [b]	14	1	4	2
1922–23	16	6	1	4	3	1	2	..	..	1
1923–24	10	3	2	1	..	1	1	1	..	..
1924–29	63	20	1	16	6	3	13	1	..	..
1929–31	36	7	4	1	..	1	2	4	1	1
1931–35	62	10	..	9	..	1	10	..	..	..
1935–45	219	30	..	29	..	..	13	1	17	..
1945–50	52	3	3	..	..	..	..	..	..	3
1950–51	16	..	..	..	..	..	..	..	..	..
1951–55	48	1	1	..	..	..	..	1	..	..
1955–59	52	6	1	4	1	1	4	..	..	1
1959–64	62	9	2	7	1	..	6	2	..	..
1964–66	13	2	1	1	1	..	..	1	..	..
1966–70	38	16	12	1	1	..	..	15	3	..
1970–74	30	9	..	5	5	..	2	3	2	1
1974	1	..	..	..	..	..	..	..	..	..

[a] Up to 1918, and to a lesser extent to 1926, the number of by-elections is inflated by the necessity for Ministers to stand for re-election on appointment. In 53 such cases the returns were unopposed.
[b] In 1918–22 Opposition Liberals won 5 seats and lost 2. Coalition Liberals lost 9.

Seats Changing Hands at By-elections

Date	Constituency	General Election	By-election
26 Sep 01	N.E. Lanark.	Lib.	Con.
21 Nov 01	Galway	Con.	Nat.
10 May 02	Bury	Con.	Lib.
29 Jul 02	Leeds N.	Con.	Lib.
1 Aug 02	Clitheroe	Lib.	Lab.
18 Aug 02	S. Belfast	Con.	Ind. U.
22 Oct 02	†Devonport	Lib.	Con.
19 Nov 02	Orkney & Shetland	Con.	Ind. Lib.
2 Jan 03	E. Cambs.	Con.	Lib.
1 Mar 03	Woolwich	Con.	Lab.
17 Mar 03	†E. Sussex	Con.	Lib.
20 Mar 03	†N. Fermanagh	Con.	Ind. Con.
24 Jul 03	Barnard Castle	Lib.	Lab.
26 Aug 03	Argyll	Con.	Lib.
17 Sep 03	†St. Andrews	Con.	Lib.
15 Jan 04	Norwich	Con.	Lib.
30 Jan 04	†Ayr	Con.	Lib.
12 Feb 04	†Mid-Herts.	Con.	Lib.
17 Mar 04	E. Dorset	Con.	Lib.
6 Apr 04	Isle of Wight	Con.	Ind. Con.
20 Jun 04	Devonport	{ Con. 02 / Lib. 00 }	Lib.
26 Jul 04	†W. Shropshire	Con.	Lib.
10 Aug 04	N.E. Lanark.	{ Con. 01 / Lib. 00 }	Lib.
7 Jan 05	Stalybridge	Con.	Lib.
26 Jan 05	N. Dorset	Con.	Lib.
3 Mar 05	Bute	Con.	Lib.
5 Apr 05	Brighton	Con.	Lib.
1 Jun 05	†Whitby	Con.	Lib.
29 Jun 05	Finsbury E.	Con.	Lib.
13 Oct 05	†Barkston Ash	Con.	Lib.

General Election 12 Jan–7 Feb 06

Date	Constituency	General Election	By-election
3 Aug 06	Cockermouth	Lib.	Con.
31 Dec 06	Mid-Cork	Nat.	I. Nat.
30 Jan 07	N.E. Derbyshire [a]	Lib.	Lab.
26 Feb 07	†Brigg	Lib.	Con.
4 Jul 07	†Jarrow	Lib.	Lab.
18 Jul 07	†Colne Valley	Lib.	I. Lab.
31 Jul 07	N.W. Staffs. [a]	Lib.	Lab.
17 Jan 08	†Mid-Devon	Lib.	Con.
31 Jan 08	S. Hereford	Lib.	Con.
24 Mar 08	Peckham	Lib.	Con.
24 Apr 08	†Manchester N.W.	Lib.	Con.
20 Jun 08	†Pudsey	Lib.	Con.
1 Aug 08	†Haggerston	Lib.	Con.
24 Sep 08	†Newcastle-o-T.	Lib.	Con.
2 Mar 09	Glasgow C.	Lib.	Con.
1 May 09	Cork City	Nat.	I. Nat.
4 May 09	Attercliffe	Lib.	Lab.
4 May 09	Stratford-on-Avon	Lib.	Con.
15 Jul 09	Mid-Derbyshire	Lib.	Lab.
28 Oct 09	†Bermondsey	Lib.	Con.

General Election 14 Jan–9 Feb 10
1910—no change

General Election 2–19 Dec 10

Date	Constituency	General Election	By-election
28 Apr 11	Cheltenham	Lib.	Con.
13 Nov 11	Oldham	Lib.	Con.
21 Nov 11	S. Somerset	Lib.	Con.

Date	Constituency	General Election	By-election
20 Dec 11	N. Ayrshire	Lib.	Con.
5 Mar 12	Manchester S.	Lib.	Con.
13 Jul 12	Hanley	Lab.	Lib.
26 Jul 12	Crewe	Lib.	Con.
8 Aug 12	Manchester N.W.	Lib.	Con.
10 Sep 12	Edinburghshire	Lib.	Con.
26 Nov 12	Bow & Bromley	Lab.	Con.
30 Jan 13	Londonderry	Con.	Lib.
18 Mar 13	S. Westmorland	Con.	Ind. Con.
16 May 13	E. Cambs.	Lib.	Con.
20 Aug 13	Chesterfield	Lab.	Lib.
8 Nov 13	Reading	Lib.	Con.
12 Dec 13	S. Lanarkshire	Lib.	Con.
19 Feb 14	Bethnal Green S.W.	Lib.	Con.
26 Feb 14	Leith	Lib.	Con.
20 May 14	N.E. Derbyshire	Lab.	Con.
23 May 14	Ipswich	Lib.	Con.
9 Dec 14	Tullamore	Nat.	I. Nat.
25 Nov 15	Merthyr Tydfil	Lab.	Ind.
9 Mar 16	E. Herts.	Con.	Ind.
15 Nov 16	W. Cork	I. Nat.	Nat.
23 Dec 16	†Ashton-u-Lyne	Con.	Lib. (Unop.)
3 Feb 17	N. Roscommon	Nat.	S.F.
10 May 17	S. Longford	Nat.	S.F.
10 Jul 17	E. Clare	Nat.	S.F.
10 Aug 17	Kilkenny	Nat.	S.F.
2 Nov 17	Salford N.	Lib.	Lab.
19 Apr 18	Tullamore	{ I. Nat. 14 / Nat. 10 }	S.F.
20 Jun 18	E. Cavan	Nat.	S.F.

General Election 14 Dec 18

Date	Constituency	General Election	By-election
1 Mar 19	†Leyton W.	Co. U.	Lib.
29 Mar 19	Hull C.	Co. U.	Lib.
16 Apr 19	C. Aberdeen & Kincardine	Co. U.	Lib.
27 May 19	E. Antrim	Con.	Ind. U.
16 Jul 19	Bothwell	Co. U.	Lab.
30 Aug 19	†Widnes	Co. U.	Lab.
20 Dec 19	Spen Valley	Co. Lib.	Lab.
7 Feb 20	Wrekin	Co. Lib.	Ind.
27 Mar 20	†Dartford	Co. Lib.	Lab.
27 Mar 20	Stockport	Co. Lab.	Co. U.
3 Jun 20	Louth	Co. U.	Lib.
27 Jul 20	S. Norfolk	Lib.	Lab.
12 Jan 21	†Dover	Co. U.	Ind.
2 Mar 21	†Woolwich E.	Lab.	Co. U.
3 Mar 21	†Dudley	Co. U.	Lab.
4 Mar 21	†Kirkcaldy	Co. Lib.	Lab.
5 Mar 21	Penistone	Lib.	Lab.
7 Jun 21	Westminster, St. George's	Co. U.	Ind.
16 Jun 21	Hertford	Ind.	Ind.
8 Jun 21	†Heywood & Radcliffe	Co. Lib.	Lab.
14 Dec 21	†Southwark, S.E.	Co. Lib.	Lab.
18 Feb 22	†Manchester, Clayton	Con.	Lab.
20 Feb 22	Camberwell N.	Co. U.	Lab.
24 Feb 22	Bodmin	Co. U.	Lib.
30 Mar 22	†Leicester E.	Co. Lib.	Lab.

[a] Miners candidates standing as Lib-Lab, who only joined the Labour Party in 1909.
† Seats regained at subsequent General Election.

Date	Constituency	General Election	By-election
25 Jul 22	Pontypridd	Co. Lib.	Lab.
18 Aug 22	Hackney S.	Ind.	Co. U.
18 Oct 22	Newport	Co. Lib.	Con.

General Election 15 Nov 22

Date	Constituency	General Election	By-election
3 Mar 23	†Mitcham	Con.	Lab.
3 Mar 23	Willesden E.	Con	Lib.
6 Mar 23	Liverpool, Edge Hill	Con.	Lab.
7 Apr 23	Anglesey	Ind.	Lib.
31 May 23	Berwick on Tweed	Nat. Lib.	Con.
21 Jun 23	Tiverton	Con.	Lib.

General Election 6 Dec 23

Date	Constituency	General Election	By-election
22 May 24	Liverpool, W. Toxteth	Con.	Lab.
5 Jun 24	Oxford	Lib.	Con.
31 Jul 24	Holland with Boston	Lab.	Con.

General Election 29 Oct 24

Date	Constituency	General Election	By-election
17 Sep 25	Stockport	Con.	Lab.
17 Feb 26	Darlington	Con.	Lab.
12 Mar 26	English Univs.	Lib.	Con.
29 Apr 26	East Ham N.	Con.	Lab.
28 May 26	Hammersmith N.	Con.	Lab.
29 Nov 26	Hull C.	Lib.	Lab.
23 Feb 27	Stourbridge	Con.	Lab.
28 Mar 27	†Southwark N.	Lab.	Lib.
31 May 27	Bosworth	Con.	Lib.
9 Jan 28	Northampton	Con.	Lab.
9 Feb 28	†Lancaster	Con.	Lib.
6 Mar 28	St. Ives	Con.	Lib.
4 Apr 28	Linlithgow	Con.	Lab.
13 Jul 28	Halifax	Lib.	Lab.
29 Oct 28	Ashton-u-Lyne	Con.	Lab.
29 Jan 29	†N. Midlothian	Con.	Lab.
7 Feb 29	Battersea S.	Con.	Lab.
20 Mar 29	Eddisbury	Con.	Lib.
21 Mar 29	†N. Lanark	Con.	Lab.
21 Mar 29	Holland	Con.	Lib

General Election 30 May 29

Date	Constituency	General Election	By-election
31 Jul 29	Preston	Lib.	Lab.
14 Dec 29	Liverpool, Scotland	I. Nat.	Lab. (Unop.)
6 May 30	Fulham W.	Lab.	Con.
30 Oct 30	Paddington S.	Con	Ind.
6 Nov 30	Shipley	Lab.	Con.
26 Mar 31	Sunderland	Lab.	Con.
30 Apr 31	Ashton-u-Lyne	Lab.	Con.

General Election 27 Oct 31

Date	Constituency	General Election	By-election
21 Apr 32	Wakefield	Con.	Lab.
26 Jul 32	Wednesbury	Con.	Lab.
27 Feb 33	Rotherham	Con.	Lab.
25 Oct 33	†Fulham E.	Con.	Lab.
24 Apr 34	Hammersmith N.	Con.	Lab.
14 May 34	West Ham, Upton	Con.	Lab.
23 Oct 34	Lambeth N.	Lib.	Lab.
25 Oct 34	†Swindon	Con.	Lab.
6 Feb 35	†Liverpool, Wavertree	Con.	Lab.

Date	Constituency	General Election	By-election
16 Jul 35	Liverpool, W. Toxteth	Con.	Lab.

General Election 14 Nov 35

Date	Constituency	General Election	By-election
18 Mar 36	Dunbartonshire	Con.	Lab.
6 May 36	Camberwell, Peckham	Con.	Lab.
9 Jul 36	Derby	Con.	Lab.
26 Nov 36	Greenock	Con.	Lab.
27 Feb 37	Oxford Univ.	Con.	Ind. Con.
19 Mar 37	English Univs.	Con.	Ind.
29 Apr 37	Wandsworth C.	Con.	Lab.
22 Jun 37	Cheltenham	Con.	Ind. Con.
13 Oct 37	Islington N.	Con.	Lab.
16 Feb 38	Ipswich	Con.	Lab.
6 Apr 38	Fulham W.	Con.	Lab.
5 May 38	Lichfield	Con.	Lab.
7 Nov 38	Dartford	Con.	Lab.
17 Nov 38	Bridgwater	Con.	Ind.
21 Dec 38	Kinross & W. Perth	Con. (Ind.)	Con.
17 May 39	Southwark N.	Con.	Lab.
24 May 39	Lambeth, Kennington	Con.	Lab
1 Aug 39	Brecon & Radnor	Con.	Lab.
24 Feb 40	Cambridge Univ.	Con.	Ind. Con.
8 Jun 40	†Newcastle N.	Con.	Ind. Con.
25 Mar 42	Grantham	Con.	Ind.
29 Apr 42	Rugby	Con.	Ind.
29 Apr 42	†Wallasey	Con.	Ind.
25 Jun 42	Maldon	Con.	Ind.
9 Feb 43	Belfast W.	U.	Eire Lab.
7 Apr 43	†Eddisbury	Con.	C.W.
7 Jan 44	†Skipton	Con.	C.W.
17 Feb 44	W. Derbyshire	Con.	Ind.
12 Apr 45	†Motherwell	Lab.	S. Nat.
13 Apr 45	Scottish Univs.	Con.	Ind.
26 Apr 45	Chelmsford	Con.	C.W

General Election 5 Jul 45

Date	Constituency	General Election	By-election
18 Mar 46	English Univs.	Ind.	Con.
6 Jun 46	Down	Ind. U.	U.
29 Nov 46	Scottish Univs.	Ind.	Con.
28 Jan 48†	Glasgow, Camlachie	I.L.P.	Con.

General Election 23 Feb 50

1950–51—no change

General Election 25 Oct 51

Date	Constituency	General Election	By-election
13 May 53	Sunderland, S.	Lab.	Con.

General Election 26 May 55

Date	Constituency	General Election	By-election
12 Aug 55	Mid-Ulster	S.F.	U.
8 May 56	Mid-Ulster	S.F.	Ind. U.
14 Feb 57	†Lewisham N.	Con.	Lab.
28 Feb 57	Carmarthen	Lib.	Lab.
12 Feb 58	Rochdale	Con.	Lab.
13 Mar 58	†Glasgow, Kelvingrove	Con.	Lab.
27 Mar 58	†Torrington	Con.	Lib.

General Election 8 Oct 59

Date	Constituency	General Election	By-election
17 Mar 60	†Brighouse & Spenborough	Lab.	Con.
4 May 61	†ᵃBristol S.E.	Lab.	Con.
14 Mar 62	Orpington	Con.	Lib.

ᵃ Seat awarded to Con. on petition.
† Seats regained at the subsequent General Election.

Date	Constitueney	General Election	By-election
6 Jun 62	Middlesbrough W.	Con.	Lab.
22 Nov 62	Glasgow, Woodside	Con.	Lab.
22 Nov 62	†S. Dorset	Con.	Lab.
23 Aug 63	Bristol S.E.	Lab. 59 / Con.ᵃ 61	Lab.
7 Nov 63	Luton	Con.	Lab.
14 May 64	Rutherglen	Con.	Lab.
General Election 15 Oct 64			
21 Jan 65	†Leyton	Lab.	Con.
24 Mar 65	Roxburgh Selkirk & Peebles	Con.	Lib.
General Election 31 Mar 66			
14 Jul 66	†Carmarthen	Lab.	Plaid Cymru
9 Mar 67	†Glasgow Pollok	Lab.	Con.
21 Sep 67	†Walthamstow W.	Lab.	Con.
21 Sep 67	Cambridge	Lab.	Con.
2 Nov 67	†Hamilton	Lab.	S.N.P.
2 Nov 67	Leicester S.W.	Lab.	Con.
28 Mar 68	†Acton	Lab.	Con.
28 Mar 68	Meriden	Lab.	Con.

Date	Constituency	General Election	By-election
28 Mar 68	†Dudley	Lab.	Con.
13 Jun 68	†Oldham W.	Lab.	Con.
27 Jun 68	Nelson & Colne	Lab.	Con.
14 Jul 66	†Carmarthen	Lab.	Plaid Cymru
27 Mar 69	Walthamstow E.	Lab.	Con.
17 Apr 69	Mid-Ulster	U.U.	Ind. Unity
26 Jun 69	†Birmingham, Ladywood	Lab.	Lab.
30 Oct 69	†Swindon	Lab.	Con.
4 Dec 69	Wellingborough	Lab.	Con.
General Election 18 Jun 70			
27 May 71	†Bromsgrove	Con.	Lab.
13 Apr 72	Merthyr Tydfil	Ind. Lab.	Lab.
26 Oct 72	Rochdale	Lab.	Lib.
7 Dec 72	†Sutton & Cheam	Con.	Lib.
1 Mar 73	Lincoln	Lab.	Dem. Lab.
26 Jul 73	Isle of Ely	Con.	Lib.
26 Jul 73	†Ripon	Con.	Lib.
8 Nov 73	†Glasgow Govan	Lab.	S.N.P.
8 Nov 73	Berwick on Tweed	Con.	Lib.

General Election 28 Feb 74
1974—no change

General Election 10 Oct 74

ᵃ Seat awarded to Cons. on petition.
† Seats regained at the subsequent General Election.

M.P.s seeking Re-election

The following M.P.s on changing their party, or for other reasons, voluntarily resigned their seats to test public opinion in a by-election:

Date of by-election	M.P.	Constituency	Former label	New label	Whether Successful
18–19 Nov 02	J. Wason	Orkney & Shetland	L.U.	Ind. L.	Yes
6 Apr 03	J. Seely	I. of Wight	Con.	Lib.	Yes (unop.)
19 Aug 04	W. O'Brien	Cork City	Nat.	Nat.	Yes
31 Dec 06	D. Sheehan	Mid-Cork	Nat.	Ind. Nat.	Yes (unop.)
21 Dec 08	C. Dolan	N. Leitrim	Nat.	Ind. Nat.	No
4 May 09	T. Kincaid-Smith	Stratford-on-Avon	Lib.	Ind.	No
26 Nov 12	G. Lansbury	Bow and Bromley	Lab.	Ind.	No
18 Feb 14	W. O'Brien	Cork City	Ind. Nat.	Ind. Nat.	Yes (unop.)
21 Jul 14	R. Hazleton	N. Galway	Nat.	Nat.	Yes (unop.)
29 Nov 26	J. Kenworthy	Hull C.	Lib.	Lab.	Yes
28 Mar 27	L. Guest	Southwark N.	Lab.	Const.	No
31 Jul 29	Sir W. Jowitt	Preston	Lib.	Lab.	Yes
21 Dec 38	Dss of Atholl	Kinross & W. Perth	Con.	Ind.	No
26 May 55ᵃ	Sir R. Acland	Gravesend	Lab.	Ind.	No
1 Mar 73	D. Taverne	Lincoln	Lab.	Dem. Lab.	Yes

ᵃ Date of General Election which overtook the by-election.

Some members have been compelled to seek re-election because they inadvertently held a government contract of appointment, or because they voted before taking the oath. This last happened in 1925.

Until the Re-election of Ministers Acts of 1919 and 1926 there were many cases of members having to seek re-election on appointment to ministerial office. In eight instances they were unsuccessful:

5 Apr 05	G. Loder	Brighton
24 Apr 08	W. Churchill	Manchester N.W.
20 Dec 11	A. Anderson	N. Ayrshire
5 Mar 12	Sir A. Haworth	Manchester S.
19 Feb 14⟩ 23 May 14⟩	C. Masterman	⟨Bethnal Green S.W. ⟨Ipswich
3 Mar 21	Sir A. Griffith- Boscawen	Dudley
15 Jul 22	T. Lewis	Pontypridd

Electoral Administration

From 1900 to 1918 electoral arrangements were governed primarily by the *Representation of the People Act, 1867*, as modified by the *Ballot Act, 1872*, the *Corrupt Practices Act, 1883*, the *Franchise Act, 1884*, the *Registration Act, 1885*, and the *Redistribution of Seats Act, 1885*. The *Representation of the People Act, 1918*, the *Equal Franchise Act, 1928*, and the *Representation of the People Act, 1948* (consolidated in 1949), constitute the only major legislation in the century. There have been six major inquiries into electoral questions:

1908–10	Royal Commission on Electoral Systems
1917	Speaker's Conference on Electoral Reform
1930	Ullswater Conference on Electoral Reform
1934–44	Speaker's Conference on Electoral Reform
1965–68	Speaker's Conference on Electoral Law
1972–4	Speaker's Conference on Electoral Law

The Franchise. From 1885 the United Kingdom had a system of fairly widespread male franchise, limited however by a year's residence qualification and some other restrictions. Voting in more than one constituency was permitted to owners of land, to occupiers of business premises, and to university graduates. The *Representation of the People Act, 1918* reduced the residence qualification to six months and enfranchised some categories of men who had not previously had the vote. It also enfranchised women over 30. In 1928 the *Equal Franchise Act* lowered the voting age for women to 21. In 1948 the *Representation of the People Act* abolished the business and university votes for parliamentary elections; it also abolished the six months' residence qualification.

In 1969 the *Representation of the People Act* provided votes for everyone as soon as they reached the age of 18.

Redistribution. The *Redistribution of Seats Act, 1885*, left the House of Commons with 670 members. The 1885 Act, while removing the worst anomalies, specifically rejected the principle that constituencies should be approximately equal in size. This principle was, however, substantially accepted in the *Representation of the People Act, 1918*, on the recommendation of the Speaker's Conference of 1917, although Wales, Scotland and Ireland were allowed to retain disproportionate numbers of seats. The 1918

Electorate

Year	Population	Population over 21	Electorate	Electorate as % of Adult Population [a]	
				Male	Total
1900	41,155,000	22,675,000	6,730,935	58	27
1910	44,915,000	26,134,000	7,694,741	58	28
1919	44,599,000	27,364,000	21,755,583	..	78
1929	46,679,000	31,711,000	28,850,870	..	90
1939	47,762,000	32,855,000	32,403,559	..	97
1949	50,363,000	35,042,000	34,269,770	..	98
1959	52,157,000	35,911,000	35,397,080	..	99
1965	54,606,000	36,837,000	36,128,387	..	98
1970	55,700,000	44,503,000[b]	39,153,000	..	96

[a] This percentage makes allowance for plural voting. In the period before 1914 this amounted to about 500,000. After 1918 the business vote reached its peak in 1929 at 370,000. The university electorate rose from 39,101 in 1900 to 217,363 in 1945. [b] Population over 18.

Act increased the size of the House of Commons to 707 but this fell to 615 in 1922 on the creation of the Irish Free State. Population movements produced substantial anomalies in representation and the *Redistribution of Seats Act, 1944,* authorised the immediate subdivision of constituencies with more than 100,000 electors, which led to 25 new seats being created at the 1945 election and raised the size of Parliament to 640. It also provided for the establishment of Permanent Boundary Commissioners to report every three to seven years. The Boundary Commissioners' first recommendations were enacted in the *Representation of the People Act, 1948* (with the controversial addition by the Government of 17 extra seats as well as the abolition of the 12 University seats), and the 1950 Parliament had 625 members. The next reports of the Boundary Commissioners, given effect by resolutions of the House in December 1954 and January 1955, increased the number of constituencies to 630. The controversy caused by these changes led to the *Redistribution of Seats Act, 1958,* which modified the rules governing the Boundary Commissioners' decisions and asked them to report only every 10 to 15 years. The Boundary Commissioners started their revision in 1965; they reported in 1969, but the Labour Government secured the temporary rejection of their proposals. In November 1970 the Conservative Government gave effect to the 1969 proposals. The House of Commons elected in 1974 therefore had 635 constituencies.

Election Expenses

Candidates' expenses were restricted by the *Corrupt Practices Act, 1883,* on a formula based on the number of electors. Candidates still had to bear the administrative costs of the election. The *Representation of the People Act, 1918,* removed from the candidates responsibility for the Returning Officers' fees and lowered the maximum limits on expenditure. This limit was further reduced by the *Representation of the People Act, 1948,* and only slightly increased by the *Representation of the People Act, 1969*; in February 1974 the *Representation of the People Act 1974* provided a further increase. In the following table the effect of variations in the number of unopposed candidates should be borne in mind (unopposed candidates seldom spent as much as £200). It is notable how the modifications in the law have kept electioneering costs stable despite a fivefold depreciation in the value of money and a fivefold increase in the size of the electorate.

Candidates' Election Expenses

Year	Total Expenditure £	Candidates	Average per Candidate £	Con.	Lib.	Lab.
1900	777,429	1,002	776	..	..	..
1906	1,166,858	1,273	917	..	..	..
1910 Jan	1,295,782	1,315	985	1,109	1,075	881
1910 Dec	978,312	1,191	821	918	882	736
1918	No pub. returns	1,625	..	..	..	..
1922	1,018,196	1,443	706	..	..	..
1923	982,340	1,446	679	845	789	464
1924	921,165	1,428	645	..	..	..
1929	1,213,507	1,730	701	905	782	452
1931	654,105	1,292	506	..	..	..
1935	722,093	1,348	536	777	495	365
1945	1,073,216	1,682	638	780	532	595
1950	1,170,124	1,868	626	777	459	694
1951	946,018	1,376	688	773	488	658
1955	904,677	1,409	642	692	423	611
1959	1,051,219	1,536	684	761	532	705
1964	1,229,205	1,757	699	790	579	751
1966	1,130,882	1,707	667	766	501	726
1970	1,392,796	1,786	761	949	828	667
1974 Feb	2,008,660	2,135	941	1,197	745	1,127
1974 Oct	2,155,790	2,252	957	1,275	725	1,163

Lost Deposits

The Representation of the People Act 1918 provided that any Parliamentary candidate would have to deposit, on nomination, £150 in cash with the returning officer. This money would be forfeit to the state unless the candidate received one-eighth of the valid votes cast. The number of deposits lost in general elections has been as follows:

	Con.	Lab.	Lib.	Comm.	Other	Total	% of candidates
1918	3	6	44	—	108	161	9·9
1922	1	7	31	1	12	52	3·6
1923	—	17	8	—	2	27	1·9
1924	1	28	30	1	8	68	4·7
1929	18	35	25	21	14	113	6·5
1931	—	21	6	21	37	85	6·6
1935	1	16	40	—	24	81	6·0
1945	5	2	76	12	87	182	10·8
1950	5	0	319	97	40	461	24·6
1951	3	1	66	10	16	96	7·0
1955	3	1	60	15	21	100	7·1
1959	2	1	55	17	41	116	7·6
1964	5	8	52	36	85	186	10·6
1966	9	3	104	57	64	237	13·9
1970	10	6	184	58	150	408	22·2
1974 Feb	8	25	23	43	222	321	15·0
1974 Oct	28	13	125	29	247	442	19·6
All General Elections	102	190	1,248	418	1,178	3,136	11·3
By-elections 1918–74	14	14	73	33	229	363	16·2
Lost deposits 1918–74	116	204	1,321	451	1,407	3,499	11·6

Women Candidates and M.P.s

	Conservative		Labour		Liberal		Other		Total	
	Cands.	M.P.s	Cands.	M.P.s	Cands.	M.P.s	Cands.	M.P.s	Cands.	M.P.s
1918	1	..	4	..	4	..	8	1	17	1
1922	5	1	10	..	16	1	2	..	33	2
1923	7	3	14	3	12	2	1	..	34	8
1924	12	3	22	1	6	..	1	..	41	4
1929	10	3	30	9	25	1	4	1	69	14
1931	16	13	36	..	6	1	4	1	62	15
1935	19	6	35	1	11	1	2	1	67	9
1945	14	1	45	21	20	1	8	1	87	24
1950	28	6	42	14	45	1	11	..	126	21
1951	29	6	39	11	11	..	..	..	74	17
1955	32	10	43	14	12	..	2	..	89	24
1959	28	12	36	13	16	..	1	..	81	25
1964	24	11	33	17	25	..	8	..	90	28
1966	21	7	30	19	20	..	9	..	80	26
1970	26	15	29	10	23	..	21	..	99	26
1974 F.	33	9	40	13	40	..	30	1	143	25
1974 O.	30	7	50	18	49	..	32	2	161	27
						..				

SOURCE.—F. W. S. Craig, *British Parliamentary Election Statistics 1918–1970* (1970)

Successful Election Petitions

In the following constituencies election petitions have led to the original result being disallowed by the courts.[1]

Jul	00	Maidstone	Dec	10	Exeter
Jul	00	Monmouth	Dec	10	Hull C.
Jan	06	Worcester	Dec	10	N. Louth
Jan	06	Bodmin	Dec	10	West Ham N.
Jan	10	E. Dorset	Nov	22	Berwick on Tweed
Jan	10	E. Kerry	Dec	23	Oxford
Jan	10	The Hartlepools	May	55	Fermanagh & S. Tyrone
Dec	10	Cheltenham	Aug	55	Mid-Ulster
Dec	10	E. Cork	May	61	Bristol S.E.

[1] On 19 Oct 50 the House of Commons decided that the seat at West Belfast stood vacant because the successful candidate was ineligible as a minister of the Church of Ireland. On 20 Jul 55 the Mid-Ulster seat was declared vacant because the successful candidate was a felon: on 6 Feb 56 it was declared vacant again because the candidate in the ensuing by-election who was declared elected on petition was found to be ineligible because he held offices of profit under the Crown.

Sources on Electoral Matters

Official returns, listing candidates' votes and expenses, have been published as Parliamentary Papers about one year after every General Election, except 1918: *1901 (352) lix, 145; 1906 (302) xcvi, 19; 1910 (259) lxxiii, 705; 1911 (272) lxii, 701; 1924 (2) xviii, 681; 1924–5 (151) xviii, 775; 1926 (1) xxii, 523; 1929–30 (114) xxiv, 755; 1931–2 (109) xx, 1; 1935–6 (150) xx, 217; 1945–6 (128) xix, 539; 1950 (146) xviii, 311; 1951–2 (210) xxi, 841; 1955 (141) xxxii, 913; 1959–60 (173) xxiv, 1031; 1964–5 (220) xxv, 587; 1966–7 (162) liv, 1; 1970–1 (305); 1974–5 (69);*

More usable returns, identifying candidates by party and supplying supplementary data, are to be found in the following works:

Dod's Parliamentary Companion, Vacher's Parliamentary Companion, and *Whitaker's Almanack,* all issued annually (or more often).

Parliamentary Poll Book, by F. H. McCalmont (7th ed. 1910). This gives all returns from 1832 to 1910 (Jan). In 1971 it was reprinted and updated to 1918.

Pall Mall Gazette House of Commons, issued in paperback form after each election from 1892 to 1910 (Dec).

The Times House of Commons, issued after every election since 1880 except for
1918 and after 1906, 1922, 1923 and 1924.

The Constitutional Year Book, issued annually from 1885 to 1939. Up to
1920 it gives all results from 1885. Up to 1930 it gives the results for all
post-1918 contests. Thereafter it records the latest four elections.

The Daily Telegraph Gallup Analysis of Election '66 provides an exhaustive
statistical comparison of the 1964 and 1966 elections.

The most convenient and reliable source of data, giving percentages as well as
absolute figures, is provided by F. W. S. Craig in *British Parliamentary
Election Results 1885–1918* (1973), *British Parliamentary Election Results
1918–1949* (1969) and *British Parliamentary Election Results 1950–1970*
(1971). All by-election results are listed in C. Cook and J. Ramsden
(eds.), *By-elections in British Politics* (1973).

From 1945, the results of each election have been analysed in statistical
appendices to the Nuffield College series of studies, *The British General
Election of 1945* (1947), by R. B. McCallum and Alison Readman, *The
British General Election of 1950* (1951), by H. G. Nicholas, *The British
General Election of 1951* (1952), by D. E. Butler, *The British General
Election of 1955* (1955), by D. E. Butler, *The British General Election
of 1959* (1960), by D. E. Butler and Richard Rose, *The British General
Election of 1964* (1965), by D. E. Butler and Anthony King, *The British
General Election of 1966* (1966) by D. E. Butler and Anthony King, *The
British General Election of 1970* (1971) by D. E. Butler and M. Pinto-
Duschinsky, *The British General Election of February 1974* by D. E.
Butler and D. Kavanagh, 1974, *The British General Election of October
1974* by D. E. Butler and D. Kavanagh, 1975. See also A. K. Russell,
Liberal Landslide: The General Election of 1906 (1973) and N. Blewett, *The
Peers, the Parties and the People; The General Elections of 1910* (1972).

Further data is to be found in *The Electoral System in Britain since 1918,* by
D. E. Butler (2nd ed. 1963), *Parliamentary Representation,* by J. F. S.
Ross (2nd ed. 1948) and *Elections and Electors,* by J. F. S. Ross (1955);
Elections in Britain, by R. Leonard (1968), *Parliamentary Election
Statistics 1918–1970,* by F. W. S. Craig (1970), *The British Voter
(1885–1966),* by M. Kinnear (1968); and *Social Geography of British
Elections 1885–1910,* by H. Pelling (1967). See also the *Report of
the Royal Commission on Electoral Systems (Cd. 5163/1910);* evidence *Cd.
5352/1910.*

Census data arranged on a constituency basis is available for 1966 in *Census
1966; General and Parliamentary Constituency Tables* (1969). It is also
available for 1971 in duplicated form.

The problems of electoral administration are also dealt with in the reports of
the Speaker's Conferences on Electoral Reform of 1917, 1944, 1966, and
1972–4 and the Ullswater Conference of 1930 (*Cd. 8463/1917; Cmd.
3636/1930; Cmd. 6534* and *6543/1944, Cmnd. 2917* and *2932/1966,
Cmnd. 3202* and *3275/1967, Cmnd. 3550/1968, Cmnd. 5363/1973, Cmnd.
5547/1974* and in the reports of the Boundary Commissioners (*Cmnd.
7260, 7274, 7270, 7231 of 1947, Cmd. 9311–4 of 1954* and *Cmnd. 4084–7 of
1969*). See also H. L. Morris, *Parliamentary Franchise Reform in England
from 1885 to 1918* (New York 1921), *The Redistribution of Seats,* by D. E.
Butler, *Public Administration,* Summer 1955, pp. 125–47, and F. W. S.
Craig, *Boundaries of Parliamentary Constituencies 1885–1972* (1972).

Public Opinion Polls
Gallup Poll

The British Institute of Public Opinion was established in 1937. Its name was changed in 1952 to Social Surveys (Gallup Poll) Ltd. Its poll findings were published exclusively in the *News Chronicle* until October 1960. Since 1961 its findings have been published regularly in the *Daily Telegraph* and the *Sunday Telegraph*. As the years advanced, its questions on politics became increasingly systematic and detailed. Some of its early findings are collected in *Public Opinion, 1935–1946*, edited by H. Cantril (1951). Others may be found in the *News Chronicle*, in occasional pamphlets, in the 1959 *Gallup Election Handbook*, in the 1966 *Gallup Election Handbook*, and in the monthly *Gallup Political Index* available since 1960 from Social Surveys (Gallup Poll) Ltd. (now at 202 Finchley Road, London, N.W.3).

The following tables show in summary form the answers to the question 'If there were a General Election tomorrow, how would you vote?'

Voting Intention (Gallup Poll)

		Government %	Opposition %	Don't Know %
1939	Feb	50	44	6
1939	Dec	54	30	16
1940	Feb	51	27	22

		Con. %	Lab. %	Lib. %	Other %	Don't Know %	Con. lead over Lab. %
1943	Jun	31	38	9	8	14	−7
	Jul	27	39	9	9	16	−12
	Dec	27	40	10	9	14	−13
1944	Feb	23	37	10	14	16	−14
1945	Feb	24	42	11	11	12	−18
	Jun	32	45	15	7	..	−13
1946	Jan	30	49	10	4	7	−19
	May	37	40	12	3	8	−3

Voting Intention (Gallup Poll)

		Con. %	Lab. %	Lib. %	Other %	Don't Know %	Con. lead over Lab. %
1947	Jan	38	41	11	2	8	−3
	Mar	38	38	9	2	13	0
	Jun	38	38	11	2	11	0
	Jul	38	38	11	2	11	0
	Aug	37	34	9	3	17	3
	Sep	39	35	10	4	12	4
	Nov	44	33	8	2	13	11
1948	Jan	38	37	9	1	15	1
	Feb	38	35	7	3	17	3
	Mar	38	36	7	2	17	2
	Apr	36	35	9	5	15	1
	May	37	34	9	2	18	3
	Jul	42	35	8	3	12	7
	Aug	40	34	7	2	17	6
	Sep	38	33	8	1	20	5
	Oct	38	34	8	2	18	4
	Nov	38	36	7	2	17	2
1949	Jan	38	35	11	2	14	3
	Feb	38	37	8	2	15	1
	Mar	36	37	11	2	14	−1
	Apr	36	37	11	1	15	−1
	May	39	35	9	2	15	4
	Jun	37	34	10	1	18	3
	Jul	38	36	10	2	14	2
	Aug	38	36	10	2	14	2
	Sep	40	34	9	2	15	6
	Oct	43	34	8	1	14	9
	Nov	40	32	11	1	16	8
1950	Jan	38	38	10	2	12	0
	Feb	40	41	10	1	8	−1
	Mar	41	43	6	1	9	−2
	May	40	42	8	1	9	−2
	Jun	39	42	8	2	9	−3
	Jul	38	39	10	3	10	−1
	Aug	40	42	8	1	9	−2
	Sep	38	41	10	2	9	−3
	Oct	40	42	8	0	10	−2
	Dec	41	39	9	1	10	2
1951	Jan	44	33	9	1	13	11
	Feb	46	34	8	2	10	12
	Mar	44	33	8	1	14	11
	Apr	45	34	7	2	12	11
	May	42	34	9	2	13	8
	Jun	42	36	9	1	12	6
	Jul	43	34	9	1	13	9
	Aug	44	34	10	1	11	10
	Sep	47	36	5	1	11	11
	Oct	45	39	5	0	11	6
	Dec	43	41	6	1	9	2

Voting Intention (Gallup Poll)

		Con. %	Lab. %	Lib. %	Other %	Don't Know %	Con. lead over Lab. %
1952	Jan	40	43	5	2	10	−3
	Feb	35	40	10	1	14	−5
	Mar	38	43	9	1	9	−5
	May	40	44	6	1	9	−4
	Jun	38	46	9	1	6	−8
	Jul	36	45	8	2	9	−9
	Sep	37	44	8	2	9	−7
	Oct	37	43	8	1	11	−6
	Nov	38	40	8	1	13	−2
	Dec	39	40	9	1	11	−1
1953	Jan	38	41	9	1	11	−3
	Feb	38	41	9	1	11	−3
	Mar	41	39	7	1	12	2
	Apr	41	39	7	0	13	2
	May	41	39	7	1	12	2
	Jun	41	41	6	1	11	0
	Aug	39	40	7	1	13	−1
	Sep	39	42	6	1	12	−3
	Oct	39	42	7	1	11	−3
	Dec	39	41	6	1	13	−2
1954	Jan	39	40	6	1	14	−1
	Feb	39	40	7	1	13	−1
	Mar	41	40	6	1	12	1
	Apr	40	40	6	1	13	0
	May	40	41	6	1	12	−1
	Jun	39	40	7	1	13	−1
	Aug	38	43	7	1	11	−5
	Sep	38	43	7	1	11	−5
	Oct	38	38	7	1	16	0
	Nov	39	40	5	1	15	−1
	Dec	42	43	2	0	13	−1
1955	Jan	40	39	6	1	14	1
	Feb	40	39	7	1	13	1
	Mar	40	39	7	1	13	1
	Apr	41	40	4	1	14	1
	May	43	40	2	1	14	3
	Jun	42	39	2	1	16	3
	Jul	42	38	8	1	11	4
	Aug	38	41	6	1	14	−3
	Sep	43	40	6	1	10	3
	Oct	40	39	7	1	13	1
	Nov	39	40	8	1	12	−1
	Dec	40	41	6	1	12	−1
1956	Jan	40	41	6	1	12	−1
	Feb	39	40	8	1	12	−1
	Mar	36	38	6	1	19	−2
	Apr	36	40	6	1	17	−4
	May	37	40	7	1	15	−3
	Jul	36	42	7	1	14	−6
	Aug	36	42	5	1	16	−6
	Sep	40	42	1	1	16	−2
	Oct	36	40	8	1	15	−4
	Nov	38	38	7	0	17	0
	Dec	38	39	7	1	15	−1

Voting Intention (Gallup Poll)

		Con. %	Lab. %	Lib. %	Other %	Don't Know %	Con. lead over Lab. %
1957	Jan	39	44	6	1	10	−5
	Feb	34	39	7	1	19	−5
	Mar	31	41	6	1	21	−10
	Apr	36	43	5	1	15	−7
	May	35	42	6	1	16	−7
	—						
	Jul	35	42	6	1	16	−7
	Aug	36	42	4	1	17	−6
	Sep	26	39	10	0	25	−13
	Oct	31	41	11	1	16	−10
	Nov	31	40	9	1	19	−9
	Dec	35	40	8	1	16	−5
1958	Jan	33	39	10	1	17	−6
	Feb	29	36	15	1	19	−7
	—						
	Apr	31	38	12	1	18	−7
	May	28	38	15	0	19	−10
	Jun	34	37	13	1	15	−3
	—						
	Aug	36	36	13	1	14	0
	Sep	37	35	11	0	17	2
	Oct	38	35	10	1	16	3
	Nov	39	36	9	1	15	3
	Dec	40	36	8	1	15	4
1959	Jan	37	36½	7	½	19	½
	Feb	33½	36½	6½	1	22½	−3
	Mar	35½	36½	5	1	22	−1
	Apr	38	38	8½	1½	14	0
	May	38½	37½	8½	1	14½	1
	Jun	38½	37	9½	½	14½	1½
	Jul	38½	35	10½	½	15½	3½
	Aug	41	36	8½	1	13½	5
	Sep	41½	36	8	½	14	5½
	Oct	40½	39	4	½	16	1½
	Nov	43	39	6	1	11	4
	Dec	40½	37½	6	1	15	3
1960	Jan	39	35	8	1	17	4
	Feb	39½	36½	7½	½	16	3
	Mar	39	35	8½	½	17	4
	Apr	37½	35½	9½	½	17	2
	May	38½	36	9	1	15½	2½
	Jun	39	36½	9	1	14½	2½
	Jul	39	35	8	1	17	4
	Aug	40	35	8	½	16½	5
	Sep	40	34	9	1	16	6
	Oct	40½	30	10	½	19	10½
	Nov	39½	35	11½	0	14	4½
	Dec	40½	32	11½	1	15	8½
1961	Jan	36½	33½	10	1	19	3
	Feb	35½	34½	10½	1	18½	1
	Mar	38½	35	13½	1	12	3½
	Apr	35½	33	12½	1	18	2½
	May	36½	33	11½	1	18	3½
	Jun	36½	33½	12½	1	16½	3
	Jul	36	34	11½	½	18	2
	Aug	32	36	14	1	17	−4
	Sep	33½	37	10	½	19	−3½
	Oct	37	37	10½	1	14½	0
	Nov	34	34½	14½	1	16	−½
	Dec	30½	34½	14	1	20	−4

Voting Intention (Gallup Poll)

		Con. %	Lab. %	Lib. %	Other %	Don't Know %	Con. lead over Lab. %
1962	Jan	34½	34½	12	½	18½	0
	Feb	33	35	14	0	18	-2
	Mar	32½	36	13	½	18	-3½
	Apr	29	35	22	½	13½	-6
	May	28½	33	21	½	17	-4½
	Jun	30½	33½	21½	½	14	-3
	Jul	31	35	19	1	14	-4
	Aug	29	34	16	1	20	-5
	Sep	31½	38½	15	1	14	-7
	Oct	30½	35	15	1	18½	-4½
	Nov	30½	37	14	½	18	-6½
	Dec	30½	38	13	1	17½	-7½
1963	Jan	28½	40	12½	1½	17½	-11½
	Feb	28	40½	14	1	16½	-12½
	Mar	28	43½	12	½	16	-15½
	Apr	28	42	12	½	17½	-14
	May	29½	38½	12½	1	18½	-9
	Jun	29	42½	12	½	16	-13½
	Jul	26½	42	10½	1	20	-15½
	Aug	28½	41	11	1	18½	-12½
	Sep	28	40½	12	1	18½	-12½
	Oct	29	40	10	½	20½	-11
	Nov	30½	41½	10	½	17½	-11
	Dec	31	39½	9	½	20	-8½
1964	Jan	32	38	9	½	20½	-6
	Feb	34	39½	9	½	17	-5½
	Mar	32	41	9	½	17½	-9
	Apr	32½	42	8	½	17	-9½
	May	33	44½	8	0	14½	-11½
	Jun	35	43½	6½	½	14½	-8½
	Jul	35½	43	7½	0	14	-7½
	Aug	36	42	6	0	16	-6
	Sep	38	39½	6½	0	15½	-1½
	Oct	38	40½	8	½	13	-2½
	Nov	33	43½	10	0	13	-10½
	Dec	34½	43½	8	0	13½	-9
1965	Jan	36½	40	8	1	14½	-3½
	Feb	41	39	6½	0	13½	2
	Mar	37	38½	7	1	16½	-1½
	Apr	33½	40	9	0	17	-6½
	May	36½	35	9	½	19	1½
	Jun	40	35	7	1	17	5
	Jul	39	36½	5½	0	18½	2½
	Aug	42	33	6	1	18	9
	Sep	36½	42½	6½	1	13½	-6
	Oct	37	40½	7	0	15	-3½
	Nov	36	41½	6½	1	15	-5½
	Dec	34	40½	8	1	16½	-6½
1966	Jan	36½	40½	7	1	15	-4
	Feb	36	40½	5	0	18½	-4½
	Mar	34	43½	7	½	15	-9½
	Apr						
	May	32	47½	8	1	11½	-15½
	Jun	34½	45½	6	1	13	-11
	Jul	35½	42	7	1	14½	-6½
	Aug	37½	37	8	1	16½	½
	Sep	36	38	7½	1	17½	-2
	Oct	37	38	8	1	16	-1
	Nov	37½	35	9	1	17½	2½
	Dec	37	40½	8½	1½	12½	-3½

Voting Intention (Gallup Poll)

	Con. %	Lab. %	Lib. %	Other %	Don't Know %	Con. lead over Lab. %
1967 Jan	36	38½	8½	1	16	−2½
Feb	32	43	10½	1	13½	−11
Mar	34½	35	9	2½	19	−½
Apr	40	34	8	2	16	6
May	40	33½	10	1	15½	6½
Jun	39	34	7	1½	18½	5
Jul	37	36½	9½	1½	15½	½
Aug	36	32½	9	2	20½	3½
Sep	38	35	8	2	17	3
Oct	38½	33½	9	2½	16½	5
Nov	39	33	8½	4	15½	6
Dec	42		9	5	18	16
1968 Jan	37	31½	8½	4	19	5½
Feb	42½	23	8½	4	22	19½
Mar	38	24	8½	2½	27	18
Apr	44½	23	8	2½	22	21½
May	45	21	6½	3½	24	24
Jun	40½	21	10	4	19½	19½
Jul	42	22½	10	6	19½	19½
Aug	38	26	7	3½	25½	12
Sep	39	29	8½	3½	20	10
Oct	39½	32½	6½	3½	18	7
Nov	41½	26	10½	2	20	15½
Dec	43	23	7	4	23	20
1969 Jan	42	25	8½	3½	21	17
Feb	42	24	7	1½	25½	18
Mar	43	26½	7	2½	21	16½
Apr	40½	24½	9½	3	22½	16
May	41½	23½	10	2	23	18
Jun	40	27	8½	2½	22	13
Jul	45	25	7½	1½	21	20
Aug	38	27	9½	2½	23	11
Sep	38	29½	9½	2½	20½	8½
Oct	38½	36	4½	1½	19½	2½
Nov	38	33½	7	2	19½	4½
Dec	42	31½	6	1	19½	10½
1970 Jan	39½	33½	5	2½	19½	6
Feb	39½	34	6½	1½	18½	5½
Mar	39½	34	7½	2	17	5½
Apr	38	34½	5½	2	20	3½
May	35⅓	41½	6	2	15	−6
Jun	38	41½	5	1	14½	−3½
Aug	40	36½	6½	1½	15½	3½
Sep	38½	37	6	1½	17	1½
Oct	37	36½	5	½	21	½
Nov	34½	39	5	1½	20	−4½
Dec	38	37	4½	3	17½	1
1971 Jan	36	39½	7	2	15½	−3½
Feb	35	41	6	1½	16½	−6
Mar	31½	41½	5½	2	19½	−10
Apr	37	38	6	1	18	−1
May	32	43½	7	2	15½	−11½
Jun	29	43	5½	1½	21	−14
Jul	26½	46½	6	2	19	−20
Aug	33	40	5	2	20	−7
Sep	28½	44½	4½	1	21½	−16
Oct	34	42½	5½	1½	16½	−8½
Nov	35	39½	5	1½	19	−4½
Dec	33	38	5½	2	21½	−5

Voting Intention (Gallup Poll)

		Con. %	Lab. %	Lib. %	Other %	Don't Know %	Con. lead over Lab. %
1972	Jan	32½	39	6½	1½	20½	-6½
	Feb	32	39	6½	1	21½	-7
	Mar	33	40	6½	2½	19½	-7
	Apr	36	36½	7½	2	18	-½
	May	34	38	7	1½	19½	-4
	Jun	35	37	7½	1½	19	-2
	Jul	32½	41	7	2	17½	-8½
	Aug	32½	40	5	2	20½	-7½
	Sep	30	40	6½	2	21½	-10
	Oct	30½	39½	5½	3	22½	-9
	Nov	31½	37½	11½	1	18½	-6
	Dec	30½	36	8	2½	23	-5½
1973	Jan	30½	35	12	1½	21	-4½
	Feb	30½	37	8½	2	22	-6½
	Mar	33	34½	11	1½	20	-1½
	Apr	31	33	11	2½	22½	-2
	May	32	35	10½	3	19½	-3
	Jun	34	35	10½	2	18½	-1
	Jul	30	36	12½	1½	20	-6
	Aug	25½	30½	22½	1½	20	-5
	Sep	27½	34	15½	1	22	-6½
	Oct	27	32	18½	1½	21	-5
	Nov	29½	30½	16½	2	21½	-1
	Dec	29	35	14	2	20	-6
1974	Jan	33	31	14	2½	19½	2
	Feb						
	Mar	29½	37½	14½	2½	16	-8
	Apr	28	42½	13	2	14	-14½
	May	28	40	14½	3	14½	-12
	Jun	30½	38	14½	3	14	-7½
	Jul	29½	31	16½	4½	18½	-1½
	Aug	29½	33	17	3½	17	-3½
	Sep	29½	33	13½	3	21	-3½
	Oct						
	Nov	29½	39½	12	3½	15½	-10
	Dec	27½	38½	13½	2½	18	-11
1975	Jan	27	40	10½	4	18½	-13
	Feb						
	Mar						

National Opinion Polls

National Opinion Polls were established in 1957 as an affiliate of Associated Newspapers Ltd. (now at 76–88 Strand, London, W.C.2). Political findings were published in the *Daily Mail* intermittently until 1961 and regularly thereafter. In October 1963 N.O.P. switched from quota to random sampling and used larger samples (usually between 2,000 and 3,000). The monthly average of their findings in answer to the question 'How would you vote if there were a general election tomorrow?' are set out below.

Voting Intention (N.O.P.)

		Con. %	Lab. %	Lib. %	Other %	Un-decided %	Con. lead over Lab. %
1963	Oct	40·2	47·5	10·0	0·3	2·0	−7·3
	Nov	38·8	46·2	10·3	0·6	4·1	−7·4
	Dec	39·3	47·6	8·8	0·3	4·0	−8·3
1964	Jan	40·1	46·7	9·3	0.3	3·6	−6·6
	Feb	39·5	48·2	9·3	0·1	2·9	−8·7
	Mar[a]	40·6	47·9	8·2	0·4	2·9	−7·3
	Apr[a]	38·4	49·8	8·2	0·2	3·4	−11·4
	May[a]	40·2	48·0	8·1	0·4	3·3	−7·8
	June[a]	40·8	48·1	7·0	0·2	3·9	−7·3
	July[a]	43·0	46·8	7·1	0·2	2·9	−3·8
	Aug[a]	45·7	45·6	5·5	0·3	2·9	0·1
	Sep[a]	45·4	43·8	7·9	0·3	2·6	1·6
	Oct[a] (pre-election)	44·1	44·8	8·1	0·4	2·6	−0·7
	Oct (post-election)	34·7	48·1	11·4	0·6	5·2	−13·4
	Nov[a]	37·2	49·2	10·1	0·3	3·2	−12·0
	Dec	37·9	47·5	11·9	0·3	2·4	−9·6
1965	Jan	39·3	47·7	10·2	0·5	2·3	−8·4
	Feb	42·6	47·2	8·0	0·2	2·0	−4·6
	Mar	40·4	49·4	8·3	0·3	1·6	−9·0
	Apr[a]	38·8	46·1	11·8	0·4	2·9	−7·3
	May	41·0	45·5	10·4	0·6	2·5	−4·5
	Jun	40·5	45·8	10·1	1·0	2·6	−4·3
	Jul[a]	42·0	45·3	9·7	0·5	2·5	−3·3
	Aug	45·5	41·8	9·2	0·5	3·0	3·7
	Sep	42·0	45·3	10·2	0·3	2·2	−3·3
	Oct[a]	38·9	49·3	7·9	0·6	3·3	−10·4
	Nov	36·4	54·9	6·4	0·3	2·0	−18·5
	Dec[a]	37·9	51·6	7·7	0·2	2·6	−13·7
1966	Jan	37·8	51·4	7·0	0·2	3·6	−13·6
	Feb[a]	37·9	52·1	6·1	0·2	3·7	−14·2
	Mar[a]	38·2	51·0	7·0	0·4	3·4	−12·8
	Apr	35·2	54·4	8·6	0·7	1·1	−19·2
	May	33·5	54·3	9·4	1·1	1·7	−21·8
	Jun	36·4	53·9	6·6	0·8	2·3	−17·5
	Jul	35·7	52·0	8·8	0·9	2·6	−16·3
	Aug	37·8	46·9	11·1	1·7	2·5	−9·1
	Sep	38·1	47·5	10·8	1·4	2·2	−9·4
	Oct	35·0	49·9	11·1	1·3	2·7	−14·9
	Nov	39·4	45·1	10·8	1·8	2·9	−5·7
	Dec	41·3	45·6	8·4	1·8	2·9	−4·3
1967	Jan[a]	38·9	46·5	11·5	1·4	1·7	−7·6
	Feb[a]	39·9	45·4	11·0	1·9	1·8	−5·5
	Mar	41·2	46·6	9·0	1·5	1·7	−5·4
	Apr[a]	41·7	46·0	9·0	1·6	1·7	−4·3
	May	44·9	42·6	8·3	2·6	1·6	2·3
	Jun	41·7	46·1	8·4	1·8	2·0	−4·4
	Jul	42·4	43·8	9·8	2·0	2·0	−1·4
	Aug	44·6	40·2	9·8	2·6	2·8	4·4
	Sep	45·3	39·5	10·1	1·9	3·2	5·8
	Oct	41·8	41·8	11·2	2·4	2·8	0·0
	Nov	44·9	37·9	11·7	3·3	2·2	7·0
	Dec	44·5	37·0	12·2	4·1	2·2	7·5

[a] % The average figure when two or more surveys were carried out in a given month.

Voting Intention (N.O.P.)

		Con. %	Lab. %	Lib. %	Other %	Un-decided %	Con. lead over Lab. %
1968	Jan	52·2	33·9	9·6	1·7	2·6	18·3
	Feb	49·4	32·7	11·9	3·3	2·7	16·7
	Mar	48·6	34·9	10·1	3·7	2·7	13·7
	Apr	53·7	31·1	8·7	3·3	3·2	22·6
	May	50·8	31·1	11·1	4·2	2·8	19·7
	Jun	51·4	32·4	9·0	4·6	2·6	19·0
	Jul	49·0	34·7	10·0	3·7	2·6	14·3
	Aug	46·2	35·7	11·3	3·4	3·4	10·5
	Sep	47·3	37·4	9·6	3·4	2·3	9·9
	Oct	46·6	40·0	8·7	2·7	2·0	6·6
	Nov	49·2	36·8	8·4	2·9	2·7	12·4
	Dec	53·6	32·4	8·1	3·0	2·9	21·2
1969	Jan	46·0	35·9	12·3	3·2	2·6	10·1
	Feb	52·7	31·4	9·9	2·8	3·2	21·3
	Mar	53·5	30·7	9·4	2·6	3·8	22·8
	Apr	53·2	31·6	10·0	2·1	3·1	21·6
	May	53·0	31·0	11·2	2·3	2·5	22·0
	Jun	50·5	33·8	9·9	2·9	2·9	16·7
	Jul	50·8	34·9	9·5	1·4	3·4	15·9
	Aug	49·9	34·4	11·9	1·8	2·0	15·5
	Sep	51·5	32·7	10·4	1·9	3·5	18·8
	Oct	49·2	39·3	7·9	1·7	1·9	9·9
	Nov	46·4	40·4	7·8	1·6	3·8	6·0
	Dec	46·5	43·4	6·9	0·9	2·3	3·1
1970	Jan	48·4	41·7	8·4	1·5	8·8	6·7
	Feb	51·1	40·6	7·1	1·2	9·4	10·5
	Mar	49·5	42·0	7·1	1·4	10·0	7·5
—							
	May					a	
—							
	Jul	51·2	40·4	6·6	1·8	(9·4)	10·8
	Aug	47·3	44·2	6·9	1·6	(5·2)	3·1
—							
	Oct	45·8	46·6	6·7	0·9	(7·0)	− 0·8
—							
—							
1971	Jan	46·3	44·3	8·3	1·1	(8·0)	2·0
—							
	Mar	39·9	50·4	8·9	0·8	(9·2)	− 10·5
	Apr	42·0	48·8	7·3	1·9	(10·1)	− 6·8
—							
	Jun	38·3	52·0	7·9	1·8	(11·2)	− 13·7
	Jul	38·1					
—							
	Sep	41·8	49·3	7·9	1·0	(9·4)	− 7·5
—							
	Nov	38·8	51·8	8·4	1·0	(9·2)	− 13·0
—							
1972	Jan	39·1	49·8	9·6	1·5	(9·9)	− 10·7
—							
	Mar	42·3	48·6	7·6	1·5	(9·8)	− 6·3
	Apr	44·8	46·8	7·5	0·9	(10·7)	− 2·0
	May	40·9	46·9	10·8	1·4	(9·7)	− 6·0
—							
	Jul	39·5	49·0	10·0	1·5	(10·8)	− 9·5
—							
	Sep	35·7	53·5	9·1	1·7	(12·3)	− 17·8
	Oct	38·6	49·7	9·9	1·8	(12·3)	− 11·1
	Nov	40·5	45·4	12·9	1·2	(9·8)	− 4·9
	Dec	38·4	45·0	14·7	1·9	(10·3)	− 6·6

ᵃ After June 1970 the 'don't knows' are not included in the percentages.

Voting Intention (N.O.P.)

		Con. %	Lab. %	Lib. %	Other %	Un-decided %	Con. lead over Lab. %
1973	Jan	39·6	40·7	17·9	1·9	(10·8)	− 1·1
	Mar	38·0	45·2	14·9	1·9	(11·5)	− 7·2
	Apr	36·6	45·0	17·0	1·4	(10·6)	− 8·4
	May	31·9	50·1	16·9	1·1	(10·8)	− 18·2
	Jun	41·3	41·6	15·7	2·3	(12·3)	− 0·3
	Jul	39·3	43·9	14·8	2·0	(9·6)	− 4·6
	Aug	28·9	41·7	27·6	1·8	(12·0)	− 12·8
	Sep	33·9	40·9	23·8	1·4	(11·2)	− 7·0
	Oct	35·9	37·6	25·2	1·3	(10·0)	− 1·7
	Nov	36·5	39·9	21·2	2·4	(10·4)	− 3·4
	Dec	35·6	43·2	20·0	1·2	(10·5)	− 7·5
1974	Jan	39·4	42·0	16·5	2·1	(11·9)	− 2·6
	Apr	36·4	45·1	16·5	2·0	(11·1)	− 8·6
	Jun	37·7	45·8	14·0	2·4	(12·0)	− 8.1
	Jul	35·4	44·8	18·2	1·6	(8·1)	− 9·4
	Aug	39·1	37·0	19·1	4·8	(7·5)	2·1
	Sep	32·0	46·6	18·3	3·2	(11·0)	− 14·6
	Oct	36·6	43·7	15·1	4·6	(8·5)	− 7·1
	Nov	38·4	47·7	11·1	2·4	(8·0)	− 9·3
1975	Jan	32·4	47·8	15·9	3·9	(10·0)	− 15·4
	Feb	38·6	46·0	11·1	4·3	(7·2)	− 7·4
	Mar	40·8	46·4	10·3	2·5	(9·6)	− 5·6

Opinion Research Centre

The Opinion Research Centre, founded in 1965 (now at 251–9 Regent Street, London, W.1), has published a regular monthly poll in the *Evening Standard* and other newspapers since 1967.

Voting Intention (O.R.C.)
(Don't knows eliminated)

		Con. %	Lab. %	Lib. %	Other %	Con. lead over Lab.
1967	May	46	40	11	3	6
	Jun	42	46	10	2	− 4
	Jul	40	45	12	3	− 5
	Aug	44	41	12	3	3
	Sep	45	40	11	4	5
	Oct	47	41	10	2	6
	Nov	46	39	10	5	7
	Dec	47	36	12	5	11
1968	Jan	51	34	11	4	17
	Feb	50	34	11	5	16
	Mar	48	35	12	5	13
	Apr	56	28	11	5	28
	May	54	31	11	4	23
	Jun	50	34	12	4	16
	Jul	49	34	11	6	15
	Aug	49	37	10	4	12
	Sep	51	32	13	4	19
	Oct	49	37	10	4	12
	Nov	47	38	11	3	9
	Dec	55	28	13	4	27
1969	Jan	49	33	13	5	16
	Feb	55	32	10	3	23
	Mar	56	31	10	3	25
	Apr	54	31	12	3	23
	May	53	32	13	2	21
	Jun	54	33	10	3	21
	Jul	52	33	13	2	19
	Aug	51	33	13	3	18
	Sep	48	37	12	2	11
	Oct	46	42	10	2	4
	Nov	48	39	10	3	9
	Dec	49	40	8	3	9
1970	Jan	52	37	9	2	15
	Feb	50	38	9	3	12
	Mar	48	41	8	3	7
	Apr	47	41	9	3	6
	May	$44\frac{1}{2}$	$45\frac{1}{2}$	7	3	− 1
	Jun	44	47	$7\frac{1}{2}$	$1\frac{1}{2}$	− 3
	Jul	51	40	8	1	11
	Aug	49	41	8	2	8
	Sep	50	42	6	2	8
	Oct	48	43	7	2	5
	Nov	51	40	7	2	11
	Dec	$41\frac{1}{2}$	47	$9\frac{1}{2}$	2	− $5\frac{1}{2}$

Voting Intention (O.R.C.) continued

		Con. %	Lab. %	Lib. %	Other %	Con. lead over Lab.
1971	Jan	45	45	9	2	0
	Feb	41½	48	9	1½	−6½
	Mar	41	46	11	2	−5
	Apr	48½	41½	8½	1½	7
	May	45	45	8	2	0
	Jun	40	51	7	2	−11
	Jul	39	50	8	3	−11
	Aug	42	47	9	2	−5
	Sep	42	46	9	3	−4
	Oct	42	48	8	2	−6
	Nov	40	51	7½	1½	−11
	Dec	39½	49½	9	2	−10
1972	Jan	43	47	8	2	−4
	Feb	35	55	8	2	−20
	Mar	39	49	10	2	−10
	Apr	40	51	7	2	−11
	May	43	44½	10½	2	−1½
	Jun	42	46	10	2	−4
	Jul	37	50	10	2	−13
	Aug	44	49	6	1	−5
	Sep	39	46	12	3	−7
	Nov	37	45	16	2	−8
	Dec	36	45	16	3	−9
1973	Jan	39	41	17	3	−2
	Feb	39	41	17	3	−2
	Mar	38	43	16	3	−5
	Apr	36	41	20	3	−5
	May	34	41	22	3	−7
	Jun	39	37	21	3	2
	Jul	38½	39	18½	4	−½
	Aug	30	41	26	3	−11
	Sep	30½	38	29	2½	−7½
	Oct	33	37½	27½	2½	−6
	Nov	33	38½	25½	3	−5½
	Dec	35	40	23	2	−5
1974	Jan	41	37	19	3	4
	Feb	42	40	16	2	2
	Mar	35	44	17	4	−9
	Apr	35½	42½	18	4	−7
	May	35	45	16	4	−10
	Jun	34	46	18	2	−12
	Jul	37	37	22	4	0
	Aug	34	40½	21	4½	−6½
	Sep	36	42½	17	4½	−6½
	Oct	33	43	20	4	−10
	Nov					
	Dec					
1975	Jan					

Louis Harris Research Ltd

In 1969 the *Daily Express* abandoned the poll which since the 1940s it has run from within its own office and joined with the Opinion Research Centre and the American expert, Louis Harris in setting up an independent new polling organisation, Louis Harris Research Ltd (now at 251–9 Regent Street, London, W.1.).

Voting Intention (Louis Harris)

(Don't knows eliminated)

		Con. %	Lab. %	Lib. %	Other %	Con. lead over Lab.
1969	Sep	52	35	11	2	17
	Oct	51	39	9	2	12
	Nov	50	40	8	2	10
1970	Jan	51	40	8	1	11
	Feb	52	40	6	2	12
	Mar	49	42	7	2	7
	Apr	44	46	7	3	−2
	May	44½	48	6½	1	−3½
	Jun	43½	48	7½	1	−4½
	Sep	49	45	5	1	4
	Oct	48	44	7	1	4
	Nov	45	48	7	–	−3
1971	Jan	42	49	8	1	−7
	Feb	41	49	8	2	−8
	Mar	42	49	8	1	−7
	Apr	44	47	7	2	−3
	May	39	54	7	–	−15
	Jun	36	57	5	2	−24
	Jul	42	51	7	–	−9
	Aug	42	50	7	1	−8
	Sep	42	50	7	1	−8
	Oct	40	52	7	1	−12
	Nov	38	54	7	1	−16
1972	Jan	43	49	7	1	−6
	Feb	39	53	7	1	−14
	Mar	41	50	8	1	−9
	Apr	42	50	6	2	−8
	May	44	47	8	1	−3
	Jun	38	52	9	1	−14
	Jul	42	48	9	1	−6
	Aug	41	49	9	1	−8
	Sep	40	48	11	1	−8
	Oct	37	50	11	2	−13
	Nov	40	46	12	2	−6
1973	Jan	37	47	14	2	−10
	Feb	39	46	14	1	−7
	Mar	36	47	15	2	−11
	Apr	38	42	17	3	−4
	May	37	45	16	2	−8
	Jun					
	Jul					
	Aug					
	Sep					
	Oct					
	Nov					
	Dec	36	38½	23	2½	−2½

Voting Intention (Louis Harris)

(Don't knows eliminated)

		Con. %	Lab. %	Lib. %	Other %	Con. lead over Lab.
1974	Jan	41	37	20	2	4
	Feb					
	Mar					
	Apr					
	May					
	Jun	35½	42	20½	2	−6½
	Jul					
	Aug					
	Sep	36	41½	19½	3	−5½
	Oct					
	Nov					
	Dec					
1975	Jan					
	Feb					
	Mar	47½	39½	11½	1½	12

Opinion Poll Accuracy in General Elections

The following is a list of all major poll predictions of general election results.

Actual Result (G.B.)		Gallup	N.O.P.	Daily Express	Research Services
1945					
Con	39·5	+1·5			
Lab	49·0	−2·0			
Lib	9·2	+1·3			
1950					
Con	43·1	+0·4		+1·4	
Lab	46·8	−1·8		−2·8	
Lib	9·3	+1·2		+1·7	
1951					
Con	47·8	+1·7		+2·2	+2·2
Lab	49·3	−2·3		−3·3	−6·3
Lib	2·6	+0·4		+0·9	(+4·1)[a]
1955					
Con	49·3	+1·7		+1·9	
Lab	47·3	+0·2		−0·1	
Lib	2·8	−1·3		−0·6	
1959					
Con	48·8	−0·3	−0·8	+0·3	
Lab	44·6	+1·9	+0·5	+0·8	
Lib	6·1	−1·6	(+2·4)[a]	−1·1	
1964					
Con	42·9	+1·6	+1·4	+1·6	+2·1
Lab	44·8	+1·2	+2·6	−1·1	+1·2
Lib	11·4	−2·9	−3·5	−0·3	−2·4
1966					
Con	41·4	−1·4	+0·2	−4·0	+0·2
Lab	48·7	+2·3	−1·9	+5·9	+1·0
Lib	8·6	−0·6	−1·2	−0·9	−0·3
				Louis Harris	O.R.C.
1970					
Con	46·2	−4·2	−2·2	−0·2	+0·3
Lab	43·8	+5·2	+4·3	+4·2	+1·7
Lib	7·6	−0·1	−1·2	−2·6	−1·1
1974 Feb					
Con	38·6	+0·9	+0·9	+1·6	+1·1
Lab	38·0	−0·5	−2·5	−2·8	−1·3
Lib	19·8	+0·7	+2·2	+2·2	+1·4
Other	3·6	−1·1	−0·6	−0·9	−1·2
1974 Oct					
Con	36·7	−0·7	−5·7	−2·1	−2·3
Lab	40·2	+1·3	+5·3	+2·8	+1·6
Lib	18·8	+0·2	+0·7	+0·5	+0·6
Other	4·3	−0·8	−0·3	−1·2	+0·1

[a] Error in Liberal and Other vote combined.

In 1970 Marplan (on a U.K. not a G.B. basis) produced a forecast for *The Times* that overestimated Labour's lead by 9·6%.

In Oct 74 a Marplan poll in the *Sun* overestimated Labour's lead by 6·2%. A Business Decisions poll in the *Observer* overestimated Labour's lead by 1·0%.

SOURCES.—For a comprehensive description of British opinion polling see F. Teer and J. D. Spence *Political Opinion Polls* (1973); see also R. Hodder Williams, *Public Opinion Polls and British Politics* (1970). R. Rose, *The Polls and the 1970 Election* (1970) gives full documentation about the 1970 findings. For the 1974 elections see R. Rose's contributions to H. Penniman (ed.), *Britain at the Polls* (1975). Each of the Nuffield *British General Election* Series includes analyses of the polls.

V

POLITICAL PLACE-NAMES

At one time or another in the twentieth century the following place-names were sufficiently famous to be alluded to without further explanation. Any such list must necessarily be very selective. No foreign names are included here — even though that means omitting Agadir, Chanak, Munich and Suez. No venues of party conferences are included, even though that means omitting Scarborough (Labour, 1960) and Blackpool (Conservative, 1963). No constituency names are included as such, even though that means omitting some, like Bewdley or Ebbw Vale, which are indelibly associated with individuals and others where sensational elections had a lasting national impact, like Colne Valley (1907), St George's Westminster (1931), East Fulham (1933), Orpington (1962), Smethwick (1964) and Lincoln (1973).

Abbey House, Victoria St., S.W.1. Conservative Party Headquarters 1946–58.
Abingdon St., S.W.1. Site of Liberal Party Headquarters 1910–34.
Aldermaston, Berkshire. Site of Atomic Weapons Research Establishment. Starting- or finishing-point of the Campaign for Nuclear Disarmament's Easter Marches 1958–63, 1967–.
Ashridge, Herts. Site of Conservative Party College, 1929–39.
Astley Hall. Worcestershire home of S. (Earl) Baldwin 1902–47.
Bachelor's Walk, Dublin. Scene (26 Jul 1914) of disturbance in which soldiers killed three rioters.
Balmoral Castle, Aberdeenshire. Summer home of the Sovereign since 1852.
Birch Grove, Sussex. Home of H. Macmillan 1906– .
Blenheim Palace, Oxfordshire. Home of Dukes of Marlborough. Birthplace of (Sir) W. Churchill.
Bowood, Wiltshire. Home of Ms of Lansdowne.
Broadstairs, Kent. Birthplace and home of Edward Heath.
Carlton Club. London meeting place of Conservatives. Scene (19 Oct 1922) of gathering which brought down the Lloyd George Coalition.
Carmelite House, E.C.4. Headquarters of the *Daily Mail* and *Evening News*.
Chartwell, Kent. Home of (Sir) W. Churchill 1923–65.
Chatsworth, Derbyshire. Home of Ds of Devonshire.
Chequers, Buckinghamshire. Country house given to the nation by Lord Lee of Fareham in 1917 and used as country residence for Prime Ministers from 1921.
Cherry Cottage, Buckinghamshire. Home of C. (Earl) Attlee 1951–61.
Cherkley Court, Surrey. Home of Ld Beaverbrook 1916–64.
Church House, S.W.1. Meeting place of the Church Assembly since 1920; and of both Houses of Parliament, Nov–Dec 1940, May–Jun 1941, Jun–Aug 1944. Scene of United Nations preparatory meeting 1945 and of many Conservative gatherings.
Churt, Surrey. Home of D. Lloyd George (E) 1921–45.
Clay Cross, Derbyshire. Urban District Council which refused to implement 1972 Housing Act.
Cliveden, Buckinghamshire. Home of 2nd and 3rd Vt Astor. Alleged centre of 'Cliveden Set' in 1930's. Scene (1962) of events in the Profumo affair.
Congress House, Gt. Russell St., W.C.1. Headquarters of Trades Union Congress 1960– .
Criccieth, Caernarvonshire. Welsh home of D. Lloyd George (E) 1880–1945.

Crichel Down, Dorset.   The refusal to derequisition some land here led, ultimately, to the resignation of the Minister of Agriculture in Jul 1954.

Cross St., Manchester.   Headquarters of the *(Manchester) Guardian.*

Curragh, The, Co. Kildare.   Military camp; scene of 'mutiny' 20 Mar 1914.

Dalmeny, Midlothian.   Home of Es of Rosebery.

Dorneywood, Buckinghamshire.   Country house bequeathed to the nation in 1954 by Ld Courtauld-Thomson as an official residence for any Minister designated by the Prime Minister.

Downing St., S.W.1.   No. 10 is the Prime Minister's official residence.   No. 11 is the official residence of the Chancellor of the Exchequer.   No. 12 houses the offices of the Government Whips.

Dublin Castle.   Offices of the Irish Administration until 1922.

Durdans, The, Epsom.   Home of 5th E of Rosebery 1872–1929.

Eccleston Square, S.W.1.   Site of Headquarters of the Labour Party and of the Trades Union Congress 1918–29.

Euston Lodge, Phoenix Park, Dublin.   Residence of the Ld-Lieutenant of Ireland·

Falloden, Northumberland.   Home of Sir E. (Vt) Grey 1862–1933.

Fleet St., E.C.4   Location of *Daily Telegraph* and *Daily Express.*   Generic name for the London press.

Fort Belvedere, Berkshire.   Country home of Edward VIII 1930–36.

Great George St., S.W.1.   Site of the Treasury and, 1964–69, of the Department of Economic Affairs.

Hampstead.   London suburb which, during H. Gaitskell's leadership of the Labour Party, provided a generic name for the set of intellectuals associated with him.

Hatfield House, Hertfordshire.   Home of Ms of Salisbury.

Highbury, Birmingham.   Home of J. Chamberlain 1868–1914.

Hirsel, The, Berwickshire.   Home of Es of Home.

Holy Loch, Argyll.   Site of U.S. atomic submarine base 1962– .

Howth, Co. Dublin.   Scene of gun-running 26 Jul 1914.

Invergordon, Ross and Cromarty.   Site of naval protest in Sep 1931 over proposed pay reductions.

Jarrow, Durham.   Shipbuilding town where unemployment reached 73% in 1935.   Start of Jarrow to London protest march Oct 1936.

Kilmainham Jail, Dublin.   Scene of execution of the leaders of the 1916 rising.

King St., W.C.2.   Site of Communist Party Headquarters since early 1920's.

Knowsley, Lancashire.   Home of Es of Derby.

Larne, Co. Antrim.   Scene of gun-running 24 Apr 1914.

Limehouse, E.14.   Scene of speech by D. Lloyd George 30 Jul 1909 ; became generic name for political vituperation.

Londonderry House, W.1.   London home of Ms of Londonderry until 1946.

Lord North St.   Home of H. Wilson 1971–.

Lossiemouth, Morayshire.   Home of R. MacDonald, 1866–1937.

Notting Hill, W.11.   Scene of racial disturbances in Aug 1958.

Old Queen St., S.W.1   Site of Conservative Party Headquarters 1941–46.   Site of Conservative Research Department 1930– .

Olympia, W.14.   Exhibition Hall; scene (7 Jun 1934) of Mosley meeting which provoked violence.

Palace Chambers, S.W.1.   Headquarters of Conservative Party 1922–41.

Pembroke Lodge, W.8.   Home of A. Bonar Law 1909–16.

Poplar.   London borough whose Poor Law Guardians (including G. Lansbury) were imprisoned in 1921 for paying more than national rates of relief.

Portland Place, W.1.   Headquarters of the British Broadcasting Corporation 1932– .

Printing House Square, E.C.4.   Headquarters of *The Times* 1785–1974.

Relugas, Morayshire.   Fishing lodge of Sir E. Grey ; scene of 'Relugas Compact' with H. Asquith and R. Haldane Sep 1905.

St. James Palace, W.1.   Royal Palace.   Foreign Ambassadors continue to be accredited to the Court of St. James.

St. Stephen's Chambers, S.W.1.   Site of Conservative Headquarters 1900–18.

Sanctuary Buildings, S.W.1.   Site of Conservative Party Headquarters 1918–22.

Sandringham House, Norfolk.   Royal residence since 1861.

Scapa Flow, Orkney. Naval anchorage where German Fleet was scuttled 21 Jun 1919. Scene of trouble at the time of the Invergordon 'mutiny' Sep 1931.

Scilly Isles, Cornwall. Location of H. Wilson's country cottage 1959– .

Selsdon Park. Hotel in Croydon. Scene of Conservative Shadow Cabinet's weekend meeting, 30 Jan–1 Feb 1970.

Shanklin, Isle of Wight. Scene (Feb 1949) of meeting of Labour Party leaders.

Sidney St., E.1. Scene of police siege of anarchists 3 Jan 1911.

Smith Square, S.W.1. Location of the Labour Party Headquarters (Transport House) since 1928; of the Conservative Party Headquarters since 1958; and of the Liberal Party Headquarters 1965–68.

Stormont, Belfast. Site of Parliament and Government of Northern Ireland.

Sunningdale, Surrey. Location of Civil Service College where a Conference on Northern Ireland 6–9 Dec 73 produced the Sunningdale Agreement on power-sharing and a Council of Ireland.

Swinton, Yorkshire. Home of E of Swinton. Conservative Party College since 1948.

Taff Vale, Glamorgan. In 1901 the Taff Vale Railway Company successfully sued a trade union for loss due to a strike.

Threadneedle St., E.C.2. Site of the Bank of England.

Tonypandy. Scene of violent miners' strike to which W. Churchill sent troops in Nov 1910.

Transport House, S.W.1. Headquarters of the Transport and General Workers' Union and of the Labour Party since 1928 and of the Trades Union Congress 1928–60.

Westbourne, Birmingham. Home of N. Chamberlain 1911–40.

Wharf, The, Sutton Courtenay, Berkshire. Home of H. Asquith 1912–28.

Whittingehame, East Lothian. Home of A. Balfour 1848–1930.

Windsor Castle, Berkshire. Official royal residence since 11th century.

VI

POLITICAL QUOTATIONS

From time to time an isolated phrase becomes an established part of the language of political debate.   Such phrases are frequently misquoted and their origins are often obscure.   Here are a few which seem to have had an especial resonance.   The list is far from comprehensive; it merely attempts to record the original source for some well-used quotations.

When was a war not a war ? When it was carried on by *methods of barbarism* in South Africa ?

SIR H. CAMPBELL-BANNERMAN, speech to National Reform Union, 14 Jun 01

For the present, at any rate, I must proceed alone. *I must plough my furrow alone,* but before I get to the end of that furrow it is possible that I may not find myself alone.

LORD ROSEBERY, in a speech at the City Liberal Club, 19 Jul 01

To the distinguished representatives of the commercial interests of the Empire . . . I venture to allude to the impression which seemed generally to prevail among their brethren across the seas, that the old country must *wake up* if she [*England*] intends to maintain her old position of pre-eminence in her colonial trade against foreign competitors.

H.R.H. PRINCE OF WALES (later George V), at a lunch at the Guildhall to celebrate the recent completion of his tour of the Empire, 5 Dec 01

It [the Chinese Labour Contract] cannot in the opinion of His Majesty's Government, be classified as slavery in the extreme acceptance of the word without some risk of *terminological inexactitude.*

WINSTON CHURCHILL, House of Commons, 22 Feb 06

You mean it is *Mr Balfour's poodle*! It fetches and carries for him.   It barks for him.   It bites anybody that he sets it on to.

LLOYD GEORGE, replying to H. Chaplin, M.P., who had claimed, in a House of Commons debate on the House of Lords (Restoration of Powers) Bill, that the Lords was the watchdog of the Constitution, 26 Jun 07

If we believe a thing to be bad, and if we have a right to prevent it, it is our duty to try to prevent it and to *damn the consequences.*

LORD MILNER, in a speech at Glasgow in opposition to Lloyd George's 1909 Finance Bill, 26 Nov 09

Wait and see.

H. ASQUITH, repeated four times to Opposition members pressing for a statement when speaking on Parliament Act Procedure Bill, House of Commons, 4 Apr 10

We were beaten by *the Bishops and the rats.*

G. WYNDHAM, on the passing of the Parliament Bill by the House of Lords 10 Aug 11

La Grande Illusion.

Title of a book by N. ANGELL, published by Nelson (1913); republished as *The Great Illusion*

The lamps are going out all over Europe. *We shall not see them lit again in our lifetime.*	SIR E. GREY, 3 Aug 14, talking in his room at the Foreign Office, quoted in his autobiography *Twenty Five Years*, Vol II, p. 20
Your country needs YOU.	Originally cover of *London Opinion*, 5 Sep 14, designed by A. LEETE, depicting LORD KITCHENER with arresting eyes and pointing finger above the caption 'Your Country needs you'; reproduced by Parliamentary Recruiting Committee for use as recruiting poster and issued Sep 14
The maxim of the British people is '*business as usual*'.	WINSTON CHURCHILL in a speech at the Guildhall, 9 Nov 14
To secure for the producers by hand or by brain the full fruits of their industry and the most equitable distribution thereof that may be possible upon the basis of the common ownership of the means of production (, distribution and exchange).	Listed under party objects in the Constitution of the Labour Party adopted at the Annual Conference in London, 26 Feb 18 (words in brackets added at the 1928 Conference).
What is our task? To make Britain *a fit country for heroes to live in.*	D. LLOYD GEORGE, speech at Wolverhampton, 24 Nov 18
We will get everything out of her [Germany] that you can squeeze out of a lemon and a bit more. . . . *I will squeeze her until you can hear the pips squeak.*	SIR E. GEDDES, in a speech at the Drill Hall, Cambridge 9 Dec 18
They are a lot of *hard-faced men . . . who look as if they had done very well out of the war.*	A Conservative politician (often said to be Baldwin), quoted by J. M. Keynes in *Economic Consequences of the Peace* (Macmillan, 1919), p. 133
First let me insist on what our opponents habitually ignore, and indeed what they seem intellectually incapable of understanding, namely the *inevitable gradualness* of our scheme of change.	S. WEBB, in his Presidential Address to the Labour Party Conference, Queen's Hall, Langham Place, 26 Jun 25
Until our educated and politically minded democracy has become predominantly a *property-owning democracy*, neither the national equilibrium nor the balance of the life of the individual will be restored.	A. SKELTON, in *Constructive Conservatism* (Blackwood, 1924) p. 17; subsequently used by A. EDEN at Conservative Conference, Blackpool, 3 Oct 46, and by W. CHURCHILL, 5 Oct 46
Although I know that there are those who work for different ends from most of us in this House, yet there are many in all ranks and all parties who will re-echo my prayer '*give peace in our time, O Lord*'.	S. BALDWIN speaking in House of Commons on Trade Unions (Political Fund Bill), 6 Mar 25
Not a penny off the pay, not a second on the day	Slogan coined by A. J. COOK, Secretary of the National Union of Mineworkers, and used frequently in the run-up to the miners' strike of 1926

We can conquer unemployment.

Title of a pamphlet which was a potted version of the Liberal *Yellow Book* (1929)

Safety First. Stanley Baldwin, the man you can trust.

Slogan on election posters used by the Conservative Party in 1929; the slogan 'Safety First' was previously used by the Conservatives in the 1922 General Election

I remember when I was a child being taken to the celebrated Barnum's Circus ... the exhibit which I most desired to see was the one described as 'the Boneless Wonder'. My parents judged that the spectacle would be too revolting for my youthful eyes, and I have waited fifty years to see *the Boneless Wonder* sitting on the Treasury Bench.

W. CHURCHILL, referring to R. MacDonald during a debate on the Amendment Bill, 28 Jan 31

What the proprietorship of these papers is aiming at is power, and *power without responsibility — the prerogative of the harlot throughout the ages.*

S. BALDWIN, attacking the Press Lords in a speech at Queen's Hall, London, during Westminster St George's by-election campaign, 18 Mar 31

I hope you have read the Election programme of the Labour Party. It is the most fantastic and impracticable programme ever put before the electors. ... This is not Socialism. It is *Bolshevism run mad.*

P. SNOWDEN, election broadcast, 17 Oct 31

I think it is well also for the man in the street to realise that there is no power on earth that can protect him from being bombed. Whatever people may tell him, *the bomber will always get through.*

S. BALDWIN, in the House of Commons, 10 Nov 32

That this House *will in no circumstances fight for its King and Country.*

Oxford Union motion, 9 Feb 33

[You are] placing ... the Movement in an absolutely wrong position to be *hawking your conscience round from body to body* asking to be told what you ought to do with it.

E. BEVAN, attacking G. Lansbury at the Labour Party Conference, Brighton, 1 Oct 35

A Corridor for Camels.

Heading of a first leader in *The Times*, on the Hoare–Laval Pact, written by G. Dawson, 16 Dec 35

I put before the whole House my own views *with appalling frankness.* ... supposing I had gone to the country and ... said that we must rearm, does anybody think that this pacific democracy would have rallied to the cry? I cannot think of anything that would have made the loss of the election from my point of view more certain.

S. BALDWIN, speaking in the House of Commons, 12 Nov 36.

Something ought to be done to find these people employment. ... Something will be done.

EDWARD VIII, on a visit to South Wales, 18 Nov 36

How horrible, fantastic, incredible it is that we should be digging trenches and trying on gas-masks here because of *a quarrel in a faraway country between people of whom we know nothing.*

N. CHAMBERLAIN, referring to Czechoslovakia in a broadcast of 27 Sep 38

This is the second time in my history that there has come back from Germany to Downing Street, peace with honour.   I believe that it is *peace for our time*.

N. CHAMBERLAIN, referring back to Disraeli's comment on the Congress of Berlin (1878), in a speech from a window of 10 Downing Street on return from Munich 30 Sep 38

Speak for England, Arthur.

L. AMERY, R. BOOTHBY; shouted out as Arthur Greenwood rose to speak in the House of Commons, 2 Sep 39

Whatever may be the reason, whether it was that *Hitler* thought he might get away with what he had got without fighting for it, or whether it was that, after all, the preparations are not sufficiently complete, one thing is certain — he *has missed the bus*.

N. CHAMBERLAIN, speaking at Conservative Central Council 4 Apr 40

You have sat too long here for any good you have been doing.   Depart, I say, and let us have done with you. *In the name of God, go !*

L. S. AMERY, quoting Cromwell (1657) to N. Chamberlain in House of Commons, 7 May 40

I have nothing to offer but *blood, toil, tears and sweat*.

W. CHURCHILL, House of Commons, 13 May 40

We shall fight on the beaches, we shall fight on the landing grounds, we shall fight in the fields and in the streets.

W. CHURCHILL, House of Commons, 4 Jun 40

If the British nation and Commonwealth last a thousand years . . . men will still say, ' *This was their finest hour*'.

W. CHURCHILL, broadcast to the nation when the fall of France was imminent, 18 Jun 40

Guilty Men

Political tract written by Michael Foot, Frank Owen and Peter Howard, using pseudonym Cato; published Jul 40

Never in the field of human conflict was *so much owed by so many to so few*.

W. CHURCHILL, House of Commons, 20 Aug 40

Give us the tools and we will finish the job.

W. CHURCHILL, broadcast to the nation, 9 Feb 41

When I warned them [the French] that Britain would fight on alone . . . their General told their Prime Minister, . . . in three weeks England will have her neck wrung like a chicken — *some chicken, some neck*.

W. CHURCHILL, speaking to the Canadian Parliament, 30 Dec 41

I have not become the King's First Minister in order to preside over the liquidation of the British Empire.

W. CHURCHILL, speech at the Mansion House, 10 Nov 42

Pounds, shillings and pence have become quite *meaningless symbols*.

A. GREENWOOD, in the House of Commons, 16 Feb 43

Let us face the future.

Title of Labour Party Manifesto, May 45

No *Socialist* system can be established without a political police. . . . They would have to fall back on some form of *Gestapo*.

W. CHURCHILL, election broadcast, 4 Jun 45

From Stettin in the Baltic to Trieste in the Adriatic, *an iron curtain* has descended across the Continent.

W. CHURCHILL, speaking at Westminster Cottage, Fulton, U.S.A., 5 Mar 46. The phrase can be traced back to Mrs Snowden's visit to Russia in 1920.

We are the masters at the moment — and not only for the moment, but for a very long time to come.

SIR H. SHAWCROSS, in the House of Commons, during third reading of the Trade Disputes and Trade Uunion Bill, 2 Apr 46

We know that you, the organised workers of the country, are our friends. . . . As for the rest, they do not matter *a tinker's curse*.

E. SHINWELL, speaking at E.T.U. Conference, Margate, 7 May 47

For in the case of nutrition and health, just as in the case of education, *the gentleman in Whitehall really does know better* what is good for people than the people know themselves.

D. JAY, from *The Socialist Case* (1947) p. 258.

The Hon. Member asked two other questions. One of them was how many licences and permits are to be issued after the removal of the 200,000 Board of Trade licences and the 5,000 or 6,000 others which were as the result of yesterday's little *bonfire*. . . .

H. WILSON, as President of the Board of Trade, House of Commons, 5 Nov 48

I have authorised the relaxation *of controls* affecting more than 60 commodities for which the Board of Trade is responsible.

H. WILSON, House of Commons, 4 Nov 48

The Right Road for Britain.

Conservative Party policy statement, 1949

No attempt at ethical or social education can eradicate from my heart a deep burning hatred for the Tory Party. . . . So far as I am concerned, they are *lower than vermin*.

A. BEVAN, speech at Manchester, 4 Jul 49

Whose finger on the trigger?

Daily Mirror, front-page headline on eve of the election, 24 Oct 51

The right technique of economic opposition at the moment can be summed up in a slogan. The slogan is that the Opposition should keep itself on the constructive and sunny side of Mr Butskell's dilemma. Mr *Butskell* [*ism*] . . . is a composite of the present Chancellor and the previous one.

Article in *The Economist* referring to R. Butler and H. Gaitskell, 13 Feb 54

I know that the right kind of political leader for the Labour Party is a *desiccated calculating machine*.

A. BEVAN, taken as referring to H. Gaitskell, though Bevan subsequently denied this, at 'Tribune' meeting during Labour Party Conference at Scarborough, 29 Sep 54

There ain't gonna be no war.

H. MACMILLAN, at press conference, on return from Summit, 24 Jul 55

Reporter: Mr Butler, would you say that this is *the best Prime Minister we have*? R. Butler: Yes.

R. BUTLER, interviewed by a Press Association reporter at London Airport, Dec 55

And all these financiers, all the little *gnomes of Zürich* and the other financial centres about whom we keep on hearing, started to make their dispositions in regard to sterling.

H. WILSON, in the House of Commons Debate on the Address, 12 Nov 56

During the past few weeks I have felt sometimes that *the Suez Canal was flowing through my drawing-room.*

LADY EDEN, opening Gateshead Conservative Association Headquarters, 20 Nov 56

Let us be frank about it, most of our people have *never had it so good.*

H. MACMILLAN, speaking at Bedford to a Conservative Party rally, 21 Jul 57

If you carry this resolution . . . you'll send the British Foreign Secretary — whoever he was — *naked into the Conference Chamber.*

A. BEVAN, Labour Party Conference, Brighton, 3 Oct 57

And you call that statesmanship. I call it *an emotional spasm.*

A. BEVAN, speaking on unilateral disarmament, Labour Party Conference, Brighton, 3 Oct 57

I thought the best thing to do was to settle up these *little local difficulties,* and then turn to the wider vision of the Commonwealth.

H. MACMILLAN, referring to resignation of Treasury Ministers in a statement at London Airport before leaving for Commonwealth tour, 7 Jan 58

Jaw-jaw is better than war-war.

H. MACMILLAN, Canberra, 30 Jan 58; echoing CHURCHILL, 'Talking jaw to jaw is better than going to war', White House lunch, 26 Jun 54

Introducing *Super-Mac.*

VICKY, caption of cartoon depicting H. Macmillan in a Superman outfit; first appeared in *Evening Standard,* 6 Nov 58

Life's better with the Conservatives. *Don't let Labour ruin it.*

Slogan on Conservative posters in the 1959 General Election

What matters is that Mr Macmillan has let Mr Lloyd know that at the Foreign Office, in these troubled times, *enough is enough.*

Article by David Wood, *The Times* Political Correspondent, 1 Jun 59

Britain belongs to you.

Title of Labour Party election manifesto, published 18 Sep 59

The wind of change is blowing through this Continent, and whether we like it or not, this growth of national consciousness is a political fact.

H. MACMILLAN, address to Joint Assembly of Union Parliament, Cape Town, 3 Feb 60

We have developed instead an *affluent*, open and democratic *society*, in which the class escalators are continually moving and in which people are divided not so much between 'haves' and 'have-nots' as between 'haves' and 'have-mores'.

R. BUTLER, at a Conservative Political Centre Summer School, 8 Jul 60

There are some of us, Mr Chairman, who will *fight and fight and fight again* to save the party we love.

H. GAITSKELL, Labour Party Conference, Scarborough, 3 Oct 60

The present Colonial Secretary . . . has been too *clever by half*. . . . I believe that the Colonial Secretary is a very fine bridge player. . . . It is not considered immoral, or even bad form to outwit one's opponents at bridge. . . . It almost seems to me as if the Colonial Secretary, when he abandoned the sphere of bridge for the sphere of politics, brought his bridge technique with him.

M. OF SALISBURY, referring to I. MACLEOD and his policy in Africa in a debate in the House of Lords, 7 May 61

SCOTT: Do you think the Unions are going to respond to what amounts in effect to a '*wage freeze*' in the public sector?
LLOYD: Well, I said that I wasn't going to deal with every possible circumstance. This is a pause rather than a wage freeze.

S. LLOYD interviewed on B.B.C. Radio Newsreel by Hardiman Scott about the 'July measures', 25 Jul 61

And in bygone days, commanders were taught that, when in doubt, they should march their troops towards the sound of gunfire. *I intend to march my troops towards the sound of gunfire.*

J. GRIMOND, in a speech to the Liberal Assembly at Brighton, 22 Sep 62

It does mean, if this is the idea, the end of Britain as an independent European state . . . it means the end of *a thousand years of history.*

H. GAITSKELL, Labour Party Conference, Brighton, 3 Oct 62

It is *a moral issue.*

Heading of a *Times* first leader on the Profumo Affair, 11 Jun 63

A great party is not to be brought down because of a *squalid affair between a woman of easy virtue and a proven liar.*

LORD HAILSHAM, in a BBC interview with R. McKenzie about the Profumo Affair, 13 Jun 63

We are re-defining and we are re-stating our socialism in terms of *the scientific revolution* . . . the Britain that is going to be forged in *the white heat of* this revolution will be no place for restrictive practices or out-dated methods on either side of industry.

H. WILSON, Labour Party Conference, Scarborough, 1 Oct 63

I hope that it will soon be possible for the *customary processes of consultation* to be carried on within the Party about its future leadership.

H. MACMILLAN, in the letter in which he announced his resignation as P.M.; read out to the Conservative Party Conference at Blackpool by the Earl of Home, 10 Oct 63

After half a century of democratic advance, the whole process has ground to a halt with *a 14th Earl.*

H. WILSON, speech at Belle Vue, Manchester, 19 Oct 63

As far as the 14th Earl is concerned, I suppose Mr Wilson when you come to think of it, is *the 14th Mr Wilson.*

EARL OF HOME, in a television interview by Kenneth Harris on I.T.V., 21 Oct 63

Let's go with Labour.   Labour Party slogan used in
                                                 1964

If the British public falls for this [Labour policies] I   Q. HOGG, press conference at
say it will be *stark, staring bonkers.*   Conservative Central Office
                                                            during election campaign, 12
                                                            Oct 64

Smethwick Conservatives can have the satisfaction of   H. WILSON, referring to Peter
having topped the poll, of having sent a Member who,   Griffiths, M.P., who defeated
until another election returns him to oblivion, will   Patrick Gordon Walker in an
serve his time here as *a Parliamentary leper.*   allegedly racialist election
                                                         campaign at Smethwick,
                                                         House of Commons, 4 Nov
                                                         64

In this connection [use of military force in Rhodesia]   Final communiqué of Com-
the Prime Ministers noted the statement by the   monwealth Prime Ministers'
British Prime Minister that on the expert advice avail- Conference at Lagos, re-
able to him, the cumulative effects of the economic   leased 12 Jan 66; referring
and financial sanctions might well bring the rebellion   back to unreported speech by
to an end within a matter of *weeks rather than months.* H. WILSON also on 12 Jan 66

Action not words.   Title of Conservative election
                                                 manifesto, published 6 Mar
                                                 66

You know *Labour Government works.*   Labour Party slogan used in
                                                 1966 election

Now one encouraging gesture from the French   H. WILSON, Bristol, 18 Mar
Government which I welcome and the Conservative   66
leader *rolls on his back like a spaniel.*

It is difficult for us to appreciate the pressures which   H. WILSON, House of Com-
are put on men . . . in the highly organised strike com-   mons, 20 Jun 66
mittees in the individual ports by this *tightly knit
group of politically motivated men* . . . who are now
determined to exercise back-stage pressures . . . en-
dangering the security of the industry and the economic welfare of the nation.

Sterling has been under pressure for the past two and   H. WILSON, House of Com-
a half weeks.   After improvement in the early weeks   mons, 20 Jul 66
of May, we were *blown off course* by the seven weeks
seamen's strike.

Every dog is allowed one bite, but a different view is   H. WILSON, speech to Parlia-
taken of a *dog* that goes on biting all the time.   He   mentary Labour Party, 2 Mar
may not get his *licence* returned when it falls due.   67

It does not mean, of course, that *the pound* here in   H. WILSON, television and
Britain *in your pocket* or purse or in your bank has been   radio broadcast announcing
devalued.   devaluation of the pound, 20
                                                 Nov 67

As I look ahead, I am filled with foreboding.   Like   E. POWELL, speech to a Con-
the Roman, I seem to see '*the River Tiber foaming with* servative Political Central
much blood'.   Meeting in Birmingham, 21
                                                 Apr 68

In Place of Strife.   Title of Government White
                                                 Paper on industrial relations
                                                 legislation, 19 Jan 69

Selsdon Man is designing a system of society for the ruthless and the pushing, the uncaring.... His message to the rest is: you're out on your own.

H. WILSON, at a Rally of the Greater London Party in St Pancras Town Hall, 21 Feb 70; referring to the Conservative policy-forming meeting at Selsdon Park, Croydon, on 31 Jan 70

I am determined, therefore, that a Conservative Government shall introduce *a new style of government*.

E. HEATH, in foreword to Conservative manifesto, published May 70

This would, *at a stroke*, reduce the rise in prices, increase productivity and reduce unemployment.

Wrongly reported in *The Times* as having been said by E. HEATH at a press conference at Central Office, 16 Jun 70; actually taken from a Conservative Press Release (No. G.E.228) distributed at the press conference

We believe that the essential need of the country is to gear its policies to the great majority of the people, who are not *lame ducks*.

J. DAVIES, speaking in a debate on public expenditure and taxation in the House of Commons, 4 Nov 70; echoing a speech by A. BENN in the House of Commons ['the next question is, what safeguards are there against the support of lame ducks'] on 1 Feb 68

Yesterday's Men.

Slogan on Labour poster caricaturing Conservative leaders, May 70; subsequently title of B.B.C. television programme about Labour leaders in opposition, transmitted 17 Jun 71

We say that what Britain needs is a new *Social Contract*. That is what this document [*Labour's Programme 1972*] is all about.

J. CALLAGHAN, Labour Party Conference, Blackpool, 2 Oct 72. But A. Wedgwood Benn had used the phrase in a 1970 Fabian pamphlet *The New Politics*. J.-J.Rousseau's *Le Contrat Social* was published in 1762.

It is *the unpleasant and unacceptable face of capitalism*, but one should not suggest that the whole of British industry consists of practices of this kind.

E. HEATH, replying in the House of Commons to a question from J. Grimond about the Lonrho affair, 15 May 73

From 31 December, they [most industrial and commercial premises] will be limited [in the use of electricity] to *three* specified *days* each *week*.

E. HEATH, speaking in the House of Commons, 13 Dec 73

Looking around the House, one realises that *we are all minorities now* — indeed, some more than others.

J. THORPE, speaking in the House of Commons, after the election of the Speaker, 6 Mar 74

We believe that the only way in which the maximum degree of national cooperation can be achieved is for *a government of national unity* to be formed. . . .

J. THORPE in a letter to E. Heath 4 Mar 74. Later in the year the phrase became a central theme in the Conservatives' October campaign.

VII
CIVIL SERVICE

Heads of Departments and Public Offices

Except where stated otherwise, all these had the title of Permanent Secretary or Permanent Under-Secretary. The Permanent Secretary is the official head and usually the accounting officer of the Department and is responsible to the Minister for all the Department's activities. In some Departments, e.g. Defence since 1964, there are also Second Permanent Secretaries who are official heads and usually accounting officers for large blocks of work. Except where stated otherwise, all the following had the title of Permanent Secretary or Permanent Under-Secretary.

Admiralty

1884	Sir E. MacGregor
1907	Sir I. Thomas
1911	Sir G. Greene
1917	Sir O. Murray
1936	Sir R. Carter
1940	Sir H. Markham
1947	(Sir) J. Lang
1961	Sir C. Jarrett
1964	(see *Defence*)

Agriculture & Fisheries

1892	(Sir) T. Elliott
1913	Sir S. Olivier
1917	(Sir) D. Hall
1920	Sir F. Floud
1927	Sir C. Thomas
1936	(Sir) D. Fergusson
1945	Sir D. Vandepeer
1952	Sir A. Hitchman

(Agriculture, Fisheries & Food)

1955	Sir A. Hitchman
1959	Sir J. Winnifrith
1968	Sir B. Engholm
1973	Sir A. Neale

Air

1917	Sir A. Robinson
1920	(Sir) W. Nicholson
1931	(Sir) C. Bullock
1936	Sir D. Banks
1939	Sir A. Street
1945	Sir W. Brown
1947	Sir J. Barnes
1955	Sir M. Dean
1963	(Sir) M. Flett
1964	(see *Defence*)

Aircraft Production (Director-General)

1940	Sir A. Rowlands
1943	Sir H. Scott
1945 –1945	} Sir F. Tribe

Aviation

(see *Transport & Civil Aviation*)

1959	Sir W. Strath
1960	(Sir) H. Hardman
1963	Sir R. Way
1966	Sir R. Clarke
1966 –1967	} Sir R. Melville

Burma

(see *India & Burma*)

Cabinet Office (Secretary to the Cabinet)

1916	(Sir) M. Hankey
1938	Sir E. Bridges
1947	Sir N. Brook
1963	Sir B. Trend
1973	Sir J. Hunt

(Chief Scientific Adviser)

1964	Sir S. Zuckerman (Ld)
1971	Sir A. Cottrell
1974	(*post vacant*)

(Head of Government Statistical Service)

1968	(Sir) C. Moser

(Central Policy Review Staff: Director-General)

1970	Ld Rothschild
1974	Sir K. Berrill

(see p. 305 for *Economic Advisers*)

Civil Aviation (Director-General)

1941	Sir W. Hildred
1946	Sir H. Self
1947	Sir A. Overton
1953	(see *Transport & Civil Aviation*)

Civil Service Commission (First Commissioner)

1892	W. Courthope
1907	Ld F. Hervey
1910	(Sir) S. Leathers
1928	(Sir) R. Meiklejohn
1939	(Sir) P. Waterfield
1951	P. Sinker
1954	(Sir) L. Helsby
1959	Sir G. Mallaby
1965	Sir G. Abell
1968	J. Hunt
1971	K. Clucas
1974	K. Allen

Head of the Civil Service

1919	Sir W. Fisher
1939	Sir H. Wilson
1942	Sir R. Hopkins
1945	Sir E. Bridges
1956	Sir N. Brook
1963	Sir L. Helsby
1968	Sir W. Armstrong
1974	Sir D. Allen

Civil Service Department
1968   Sir W. Armstrong
1974   Sir D. Allen

Colonial Office
1897   (Sir) E. Wingfield
1900   (Sir) M. Ommaney
1907   Sir F. Hopwood
1911   Sir J. Anderson
1916   Sir G. Fiddes
1921   Sir J. Masterton-
         Smith
1925   Sir S. Wilson
1933   Sir J. Maffey
1937   Sir C. Parkinson
1940   Sir G. Gater
1940   Sir C. Parkinson
1942   Sir G. Gater
1947   Sir T. Lloyd
1956   Sir J. Macpherson
1959   Sir H. Poynton
1966   (see *Commonwealth
         Office*)

**Commonwealth Relations
Office**
1947   { Sir E. Machtig
         { Sir A. Carter
1949   Sir P. Liesching
1955   Sir G. Laithwaite
1959   Sir A. Clutterbuck
1962   } Sir S. Garner
-1966 }

**(Commonwealth
Affairs)**
1966   Sir S. Garner
1968   Sir M. James
1968   (see *Foreign &
         Commonwealth
         Office*)

**Customs Establishment
(Chairman)**
1900   (Sir) G. Ryder
1903   (Sir) T. Pittar

**(Board of Customs
and Excise)**
1909   (Sir) L. Guillemard
1919   Sir H. Hamilton
1927   Sir F. Floud
1930   J. Grigg
1930   (Sir) E. Forber
1934   Sir E. Murray
1941   Sir W. Eady

1942   Sir A. Carter
1947   Sir W. Croft
1955   Sir J. Crombie
1963   Sir J. Anderson
1965   Sir W. Morton
1969   Sir L. Petch
1973   R. Radford

Defence
1947   Sir H. Wilson Smith
1948   Sir H. Parker
1956   Sir R. Powell
1960   Sir E. Playfair
1961   Sir R. Scott
1964   Sir H. Hardman
1966   Sir J. Dunnett
1974   Sir M. Cary

**Defence (Procurement)
(Chief Executive)**
1971   (Sir) D. Rayner
1972   Sir M. Cary
1974   (Sir) G. Leitch

Dominions Office
1925   Sir C. Davies
1930   Sir E. Harding
1940   Sir C. Parkinson
1940   } Sir E. Machtig
-1947 }

Economic Affairs
1964   Sir E. Roll
1966   (Sir) D. Allen
1968   } Sir W. Nield
1969   }

**Economic Warfare
(Director-General)**
1939   Sir F. Leith-Ross
1940   { Sir F. Leith-Ross
         { E of Drogheda
1942   } E of Drogheda
-1945 }

Education (and Science)
1900   Sir G. Kekewich
1903   Sir R. Morant
1911   Sir A. Selby-Bigge
1925   Sir A. Symonds
1931   Sir H. Pelham
1937   (Sir) M. Holmes
1945   Sir J. Maud
1952   (Sir) G. Flemming
1959   Dame M. Smieton
1967   Sir H. Andrew
1970   (Sir) W. Pile

Employment (*see Labour*)

Energy
1974   Sir J. Rampton

Environment
1970   Sir D. Serpell
1972   Sir J. Jones

**Exchequer and Audit
Department
(Comptroller and
Auditor-General)**[1]
1896   R. Mills
1900   D. Richmond
1904   (Sir) J. Kempe
1911   (Sir) H. Gibson
1921   Sir M. Ramsay
1931   (Sir) G. Upcott
1946   Sir F. Tribe
1958   Sir E. Compton
1966   Sir B. Fraser
1971   Sir D. Pitblado

Food (Director-General)
1918   Sir C. Fielding
1919   } F. Coller
-1921 }
1939   Sir H. French
1945   Sir F. Tribe
1946   Sir P. Liesching
1949   (Sir) F. Lee
1951   Sir H. Hancock
1955   (see *Agriculture, Fish-
         eries & Food*)

Foreign Office
1894   Sir T. Sanderson (Ld)
1906   Sir C. Hardinge (Ld)
1910   Sir A. Nicolson
1916   Ld Hardinge
1920   Sir E. Crowe
1925   Sir W. Tyrrell
1928   Sir R. Lindsay
1930   Sir R. Vansittart
1938   Sir A. Cadogan
1946   Sir O. Sargent[2]
1949   Sir W. Strang[2]
1953   Sir I. Kirkpatrick
1957   Sir F. Hoyer Millar
1962   Sir H. Caccia
1965   Sir P. Gore-Booth[3]

**(Foreign and Common-
wealth Office)**
1969   Sir D. Greenhill
1973   Sir T. Brimelow

---

[1] The Comptroller and Auditor-General is appointed by the Crown by letters patent and is not in the ordinary sense a civil servant.
[2] Joint Permanent Under-Secretaries—Head of the German Section: 1947–9 Sir W. Strang, 1949–50 Sir I. Kirkpatrick, 1950–1 Sir D. Gainer.

Forestry Commission
(Chairman)

1920	Ld Lovat
1927	Ld Clinton
1929	Sir J. Stirling-Maxwell
1932	Sir R. Robinson (Ld)
1952	E of Radnor
1964	Earl Waldegrave
1966	L. Jenkins
1970	Ld Taylor of Gryfe

Fuel & Power

1942	Sir F. Tribe
1945	Sir D. Fergusson
1952	Sir J. Maud

(Power)

1957	Sir J. Maud
1958	(Sir) D. Proctor
1965	Sir M. Stevenson
1966	Sir D. Pitblado
1969	(see *Technology*)

Health

1919	Sir R. Morant
1920	Sir A. Robinson
1935	Sir G. Chrystal
1940	Sir J. Maude
1945	Sir W. Douglas
1951	(Sir) J. Hawton
1960	(Sir) B. Fraser
1964 -1968	(Sir) A. France

(Health & Social Security)

1968	Sir C. Jarrett
1970	Sir P. Rogers

Home Office

1895	Sir K. Digby
1903	Sir M. Chalmers
1908	Sir E. Troup
1922	Sir J. Anderson
1932	Sir R. Scott
1938	Sir A. Maxwell
1948	Sir F. Newsam
1957	Sir C. Cunningham
1966	Sir P. Allen
1972	Sir A. Peterson

Home Security

1939	{ Sir T. Gardiner / Sir G. Gater
1940	Sir G. Gater
1942	Sir H. Scott
1943 -1945	Sir W. Brown

Housing & Local Government
(see *Town & Country Planning*, 1943–51)

1951	Sir T. Sheepshanks
1955	Dame E. Sharp
1966	Sir M. Stevenson
1970	(see *Environment*)

India

1883	Sir A. Godley
1909	Sir R. Ritchie
1912	Sir T. Holderness
1920	Sir W. Duke
1924	Sir A. Hirtzel
1930	Sir F. Stewart

(India & Burma)

1937	Sir F. Stewart
1941 -1948	(Sir) D. Monteath

Industry

1974	Sir A. Part

Information
(Director of Propaganda)

1918 -1919	A. Bennett

(Director-General)

1939	Sir K. Lee
1940	F. Pick
1941	Sir C. Radcliffe
1945 -1946	E. Bamford

(Central Office of Information)
(Director-General)

1946	Sir E. Bamford
1946	Sir R. Fraser
1954	(Sir) T. Fife Clark
1971	F. Bickerton
1974	H. James

Board of Inland Revenue
(Chairman)

1899	Sir H. Primrose
1907	(Sir) R. Chalmers
1911	Sir M. Nathan
1914	Sir E. Nott-Bower
1918	W. Fisher
1919	Sir J. Anderson

1922	Sir R. Hopkins
1927	Sir E. Gowers
1930	(Sir) J. Grigg
1934	Sir E. Forber
1938	Sir G. Canny
1942	Sir C. Gregg
1948	Sir E. Bamford
1955	Sir H. Hancock
1958	Sir A. Johnston
1968	Sir A. France
1973	N. Price

Irish Office

1893	Sir D. Harrel
1902	Sir A. Macdonnell
1908	Sir J. Dougherty
1914	Sir M. Nathan
1916	Sir W. Byrne
1918	J. Macmahon
1920 -1922	J. Macmahon / Sir J. Anderson

Labour

1916	(Sir) D. Shackleton
1920	{ Sir D. Shackleton / Sir J. Masterton-Smith
1921	Sir H. Wilson
1930	Sir F. Floud
1935	Sir T. Phillips

(Labour & National Service)

1939	Sir T. Phillips
1944	(Sir) G. Ince
1956	Sir H. Emmerson

(Labour)

1959	Sir L. Helsby
1962	Sir J. Dunnett
1966	(Sir) D. Barnes

(Employment & Productivity)

1968	Sir D. Barnes

(Employment)

1970	Sir D. Barnes
1974	C. Heron

Land & Natural Resources

1964	F. Bishop
1965 -1966	Sir B. Fraser

Local Government Board

1898	(Sir) S. Provis
1910 -1919	(Sir) H. Monro

Secretary to the Ld Chancellor[1]

1885 Sir K. Mackenzie
1915 Sir C. Schuster
1944 Sir A. Napier
1954 Sir G. Coldstream
1968 Sir D. Dobson

Materials

1951 A. Hitchman
1952 Sir J. Helmore
1953 }
-1954 } Sir E. Bowyer

Munitions

1915 Sir H. Llewellyn Smith
1916 E. Phipps
1917 Sir G. Greene
1920 { Sir S. Dannreuther
-1921 { D. Neylan

Unemployment Assistance Board (Chairman)

1934 Sir H. Betterton (Ld Rushcliffe)

(Assistance Board)

1940 Ld Rushcliffe
1941 Ld Soulbury

(National Assistance Board)

1948 G. Buchanan
1954 Sir G. Hutchinson (Ld Ilford)
1964 }
-1966 } Ld Runcorn

National Insurance

1944 Sir T. Phillips
1949 Sir H. Hancock
1951 Sir G. King
1953 (see *Pensions & National Insurance*)

National Service

1917 S. Fawcett
1918 }
-1919 } W. Vaughan

Northern Ireland

1972 Sir W. Nield
1973 (Sir) F. Cooper

Overseas Development

1964 Sir A. Cohen
1968 Sir G. Wilson
1970 (see *Foreign &*
-1974 *Commonwealth Office*)
1974 R. King

Parliamentary Commissioner

1967 Sir E. Compton
1971 Sir A. Marre

Pensions

1916 Sir M. Nathan
1919 Sir G. Chrystal
1935 Sir A. Hore
1941 (Sir) A. Cunnison
1946 Sir H. Parker
1948 Sir A. Wilson

(Pensions & National Insurance)

1953 Sir G. King
1955 Sir E. Bowyer
1965 Sir C. Jarrett
1966 (see *Social Security*)

Post Office

1899 Sir G. Murray
1903 Sir H. Babington-Smith
1909 Sir M. Nathan
1911 Sir A. King
1914 (Sir) E. Murray

(Director-General)

1934 (Sir) D. Banks
1936 Sir T. Gardiner
1946 Sir R. Birchall
1949 (Sir) A. Little
1955 (Sir) G. Radley
1960 Sir R. German
1966 { (Sir) J. Wall (*Deputy*
-1968 { *Chairman of Post Office Board*)

Power

(see *Fuel & Power*)

Prices and Consumer Protection

1974 K. Clucas

Privy Council (Clerk of the Council)

1899 (Sir) A. FitzRoy
1923 Sir M. Hankey

1938 Sir R. Howorth
1942 (Sir) E. Leadbitter
1951 F. Fernau
1953 (Sir) W. Agnew
1974 N. Leigh

Production

1942 Sir H. Self
1943 }
-1945 } J. Woods

Reconstruction

1943 }
-1945 } N. Brook

General Register Office (Registrar-General for England and Wales)

1880 Sir B. Henniker
1900 R. MacLeod
1902 (Sir) W. Dunbar
1909 (Sir) B. Mallet
1921 (Sir) S. Vivian
1945 (Sir) G. North
1959 E. Firth
1964 M. Reed
1972 G. Paine

Department of Scientific and Industrial Research (Secretary)

1916 (Sir) F. Heath
1927 H. Tizard
1929 (Sir) F. Smith
1939 (Sir) E. Appleton
1949 Sir B. Lockspeiser
1956 (Sir) H. Melville

(Science Research Council (Chairman))

1965 Sir H. Melville
1967 (Sir) B. Flowers
1973 S. Edwards

Office of the Minister for Science

1962 }
-1964 } F. Turnbull

Scottish Office

1892 Sir C. Scott-Moncrieff
1902 Sir R. Macleod
1909 Sir J. Dodds
1921 Sir J. Lamb
1933 Sir J. Jeffrey
1937 J. Highton
1937 Sir H. Hamilton

---

[1] Full title, Permanent Secretary to the Ld Chancellor and Clerk of the Crown in Chancery. The Clerk of the Crown is not in the ordinary sense a civil servant and is, among other things, an officer of both Houses of Parliament.

1946 (Sir) D. Milne
1959 Sir W. Murie
1965 (Sir) D. Haddow
1973 (Sir) N. Morrison

Shipping
1917 (Sir) J. Anderson
1919 ⎱ T. Lodge
–1920 ⎰
1939 ⎱ Sir C. Hurcomb
–1941 ⎰

Social Security
1966 Sir C. Jarrett
1968 (see *Health & Social Security*)

Supply
1939 Sir A. Robinson
1940 Sir G. Gater
1940 Sir W. Brown
1942 Sir W. Douglas
1945 O. Franks
1946 Sir A. Rowlands
1953 Sir J. Helmore
1956 Sir C. Musgrave
1959 ⎱ Sir W. Strath
–1959 ⎰

Technology
1964 Sir M. Dean
1966 Sir R. Clarke
1970 (see *Trade & Industry*)

Town & Country Planning
1943 Sir G. Whiskard
1946 Sir T. Sheepshanks

(Local Government & Planning)
1951 Sir T. Sheepshanks
1951 (see *Housing & Local Government*)

Board of Trade
1893 Sir C. Boyle
1901 Sir F. Hopwood
1907 (Sir) H. Llewellyn Smith
1913 ⎰ Sir G. Barnes
    ⎱ Sir H. Llewellyn Smith
1916 ⎰ Sir H. Llewellyn Smith
    ⎱ (Sir) W. Marwood
1919 ⎰ Sir S. Chapman
    ⎱ Sir W. Marwood
1919 ⎰ Sir S. Chapman
    ⎱ Sir H. Payne

1920 Sir S. Chapman
1927 Sir H. Hamilton
1937 Sir W. Brown
1941 Sir A. Overton
1945 Sir J. Woods
1951 Sir F. Lee
1960 Sir R. Powell
1968 Sir A. Part

(Trade & Industry)
1970 Sir A. Part

(Trade)
1974 Sir P. Thornton

Transport
1919 Sir F. Dunnell
1921 Sir W. Marwood
1923 Sir J. Brooke
1927 C. Hurcomb
1937 Sir L. Browett

(Director-General of War Transport)
1941 Sir C. Hurcomb

(Transport)
1946 Sir C. Hurcomb
1947 Sir G. Jenkins

(Transport & Civil) Aviation
1953 Sir G. Jenkins

(Transport) (and see *Aviation*)
1959 Sir J. Dunnett
1962 Sir T. Padmore
1968 Sir D. Serpell
1970 (see *Environment*)

Treasury
1894 Sir F. Mowatt
1902 ⎰ Sir F. Mowatt
    ⎱ Sir E. Hamilton
1903 ⎰ Sir E. Hamilton
    ⎱ Sir G. Murray
1908 Sir G. Murray
1911 Sir R. Chalmers
1913 ⎰ Sir T. Heath
    ⎱ Sir J. Bradbury
1916 ⎰ Sir T. Heath
    ⎰ Sir J. Bradbury
    ⎱ Sir R. Chalmers
1919 Sir W. Fisher
1939 Sir H. Wilson
1942 Sir R. Hopkins
1945 Sir E. Bridges

1956 ⎰ Sir N. Brook
    ⎱ Sir R. Makins
1960 ⎰ Sir N. Brook
    ⎱ Sir F. Lee
1962 ⎰ Sir N. Brook
    ⎱ W. Armstrong
1963 ⎰ Sir L. Helsby
    ⎱ (Sir) W. Armstrong
1968 ⎰ Sir W. Armstrong
    ⎱ Sir D. Allen
1968 Sir D. Allen
1974 (Sir) D. Wass

University Grants Committee (Chairman)
1919 Sir W. McCormick
1930 Sir W. Buchanan-Riddell
1935 Sir W. Moberly
1949 (Sir) A. Trueman
1953 (Sir) K. Murray
1968 (Sir) K. Berrill
1973 Sir F. Dainton

War Office
1897 Sir R. Knox
1901 Sir E. Ward
1914 Sir R. Brade
1920 Sir H. Creedy
1939 Sir J. Grigg
1942 ⎰ Sir F. Bovenschen
    ⎱ Sir E. Speed
1945 Sir E. Speed
1949 Sir G. Turner
1956 Sir E. Playfair
1960 (Sir) R. Way
1963 (Sir) A. Drew
1964 (see *Defence*)

Welsh Office
1964 (Sir) G. Daniel
1969 (Sir) I. Pugh
1971 H. Evans

Works
1895 Sir R. Brett (Vt Esher)
1902 Sir S. McDonnell
1912 Sir L. Earle
1933 Sir P. Duff
1941 Sir G. Whiskard
1943 Sir P. Robinson
1946 Sir H. Emmerson
1956 Sir E. Muir

(Public Building & Works)
1962 Sir E. Muir
1965 (Sir) A. Part
1968 Sir M. Cary
1970 (see *Environment*)

	Prime Minister's Principal Private Secretary		
1900	S. McDonnell	1939	A. Rucker
1902	J. Sandars	1940	E. Seal
1905	A. Ponsonby	1941	J. Martin
1908	V. Nash	1945	L. Rowan
1912	M. Bonham-Carter	1947	L. Helsby
1916	{ J. Davies	1950	D. Rickett
	{ Miss F. Stevenson	1951	D. Pitblado
1922	(Sir) R. Waterhouse	1952	{ D. Piblado
1928	R. Vansittart		{ J. Colville
1930	P. Duff	1955	D. Pitblado
1933	J. Barlow	1956	F. Bishop
1934	H. Vincent	1959	T. Bligh
1937	O. Cleverly	1964	D. Mitchell
		1966	A. Halls
		1970	A. Isserlis
		1970	R. Armstrong

Salary of Permanent Secretary to the Treasury

1900	£2,500	1950	£3,750
1910	£2,500	1960	£7,500
1920	£3,500	1970	£12,700
1930	£3,500	1974	£16,750
1940	£3,500	1975	£20,175[a]

[a] A salary increase to £23,000 was deferred from 1 Jan 75 to 1 Jan 76.

Size of Civil Service

Adequate statistics of the number of civil servants engaged in each branch of government activity since 1900 are not readily available. Moreover, the transfer of functions between departments makes comparisons of one year with another potentially misleading. An analysis of civil service strength for certain years is to be found in *The Organisation of British Central Government, 1914–1956*, by D. N. Chester and F. M. G. Wilson. The figures in heavy type in the following table are taken from the statement *Staffs Employed in Government Departments* which has been published annually, or more frequently, by the Treasury as a Command Paper since 1919 (with retrospective figures for 1914 included in the first issue). The figures in light type in the table are taken from the *Annual Estimates* presented to Parliament by the Civil Service and Revenue Departments, and the *East India Home Accounts*. These figures are liable to slight error as they are estimates and not reports of the actual staff employed. In each case they are estimates for the year ending March 31 of the following year (e.g. under the third column headed '1 Apr 1920' the estimates are for 1920–21). The source for the 1971 figures are departmental returns made to the Civil Service Department. The figures in this table should be used with great caution because of the considerable differences in the sources.

Number of Civil Servants

	1900–01	1 Aug 1914	1 Apr 1920	1 Apr 1930	1 Apr 1938	1 Apr 1950	1 Apr 1960	1 Apr. 1971
Total Non-industrial Staff	n.a.	282,420	380,963	306,154	376,491	575,274	637,374	498,425
Total Industrial Staff	n.a.	497,100	n.a.	483,100	204,400	396,900	358,900	201,660
Total Civil Service Staff	n.a.	779,520	n.a.	789,254	580,891	972,174	996,274	700,085
Admiralty	n.a.	4,366	13,432	7,433	10,609	30,801	30,731	f
War Office	n.a.	1,636	7,434	3,872	7,323	33,493	47,244	f
Air	..	..	2,839	1,704	4,317	24,407	27,563	f
Defence (Navy)	..	..	..	..	..	..	..	33,001
Defence (Army)	..	..	..	..	..	..	..	44,732
Defence (Air Force)	..	..	..	..	..	..	..	19,976
Defence (Centre)	..	..	..	..	..	..	..	14,131
Aviation Supply	..	..	..	..	..	5,271	24,756	16,963
Foreign Office[a]	142	187	885	730	902	6,195	5,992	g
Diplomatic Service	..	..	..	..	..	..	..	10,353
Overseas Development Administration								2,449
Colonial Office	109	214	256	365	438	1,286	1,211	.. g
Dominions & C.R.O.	..	..	..	52	91	904	847	..
India Office	589	554	342	n.a.	539	..	..	.. i
Irish Office	559	1,007	829	..	..	..	..	..
Scottish Office	159	401	517	68	n.a.	749	887	3,006
Welsh Office[h]	..	..	..	..	..	..	..	903
Treasury[b]	120	140	291	299	344	1,396	1,322	1,012
Home Office	297	773	926	1,024	1,688	3,953	3,534	21,743
Agriculture	182	2,976	3,446	2,463	4,588	16,842	14,938	14,874
Education (and Science)	864	2,187	1,522	1,041	1,435	3,280	2,738	4,127
Environment	..	..	..	..	..	..	..	38,806 j
Food	..	..	4,142	..	..	30,785	c	.. k
(Fuel and) Power	..	..	..	..	..	6,358	1,768	.. k
Health (and Social Security)	a	a	5,820	6,711	6,771	5,893	4,993	71,811 l
Labour	..	4,428	17,835	18,076	26,934	29,902	21,394	.. m
Employment	..	..	..	..	..	..	..	31,099 m
(Housing and) Local Government	425	963	d	d	d	1,312	2,802	j
Munitions	..	1,250	11,440	..	..	..	..	.. i
National Insurance	..	1,957	2,263	n.a.	n.a.	35,539	e	.. i
Pensions	..	..	24,169	6,175	3,147	10,954	36,323	.. i
Post Office	79,482	208,889	209,269	194,933	224,374	249,869	254,919	..
Supply	..	..	..	..	..	13,312	..	k
Board of Trade	1,359	2,535	5,410	4,398	4,611	10,136	6,735	k
Trade & Industry	..	..	..	..	..	..	..	24,549 k
Transport	..	..	876	759	2,820	6,906	6,909	.. j
Works	140	679	580	2,054	3,584	17,573	10,693	.. j

a Home civil servants only.
b Not including subordinate departments (e.g. Committee of Imperial Defence, University Grants Commission).
c Combined with Ministry of Agriculture and Fisheries.
d The functions of the Local Government Board passed to the Ministry of Health in 1919. In 1943 the Ministry of Town and Country Planning (later becoming the Ministry of Housing and Local Government) took back many of these functions from the Ministry of Health.
e National Insurance merged with the Ministry of Pensions, and in 1966 together with the N.A.B. became the Ministry of Social Security.
f In 1964 the Admiralty, War Office and Air Office were combined into the Ministry of Defence.
g In 1965 the Foreign Office, Commonwealth Relations Office, Trade Commission Service and attachés abroad were combined into the Diplomatic Service.
h The Welsh Office was set up in 1964.
i The Northern Ireland Office was set up in 1972.
j In 1970 Ministry of Housing and Local Government, Ministry of Public Building and Works, and the Ministry of Transport were combined into the Department of the Environment.
k In 1970 the Board of Trade and Ministry of Technology combined into the Department of Trade and Industry.
l In 1968 the Ministry of Social Security and Ministry of Health combined into the Department of Health and Social Security.
m The Ministry of Labour is now the Department of Employment.

Number of Civil Servants (*contd.*)

	1900–01	1 Aug 1914	1 Apr 1920	1 Apr 1930	1 Apr 1938	1 Apr 1950	1 Apr 1960	1 Apr 1971
Customs and Excise	3,792	10,256	12,602	11,659	14,669	14,236	15,338	17,949
Exchequer and Audit Department	230	269	269	331	369	501	532	577
Inland Revenue Board	5,345	9,753	19,446	21,059	24,342	49,740	56,026	69,765 }
National Assistance	..	..	..	..	8,105	8,516	10,509	
Stationery Office	100	517	728	1,660	1,947	3,241	2,903	3,480
Civil Service Department	..	..	..	..	..	..	..	2,070[n]

[j] In 1970 Ministry of Housing and Local Government, Ministry of Public Building and Works, and the Ministry of Transport were combined into the Department of the Environment.

[n] The Civil Service Department was formed in 1968 by the merger of the Civil Service Commission and the pay and management side of the Treasury.

SOURCES.—*Staffs Employed in Government Departments* (H.M.S.O., first published in 1919) figures in heavy type. *Civil Estimates, Estimates for Revenue Departments, Service Estimates,* and *East India Home Accounts*) (H.M.S.O. annually), figures in light type. Figures for 1960–71 collected by the Civil Service Department, in italics.

VII

ROYAL COMMISSIONS, COMMITTEES OF INQUIRY AND TRIBUNALS

Investigatory Processes

THE public investigation of problems can take a number of forms — Royal Commissions, Tribunals, *ad hoc* departmental Committees and special parliamentary conferences or committees. We do not deal here with purely parliamentary bodies like the Speaker's Conferences (on Electoral Reform — see p. 199 — and on Devolution) or like the Select Committees set up from time to time by the House of Commons and/or the House of Lords. But we attempt an exhaustive listing of all domestic Royal Commissions and of all Tribunals of Inquiry appointed under the *Tribunals of Inquiry Act, 1921*, as well as an arbitrary selection from the 1,000 or so *ad hoc* and statutory Committees of Inquiry appointed since 1900. It is, however, important to remember that the decision whether to refer a problem to a Royal Commission or a Committee is not necessarily determined by the importance of the subject. Royal Commissions are listed fully here because the number is not excessive. Departmental Committees, which have been much more numerous, often deal with relatively narrow and limited matters; we have selected only a few which seemed plainly as important as the average Royal Commission. We have also omitted any reference to committees and sub-committees appointed by Royal Commissions and by standing governmental advisory bodies, though these include some reports of importance, such as the Report to the Central Advisory Council on Education by Lady Plowden's Committee on Primary Education (1967).

Advisory Committees appointed by the Government fall into two basic kinds (apart from those which are just internal committees of civil servants): (*a*) standing committees, set up to give advice on such matters, usually within some general class of subjects, as may from time to time be referred to them or otherwise come to their attention; and (*b*) *ad hoc* committees, which are appointed to carry out some specific mandate and which come to an end when that mandate is discharged. These committees may be appointed directly by the Minister in his own name or indirectly in the name of the Crown. Finally, standing and *ad hoc* committees may both be appointed in two different ways: namely, by virtue of conventional or (in the case of the Crown) prerogative powers, or by virtue of authority conferred by Parliament by means of a statute.

Royal Commissions

Royal Commissions are *ad hoc* advisory committees formally appointed by the Crown by virtue of its prerogative powers. All such committees appointed since the turn of the century are listed in the table below, along with the name of their chairman, their size, the dates of their appointment and adjournment, and the Command number of their final report. There is no 'official' title for a Royal Commission, so that usage may vary slightly from that given below. Where there were two successive chairmen for a single committee, both are listed. The size of a Royal Commission is given as of the date of its appointment; subsequent changes in membership are not shown. The date of appointment is the date on which the Royal Warrant appointing the committee was signed, and the date of adjournment is the date of signature of the last report issued (or, failing that, the date of its presentation to the House of Commons). Command numbers form part of three successive series, each of which is marked by a different abbreviation of the word 'Command' as follows:

1900–18: Cd. 1 to Cd. 9239
1919–56: Cmd. 1 to Cmd. 9899
1956– : Cmnd. 1, which had reached Cmnd. 5900 by Feb 75

Title	Chairman	Size	Date appointed	Date of Report	Command number
Military and Civil Expenditure of India	Ld Welby	14	Aug 96	Apr 00	131
Local Taxation	Ld Balfour	14	Aug 96	May 01	638
University of London Act	Ld Davy	8	Aug 98	Feb 00	83
Newfoundland. Operation of Certain Treaties	Sir J. Bramston	2	Aug 98	Report not published	
Accidents to Railway Servants	Ld Hereford	14	May 99	Jan 00	41
Salmon Fisheries	E of Elgin	9	Mar 00	Jul 02	1188
Administration of the Port of London	E Egerton	7	Jun 00	..	
	Ld Revelstoke	7	..	Jun 02	1151
South African Hospitals	Sir R. Romer	5	Jul 00	Jan 01	453
Poisoning by Arsenic (Arsenic in Beer and Other Articles of Diet)	Ld Kelvin	6	Feb 01	Nov 03	1848
University Education (Ireland)	Ld Robertson	11	Jul 01	Feb 03	1483
Tuberculosis	Sir M. Foster	5	Aug 01	..	
	W. H. Power	5	..	Jun 11	5761
Coal Supplies	Ld Allerton	15	Dec 01	Jan 05	2353
Alien Immigration	Ld James	7	Mar 02	Aug 03	1741
Physical Training (Scotland)	Ld Mansfield	9	Mar 02	Mar 03	1507
Martial Law Sentences in S. Africa	Ld Alverstone	3	Aug 02	Oct 02	136
South African War	E of Elgin	7	Sep 02	Jul 03	1789
Superannuation in the Civil Service	L. Courtney	9	Nov 02	Aug 03	1744
Locomotion and Transport in London	Sir D. Barbour	12	Feb 03	Jun 05	2597
Militia and Volunteer Forces	D of Norfolk	10	Apr 03	May 04	2061
Food Supply in Time of War	Ld Balfour of Burleigh	17	Apr 03	Aug 05	2643
Trade Disputes and Trade Combinations	A Murray (Ld Dunedin)	5	Jun 03	Jan 06	2825
Ecclesiastical Discipline	Sir M. Hicks Beach	14	Apr 04	Jun 06	3040
The Feeble-Minded	M of Bath	10	Sep 04	..	..
Churches (Scotland)	E of Elgin	3	Dec 04	Apr 05	2494
War Stores in South Africa	Sir G. Farwell	5	Jun 05	Jul 06	3127
Motor-Car	Ld Selby	7	Sep 05	Jul 06	3080
Poor Laws	Ld Hamilton	18	Dec 05	Feb 09	4498
Canals and Inland Navigation of the United Kingdom	Ld Shuttleworth	15	Mar 06	Dec 09	4979
Duties of the Metropolitan Police	D. B. Jones	5	May 06	Jun 08	4156
	A. Lyttelton				
Registration of Title	Ld Dunedin	8	May 06	Jul 10	5316

Title	Chairman	Size	Date appointed	Date of Report	Command number
Safety in Mines	Ld Monkswell H. Cunynghame	9	Jun 06	..	..
Trinity College Dublin	Sir E. Fry	9	Jun 06	Jan 07	3311
Coast Erosion	I. Guest	13	Jul 06	reconstituted	..
Congested Districts in Ireland	E of Dudley	9	Jul 06	May 08	4097
Lighthouse Administration	G. Balfour	5	Aug 06	Jan 08	3923
Vivisection	Ld Selby A. Ram	10	Sep 06	Mar 12	6114
Care and Control of the Feeble-Minded	E of Radnor	12	Nov 06	Jul 08	4202
Shipping 'Rings' or Conferences generally	A. Cohen	21	Nov 06	reconstituted	..
Mines and Quarries	Ld Monkswell	9	May 07	Feb 11	5561
Church of England in Wales and Monmouthshire	Sir R. Vaughan-Williams	9	Jun 07	Nov 10	5432
Indian Decentralisation	Sir H. Primrose C. Hobhouse	6	Sep 07	Feb 09	4360
Whisky and other potable Spirits	Ld Hereford	8	Feb 08	Jul 09	4796
Coast Erosion and Afforestation	I. Guest	19	Mar 08	May 11	5708
Land Transfer Acts	Ld St. Aldwyn	12	Jul 08	Jan 11	5483
Systems of Election	Ld R. Cavendish	8	Dec 08	May 10	5163
University Education in London	Ld Haldane	8	Feb 09	Mar 13	6717
Mauritius	Sir F. Smettenham	3	May 09	Apr 10	5185
Trade Relations between Canada and the West Indies	Ld Balfour	5	Aug 09	Aug 10	5369
Selection of Justices of the Peace	Ld James	16	Nov 09	Jul 10	5250
Divorce and Matrimonial Causes	Ld Gorell	14	Nov 09	Nov 12	6478
Metalliferous Mines and Quarries	Sir H. Cunynghame	9	May 10	Jun 14	7476
Public Records	Sir F. Pollock	9	Oct 10	Apr 18	367
Railways Conciliation and Arbitration Scheme of 1907	Sir D. Hamel	5	Aug 11	Oct 11	5922
Malta	Sir F. Mowatt	3	Aug 11	May 12	6090
Civil Service	Ld MacDonnell H. Smith	19	Mar 12	Nov 15	7832
The Natural Resources, Trade and Legislation of the Dominions	E. Vincent	10	Apr 12	Feb 17	8462
Public Services (India)	Ld Islington	12	Sep 12	Aug 15	8382
Housing of the Industrial Population of Scotland, rural and urban	G. Ballantyne	12	Oct 12	Sep 17	8731
Delay in the King's Bench Division	Ld St. Aldwyn	11	Dec 12	Nov 13	7177
Finance and Currency (East Indies)	A. Chamberlain	10	Apr 13	Feb 14	7236
Venereal Diseases	Ld Sydenham	15	Nov 13	Feb 16	8189
Meat Export Trade of Australia	P. Street	1	Jun 14	Apr 15	7896
The Circumstances connected with the Landing of Arms at Howth July 26th, 1914	Ld Shaw	3	Aug 14	Sep 14	7631
University Education in Wales	Ld Haldane	9	Apr 16	Feb 18	8991
The Rebellion in Ireland	Ld Hardinge	3	May 16	Jun 16	8729
The Arrest and subsequent treatment of Mr Francis Sheehy of Skeffington, Mr Thomas Dickson, and Mr Patrick James McIntyre	Sir J. Simon	3	Aug 16	Sep 16	8376
Allegations against Sir John Jackson, Limited	A. Chamel	3	Nov 16	Mar 17	8518
Proportional Representation	J. Lowther	5	Feb 18	Apr 18	9044
Decimal Coinage	Ld Emmott	20	Aug 18	Feb 20	628
Income Tax	Ld Colwyn	21	Apr 19	Mar 20	615
Agriculture	H. Peat	23	Jul 19	Dec 19	473[1]
Oxford and Cambridge Universities	H. Asquith	19	Nov 19	Mar 22	1588

[1] Interim Report only; no Final Report published.

Title	Chairman	Size	Date appointed	Date of Report	Command number
The University of Dublin (Trinity College)	A. Geikie	5	Mar 20	Nov 20	1078
Fire Brigades and Fire Prevention	Sir P. Laurence	14	Jan 21	Jul 23	1945
The Importation of Store Cattle	Ld Finlay	5	May 21	Aug 21	1139
Local Government of Greater London	Vt Ullswater	8	Oct 21	Feb 23	1830
Honours	Ld Dunedin	7	Sep 22	Dec 22	1789
Local Government	E of Onslow	12	Feb 23	Nov 29	3436
Mining Subsidence	Ld Blanesburgh	13	Jun 23	Jun 27	2899
Superior Civil Services India	H. Lee	9	Jun 23	Mar 24	2128
Lunacy and Mental Disorder	H. Macmillan	10	Jul 24	Jul 26	2700
National Health Insurance	Ld Lawrence	13	Jul 24	Feb 26	2596
Food Prices	Sir A. Geddes	16	Nov 24	Apr 25	2390
Indian Currency and Finance	E. Hilton Young	9	Aug 25	Jul 26	Parl. paper
The Coal Industry	Sir H. Samuel	4	Sep 25	Mar 26	2600
Court of Session and the Office of Sheriff Principal (Scotland)	Ld Clyde	9	Jan 26	Jan 27	2801
Agriculture in India	M of Linlithgow	10	Apr 26	Apr 28	3132
Cross-River Traffic in London	Ld Lee of Fareham	6	Jul 26	Nov 26	2772
Land Drainage in England and Wales	Ld Bledisloe	11	Mar 27	Dec 27	2993
National Museums and Art Galleries	Ld d'Abernon	11	Jul 27	Jan 30	3463
London Squares	M of Londonderry	14	Aug 27	Sep 28	3196
Police Powers and Procedure	Ld Lee	8	Aug 28	Mar 29	3297
Transport	Sir A. Griffith-Boscowen	12	Aug 28	Dec 30	3751
Labour in India	J. Whitley	11	Jul 29	Mar 31	3583
Licensing (England and Wales)	Ld Amulree	19	Sep 29	May 31	3988
Civil Service	Ld Tomlin	16	Oct 29	Jul 31	3909
Licensing (Scotland)	Ld Mackay	14	Oct 29	May 31	3894
Unemployment Insurance	H. Gregory	7	Dec 30	Oct 32	4185
Malta	Ld Askwith	3	Apr 31	Jan 32	3993
Lotteries and Betting	Sir S. Rowlatt	12	Jun 32	Jun 33	4341
Newfoundland	Ld Amulree	3	Feb 33	Oct 33	4480
The University of Durham	Ld Moyne	8	Mar 34	Jan 35	4815
Tithe Rentcharge in England and Wales	J. Williams	4	Aug 34	Nov 35	5095
Despatch of Business at Common Law	Earl Peel	7	Dec 34	Jan 36	5065
Private Manufacture of and Trading in Arms	J. Bankes	7	Feb 35	Sep 36	5292
Local Government in the Tyneside Area	Sir A. Scott	5	May 35	Feb 37	5402
Merthyr Tydfil	Sir A. Lowry	2	May 35	Nov 35	5039
Safety in Coal Mines	Ld Rockley	10	Dec 35	Dec 38	5890
Palestine	Earl Peel	1	Aug 36	Jun 37	5479
The Distribution of the Industrial Population	Sir M. Barlow	13	Jul 37	Dec 39	6153
Rhodesia-Nyasaland	Vt Bledisloe	1	Mar 38	Mar 39	5949
West Indies	Ld Moyne	1	Aug 38	Dec 39	6607
Workmen's Compensation	Sir H. Hetherington	15	Dec 38	Dec 44	658
Population	Vt Simon	16	Mar 44	..	
	Sir H. Henderson	14	May 46	Mar 49	7695
Equal Pay	C. Asquith	9	Oct 44	Oct 46	6937
Justices of the Peace	Ld du Parcq	16	Jun 46	May 48	7463
The Press	Sir D. Ross	17	Apr 47	Jun 49	7700
Betting, Lotteries and Gaming	H. Willink	13	Apr 49	Mar 51	8190
Capital Punishment	Sir E. Gowers	12	May 49	Sep 53	8932
Taxation of Profits and Income	Ld Cohen	14	Jan 51		
	Ld Radcliffe	14	..	May 55	9474
University Education in Dundee	Ld Tedder	9	Mar 51	Apr 52	8514
Marriage and Divorce	Ld Morton of Henryton	18	Sep 51	Dec 55	9678
Scottish Affairs	E of Balfour	15	Jul 52	Jul 54	9212
East Africa	Sir H. Dow	8	Jan 53	May 55	9475

Title	Chairman	Size	Date appointed	Date of Report	Command number
The Civil Service	Sir R. Priestley	12	Nov 53	Nov 55	9613
The Law Relating to Mental Illness and Mental Deficiency	Ld Percy of Newcastle	11	Feb 54	May 57	169
Common Land	Sir I. Jennings	12	Dec 55	Jul 58	462
Doctors' and Dentists' Remuneration	Sir H. Pilkington	9	Mar 57	Feb 60	939
Local Government in Greater London	Sir E. Herbert	7	Dec 57	Oct 60	1164
The Police	Sir H. Willink	15	Jan 60	Apr 62	1728
The Press	Ld Shawcross	5	Mar 61	May 62	1811
The Penal System in England and Wales	Vt Amory	16	Jul 64	*wound up* May 66	
Reform of the Trade Unions and Employers' Associations	Ld Donovan	12	Apr 65	Jun 68	3623
Medical Education	Ld Todd	16	Jun 65	Mar 68	3569
Tribunals of Inquiry	Sir C. Salmon	7	Feb 66	Nov 66	3121
The Examination of Assizes and Quarter Sessions	Ld Beeching	8	Nov 66	Sep 69	4153
Local Government, England	Sir J. Maud (Ld)	11	May 66	May 69	4040
Local Government, Scotland	Ld Wheatley	9	May 66	Sep 69	4150
The Constitution	Ld Crowther Ld Kilbrandon	16	Apr 69 ..	Oct 73	5460
The Press	Sir M. Finer O. McGregor	11	Jun 74 ..		
Distribution of Income	Ld Diamond	8	Jul 74		
Standards of Conduct in Government	Ld Salmon	12	Jul 74		

Permanent and Operating Commissions

Certain Royal Commissions have an enduring existence:

The Royal Commission on Historical Manuscripts set up in 1869 sits under the *ex officio* Chairmanship of the Master of the Rolls. It was reconstituted with extended powers in 1959. Its task is to advise and assist in the preservation of historical manuscripts and to publish them.

The *Royal Commission on Historical Monuments* was set up for England in 1908 with similar bodies for Scotland (reconstituted 1948) and Wales and Monmouthshire. Their task is to maintain an inventory of Ancient Monuments.

The *Royal Fine Arts Commission* was set up in 1924 (re-constituted in 1933 and 1946) and the *Royal Fine Art Commission for Scotland* in 1927 (reconstituted 1948): their task is to inquire into questions of public amenity and artistic importance.

The *Royal Commission for the Exhibition of 1851*, surviving from the winding up of the affairs of the Great Exhibitions, still distributes the income from surplus funds to promote scientific and artistic education. There was also the *Royal Commission for the Patriotic Fund (1854–1904)*. In addition, there have been operating Commissions for the *Paris Exhibition of 1900*, the *St Louis Exhibition of 1904*, and for the *International Exhibitions at Brussels, Rome, and Turin in 1910 and 1911*. Another miscellaneous group of operating Royal Commissions covered *Sewage Disposal (1898–1915)*, *Horse-Breeding (1887–1911)*, and *Crofter Colonisation (1888–1906)*.

War produced another group of operating or semi-permanent Royal Commissions, *Sugar Supply* (1914–21), *Wheat Supplies* (1916–25), *Paper and Paper making materials* (1917–[1]). *Defence of the Realm Losses* (1915–20), *Compensation for Suffering Damage by Enemy Action* (1921–24), and *Awards to Inventors* (1919–35, 1946–56).

[1] No Final Report.

Other Crown Committees

The Crown has also appointed a number of other advisory committees, some of which are called 'Royal Commissions' but all of which are different from those listed above. Some of them are different because they are standing, not *ad hoc*, in nature. Two of these appointed in the nineteenth century are still in existence: the Commission on the Exhibition of 1851 (appointed in 1850) and the Historical Manuscripts Commission (appointed in 1869). In the present century there have been thirteen others appointed (see table below), of which six are still in existence. All of them were appointed by virtue of prerogative powers. Other Crown advisory committees are different from those listed above because they were appointed by virtue of statutory, not prerogative, powers. Four, all of them *ad hoc* in nature, have been appointed in this century; they dealt with Property of the Free Church of Scotland (1905–10, Cd. 5060), the Election in Worcester in 1906 (1906, Cd. 3262), the Coal Industry (1919, Cmd. 360), and Indian Government (1927–30, Cmd. 3568). Finally, the Government in Ireland prior to 1922 appointed a special kind of committee in the name of the Crown called a 'Vice-Regal Commission'; thirteen were appointed in this century (see table below).

Standing Advisory Committees Appointed by the Crown since 1900

Title	Date of appointment		Date of adjournment		Report
Ancient and Historical Monuments and Constructions in Scotland	Feb	08	*		Cmnd. 4808
Ancient Monuments and Constructions of Wales and Monmouthshire	Aug	08	*		Cmnd. 2551
Ancient and Historical Monuments and Constructions of England	Oct	08	*		Cmnd. 4979
Supply of Sugar	Aug	14	Apr	21	Cmd. 1300
Defence of the Realm Losses	Mar	15	Nov	20	Cmd. 1044
Supply of Paper	Feb	16	Feb	18	None issued
Supply of Wheat	Oct	16	Jul	25	Cmd. 2462
Awards to Inventors	Mar	19	Nov	37	Cmd. 5594
Compensation for Suffering and Damage by Enemy Action	Aug	21	Feb	24	Cmd. 2066
Fine Art	May	24	*		Cmnd. 4832
Fine Art for Scotland	Aug	27	*		Cmnd. 4317
Awards to Inventors	May	46	Apr	56	Cmd. 9744
Environmental Pollution	Feb	70	*		Cmnd. 5054

* Committee still in existence; report is latest issued.

Irish Vice-Regal Commissions

Title	Chairman	Size	Date appointed	Date of Report	Command number
Irish Inland Fisheries	S. Walker	7	Aug 99	Jan 01	448
Poor Law Reform in Ireland	W. L. Micks	3	May 03	Oct 06	3202
Trinity College, Dublin, Estates Commission	G. Fitzgibbon	3	Jun 04	Apr 05	2526
Arterial Drainage (Ireland)	A. Binnie	5	Sep 05	Feb 07	3374
Irish Railways, Including Light Railways	C. Scotter	7	Jul 06	Jul 10	5247
Circumstances of the Loss of the Regalia of the Order of St. Patrick	J. Shaw	3	Jan 08	Jan 08	3936
Irish Milk Supply	P. O'Neill	9	Nov 11	Oct 13	7129
Primary Education (Ireland) System of Inspection	S. Dill	8	Jan 13	Jan 14	7235
Dublin Disturbances	D. Henry	2	Dec 13	Feb 14	7269
Primary Education (Ireland) 1918	Ld Killanin	17	Aug 18	Feb 19	60
Intermediate Education (Ireland)	T. Molony	14	Aug 18	Mar 19	66
Under Sheriffs and Bailiffs (Ireland)	T. O'Shaughnessy	5	Oct 18	May 19	190
Reorganisation and Pay of the Irish Police Forces	J. Ross	6	Oct 19	Dec 19	603
Clerk of the Crown and Peace, Etc. (Ireland)	J. Wakely	7	Oct 19	Jun 20	805

Departmental Committees

Departmental Committees are *ad hoc* advisory committees appointed by Ministers by virtue of their conventional powers. As such they are the direct counterpart of Royal Commissions. In the table below are listed some of the more important Departmental Committees appointed since the turn of the century. As with Royal Commissions, there is no 'official' title for a Departmental Committee, so usage may vary slightly; where there were two successive chairmen, both are listed; and the dates of appointment and report as well as the Command number are derived in the same manner as for Royal Commissions.

A Select List of Departmental Committees 1900-

In the absence of any single official title for a Committee we have tried to select the most commonly used short title. The Command number given is that of the final report.

Title	Chairman	Date appointed	Date of Report	Command number
Compensation for injuries to workmen	K. Digby	Nov 03	Aug 04	2208
Motor Cars	R. Hobhouse	Jan 04	Apr 04	2069
Income Tax	C. Ritchie	..	Jun 05	2575
Company and Commercial law and Practice	C. Warmington	Feb 05	Jun 06	3052
Accounts of local authorities	W. Runciman	Jan 06	Jul 07	3614
Law of Copyright	Ld Gorell	Mar 09	Dec 09	4967
Probation of Offenders Act '07	H. Samuel	Mar 09	Dec 09	5001
Procedure of Royal Commissions	Ld Balfour of Burleigh	Apr 09	Jun 10	5235
Railway Agreements and amalgamations	R. Rea	June 09	Apr 11	5631
Alien Immigrants at the Port of London	R. Lehmann	..	Mar 11	5575

Title	Chairman	Date appointed	Date of Report	Command number
Educational Endowments	C. Trevelyan	..	Mar 11	5662
National Guarantee for the War Risks of Shipping	A. Chamberlain	..	..	7560
Local Taxation	Sir J. Kempe	Nov 12	Mar 14	7315
Retrenchment in the public expenditure	R. McKenna	Jul 15	Sep 15	8068
Royal Aircraft Factory	R. Burbridge	Mar 16	Jul 16	8191
Increase of Prices of Commodities since the beginning of the War	J. Robertson	Jun 16	Sep 16	8358
Summer Time	J. Wilson	Sep 16	Feb 17	8487
Commercial and Industrial Policy. Imperial Preference	Ld Balfour of Burleigh	..	Feb 17	8482
Currency and Foreign Exchanges	Ld Cunliffe	Jan 18	Dec 19	464
National Expenditure	Ld Geddes	Aug 21	Feb 22	1589
Broadcasting	Sir M. Sykes	Apr 23	Aug 23	1951
Imperial Wireless Telegraphy	Sir R. Donald	Jan 24	Feb 24	2060
National Debt and Taxation	H. Colwyn	Mar 24	Nov 26	2800
Broadcasting	Ld Crawford and Balcarres	Aug 25	Mar 26	2599
Ministers' Powers	E of Donoughmore	Oct 29	Apr 32	4060
Finance and Industry	H. Macmillan (Ld)	Nov 29	Jun 31	3897
Regional Development	H. Chelmsford	Jan 31	Mar 31	3915
National Expenditure	Sir G. May	Mar 31	Jul 31	3920
Depressed Areas	(3 Area Chairmen)	Apr 34	Nov 34	4728
Broadcasting	Vt Ullswater	Apr 35	Mar 36	5091
Parliamentary Pensions	Sir W. Fisher	Jul 35	Nov 37	5624
Compensation and Betterment	Sir A. Uthwatt	Jan 41	Sep 42	6291
Social Insurance and Allied Services	Sir W. Beveridge	Jun 41	Nov 42	6404
Training of Civil Servants	R. Assheton	Feb 43	Apr 44	6525
Company Law Amendment	Sir L. Cohen	Jun 43	Jun 45	6659
Television	Ld Hankey	Sep 43	Dec 44	Non-parl
Rent Control	Vt Ridley	Nov 43	Feb 45	6621
Legal Aid and Legal Advice in England and Wales	Ld Rushcliffe	May 44	May 45	6641
Gas Industry	G. Heyworth	Jun 44	Nov 45	6699
Social and Economic Research	Sir J. Clapham	Jan 45	Jun 46	6868
Care of Children	Miss M. Curtis	Mar 45	Aug 46	6922
National Parks (England and Wales)	Sir A. Hobhouse	Jul 45	Mar 47	7121
New Towns	Ld Reith	Oct 45	Jul 46	6876
Port Transport Industry	R. Evershed	Nov 45	Dec 45	Non-parl
Shops and Non-Industrial Employment	Sir E. Gowers	Jan 46	Mar 49	7664
Resale Price Maintenance	Sir G. Lloyd-Jacob	Aug 47	Mar 49	7696
Higher Civil Service Remuneration	Ld Chorley	Jan 48	Sep 48	7635
Leasehold	Ld Uthwatt Ld Jenkins	Feb 48 ..	Jun 50	7982
Political Activities of Civil Servants	J. Masterman	Apr 48	Apr 49	7718
Intermediaries	Sir E. Herbert	Feb 49	Oct 49	7904
Broadcasting	Ld Beveridge	Jun 49	Dec 50	8116
Fuel and Power Resources	Vt Ridley	Jul 51	Jul 52	8647
Departmental Records	Sir J. Grigg	Jun 52	May 54	9163
National Health Service	C. Guillebaud	May 53	Nov 55	9663
Air Pollution	Sir H. Beaver	Jul 53	Nov 54	9322
Crichel Down	A. Clark	Nov 53	May 54	9176
Electricity Supply Industry	Sir E. Herbert	Jul 54	Dec 55	9672
Homosexual Law Reform	Sir J. Wolfenden	Aug 54	Aug 57	247
Crown Lands	Sir M. Trustram Eve	Dec 54	May 55	9843
Dock Workers' Scheme	Sir P. Devlin	Jul 55	Jun 56	9813
Administrative Tribunals and Inquiries	Sir O. Franks	Nov 55	Jul 57	218
Children and Young People	Vt Ingleby	Oct 56	Oct 60	1191
Damage and Casualties in Port Said	Sir E. Herbert	Dec 56	Dec 56	47
Working of the Monetary System	Ld Radcliffe	May 57	Jul 59	827
Interception of Communications	Sir N. Birkett	Jun 57	Sep 57	283
Preservation of Downing Street	E of Crawford	Jul 57	Mar 58	457
The Structure of the Public Library Service in England and Wales	Sir S. Roberts	Sep 57	Dec 58	660
The Youth Service in England and Wales	Ctee of Albemarle	Nov 58	Oct 59	929
Consumer Protection	J. Molony	Jun 59	Apr 62	1781
Control of Public Expenditure	Ld Plowden	Jul 59	Jun 61	1432
Company Law Committee	Ld Jenkins	Dec 59	May 62	1749

Title	Chairman	Date appointed	Date of Report	Command number
Broadcasting	Sir H. Pilkington	Jul 60	Jun 62	1753
Higher Education	Ld Robbins	Feb 61	Sep 63	2154
Major Ports of Great Britain	Vt Rochdale	Mar 61	Jul 62	1824
Security in the Public Service	Ld Radcliffe	May 61	Nov 61	1681
Economy of Northern Ireland	Sir R. Hall	May 61	Jun 62	1835
Sunday Observance	Ld Crathorne	Jul 61	Sep 64	2528
Decimal Currency	E of Halsbury	Dec 61	Jul 63	2145
Organisation of Civil Science	Sir B. Trend	Mar 62	Sep 63	2171
The Vassall Case	Sir C. Cunningham	Oct 62	Nov 62	1871
Security Service and Mr Profumo	Ld Denning	Jun 63	Sep 63	2152
Remuneration of Ministers and M.P.s	Sir G. Lawrence	Dec 63	Oct 64	2516
Social Studies	Ld Heyworth	Jun 63	Feb 65	2660
Housing in Greater London	Sir M. Holland	Aug 63	Mar 65	2605
Port Transport Industry	Ld Devlin	Oct 64	Nov 64	2523
Aircraft Industry	Ld Plowden	Dec 64	Dec 65	2853
Shipbuilding	R. Geddes	Feb 65	Feb 66	2939
Age of Majority	Sir J. Latey	Jul 65	Jun 67	3342
Local Authority Personal Social Services	F. Seebohm	Dec 65	Jul 68	3703
Death Certification and Coroners	N. Brodrick	Mar 65	Sep 71	4810
Civil Service	Ld Fulton	Feb 66	Jul 68	3638
Prison Security	E. Mountbatten	Oct 66	Dec 66	3175
Fire Service	Sir R. Holroyd	Feb 67	May 70	4371
Shipping	Vt Rochdale	Jul 67	Feb 70	4337
Intermediate Areas	Sir J. Hunt	Sep 67	Feb 69	3998
Civil Air Transport	Sir E. Edwards	Nov 67	Apr 69	4018
Legal Education	Sir R. Ormrod	Dec 67	Jan 71	4595
Commercial Rating	D. Anderson	Aug 68	Apr 70	4366
Overseas Representation	Sir V. Duncan	Aug 68	Jun 69	4107
Consumer Credit	Ld Crowther	Sep 68	Dec 70	4596
Adoption of Children	Sir W. Houghton	Jul 69	Jul 72	5107
	F. Stockdale	..		
Small Firms	J. Bolton	Jul 69	Sep 71	4811
Rent Acts	H. Francis	Oct 69	Jan 71	4609
Privacy	K. Younger	May 70	May 72	5012
Safety and Health at Work	Ld Robens	May 70	Jun 72	5034
Defence Procurement	D. Rayner	Oct 70	Mar 71	4641
Dispersal of Government Work from London	Sir H. Hardman	Oct 70	Jun 73	5322
Lotteries	K. Witney	Jan 71	Dec 73	5506
Abuse of Social Security	Sir H. Fisher	Mar 71	Mar 73	5228
Liquor Licensing	Ld Erroll of Hale	Apr 71	Oct 72	5154
Scottish Licencing Laws	G. Clayson	Apr 71	Aug 73	5354
Official Secrets Act	Ld Franks	Apr 71	Sep 72	5104
Public Trustee Office	H. Hutton	May 71	Nov 71	4913
Contempt of Court	Ld Phillimore	Jun 71	Dec 74	5794
National Savings	Sir H. Page	Jun 71	Jun 73	5273
Brutality in Northern Ireland	Sir E. Compton	Aug 71	Nov 71	4823
Interrogation of Terrorists	Ld Parker of Waddington	Nov 71	Jan 72	4901
Probation Officers and Social Workers	J. Butterworth	Dec 71	Aug 72	5076
Psychiatric Patients	Sir C. Aarvold	Jun 72	Jan 73	5191
Legal Procedures to deal with Terrorists in Northern Ireland	Ld Diplock	Oct 72	Nov 72	5185
Handling of Complaints against Police	A. Gordon-Brown	Apr 73	Mar 74	5582
Export of Animals for Slaughter	Ld O'Brien	Jul 73	Mar 74	5566
Conduct in Local Government	Ld Redcliffe-Maud	Oct 73	May 74	5636
Pay of Non-University Teachers	Ld Houghton	Jun 74	Jan 75	5848
Civil Liberties in Northern Ireland	Ld Gardiner	Jun 74	Jan 75	5879

Inquiries held under the Tribunals of Inquiry (Evidence) Act, 1921

Tribunals of Inquiry (Evidence) Act, 1921

Upon a resolution of both Houses of Parliament on a matter of urgent public importance a tribunal might be appointed by the Sovereign or a Secretary of State with all the powers of the High Court as regards examination of witnesses and production of documents, for the objective investigation of facts.

Title	Members of Tribunal	Year	Command number
Destruction of documents by Ministry of Munitions officials	Ld Cave Ld Inchape Sir W. Plender	1921	1340
Royal Commission on Lunacy and Mental Disorder given powers under the Act	H. Macmillan + 9	1924	2700
Arrest of R. Sheppard, R.A.O.C. Inquiry into conduct of Metropolitan Police	J. Rawlinson	1925	2497
Allegations made against the Chief Constable of Kilmarnock in connection with the dismissal of Constables Hill and Moore from the Burgh Police Force	W. Mackenzie	1925	2659
Conditions with regard to mining and drainage in an area around the County Borough of Doncaster	Sir H. Monro (Ch)	1926/8	..
Charges against the Chief Constable of St. Helens by the Watch Committee	C. Parry T. Walker	1928	3103
Interrogation of Miss Irene Savidge by Metropolitan Police at New Scotland Yard	Sir J. Eldon Banks H. Lees-Smith J. Withers	1928	3147
Allegations of bribery and corruption in connection with the letting and allocation of stances and other premises under the control of the Corporation of Glasgow	Ld Anderson Sir R. Boothby J. Hunter	1933	4361
Unauthorised disclosure of information relating to the Budget	Sir J. Porter G. Simonds R. Oliver	1936	5184
The circumstances surrounding the loss of H.M. Submarine "Thetis"	Sir J. Bucknill	1939	6190
The conduct before the Hereford Juvenile Court Justices of the proceedings against Craddock and others	Ld Goddard	1943	6485
The administration of the Newcastle upon Tyne Fire, Police and Civil Defence Services	R. Burrows	1944	6522
Bribery of Ministers of the Crown or other public servants in connection with the grant of licences, etc.	Sir J. Lynskey G. Russell Vick G. Upjohn	1948	7616
Allegations of improper disclosure of information relating to the raising of the Bank Rate	Ld Parker E. Holland G. Veale	1957	350
Allegations that John Waters was assaulted on 7th December, 1957, at Thurso and the action taken by Caithness Police in connection therewith	Ld Sorn Sir J. Robertson J. Dandie	1959	718
The circumstances in which offences under the Official Secrets Act were committed by William John Christopher Vassall	Ld Radcliffe Sir J. Barry Sir E. Milner Holland	1962	2009
The events on Sunday, 30th January 1972 which led to loss of life in connection with the procession in Londonderry on that day	Ld Widgery	1972	H.C. 220/72

SOURCES.—P. and G. Ford, *A Breviate of Parliamentary Papers* (3 vols, 1951–61); H. M. Clokie and J. W. Robinson, *Royal Commissions of Inquiry: the Significance of Investigations in British Politics* (1937); R. V. Vernon and N. Mansergh, *Advisory Bodies* (1937); C. J. Hanser, *Guide to Decision: the Royal Commission* (1966); G. W. Keeton, *Trial by Tribunal* (1960); S. A. de Smith, *Constitutional and Administrative Law* (1971); R. Chapman, *The Role of Commissions in Policy Making* (1973); T. J. Cartwright, *Royal Commissions and Departmental Committees in Britain* (1974); and the Report of the Royal Commission on the Tribunals of Inquiry (Evidence) Act, 1921 (Cmnd. 3121, published Feb 1966).

Tribunals and Inquiries

Ministers may also appoint *ad hoc* advisory committees by virtue of statutory authority. Such authority may be general in nature, referring to certain circumstances which, whenever they occur, permit or require a Minister to appoint a committee; or statutory authority may be specific in nature, dealing with the appointment of a single committee at a single time. In either case, the authorisation may be mandatory or discretionary. The total number of statutory *ad hoc* advisory committees is enormous. Reliable estimates put the number currently appointed in excess of 10,000 per year. The vast majority of these are of two kinds: tribunals and inquiries.

Select Examples of Tribunals and Inquiries

A large number of statutory tribunals, with jurisdiction to decide quasi-legal disputes, have been created since 1900. By 1960 there were over 2,000 tribunals within the supervisory role of the *Council on Tribunals*. The fifteen-member *Council on Tribunals* was set up under the *Tribunals and Inquiries Act, 1958*, following the report of the Franks Committee (*Cmnd. 218/1957*). Its role is purely advisory, but it has to report annually to Parliament.

The Schedule to the *Tribunals and Inquiries Act, 1958* gives the list of tribunals under the supervision of the Council on Tribunals. Others have been added by subsequent legislation, e.g. by the *Mental Health Act, 1959*, the *Finance Act, 1960*, the *Civil Aviation Licensing Act, 1960*, the *Betting, Gaming and Lotteries Act, 1963*, and the *Rent Act, 1965*.

These are some of the more important tribunals:

The National Health Service Tribunals

These hear complaints against medical practitioners and dentists under the National Health Service Acts.

Industrial Courts of Inquiry (Industrial Courts Act, 1919)

The Minister of Labour empowered to refer any matter relevant to a trade dispute to these.

The Lands Tribunal (Lands Tribunal Act, 1949)

This has varied jurisdiction, including questions relating to compulsory acquisition of land by Government Departments and local authorities, such as the value of land and compensation payable under the different compensation acts.

The Transport Tribunal (Transport Acts, 1947 and 1962)

This had jurisdiction over railway charges, road transport, harbours and canals and hears appeals from various transport licensing authorities. The tribunal's jurisdiction over railway charges were removed as far as the British Railways are concerned (but not the London Transport Commission) by the Transport Act, 1962.

National Assistance Appeal Tribunals (National Assistance Act, 1948)

These used to hear appeals against the National Assistance Board on such questions as refusal to give assistance, and the nature and amount of assistance.

Supplementary Benefits Appeals Tribunals (Social Security Act, 1965)

These hear appeals against the Supplementary Benefits Commission on such questions as refusal to pay supplementary pensions or allowances or for any decision on a claim for supplementary benefits.

National Insurance Tribunals

These decide questions concerning rights to benefit under the *National Insurance Act, 1946*, and the *National Insurance (Industrial Injuries) Act, 1946*. (These questions were determined in the first instance by insurance officers of the Ministry of National Insurance until 1966 and since 1966 of the Ministry of Social Security.)

Rent Tribunals

These determine the fair rent for furnished houses under the *Furnished Houses (Rent Control) Act, 1946*.

Pensions Appeal Tribunals (*Pensions Appeal Act, 1943*)

These hear appeals against the Minister of Pensions concerning war pensions.

Rent Assessment Committees (*Rent Act, 1965*)

These fix fair rents for houses with rateable value not exceeding £200 (£400 in London) on appeal from the decision of a Rent Officer.

IX

ADMINISTRATION OF JUSTICE

Major Criminal Justice Legislation 1900-

Poor Prisoners' Defence Act, 1903. This was the first Act which made provision for legal aid, which was limited to trials on indictment.

The Probation of Offenders Act, 1907. This extended courts' probation powers and allowed appointment of official probation officers.

The Criminal Appeal Act, 1907. This created the Court of Criminal Appeal.

The Prevention of Crime Act, 1908. This provided for 'borstal training' of young recidivists and 'preventive detention' for adult habitual criminals.

The Children Act, 1908. This created 'places of detention' (later 'Remand Homes') and Juvenile Courts; it also prohibited imprisonment of those under 14, restricted imprisonment of those from 14–17 and abolished death sentence for those under 17.

The Criminal Justice Administration Act, 1914. This required Summary Courts to give time for payment of fines.

Poor Prisoners' Defence Act, 1930. This Act provided a comprehensive system of legal aid, extending aid to preliminary inquiries and to cases heard summarily before magistrates' courts.

Summary Jurisdiction (Appeals) Act, 1933. This Act made provision for free legal aid for criminal cases, payable out of county or borough funds at the discretion of the magistrates.

The Children and Young Persons Act, 1933. This Act which followed the 1927 Report of the Cecil Committee on the treatment of young offenders, codified and extended 'care and protection' law; it also raised the age of criminal responsibility from 7 to 8.

The Administration of Justice (Miscellaneous Provisions) Act, 1933. This abolished Grand Juries.

The Criminal Justice Act, 1948. Following the lines of a 1938 Bill abandoned through the onset of war, this extended the fining powers of higher courts; it further restricted imprisonment of juveniles and abolished distinction between penal servitude, imprisonment, etc.; it also improved law on probation, introduced corrective training and a new form of preventive detention and it provided for remand centres, attendance centres, and detention centres. It also abolished the right of peers to be tried by the House of Lords.

Legal Aid and Advice Act, 1949. This introduced a new system of aid for civil cases. It provided for the establishment of a network of local committees, composed of solicitors and some barristers to grant legal aid under regulations made by the Lord Chancellor. By this Act, aid was extended to cover all proceedings in civil courts and civil proceedings in magistrates' courts, except for certain types of action (of which defamation and breach of promise were the most important).

Cost in Criminal Cases Act, 1952. This Act empowered the courts, in the case of an indictable offence, to order reasonable defence costs to be paid out of public funds, when the accused was discharged or acquitted.

The Homicide Act, 1957. This amended the law on murder, distinguishing capital and non-capital murder and introducing the defence of diminished responsibility.

The First Offenders Act, 1958. This restricted imprisonment of adults by Summary Courts.

Administration of Justice Act, 1960. This gave a greatly extended right of appeal to the House of Lords in criminal matters and reformed the law relating to habeas corpus and to contempt of court.

Legal Aid Act, 1960. This relates financial conditions for legal aid and makes further provision for the remuneration of counsel and solicitors.

The Criminal Justice Act, 1961. This provided compulsory supervision after release from detention centres and rationalised custodial sentences for 17–21 age-group.

The Children and Young Persons Act, 1963. This raised the age of criminal responsibility from 8 to 10, and redefined the need for 'care, protection, and control'.

The Criminal Injuries Compensation Board was set up in 1964, under an ex gratia State Scheme for compensating victims of crimes of violence.

The Murder (Abolition of Death Penalty) Act, 1965. This suspended death penalty until 1970, and substituted a mandatory 'life' sentence. In 1969 Parliament voted to continue the suspension indefinitely.

Criminal Appeal Act, 1966. This amalgamated the Court of Criminal Appeal and the Court of Appeal.

The Criminal Justice Act, 1967. This introduced suspended sentences, parole, a new type of sentence for recidivists and further restricted imprisonment of adults. It allowed majority verdicts (10–2) by juries.

The Theft Act, 1967. This rationalised definitions of theft and other dishonesty.

The Criminal Law Act, 1967. This replaced the distinction between felonies and misdemeanours, with a distinction between arrestable and non-arrestable offences.

The Children and Young Persons Act, 1969. Redefined the circumstances in which juvenile courts could make orders dealing with children and young persons, and simplified the nature of such orders; it also provided for the raising of the minimum age of liability to prosecution (although this has not yet been implemented) and for the reorganisation of approved schools, children's homes, etc., into a system of 'community homes' controlled by local authorities.

The Courts Act, 1971, replaced Assizes and Quarter Sessions with a system of Crown Courts.

The Criminal Justice Act, 1972. Provided courts with several new means of dealing with offenders, including criminal bankruptcy orders, community service orders, deferment of sentence, day centres for probationers; and further restricted the imprisonment of adults.

The Rehabilitation of Offenders Act, 1974. This made it an offence to refer to criminal proceedings after the lapse of a certain period. This involved consequential amendments to the law of defamation.

SOURCES.—R. M. Jackson, *Enforcing the Law* (1967); N. D. Walker, *Crime and Punishment in Britain* (1965); K. Smith and D. J. Keenan, *English Law* (1963); G. Rose, *The Struggle for Penal Reform* (1961); J. Smith and B. Hogan, *Criminal Law* (1973); L. Blom-Cooper and G. Drewry, *Final Appeal: The House of Lords in its Judicial Capacity* (1972).

Major Legislation Relating to the Administration of Civil Justice, 1900–

Industrial Courts Act, 1919. This Act provided a standing body for voluntary arbitration and inquiry in cases of industrial dispute (see p. 251).

Supreme Court of Judicature (Consolidation) Act, 1925. This is still the principal Act defining the structure, composition and jurisdiction of the High Court and the Court of Appeal.

Administration of Justice (Miscellaneous Provisions) Act, 1933. This restricted the right to jury trial in King's Bench civil proceedings.

Administration of Justice (Appeals) Act, 1934. This made it necessary to obtain leave to appeal to the House of Lords in civil matters arising in English courts.

County Courts Act, 1934. This effectively abolished jury trials in county courts and rationalised the procedure for appointing registrars.

Summary Jurisdiction (Domestic Proceedings) Act, 1937. This rationalised procedure in matrimonial, guardianship and affiliation proceedings before magistrates.

Administration of Justice (Miscellaneous Provisions) Act, 1938. This Act made important changes relating in particular to the King's Bench Division of the High Court and to Courts of Quarter Sessions.

Juries Act, 1949. This abolished special juries outside the City of London.

Justices of the Peace Act, 1949. This Act brought about extensive revision of the functions and organisation of magistrates' courts.

County Courts Act, 1955. This fixed the general limit of county court jurisdiction at £400 (it was raised by Order in Council to £500 in 1956).

County Courts Act, 1959. This consolidated existing legislation on county courts.

Judicial Pensions Act, 1959. This fixed a retiring age of 75 for the higher judiciary and revised the system of judicial pensions.

Legal Aid Act, 1964. This gave limited powers for a non-legally aided litigant to be awarded his costs out of the legal aid fund where his unsuccessful opponent is in receipt of legal aid.

Justices of the Peace Act, 1968. This abolished *ex officio* J.P.s and redefined the powers and functions of magistrates' clerks.

Administration of Justice Act, 1969. This increased the jurisdiction of county courts to £750 and allowed certain categories of civil case in the High court to 'leapfrog' directly to the House of Lords.

Administration of Justice Act, 1970. This Act rearranged the jurisdictions of the three divisions of the High Court (the Probate, Divorce and Admiralty Division becoming the Family Division) and abolished imprisonment for debt.

Courts Act, 1971. This replaced Courts of Assize and Quarter Sessions by Crown Courts staffed by Recorders and circuit judges; it rationalised the location of civil and criminal courts throughout England and Wales; it made sweeping changes in the administration of courts of intermediate jurisdiction and it abolished the use of juries in civil proceedings.

Industrial Relations Act, 1971. This established the National Industrial Relations Court (see pp. 286–7).

Legal Aid and Advice Act, 1972. This Act empowered solicitors to do up to £25 worth of work for a client without the latter first having to obtain a certificate from the Law Society.

SOURCES.—R. M. Jackson, *The Machinery of Justice in England* (6th ed. 1972); P. S. James, *Introduction to English Law* (8th ed. 1972).

Principal Judges

Lord Chief Justice

1894	Ld Russell of Killowen
1900	Ld Alverstone
1913	Ld Reading (Vt) (E)
1921	Ld Trevethin
1922	Ld Hewart
1940	Vt Caldecote
1946	Ld Goddard
1958	Ld Parker of Waddington
1971	Ld Widgery

Master of the Rolls

1897	Sir N. Lindley (Ld)
1900	Sir R. Webster (Ld Alverstone)
1900	Sir A. Smith
1901	Sir R. Collins
1907	Sir H. Cozens-Hardy (Ld)
1918	Sir C. Eady
1919	Ld Sterndale
1923	Sir E. Pollock (Ld Hanworth)
1935	Ld Wright
1937	Sir W. Greene (Ld)
1949	Sir R. Evershed (Ld)
1962	Ld Denning

President of the Probate, Divorce and Admiralty Division (since 1971 the Family Division)

1892	Sir F. Jeune
1905	Sir G. Barnes
1909	Sir J. Bigham
1910	Sir S. Evans
1918	Ld Sterndale
1919	Sir H. Duke (Ld Merrivale)
1933	Sir B. Merriman (Ld)
1962	Sir J. Simon
1971	Sir G. Baker

Lord President of the Court of Session

1899	Ld Kinross
1905	Ld Dunedin
1913	Ld Stratchlyde
1920	Ld Clyde
1935	Ld Normand
1947	Ld Cooper
1955	Ld Clyde
1972	Ld Emslie

Lord Justice Clerk

1889	Ld Kingburgh
1915	Ld Dickson
1922	Ld Alness
1933	Ld Aitchison
1941	Ld Cooper
1947	Ld Thomson
1962	Ld Grant
1972	Ld Wheatley

Lord Chief Justice of Ireland

1889	Ld O'Brien
1914	R. Cherry
1917	Sir J. Campbell
1918	T. Molony
	(Office abolished 1922

Lord Chief Justice of Northern Ireland

1921	(Sir) D. Henry
1925	(Sir) W. Moore
1937	(Sir) J. Andrews
1951	Ld MacDermott
1971	Sir R. Lowry

Lords of Appeal in Ordinary

1887–1910	Ld Macnaghten	1913–1918	Ld Parker
1894–1907	Ld Davey	1913–1930	Ld Sumner (Vt)
1899–1909	Ld Robertson	1913–1932	Ld Dunedin (Vt)
1899–1905	Ld Lindley	1918–1922	Vt Cave
1905–1928	Ld Atkinson	1921–1929	Ld Carson
1907–1910	Ld Collins	1923–1937	Ld Blanesburgh
1909–1929	Ld Shaw	1928–1944	Ld Atkin
1910–1912	Ld Robson	1929–1935	Ld Tomlin
1912–1921	Ld Moulton	1929–1946	Ld Russell of Killowen

1929–1948	Ld Thankerton	1953–1961	Ld Keith of Avonholm
1930–39 & 1941–47		1954–1960	Ld Somervell of
	Ld Macmillan		Harrow
1932–35 & 1937–47	Ld Wright	1957–1962	Ld Denning
1935–38 & 1939–41		1959–1963	Ld Jenkins
	Ld Maugham (Vt)	1960–1975	Ld Morris of Borth-
1935–1938	Ld Roche		y-Gest
1938–1944	Ld Romer	1960–1971	Ld Hodson
1938–1954	Ld Porter	1961–1971	Ld Guest
1944–51 & 1954–62		1961–1964	Ld Devlin
	Ld Simonds (Vt)	1962–1969	Ld Pearce
1944–1946	Ld Goddard	1962–1965	Ld Evershed
1946–1949	Ld Uthwatt	1963–1971	Ld Upjohn
1946–1949	Ld du Parcq	1963–1971	Ld Donovan
1947–1951	Ld MacDermott	1964–	Ld Wilberforce
1947–1953	Ld Normand	1965–1974	Ld Pearson
1947–1957	Ld Oaksey	1968–	Ld Diplock
1947–1959	Ld Morton of	1969–	Vt Dilhorne
	Henryton	1971–	Ld Cross of Chelsea
1948–1975	Ld Reid	1971–	Ld Simon of Glaisdale
1949–1950	Ld Greene	1971–	Ld Kilbrandon
1949–1964	Ld Radcliffe	1972–	Ld Salmon
1950–1961	Ld Tucker	1974–	Ld Edmund-Davies
1951–1954	Ld Asquith of	1975–	Ld Fraser of Tully-
	Bishopstone		bolton
1951–1960	Ld Cohen		

and such peers of Parliament as are holding, or have held, high judicial office.

Lords Justices of Appeal

1892–1900	Sir A. Levin Smith	1944–1947	Sir F. Morton
1894–1901	Sir J. Rigby	1945–1950	Sir F. Tucker
1897–1901	Sir R. Collins	1945–1951	Sir A. Bucknill
1897–1914	Sir R. Williams	1946–1954	Sir D. Somervell
1899–1906	Sir R. Romer	1946–1951	Sir L. Cohen
1900–1906	Sir J. Stirling	1946–1951	Sir C. Asquith
1901–1906	Sir J. Mathew	1947–1948	Sir F. Wrottesley
1901–1907	Sir H. Cozens-Hardy	1947–1949	Sir R. Evershed
1906–1912	Sir J. Moulton	1948–1957	Sir J. Singleton
1906–1913	Sir G. Farwell	1948–1957	Sir A. Denning
1906–1915	Sir H. Buckley	1949–1959	Sir D. Jenkins
1907–1915	Sir W. Kennedy	1950–1957	Sir N. Birkett
1912–1913	Sir J. Hamilton	1951–1960	Sir F. Hodson
1913–1918	Sir C. Eady	1951–1960	Sir J. Morris
1913–1916	Sir W. Phillimore	1951–1960	Sir C. Romer
1914–1919	Sir W. Pickford	1954–1958	Sir H. Parker
1915–1927	Sir J. Bankes	1957–1968	Sir F. Sellers
1915–1926	Sir T. Warrington	1957–1963	Sir B. Ormerod
1916–1934	Sir T. Scrutton	1957–1962	Sir H. Pearce
1918–1919	Sir H. Duke	1958–1968	Sir H. Willmer
1919–1928	Sir J. Atkin	1959–1970	Sir C. Harman
1919–1923	Sir R. Younger	1960–1961	Sir P. Devlin
1923–1928	Sir C. Sargant	1960–1965	Sir G. Upjohn
1926–1934	Sir P. Lawrence	1960–1963	Sir T. Donovan
1927–1938	Sir F. Greer	1961–1969	Sir H. Danckwerts
1928–1929	Sir J. Sankey	1961–1974	Sir W. Davies
1928–1929	F. Russell	1961–1968	Sir K. Diplock
1929–1940	Sir H. Slesser	1962–	Sir C. Russell
1929–1938	Sir M. Romer	1964–1972	Sir C. Salmon
1934–1935	Sir F. Maugham	1965–1972	Sir E. Winn
1934–1935	Sir A. Roche	1966–1974	Sir E. Davies
1935–1937	Sir W. Greene	1966–1971	Sir E. Sachs
1935–1948	Sir L. Scott	1968–1971	Sir J. Widgery
1937–1946	Sir F. MacKinnon	1968–1971	Sir F. Atkinson
1938–1942	Sir A. Clauson	1968–1974	Sir H. Phillimore
1938–1945	Vt Finlay	1968–1973	Sir S. Karminski
1938–1944	Sir F. Luxmoore	1969–	Sir J. Megaw
1938–1944	Sir R. Goddard	1970–	Sir D. Buckley
1938–1946	Sir H. du Parcq	1970–	Sir D. Cairns
1944–1947	Sir G. Lawrence	1971–	Sir B. Stamp

1971–	Sir J. Stephenson	1973–	Sir A. James
1971–	Sir A. Orr	1974–	Sir R. Ormrod
1971–	Sir E. Roskill	1974–	Sir P. Browne
1972–	Sir F. Lawton	1974–	Sir G. Lane
1973–	Sir L. Scarman		

and ex officio *the Lord High Chancellor (President), the Lord Chief Justice, the Master of the Rolls, and the President of the Family Division.*

SOURCES.—*The Law List 1900–; Who Was Who 1900–,* and *Who's Who; Whitaker's Almanack 1900–.*

	Law Commission (*Chairman*)		*Monopolies and Restrictive Practices Commission* (*Chairman*)
1965	Sir L. Scarman	1948	Sir A. Carter
1973	Sir S. Cooke	1954	Sir D. Cairns
			(*Monopolies Commission*)
		1956	R. Levy
		1965	(Sir) A. Roskill

Judge Power by Type of Judge and Population

Year	Population (aged 15–64) in millions	Lords of Appeal Lord Justices and ex officio judges		High Court Judges		County Court Judges[a]	
		No.	No. per million of pop.	No.	No. per million of pop.	No.	No. per million of pop.
1910	23·1	12	0·52	24	1·04	57	2·47
1920	25·1	14	0·56	24	0·96	54	2·15
1930	27·5	15	0·55	26	0·95	57	2·07
1940	29·3	18	0·61	29	0·99	59	2·01
1950	29·6	20	0·68	35	1·18	60	2·03
1960	29·8	24	0·81	57	1·91	75	2·52
1970	31·1	26	0·84	68	2·19	103	3·31

[a] Now Circuit Judges.

SOURCE.—*Civil Judicial Statistics for 1970* (Cmnd. 47721/1970).

Volume of Civil Proceedings

Year	Total No. of Proceedings	Number of proceedings commenced per 100,000 population (age group 15–64)[a]				
		Chancery Division	Queen's Bench Division	Divorce	County Court	All Courts
1909	1,511,637	27	290	4	6,228	6,748
1919	512,407	32	230	28	2,188	2,524
1929	1,316,903	24	343	15	4,217	4,896
1939	1,289,755	37	281	31	3,907	4,494
1949	612,627	32	340	123	1,574	2,135
1959	1,482,188	33	314	90	4,494	5,024
1969	1,968,678	80	671	198	5,284	6,330

[a] Most actions that are commenced are in fact settled or withdrawn before coming to trial.

SOURCE.—*Civil Judicial Statistics for 1969* (Cmnd. 4414/1970).

Appeal Proceedings

Year	Court of Appeal			House of Lords		
	No. of Appeals heard	No. of reversals or or variations	%	No. of Appeals heard	No. of reversals or variations	%
1909	533	184	35	69	20	29
1919	392	135	34	60	21	35
1929	405	144	36	53	20	38
1939	433	149	34	40	20	50
1949	612	225	37	32	12	38
1959	441	147	33	58	29	50
1969	680	261	38	60	31	51

SOURCE.—*Civil Judicial Statistics for 1970* (Cmnd. 4721/1970).

Criminal Statistics: England and Wales

HIGHER COURTS: ALL AGES

	No. for trial				Sentences as percentage of those found guilty					
	Total	Male	Female	No. found guilty[b]	Death[k]	Custodial measure[c]	Probation	Fine	Nominal penalties[d]	Otherwise dealt with[a]
1900	10,149	8,928	1,219	7,975	0·3	90·5	—	1·1	8·1	2([n])
1910	13,680	12,522	1,157	11,337	0·2	83·6	5·2	0·6	10·2	0·2
1920	9,130	8,141	989	7,225	0·5	76·5	8·1	0·8	13·4	0·7
1930	8,384	7,781	601	6,921	0·2	71·4	11·3	1·6	15·0	0·5
1938	10,003	9,322	681	8,612	0·3	62·4	19·2	1·3	16·0	0·8
1950	18,935	17,990	945	17,149	0·2	62·6	17·2	6·6	13·2	0·2
1960	30,591	29,462	1,129	27,830	0·1	53·8	22·5	13·8	9 3	0·6
1968	32,347	30,690	1,657	27,395	—	{50·7 / 16·3†	14·6	12·8	5·0	1·2

† Suspended prison sentences.

SUMMARY COURTS: INDICTABLE OFFENCES

	Adults[tg]		Sentences as a percentage of those found guilty				Juveniles[i]	
	No. proceeded against	No. found guilty or charge proved[b]	Custodial measure[c]	Probation	Fine	Other[e]	No. proceeded against	No. found guilty or charge proved[b]
1900[h]	43,479	30,736	47·1	14·0	26·7	12·8	n.a.	n.a.
1910	40,434	36,094	47·5	11·3	22·1	19·1	12,275	10,786
1920	37,107	32,942	31·7	11·3	38·6	28·4	14,380	12,919
1930	43,464	38,709	25·6	21·1	28·3	25·0	12,198	11,137
1938	46,014	41,976	22·0	22·2	28·9	25·9	29,388	27,875
1950	61,701	57,102	18·5	11·9	48·8	20·8	43·823	41,910
1960	84,523	79,538	13·4	12·5	56·1	18·0	58,350	56,114
1968	209,498	166,512	{7·8 / 11·0†	10·0	53·2	18·0	68,220	63,420

† Suspended prison sentences.

See Notes overleaf.

NON-INDICTABLE OFFENCES OTHER THAN HIGHWAY OFFENCES

TRAFFIC OFFENCES[j] (all courts)

	Adults[g]		Juveniles[i]			
	No. proceeded against	No. found guilty or charge proved[b]	No. proceeded against	No. found guilty or charge proved[b]	No. found guilty	As % of all found guilty of offences
1900	672,989[h]	557,489	n.a.	n.a.	2,548	0·4
1910	551,395	483,111	18,959	14,694	55,633	9·1
1920	427,556	374,565	16,953	14,956	157,875	24·9
1930	317,231	287,691	8,842	7,577	267,616	42·8
1938	236,752	216,759	16,873	15,310	475,124	60·3
1950	220,188	202,286	19,810	18,410	357,932	52·6
1960	247,133	232,992	28,025	26,337	622,551	60·1
1968	327,657	295,783	21,314	19,457	1,014,793	64·4

[a] Including the Central Criminal Court and the Crown Courts.

[b] Excluding those found guilty but insane or (since 1964) acquitted by reason of insanity.

[c] Including imprisonment, or committal to a reformatory, approved school, remand home or (since 1952) detention centre, or (in the case of Assizes and Quarter Sessions) borstal training.

[d] Includes absolute and conditional discharge and binding over with recognisances.

[e] Includes whipping (abolished 1948), fit person orders (introduced 1934), as well as days in prison cells, admission to institutions for the mentally disordered, and other miscellaneous and numerically unimportant methods of disposal.

[f] Until 1932, persons aged 16 or older were tried and sentenced as adults (although in some cases sent to establishments reserved for younger offenders, e.g. borstals). From 1933, however, 'adult' means a person aged 17 or older.

[g] Includes small numbers of juveniles tried jointly with adults.

[h] The published tables for 1900 unfortunately do not distinguish adults from juveniles, although one table shows that those found guilty include 9,450 persons under 16. Consequently the figures showing the disposal of adult offenders in 1900 include unknown numbers of juveniles. Almost certainly most of the 3,218 who were whipped in 1900 were boys.

[i] From 1908 there were in effect 'juvenile courts', although lacking many special features which were introduced later.

[j] From 1900 to 1938 'highway offences' have been taken to include all offences under the Highway Acts together with offences against regulations, etc., dealing with stage coaches, trams, trolleybuses and so on. For 1950 they have been taken to include offences numbered 123–38, 173 and 180 in the Home Office code, and for 1960 and 1968 offences numbered 124, 130, 135–8, 173 and 180.

[k] The death penalty was, in practice, confined to murder throughout this period (except for war-time executions for treason or similar offences). 'Infanticides' were excluded from 'murder' from 1922, and from 1957 murders in certain circumstances became 'non-capital': the death penalty for murder was completely suspended from 1965. A large proportion of the murderers who were sentenced to death were subsequently reprieved.

SOURCE.—N. D. Walker in A. H. Halsey (ed.), *Trends in British Society since 1900* (1972).

Rates of Change for Different Classes of Offence in Selected Years from 1901 to 1963

(Rates: Annual Average 1901–05 = 100)[a]

England and Wales

Classification of offences according to relative magnitude of percentage increase between 1901–5 and 1963 (annual average 1901–5=100)	Rate of change (annual average 1901–5=100)				
	1921	1938	1948	1961	1963
1. HIGH INCREASE (> 1700)					
Malicious woundings	56	174	386	1,520	1,779
Homosexual offences	178	572	1,405	2,513	2,437
Shopbreaking	206	556	1,464	1,990	2,568
Attempted breakings	218	1,088	2,392	3,213	4,186
Larceny from dwelling house	140	767	2,428	3,068	3,903
Forgery	138	396	1,449	1,688	2,106
2. MEDIUM HIGH INCREASE (1300 < 1700)					
Housebreaking	141	377	710	1,051	1,427
Receiving	160	295	777	1,184	1,527
Malicious damage	108	113	737	1,110	1,373
3. AVERAGE INCREASE (900 < 1300)					
Heterosexual offences[b]	155	282	588	1,218	1,248
Robbery	86	117	449	959	1,013
Simple and minor larcenies[c]	115	335	557	879	1,053
Frauds and false pretences	187	420	506	1,042	1,204
4. MEDIUM LOW INCREASE (500 < 900)	nil	nil	nil	nil	nil
5. LOW INCREASE (< 500) OR DECREASE					
Murder	88	74	110	94	98
Felonious woundings, etc.[d]	84	127	194	440	450
Larceny by servant and embezzlement	90	141	281	331	360
Larceny from the person	46	61	121	136	146
Total indictable crimes	118	323	597	921	1,117
Males aged 15–49[e]	115	130	135	131	130

[a] Based on figures extracted from relevant volumes of *Criminal Statistics, England and Wales*.
[b] Including Home Office Statistical Classes 19–23.
[c] Including Home Office Statistical Classes 44–9.
[d] Including Home Office Statistical Classes 2, 4 and 5.
[e] Not in McClintock and Avison's table. Figures supplied by N. D. Walker.

SOURCE.—F. H. McClintock and N. H. Avison, *Crime in England and Wales* (1968); but see note (e) above.

Prison Sentences and Prison Populations, 1901–

England and Wales

	Prisoners received under sentence[a]		Daily average prison population[b]		
			Male	Female	Total
1901	149,397		14,459	2,976	17,435
1910	179,951		19,333	2,685	22,018
1920	35,439		8,279	1,404	9,683
1930	38,832		10,561	785	11,346
1940	24,870		8,443	934	9,377
1950	33,875		19,367	1,107	20,474
1960	42,810		26,198	901	27,099
1970	62,021		38,040	988	39,028

[a] This column excludes those sentenced by courts martial and those under sentence of death or recalled under licence; but includes sentences of penal servitude (which were abolished in 1948), borstal training and committals to Detention Centres from 1952. Civil prisoners are not included as they are not 'under sentence'.
[b] Figures are for daily average population of penal establishments in prisons, borstals and (from 1952) detention centres.

SOURCE.—*Annual Reports* of the Prison Commissioners (changed in 1964 to the Prison Department of the Home Office).

Police Force

	England & Wales		Scotland		Ireland (N. Ireland only from 1930)	
	No. of forces	No. of Police	No. of forces	Authorised no. of Police	No. of forces	No. of Police
1900	179	41,900	64	4,900	1	12,300
1910	190	49,600	63	5,600	1	11,900
1920	191	56,500	59	6,500	1	11,600
1930	183	58,000	49	6,600	1	2,800
1940	183	57,300	48	6,800	1	2,900
1950	129	62,600	33	7,200	1	2,800
1960	125	72,300	33	8,700	1	2,900
1965	120	83,300	31	10,200	1	3,000
1970	47	92,700	20	11,200	1	3,800

SOURCES.—*The War Against Crime in England and Wales 1959–1964*, Cmnd. 2296/1964; C. Reith, *A Short History of the British Police* (1948); J. M. Hart, *The British Police* (1951); B. Whitaker, *The Police* (1965); M. Banton, *The Police and the Community* (1964); Sir F. Newsam, *The Home Office* (2nd ed. 1955); Sir J. Moylan, *New Scotland Yard* (1934); Ld Devlin, *The Criminal Prosecution in England* (1966); Sir C. Allen, *The Queen's Peace* (1953); C. Reith, *A New Study of Police History* (1954); *Royal Commission on Police Powers and Procedure*, Cmd. 3297/1929; *Royal Commission on the Police*, Cmnd. 1728/1962; G. Marshall, *Police and Government* (1965). Much information on the police is available in three reports from the House of Commons Estimates Committee H.C. 307 of 1957–8, H.C. 293 of 1962–3, and H.C. 145 of 1966–7. Annual Reports of H.M. Inspectors of Constabulary.

X

SOCIAL CONDITIONS

Population

U.K. POPULATION 1901–
(thousands)

1901	41,459	1921	47,123	1941	48,216	1961	52,807
1902	41,893	1922	44,372	1942	48,400	1962	53,274
1903	42,237	1923	44,597	1943	48,789	1963	53,553
1904	42,611	1924	44,916	1944	49,016	1964	53,885
1905	42,981	1925	45,060	1945	49,182	1965	54,218
1906	43,361	1926	45,233	1946	49,217	1966	54,500
1907	43,738	1927	45,389	1947	49,571	1967	54,800
1908	44,124	1928	45,578	1948	50,065	1968	55,049
1909	44,519	1929	45,672	1949	50,363	1969	55,263
1910	44,916	1930	45,866	1950	50,616	1970	55,421
1911	45,222	1931	46,038	1951	50,225	1971	55,610
1912	45,436	1932	46,335	1952	50,444	1972	55,793
1913	45,648	1933	46,520	1953	50,611	1973	55,933
1914	46,048	1934	46,666	1954	50,784		
1915	44,333	1935	46,869	1955	50,968		
1916	43,710	1936	47,081	1956	51,208		
1917	43,280	1937	47,289	1957	51,456		
1918	43,116	1938	47,494	1958	51,680		
1919	44,599	1939	47,762	1959	51,986		
1920	46,472	1940	48,226	1960	52,383		

SOURCE.—

1. Census figures for 1901, 1911, 1921, 1931, 1951 and 1971. Figures for other years are mid-year estimates. Figures for 1900–21 inclusive include S. Ireland. Figures for 1915–20 and for 1940–50 relate to civil population only. *Annual Reports of the Registrars-General for England and Wales, Scotland, and N. Ireland. Annual Abstract of Statistics. Monthly Digest of Statistics.*

INTERCENSAL CHANGES IN POPULATION
(thousands)

	Population at beginning of period	Actual increases	Excess of births over deaths	Net gain or loss by migration
1901–1911	38,237	3,846	4,666	− 820
1911–1921	42,082	1,945	2,863	− 919
1921–1931	44,027	2,011	2,683	− 672
1931–1951	46,038	4,244	3,809	+ 4
1951–1961	50,282	2,518	2,461	+ 57
1961–1971	52,800	2,770	3,245	− 475

SOURCE.—*Annual Abstract of Statistics.*

POPULATION OF COMPONENTS OF U.K.
(thousands)

	Area (sq. kilometres)	1911	1921	1931	1951	1961	1971
England: Standard Regions[a]							
North	19,349	2,814	3,019	3,037	3,138	3,250	3,292
Yorkshire and Humberside	14,196	3,896	4,095	4,307	4,527	4,635	4,792
East Midlands	12,179	2,247	2,337	2,511	3,100	3,100	3,385
East Anglia	12,566	1,193	1,211	1,233	1,382	1,470	1,665
South East	27,414	11,739	12,317	13,537	15,127	16,271	17,143
South West	23,660	2,688	2,725	2,794	3,229	3,411	3,771
West Midlands	13,013	3,278	3,504	3,743	4,423	4,758	5,103
North West	7,992	5,793	6,022	6,196	6,447	6,567	6,729
Wales	20,762	2,421	2,656	2,593	2,599	2,644	2,724
Scotland	78,767	4,761	4,882	4,843	5,096	5,179	5,228
N. Ireland	14,120	1,251	1,258	1,243	1,371	1,425	1,528
Conurbations[a]							
Greater London	1,596	7,256	7,448	8,216	8,348	8,183	7,393
West Midlands	696	1,634	1,773	1,933	2,237	2,347	2,368
West Yorkshire	1,255	1,590	1,614	1,655	1,693	1,704	1,725
South-East Lancashire	983	2,328	2,361	2,427	2,423	2,428	2,387
Merseyside	389	1,157	1,263	1,347	1,382	1,384	1,264
Tyneside	234	761	816	827	836	855	805
Central Clydeside	778	(1,461)	1,638	1,690	1,760	1,802	1,728

[a] Standard Regions and conurbations are based on 1969 boundaries.

SOURCE.—*Annual Abstract of Statistics.*

BIRTH RATES, DEATH RATES, AND MARRIAGES IN THE U.K.

	Total Births per 1000 Population	Infant Mortality (under 1 year) per 1000 live births	Total Deaths per 1000 Population	Total Marriages per 1000 Population
1900	28·2	142·0	18·4	15·1
1910	25·0	110·0	14·0	14·3
1920	25·4	82·0	12·9	19·4
1930	16·8	67·0	11·7	15·5
1940	14·6	61·0	14·4	22·2
1950	16·2	31·2	11·8	16·1
1960	17·5	22·4	11·5	15·0
1970	16·0	18·5	11·7	17·0

Figures for 1900, 1910 and 1920 (except for infant mortality) include Southern Ireland. Death rate in 1940 based on civil deaths and population only.

SOURCE.—*Annual Reports of the Registrars-General.*

AGE DISTRIBUTION OF THE POPULATION OF THE U.K.
(Percentages)

Age Groups	1901	1911	1921 [a]	1931	1939	1951	1960	1971
Under 10	22·2	21·0	18·2	16·1	14·1	16·0	15·1	16·6
10-19	20·3	19·1	19·0	16·8	16·3	12·9	14·9	14·6
20-29	18·3	17·3	16·2	17·1	15·6	14·2	12·7	14·3
30-39	13·9	15·1	14·5	14·5	16·0	14·5	13·7	11·6
40-49	10·5	11·4	13·1	12·9	13·1	14·8	13·5	12·3
50-59	7·3	7·9	9·6	11·1	11·3	11·9	13·2	11·9
60-69	4·7	5·1	6·0	7·3	8·5	8·9	9·4	10·6
70-79	2·2	2·5	2·7	3·4	4·1	5·3	5·6	5·9
80 and over	0·6	0·6	0·7	0·8	1·0	1·5	1·9	2·2
Total	100·0	100·0	100·0	100·0	100·0	100·0	100·0	100·0

[a] Percentages for 1921 are for England, Wales and Scotland only.

SOURCES.—Census figures for 1901, 1911, 1921, 1931, 1951. Mid-year estimate 1939, 1960 and 1971. Registrars-General of England and Wales, and Scotland, *Censuses of Population*, and the *Annual Abstract of Statistics*.

EXPECTATION OF LIFE
England and Wales
(Average future expected lifetime at birth)

Years	Male	Female	Years	Male	Female
1900–02	46	50	1938	61	66
1910–12	52	55	1950–52	66	72
1920–22	56	60	1960–62	68	74
1930–32	59	63	1969–71	69	75

SOURCES.—*Annual Reports of the Registrar-General for England and Wales*, and the *Government Actuary's Department, Annual Abstract of Statistics*.

MAIN CAUSES OF DEATH
England and Wales
(thousands)

	1900	1910	1920	1930	1940	1950	1960	1970
Total deaths	588	483	466	455	572	510	526	575
Due to:								
Tuberculosis	61	51	43	36	27	16	3	2
Cancer	27	35	44	57	69	83	96	114
Vascular lesions of the nervous system[a]	41	30	49	41	52	65	76	79
Heart diseases	n.a.	49	53	90	136	146	153	179
Pneumonia	44	40	37	28	29	18	24	43
Bronchitis	54	34	38	19	46	28	26	29
Violent Causes	20	19	17	22	47[b]	19	23	23

[a] All diseases of the nervous system, 1900–30.
[b] Including 22,000 deaths of civilians due to operations of war.

Infant mortality (i.e. deaths under 1 year) per 1000 live births: 1900 — 154; 1910 — 105; 1920 —80; 1930 — 64; 0 — 57; 1950 — 30; 1960 — 22; 1964 — 20.

SOURCE.—*Annual Reports and Statistical Reviews of the Registrars-General for England and Wales*.

AVERAGE AGE AT FIRST MARRIAGE
England and Wales

Years	Bachelors	Spinsters
1901–05	26·9	25·4
1911–15	27·5	25·8
1921–25	27·5	25·6
1931–35	27·4	25·5
1941–45	26·8	24·6
1951–55	26·5	24·2
1961–65	25·5	22·9
1966–70	24·6	22·4

SOURCE.—*Annual Reports of Registrars-General for England and Wales.*

DIVORCES
Great Britain
Decrees made absolute

1910	.	.	801	1950 . . 32,516
1920	.	.	3,747	1960 . . 25,672
1930	.	.	3,944	1970 . . 62,010
1940	.	.	8,396	1973 . . 107,471

SOURCE.—*Annual Reports of Registrars-General for England, Wales and Scotland.*

NET EMIGRATION FROM GREAT BRITAIN AND IRELAND
Commonwealth citizens travelling by the long sea routes to non-European countries,
1900–59 ; all routes 1970

	1900	1910	1920	1931	1938	1946	1950	1959	1970
All Countries	71,188	241,164	199,047	− 39,056	− 6,467	103,504	54,153	28,400	65,100
U.S.A.	47,978	75,021	60,067	− 10,385	− 1,432	45,751	8,541	4,500	4,500
Canada	7,803	115,955	94,496	− 10,464	− 3,974	43,414	6,464	− 400	12,700
Australasia	6,259	34,657	28,405	− 8,760	2,204	8,443	54,581	28,800	56,000
S. Africa	7,417	8,314	7,844	− 1,263	2,037	2,242	1,912	− 800	19,400

Southern Ireland excluded from 1938 onwards.

SOURCES.—1900–1950 *External Migration 1815–1950*, N. H. Carrier and J. R. Jeffrey, *Studies on Medical and Populatio Subjects No. 6*, General Register Office (1953). 1959 and 1970 figures are from the *Annual Abstract of Statistics.*

PEOPLE BORN OVERSEAS
Great Britain

	1931		1951		1961		1971	
Birthplace Number of people (thousands)[a]	’000s	% of population	’000s	% of population	’000s	% of population	’000s	% of population
Foreign countries[b]	347	0·8	722	1·5	842	1·6	984	1·7
Canada, Australia, New Zealand	75	0·2	99	0·2	110	0·2	136	0·4
Other Commonwealth	137	0·3	218	0·4	541	1·1	1,140	2·1
Irish Republic[c]	362	0·8	532	1·1	709	1·4	718	1·3
Total born overseas	921	2·0	1,571	3·2	2,202	4·3	2,976	5·5

[a] Persons resident in Great Britain at the time of the Census who had been born outside the United Kingdom; including United Kingdom citizens born overseas but excluding short-term visitors.
[b] Including South Africa.
[c] Including Ireland (part not stated).

SOURCE.—*Social Trends 1972.*

ALIENS IN GREAT BRITAIN
(thousands)

	1901	1931	1961
Russia, Poland, Finland	93	71	128
Austro-Hungarian group	11	5	23
Balkans	6	6	15
Germany	52	16	37
France	22	16	14
Italy	24	22	70
Low Countries	12	12	18
Sweden, Norway, Denmark	17	11	8
Spain and Portugal	3	3	19
Switzerland	9	10	9
Total Europe	249	174	327
USA	17	13	80
All other countries	4	14	30
Total	270	210	447

SOURCES.—N. H. Carrier and J. R. Jeffrey *External Migration 1815-1950* (1953). 1961 Census *Summary Tables* (1966). Statistics are also available in Annual Home Office returns (summarised in the *Annual Abstracts of Statistics*) for the number of aliens registered with the police. In 1961 this number fell from 406,000 to 125,000 when permanently resident aliens were no longer required to register.

NATURALISATION
Total certificates granted by the Home Department or oaths taken in period

1901–10	. .	7,997	1941–50 . .	51,132
1911–20	. .	11,293	1951–60 . .	44,977
1921–30	. .	9,849	1961–70 . .	40,252
1931–40	. .	15,454		

SOURCES.—N. H. Carrier and J. R. Jeffrey, *External Migration, 1815-1950, Studies on Medical and Population Subjects, No. 6*, General Register Office (H.M.S.O., 1953), and *Whitaker's Almanack*.

MIGRANT FLOWS
United Kingdom
(thousands)

		Mid-year to mid-year							
		1964 –65	1965 –66	1966 –67	1967 –68	1968 –69	1969 –70	1970 –71	1971 –72
Citizenship									
Aliens:	In	60	59	69	62	61	66	61	53
	Out	38	35	39	38	40	42	40	38
	Net	+22	+24	+30	+24	+21	+24	+21	+15
Canada, Australia,	In	16	15	17	15	16	15	18	19
New Zealand:	Out	15	17	12	25	17	19	23	13
	Net	+1	−2	+5	−10	−2	−3	−5	+6
Other	In	73	61	66	87	76	64	61	54
Commonwealth:	Out	18	19	21	17	19	21	19	17
Commonwealth:	Net	+55	+42	+45	+70	+57	+43	+42	+37
British (U.K.):	In	74	74	79	78	76	77	87	74
	Out	210	215	254	206	220	223	185	171
	Net	−136	−141	−175	−128	−144	−146	−98	−97
All migrants:	In	223	209	231	242	228	224	227	201
beyond the	Out	281	286	326	286	296	306	266	240
British Isles[ab]:	Net	−58	+77	−95	−44	−68	−82	−39	−39

Note: All figures are subject to revision in the light of finalised 1971 Census results.
[a] Including United Kingdom passport holders from East Africa from mid-1967.
[b] Net immigration due to direct traffic with the Republic of Ireland may have averaged some 10,000 persons per annum during the 1961–71 intercensal period.
SOURCE.—*Social Trends 1972*.

Commonwealth Immigration

Commonwealth immigration came under systematic control under the Commonwealth Immigrants Act of 1962. This act was strengthened by the Commonwealth Immigrants Act of 1968. The Race Relations Acts of 1965 Commonwealth Immigrants Act of 1968 and largely replaced by the Immigration Act of 1971.

ANNUAL NET COMMONWEALTH IMMIGRATION INTO THE UNITED KINGDOM 1956–72

Year	West Indians[a]	Indians	Pakistanis[a] (Bangladeshis)	Australians[b]	Others[b]	Total
1956	29,800	5,600	2,100	n.a.	n.a.	n.a.
1957	23,000	6,000	5,200	n.a.	n.a.	n.a.
1958	15,000	6,200	4,700	n.a.	n.a.	n.a.
1959	16,400	2,900	900	n.a.	n.a.	n.a.
1960	49,700	5,900	2,500	n.a.	n.a.	n.a.
1961	66,300	23,750	25,100	n.a.	n.a.	n.a.
1962						
Jan/June	31,800	19,050	25,080	n.a.	n.a.	n.a.
Jul/Dec	3,241	3,050	− 137	− 2,082	− 1,569	2,503
1963	7,928	17,498	16,330	3,774	20,464	66,000
1964[c]	14,848	15,513	10,980	5,562	28,596	75,499
1965	13,400	18,815	7,432	6,367	17,805	63,819
1966	9,023	18,402	8,008	2,056	13,859	51,348
1967	9,109	22,638	21,176	−5,236	11,219	36,368
1968	4,801	28,340	14,876	− 4,445	− 5,074	38,498
1969	688	12,238	− 12,812	− 2,579	− 4,061	19,098
1970	4,291	8,416	9,888	− 9,873	− 5,515	7,207
1971	− 1,163	6,584	190	− 19,687	− 17,777	− 31,853
1972	1,176	3,634	− 3,515	− 23,589	− 8,345	− 30,589

[a] Fuller statistics became available under the Commonwealth Immigrants Act, 1962.
[b] No reliable estimates for individual years prior to the Act.
[c] 1964 figures include diplomats exempt from control under the Act.

COMMONWEALTH IMMIGRANTS IN THE U.K.

according to the 1961 and 1971 Censuses and the 1966 Sample Census

Year	W. Indians	Indians and Pakistanis	Australians	Others in British Territories	Total
1961	173,076	115,982[a]	23,390[a]	285,962[b]	596,755
1966	267,850	205,340[a]	44,480	324,640[b]	942,310
1971	302,970	462,125	32,400	496,410[b]	1,293,905

[a] Persons born in these countries but British by birth or descent have been deducted for 1961. No nationality data were included in the 1966 Sample Census, and therefore, on the basis of past data, the estimate for those born in the Indian subcontinent has been reduced by 100,000.
[b] The largest contributors to this total are Cypriots, New Zealanders, Maltese, Canadians and South Africans.

TYPES OF COMMONWEALTH ENTRANT
1962–1972

	Holders of Ministry of Labour Vouchers	Dependants	Students
Jul–Dec 62	51,121	8,832	12,596
1963	30,125	26,234	18,484
1964	14,705	37,460	17,705
1965	12,880	41,214	12,880
1966	5,461	42,026	13,831
1967	4,978	52,813	10,988
1968	4,691	48,650	13,196
1969	4,021	33,820	14,523
1970	4,098	27,407	16,639
1971	3,477	28,114	18,412
1972	1,803	45,494	19,671

SOURCE.—Home Office Statistics under the Commonwealth Immigrants Act 1962, published annually since 1963.

Race Relations Legislation

Race Relations Act, 1965, set up the Race Relations Board to receive complaints of unlawful discrimination and to investigate them.

Race Relations Act, 1968, enlarged the Race Relations Board and extended its scope. It also set up the Community Relations Commission to establish harmonious race relations.

Race Relations Board
Chairman
17 Feb 66	M. Bonham Carter
1 Jan 71	Sir R. Wilson (Acting)
1 Oct 71	Sir G. Wilson

Community Relations Commission
Chairman
17 Feb 68	F. Cousins
1 Jan 71	M. Bonham Carter

Housing

(a) Major Housing Acts

Housing and Town Planning Act, 1909. This amended the law relating to the housing of the working classes, and provided for town-planning schemes. It also provided for the establishment of public health and housing committees of county councils.

Housing Acts, 1919, 1923, and *1924.* These Acts provided for varying subsidies to encourage the building of new houses for the working classes.

Housing Act, 1930. This Act extended subsidies and provided wider powers for slum clearance.

Housing (Financial Provisions) Act, 1933. This reduced the general subsidies, but increased subsidies for slum clearance.

Housing (Financial Provisions) Act, 1938. This Act regulated subsidies to housing.

Housing (Financial Provisions) Act, 1958. This Act provided grants for improvements to private houses.

House Purchase and Housing Act, 1959. This extended grants for improvements.

Housing Act, 1961. Lays down regulations for landlords leasing houses for less than 7 years to keep the structure, exterior, installations, etc., of the house in repair and proper working order.

Housing Act, 1964. Sets up the Housing Corporation to assist Housing Societies to provide housing accommodation and confers powers and duties on local authorities with regard to housing improvements.

Building Control Act, 1966. Controlled and regulated building and constructional work.

Housing Subsidies Act, 1967. Provided for financial assistance towards the provision, acquisition or improvement of dwellings and the provision of hostels.

Housing Act, 1969. Made further provision for grants by local authorities towards the cost of improvements and conversions; made provision as to houses in multiple occupation; altered the legal standard of fitness for human habitation; and amended the law relating to long tenancies.

Housing Act, 1971. Increased the amount of financial assistance available for housing subsidies in development or intermediate areas.

Housing Finance Act, 1972. Altered the system for the allocation of housing subsidies and obliged local authorities to use a profit-related system in evaluating council house rents, and to introduce an income-assisted benefit for tenants below a minimum income level.

Housing Finance Act, 1974. Increased financial help to local authorities needing to clear slums, provided national rent rebate scheme for Council tenants and rent loans for private tenants of unfurnished accommodation, and based rent of public sector and private unfurnished accommodation on the 'fair rent' principle.

(b) Major Rent and Mortgage Interest Restriction Acts

Increase of Rent and Mortgage Interest (Restrictions) Acts, 1914 and 1920. These acts established a limit to the rent of small houses, and protected tenants from eviction.

Rent Acts, 1919–39. These altered the exact limits on rents.

Rent Act, 1939. This extended rent restriction and security of tenure to houses which had become decontrolled and to new houses.

Furnished House Rent Control Act, 1946. This Act created rent tribunals to fix the prices of furnished lettings.

Landlord and Tenant Rent Control Act, 1949. Rent tribunals were authorised to determine 'reasonable' rents, on the application of the tenants, who could also apply for the recovery of premiums. The Act applied to unfurnished houses and flats.

Housing Repairs and Rents Act, 1954. This Act authorised landlords to increase rents where sufficient repairs to their property had been carried

PERMANENT DWELLINGS BUILT
England and Wales

	Private Enter-prise[a] ('000s)	Local Authori-ties ('000s)	Total[b] ('000s)		Private Enter-prise[a] ('000s)	Local Authori-ties ('000s)	Total ('000s)[b]
				1951	30·3	141·6	171·9
				1952	43·4	165·6	209·0
No figures available 1900–1919				1953	76·3	202·9	279·2
1919[c]		0·6		1954	109·4	199·6	309·0
1920	97·5	15·6	252·0	1955	120·8	162·5	283·3
1921		80·8		1956	128·7	140·0	268·7
1922		57·5		1957	131·1	137·6	268·7
1923	71·8	14·3	86·1	1958	128·4	113·1	241·5
1924	116·2	20·7	136·9	1959	149·9	99·5	249·4
1925	129·2	44·2	173·4	1960	166·0	103·2	269·2
1926	143·5	74·1	217·6	1961	175·9	92·9	268·8
1927	134·9	104·1	239·0	1962	173·4	105·3	278·7
1928	113·8	55·7	169·5	1963	173·6	97·0	270·7
1929	140·3	61·8	202·1	1964	217·0	119·5	336·5
1930	128·0	55·9	183·9	1965	206·2	133·0	347·2
1931	130·7	70·1	200·8	1966	207·1	142·4	349·5
1932	144·5	55·9	200·4	1967	203·6	159·3	362·9
1933	210·7	56·0	266·7	1968	223·7	148·0	371·7
1934	287·5	40·2	327·7	1969	184·4	139·9	324·2
1935	271·9	53·5	325·4	1970	172·4	134·9	307·3
1936	275·2	71·8	347·0	1971	192·6	117·2	309·8
1937	259·7	78·0	337·7	1972	193·5	93·6	287·1
1938	230·6	100·9	331·5	1973	184·2	79·3	263·5
1939	145·5	50·5	196·0	1974	139·6	129·3	268·9
1940	27·1	15·4	42·5				
1941	6·9	2·9	9·8				
1942	8·2	1·4	9·6				
1943	3·3	2·5	5·8				
1944	3·2	2·4	5·6				
1945	0·9	0·5	1·4				
1946	29·9	21·2	51·1				
1947	40·9	86·6	127·5				
1948	35·6	170·8	206·4				
1949	30·0	141·8	171·8				
1950	33·0	139·4	172·4				

[a] Including houses built for families of police, prison staff, armed services and other services.
[b] Flats are included, and each is counted as one unit.
[c] 1919–44 years ending 31 Mar of following year. 1945 Apr–Dec. 1946 onwards calendar years.

SOURCES.—1919–38 M. E. Bowley, *Housing and the State, 1919–44* (1945); 1939 onwards *Annual Abstract of Statistics.* For conflicting figures for G.B. see B. Weber, 'A New Index of Residential Construction, 1838–1950', *Scottish Journal of Political Economy*, No. 2, June 1955.

NUMBER OF HOUSES
England and Wales

Occupied and Unoccupied (to nearest '000)			
1901 . .	6,710	1939 . .	11,263
1911 . .	7,550	1951 . .	12,389
1921 . .	7,979	1961 . .	14,648 [a]
1931 . .	9,400	1971 . .	18,196 [a]

[a] Excluding vacant dwellings.

SOURCES.—1901, 1911, 1921, 1931, 1951, 1961, 1971 *Population Censuses*; 1939 estimates in M. E. Bowley, *Housing and the State, 1919–1944* (1945).

out. Rent could also be increased to cover the increase in cost since 1939 of other services provided by the landlord.

Rent Act, 1957. This decontrolled many houses in 1958 and permitted substantial increases on controlled rents.

Rent Act, 1965. Provides for the registration of rents, introduces controls, and provides security of tenure subject to certain conditions. A landlord cannot enforce a right to possession against a tenant without a court order

Leasehold Reform Act, 1967. Enabled tenants of houses held on long leases at low rents to acquire the freehold or an extended lease.

Rent Act, 1968. Consolidated the statute law relating to protected or statutory tenancies, rents under regulated or controlled tenancies and furnished tenancies.

Rent Act, 1974. Extended indefinite security of tenure and access to rent tribunals to furnished tenants. Landlords resident on the premises exempt from provisions of the Act.

HOUSING BY TENANCY

Great Britain

	% Owner-Occupied	% Local Authority[a]	Rented from Private Landlord %	Other[b]		Total Stock (millions)
1914	10[c]	—[d]		90	100%	9·0
1938	25	10		65	100%	12·7
1945	26	12	54	8	100%	12·9
1951	29	18	45	8	100%	13·9
1956	34	23	36	7	100%	15·1
1960	42	26	26	6	100%	16·2
1965	47	28	20	5	100%	17·4
1970	50	30	15	5	100%	18·7

[a] Includes New Towns.
[b] Includes dwellings rented with farm and business premises, or occupied by virtue of employment.
[c] Approximate only: true figure probably lies between 8% and 15%.
[d] Included under private landlord.

Social Security

Old Age Pensions Act, 1908. This granted non-contributory pensions ranging from one to five shillings a week to be paid from national funds, subject to a means test, at the age of 70, where income was under £31 p.a.

National Insurance Act, 1911 (National Health Insurance, Pt. I). This was the first part of an act providing insurance against both ill-health and unemployment. The Act covered all those between the ages of 16 and 70 who were manual workers or earning not more than £160 p.a. (This income limit was raised in 1920 and 1942.) The self-employed, non-employed, and those already provided for by other health insurance schemes were not insurable under this Act. The scheme was administered through independent units, or 'approved societies'. Local insurance committees were set up. The insurance included benefits for sickness, maternity, and medical needs. A weekly contribution was made by the insured person, his employer, and the government. The basic weekly sickness benefit was 10s. for men, 7s. 6d. for women. It also set up general medical and pharmaceutical services.

Widows', Orphans' and Old Age Contributory Pensions Act, 1925. This provided for a contributory scheme, covering almost the same field as the national health insurance scheme. Pensions were payable to the widows of insured persons, and to insured persons and their wives over the age of 70. This age limit was reduced to 65 in 1928. The weekly rates were 10s. for widows, with additional allowances of 5s. for the first child and 3s. for each other child, 7s. 6d. for orphans and 10s. for old age pensioners.

Widows', Orphans' and Old Age Contributory Pensions Act, 1929. This Act provided a pension at age 55 for certain widows who could not satisfy the conditions of the 1925 Act.

Widows', Orphans' and Old Age Contributory Pensions (Voluntary Contributors) Act, 1937. This Act created a new scheme of voluntary insurance for old age, widows' and orphans' benefits open to certain persons who were not within the scope of the main scheme.

Old Age and Widows' Pensions Act, 1940. This reduced to 60 the age at which a woman who was herself insured or who was the wife of an insured man could become entitled to an old age pension. The Act also introduced supplementary pensions in cases of need for widow pensioners over the age of 60 and for old age pensioners. The Unemployment Assistance Board was renamed the Assistance Board and became responsible for payment of these supplementary pensions.

National Health Insurance, Contributory Pensions and Workmen's Compensation Act, 1911. This raised the income limit for compulsory insurance of non-manual workers for pensions purposes to £420 p.a.

Public Health Act, 1936. This replaced the 1875 Act, and consolidated the existing legislation.

Family Allowances Act, 1945. This granted a non-contributory allowance, to be paid to the mother, for each child other than the first. 1945–52 5s. per week; 1952–68 8s. per week; 1956–68 10s. per week for third and subsequent children; 1968 15s. (75p) per week for second, £1 per week for third and subsequent children.

National Health Service Act, 1946. By this Act, hospitals were transferred from local authorities and voluntary bodies and were to be administered by the Minister through regional hospital boards, general medical and dental services through executive councils, and other health services by county and county borough councils. Health centres were to be provided by local authorities for general, mental, dental, and pharmaceutical services, but few were built. Almost all services under the Act were to be free.

National Health Service (Amendment) Act, 1949; National Health Service Acts, 1951 and 1952, and National Health Service Contributions Acts, 1957–1958. These made modifications in the original scheme by imposing charges for certain parts of the scheme (prescriptions, dental treatment, etc.).

National Insurance Act, 1946. This Act provided a new scheme of insurance replacing the national health insurance and contributory pensions schemes with effect from 5 Jul 1948. All persons over school-leaving age, except certain married women, became compulsorily insurable. In addition to provisions for unemployment (see p. 289) benefits payable were retirement pension, widow's benefit, and death grant.

National Insurance Act, 1951. This Act introduced an allowance payable with widows' benefits for each dependent child in the family.

Family Allowances and National Insurance Act, 1956. Enabled allowances for dependent children to be paid in certain cases up to the age of 18; introduced new personal rate of widowed mother's allowance, reduced length of marriage condition for widow's pension, and introduced amendments to widows' pensions.

National Insurance Act, 1957. This introduced the child's special allowance for the children of divorced parents payable on the death of the father if he had been contributing towards their support and the mother had not remarried.

National Insurance Act, 1959. This introduced a state scheme of graduated pensions, requiring that both contributions and pensions should be graduated according to salary level.

Mental Health Act, 1959. The Board of Control was abolished and its functions passed to the new Mental Health Review Tribunals, local authorities, and the Minister of Health. The Act redefined the classifications of mental disorders, provided for further safeguards against improper detention, and extended the provisions for voluntary and informal treatment of patients.

Family Allowances and National Insurance Act, 1964. This increased from 18 to 19 the age limit up to which a person could be regarded as a child for the purposes of an increase of benefit or widowed mother's allowance.

Prescription Charges were ended in 1965. They were reimposed in 1968 with exemptions for some categories.

National Insurance Act, 1966. This extended the period of widow's allowance, introduced a scheme of earnings-related supplements to unemployment and sickness benefits and included a widow's supplementary allowance.

Ministry of Social Security Act, 1966 repealed and amended much previous legislation. It provided for the abolition of the Ministry of Pensions and National Insurance and the National Assistance Board and the establishment of the Ministry of Social Security. The Act also provided for a scheme of supplementary benefits to replace the system of allowances which had previously been administered by the National Assistance Board. The benefits are paid as of right to those people whose incomes are below the levels set in the Act and not according to national insurance contribution records.

Chronically Sick and Disabled Persons Act, 1970. This placed more stringent obligations on local authorities to seek out and provide for the chronically sick and disabled.

OLD AGE PENSIONS
Maximum rate for a single person

Jan 1909	. .	5/–
Feb 1920	. .	10/–
Oct 1946	. .	26/–
Sep 1952	. .	32/6
Jan 1958	. .	50/–
Apr 1961	. .	57/6
Mar 1963	. .	67/6
Mar 1965	. .	81/–
Oct 1967	. .	90/–
Nov 1969	. .	100/–
Sep 1971	. .	£6·00
Oct 1972	. .	£6·75
Oct 1973	. .	£7·35
Jul 1974	. .	£10·00
Apr 1975	. .	£11·60

SOURCES.—Sir E. Wilson and G. S. Mackay, *Old Age Pensions* (1941); *Keesings Contemporary Archives 1931–*; *Report on Social Insurance and Allied Services* (Beveridge), Cmd. 6404/1944, Appendix B, *National Superannuation and Social Insurance*, Cmnd. 3883/1969, and the Department of Health and Social Security.
In 1972 a £10 Christmas bonus for pensioners was instituted.

Women and Children

Women's Rights

Representation of the People Act, 1918, gave women over 30 the right to vote.

The Sex Disqualification (Removal) Act, 1919, abolished disqualification by sex or marriage for entry to the professions, universities, and the exercise of any public function.

Matrimonial Causes Act, 1923, relieved a wife petitioner of necessity of proving cruelty, desertion etc. in addition to adultery as grounds for divorce. (Further acts in 1927 and 1950 extended grounds for divorce and codified the matrimonial law.)

Guardianship of Infants Act, 1924, vested guardianship of infant children in the parents jointly. If parents disagree either may apply to court, the Court's subsequent decision being guided solely by consideration of the infant's interest.

New English Law of Property, 1926, provided that both married and single women may hold and dispose of their property, real and personal, on the same terms as a man.

Representation of the People Act, 1928, gave women over 21 the right to vote.

Law Reform (Married Women and Tortfeasors) Act, 1935, empowered a married woman to dispose by will of all her property as if she were single.

British Nationality of Women Act, 1948, gave British women the right to retain British nationality on marriage to a foreigner, and ended right of alien women to acquire automatic British nationality when marrying.

Equal Pay Act, 1970. (See p. 285).

Maternity and Child Welfare

Midwives Act, 1902. This Act sought to improve the standards of mid-wifery. It only became fully operative in 1910. Further Acts were passed in 1936 and 1951.

Notification of Births Act, 1907. This gave powers to local authorities to insist on compulsory notification of births.

Notification of Births Extension Act, 1915. This made notification universally compulsory.

Children Act, 1908. This Act consolidated the existing law and recognised the need for legal protection of children. It provided legislation covering negligence to children. Imprisonment of children was abolished, and remand homes were set up for children awaiting trial. This was to be only in special juvenile courts.

Education (Choice of Employment) Act, 1910. This empowered authorities to set up their own juvenile employment bureaux.

Maternity and Child Welfare Act, 1918. This empowered authorities to set up 'home help' schemes and clinics.

Children and Young Persons Act, 1933. This extended responsibility for children until the age of 17 and included a careful definition of the meaning of the need for care and protection. It established approved schools, and made detailed regulations about juvenile court procedure.

Children Act, 1948. This gave local authorities new responsibilities, with children's officers to administer the children's service (see *Local Government section*).

Children and Young Persons Act, 1963. This extended the power of local authorities to promote the welfare of children and dealt with children and young persons in need of supervision, ordered approved schools, employment of children and young persons (amended by *Children and Young Persons Act, 1969*).

Abortion Act, 1967. Made it legal for a registered medical practitioner to perform an abortion provided two registered practitioners are of the opinion termination is justifiable, either because continuance of the pregnancy would involve more risk to the life of the pregnant woman or injury to her physical or mental health or any existing children, than if the pregnancy were terminated, or because there is a substantial risk that if the child were born it would be seriously physically or mentally handicapped.

Legal Abortions, England and Wales

	Married	Single	Others[a]	Total
1968[b]	10,497	11,120	2,024	23,641
1969	24,403	25,499	4,917	54,819
1970	38,096	40,734	7,735	86,565
1971	55,358	61,036	10,383	126,777
1972	67,840	75,858	12,889	156,714
1972	69,327	77,293	13,264	159,884
1973	83,001	72,454	13,907	169,362

[a] Widowed, divorced, separated, or women whose marital status was unknown.
[b] The 1968 figures are from the 27th April when the Act came into effect.
SOURCE.—*Registrar General.*

Sexual Offences Act, 1967. Amended the law in England and Wales relating to homosexual acts and permitted homosexual acts in private by consenting adults.

Family Law Reform Act, 1969. This reduced the age of majority from 21 to 18. It also secured rights for illegitimate children.

Education

Education Act, 1902. This abolished school boards, gave powers to local authorities to provide secondary education, and made provisions for rate aid to voluntary schools (see Local Government section).

Education (Provision of Meals) Act, 1906. By this Act cheap school meals for children attending public elementary schools were given statutory recognition. Local authorities were to use voluntary organisations, contributing only to the cost of administration. In 1914 half the cost of the meals was provided by the Exchequer.

Education (Administrative Provisions) Act, 1907. This provided for medical inspection for elementary schools. In 1912 the Board of Education made grants to Local Education Authorities to make the treatment of children possible.

Education Act, 1918. Compulsory attendance was made universal until the age of 14. Day continuation (part-time compulsory) education was introduced for children between school-leaving age and 18. This almost disappeared under the economies proposed by Geddes but was revived in 1944.

Free milk was supplied to children in need in 1921. In 1934 it was subsidised by the Milk Marketing Board. From 1946 to 1971 it was free to all.

Education Act, 1936. Provision was made for the school-leaving age to be raised to 15 in Sep 1939 but this was not implemented. 1940–41, the school meal service was expanded and subsidised to meet war-time needs. These provisions were continued after the war, by the *Education Act, 1944.*

Education Act, 1944. This Act changed the title of the President of the Board of Education to the Minister of Education. Primary and secondary education was divided at '11 plus', and secondary education was generally provided under this Act in three types of schools, grammar, technical, and modern. Some local authorities preferred to use their powers to amalgamate these into comprehensive schools. Provision was made for compulsory part-time education between the school-leaving age and 18 in county colleges, but this has not been implemented. The minimum school-leaving age was raised to 15 (in 1947) and provision was made for raising it to 16. Powers were granted under this Act, which led to a great expansion of technical colleges. No fees were to be charged in schools which were publicly provided or aided by grants from the local authority.

School-leaving Age. It was announced in 1964 that the school-leaving age be raised to 16 in the educational year 1970–71. In 1968 this date was put back for four years. The change was made in 1973.

Comprehensive Schools.   In 1965 the Department of Education asked all
local authorities to submit plans for reorganising secondary education on comprehensive lines, with a view to ending selection at 11-plus and the tripartite
system.   The policy of universal comprehensivisation was suspended in 1970
but revived in 1974.

Nursery Schools.   In 1972 the Department of Education (Cmnd 5174)
accepted that within ten years it should provide nursery education for 90 per
cent of 4-year-olds and 50 per cent of 3-year-olds.

PUPILS IN SCHOOLS
England and Wales ('000s)

	Public Elementary	On Grant List	Efficient Independent	Other Independent
1900	5,709	n.a.	n.a.	n.a.
1910	6,039	151	22	n.a.
1920	5,878	340	46	n.a.
1930	4,936	411	82	n.a.
	Maintained	Direct Grant		
1950	5,710	95	204	n.a.
1960	6,924	111	294	203
1970	7,960	143	308	111

SOURCE.—*Annual Abstract of Statistics.*

PERCENTAGE OF VARIOUS AGE-GROUPS IN GRANT-AIDED SCHOOLS
England and Wales

	1938	1950	1960	1970
Age 2–4	10·5	7·7	9·8	10·3
Age 5–14	86·7	92·3	94·2	95·4
Age 15–18	6·1	10·0	13·8	23·8

SOURCE.—*Annual Abstract of Statistics.*

PERCENTAGE OF VARIOUS AGES RECEIVING FULL-TIME EDUCATION
Great Britain

	0–5 year olds	10 year olds	14 year olds	17 year olds	19 year olds
1870	3	40	2	1	1
1902	n.a.	100	9	2	1
1938	10	100	38	4	2
1962	10	100	100	15	7
1970	11	100	100	20	10

SOURCE.—*Report on Higher Education* (Robbins), Cmnd. 2154/1963; *Social Trends* (1971).

STUDENTS IN FULL-TIME HIGHER EDUCATION
Great Britain

	University	Teacher Training	Further Education
1901	20,000	5,000	—
1925	42,000	16,000	3,000
1939	50,000	13,000	6,000
1955	82,000	28,000	12,000
1963	118,000	55,000	43,000
1970	236,000	124,000	98,000

SOURCE.—*Report on Higher Education* (Robbins), Cmnd. 2154/1963. For 1967–8, Department of Education and Science and Scottish Education Department.

EXPENDITURE ON EDUCATION (U.K.)
(current prices)

	Net public expenditure on education (£m)	(as % of G.N.P.)	Private expenditure on education (£m)	Total expenditure of universities (£m)	% of university expenditure from parliamentary grants
1920	65·1	(1·2)	8·4	4·2	34
1930	92·8	(2·3)	8·3	7·0	36
1940	107·5	(2·0)	10·0	8·6	36
1950	272·0	(2·7)	27·8	24·1	64
1955	410·6	(2·8)	30·9	35·1	73
1965	1,114·9	(4·1)	60·0	124·2	80

SOURCES.—The main facts on education may be found in a series of official reports from *ad hoc* committees or from sub-committees of the Consultation Committee of the Board of (Ministry of) Education.
    Education of the Adolescent (Hadow) (1926); *The Primary School* (Hadow) (1931); *Secondary Education* (Spens) (1938); *The School Curriculum* (Norwood) (1943); *Education Reconstruction* (Cmd. 6458/ 1942–3); *Public Schools* (Flemming) (1944); *Education from 15 to 18* (Crowther) (1959); *Half Our Future* (Newsom) (1963); *Higher Education* (Robbins) (Cmnd. 2154/1963); *Primary Education* (Plowden) (1967). Since 1947 the Ministry of Education has published an *Annual Report* and *A Guide to the Educational Structure of England and Wales*. Among books on the educational system are the following: H. C. A. Barnard, *A Short History of English Education 1760–1944* (new ed. 1959); G. Baron, *A Bibliographical Guide to the English Educational System* (2nd rev. ed. 1960); H. C. Dent, *The Educational System of England and Wales* (1961); G. Kalton, *The Public Schools: a Factual Survey* (1966); J. S. McClure, *Educational Documents 1816–1963* (1965); L. Selby-Bigge, *The Board of Education* (1934); N.F.E.R., *Comprehensive Schools*; A. H. Halsey, *Educational Priority*, vol. 1, H.M.S.O. 1972; J. Vaizey and J. Sheehan, *Resources for Education* (1968). See also Annual Reports of University Grants Committee, and *Educational Statistics* published annually by the Department of Education.

PUBLIC LIBRARY SERVICE

	Books in stock ('000s)	No. of book issues ('000s)	Total expenditure (£'000)
1906	4,450	26,255	286
1911	10,874	54,256	805
1924	14,784	85,668	1,398
1939	32,549	247,335	3,178
1953	56,056	359,700	11,183
1962	77,200	460,504	24,431
1971–2	114,472	628,000[a]	73,436

[a] 1970–1.

SOURCE.—A. H. Halsey (ed.), *Trends in British Society* (1972). See also The Library Association, *A Century of Public Libraries 1850–1950*.

Transport and Communications
CURRENT VEHICLE LICENCES [a]

	Cars[b]	Public Transport[c]	Goods Vehicles[d]	Total
1905	15,895	7,491[e]	9,000	32,386
1910	89,411	24,466[e]	30,000	143,877[e]
1915	277,741	44,480[e]	84,600	406,821[e]
1920	474,540	74,608[e]	101,000	650,148[e]
1925	1,151,453	113,267	259,341	1,524,061
1930	1,700,533	114,796	391,997	2,287,326
1935	1,973,945	96,419	490,663	2,581,027
1938	2,406,769	96,718	590,397	3,093,884
1940	1,701,500	88,200	542,200	2,331,900
1945	1,795,700	110,800	740,500	2,647,000
1946	2,232,279	110,704	769,747	3,112,930
1950	3,009,611	141,091	1,263,131	4,413,833
1955	4,781,741	104,664	1,581,814	6,468,219
1960	7,387,075	93,942	1,958,856	9,439,873
1965	10,623,900	96,500	2,219,500	12,939,900
1970	12,687,000	103,000	2,068,000	14,950,000

[a] 1905–1920—Figures at 31 Mar 1925 and 1945 at 31 Aug. 1930–38 and 1946–65 during quarter ending 30 Sep. [b] Cars, motor-cycles, tricycles and pedestrian controlled vehicles.
[c] Buses, coaches, and trams.
[d] Goods vehicles, haulage including agricultural vehicles, exempt including Government vehicles.
[e] These figures do not include trams. In 1920 there were 14,000 trams.

SOURCES.—*Census of mechanically propelled vehicles* (Ministry of Transport), 1926–62 *Highway Statistics* (Ministry of Transport), 1963 onwards, *The Motor Industry of Great Britain* (Soc. of Motor Manufacturers and Traders). Reports of the Steering Group appointed by the Ministry of Transport, *Traffic in Towns* (Buchanan Report), H.M.S.O.

DRIVING LICENCES, ROAD DEATHS, AND TRAFFIC OFFENCES

	Driving licences	Road deaths involving motor vehicles or bicycles	Persons found guilty of traffic offences
1900	92,168[a]	n.a.	2,548
1910		1,277	55,633
1920		2,937	157,875
1930		7,305	267,616
1938	(4,500,000)	6,648	475,124
1950	5,993,000	4,840	357,932
1960	11,700,000	7,496	622,551
1970	17,520,000	6,689	1,014,793

[a] The only pre-war figures available are for 1905 in the Report of the Royal Commission on Motor Cars (Cd. 3080-1/1906).

SOURCE.—*Annual Abstract of Statistics.*

RAILWAYS
Great Britain

	Standard Gauge Route Miles	Train Miles (million miles)	Passengers Carried (millions)	Freight[a]	
				Tons (millions)	Ton Miles (millions)
1900	18,680	379·3	962·3	461·1	n.a.
1910	19,986	386·7	936·0	504·7	n.a.
1920	20,147	355,7	1,243·2	332·2	19·2
1930	20,243	397·5	844·9	304·3	17·8
1938	19,934	420·9	1,237·2	265·7	16·3
1950	19,471	384·1	981·7	281·3	22·1
1960	18,369	375·4	1,036·7	248·5	18·6
1970	11,799	195·8	823·8	198·9	15·0

Excluding operations of London Electric Railway, London Passenger Board, and London Transport throughout.   Standard-gauge Railways only (except 1900 and 1910).

[a] Excluding free-hauled traffic.

SOURCE.—British Railways, *Annual Reports*.

SHIPPING
Tonnage registered
(United Kingdom)

	'ooo gross tons	% of World tonnage
1900	11,514	51·5
1910	16,768	45·0
1920	18,111	33·6
1930	20,322	29·9
1939	17,891	26·1
1950	18,219	21·5
1960	21,131	16·3
1970	25,825	11·0

Steam and motor ships of 100 gross tons and over.

SOURCE.—*Lloyd's Register of Shipping* (Statistical Tables), published annually.

VOLUME OF POSTAL TRAFFIC

Letters, postcards, parcels, registered letters (excluding football pools). Number of inland deliveries.

1903–4	4,300 million	1946–7	6,601
1911–12	5,508	1951–2	7,964
1922–2	5,638	1956–7	8,753
1929–30	6,622	1959–60	9,244
1935–6	7,569	1965–6	10,461
1939–40	7,624	1972–3	10,790

COST OF FIRST CLASS LETTER MAIL
(inland)

6 May 1840	1*d.*
3 Jun 1918	1½*d.*
1 Jun 1920	2*d.*
29 May 1922	1½*d.*
1 May 1940	2½*d.*
1 Oct 1957	3*d.*
17 May 1965	4*d.*
16 Sep 1968	5*d.*[a]
15 Feb 1971	3*p.*
10 Sep 1973	3½*p.*
24 Jun 1974	4½*p.*
17 Mar 1975	7*p.*

[a] Two-tier postal pricing introduced.

TELEPHONES

United Kingdom [a]	
	('000s)
1900	3
1910	122
1920	980
1930	1,996
1940	3,339
1950	5,171
1960	7,864
1970	13,844

[a] Including Southern Ireland, 1900–20.

SOURCES.—General Post Office, *Post Office Commercial Accounts*, published annually, and *Annual Abstracts of Statistics*. Since 1969 *Annual Reports* of the Post Office Corporation.

XI

EMPLOYMENT AND TRADE UNIONS

Major Employment Legislation[1]

Factory and Workshop Act, 1901. This consolidated, with amendments, all previous Factory and Workshop Acts.

Unemployed Workmen Act, 1905. This established 'Distress Committees' to investigate needs and to provide employment or assistance. Funds were to be partly voluntary, and partly from the local rates.

Labour Exchanges Act, 1909. These were established in 1909 and renamed Employment Exchanges in 1919.

National Insurance Act, 1911. This Act covered all those between the ages of 16 and 70 years, but was limited to manual workers in industries known to be subject to severe and recurrent unemployment. (The Act covered about 2¼ million men.) Within these limits it was compulsory, and financed by a triple weekly levy, from the workman, the employer, and the government. Payment of benefit continued only for a limited period, after which responsibility for the unemployed person lapsed to the poor law. In 1916 the Act was extended to include munitions workers.

Industrial Courts Act, 1919. This provided for the establishment of an Industrial Court and Courts of Inquiry in connection with Trade disputes, and made other provisions for the settlement of such disputes.

Unemployment Insurance Act, 1920. The scheme was extended to cover the same field as the National Health Insurance scheme, and included non-manual workers with an income of under £250 p.a. Workers in agriculture or domestic service were excluded from the insurance scheme until 1936–37. It was administered through the local employment exchanges of the Ministry of Labour. The basic unemployment benefit was 7s. in 1911, increased to 15s. in 1920. It was increased in 1921, and in 1924 was 18s. It was reduced in 1928 and 1931. Additional allowances for dependants were introduced in 1921.

Unemployment Insurance Act, 1927. By this Act the original scheme was completely revised in accordance with the recommendations of the Blanesburgh Committee Report. The new scheme was to provide unlimited benefits after the insured person had satisfied certain qualifying contribution conditions.

Local Government Act, 1929. This Act abolished the Poor Law Guardians, and their responsibilities passed to county councils and county borough councils, who were so far as possible to administer the specialised branches through separate committees.

Poor Law Act, 1930. By this Act poor law was renamed Public Assistance. The existing law was consolidated.

[1] This list of major legislation since 1900 excludes temporary wartime measures. The most important example was the Conditions of Employment and National Arbitration Order, 1940, commonly known as Order 1305; this imposed legal restrictions upon strikes and lockouts and imposed a system of compulsory arbitration; in 1951 it was replaced by Order 1376 which retained only the compulsory arbitration system; Order 1376 was revoked in 1958.

Unemployment Insurance Act, 1930. This made qualification easier for transitional benefit, and abolished the requirement that the unemployed receiving benefits should be 'genuinely seeking work'. Transitional benefits were made to claimants in need of assistance, but unable to fulfil the usual qualifying conditions. Responsibility for the long-term unemployed was placed directly on the Exchequer in 1931, though receipt of benefit was made subject to a 'means test'. Dependants' benefits were increased.

Unemployment Act, 1934. An amended scheme was introduced distinguishing between 'unemployed benefit' paid from the Fund (at the basic rate of 17s. a week) for a limited period to those satisfying contribution conditions, and 'unemployment assistance' which was paid, subject to a 'means test', to those still needing assistance after exhausting their title to benefit, or those who were not entitled. These long-term unemployed were paid directly by the Exchequer through the newly created *Unemployment Assistance Board* (known as Assistance Board from 1940 and from 1948 until 1966 as National Assistance Board). In 1937 juveniles between the ages of 14 and 16 were brought into the scheme for medical benefits only.

Unemployment Insurance (Agriculture) Act, 1936. A separate insurance scheme was set up for agricultural workers granting lower rates of benefit than the general scheme. In 1937, the benefits of voluntary insurance for widows, orphans, etc. (see *Contributory Pensions Act, 1925*), were extended to those with small incomes, without the qualifications of insurable employment essential to insurance under the main scheme. For the first time married women could become voluntary contributors for pensions.

Control of Employment Act, 1939. This gave the government wide powers for the organisation of labour in war-time. Its aim was to make the best use of labour and to direct it to the most vital work.

Determination of Needs Act, 1941. This abolished the household 'means test'.

National Insurance (Industrial Injuries) Act, 1946. This covered all those in insurable employment against injuries and industrial diseases arising from their employment. It was financed by contributions from the insured person, his employer, and the government.

National Insurance Act, 1946. This Act covered all contributors between school-leaving age and pensionable age, for benefits for unemployment, sickness, maternity, retirement, widow's pensions, guardians' allowances, and death grants. The self-employed and non-employed were entitled to fewer benefits. The basic weekly rate for unemployment benefit was raised to 26s.

The national insurance scheme was amended by Acts in 1949, 1951, 1953, 1954, 1955, 1956, 1957, 1959, 1960, 1961, 1964, 1965, 1967, 1969, 1971, and 1973 (for rates, see p. 289).

National Assistance Act, 1948. This Act repealed all the poor law still in existence and it established a comprehensive scheme to be financed from government funds, to cover all the arrangements for assistance then in force. Provision was also made for those not qualified for benefits under national insurance schemes, or where the benefits were insufficient.

Local Employment Act, 1960, makes provision for promoting employment in areas of persistent or threatened unemployment.

Payment of Wages Act, 1960 removes certain restrictions on methods of payment of wages and permits them to be paid otherwise than in cash by payment into a banking account in the name of the employee, by Postal Order, by Money Order or by Cheque.

The Contracts of Employment Act, 1963, laid down the notice required to be given by an employer to terminate the contract of a person who has been continuously employed for 26 weeks or more (reduced to 13 weeks in 1974), the length of notice to be given varying according to the length of continuous employment.

Offices, Shops and Railway Premises Act, 1963, contained sweeping provisions relating to the health, safety, and welfare of employees, fire precautions, accidents and other matters in connection with office, shop and railway premises.

The Industrial Training Act, 1964, gave power to establish an industrial training board for the training of persons over compulsory school age for employment in any activities of industry or commerce.

Redundancy Payments Act, 1965, obliged employers in certain industries to make payment to redundant workers and set up a Redundancy fund to which employers must contribute.

Equal Pay Act, 1970, made provision for the application to all workers of the principle of equal remuneration for men and women for work of equal value and requires that terms and conditions of employment applicable to one sex should not be in any respect less favourable than those applicable to the other.

Employment and Training Act, 1973, extended provisions for public authorities to provide work or training for unemployed persons.

Health and Safety at Work Act, 1974, provided a comprehensive system of law to deal with health and safety at work and established a Health and Safety Commission and Executive.

Major Trade Union Legislation and Litigation

Taff Vale Railway Co. v. *Amalgamated Society of Railway Servants,* [1901] A.C. 426 (H.L.)

A trade union, registered under the *Trade Union Acts, 1871* and *1876,* may be sued in its registered name. Lord Hailsbury said, 'If the legislature has created a thing which can own property, which can employ servants, or which can inflict injury, it must be taken, I think, to have impliedly given the power to make it suable in a court of law, for injuries purposely done by its authority and procurement.'

The Trade Disputes Act, 1906, reversed the Taff Vale decision and freed trade unions from liability caused by the calling of a strike.

Amalgamated Society of Railway Servants v. *Osborne,* [1910] A.C. 87 (H.L.)

There is nothing in the Trade Union Acts from which it can reasonably be inferred that trade unions as defined by Parliament were meant to have the power of collecting and administering funds for political purposes. Exercise of such powers is *ultra vires* and illegal.

The Trade Union Act, 1913, reversed the Osborne judgment and laid down the conditions under which political objects could be included in the rules of a Union by its members' consent.

The Trades Disputes and Trade Unions Act, 1927, made a sympathetic strike or a lockout designed to coerce the government illegal; it also severed the connection between civil service organisations and other unions, and it imposed new restrictions on the unions' political activities and their conduct of trade disputes. The political levy could only be raised from workers who 'contracted in'.

The Trade Unions Act, 1946, repealed the 1927 Act.

Bonsor v. *Musicians' Union,* [1956] A.C. 104 (H.L.)

A member of a registered trade union wrongfully expelled from it was entitled to maintain an action for damages for breach of contract against the union in its registered name.

Rookes v. *Barnard,* [1964] A.C. 1129

Threats to strike in breach of a contractual agreement for the purpose of injuring a third party were unlawful and were, even if done in furtherance of a trade dispute, not protected by the Trade Disputes Act, 1906.

Stratford v. *Lindley,* [1964] 3 All E.R. 102

Strike Action not taken in pursuance of a trade dispute about terms of employment with the plaintiff's firm was not prima facie protected by the 1906 Trade Disputes Act.

Trades Disputes Act, 1965, reversed the Rookes v. Barnard case and disallowed actions for tort or reparation being brought in respect of some kinds of activities in the conduct of industrial disputes.

Industrial Relations Act, 1971, introduced fundamental and wide ranging changes into the legal framework of industrial relations. It repealed the *Trade Union Acts, 1871 and 1876,* and the *Trade Disputes Acts, 1905 and 1965.* Its provisions established new legal rights for the individual mainly in relation to trade union membership and activity, protection from unfair dismissal, information about his employment, and improved terms of notice. The Act introduced a new concept of 'unfair industrial practice'. It established a National Industrial Relations Court which, together with the industrial tribunals, was required to maintain these standards and rights by hearing complaints of unfair industrial practice and determining rights and liabilities. The Act also provided for a new system of registration and restricted legal immunities to registered trade unions; new methods of settling disputes over trade union recognition to be administered by a Commission on Industrial Relations; and new powers to be exercised by the Secretary of State for Employment to deal with emergency situations (i.e. the 'cooling off period' and ballots of membership).

Trade Unions and Labour Relations Act, 1974, repealed the *Industrial Relations Act, 1971,* except for the provisions on unfair dismissal. The Act abolished the National Industrial Relations Court and the Commission on Industrial Relations.

National Industrial Relations Court 1971–4
President
1971   Sir J. Donaldson

Commission on Industrial Relations 1971–4
Chairman
1969   G. Woodcock
(*Made a Statutory Body*, 1 Nov 71)
1971   (Sir) L. Neal

Conciliation and Arbitration Service 1974–
Chairman
1974   J. Mortimer

EARNINGS AND HOURS WORKED
Great Britain

Year	Average Weekly Earnings		Average Weekly Hours Worked	
	All Operatives	Men aged 21 and over	All Operatives	Men aged 21 and over
	s. d.	s. d.		
1924	47 9 [a]	56 3 [a]	n.a.	n.a.
1935	48 11	64 6	n.a.	n.a.
1938	53 3	69 0	46·5	47·7
1940	69 2	89 0	n.a.	n.a.
1941	75 10	99 5	n.a.	n.a.
1942	85 2	111 5	n.a.	n.a.
1943	93 7	121 3	50·0	52·9
1944	96 8	124 4	48·6	51·2
1945	96 1	121 4	47·4	49·7
1946	101 0	120 9	46·2	47·6
1947	108 2	128 1	45·0	46·3
1948	117 4	137 11	45·3	46·5
1949	121 9	142 8	45·3	46·6
1950	124 1	145 9	45·6	47·0
1951	136 2	160 2	46·3	47·9
1952	147 3	173 7	45·6	47·3
1953	157 5	185 11	46·2	47·8
1954	166 6	197 8	46·5	48·3
1955	182 3	217 5	46·9	48·9
1956	197 9	235 4	46·7	48·6
1957	204 7	241 6	46·6	48·5
1958	214 2	253 2	46·2	48·0
1959	222 6	262 11	46·3	48·0
1960	n.a.	282 1	n.a.	48·0
1961	n.a.	317 10	n.a.	47·6
1962	n.a.	313 0	n.a.	47·3
1963	n.a.	323 0	n.a.	46·9
1964	n.a.	352 0	n.a.	47·8
1965	n.a.	378 0	n.a.	47·5
1966	n.a.	405 0	n.a.	46·4
1967	n.a.	411 3	n.a.	46·1
1968	n.a.	445 3	n.a.	46·2
1969	n.a.	478 2	n.a.	46·0

(NEW SERIES, 1970)

	Average weekly earnings men aged 21 and over	Average weekly hours men aged 21 and over
1970	£26·80	45·8
1971	£29·40	45·0
1972	£32·80	46·0
1973	£38·10	46·7
1974	£43·60	46·5

Figures cover manufacturing industry and some non-manufacturing industries and services, but exclude coal mining, dock labour, railways, agriculture, shipping, distributive trades, catering, entertainments, and domestic services. 1935, 1938, and 1946 figures are for October, 1940–45 for July, 1947 onwards for April.

ª Average of four weeks during 1924.

SOURCES.—*Ministry of Labour Gazette* (–1968); *Employment (and Productivity 68–70) Gazette* (1968–) G. C. Routh, *Occupation and Pay in Great Britain 1906–60* (1966).

SIZE OF LABOUR FORCE

Great Britain
(to nearest '000)

Year	Total	Male	Female
1901	16,312	11,548	4,763
1911	18,354	12,930	5,424
1921	19,357	13,656	5,701
1931	21,055	14,790	6,265
1939	19,750	14,656	5,094
1951	24,600	15,649	9,661
1960	24,436	16,239	8,197
1970	25,082	16,061	9 021
1972	24,782	15,852	8'930

1901, 1911, and 1921 figures cover persons aged 10 years and over.

1931 and 1939 figures cover persons aged 14 years and over.

1951 and 1960 figures cover persons aged 15 years and over.

SOURCES.—*Censuses of Population*, except 1939, 1960, 1966 and 1967; *Ministry of Labour Gazette* (–1968); *Employment (and Productivity 68–70) Gazette* (1968–).

RATES OF UNEMPLOYMENT BENEFIT
(other than agricultural)

		Men over 18	Women over 18
15 Jan	13	7/–	Nil
25 Dec	19	11/–	Nil
8 Nov	20	15/–	12/–
3 Mar	21	20/–	16/–
30 Jun	21	15/–	12/–
14 Aug	24	18/–	15/–
19 Apr	28	17/–	15/–
8 Oct	31	15/3	13/6
26 Jul	34	17/–	15/–
1 Aug	40	20/–	18/–
2 Nov	44	24/–	22/–
3 Jun	48	26/–	26/–
24 Jul	52	32/6	26/–
19 May	55	40/–	26/–
6 Feb	58	50/–	50/–
6 Apr	61	57/6	57/6
7 Mar	63	67/6	67/6
28 Jan	65	80/–	80/–
30 Oct	67	90/–	90/–
6 Nov	69	100/–	100/–
23 Sep	71	£6·00	£6·00
20 Oct	72	£6·75	£6·75
4 Oct	73	£7·35	£7·35
22 Jul	74	£8·60	£8·60

After 6 Oct 66 flat rate unemployment benefit was supplemented by earnings related benefit.

SOURCE.—Information from Ministry of Social Security.

INDUSTRIAL ANALYSIS OF THE OCCUPIED POPULATION
Great Britain
(thousands)

	1911	1921	1931	1940	1950	1960	1970
Total Working Population	18,351	19,369	21,074	20,676	22,982	24,526	25,082
H.M. Forces	n.a.	n.a.	n.a.	2,273	697	518	372
Total in Civil Employment	n.a.	n.a.	n.a.	17,758	22,013	23,711	24,710
Agriculture & Fishing	1,493	1,373	1,259	925	785	596	370
Mining & Quarrying	1,308	1,469	1,385	886	858	766	415
Manufacturing Industries	6,147	6,723	7,006	7,128	8,318	8,663	8,727
Building & Contracting	950	826	1,149	1,064	1,294	1,423	13,22
Gas, Electricity & Water	117	180	246	213	354	371	382
Transport & Communications	1,260	1,359	1,443	1,146	1,738	1,634	1,567
Distributive Trades	n.a.	n.a.	n.a.	2,639	2,082	2,774	2,651
Insurance, Banking & Finance	n.a.	n.a.	n.a	370	430	538	954
Public Administration:							
National	452[a]	706[a]	610[a]	} 1,793	619	502	549
Local	555	773	1,019		743	741	842
Professional Service	2,678[b]	2,225[b]	2,629[b]	n.a.	1,421	1,973	2,818
Miscellaneous	n.a.	n.a.	n.a.	1,594	1,657	1,965	1,808
Registered wholly unemployed	n.a.	n.a.	n.a.	645	272	297	524

The Table shows only the changes in the general pattern of industry over the period. The figures for 1911–31 are based on the Census of Population figures published by the Registrar-General. The figures for 1940–70 are compiled by the Ministry of Labour. The figures are in no cases completely comparable owing to changes in the methods of classification and changes in the age-limits. The analysis excludes unemployed and self-employed.

[a] Including members of the armed forces stationed in Great Britain.   [b] Personal Service.
[c] Financial, Professional and Scientific Services calculated together.

SOURCE.—Annual Abstract of Statistics, 1935–46, 1938–50, 1958, 1961, and 1966; British Labour Statistics Historical Abstract.

Trades Union Congresses 1900–1967

Date	Place	President	General Secretary	No. of Delegates	Members represented ('000s)
3–8 Sep 00	Huddersfield	W. Pickles	S. Woods	386	1,250
2–7 Sep 01	Swansea	C. Bowerman	,,	407	1,200
1–6 Sep 02	London	W. Steadman	,,	485	1,400
6–11 Sep 03	Leicester	W. Hornidge	,,	460	1,500
5–10 Sep 04	Leeds	R. Bell	,,	453	1,423
4–9 Sep 05	Hanley	J. Sexton	W. Steadman	457	1,541
3–8 Sep 06	Liverpool	D. Cummings	,,	491	1,555
2–7 Sep 07	Bath	A. Gill	,,	521	1,700
7–12 Sep 08	Nottingham	D. Shackleton	,,	522	1,777
6–11 Sep 09	Ipswich	,,	,,	598	1,705
12–17 Sep 10	Sheffield	J. Haslam	,,	505	1,648
4–9 Sep 11	Newcastle	W. Mullin	C. Bowerman	523	1,662
2–7 Sep 12	Newport	W. Thorne	,,	495	2,002
1–6 Sep 13	Manchester	W. Davis	,,	560	2,232
6–11 Sep 15	Bristol	J. Seddon	,,	610	2,682
4–9 Sep 16	Birmingham	H. Gosling	,,	673	2,851
3–8 Sep 17	Blackpool	J. Hill	,,	697	3,082
2–7 Sep 18	Derby	J. Ogden	,,	881	4,532
8–13 Sep 19	Glasgow	G. Stuart-Bunning	,,	851	5,284
6–11 Sep 20	Portsmouth	J. Thomas	,,	955	6,505
5–10 Sep 21	Cardiff	E. Poulton	,,	810	6,418
4–9 Sep 22	Southport	R. Walker	,,	723	5,129
3–8 Sep 23	Plymouth	J. Williams	F. Framley	702	4,369
1–6 Sep 24	Hull	A. Purcell	,,	724	4,328
7–12 Sep 25	Scarborough	A. Swales	,,	727	4,351
6–11 Sep 26	Bournemouth	A. Pugh	W. Citrine	696	4,366
5–10 Sep 27	Edinburgh	G. Hicks	,,	646	4,164
3–8 Sep 28	Swansea	B. Turner	,,	621	3,875
2–6 Sep 29	Belfast	B. Tillett	,,	592	3,673
1–5 Sep 30	Nottingham	J. Beard	,,	606	3,744
7–11 Sep 31	Bristol	A. Hayday	,,	589	3,719
5–9 Sep 32	Newcastle	J. Bromley	,,	578	3,613
4–8 Sep 33	Brighton	A. Walkden	,,	566	3,368
3–7 Sep 34	Weymouth	A. Conley	,,	575	3,295
2–6 Sep 35	Margate	W. Kean	Sir W. Citrine	575	3,389
7–11 Sep 36	Plymouth	A. Findlay	,,	603	3,615
6–10 Sep 37	Norwich	E. Bevin	,,	623	4,009
5–9 Sep 38	Blackpool	H. Elvin	,,	650	4,461
4–5 Sep 39	Bridlington	J. Hallsworth	,,	490[a]	4,669
7–9 Oct 40	Southport	W. Holmes	,,	667	4,867
1–4 Sep 41	Edinburgh	G. Gibson	,,	683	5,079
7–11 Sep 42	Blackpool	F. Wolstencroft	,,	717	5,433
6–10 Sep 43	Southport	Anne Loughlin	,,	760	6,024
16–20 Oct 44	Blackpool	E. Edwards	,,	730	6,642
10–14 Sep 45	Blackpool	,,	,,	762	6,576
21–25 Oct 46	Brighton	C. Dukes	V. Tewson	794	6,671
1–5 Sep 47	Southport	G. Thomson	,,	837	7,540
6–10 Sep 48	Margate	Florence Hancock	,,	859	7,791
5–9 Sep 49	Bridlington	Sir W. Lawther	,,	890	7,937
4–8 Sep 50	Brighton	H. Bullock	Sir V. Tewson	913	7,883

Date	Place	President	General Secretary	No. of Delegates	Members represented ('000s)
3–7 Sep 51	Blackpool	A. Roberts	,,	927	7,828
1–5 Sep 52	Margate	A. Deakin	,,	943	8,020
7–11 Sep 53	Douglas	T. O'Brien	,,	954	8,088
6–10 Sep 54	Brighton	J. Tanner	,,	974	8,094
5–9 Sep 55	Southport	C. Geddes	,,	984	8,107
3–7 Sep 56	Brighton	W. Beard	Sir V. Tewson	1,000	8,264
2–6 Sep 57	Blackpool	Sir T. Williamson	,,	995	8,305
1–5 Sep 58	Bournemouth	T. Yates	,,	993	8,337
7–11 Sep 59	Blackpool	R. Willis	,,	1,017	8,176
5–9 Sep 60	Douglas	C. Bartlett	G. Woodcock	996	8,128
4–8 Sep 61	Portsmouth	E. Hill	,,	984	8,299
3–7 Sep 62	Blackpool	A. Godwin	,,	989	8,313
2–6 Sep 63	Brighton	F. Hayday	,,	975	8,315
7–11 Sep 64	Blackpool	G. Lowthian	,,	997	8,326
6–10 Sep 65	Brighton	H. Collison	,,	1,013	8,771
5–9 Sep 66	Blackpool	J. O'Hagan	,,	1,048	8,868
4–8 Sep 67	Brighton	Sir H. Douglass	,,	1,059	8,787
2–6 Sep 68	Blackpool	Ld Wright	,,	1,051	8,726
1–5 Sep 69	Portsmouth	J. Newton	,,	1,034	8,875
7–11 Sep 70	Brighton	Sir S. Greene	V. Feather	1,064	9,402
6–10 Sep 71	Blackpool	Ld Cooper	,,	1,064	10,002
4–8 Sep 72	Brighton	G. Smith	,,	1,018	9,895
3–7 Sep 73	Blackpool	J. Crawford	,,	991	10,001
2–6 Sep 74	Brighton	Ld Allen	L. Murray	1,027	10,001

ᵃ Actual attendance owing to the outbreak of war. Credentials were issued to 659 delegates.
SOURCE.—*Trades Union Congress Report, 1900–.*

The Eight Largest Unions

Amalgamated Union of Engineering Workers	1920 (1970)	Amalgamated Society of Engineers (founded 1851) merged with other unions to form the Amalgamated Engineering Union (A.E.U.) in 1920. In 1968 the A.E.U. merged with the Amalgamated Union of Foundry Workers to (A.E.F.) which in 1970 merged with the Construction Engineering Workers and the Draughtsmen and Allied Technicians Association.

President

1920	J. Brownlie		1939	J. Tanner
1930	W. Hutchinson		1954	R. Openshaw
1933	J. Little		1956	(Sir) W. Carron (Ld)
			1967	H. Scanlon

Electrical Trades Union	1889	Electrical Trades Union and others. In 1968 following mergers it became the Electrical, Electronic and Telecommunications Union–Plumbing Trades Union and then the Electrical, Electronic Telecommunication and Plumbing Trade Union.

President

1907	J. Ball		1944	F. Foulkes
1931	E. Bussey		1963	(Sir) L. Cannon
1940	H. Bolton		1971	F. Chapple

| National and Local Government Officers' Association | 1905 | National Association of Local Government Officers. 1930 amalgamated with National Poor Law Officers' Association and in 1963 with the British Gas Staffs Association. 1952 changed name to National and Local Government Officers' Association. Affiliated to T.U.C. in 1965. |

Secretary

1905	F. Ginn	1945	H. Corser (*Acting*)
1909	L. Hill	1946	J. Warren
1943	J. Simonds	1957	W. Anderson
		1973	G. Drain

| National Union of General and Municipal Workers | 1924 | National Union of General Workers (founded 1889 as the National Union of Gasworkers and General Labourers of G.B. and Ireland), National Amalgamated Union of Labour (founded 1889 as Tyneside and General Labourers' Union), and Municipal Employees' Association (founded 1894). Became National Union of General and Municipal Workers in 1924. Changed name to General and Municipal Workers for popular use in 1965. |

Secretary

1924	W. Thorne	1946	(Sir) T. Williamson
1934	C. Dukes	1962	J. (Ld) Cooper
		1972	D. Basnett

| National Union of Mineworkers | 1889 (1945) | Formed as the Miners' Federation of G.B., amalgamated with specialist unions, renamed N.U.M. in 1945. |

Secretary

1920	F. Hodges	1946	A. Horner
1924	A. Cook	1959	W. Paynter
1932	E. Edwards	1969	L. Daly

| National Union of Railwaymen | 1913 | Amalgamated Society of Railway Servants, and General Railway Workers' Union, and others. |

Secretary

1920	J. Thomas and C. Cramp	1943	J. Benstead
1931	C. Cramp	1948	J. Figgins
1933	(*Acting Secretary*)	1953	J. Campbell
1934	J. Marchbank	1958	(Sir) S. (Ld) Greene
		1975	S. Weighell

| Transport and General Workers' Union | 1922 | Dock, Wharf, Riverside and General Workers' Union, National Union of Dock Labourers and other dockers' unions, United Vehicle Workers, National Union of Vehicle Workers and others. 1928 amalgamated with the Workers' Union. |

Secretary

1921	E. Bevin	1956	F. Cousins
1940	A. Deakin[1]	1964	H. Nicholas (*Acting*)
1955	A. Tiffin	1966	F. Cousins
		1969	J. Jones

[1] Acting Secretary until March 1946.

Union of Shop, Distributive and Allied Workers	1921 (1946)	Co-operative Employees, and Warehouse and General Workers amalgamated in 1921 to form the National Union of Distributive and Allied Workers. 1946 fusion with National Amalgamated Union of Shop Assistants, Warehousemen and Clerks.

Secretary

1921 J. Hallsworth and W. Robinson	1947 (*Acting Secretary*)
1924 (Sir) J. Hallsworth	1949 (Sir) A. Birch
	1962 A. (Ld) Allen

SOURCES.—*Trade Union Congress Reports, 1920–* ; *Amalgamated Engineering Union Monthly Journal and Report, 1920– .*

Membership[1]

(to nearest '000)

Year	AUEW	ETU	NALGO	NUGMW	NUM	NUR	T & GWU	USDAW
1920	407	57	36	..	900	458	..	..
1921	357	46	36	..	800	341	300	100
1922	256	31	33	..	750	327	300	90
1923	246	26	33	..	750	327	300	90
1924	206	28	34	327	800	327	300	93
1925	205	29	37	320	800	327	300	95
1926	162	29	40	300	800	327	300	94
1927	146	26	44	278	725	327	300	100
1928	151	26	46	258	600	313	286	109
1929	155	29	49	261	600	310	389	115
1930	154	31	61	258	600	321	384	119
1931	146	31	65	240	600	310	390	121
1932	136	31	68	220	500	285	390	127
1933	135	31	73	230	500	272	370	131
1934	146	34	79	252	500	291	403	134
1935	164	40	86	280	500	306	460	145
1936	248	48	93	340	518	338	523	158
1937	299	58	101	405	538	365	611	172
1938	334	64	106	417	584	367	635	183
1939	376	70	114	430	589	350	648	194
1940	454	80	111	441	589	362	650	223
1941	550	97	113	548	580	376	680	234
1942	645	113	121	721	599	394	806	254
1943	825	124	127	726	603	406	1,089	268
1944	811	132	133	661	605	404	1,017	272
1945	704	133	134	605	533	410	975	275
1946	723	162	146	795	538	414	1,230	374
1947	742	170	171	824	572	448	1,264	343
1948	743	182	176	816	611	455	1,271	342
1949	714	188	189	805	609	421	1,253	340
1950	716	192	197	785	602	392	1,242	343
1951	756	198	212	809	613	396	1,285	348
1952	796	203	222	808	641	397	1,277	346
1953	810	212	225	790	669	378	1,259	339
1954	823	216	230	787	675	372	1,240	344
1955	854	223	236	805	675	368	1,278	347
1956	860	228	243	808	674	369	1,264	349
1957	900	239	247	804	681	371	1,244	352
1958	888	230	252	775	674	355	1,225	353
1959	908	233	263	769	639	334	1,241	351
1960	973	243	274	769	586	334	1,302	355
1961	982	253	285	786	545	317	1,318	351
1962	986	257	295	781	529	311	1,331	356
1963	981	272	226	782	501	283	1,374	355
1964	1,011	282	338	785	479	264	1,426	352
1965	1,049	293	349	796	446	255	1,444	349
1966	1,055	293	361	793	413	220	1,428	336
1967	1,107	352	367	782	380	218	1,451	321
1968	1,136	365	373	798	344	199	1,476	311
1969	1,195	392	397	804	297	191	1,532	316
1970	1,295	421	440	853	279	198	1,629	330
1971	1,284	420	464	842	276	194	1,643	319
1972	1,340	417	498	848	271	184	1,747	325
1973	1,173	420	518	864	261	174	1,785	326

[1] By 1973 four other unions had larger membership. The National Union of Public Employees had 470,000, the National Union of Teachers had 250,000, the Union of Construction, Allied Trades and Technicians had 257,000 and the Association of Scientific, Technical and Managerial Staffs 310,000 members.

SOURCE.—*Trade Union Congress Reports 1920– .*

Income, Expenditure and Funds of Registered Trade Unions
(in shillings per member)

Year	Income from members	Expenditure					Funds
		Dispute benefit	Unemployment benefit	Other Welfare benefits	Political	Working Expenses	
1910	27·8	5·3	6·8	11·1	..	8·1	59·3
1920	32·4	9·3	4·5	5·1	0·5	17·2	45·8
1930	37·6	1·6	9·7	12·1	0·5	16·6	62·0
1940	36·0	0·2	3·0	10·4	0·4	14·8	92·2
1950	39·6	0·6	0·4	10·4	1·1	22·8	156·4
1960	58·8	1·1	0·4	15·5	1·2	34·9	211·6
1964	74·2	1·1	0·5	17·5	2·3	44·5	258·3

SOURCE.—A. Flanders, *Trade Unions* (1967), and *Ministry of Labour Gazette.*

Density of Union Membership in Total Labour Force
United Kingdom

1901	12·6%	1933	30·5%
1911	17·7	1951	45·0
1920	45·2	1951	42·8
1933	22·6	1970	46·9

SOURCE.—G. S. Bain, *The Growth of White-Collar Unionism* (1970); G. S. Bain and R. Price, 'Union Growth and Employment Trends in the U.K., 1964–70' *British Journal of Industrial Relations* (1972), pp. 366–81.

White-Collar Unions

Much of the expansion of union membership during the twentieth century has occurred among white-collar workers. Prior to 1900 few of these workers were unionised, but by 1920 the Webbs estimated that close to three-quarters of a million white-collar employees belonged to trade unions. More recently, there has been a further dramatic increase in union membership among white-collar employees. While union membership among manual workers increased by only 0·9 per cent between 1948 and 1970 union membership among white-collar workers increased by 79·8 per cent. In 1970 there were approximately 300 unions catering for white-collar employees with a total membership of 3·5 million, and union density among white-collar workers was 38 per cent compared with 53 per cent among manual workers.

SOURCE.—G. S. Bain, *The Growth of White-Collar Unionism* (1970).

Major Industrial Disputes

(in which more than 500,000 working days were lost)

Dispute Began	Industrial group	Area	Numbers affected ('000s)	Working days lost ('000s)[a]
1900 Apr	Potters	N. Staffs.	20	640
Nov	Quarrymen	Bethesda	3	505
1902 Jul	Miners	Federated districts	103	872
1906 Oct	Shipyard workers	Clyde	15	592
1908 Feb	Shipyard workers	Humber, Barrow, Birkenhead, Clyde, E. Scotland	35	1,719
Feb	Engineers	N.E. Coast	11	1,706
Sep	Cotton operatives	Lancs., Cheshire, Derby	120	4,830
1909 Jul	Miners	S. Wales and Mon.	55	660
1910 Jan	Miners	Durham	85	1,280
Jan	Miners	Northumberland	30	1,080
Apr	Miners	Rhondda	13	2,985
Jun	Cotton operatives	Lancs. and Cheshire	102	600
Sep	Shipyard workers	N.E. Coast and Scotland	35	2,851
1911 Jun	Seamen and dockers	U.K.	120	1,020
Aug	Dockers and carters	London	22	500
Aug	Railwaymen	U.K.	145	500
Dec	Cotton weavers	N.E. Lancs.	160	2,954
1912 Feb	Miners	U.K.	1,000	30,800
Feb	Jute workers	Dundee	28	726
May	Dockers and carters	Port of London and Medway	100	2,700
1913 Jan	Cab drivers	London	11	637
Apr	Tube and metal workers	S. Staffs. and N. Worcs	50	1,400
Aug	Transport workers	Dublin	20	1,900
1914 Jan	Builders	London	20	2,500
Feb	Miners	Yorks.	150	2,654
1915 Jul	Miners	S. Wales	232	1,400
1916 Mar	Jute workers	Dundee	30	500
1917 May	Engineers	U.K.	160	2,880
1918 May	Miners	S. Wales and Mon.	40	760
Dec	Cotton spinners	Lancs. and Cheshire	100	900
1919 Jan	Miners	Yorks.	150	1,950
Jan	Shipyard workers	N.E. Coast	40	820
Mar	Miners	Various districts	100	600
Jun	Cotton operatives	Lancs. and adjoining counties	450	7,500
Jul	Miners	Yorks.	150	4,050
Sep	Ironfounders	England, Wales, and Ireland	50	6,800
Sep	Railwaymen	U.K.	500	3,850
1920 Sep	Cotton operatives	Oldham and district	400	620
Oct	Miners	U.K.	1,100	16,000
1921 (Dec 1920)	Shipyard carpenters	U.K.	10	2,200
Apr	Miners	U.K.	1,100	72,000
Jun	Cotton operatives	Lancs. and adjoining counties	375	6,750
1922 Mar	Engineers	U.K.	250	13,650
1922 Mar	Shipyard workers	Various districts	90	3,400

Dispute Began	Industrial group	Area	Numbers affected ('000s)	Working days lost ('000s)[a]
1923 Feb	Jute workers	Dundee	29	950
Apr	Boilermakers	Clyde, E. Scotland, N.E. Coast, Hull, South-ampton, Birkenhead, Barrow	30	5,725
1924 Jan	Railwaymen	U.K.	69	500
Feb	Dockers	U.K.	110	510
Jul	Builders	U.K.	100	2,970
1925 Jul	Wool textile workers	W. Riding of Yorks. and part of Lancs.	165	3,105
1926 May	Miners	U.K.	1,050	145,200
May	General Strike	U.K.	1,580 [b]	15,000 [b]
1928 May	Cotton weavers	Nelson	17	600
1929 Jul	Cotton operatives	Lancs. and adjoining counties	388	6,596
1930 Apr	Wool textile workers	W. Riding of Yorks. and part of Lancs.	120	3,258
1931 Jan	Cotton weavers	Lancs. and adjoining counties	145	3,290
Jan	Miners	S. Wales and Mon.	150	2,030
1932 Aug	Cotton weavers	Lancs. and Yorks.	148	4,524
Oct	Cotton spinners	Lancs. and adjoining counties	130	760
1937 May	Busmen	London	24	565
1944 Mar	Miners	Wales and Mon.	100	550
Mar	Miners	Yorkshire	120	1,000
1945 Sep	Dockers	Birkenhead, Liverpool, Hull, Manchester, London	50	1,100
1953 Dec	Engineers and Ship-yard workers	U.K.	1,070	1,070
1954 Sep	Dockers	Port of London and sym-pathy strikes	45	726
1955 May	Dockers	Various ports of England	21	673
May	Railwaymen	U.K.	70	865
1957 Mar	Engineers	U.K.	615	4,000
Mar	Shipyard workers	U.K.	165	2,150
Jul	Busmen	Provinces	100	770
1958 Apr	Dockers, transport and market workers	London	24	515
May	Busmen	Greater London	49	1,604
1959 Jun	Printing workers	U.K.	120	3,500
1962 Feb	Engineering & Ship-building	U.K.	1,750	1,750
Mar	Engineering & Ship-building	U.K.	1,750	1,750
1966 May	Shipping	U.K.	30	850
1968 May	Engineering	U.K.	1,500	1,500
1969 Feb	Motor Vehicles	Various districts	38	561
Oct	Miners	Various districts	121	979
1970 Jul	Dockers	U.K.	42	502
Sep	Local authority workers	England and Wales	134	1,216
Oct	Miners	Various	99	1,050

[a] Where figures for working days lost are not given in the *Gazettes*, they have been estimated.
[b] Excluding Miners.

Dispute Began	Industrial group	Area	Number affected ('000s)	Working days lost ('000s)[a]
1971 Jan	Motor vehicles	Various districts	42	1,909
Jan	Post Office workers	U.K.	180	6,229
1972 Jan	Miners	U.K.	309	10,726
Jun	Construction	England and Wales	120	2,904
Jun	Construction	Scotland	36	933
Jul	Dockers	U.K.	35	548
1974 Feb	Miners	U.K.	250	5,567

[a] Where figures for working days lost are not given in the *Gazettes*, they have been estimated.

SOURCES.—*The Board of Trade Labour Gazette, 1900–17; The Ministry of Labour Gazette* (1918–68); *Employment and Productivity Gazette* (1968–).

Emergency Powers

Under the *Emergency Powers Act, 1920,* the government may proclaim a State of Emergency if the essentials of life of the country are threatened.   The Act then empowers the Government to make regulations by Order-in-Council which have the full force of law.   All the occasions on which States of Emergency have been proclaimed under the Act have been associated with strikes.

31 Mar	21	Coal
26 Mar	24	London Transport[1]
2 May	26	General strike
29 Jun	48	Docks
11 Jul	49	Docks
31 May	55	Rail
23 May	66	Seamen
16 Jul	70	Docks
12 Dec	70	Electricity
9 Feb	72	Coal
3 Aug	72	Docks
13 Nov	73	Coal and Electricity (also Middle East oil crisis)

[1] It is doubtful whether this proclamation was ever made.

Unemployment, Industrial Disputes, and Trade Union Statistics

	Unemployment[b]		Industrial Disputes[c]			Total No. of Trade Unions	Total No. of Trade Union Members ('000s)	Total No of Trade Unions affiliated to T.U.C.	Total No. of members of Trade Unions affiliated to T.U.C. ('000s)
	Maximum ('000s)	Minimum ('000s)	Working Days Lost[d] ('000s)	No. of Stoppages beginning in year[e]	Workers involved[d] ('000s)				
1900			3,088	633	185	1,325	1,911	184	1,250
1901			4,130	631	179	1,323	2,022	191	1,200
1902			3,438	432	255	1,322	2,025	198	1,400
1903			2,320	380	116	1,297	2,013	204	1,500
1904			1,464	346	87	1,285	1,994	212	1,423
1905			2,368	349	92	1,256	1,967	205	1,541
1906			3,019	479	218	1,244	1,997	226	1,555
1907			2,148	585	146	1,282	2,210	236	1,700
1908			10,785	389	293	1,283	2,513	214	1,777
1909			2,687	422	297	1,268	2,485	219	1,705
1910			9,867	521	514	1,260	2,477	212	1,648
1911			10,155	872	952	1,269	2,565		
1912			40,890	834	1,462	1,290	3,139	202	1,662
1913			9,804	1,459	664	1,252	3,416	201	2,002
1914			9,878	972	447	1,269	4,135	207	2,232
1915			2,953	672	448	1,260	4,145	215	2,682
1916			2,446	532	276	1,229	4,359	227	2,851
1917			5,647	730	872	1,225	4,644	235	3,082
1918			5,875	1,165	1,116	1,241	5,499	262	4,532
1919			34,969	1,352	2,591	1,264	6,533	266	5,284
1920			26,568	1,607	1,932	1,360	7,926	215	6,505
1921	2,038[a]		85,872	763	1,801	1,384	8,348	213	6,418
1922	2,015 Jan	1,443 Oct	19,850	576	552	1,275	6,633	206	5,129
1923	1,525 Jan	1,229 Dec	10,672	628	405	1,232	5,625	194	4,369
1924	1,374 Jan	1,087 Jun	8,424	710	613	1,192	5,429	203	4,328
1925	1,443 Aug	1,243 Dec	7,952	603	441	1,194	5,544	205	4,351
1926	1,432 Dec	1,094 Apr	162,233	323	2,734	1,176	5,506	207	4,366
1927	1,451 Jan	1,059 May	1,174	308	108	1,164	5,219	204	4,164
1928	1,375 Aug	1,127 Mar	1,388	302	124	1,159	4,919	196	3,875
1929	1,466 Jan	1,164 Jun	8,287	431	533	1,142	4,866	202	3,673
1930	2,500 Dec	1,520 Jan	4,399	422	307	1,133	4,858	210	3,744
1931	2,880 Sep	2,578 May	6,983	420	490	1,121	4,842	210	3,719
1932	2,955 Jan	2,309 Nov	6,488	389	379	1,108	4,624	209	3,613
1933	2,407 Jan	1,858 Dec	1,072	357	136	1,081	4,444	208	3,368
1934	2,295 Jan	2,080 Sep	959	471	134	1,081	4,392	210	3,295
1935	2,333 Jan	1,888 Dec	1,955	553	271	1,063	4,590	211	3,389
1936	2,169 Jan	1,640 Aug	1,829	818	316	1,049	4,867	214	3,615
1937	1,739 Dec	1,373 Sep	3,413	1,129	597	1,036	5,295	214	4,009
1938	1,912 Dec	1,818 Apr	1,334	875	274	1,032	5,842	216	4,461
1939	2,032 Jan	1,230 Aug	1,356	940	337	1,024	6,053	217	4,669
1940	1,471 Jan	683 Dec	940	922	299	1,019	6,298	223	4,867
1941	653 Jan	151 Dec	1,079	1,251	360	1,004	6,613	223	5,079
1942	162 Jan	100 Dec	1,527	1,303	456	996	7,165	232	5,433
1943	104 Jan	..	1,808	1,785	557	991	7,867	230	6,024
1944	84 Jan	..	3,714	2,194	821	987	8,174	190	6,642
1945	111 Jan	..	2,835	2,293	531	963	8,087	191	6,576

Unemployment, Industrial Disputes, and Trade Union Statistics

	Unemployment[b]		Industrial Disputes[c]			Total No. of Trade Unions	Total No. of Trade Union Members ('000s)	Total No. of Trade Unions affiliated to T.U.C.	Total No. of members of Trade Unions affiliated to T.U.C. ('000s)
	Maximum ('000s)	Minimum ('000s)	Working Days Lost[d] ('000s)	No. of Stoppages beginning in year	Workers involved[e] ('000s)				
1946	408 Jan	360 Jan	2,158	2,205	526	781	7,875	192	6,671
1947	1,916 Feb	262 Sep	2,433	1,721	620	757	8,803	187	7,540
1948	359 Dec	299 Jun	1,944	1,759	424	734	9,145	188	7,791
1949	413 Jan	274 Jul	1,807	1,426	433	735	9,319	187	7,937
1950	404 Jan	297 Jul	1,389	1,339	302	726	9,274	186	7,883
1951	367 Jan	210 Jul	1,694	1,719	379	732	9,289	186	7,828
1952	468 Apr	379 Jan	1,792	1,714	415	735	9,535	183	8,020
1953	452 Feb	273 Jul	2,184	1,746	1,370	719	9,583	183	8,088
1954	387 Feb	220 Jul	2,457	1,989	448	717	9,523	184	8,094
1955	298 Jan	185 Jul	3,781	2,419	659	703	9,556	183	8,107
1956	297 Dec	223 Jun	2,083	2,648	507	694	9,726	186	8,264
1957	383 Jan	244 Jul	8,412	2,859	1,356	685	9,829	185	8,305
1958	536 Nov	395 Jan	3,462	2,629	523	675	9,639	185	8,337
1959	621 Jan	395 Jul	5,270	2,093	645	668	9,623	186	8,176
1960	461 Jan	292 Jul	3,024	2,832	817	664	9,835	184	8,128
1961	419 Jan	259 Jul	3,046	2,686	771	646	9,897	183	8,299
1962	566 Dec	397 Jun	5,795	2,449	4,420	626	9,887	182	8,313
1963	878 Feb	449 Jul	1,755	2,068	591	607	9,934	176	8,315
1964	501 Jan	318 Jul	2,277	2,524	871	598	10,079	175	8,326
1965	376 Jan	276 Jun	2,925	2,354	871	583	10,181	172	8,771
1966	564 Dec	261 Jun	2,398	1,937	530	575	10,111	170	8,868
1967	603 Feb	497 Jul	2,787	2,116	734	556	10,034	169	8,787
1968	631 Jan	515 Jul	4,690	2,378	2,258	534	10,036	160	8,726
1969	595 Jan	499 Jun	6,846	3,116	1,665	509	10,307	155	8,875
1970	628 Jan	547 Jun	10,980	3,906	1,801	481	11,000	150	9,402
1971	868 Dec	655 Jan	13,551	2,228	2,228	f	f	142	10,002
1972	929 Jan	745 Dec	23,909	2,497	1,734	f	f	132	9,895
1973	785 Jan	486 Dec	7,197	2,873	1,528	f	f	126	10,001
1974	656 Aug	515 Jun	14,740	2,882	1,601				

a Figures for Dec available only.
b 1900–20, unemployment figures for certain skilled trade unions available in *Ministry of Labour Gazettes*, figures are given as percentages. No comparable figures of total unemployed before 1921. Figures for insured workers registered as unemployed. Agricultural workers, insurable in 1936, are included from that date. Numerous changes in coverage throughout.
c Disputes involving less than 10 work-people and those lasting less than one day are omitted, except where aggregate duration exceeded 100 working days. d S. Ireland included from 1900 to 1907.
e Workers involved directly and indirectly. 'Indirectly' involved means those unable to work at establishments where disputes occurred, though not themselves parties to the dispute.
f After the passage of the *Industrial Relations Act, 1971*, many trade unions ceased to be registered and as a result many trade union statistics for the following years are non-existent or non-comparable.

SOURCES.—*Annual Abstract of Statistics*, *Ministry of Labour Gazette*, *Employment Gazette* and *Abstract of Labour Statistics*. *T.U.C. Congress Reports*.

For a general introductory survey of industrial relations see: A. Flanders, *Trade Unions* (1967) (contains a useful bibliography); H. A. Clegy (ed.), *The System of Industrial Relations in Great Britain* (1972); B. C. Roberts (ed.), *Industrial Relations: Contemporary Problems and Perspectives* (1962); Ministry of Labour, *Industrial Relations Handbook* (H.M.S.O., 1961); Ministry of Labour, *Evidence to the Royal Commission on Trade Unions and Employers' Associations* (H.M.S.O., 1965); G. D. H. Cole, *An Introduction to Trade Unionism* (1953); G. S. Bain, *The Growth of White-Collar Unionism* (1970).

A comprehensive study of the whole field is to be found in the *Report* of the Royal Commission on Trade Unions and Employers' Associations (Cmnd. 3623/1968) and the eleven *Research Papers* which were published in connection with it.

For a discussion of contemporary problems see: A. Flanders, *Industrial Relations: What Is Wrong With the System?* (1965); A. Flanders, *Collective Bargaining: Prescription for Change* (1967); PEP, 'Trade Unions in a Changing Society', *Planning*, No. 472 (1963); J. Hughes, *Change in the Trade Unions*, Fabian Research Series 244 (1964); W. E. J. McCarthy, *The Future of the Unions*, Fabian Tract No. 339 (1962); E. Wigham, *What's Wrong With the Unions?* (1961); and the research papers published by the Royal Commission on Trade Unions and Employers' Associations.

The definitive history of British trade unionism is H. A. Clegg *et al.*, *A History of British Trade Unions Since 1889* (Vol. 1, 1889–1910 (1964), Vols 2 and 3 are still to be published). For the period prior to 1889 see S. and B. Webb, *The History of Trade Unionism* (1920). The most useful short history is H. Pelling, *A History of British Trade Unionism* (1963) (contains an excellent bibliography, including references to the histories of individual unions).

For recent developments, see *In Place of Strife* (Cmnd. 3888/1969); P. Jenkins, *The Battle of Downing Street* (1970); W. E. J. McCarthy and N. D. Ellis, *Management Agreement; An Alternative to the Industrial Relations Act* (1973); M. A. Clegg, *How to Run an Incomes Policy* (1971).

For the legal aspects of trade unionism and industrial relations see K. W. Wedderburn, *The Worker and the Law* (1972) (contains a very comprehensive bibliography); C. Granfeld, *Modern Trade Union Law* (1970); O. Kahn-Freund, *Labour and the Law* (1972); R. W. Rideout, *Principles of Labour Law* (1972).

The most extensive work on trade union government and administration is B. C. Roberts, *Trade Union Government and Administration* (1956). See also: H. A. Clegg *et al.*, *Trade Union Officers* (1961); V. L. Allen, *Power in Trade Unions* (1954); PEP, 'The Structure and Organisation of British Trade Unions', *Planning*, No. 477 (1963); PEP, 'Trade Union Membership', *Planning*, No. 463 (1962); and TUC, *Written Evidence to the Royal Commission on Trade Unions and Employers' Associations* (1966).

For the relations between trade unions and the government see: D. F. Macdonald, *The State and the Trade Unions* (1960); V. L. Allen, *Trade Unions and the Government* (1960); and M. Harrison, *Trade Unions and the Labour Party Since 1945* (1960).

Other useful books include: W. E. J. McCarthy, *The Closed Shop* (1964); F. J. Bayliss, *British Wages Councils* (1962); and K. G. J. C. Knowles, *Strikes* (1952); B. Wootton, *The Social Foundations of Wage Policy* (1955); J. Corina, *Incomes Policy — Problems and Prospects*, Institute of Personnel Management (1966), Parts 1 and 2. A Marsh, *Industrial Relations in Engineering* (1965); E. H. Phelps Brown, *The Growth of Industrial Relations* (1959); H. A. Turner, *Trade Union Growth, Structure and Policy* (1962); R. Hyman, *Strikes* (1972); W. Brown, *Piecework Beginning* (1973); R. B. Mackenzie and L. C. Hunter, *Pay, Productivity and Collective Bargaining* (1973).

Bibliographies and details of current work on labour history and industrial relations may be found in the *Bulletin* of the Society for the Study of Labour History. Useful articles on various aspects of industrial relations as well as a chronicle of events may be found in the *British Journal of Industrial Relations*. Most of the basic statistics of industrial relations are to be found in the *Ministry of Labour/Employment Gazette*.

XII

THE ECONOMY

Some Landmarks in British Economic Policy

1 Aug	14	War emergency measures, including temporary increase in Bank Rate to 10%.
Dec	16	Exchange rate pegged at $4·77 to £.
15 Aug	18	Report of Cunliffe Committee on Currency and Foreign Exchanges (Cd. 9182) recommended eventual return to an effective gold standard at pre-war par value.
20 Mar	19	Withdrawal of official peg from sterling–dollar exchange ; exchange rates allowed to fluctuate.
Jan	21	Post-war trade slump. Unemployment exceeded 1 million (it remained above that level until 1939).
28 Apr	25	Return to fixed gold parity, at pre-1914 level ($4·86=£1). Britain now on gold bullion standard.
May	26	General Strike.
23 Jun	31	Report of Macmillan Committee on Finance and Industry (Cmd. 3897).
24 Jul	31	Report of May Committee on National Expenditure (Cmd. 3920), recommended big cuts in Government expenditure.
21 Sep	31	Gold Standard suspended ; sterling on fluctuating rate.
29 Feb	32	Import Duties Act set up Import Duties Advisory Council.
25 Apr	32	Exchange Equalisation Fund established to smooth variations in exchange rates.
30 Jun	32	Bank rate reduced to 2% and held at this level until 1939.
21 Aug	32	Ottawa Agreements on Imperial Preference.
21 Dec	33	Agricultural Marketing Act authorises quota controls on agricultural imports.
21 Dec	34	Special Areas (Development and Improvement) Act recognised problems of distressed areas.
12 Oct	36	Tripartite Agreement between Britain, France, and the U.S.A. to promote greater exchange stability by inter-Treasury Co-operation.
4 Sep	39	War emergency measures including imposition of exchange control with formal definition of the Sterling Area. Exchange rate fixed at $4·03=£.
21 Aug	41	Start of Lend-Lease.
26 Aug	44	White Paper on Employment Policy (Cmd. 6527) accepts Government responsibility for 'maintenance of a high and stable level of employment'.
21 Aug	45	End of Lend-Lease followed by U.S. and Canadian loans to Britain.
1 Jan	46	Nationalisation of Bank of England.
Feb	47	Fuel Crisis.
5 Jun	47	Gen. Marshall's speech leading to establishment of Marshall Aid (Jul 48) and of Organisation for European Economic Co-operation (Apr 48).
15 Jul	47	Sterling made convertible. Convertibility suspended 20 Aug.
4 Oct	47	Agriculture Act put the policy of agricultural subsidy and protection on a permanent basis.
4 Feb	48	'Wage Freeze' and dividend restraint.
30 Jul	48	Monopolies and Restrictive Practices (Inquiry and Control) Act established Monopolies Commission.
18 Sep	49	Devaluation of £ from $4·03 to $2·80.
13 Dec	50	Marshall Aid suspended as no longer necessary.
7 Nov	51	Bank rate increase from 2% to 2½% signals the revival of use of monetary policy. Import liberalisation rescinded to check record dollar drain.
25 Oct	55	Autumn budget following balance-of-payments crisis.
2 Aug	56	Restrictive Trade Practices Act established Restrictive Trade Practices Court.
11 Dec	56	Stand-by credits arranged following post-Suez balance-of-payments crisis.
12 Aug	57	Council on Prices Productivity and Incomes ('Three Wise Men') set up. (Disbanded 1961.)
19 Sep	57	Bank rate raised to 7% to meet sterling crisis.
27 Dec	57	Convertibility announced for non-resident sterling on current account.

20 Aug	59	Report of Radcliffe Committee on the working of the monetary system (Cmnd. 827).
20 Nov	59	European Free Trade Association Treaty signed.
4 Dec	60	O.E.E.C. reconstituted and broadened to include U.S.A. and Canada and retitled O.E.C.D.
20 Jul	61	Plowden Report on Control of Public Expenditure.
25 Jul	61	'Pay Pause' measures of S. Lloyd following balance-of-payments crisis. Establishment of National Economic Development Council.
10 Aug	61	Britain applies to join European Economic Community (negotiations terminated Jan 63).
16 Jul	64	Resale Prices Act greatly limits resale price maintenance.
26 Oct	64	New Government meets balance-of-payments deficit by imposing 15% import surcharge (reduced to 10% in Apr 65 and ended Nov 66).
18 Mar	65	Establishment of Prices and Incomes Board.
5 Aug	65	Monopolies and Mergers Act extended 1948 Monopolies Act to cover services as well as goods.
16 Sep	65	Publication of first National Economic Plan (Cmnd. 2764).
25 Jan	66	Industrial Reorganisation Corporation established to encourage 'concentration and rationalisation and to promote the greater efficiency and international competitiveness of British Industry'. (Cmnd. 2889.)
6 Mar	66	Announcement that Decimal Currency would be adopted in 1971.
20 Jul	66	Sterling crisis leads to Bank rate 7%, tax increases, credit restraints, and prices and incomes standstill (Cmnd. 3073).
12 Aug	66	Prices and Incomes Act becomes law (Part IV actuated 6 Oct 66).
11 May	67	Britain applies (for second time) to join European Economic Community. (De Gaulle gives second veto 27 Nov 67.)
18 Nov	67	Devaluation of £ from $2.80 to $2.40. Bank Rate 8%.
19 Jan	68	Major cuts in Government expenditure announced, followed by drastically deflationary Budget 19 Mar.
17 Mar	68	Two-tier gold system announced by World Central Banks.
30 Mar	68	Agreement on Special Drawing Rights in International Monetary Fund.
27 Oct	70	Expenditure cuts of £330m. announced, together with tax cuts.
15 Feb	71	Changeover to decimal currency.
30 Mar	71	Budget announces switch from surtax to graduated tax and to adopt Value Added Tax in 1973.
15 Aug	71	U.S.A. ends dollar–gold convertibility and, thereby, the Bretton Woods era.
23 Aug	71	£ floated.
19 Dec	71	General currency realignment under the Smithsonian agreement.
18 Feb	72	Wilberforce Court of Enquiry (Cmnd 4903) ends six-week miners' strike with 22% pay increase recommendation.
26 Sep	72	Anti-inflation programme announced including pay and prices freezes and establishment of Prices Commission and Pay Board.
1 Jan	73	Britain joins European Economic Community.
4 Mar	73	European currencies floated against £.
1 Apr	73	Value Added Tax supplants other excise duties and Selective Employment Tax.
6 Oct	73	Outbreak of Middle East War followed by short term cut in Middle East oil supplies and quadrupling of world oil prices.
8 Oct	73	Announcement of 'Phase 3' anti-inflation proposals.
13 Dec	73	Announcement of 3-day week for industry, starting in January, to cope with miners' overtime ban since 12 Nov.
11 Feb	74	Complete mine stoppage until 11 Mar. 3-day week ended 8 Mar.
31 Dec	74	End of year during which retail prices rose by 19% and wage rates by 29% while total industrial production fell by 3% (each figure a post-war record.)
30 Jan	75	*Financial Times* Index of leading shares price touched 252 having been at 146 on 9 Jan 75 and at 339 on 28 Feb 74.

SOURCES.—A. Shonfield, *British Economic Policy Since The War* (1958); J. C. R. Dow, *The Management of the British Economy 1945–60* (1964); A. C. Pigou, *Aspects of British Economic History 1918–1925* (1948); E. V. Morgan, *Studies in British Financial Policy 1914–1925*; S. Brittan, *Steering the Economy* (1971); R. S. Sayers, 'Co-operation between Central Banks', *The Three Banks Review* (Sep 1963); R. S. Sayers, *Central Banking after Bagehot* (1959).   Since 1960 an economic chronology has been provided in successive issues of the *National Institute Economic Review*.

Sources of Government Economic Advice

The Treasury and, from 1964–69, the Department of Economic Affairs have provided governments with their main official guidance (see p. 234 for

Permanent Secretaries). In addition, under the Cabinet Office or the Treasury, there have been the following official economic advisers.

Economic Section of the Cabinet Office (1941–53)
Director

1941	J. Jewkes	1946	J. Meade
1941	L. Robbins	1947	R. Hall

Economic Adviser to the Government (1953–64)

1953	(Sir) R. Hall	1961	A. Cairncross

Head of Government Economic Service (1964–)

1964	(Sir) A. Cairncross	1973	Sir K. Berrill
1969	Sir D. MacDougall	1974	Sir B. Hopkin

Outside the Civil Service there have been the following official bodies:

Bank of England (1696–)
Governor

1899	S. Gladstone	1920	M. Norman (Ld)
1901	(Sir) A. Prevost	1944	Ld Catto
1903	S. Morley	1949	C. Cobbold (Ld)
1905	A. Wallace	1964	E of Cromer
1908	R. Johnston	1966	(Sir) L. O'Brien (Ld)
1913	W. Cunliffe (Ld)	1973	G. Richardson
1918	Sir B. Cokayne (Ld Cullen of Ashbourne)		

Economic Advisory Council (1930–39)
(No full meeting of this body was held after the first year, but until 1939 its Standing Committee on Economic Information was active under Sir J. Stamp (Ld).)

Import Duties Advisory Council (1932–39)
Chairman

1932 Sir F. May (Ld)

Economic Planning Board (1947–62)
Chairman

1947–53 Sir E. Plowden

(After 1953, when some of its functions were merged with the Economic Section of the Treasury, the Permanent Secretary of the Treasury was made *ex officio* Chairman of the Board of outside advisers.)

National Economic Development Council (1961–)
Director–General of National Economic Development Office

1962	Sir R. Shone	1966	Sir F. Figgures
1966	(Sir) F. Catherwood	1973	(Sir) R. McIntosh

Council on Pay, Productivity, and Incomes (1957–61)
Chairman

1957	Ld Cohen	1960	Ld Heyworth

National Incomes Commission (1961–64)
Chairman

1962 Sir G. Lawrence

Prices and Incomes Board (1965–70)
Chairman

1965 A. Jones

Prices Commission (1973–)
Chairman

1973 Sir A. Cockfield

Pay Board (1973–4)
Chairman

1973 Sir F. Figgures

Industrial Adviser to the Government (1974–   )

1974 Sir D. Ryder

(see also *Monopolies Commission,* p. 330; Royal Commissions and Committees of Inquiry, pp. 241–2; Central Policy Review Staff p. 233.)

Select Statistics

	Net National Income (at factor cost)ª (£m.)	Income Tax (Standard Rate in £)	Amount Retained of Bachelor's £10,000 earned income after Income Tax and Surtax	Wholesale Price Index Number (1963=100)	Retail Price Index Number (1963=100)	Purchasing Power of £ (1900 =20/-)	Real gross domestic product per head (1963 =100)
	1	2	3	4	5	6	7
1900	1,750	8	9,667	22	19	20/–	53
1901	1,727	1/–	9,500	21	19	19/9	54
1902	1,740	1/2	9,417	21	19	19/7	54
1903	1,717	1/3	9,375	21	19	19/4	52
1904	1,704	11	9,542	22	19	19/1	52
1905	1,776	1/–	9,500	21	19	19/4	53
1906	1,874	1/–	9,500	22	19	19/4	53
1907	1,966	1/–	9,500	23	20	18/8	53
1908	1,875	1/–	9,500	23	20	18/4	49
1909	1,907	1/–	9,500	23	20	18/4	51
1910	1,984	1/2	9,242	24	20	18/1	52
1911	2,076	1/2	9,242	24	21	17/11	53
1912	2,181	1/2	9,242	25	21	17/3	53
1913	2,265	1/2	9,242	26	21	17/3	54
1914	2,209	1/2	9,242	26	21	17/5	54
1915	(2,591)	1/8	8,669	31	26	14/2	..
1916	(3,064)	3/–	7,721	41	30	11/11	..
1917	(3,631)	5/–	6,721	53	37	9/11	..
1918	(4,372)	5/–	6,721	59	42	8/7	..
1919	(5,461)	6/–	5,813	66	46	8/1	..
1920	5,664	6/–	5,813	79	52	7/–	..
1921	4,460	6/–	5,672	50	47	7/8	48
1922	3,856	6/–	5,672	41	38	9/6	48
1923	3,844	5/–	6,150	41	37	10/–	49
1924	3,919	4/6	6,389	43	37	9/11	49
1925	3,980	4/6	6,389	41	37	9/11	54
1926	3,914	4/–	6,968	38	36	10/1	50
1927	4,145	4/–	6,968	36	35	10/5	54
1928	4,154	4/–	6,968	36	35	10/6	56
1929	4,178	4/–	6,968	35	35	10/7	57
1930	3,957	4/–	6,968	30	33	11/–	56
1931	3,666	4/6	6,487	27	31	11/10	52
1932	3,568	5/–	6,103	26	30	12/1	52
1933	3,728	5/–	6,103	26	30	12/5	52
1934	3,881	5/–	6,103	27	30	12/4	56
1935	4,109	4/6	6,340	27	30	12/2	59
1936	4,388	4/6	6,341	29	31	11/10	60
1937	4,616	4/9	6,222	33	32	11/4	63
1938	4,671	5/–	6,103	30	33	11/2	65
1939	5,037	5/6	5,867	31	34	10/10	..
1940	5,980	7/–	4,965	42	38	8/11	..

	Net National Income (at factor cost)[a] (£m.)	Income Tax (Standard Rate in £)	Amount Retained of Bachelor's £10,000 earned income after Income Tax and Surtax	Wholesale Price Index Number (1963=100)	Retail Price Index Number (1963=100)	Purchasing Power of £ (1900 =20/-)	Real gross domestic product per head (1963 =100)
	1	2	3	4	5	6	7
1941	6,941	8/6	3,921	47	42	8/-	..
1942	7,664	10/-	3,138	48	45	7/5	..
1943	8,171	10/-	3,138	50	47	7/2	..
1944	8,366	10/-	3,138	51	47	7/-	..
1945	8,340	10/-	3,138	53	49	6/10	..
1946	7,974	10/-	3,138	58	51	6/7	..
1947	8,587	9/-	3,637	67	54	6/2	..
1948	9,669	9/-	3,501	63	57	5/9	72
1949	10,240	9/-	3,587	66	59	5/7	73
1950	10,784	9/-	3,587	71	61	5/5	75
1951	11,857	9/-	3,598	80	67	5/-	78
1952	12,763	9/6	3,361	84	73	4/8	78
1953	13,766	9/6	3,411	84	75	4/8	81
1954	14,573	9/-	3,646	83	76	4/7	84
1955	15,511	9/-	3,646	86	80	4/5	86
1956	16,827	8/6	3,873	89	84	4/2	87
1957	17,831	8/6	3,873	92	87	4/1	89
1958	18,591	8/6	4,341	93	90	4/-	88
1959	19,546	8/6	4,341	93	90	4/-	90
1960	20,798	7/9	4,648	94	91	3/11	94
1961	22,254	7/9	4,648	97	94	3/10	97
1962	23,272	7/9	4,648	99	98	3/8	97
1963	24,781	7/9	4,648	100	100	3/7	100
1964	26,854	7/9	4,845	103	103	3/6	105
1965	28,674	8/3	5,922	107	108	3/5	107
1966	30,275	8/3	5,922	110	112	3/3	108
1967	31,878	8/3	5,715	111	115	3/2	111
1968	34,015	8/3	5,715	115	121	3/-	114
1969	35,710	8/3	5,715	120	127	2/10	116
1970	39,019	7/9	5,715	128	135	2/8	118
1971	43,784	38·75%	6,188	140	148	12½p	119
1972	48,962	38·75%	6,141	147	159	11½p	120
1973	56,259	30%	6,377	158	173	11p	126
1974	..	33%	6,088	195	201	9½p	..

[a] Changes in sources at 1914 and 1947.

SOURCES.—
1. 1900–14, C. H. Feinstein, 'Income and Investment in the U.K. 1856–1914', *Economic Journal*, June 1961: 1914–46, A. R. Prest, 'National Income of the U.K. 1870–1946', *Economic Journal*, March 1948. 1947 onwards, *National Income and Expenditure* Annual Blue Books.
2. *Reports of the Commissioners for Inland Revnue.*
3. *Reports of the Commissioners for Inland Revenue* and information received from the Inland Revenue.
4 and 5. *The British Economy: Key Statistics 1900–1970* and *Annual Abstract of Statistics.*
6. 1900–14 based on unofficial price index compiled by G. H. Wood, in W. T. Layton and G. Crowther, *An Introduction to the Study of Prices* (1938); 1914–38 based on Ministry of Labour *Cost of Living Index (Min. of Labour Gazette)*; 1938 onwards based on figures in *Annual Abstract of Statistics.*
7. Based on *The British Economy: Key Statistics 1900–1970* and *Annual Abstract of Statistics, 1970–.*

	Index Number of Industrial Production (1963=100)	Steel Production[a] ('000 tons)	Coal Production[b] (million tons)	Raw Cotton Consumption[c] U.K. (million lbs.)	Agriculture			Price of 2½% Consols (Average for year)	Bank Rate % (Maximum and Minimum for year)
					Cultivated Areas[d] ('000 acres)	Agricultural Output (1963=100)	Employment in Agriculture ('000)		
	1	2	3	4	5	6	7	8	9
1900	27	4,900	225	1,737	47,795	52	2,243	99·6	6 3
1901	27	4,900	219	1,569	47,761	52	..	94·3	5 3
1902	28	4,910	227	1,633	47,753	53	..	94·4	4 3
1903	28	5,030	230	1,617	47,708	52	..	90·8	4 3
1904	28	5,030	232	1,486	47,671	52	..	88·3	4 3
1905	28	5,810	236	1,813	47,673	54	..	89·8	3 2½
1906	29	6,460	251	1,855	47,193	54	..	88·3	6 3½
1907	30	6,520	268	1,985	46,998	53	..	84·1	7 4
1908	28	5,290	262	1,917	47,002	53	..	86·0	7 2½
1909	29	5,880	264	1,824	46,888	55	..	83·9	5 2½
1910	29	6,370	264	1,632	46,932	56	..	81·1	5 3
1911	30	6,460	272	1,892	46,927	54	2,205	79·3	4½ 3
1912	31	6,800	260	2,142	46,794	55	..	76·2	5 3
1913	33	7,664	287	2,178	46,741	56	..	73·6	5 4½
1914	31	7,835	266	2,077	46,643	54	..	74·8	10 3
1915	..	8,550	253	1,931	46,554	..	..	65·5	5
1916	..	8,992	256	1,972	46,564	..	..	58·0	6 5
1917	..	9,717	249	1,800	46,212	..	..	54·7	6 5
1918	..	9,539	228	1,499	46,142	..	..	56·9	5
1919	30	7,894	230	1,526	46,206	51	..	54·1	6 5
1920	33	9,067	230	1,726	45,953	49	1,553	47·0	7 6
1921	27	3,703	163	1,066	45,581	50	1,488	48·0	7 5
1922	31	5,801	250	1,409	45,458	50	1,453	56·5	5 3
1923	33	8,482	276	1,362	33,106	52	1,415	58·0	4 3
1924	36	8,201	267	1,369	33,057	50	1,423	57·0	4
1925	38	7,385	243	1,609	32,920	53	1,420	56·3	5 4
1926	36	3,596	126	1,509	32,830	55	1,407	55·0	5
1927	41	9,097	251	1,557	32,724	55	1,389	54·8	5 4½
1928	40	8,520	238	1,520	32,617	58	1,380	55·9	4½
1929	42	9,636	258	1,498	32,547	58	1,372	54·3	6 4½
1930	40	7,326	244	1,272	32,459	60	1,340	55·8	5 3
1931	38	5,203	220	985	32,374	54	1,312	56·9	6 2½
1932	37	5,261	209	1,257	32,284	57	1,300	66·8	6 2
1933	46	7,024	207	1,177	32,193	62	1,296	73·7	2
1934	44	8,850	221	1,322	32,096	62	1,279	80·6	2
1935	47	9,859	222	1,261	32,024	60	1,260	86·6	2
1936	52	11,785	228	1,366	31,932	60	1,232	85·1	2
1937	55	12,984	240	1,431	31,827	59	1,213	76·3	2
1938	53	10,398	227	1,109	31,755	58	1,180	74·1	2
1939	..	13,221	231	1,317	31,679	..	1,168	67·2	4 2
1940	..	12,975	224	1,389	31,430	..	1,128	73·5	2

	Index Number of Industrial Production (1963=100)	Steel Production[a] ('000 tons)	Coal Production[b] (million tons)	Raw Cotton Consumption[e] U.K. (million lbs.)	Agriculture Cultivated Areas[d] ('000 acres)	Agricultural Output (1963=100)	Employment in Agriculture ('000)	Price of 2½% Consols (Average for year)	Bank Rate % (Maximum and Minimum for year)
	1	2	3	4	5	6	7	8	9
1941	..	12,312	206	965	31,353	..	1,177	80·0	2
1942	..	12,942	205	939	31,204	..	1,192	82·6	2
1943	..	13,031	199	885	31,058	..	1,235	80·7	2
1944	..	12,142	193	804	31,008	..	1,226	79·6	2
1945	..	11,824	183	717	31,023	..	1,207	85·5	2
1946	55	12,695	190	813	31,010	65	1,240	96·3	2
1947	58	12,725	197	815	31,022	62	1,231	90·7	2
1948	62	14,877	209	977	31,062	67	1,274	78·0	2
1949	66	15,553	215	979	31,056	72	1,274	75·9	2
1950	70	16,293	216	1,017	31,126	73	1,258	70·5	2
1951	72	15,639	223	1,024	31,131	75	1,232	66·1	2½ 2
1952	71	16,418	227	686	31,163	77	1,203	59·1	4 2½
1953	75	17,609	224	831	31,177	79	1,177	61·3	4 3½
1954	79	18,520	224	892	31,128	81	1,164	66·6	3½ 3
1955	83	19,791	222	778	31,103	80	1,155	60·0	4½ 3
1956	83	20,659	222	714	31,092	84	1,121	52·8	5½ 4½
1957	85	21,699	224	744	31,030	86	1,111	50·2	7 5½
1958	84	19,566	216	628	31,001	84	1,091	50·2	7 4
1959	88	20,186	206	623	30,873	87	1,044	51·8	4
1960	95	24,305	194	599	30,854	93	1,017	46·1	6 4
1961	96	22,086	192	536	30,637	93	985	46·1	7 5
1962	97	20,491	199	473	30,655	96	951	40·7	6 4½
1963	100	22,520	197	483	30,644	100	929	44·8	4½ 4
1964	108	26,230	195	508	30,686	104	890	41·5	7 4
1965	112	27,006	187	492	30,660	107	846	39·0	7 6
1966	114	24,315	175	454	30,683	106	814	36·7	7 6
1967	115	23,895	175	384	30,653	110	789	37·4	8 5½
1968	122	25,862	167	382	30,437	109	757	33·8	8 7
1969	125	26,422	153	376	30,291	110	727	28·2	8 7
1970	125	27,869	145	366	30,005	116	707	27·3	7½ 7
1971	126	23,793	147	316	30,029	123	..	27·6	7 5
1972	128	24,992	120	291	27,978	125	..	27·5	9 5
1973	138	26,229	130	278	29,846	129	..	23·2	13 7½
1974	134	22,424	109	..	29,866	..	..	16·8	13 11½

..... Change in basis of calculation.

[a] Great Britain only. [b] including S. Ireland, 1900–21 inclusive.
[c] From 1958 a revised bale weight was used in calculations.
[d] Total area under all crops and grass. For Great Britain excluding all holdings under one acre before 1970, for N. Ireland excluding all holdings under ¼ acre until 1953, and under one acre from 1954 to 1972.
[e] Includes forestry and fishing.

SOURCES—
1. *The British Economy, Key Statistics 1900–1970* and *Annual Abstract of Statistics.*
2. British Iron and Steel Federation, Annual Abstract of Statistics.
3. Ministry of Power, *Annual Abstract of Statistics.*
4. R. Robson, *The Cotton Industry in Britain* (1957), p. 332, Statistics table 1, and information supplied by the Cotton Board.
5. Figures for June each year, 1900–13 including Isle of Man and Channel Islands. 1914 onwards excluding Isle of Man and Channel Islands. 1900–22 including S. Ireland. *Annual Abstract of Statistics*, Agricultural Departments.
6 and 7. *The British Economy, Key Statistics 1900–1970* and *Annual Abstract of Statistics.*
8 and 9. Bank of England and *Annual Abstract of Statistics.*

	Net Balance of Payments of the U.K. on current account[a] (£m.)	Terms of Trade[b] Index No. (1963 =100)	Imports and Exports of the U.K.			Imports and Exports of the U.K. Volume Indices		Foreign Exchange Rates		
			Imports[c] c.i.f. (£m.)	Exports of U.K. Products[c] f.o.b. (£m.)	Re-exports[c] f.o.b. (£m.)	Imports[d]	Exports[d]	U.S.A. ($ to £)	France (Francs to £)	Germany (Marks to £)
	1	2	3	4	5	6	7	8	9	10
1900		72	523	291	63	48	44	4·84	25·1	20·4
1901		71	522	280	68	49	44	4·85	25·2	20·4
1902		69	528	283	66	51	47	4·85	25·2	20·5
1903		67	543	291	70	51	48	4·85	25·1	20·4
1904		69	551	301	70	52	49	4·85	25·2	20·4
1905		68	565	330	78	53	54	4·85	25·2	20·5
1906		68	608	376	85	54	58	4·82	25·1	20·5
1907		68	646	426	92	55	63	4·84	25·1	20·5
1908		69	593	377	80	53	58	4·85	25·1	20·4
1909		65	625	378	91	54	60	4·86	25·2	20·4
1910		65	678	430	104	56	65	4·84	25·2	20·4
1911		67	680	454	103	57	68	4·84	25·3	20·4
1912		66	745	487	112	61	72	4·85	25·2	20·5
1913	237	69	769	525	110	64	75	4·83	25·2	20·4
1914		..	697	431	95	..	..	4·87	25·2	20·5
1915		..	852	385	99	..	..	4·77	26·3	..
1916		..	949	506	98	..	..	4·76	28·2	..
1917		..	1,064	527	70	..	..	4·76	27·4	..
1918		..	1,316	501	31	..	..	4·76	27·2	..
1919	− 128	79	1,626	799	165	56	41	4·60	29·7	..
1920	235	86	1,933	1,334	223	56	53	3·97	47·9	145
1921	119	87	1,086	703	107	47	37	3·73	46·7	268
1922	173	90	1,003	720	104	54	51	4·41	52·8	1,654
1923	169	89	1,096	767	119	59	56	4·58	75·2	720,000
1924	72	86	1,277	801	140	66	57	4·33	81·8	18 billion
1925	46	85	1,321	773	154	69	56	4·86	106·1	20·4
1926	− 15	87	1,241	653	125	70	50	4·87	167·5	20·4
1927	82	86	1,218	709	123	72	58	4·85	124·0	20·5
1928	123	82	1,196	724	120	69	60	4·87	124·2	20·4
1929	103	85	1,221	729	110	73	61	4·84	124·0	20·4
1930	28	92	1,044	571	87	71	50	4·86	123·7	20·4
1931	− 104	102	861	391	64	72	38	4·86	124·2	20·5
1932	− 51	102	702	365	51	63	38	3·58	91·1	15·0
1933	—	104	675	368	49	63	39	4·30	86·2	14·3
1934	− 77	103	731	396	51	66	41	5·04	76·6	13·3
1935	32	100	756	426	55	67	45	4·94	74·5	12·2
1936	− 18	99	848	441	61	72	45	5·01	75·7	12·4
1937	− 56	93	1,028	521	75	76	49	4·94	120	12·3
1938	− 70	102	920	471	62	72	43	4·95	178	12·3
1939	− 250	99	886	440	46	69	40	4·68	177	11·7
1940	− 804	85	1,152	411	26	61	31	4·03	177	..
1941	− 816	93	1,145	365	13	50	21	4·03	..	..
1942	− 663	94	997	271	5	47	16	4·03	..	..
1943	− 680	94	1,234	234	6	50	12	4·03	..	..
1944	− 659	100	1,309	266	16	54	13	4·03	..	..
1945	− 875	94	1,104	399	51	44	20	4·03	203·8	..

..... Change in basis of calculation.   (   ) Estimated figures.

	Net Balance of Payments of the U.K. on current account[a] (£m.)	Terms of Trade[b] No. (1963 =100)	Imports and Exports of the U.K.			Imports and Exports of the U.K. Volume Indices		Foreign Exchange Rates		
			Imports[c] c.i.f. (£m.)	Exports of U.K. Products[c] f.o.b. (£m.)	Re-exports[c] f.o.b. (£m.)	Imports[d] (1963 =100)	Exports[d] (1963 =000)	U.S.A. ($ to £)	France (Francs to £)	Germany (Marks to £)
	1	2	3	4	5	6	7	8	9	10
1946	− 230	95	1,298	912	50	49	43	4·03	480·0	··
1947	− 381	88	1,798	1,142	59	55	47	4·03	480·0	··
1948	26	85	2,075	1,578	61	57	60	4·03	f	··
1949	− 1	86	2,279	1,789	58	61	66	e	g	··
1950	307	80	2,609	2,174	85	61	75	2·80	980·0	··
1951	− 369	73	3,905	2,582	127	69	74	2·80	979·7	··
1952	163	80	3,456	2,567	142	63	69	2·79	981·5	West Germany only
1953	145	87	3,328	2,558	103	68	71	2·81	982·8	11·7
1954	117	87	3,359	2,650	98	69	74	2·81	981·6	11·7
1955	− 155	84	3,861	2,877	116	76	80	2·79	978·1	11·7
1956	208	86	3,862	3,143	144	75	84	2·80	982·7	11·7
1957	233	87	4,044	3,295	130	78	86	2·79	h	11·7
1958	344	95	3,748	3,176	141	79	83	2·81	i	11·7
1959	152	97	3,983	3,330	131	84	86	2·81	13·77[j]	11·7
1960	− 255	97	4,557	3,536	141	94	90	2·81	13·77	11·7
1961	6	99	4,398	3,682	158	93	93	2·80	13·74	11·17
1962	122	101	4,492	3,792	158	96	95	2·81	13·76	11·22
1963	124	100	4,820	4,080	154	100	100	2·80	13·72	11·16
1964	− 382	99	5,696	4,412	153	111	103	2·79	13·68	11·10
1965	− 49	101	5,751	4,724	173	112	108	2·80	13·70	11·17
1966	84	103	5,949	5,047	194	114	112	2·79	13·72	11·17
1967	− 313	104	6,437	5,029	185	123	112	2·79[k]	13·68[l]	11·10[m]
1968	− 280	101	7,897	6,182	220	135	126	2·39	11·86	9·56
1969	449	101	8,315	7,039	259	138	140	2·39	12·43[n]	9·38
1970	685	104	9,051	7,741	323	144	143	2·40	13·24	8·74
1971	1,050	105	9,834	9,176		151	156	2·44	13·47	8·61
1972	72	105	11,155	9,745		167	160	2·50	12·61	7·97
1973	− 1,198	94	15,854	12,455		191	182	2·45	10·90	6·54
1974	− 3,731	78	23,160	16,500		194	191	2·34	11·25	6·05

[a] Changes in sources and methods in 1924.
[b] Export price index as a percentage of the import price index. A fall indicates an adverse movement.
[c] 1900–22 inclusive, S. Ireland is included. From 1923 direct foreign trade of S. Ireland is excluded, and Imports and Exports include trade of Great Britain and N. Ireland with S. Ireland. There are small changes in coverage from time to time.
[d] 1900–23 inclusive, including S. Ireland.
[e] 4·03 to 19 Sep, 2·80 thereafter.
[f] 480 to 25 Jan, 864 from 26 Jan to 17 Oct, 1,062 thereafter.
[g] 1,062 to 26 Apr, 1,097 from 27 Apr to 20 Sep, 980 thereafter.
[h] 984·9 to 10 Aug, 1,177·1 thereafter.
[i] 1,775·5 to 24 Dec, 13·74 from 29 Dec (in units of 100 francs).
[j] In units of 100 francs (100 francs = 1 New Franc)
[k] 2·79 to 18 Nov, 240 thereafter.
[l] 13·68 to 18 Nov, 11·88 thereafter.
[m] 11·10 to 18 Nov, 9·50 thereafter.
[n] 11·86 to 11 Aug., 13·31 thereafter.

SOURCES—
1. *Key Statistics* and *Balance of Payments Pink Books*.
2. *The British Economy, Key Statistics 1900–70*.
3, 4, and 5. *Trade and Navigation Accounts of the U.K.*, Board of Trade, annually. From 1965 *Overseas Trade Accounts of the U.K.*
6 and 7. *The British Economy, Key Statistics 1900–1970*.
8, 9, and 10. 1900–39, *The Economist*, figures for the end of June; 1940 onwards *Annual Abstract of Statistics*. Figures are average for the year.

	Total Central Government Revenue[a] (£m.)	Main Sources of Revenue				
		Income tax[b] (£m.)	Surtax (£m.)	Customs (£m.)	Excise (£m.)	Death Duties (£m.)
	1	2	3	4	5	6
1900	140	28	..	26	38	17
1901	153	35	..	31	37	19
1902	161	39	..	35	37	18
1903	151	31	..	34	37	17
1904	153	31	..	36	36	17
1905	154	31	..	35	36	17
1906	155	31	..	33	36	19
1907	157	31	..	32	36	19
1908	152	34	..	29	34	18
1909	132	13	..	30	31	22
1910	204	60	3	33	40	25
1911	185	42	3	34	38	25
1912	189	41	4	33	38	25
1913	198	44	3	35	40	27
1914	227	59	10	39	42	28
1915	337	112	17	60	61	31
1916	573	186	19	71	56	31
1917	707	216	23	71	39	32
1918	889	256	36	103	59	30
1919	1,340	317	42	149	134	41
1920	1,426	339	55	134	200	48
1921	1,125	337	62	130	194	52
1922	914	315	64	123	157	57
1923	837	269	61	120	148	58
1924	799	274	63	99	135	59
1925	812	259	69	103	135	61
1926	806	235	66	108	133	67
1927	843	251	61	112	139	77
1928	836	238	56	119	134	81
1929	815	238	56	120	128	80
1930	858	256	68	121	124	83
1931	851	287	77	136	120	65
1932	827	252	61	167	121	77
1933	809	229	53	179	107	85
1934	805	229	51	185	105	81
1935	845	238	51	197	107	88
1936	897	257	54	211	110	88
1937	949	298	57	222	114	89
1938	1,006	336	63	226	114	77
1939	1,132	390	70	262	138	78
1940	1,495	524	76	305	224	81
1941	2,175	770	75	378	326	91
1942	2,922	1,007	75	460	425	93
1943	3,149	1,184	76	561	482	100
1944	3,355	1,317	74	579	497	111
1945	3,401	1,361	69	570	541	120
1946	3,623	1,156	76	621	564	148
1947	4,011	1,189	91	791	629	172
1948	4,168	1,368	98	824	734	177
1949	4,098	1,438	115	813	706	190
1950	4,157	1,404	121	905	724	185

	Total Central Government Revenue[a] (£m.)	Main Sources of Revenue				
		Income tax[b] (£m.)	Surtax (£m.)	Customs (£m.)	Excise (£m.)	Death Duties (£m.)
	1	2	3	4	5	6
1951	4,629	1,669	130	998	753	183
1952	4,654	1,736	131	1,024	739	152
1953	4,606	1,731	132	1,042	722	165
1954	4,987	1,893	135	1,100	772	188
1955	5,160	1,943	139	1,149	865	176
1956	5,462	2,114	158	1,199	902	169
1957	5,679	2,208	157	1,207	942	171
1958	5,850	2,322	167	1,262	930	187
1959	6,016	2,243	181	1,373	909	227
1960	6,344	2,433	189	1,457	933	236
1961	6,644	2,727	224	1,616	978	262
1962	6,794	2,818	184	1,639	1,208	270
1963	6,890	2,745	177	1,723	1,043	310
1964	8,157	3,088	184	2,008	1,166	297
1965	9,144	3,678	203	3,401		292
1966	10,219	3,246	242	3,536		301
1967	11,177	3,825	239	3,721		330
1968	13,363	4,349	225	4,601		382
1969	15,266	4,907	255	4,933		365
1970	15,843	5,731	248	4,709		357
1971	16,932	6,433	348	5,325		451
1972	17,178	6,477	341	5,744		459
1973	18,226	7,137	307	6,220		412

[a] Total national revenue includes Ordinary and Self-Balancing Revenue. Figures relate to year ending 31 Mar of following year.
[b] 1900–10, 'Income tax' covers Property and Income tax. 1910 figure includes arrears for 1909.

SOURCES—
1, 2, 3, 4, 5, and 6. *Finance Accounts of the U.K.*, published annually by the Treasury.

	Main Heads of Expenditure			Specimen Tariffs		Excise Duty on Beer[d] (per barrel of 36 gallons)	National Debt[e]
	Defence (£m.)	Health, Labour and Insurance[a] (£m.)	Pensions[b] (£m.)	Sugar[c] (per cwt.)	Tea[c] (per lb.)		
	1	2	3	4	5	6	7
				s. d.	s. d.	s. d.	
1900	121	..	..	..	6	6/9	628·9
1901	124	..	..	4/2	6	7/9	689·5
1902	101	..	..	4/2	6	7/9	745·0
1903	72	..	..	4/2	6	7/9	770·8
1904	66	..	..	4/2	8	7/9	762·6
1905	62	..	..	4/2	6	7/9	755·1
1906	59	..	..	4/2	5	7/9	743·3
1907	58	..	..	4/2	5	7/9	724·5
1908	59	..	..	1/10	5	7/9	709·0
1909	63	..	..	1/10	5	7/9	702·7
1910	67	..	..	1/10	5	7/9	713·2
1911	70	..	..	1/10	5	7/9	685·2
1912	72	..	..	1/10	5	7/9	668·3
1913	77	14	1	1/10	5	7/9	656·5
1914	437	14	1	1/10	5	7/9	649·8
1915	1,424	14	1	1/10	8	23/-	1,105·0
1916	2,007	14	1	14/-	1/-	24/-	2,133·1
1917	2,436	14	1	14/-	1/-	25/-	4,011·4
1918	2,238	15	1	25/8	1/-	50/-	5,871·9
1919	692	74	100	25/8	1/-	70/-	7,434·9
1920	292	73	110	25/8	1/-	100/-	7,828·8
1921	189	73	96	25/8	1/-	100/-	7,574·4
1922	111	61	83	25/8	8	100/-	7,654·3
1923	105	59	72	25/8	8	100/-	7,742·2
1924	114	65	71	11/8	4	100/-	7,641·0
1925	119	65	70	11/8	4	100/-	7,597·8
1926	116	75	65	11/8	4	100/-	7,558·6
1927	117	73	62	11/8	4	100/-	7,554·6
1928	113	76	59	11/8	4	100/-	7,527·8
1929	113	86	56	11/8	..	100/-	7,500·3
1930	110	108	55	11/8	..	103/-	7,469·0
1931	107	121	52	11/8	..	103/-	7,413·3
1932	103	155	49	11/8	4	134/-	7,433·9
1933	107	151	49	11/8	4	24/-	7,643·8
1934	113	151	47	11/8	4	24/-	7,822·3
1935	136	162	46	11/8	4	24/-	6,763·9
1936	186	162	45	11/8	6	24/-	6,759·3
1937	197	162	44	11/8	6	24/-	6,764·7
1938	254	166	43	11/8	8	24/-	6,993·7
1939	626	167	42	11/8	8	24/-	7,130·8
1940	3,220	165	41	23/4	8	90/-	7,899·2
1941	4,085	170	41	23/4	8	90/-	10,366·4
1942	4,840	186	40	23/4	8	118/1½	13,041·1
1943	4,950	199	39	23/4	8	138/4½	15,822·6
1944	5,125	208	40	23/4	8	140/7½	18,562·2
1945	4,410	219	42	23/4	8	140/7½	21,365·9

..... Change in basis of calculation.

	Main Heads of Expenditure			Specimen Tariffs		Excise Duty on Beer^d (per barrel of 36 gallons)	National Debt^e (£m.)
	De- fence (£m.)	Health, Labour and In- surance^a (£m.)	Pen- sions^b (£m.)	Sugar^c (per cwt.)	Tea^c (per lb.)		
	1	2	3	4	5	6	7
				s. d.	s. d.	s. d.	
1946	1,653	334	97	23/4	8	140/7½	23,636·5
1947	854	380	91	23/4	8	140/7½	25,630·6
1948	753	598	96	23/4	8	178/10½	25,620·8
1949	741	806	97	11/8	2	157/10½	25,167·6
1950	777	835	94	11/8	2	155/4½	25,802·3
1951	1,110	810	91	11/8	2	155/4½	25,921·6
1952	1,404	884	100	11/8	2	155/4½	25,890·5
1953	1,365	903	97	11/8	2	155/4½	26,051·2
1954	1,436	619	419	11/8	2	155/4½	26,583·0
1955	1,405	652	433	11/8	2	155/4½	26,933·7
1956	1,525	750	463	11/8	2	155/4½	27,038·9
1957	1,430	782	490	11/8	2	155/4½	27,007·5
1958	1,468	794	575	11/8	2	155/4½	27,232·0
1959	1,475	1,209	610	11/8	2	111/9½	27,376·3
1960	1,596	1,384	634	11/8	2	111/9½	27,732·6
1961	1,689	1,417	659	11/8^f	2	111/9½	28,251·7
1962	1,767	1,549	705	..	2	123/-	28,674·4
1963	1,792	1,716	772	..	2^g	123/-	29,847·6
1964	1,909	1,897	792	..	..	147/-	30,226·5
1965	2,055	..^h	..^h	..	..	171/-	30,440·6
1966	2,145	..	..	..	..	171/-	31,340·2
1967	2,274	..	..	..	..	188/8	31,935·6
1968	2,232	..	..	..	..	188/8	34,193·9
1969	2,204	..	..	..	..	207/6	33,982·6
1970	2,488	..	..	..	..	207/6	33,079·4
1971	2,786	..	..	..	..	£10·37½	33,441·7
1972	3,079	..	..	..	..	£10·37½	35,839·1
1973	3,447	..	..	..	..	£6·90^i	36,910·0
1974	..	..	..	..	..	£9·36	40,124·5

.... Change in basis of calculation.

^a 1900–13, the system of classification prevents entries comparable with those for later years. 1949–53, figures cover Housing, Local Government, Health, Labour, National Insurance and National Assistance. From 1954 figures cover Health, Housing and Local Government.

^b 1900–13, the system of classification prevents entries comparable with those for later years. Before 1954, 'Pensions' equivalent to 'non-effective' charges. 1954 onwards figures cover Pensions, National Insurance and National Assistance.

^c Full Customs duty given. In many cases preferential rates apply to Commonwealth trade. Sugar: exceeding 98° of polarisation.

^d 1900–32 beer of 1,055° specific gravity. 1933–49 beer of 1,027° specific gravity. 1950–60 beer of 1,030° specific gravity.

^e Debt of U.K. Exchequer, debt created by N. Ireland Exchequer excluded. Bonds tendered for death duties and held by National Debt Commissioners excluded from 1920. External debt arising out of 1914–18 war, excluded from 1935, when it was £1,035·5 m. at 31 Mar.

^f April 1962 Excise Duty on sugar was repealed.

^g June 1963 tariffs on tea ceased to be direct revenue and became chargeable under the Import Duties Act 1958.

^h From 1965 onwards figures no longer collected in this form.

^i Subject to VAT at standard rate from 1/4/73.

SOURCES—
1, 2 and 3. Annual Abstract of Statistics. 2, 3, 4. 1961–64 Central Statistical Office.
4 and 5. Customs Tariff of the U.K. (Annual Reports of Commissioners for Customs and Excise.)
6. Reports of Commissioners for Customs and Excise.
7. Finance Accounts of the U.K. from 1869 Consolidated Fund and National Loans Fund Accounts and Financial Statistics.

PATTERN OF U.K. EXPORTS

(percentages)

	Western Europe	Sterling Area	North America	Rest of World	Total %	Total £m
1900	37	30	10	23	100	291
1910	32	29	12	27	100	430
1921	29	36	9	26	100	703
1930	30	38	10	22	100	571
1938	30	38	10	22	100	471
1950	26	45	9	20	100	2,160
1960	29	39	16	16	100	3,648
1970	41	28	15	16	100	7,741

SOURCE.—Based on *The British Economy: Key Statistics 1900–1970*

PERCENTAGE SHARES IN NET NATIONAL INCOME (BASED ON CURRENT PRICES) 1900–1970
United Kingdom (percentages)

Year	Wages	Salaries	Income from self-employment	Gross Trading Profits of:		Rent
				Private companies	Public corporation	
1900	41·4	9·1		36·4		12·5
1910	39·0	10·6		34·6		12·1
1921	43·6	17·9	13·4	5·7	0·5	5·8
1930	39·4	21·1	14·8	11·3	1·2	8·5
1938	40·8	21·9	13·4	14·3	1·4	9·3
1950	44·8	25·5	12·8	19·6	3·0	4·9
1960	42·8	29·2	9·5	17·7	3·4	5·9
1970	68·6		8·3	12·0	3·5	7·5

SELECTED ITEMS OF CONSUMER EXPENDITURE AS PERCENTAGES OF TOTAL CONSUMER EXPENDITURE
1900–1970 United Kingdom

Year	Food	Alcoholic drink	Tobacco	Furniture, electrical and other durables	Cars and motor-cycles	Clothing and footwear
1900	27·3	20·8	3·7	2·5	0·0	10·0
1910	28·7	16·0	4·0	2·5	0·1	10·1
1921	29·9	12·4	6·0	3·4	0·2	9·4
1930	30·2	8·4	5·7	4·7	0·8	9·8
1938	29·0	7·2	6·3	4·7	1·2	9·3
1950	31·1	6·2	6·6	4·0	0·7	9·8
1960	24·9	5·9	7·0	4·8	2·7	9·6
1970	20·3	7·4	5·5	4·3	3·1	8·5

INCOME DISTRIBUTION AFTER TAX IN
'MONEY' TERMS
United Kingdom
(absolute numbers – 000's)

Year	−£250	£250–500	£500–750	£750–1,000	£1,000–2,000	£2,000–10,000	£10,000–
1938	n.a.	1,940	375	132	142	73	0
1949	12,270	9,940	1,940	442	368	90	0
1959	6,200	7,400	6,630	3,880	2,052	298	0
1967	2,338	5,906	5,418	4,822	8,198	1,017	1

PERCENTAGE OF PERSONAL NET CAPITAL OWNED
BY VARIOUS GROUPS OF POPULATION (OVER 25)
IN ENGLAND AND WALES, 1911–1956

	1911–13	1924–30	1936	1951–56
1%	65·5	59·5	56·0	42·0
5%	86·0	82·5	81·0	56·7
10%	90·0	89·5	88·0	79·8
20%	—	96·0	94·0	89·0

SOURCE.—A. H. Halsey (ed.), *Trends in British Society since 1900* (1972). Personal capital figures based on H. F. Lydall and D. G. Tipping, 'The Distribution of Personal Wealth in Britain', *Bulletin of the Oxford University Institute of Statistics* (1961).

OUTPUT PER MAN
(1913 = 100)

	U.K.	U.S.	France	Germany (F.R.)	Italy	Sweden
1900	98·1	79·8	90·0	85·5	77·3	70·1
1913	100·0	100·0	100·0	100·0	100·0	100·0
1929	121·6	126·7	135·6	96·5	126·3	101·6
1938	143·6	136·0	125·7	122·4	145·2	127·5
1950	159·4	177·1	146·1	124·1	153·2	171·1
1960	193·1	217·3	215·8	207·5	229·4	223·6
1970	247·6	271·8	352·8	321·2	418·2	315·1
1970 (U.K. = 100·0)	100·0	251	146	142	100	166

SOURCE.—Adapted from A. Maddison, *Economic Growth in the West* (1964) and updated with O.E.C.D. data.

INDUSTRIAL OUTPUT OF THE U.K.
(Census of Production figures)

All census Industries	Value of Production (Gross Output) (£m.)
1907 [a]	1,765
1924	3,747 [b]
1930	3,371 [b]
1935	3,543 [b]
1948 [c]	12,961
1951	18,733
	- - - [d]
1958	25,465
1963	31,970
1968	44,861

[a] Including firms in the Irish Republic.
[b] Firms employing more than 10 persons only.   [c] Great Britain only.
[d] Prior to 1951 classified according to the 1948 edition of the *Standard Industrial Classification*. Figures below the line classified according to the 1958 *Standard Industrial Classification*.

SOURCE.—*Annual Abstract of Statistics.*

SURTAX, 1909–1972

Year of Change	Income Level at which Surtax Payable	Maximum Rate in £ Payable		
	Exceeding £			£
1909	5,000	6d. on amount in excess of 3,000		
1914	3,000	1/9½	,, ,,	8,000
1915	3,000	3/6	,, ,,	10,000
1918	2,500	4/6	,, ,,	10,000
1920	2,000	6/–	,, ,,	30,000
1929	2,000	7/6	,, ,,	50,000
1930	2,000	8/3	,, ,,	50,000
1938	2,000	9/6	,, ,,	30,000
1939	2,000	9/6	,, ,,	20,000
1946	2,000	10/6	,, ,,	20,000
1951	2,000	10/–	,, ,,	15,000
1961	2,000 [a]	10 -	,, ,,	15,000
1969	2,500	50%	,, ,,	15,000
1971	3,000	50%	,, ,,	15,000

[a] In 1961 special reliefs introduced for earned incomes made the surtax threshold effectively £5,000.

In 1973 the system of personal income tax and surtax was replaced by a single graduated tax. In consequence surtax ceased to be charged after 1972–3.

SOURCE.—*Annual Reports of Commissioners for Inland Revenue.*

ESTATE DUTY

Payable on estate of net capital value £100,000

Death occurred in Period	Rate of Duty %	Duty Payable £
Before 1909	5·5	5,500
1909–1914	8	8,000
1914–1919	9	9,000
1919–1925	14	14,000
1925–1939	19	19,000
1939–1939	20·9	20,900
1939–1940	22·8	22,800
1940–1946	24·7	24,700
1946–1949	30	30,000
1949–1969	45	45,000
1969–1972	65 [a]	47,125
1972–	55 [a]	37,250

Where death occurred before 30 Jul 49 additional legacy and succession duties were also payable.   [a] Marginal rate.

SOURCE.—*Annual Reports of Commissioners of Inland Revenue.*

MAXIMUM RATES OF DEATH DUTY

Death occurred in Period	Rate of Duty %	Net Capital Value of Estate £m.
1894–1907	8	1
1907–1909	15	3
1909–1914	15	1
1914–1919	20	1
1919–1925	40	2
1925–1930	40	2
1930–1939	50	2
1939–1939	55	2
1939–1940	60	2
1940–1946	65	2
1946–1949	75	2
1949–1969	80	1
1969–1972	85	0·75
1972–	75	0·5

SOURCE.—*Annual Reports of Commissioner of Inland Revenue.*

HIRE PURCHASE

Hire Purchase and other instalment credit (Finance Houses, Durable Goods Shops and Department Stores) — total outstanding business at end of period.

£ million

1947	68	1961	934
1948	105	1962	887
1949	128	1963	959
1950	167	1964	1,115
1951	208	1965	1,196
1952	241	1966	1,104
1953	276	1967	1,058
1954	384	1968	1,089
1955	461	1969	1,063
1956	376	1970	1,127
1957	448	1971	1,377
1958	556	1972	1,769
1959	849	1973	2,151
1960	935		

SOURCE.—*Key Statistics 1900–1970* and *Annual Abstract of Statistics 1970–*.

BUDGET DATES

1900	5 Mar	1921	25 Apr	1941	7 Apr	1961	17 Apr
1901	18 Apr	1922	1 May	1942	14 Apr	1962	8 Apr
1902	14 Apr	1923	17 Apr	1943	12 Apr	1963	3 Apr
1903	23 Apr	1924	29 Apr	1944	25 Apr	1964	14 Apr
1904	19 Apr	1925	28 Apr	1945	24 Apr		11 Nov
1905	10 Apr	1926	26 Apr		23 Oct	1965	6 Apr
1906	30 Apr	1927	11 Apr	1946	9 Apr	1966	5 May
1907	18 Apr	1928	24 Apr	1947	15 Apr	1967	11 Apr
1908	7 May	1929	15 Apr		12 Nov	1968	19 Mar
1909	29 Apr	1930	14 Apr	1948	6 Apr	1969	15 Apr
1910	30 Jun	1931	27 Apr	1949	6 Apr	1970	14 Apr
1911	16 May		10 Sep	1950	18 Apr	1971	30 Mar
1912	2 Apr	1932	19 Apr	1951	10 Apr	1972	21 Apr
1913	22 Apr	1933	25 Apr	1952	11 Apr	1973	6 Mar
1914	4 May	1934	17 Apr	1953	14 Apr	1974	26 Mar
	17 Nov	1935	15 Apr	1954	6 Apr		12 Nov
1915	4 May	1936	21 Apr	1955	19 Apr		
	21 Sep	1937	20 Apr	1955	26 Oct	1975	15 Apr
1916	4 Apr	1938	26 Apr	1956	17 Apr		
1917	3 May	1939	25 Apr	1957	9 Apr		
1918	22 Apr		27 Sep	1958	15 Apr		
1919	30 Apr	1940	23 Apr	1959	7 Apr		
1920	19 Apr		23 Jul	1960	4 Apr		

XII

NATIONALISATION

PUBLIC boards of a commercial character are defined by the Treasury as the
boards of undertakings which are empowered by statute to engage in substantial trading operations. Nationalised industries are included in this
category, but so are a number of other bodies listed on p. 330. Public boards
of a non-commercial category are given on pp. 330–.

There is no clear definition of the group known as 'nationalised industries'.
They are generally taken to include those public boards with a statutory
responsibility for the supply of energy — other than petroleum products —
and of steel; the provision of postal and telecommunication services other
than broadcasting; and the provision of transport services.

Although this is the definition used by the Treasury, it does not cover
all the public corporations which have been investigated by the Select
Committee on Nationalised Industries.

Main Landmarks

1908 **The Port of London Authority** was set up in 1909 under the *Port
of London Act, 1908* (but it only followed the pattern of the Mersey
Docks and Harbour Board, set up in 1874).

1926 **The Central Electricity Board** was set up by the *Electricity (Supply)
Act, 1926*, to operate and regulate the central generation of electricity.

1926 **The British Broadcasting Corporation** was granted its first charter
as a public corporation.

1933 **The London Passenger Transport Board** was established.

1946 **The Bank of England** was taken into public ownership.

1946 **The Coal Industry** was nationalised by the *Coal Industry Nationalisation Act, 1946*, which set up the National Coal Board.

1946 **Civil Aviation** was reorganised by the *Civil Aviation Act, 1946*. This
covered the British Overseas Airways Corporation (set up in 1939), and
two new corporations, British European Airways and British South
American Airways. B.S.A.A. was merged with B.O.A.C. in 1949.
B.O.A.C. and B.E.A. were merged into British Airways in 1972–4.

1947 **Electricity** was fully nationalised by the *Electricity Act, 1947*, which
set up the British Electricity Authority. The *Electricity Act, 1957*, set
up the Electricity Council and the Central Electricity Generating
Board. The twelve area boards remained financially autonomous.

1948 **Railways, Canals** (and some other transport) were nationalised by
the *Transport Act, 1947*. The British Transport Commission was
established, and the Docks and Inland Waterways, Hotels, Railways,

London Transport, Road Haulage, and Road Passenger Transport were administered by six executive boards. The *Transport Act, 1953*, denationalised Road Haulage. *The Transport Act, 1962*, reorganised nationalised transport undertakings and provided for the establishment of separate Boards for Railways, London Transport, Docks and Waterways, and for a Transport Holding Company, as successors to the British Transport Commission.

1948 **Gas** was nationalised by the *Gas Act, 1948*, which established twelve Area Gas Boards and the Gas Council. *The Gas Act, 1972*, established the British Gas Corporation which replaced the Gas Council but had larger powers.

1949 **Iron and Steel** were nationalised by the *Iron and Steel Act, 1949*, and the Iron and Steel Corporation of Great Britain was established. The vesting date of the Act was 15 Feb 51. The *Iron and Steel Act, 1953*, denationalised the industry, and set up the Iron and Steel Board. In 1967 the *Iron and Steel Act* renationalised the industry, as from 28 Jul 67.

1954 **The U.K. Atomic Energy Authority** was established by the *U.K. Atomic Energy Authority Act, 1954*.

1969 **The Post Office** ceased to be a Government Department and became a public corporation.

1971–3 **Hiving-off.** The Conservative Government began to hive-off some concerns of nationalised industries. In 1971–2 some B.O.A.C. routes were allotted to British Caledonian. In 1973 Thomas Cook's travel agency and the Carlisle state breweries were sold to the private sector.

1971 **Rolls-Royce Ltd** was established following the company's bankruptcy.

1974 **The National Enterprise Board** and the **British National Oil Corporation** were proposed in the Queen's Speech of 29 Oct 1974, together legislation to take shipbuilding, aircraft manufacture and development land into public ownership.

Public Boards of a Commercial Character
(a) Nationalised Industries

Air

		Responsible Minister 1939–74		Chairman/Deputy-Chairman Chairman		Established under the *Air Corporations Act, 1939* as successor to Imperial Airways
British Overseas Airways Corporation (B.O.A.C.)	1939	Sec. of State for Air	26 May 43	Vt Knollys		In 1946 became one of the three corporations set up under the *Civil Aviation Act 1946* to provide passenger and cargo flights to all parts of the world, other than Europe and Latin America. Under the *Civil Aviation Act 1971* merged with BEA in April 1974 to form British Airways.
	1944	Min. for Civil Aviation	1 Jul 47	Sir H. Hartley		
	1951	Min. of Transport and Civil Aviation	1 Jul 49	Sir M. Thomas		
			1 May 56	(Sir) G. d'Erlanger		
	1959	Min. of Civil Aviation				
	1964	Min. of Aviation	29 Jul 60	Sir M. Slattery		
	1968	Min. of State at Board of Trade	1 Jan 64	Sir G. Guthrie		
			1 Jan 69	(Sir) C. Hardie		
	1970	Min. of Aviation at the Dept. of Trade and Industry	1 Jan 71	K. Granville		
			1 Sep 72	J. Stainton		

		Responsible Minister	*Chairman/Deputy-Chairman*

			Deputy Chairman
1971	Min. for Aerospace (and Shipping 1972) at the Dept. of Trade and Industry	1 Aug 46	Sir H. Howitt
		1 Apr 48	Sir M. Thomas
		1 Jul 49	W. Straight
1974	Sec. of State for Trade	(1 Aug 49–30 Apr 50, *additional Deputy Chairman*, J. Booth)
		21 Nov 55	Ld Rennell
		1 May 56	Sir G. Cribbett
		20 Jun 60	Sir W. Neden
		3 Apr 64–	{K. Granville
		31 Dec 68	{C .Hardie
		1 Jan 68	K. Granville
		1 Apr 71	Sir A. Norman
		21 Dec 71	J. Stainton
		1 Sep 72	W. Bray

British European Airways Corporation (B.E.A.)

		1946–74		*Chairman*	
	1946	Min. for Civil Aviation	1 Aug 46	Sir H. Hartley
	1951	Min. of Transport and Civil Aviation	1 Apr 47	G. d'Erlanger
			14 Mar 49	Ld Douglas
	1959	Min. of Civil Aviation	3 May 56	(Sir) A. Milward
	1964	Min. of Aviation	1 Jan 71	H. Marking
	1968	Min. of State at the Board of Trade	1 Sep 72	P. Lawton
	1970	Min. of Aviation Supply		*Deputy Chairman*
			1 Aug 46	W. Straight
	1971	Min. for Aerospace (and Shipping 1972) at the Dept. of Trade and Industry	1 Apr 47	(Sir) J. Keeling
			1 Oct 65	(Sir) K. Keith
			22 Dec 71	K. Wilkinson
			1 Dec 72	R. Watts
	1974	Sec. of State for Trade		

Established under the *Civil Aviation Act 1946* to take over European, domestic and some North African flights. In April 1974, under the *Civil Aviation Act 1971* merged with B.O.A.C. to form British Airways.

British South American Airways Corporation (B.S.A.A.)

		1946–49		*Chairman*	
	1946	Min. for Civil Aviation	1 Aug 46	J. Booth
			1 May 50	Sir M. Thomas
				Deputy Chairman
			1 Aug 46	(Sir) J. Stephenson
			1 Apr 49	Sir F. Brake

Established under the *Civil Aviation Act 1946* to take over Central and South American routes from BOAC. Merged with BOAC 1949.

British Airways Board

		1974–		*Chairman*	
	1972	Min. for Aerospace and Shipping at the Dept. of Trade and Industry	7 Oct 71	D. Nicolson
				Deputy Chairman
	1974	Sec. of State for Trade	1 Sep 72	{(Sir) K. Granville
				{H. Marking

Established under the *Civil Aviation Act 1971* to take overall responsibility for the activities of BEA and BOAC from 1 Apr 72. Became fully operational from 1 Apr 74.

	Responsible Minister 1966–	*Chairman/Deputy-Chairman*	
British Airports Authority	1966 Min. of Aviation 1968 Min. of State at the Board of Trade 1970 Min. of Aviation Supply at the Dept. of Trade and Industry 1971 Min. for Aerospace (and Shipping 1972) at the Dept. of Trade and Industry 1974 Sec. of State for Trade	*Chairman* 3 Jun 65 (Sir) P. Maxfield 9 Jan 72 N. Foulkes *Deputy Chairmen* 2 Aug 65 R. MacLellan	Established under *Airport Authority Act 1965* to ru Gatwick, Heathrow and Stan sted, and since 1971, Edi burgh Turnhouse air-ports.

Fuel and Power

	1947–55	*Chairman*	
British Electricity Authority (Central Electricity Authority 1955–57)	1947 Min. of Fuel and Power 1956 Min. of Power	15 Aug 47– Ld Citrine 31 Dec 57 *Deputy Chairman* 15 Aug 47–⎰Sir H. Self 16 Dec 53 ⎱Sir J. Hacking 16 Dec 53–⎰Sir H. Self 31 Aug 57 ⎱J. Eccles	Established under the *Electricity Act, 1947*, to take ov 500 undertakings and to d velop and maintain electri ity supply throughout Gre Britain except the North Scotland. The major respon sibility for distribution w left to the Area Boards. I 1955 the west of Scotland w transferred to the South Scotland Electricity Board.

	1957–	*Chairman*	

Electricity Council	1957 Min. of Power
	1970 Min. of Technology
	1971 Sec. of State for Trade and Industry
	1974 Sec. of State for Energy
		1 Sep 57 Sir H. Self
		1 Sep 59 (Sir) R. King
		1 Jan 66 Sir R. Edwards
		1 Nov 68 Sir N. Elliott
		1 Apr 72 Sir P. Menzies
		
		Deputy Chairman
		1 Sep 57 Sir J. Eccles
		1 Sep 57 R. Edwards
		    (*whole-time from* 1 *Oct* 59)
		1 Jan 66 N. Marsh
		1 Jan 66 Sir A. Wilson
		1 Jan 72⎰Sir A. Wilson
		    ⎱R. Richardson
			Established under the *Electricity Act, 1957*, to co ordinate development of th industry. Consists of statutory corporations: th Electricity Council, the CEG and 12 Area Electrici Boards.

	1957–	*Chairman*	
Central Electricity Generating Board (C.E.G.B.)	1957 Min. of Power 1970 Min. of Technology 1971 Sec. of State for Trade and Industry 1974 Sec. of State for Energy	1 Sep 57 Sir C. Hinton 1 Jan 65 (Sir) S. Brown 1 Jul 72 A. Hawkins *Deputy Chairman* 1 Sep 57 C. King 1 Sep 59 S. Brown 1 Jan 65 O. Francis 15 May 72 W. Fenton	Established under the *Electricity Act, 1957*, to own ar operate the power stations ar to provide electricity in bu to the Area Boards.

		Responsible Minister	Chairman/Deputy-Chairman	
orth of cotland ydro-lectricity oard	1943	1943– Sec. of State for Scotland	Chairman 1 Sep 43 E of Airlie 1 Apr 46 T. Johnston 1 Jul 59 Ld Strathclyde 1 Sep 69 T. Fraser 30 Apr 73 Sir D. Haddow Deputy Chairman 1 Sep 43 Sir E. McColl 1 Jun 51 Sir H. Mackenzie 1 Jan 60 Sir J. Erskine 1 Jan 62 A. Mackenzie 1 Jan 70 I. Duncan Millar 1 Jan 73 K. Vernon	Established under the *Hydro-Electric Development (Scotland) Act, 1943*, to supply electricity and to develop water power in the Highlands and Islands. In 1947 became responsible for all public generation and distribution of electricity in the North of Scotland.
outh of cotland lectricity oard	1955	1955– Sec. of State for Scotland	Chairman 1 Dec 54 (Sir) J. Pickles 20 Feb 62 N. Elliot 1 Apr 67 C. Allan 1 Jan 74 F. Tombs Deputy Chairman 1 Dec 54 Sir N. Duke 1 Feb 56 W. Hutton 1 Jan 64 C. Allan 1 Apr 67 A. Christianson	Established under the *Electricity Reorganization (Scotland) Act, 1954*, to generate and distribute electricity throughout S. of Scotland.
ational oal Board N.C.B.)	1946 1956 1969 1970 1974	1946– Min. of Fuel and Power Min. of Power Min. of Technology Sec. of State for Trade and Industry Sec. of State for Energy	Chairman 15 Jul 46 Ld Hyndley (Vt) 1 Aug 51 Sir H. Houldsworth 1 Feb 56 (Sir) J. Bowman 7 Feb 61 A. Robens (Ld) 3 Jul 71 (Sir) D. Ezra Deputy Chairman 15 Jul 46 Sir A. Street 1 Aug 51 W. Drummond & Sir E. Coates 1 Feb 55 J. Bowman 21 Feb 56 (Sir) J. Latham 1 Sep 60 E. Browne 1 Oct 60 A. Robens 1 Feb 61 E. Browne 3 May 67 D. Ezra 8 Jul 71 W. Sheppard 1 Oct 73 { W. Sheppard { N. Siddall	Established under the *Coal Industry Nationalization Act, 1946*, to own and run the coal industry and certain ancillary activities.
as ouncil nd oards	1948 1956 1969 1970	1948–73 Min. of Fuel and Power Min. of Power Min. of Technology Sec. of State for Trade and Industry	Chairman 23 Nov 48 Sir E. Sylvester 1 Jan 52 (Sir) H. Smith 1 Jan 60 Sir H. Jones 1 Jan 72 A. Hetherington Deputy Chairman 25 Nov 48 H. Smith 1 Feb 52 (Sir) H. Jones 1 Jan 60 (Sir) K. Hutchison 1 Jan 67 A. Hetherington 1 Jan 72 D. Rooke	Established by the *Gas Act, 1948*, to co-ordinate 12 Area Gas Boards which were set up to manufacture and retail town gas. The Gas Council was responsible for the purchase and distribution of natural gas.

		Responsible Minister	Chairman/Deputy Chairman	Established under the *Gas*

British Gas Corporation

		Responsible Minister	Chairman/Deputy Chairman	
		1973–	*Chairman*	Established under the *Gas Act, 1972*, to take over responsibilities of Gas Council and Area Gas Boards.
	1973	Sec. of State for Trade and Industry	1 Jan 73 (Sir) A. Hetherington	
	1974	Sec. of State for Energy		
			Deputy Chairman	
			1 Jan 73 D. Rooke	

United Kingdom Atomic Energy Authority (U.K.A.E.A.)

		1954–	*Chairman*	Established under the *Atomic Energy Authority Act, 1972*, to be responsible for the development of nuclear energy and its applications.
	1954	Ld President	1 Aug 54 Sir E. Plowden (Ld)	
	1956	Prime Minister		
	1959	Min. of Science	1 Jan 60 Sir R. Makins	
	1963	Ld President	10 Feb 64 Sir W. Penney (Ld)	
	1964	Min. of Technology	16 Oct 67 (Sir) J. Hill	
	1970	Sec. of State for Trade and Industry		
	1974	Sec. of State for Energy		

Transport

London Passenger Transport Board (L.P.T.B.)

		1933–47	*Chairman*	Established under the *London Passenger Transport Act, 1933*, to take over railway, tramway, bus and coach undertakings within the London area. Under the *Transport Act, 1947*, responsibilities transferred to the British Transport Commission operating through a London Transport Executive.
	1933	Min. of Transport	1933 Ld Ashfield	
	1941	Min. of War Transport		
	1946	Min. of Transport		

London Transport Board 1963–70

			Chairman	Established under the *Transport Act, 1962*, to replace part of the British Transport Commission, to provide an adequate and properly co-ordinated system of passenger transport for the London area. Under the *Transport (London) Act, 1969*, responsibilities transferred to the Greater London Council.
	1963	Min. of Transport	1 Jan 63 (Sir) A. Valentine	
			1 Apr 65 (Sir) M. Holmes	
			Vice-Chairman	
			1 Jan 63 A. Grainger	
			1 Oct 65 A. Bull	

British Transport Commission (B.T.C.)

		1947–62	*Chairman*	Established under the *Transport Act, 1947*, to provide an integrated system of transport and port facilities (excluding air). The separate executives were wound up in 1953. The *Transport Act, 1962*, transferred the whole of the B.T.C. to new separate Corporations.
	1947	Min. of Transport	8 Sep 47 Sir C. Hurcomb (Ld)	
	1953	Min. of Transport and Civil Aviation	15 Sep 53 Sir B. Robertson	
	1959	Min. of Transport	1 Jun 61 R. Beeching (Ld)	
			Deputy Chairman	
			1 Jan 49 (Sir) J. Benstead	
			1 Oct 61 Sir P. Warter	
			Chairmen of Executives of BTC	
			Docks and Inland Waterways Executive	
			1947–53 Sir R. Hill	

Responsible Minister   *Chairman/Deputy Chairman*

Hotels Executive

1948–51   Ld Inman (*part-time from* 1950)

1951–53   Sir H. Methven (*part-time*)

Railway Executive

1947–51   Sir E. Missenden

1951–53   J. Elliot

Road Haulage Executive

1948–53   G. Russell

London Transport Executive

1947–53   Ld Latham

1953–59   (Sir) J. Elliot

1959–62   A. Valentine

Road Passenger Service

1948–52   G. Cardwell

British Railways Board (B.R.)	1962 1970	1963– Min. of Transport Sec. of State for the Environment	*Chairman* 1 Jan 63 R. Beeching (Ld) 1 Jun 65 (Sir) S. Raymond 1 Jan 68 (Sir) H. Johnson 13 Sep 71 R. Marsh	Established under the *Transport Act, 1962*, to take over the B.T.C.'s rail services.
			Vice-Chairman 1 Aug 64 Sir S. Mitchell 1 Aug 64 (Sir) S. Raymond 1 Aug 64 P. Shirley 17 Jun 68 M. Bosworth	
			Deputy Chairman 1 Oct 72 M. Bosworth	
British Transport Docks Board 1963–	1962 1970	Min. of Transport Sec. of State for the Environment	*Chairman* 3 Dec 62 Sir A. Kirby 15 Jun 67 S. Finnis 6 Aug 69 R. Wills 25 Sep 69 C. Cory (*acting*) 19 Jan 70 Sir C. Dove 1 May 71 Sir H. Browne	Established under the *Transport Act, 1962*, to administer publicly owned ports throughout the country. Under *Docks and Harbours Act, 1966*, became licensing authority for all but three ports.
			Vice-Chairman 10 Dec 62 Sir A. Crichton 1 Jan 68 R. Wills 15 Sep 69 C. Cory	
British Waterways Board	1963 1970	1963– Min. of Transport Sec. of State for the Environment	*Chairman* 1 Jan 63 F. Arney 1 Jul 63 Sir J. Hawton 1 Jul 68 Sir F. Price	Established under the *Transport Act, 1962*, to take over inland waterways from the B.T.C. The *Transport Act, 1968*, extended its powers particularly in regard to recreation and amenities.
			Vice-Chairman 1 Jan 63 Sir J. Hawton 11 Aug 63 Sir F. Parham 1 Jul 68 Sir J. Hawton	
National Bus Company	1968 1970	1968– Min. of Transport Sec. of State for the Environment	*Chairman* 28 Nov 68 A. Todd 1 Jan 72 F. Wood	Established under the *Transport Act, 1968*, to take over responsibility for state-owned bus companies and bus-manufacturing interests from the Transport Holding Company.

		Responsible Minister	*Chairman/Deputy Chairman*	
		1968–	*Chairman*	Established under the *Trans-*
National	1968	Min. of Transport	1 Jan 69 Sir R. Wilson	*port Act, 1968*, to take over road
Freight	1970	Sec. of State for the	1 Jan 71 (Sir) D. Pettit	haulage and shipping interests
Corpora-		Environment		of the Transport Holding
tion				Company. Shipping interests
				terminated in 1971.

Scottish	1968	Sec. of State for	*Chairman*	Established under the *Trans-*
Transport		Scotland	18 Nov 68 P. Thomas	*port Act, 1968*, to control
Group				various transport activities in
1968–				Scotland, including road pas-
				senger, insurance, tourism and
				shipping.

		1962–72	*Chairman*	Established by the *Transport*
Transport	1962	Min. of Transport	15 Nov 62 Sir P. Warter	*Act, 1962*, to take over all
Holdings			15 Nov 67 Sir R. Wilson	B.T.C. investments not given
Company			1 Jan 71 L. Whyte	to British Rail, London Trans-
				port, Docks or Waterways
			Deputy Chairman	Boards. The *Transport Act,*
			16 Nov 62– Sir R. Wilson	*1968*, transferred its road
			15 Nov 67	interests to the National
				Freight Corporation and the
				National Bus Company. Its
				residual interests (Thos.
				Cook, Lunn-Poly, etc.) were
				sold 1970–72.

Miscellaneous

Iron and	1950	Min. of Supply	*Chairman*	Established under the *Iron*
Steel			2 Oct 50 S. Hardie	*and Steel Act, 1949*, to take
Corpora-			25 Feb 52 Sir J. Green	over 298 Companies in the
tion				Iron and Steel Industries.
1950–53			*Deputy Chairman*	Wound up by the *Iron and*
			2 Oct 50 Sir J. Green	*Steel Act, 1953.*
			25 Feb 52 (*vacant*)	

		1968–		
British	1967	Min. of Power	*Chairman*	Established under the *Iron*
Steel	1969	Min. of Technology	28 Jul 67 Ld Melchett	*and Steel Act, 1967*, to take
Corpora-	1970	Sec. of State for Trade	18 Jun 73 (Sir) M. Finnis-	over the management of the
tion		and Industry	ton	major part of the steel industry.
	1974	Sec. of State for		
		Industry	*Deputy Chairman*	
			28 Jul 67– A. Peach	
			31 Dec 69	
			28 Jul 67– M. Finniston	
			18 Jun 73	
			28 Jul 67– (Sir) M. Milne-	
			30 Sep 69 Watson	
			1 Jan 70– M. Littman	
			10 Sep 73– P. Matthews	

		Responsible Minister	*Chairman/Deputy Chairman*	

ost Office orpora-ion

		1970–	*Chairman*	
	1970	Min. of Posts and Telecommunications	1 Oct 69	Vt Hall
	1974	Sec. of State for Industry	22 Apr 71	(Sir) W. Ryland

Established under the *Post Office Act, 1969,* to take over from the office of the Postmaster General, responsibility for postal services, Giro and remittance services and telecommunications throughout the U.K. In March 1974 all broadcasting functions transferred to Home Office supervision.

olls Royce td

		1971–	*Chairman*	
	1971	Min. for Aerospace at the Dept. of Trade and Industry	22 May 71	Ld Cole
	1974	Sec. of State for Industry	6 Oct 72	Sir K. Keith

Established in Feb 1971 under the *Companies Act, 1960,* with the Government as the sole shareholder to ensure the continuance of those activities of Rolls Royce Ltd. which are essential to national defence and to main air forces and airlines all over the world.

Nationalised Industries: Assets and Employees, 1950–1970

	1950		1960		1970	
	Net Assets[a] (£m.)	Total Employed ('000)	Net Assets (£m.)	Total Employed ('000)	Net Assets (£m.)	Total Employed ('000)
British Overseas Airways Corporation	42	16	132	21	251	23
British European Airways	6	7	58	13	116	25
British Airports Authority	—	—	—	—	73	4
British Electricity Authority and Area Electricity Council[b] Boards	686	161	1,948	189	4,921	197
North of Scotland Hydro-Electricity Board	53	3	197	3	267	4
South of Scotland Hydro-Electricity Board	—	—	153	13	418	15
Area Gas Boards and Gas Council	269	132	585	127	1,658	119
National Coal Board	337	749	910	631	666	356
U.K. Atomic Energy Authority	—	—	488	39	256	30
British Transport Commission	1,226	889	1,828	729	—	—
British Rail	—	—	—	—	439	273
National Bus Company	—	—	—	—	93	84
National Freight Corporation	—	—	—	—	116	65
British Transport Docks	—	—	—	—	123	11
Iron and Steel Corporation British Steel Corporation	492[c]	292[c]	—	—	1,222	250
Post Office Corporation	—	—	—	—	2,521	407

[a] Net assets should be treated with caution, as accounting methods and the definition of net assets vary from industry to industry.
[b] Including Central Electricity Generating Board.   [c] Figures for 1951.
SOURCE.—*Annual Reports and Accounts* of the individual Boards and from additional information supplied by the Boards themselves.

(b) Others

Central Electricity Board	1926–47
Cable & Wireless Ltd.	1947–
Housing Industry Board	1935–
Sugar Board	1956–
White Fish Authority	1951–
Colonial (1963– Commonwealth) Development Corporation	1948–

Public Boards of a Non-Commercial Character

There are a large number of public bodies set up by statute which are neither branches of the government departments listed on pp. 62–3, nor nationalised industries listed on pp. 322–9. They have been established in the fields of industry, commerce, the social sciences and research to carry out a variety of administrative, regulatory, and executive or managerial functions. Important examples of such bodies (as of 1 Jan 75) classified loosely by their main functions are as follows:

Advisory:
Computer Board for Universities and Research Councils
Law Commission
Monopolies Commission
Pay Board

Prices Commission
National Economic Development Council
Water Resources Board

Regulatory:

Air Transport Licensing Board
Independent Broadcasting Authority
British Board of Film Censors
Horserace Totalisator Board

Executive or Managerial:

Agricultural Marketing Boards (Wool, Hops, Milk, Potato)
British Sugar Corporation Ltd.
Forestry Commission
Land Commission
National Dock Labour Board
National Research and Development Corporation
New Towns Development Corporations
Covent Garden Market Authority
Housing Corporations

SOURCES.—For an analysis of the statutory provisions of the nationalised industries, see D. N. Chester, *The Nationalised Industries* (1951). Other studies of the nationalised industries include: Acton Society Trust, *Twelve Studies on Nationalised Industries* (1950–3); H. A. Clegg and T. E. Chester, *The Future of Nationalisation* (1953); W. A. Robson (ed.), *Problems of Nationalised Industries* (1952); W. A. Robson, *Nationalised Industry and Public Ownership* (1960); A. H. Hanson (ed.), *Nationalisation: A Book of Readings* (1963); D. Coombes, *The Member of Parliament and the Administration: The Case of the Select Committee on Nationalised Industries* (1966); G. L. Reid and K. Allen, *The Nationalised Industries* (1970); R. Pryke, *Public Enterprise in Practice* (1971); L. Tivey (ed.), *The Nationalised Industries since 1960* (1973); M. Rees, *The Public Sector in the Mixed Economy* (1973).

The table on p. 330 was compiled from the *Annual Reports and Accounts* of the individual Boards and from additional information supplied by the Boards themselves. See also: *Committee Report on the Coal Industry* (Reid), Cmd. 6610/1945; *Committee Report on the Gas Industry* (Heyworth), Cmd. 6699/1945–6; *Report of the Advisory Committee on the Organisation of the National Coal Board* (Fleck), N.C.B., 18 Jan 1955; *Report of the Committee of Inquiry into the Electricity Supply Industry* (Herbert), Cmd. 9672/1956.

White Paper, *Nationalised Industries: A Review of Economic and Financial Objectives*, Cmd. 3437/1967; White Paper, *Ministerial Control of Nationalised Industries*, Cmd. 4027/1969; N.B.P.I. paper on *Top Salaries in the Private Sector and Nationalised Industries*, Cmd. 3870/1969. See also reports of the Select Committee on Nationalised Industries. A list of Public Bodies is to be found each year in *Whitaker's Almanack*. A list of Members of Public Boards of a Commercial Character is published annually by H.M.S.O. See also D. N. Chester, 'Public Corporations and the Classification of Administrative Bodies', *Political Studies* (1953) p. 34; J. F. Garner, *New Public Corporations' Public Law* (1966) p. 324.

XIV

LOCAL GOVERNMENT

Structure

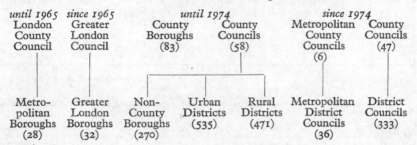

London

until 1965	since 1965
London County Council	Greater London Council

| Metro-politan Boroughs (28) | Greater London Boroughs (32) |

Rest of England & Wales

until 1974
County Boroughs (83)   County Councils (58)

since 1974
Metropolitan County Councils (6)   County Councils (47)

Non-County Boroughs (270)   Urban Districts (535)   Rural Districts (471)

Metropolitan District Councils (36)   District Councils (333)

Scotland

until 1975

Counties of a City (4)   County Councils (33)

Large Burghs (20)   Small Burghs (126)   Districts (198)

1975–

Regional Councils (9)   Island Councils (3)

District Councils (53)

Number of Councils: England & Wales

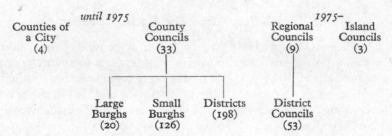

	County Councils inc. London	County Boroughs[a]	Non-County Boroughs	Urban District Councils	Rural District Councils	London Boroughs and City of London
1900	62	67	250	800	663	29
1910	62	75	249	812	657	29
1920	62	82	246	799	649	29
1930	62	83	300	780	638	29
1940	61	83	256	581	476	29
1950	61	83	309	572	475	29
1960	62	83	319	564	473	29
1973	58	83	270	535	471	33
1974	County Councils inc. London 54		District Councils 369			33

[a] The figures in this column are deceptively constant. In the 1960s a few County Boroughs disappeared through local government amalgamation (almost all in Greater London), while a few more non-County Boroughs were promoted to county status.

Parish Councils. This table does not include parish councils. No exact figures for their numbers are available. In 1900 there were about 8,000, in 1920 about 7,000 and in 1966 about 7,700. Following the 1973 reorganisation of local government a number of the smaller authorities that had been abolished applied for parish council status.

Local Government Finance — England and Wales

Year (ending 31 Mar)	Total Receipts from Rates £000s	Assessable Value of all Rateable Property £000s	Average Rates collected per £ of Assessable Value	Government Grants (£000s) [b]	Total Expenditure (£000s)
1900	40,734	175,623	4s. 11·8d.	12,249	100,862
1910	63,261	215,310	6s. 2·8d.	20,915	166,105
1920	105,590	220,714	9s. 6·8d.	48,263	289,353
1930	156,312	284,937	11s. 6·8d.	107,828	423,655 [c]
1940	200,567	318,834	12s. 7·5d.	181,900	578,798 [c]
1950	280,195	325,262	17s. 3·0d.	294,358	849,099 [c]
1960	646,608	687,618	18s. 10·0d.	705,590	1,865,718 [c]
1965	988,054	2,099,034	9s. 6·0d. [a]	1,102,989	2,902,829 [c]
1970	1,515,184	2,440,500	12s. 4·8d. [a]	1,954,931	5,405,264 [c]

[a] Spectacular fall partly due to re-rating of Industry and partly to general revaluation 1 Apr 63.
[b] Consisting partly of grants in aid, and partly of receipts from Local Taxation Account and from the local Taxation Licence Duties, not including capital receipts.
[c] Expenditure other than out of loans for capital works. Including the repayment of loans by various local authorities to the L.C.C. Consolidated Loans Fund.

SOURCES.—*Annual Local Taxation Returns*; *Annual Reports of the Local Government Board, Ministry of Health, and Ministry of Housing and Local Government*; also summarised in the *Annual Abstract of Statistics, 1900. Rates and Rateable Values in England and Wales* (annually from the Ministry of Health, 1919–43, Town and Country Planning, 1943–51, Local Government and Planning, 1951, Housing and Local Government, 1951–74).

Major Legislation Affecting Local Government

Education Act, 1902. This transferred the responsibility for education from school boards and school attendance committees to county councils, county borough councils, and some of the larger county districts.

Housing Acts. A series of acts from 1919 to 1973 provided for the building of houses by local authorities with varying rates of subsidy from the Exchequer and from the rates.

Local Government Act, 1929. This abolished the guardians of the poor, and transferred their responsibilities for poor law and registration to county councils and county borough councils. It also reorganised the system of grants in aid, creating the general grant, partly as compensation for the complete de-rating of agriculture and the de-rating of industry to 25 per cent.

Town and Country Planning Act, 1932. This established a general system of planning control which could be adopted by second tier local authorities.

Local Government Act, 1933. This was a codifying Act covering the structure and constitution of local authorities of all sorts, but making no fundamental change in the law.

Local Government (Boundary Commission) Act, 1945. This provided for the establishment of a local government boundary commission, which was later abolished by the *Local Government Boundary Commission (Dissolution) Act, 1949.* (But see *Local Government Boundary Commission Act, 1958.*)

New Towns Act, 1946. This provided for the establishment of new towns to be built by development corporations appointed by the Ministry, and was succeeded by further Acts which were consolidated in the *New Towns Act, 1965*.

National Health Service Act, 1946. This transferred local authority hospitals to the Ministry of Health. It made counties and county boroughs responsible for ambulance service, maternity and child welfare, health visiting, home helps, prevention of illness, and after-care, etc.

Town and Country Planning Act, 1947. This applied planning control to the whole country, transferred responsibility to county councils and county borough councils, and introduced development charges balanced by a compensation fund of £300 m. Development charges and the £300 m. fund were abolished by the *Town and Country Planning Act, 1953*.

Children Act, 1948. After the Curtis Committee Report, this Act made counties and county boroughs responsible for all children without proper homes.

National Assistance Act, 1948. This repealed the existing poor law. It made counties and county boroughs responsible for accommodation of the aged and those temporarily homeless, also for welfare services for the blind, deaf, dumb, etc. Financial assistance and residual responsibilities were passed to the National Assistance Board.

Local Government Act, 1948. This replaced the block grant by the Exchequer Equalisation grant. It transferred responsibility for valuation from local authorities to Inland Revenue and it provided for revaluation : small houses being valued on pre-war building costs, other houses by reference to pre-war rents.

Local Government Act, 1958. This abolished most percentage grants and the Exchequer Equalisation grant, substituting a general grant and a rate deficiency grant.

Local Government Boundary Commission Act, 1958. This set up local boundary commissions, produced a number of reports before being wound up in 1966. The main recommendations put into effect were in the Black Country and Tees-side.

Town and Country Planning Act, 1959. This Act altered the basis of compensation for compulsory acquisition.

Rating and Valuation Act, 1961. This Act ended the derating of industrial and freight-transport property, empowered the Minister to reduce by order the rateable value of dwellings in valuation lists, offered 50% relief from rates on property occupied by charities, and introduced a new method of rating statutory water undertakings. Industry and Commerce re-rated to 100% values.

Town and Country Planning Act, 1962. This consolidates enactments for England and Wales from 1944 onwards and incorporates planning sections of other Acts.

London Government Act, 1963. This Act replaced the old LCC with a Greater London Council which covered, in addition to the old LCC area, almost all of Middlesex and some suburban portions of Surrey, Kent, Essex, and Hertfordshire. All the existing 85 local authorities in the GLC area were merged into 32 new boroughs (the City of London alone preserved its complete independence). The first GLC election took place on 9 Apr 64, two, three and four councillors being chosen *en bloc* from each of the 32 boroughs. The GLC formally took over from the LCC on 1 Apr 65.

Local Government (Financial Provision) Act, 1963. This extends the powers of local authorities to defray expenses incurred by their members and officers, and to contribute to other local authorities and to bodies having activities connected with local government, and makes further provision with respect to borrowing by local authorities; the management of local authority debt, the application by local authorities of capital funds, renewal and repair funds, unexpended balances of loans, and capital money received by way of financial adjustment.

Housing Act, 1964. This set up a new Housing Corporation to assist Housing Societies, conferred new compulsory powers on local authorities to secure improvement of houses, amended the improvement grant system and strengthened the powers of local authorities in dealing with houses in multi-occupation.

Protection from Eviction Act, 1964. This Act prevents a landlord of residential premises from recovering possession without an order of the county court. The court is given power to suspend an order for possession.

Rating Act, 1966. This confers on rateable occupiers of dwellings the right to pay rates in monthly instalments and provides for the granting of rebates in respect of such rates.

Town and Country Planning Act, 1968. This introduced a fundamental change in the land-use planning system in the direction of greater flexibility and speed of action and a greater degree of public participation. The development plan was replaced by the 'structure, action area' and 'local' plans.

Local Authority Social Services Act, 1970. This required counties and county boroughs to combine, under one social services department, the child care, personal health, and welfare services.

Housing Finance Act, 1972. This changed the whole basis of financing public housing and controlling the rents of privately rented housing. It extended the concept of the 'fair' rent to cover council house tenants and introduced rent allowances for private tenants.

Local Government Act, 1972. This is the first full-scale reorganisation of the local government structure of England and Wales since 1889. It abolished the existing system entirely (outside Greater London) and replaced it with a top tier of metropolitan counties in the six conurbations and 47 non-metropolitan counties in the rest of the country. The new second tier comprises 36 metropolitan districts within the areas of the metropolitan counties and 333 districts in the rest of the country.

New Towns

The *New Towns Act, 1946*, with subsequent amendments, as consolidated in the *New Towns Act, 1965*, provided for New Towns to be built by development corporations appointed by the Minister. The *New Towns Act, 1959*, set up a Commission for the New Towns to take over responsibility for New Towns as soon as the development corporations' purposes were substantially achieved.

New Towns	Development Corporation Formed	Handed over to Commission	Area (acres)	Population ('000s)		
				1951	1961	1971
Aycliffe, Durham	1947		2,508	0·6	12	24
Basildon, Essex	1949		7,818	24	54	85
Bracknell, Berks.	1949		3,303	5	20	34
Central Lancs.	1970		35,225			25
Corby, Northants.	1950		4,296	15	36	48
Crawley, Sussex	1947	1962	6,047	10	54	68
Cwmbran, Mon.	1949		3,157	13	30	46
Harlow, Essex	1947		6,395	5	53	71
Hatfield, Herts.	1948	1966	2,340	9	20	26
Hemel Hempstead, Herts.	1947	1962	5,910	21	55	70
Milton Keynes, Bucks.	1967		22,000			46
Peterborough	1968		15,940			87
Peterlee, Durham	1948		2,799	0·2	14	22
Redditch, Worcs.	1964		7,200			38
Runcorn, Cheshire	1964		7,234			36
Skelmersdale, Lancs	1962		4,100			27
Stevenage, Herts.	1946		6,256	7	42	68
Telford, Salop.	1963		10,243			80
Warrington	1968		19,000			125
Washington, Durham	1964		5,300			25
Welwyn, Herts.	1948	1966	4,317	19	35	44
Cumbernauld, Dunbarton	1956		4,017		5	32
East Kilbride, Lanarks.	1947		13,679	6	32	64
Glenrothes, Fife	1948		5,696	2	13	27
Irvine, Ayrshire	1966		3,989			42
Livingston, W. Lothian	1962		3,641			14

New Towns Commission

Chairmen

1961 Sir D. Anderson
1964 Sir M. Wells
1971 (Sir) C. Pilcher

SOURCE.—F. J. Osborn and A. Whittick, *The New Towns* (1963). See also *Annual Reports* of New Towns.

Local Government Elections

After the Second World War the results of Local Government Elections became increasingly accepted as barometers to the national political mood. They could be misleading. The custom of fighting under national party labels spread only gradually and sporadically. The fact that, under the triennial system, only a third of the seats on borough and district councils were fought each year caused much confusion (a party might claim a great trend in its favour because it was gaining compared to three years before, even though it was losing compared to the previous year). Moreover the results were very patchily reported and no altogether satisfactory statistics are available. However, the results in the boroughs of England and Wales (excluding London), both county and non-county, provided some pointer to the national mood (even though the smaller non-county boroughs introduced a very distorting element). Between 3,300 and 3,500 seats used to be fought each year, usually on a party basis; after 1964 the number of seats at risk was between 3,000 and 3,200 owing to the merging of councils under the London Government Act. After 1946 the outcome of these borough contests was fairly accurately reported, although it was not until 1965 that the first really detailed analyses of the voting figures appeared (see *The Economist* for the Saturday nine days after the elections each year since 1945).

Borough Council Election Results, 1949-72

	Conservative and Conservative-supported Independent	Independent without Conservative Support	Labour	Liberal	Total	Labour % of vote (County Boroughs only)	Turnout % (County Boroughs only)
1947	1,892	359	776	97	3,124	41·7	52·6
1949	1,749	426	1,091	79	3,345	43·2	52·2
1950	1,610	510	1,132	72	3,324	46·2	45·5
1951	1,893	548	883	79	3,403	n.a.	44·4
1952	1,138	488	1,718	53	3,397	55·4	49·9
1953	1,571	447	1,448	60	3,562	52·0	45·2
1954	1,498	511	1,438	74	3,521	49·2	42·8
1955	1,604	514	1,470	56	3,644	47·6	43·8
1956	1,358	454	1,614	72	3,498	51·1	37·6
1957	1,292	435	1,642	89	3,458	50·0	40·0
1958	1,307	460	1,705	118	3,590	49·3	40·3
1959	1,545	441	1,399	103	3,488	45·5	41·0
1960	1,750	449	1,137	130	3,466	40·0	35·4
1961	1,453	470	1,387	196	3,506	43·3	40·6
1962	995	465	1,571	454	3,485	42·4	40·2
1963	973	524	1,733	255	3,485	46·0	41·3
1964	967	474	1,494	149	3,084	47·0	40·5
1965	1,140	476	1,027	154	2,797	38·3	37·7
1966	1,107	467	1,259	151	2,984	43·1	35·6
1967	1,690	466	846	148	3,150	36·4	40·3
1968	2,184	436	450	152	3,222	29·8	35·8
1969	1,972	453	542	168	3,135	33·1	35·6
1970	1,382	406	1,207	133	3,128	44·0	37·6
1971	823	391	1,848	128	3,180	55·7	39·2
1972	890	375	1,643	155	3,063	52·6	36·7

SOURCE.—Conservative Central Office. Turnout figures which are drawn from the Annual Reports of the Registrar-General for England and Wales.

Party Control in Major Cities, 1945–

Party politics in many cities goes back to the first half of the nineteenth century but, although in most sizeable towns (practically all over 50,000) councillors have worn political labels throughout this century, in only a few larger councils did a majority of councillors of one party mean that that party exercised control. Labour successes after the first World War introduced a more organised form of party politics into some councils. After the Second World War, the local government franchise was extended to practically the same basis as that for parliamentary elections (it had hitherto been confined to ratepayers) and, with sweeping Labour successes in the 1945 municipal elections and an organised Conservative counter-attack in the succeeding years, party politics extended their hold to most urban authorities, including practically all those with more than 20,000 inhabitants. Here is the record since 1945 of the party control in cities which in 1972 had more than 200,000 inhabitants: 'Citizen' in Bristol, 'Ratepayers' in Southampton and 'Progressive' (also called 'Moderate') in Scottish cities and Newcastle refers to local anti-Socialist, Conservative-supported parties. For England and Wales the 1974 entries refer to the district councils elected in 1973 (in some cases on enlarged boundaries).

Belfast. 1945– Unionist.
Birmingham
    1945 No clear majority.[1] 1946–67 Labour. 1947–49 No majority. 1949–52 Conservative. 1952–66 Labour. 1966–72 Conservative. 1972– Labour.
Bradford
    1945–51 Labour. 1951–52 No clear majority. 1952–59 Labour. 1959–61 No clear majority. 1961–62 Conservative and National Liberal. 1962–63 No clear majority. 1963–67 Labour. 1967–72 Conservative. 1972–74 Labour. 1974– Conservative.
Bristol
    1945–49 Labour. 1949–51 No clear majority. 1951–52 Citizen. 1952–60 Labour. 1960–63 Citizen. 1963–67 Labour. 1967–72 Citizen. 1972– Labour.
Cardiff
    1945–58 anti-Labour coalition. 1958–61 Labour. 1961–63 No clear majority. 1963–65 Labour. 1965–66 No clear majority. 1967–74 Conservative. 1974– Labour.
Coventry
    1945–67 Labour. 1967–72 Conservative. 1972– Labour.
Edinburgh
    1945–62 Progressive. 1962–65 No clear majority. 1965–71 Progressive.[1] 1971– No clear majority.
Glasgow
    1945–47 Labour. 1947–50 No clear majority. 1950–52 Progressive. 1952–68 Labour.[1] 1968–69 No clear majority. 1969–70 Progressive. 1970– Labour.
Leeds
    1945–51 Labour. 1951–53 Conservative. 1953–67 Labour. 1967–72 Conservative. 1972–74 Labour. 1974– No clear majority.
Leicester
    1945–49 Labour. 1949–52 Conservative. 1952–61 Labour. 1961–62 Conservative. 1962–63 No clear majority. 1963–66 Labour. 1966–67 No continuous majority. 1967–72 Conservative. 1972– Labour.
Liverpool
    1945–54 Conservative. 1954–55 Conservative with Protestant support. 1955–61 Labour. 1961–63 Conservative. 1963–67 Labour. 1967–72 Conservative. 1972–74 Labour. 1974– No clear majority (Liberal largest party).
Manchester
    1945–47 Labour. 1947–49 No clear majority. 1949–52 Conservative. 1952–53 No clear majority. 1953–67 Labour. 1967–71 Conservative. 1971– Labour.
Newcastle
    1945–49 Labour. 1949–58 Progressive. 1958–67 Labour. 1967–74 Conservative. 1974– Labour.
Nottingham
    1945–50 Labour. 1950–51 No clear majority. 1951–52 Conservative. 1952–53 No clear majority. 1953–60 Labour. 1960–61 No clear majority. 1961–63 Conservative. 1963–67 Labour. 1967–72 Conservative. 1972– Labour.
Plymouth
    1945–53 Conservative. 1953–59 Labour. 1959–63 Conservative. 1963–66 Labour. 1966– Conservative.
Portsmouth
    1949–64 Conservative. 1964–65 Labour. 1965– Conservative.
Sheffield
    1945–68 Labour. 1968–69 Conservative. 1969– Labour.

---

[1] 'No clear majority' is shown wherever no party had a clear overall majority of seats; frequently a party holding half the seats was able to exercise some control in this situation with the aid of the mayoral vote and in other cases a party exercised control in alliance with a minor group.
[1] The position in Edinburgh and Glasgow is complicated by two ex-officio councillors who make clear definition of overall majority difficult.

Southampton
  1945–50 Labour. 1950–54 Ratepayers. 1954–61 Labour. 1961–62 Conservative.
  1962–67 Labour. 1967–72 Conservative. 1973– Labour.
Stoke on Trent
  1945–70 Labour. 1970–71 Conservative. 1971– Labour.
Sunderland
  1945–68 Labour. 1968–72 Conservative. 1972– Labour.
Tees-side (created 1967, abolished 1974)
  1967–72 Conservative. 1972–74 Labour.
Wolverhampton
  1945–49 Labour. 1949–52 Conservative and allies. 1952–67 Labour. 1967–72
  Conservative. 1972– Labour.

Local Government Elections, 1973

Under the *Local Government Act, 1972*, elections took place in the spring
of 1973 for the new authorities that were to take power in England and
Wales in 1974.

Local Elections, 1973: Overall Results

		Party control			Seats			
		Con.	Lab.	No clear control or Ind.	Con.	Lab.	Lib.	Other
Metropolitan counties	12 Apr	—	6	—	142	402	49	8
Other counties	12 Apr	18	11	18	1,598	1,375	210	513
Metropolitan districts	10 May	5	26	5	699	1,573	178	48
Other districts (Wales)	10 May	1	19	17	136	648	42	704
Other districts (England)	7 Jun	86	73	137	4,286	4,327	919	3,983

Metropolitan Counties

	Seats				Votes (%)			
	Con.	Lab.	Lib.	Other	Con.	Lab.	Lib.	Other
Greater Manchester	24	69	13	—	38·7	45·1	14·9	1·3
Merseyside	26	53	19	1	33·7	41·3	22·0	3·0
South Yorkshire	13	82	1	4	25·5	55·8	11·3	7·4
Tyne & Wear	27	74	1	2	36·3	55·7	4·6	3·4
West Midlands	27	73	4	—	32·1	57·1	9·1	1·7
West Yorkshire	25	51	11	1	37·3	44·8	14·6	3·3
Greater London	32	58	2	—	38·0	47·4	12·5	2·1

Party Representation on the London County Council, 1898–1964

Year	Councillors (elected)				Total	Aldermen				Total	Majority
	Pr.	MRM	Lab.	Ind.		Pr.	MRM	Lab.	Ind.		
1898	84	34	..	..	118	13	6	..	..	137	Pr.
1901	87	31	..	..	118	14	5	..	..	137	Pr.
1904	83	35	..	..	118	15	4	..	..	137	Pr.
1907	38	79	..	I	118	9	10	..	..	137	MRM
1910	55	60	3	..	118	2	15	..	2	137	MRM
1913	50	67	I	..	118	3	14	..	2	137	MRM
1919	40	68	15	I	124	6	12	2	..	144	MRM
1922	25	82	17	..	124	5	12	3	..	144	MRM
1925	6	83	35	..	124	3	13	4	..	144	MRM
1928	5	77	42	..	124	I	12	6	I	144	MRM
1931	6	83	35	..	124	..	13	6	I	144	MRM
1934	..	55	69	..	124	..	9	11	..	144	Lab.
1937	..	49	75	..	124	..	8	12	..	144	Lab.
	Lib.	Con.	Lab.	Comm.		Lib.	Con.	Lab.	Comm.		
1946	2	30	90	2	124	..	6	14	..	144	Lab.
1949	I	64	64	..	129	..	5	16	..	150 a	Lab.
1952	..	37	92	..	129	..	6	15	..	150	Lab.
1955	..	52	74	..	126	..	8	13	..	147	Lab.
1958	..	25	101	..	126	..	7	14	..	147	Lab.
1961	..	42	84	..	126	..	7	14	..	147	Lab.

a Plus Chairman, an outsider and Labour nominee.

Pr.—Progressives (Lib.).   Ind.—Independent.
MRM—Municipal Reform Moderates (Con).   Comm.—Communist.
Lab.—Labour.   Lib.—Liberal.

SOURCES.—Sir G. Gibbon and R. W. Bell, *History of the London County Council, 1889–1939* (1939); *General Election of County Councillors* (published after each election by the L.C.C.), 1919–61.

Party Representation in the Greater London Council, 1964–

Year	Councillors			Aldermen		
	Con.	Lab.	Lib.	Con.	Lab.	Lib.
1964	36	64	—	5	11	—
1967	82	18	—	10	6	—
1970	65	35	—	11	5	—
1973	32	58	2	*(Aldermen abolished)*		

Control and Representation in London Boroughs, 1964–

Year	Control			Councillors			
	Con.	Lab.	No clear control	Con.	Lab.	Lib.	Other
1964	9	20	3	668	1,112	13	66
1968	27	4	I	1,441	350	10	57
1971	10	21	I	601	1,221	9	32
1974	13	18	I	713	1,090	27	37

SOURCES —J. Redlich and F. W. Hirst (ed. B. Keith-Lucas), *The History of Local Government in England* (1958); *Report of Royal Commission on Local Taxation 1901*, XXIV; *Report of Royal Commission on the Poor Law 1909*, XXXVII; *Report of Royal Commission on Local Government 1924–25*, XIV; *1928–29*, VIII, *1929–30*, XV; *Proposals for Reform in Local Government 1928*, XIX; *Social Insurance and Allied Services 1942–43* (The Beveridge Report); *A National Health Service 1943–44*, VIII; *Report of Interdepartmental Committee on the Care of Children 1945–46*, X (The Curtis Report); *Report of the Local Government Boundary Commission for the year 1947, 1947–48*, XIII; *Local Government: Areas and Status of Local Authorities in England and Wales, 1956*, Cmd. 9831; *Local Government: Functions of County Councils and County District Councils in England and Wales 1957*, Cmnd. 161; *Local Government Finance (England and Wales) 1957*, Cmnd. 209. T. W. Freeman, *The Conurbations of Great Britain* (1966). *Report of the Royal Commission on Local Government in Greater London* (1960) Cmnd. 1164. *Staffing of Local Government* (Mallaby) (1967); *Management of Local Government* (Maud) (5 vols 1967). *Report of the Royal Commission on Local Government in England*, Cmnd 4040, 1969; *The New Local Authorities: Management and Structure* (H.M.S.O., 1972); P. G. Richards, *The Reformed Local Government System* (1973).

XV

ROYALTY

British Kings and Queens, 1900–

Name	Accession		Coronation		Died		Age	Reigned
Victoria	20 Jun	1837	28 Jun	1838	22 Jan	1901	81	63 yrs
Edward VII	22 Jan	1901	9 Aug	1902	6 May	10	68	9 yrs
George V	6 May	10	22 Jun	11	20 Jan	36	70	25 yrs
Edward VIII	20 Jan	36	..		(Abdicated)		..	325 days
George VI	11 Dec	36	12 May	37	6 Feb	52	56	15 yrs
Elizabeth II	6 Feb	52	2 Jun	53	..		..	..

Use of Royal Power

Throughout this century great efforts have been made to avoid involving the Crown in politics. But there have been a few occasions when, unavoidably or deliberately, the Sovereign has been involved in decision making. No list of such occasions can be very satisfactory. It may omit times when in private audience the Sovereign expressed strong views to the Prime Minister. It may include times when, despite all the formality of consultation, the Sovereign had no real opportunity of affecting the outcome. The following list of incidents is compiled primarily from *Cabinet Government*, by Sir Ivor Jennings, *King George V*, by Sir Harold Nicolson, and *King George VI*, by Sir J. W. Wheeler-Bennett.

Dec 1909 Edward VII's refusal to promise to create peers until after a second general election.
Jul 1910 George V's sponsorship of the Constitutional Conference.
Nov 1910 George V's secret pledge to create peers, if necessary.
Jul 1914 George V's sponsorship of Buckingham Palace Home Rule Conference.
Mar 1917 George V's support for General Haig, when in danger of being dismissed.
May 1923 George V's summons of S. Baldwin as Prime Minister.
Jan 1924 George V's request to J. R. MacDonald to form government.
Aug 1931 George V's invitation to J. R. MacDonald to form National Government.
May 1940 George VI's invitation to W. Churchill to form Coalition Government.
Jul 1945 George VI's advice on switching appointment of Bevin and Dalton (a disputed allegation).
Jan 1957 Elizabeth II's summons of H. Macmillan as Prime Minister.
Oct 1963 Elizabeth II's invitation to E of Home to form a Government.
Nov 1965 Elizabeth II's award of G.C.V.O. to Governor of Rhodesia.

Regency Acts, 1937 and 1953

These Acts provide that if the Sovereign is under 18 years of age, the royal functions shall be exercised by a Regent appointed under the provisions of the Acts. (Formerly the appointment of a Regent was *ad hoc*.) The Regent may not give assent to Bills altering the succession to the throne or repealing the Acts securing the Scottish Church.

The Acts provide for Counsellors of State to be appointed during the Monarch's absence from the U.K., or infirmity; and empower certain high officials of the state to declare that 'the Sovereign is by infirmity of mind or body incapable for the time being of performing the royal function'.

The Royal Family

Children of Queen Victoria

1. H.R.H. Princess Victoria (Princess Royal). Born 21 Nov 1840, married Prince Frederick of Prussia (1858), afterwards Kaiser Frederick III, died 5 Aug 1901.
2. **H.M. King Edward VII.** Born 9 Nov. 1841, married H.R.H. Princess Alexandra (eldest daughter of King Christian IX of Denmark), 10 Mar 1863, succeeded to the throne 22 Jan 1901, crowned at Westminster Abbey 9 Aug 1902, died 6 May 1910 (*for children, see below*).
3. H.R.H. Princess Alice. Born 25 Apr 1843, married Prince Louis (1862), afterwards Grand Duke of Hesse, died 14 Dec 1878.
4. H.R.H. Prince Alfred, D of Edinburgh. Born 6 Aug 1844, married Marie Alexandrovna (1874) only daughter of Alexander II, Emperor of Russia. Succeeded as D of Saxe-Coburg and Gotha 22 Aug 1893, died 30 Jul 1900.
5. H.R.H. Princess Helena. Born 25 May 1846, married H.R.H. Prince Christian of Schleswig-Holstein (1866), died 9 Jun 1923.
6. H.R.H. Princess Louise. Born 18 Mar 1848, married M of Lorne (1871), afterwards 9th D of Argyll, died 3 Dec 1939.
7. H.R.H. Prince Arthur, D of Connaught. Born 1 May 1850, married H.R.H. Princess Louisa of Prussia (1879), died 16 Jan 1942.
8. H.R.H. Prince Leopold, D of Albany. Born 7 Apr 1853, married Princess Helena of Waldeck (1882), died 28 Mar 1884.
9. H.R.H. Princess Beatrice. Born 14 Apr 1857, married H.R.H. Prince Henry of Battenberg (1885), died 26 Oct 1944.

Children of Edward VII

1. H.R.H. Prince Albert, D of Clarence and Avondale (1891). Born 8 Jan 1864, died 14 Jan 1892.
2. **H.M. King George V.** H.R.H. Prince George, D of York (1893), Prince of Wales (1901–1910). Born 3 Jun 1865, married (6 July 1893) H.R.H. Princess Mary of Teck (Queen Mary, died 24 Mar 1953), succeeded to the throne 6 May 1910, crowned at Westminster Abbey 22 Jun 1911,

assumed by Royal Proclamation (17 Jun 1917) the name of Windsor for his House and family, died 20 Jan 1936 (*for children, see below*).

3. H.R.H. Princess Louise (Princess Royal). Born 20 Feb 1867, married to 1st D of Fife (1889), died 4 Jan 1931. Children: (i) H.H. Princess Alexandra, Duchess of Fife. Born 17 May 1891, married H.R.H. Prince Arthur of Connaught (1913), died 26 Feb 1959. Child: Alastair, D of Connaught, born 9 Aug 1914, died 26 Apr 1943. (ii) H.H. Princess Maud. Born 3 Apr 1893, married to 11th E of Southesk (1923), died 14 Dec 1945. Child: D of Fife, born 23 Sep 29, married (1956) Hon. Caroline Dewar.

4. H.R.H. Princess Victoria. Born 6 Jul 1868, died 2 Dec 1935.

5. H.R.H. Princess Maud. Born 26 Nov 1869, married Prince Charles of Denmark (1896), afterwards King Haakon VII of Norway, died 20 Nov 1938. Child: H.M. Olaf V, King of Norway. Born 2 Jul 1903, married (1929) H.R.H. Princess Marthe of Sweden. Children: (i) H.R.H. Princess Ragnhild, born 9 Jun 1930, married (1953) to E. Lorentzen. (ii) H.R.H. Princess Astrid, born 12 Feb 1932. (iii) H.R.H. Harald, Crown Prince of Norway, born 21 Feb 1937, married (1968) Miss S. Haraldsen. Child: H.R.H. Princess Martha Louise, born 22 Sep 1971.

Children of George V

1. H.R.H. Prince Edward, D of Windsor (1936), Prince of Wales (1910–36). Born 23 Jun 1894, succeeded to the throne as **King Edward VIII** on 20 Jan 1936, abdicated 11 Dec 1936. Married Mrs W. Simpson on 3 Jun 1937. Died 28 May 1972.

2. **H.M. King George VI.** H.R.H. Prince Albert, D of York (1920). Born 14 Dec 1895, married Lady Elizabeth Bowes-Lyon, daughter of 14th E of Strathmore and Kinghorne on 26 Apr 1923, succeeded to the throne on 11 Dec 1936, crowned at Westminster Abbey 12 May 1937, died 6 Feb 1952 (*for children, see below*).

3. H.R.H. Princess Victoria (Princess Royal). Born 25 Apr 1897, married (1922) to 6th E of Harewood, died 28 Mar 1965. Children: (i) George, 7th E of Harewood. Born 7 Feb 1923, married (1949) Marion, daughter of E. Stein. Divorced, 7 Jul 1967. Married (1967) Patricia Tuckwell. Children: David, Vt Lascelles, born 21 Oct 1950; J. Lascelles, born 5 Oct 1953; R. Lascelles, born 14 Feb 1955; M. Lascelles, born 5 Jul 1964. (ii) G. Lascelles, born 21 Aug 1924, married (1952) Miss A. Dowding. Child: H. Lascelles, born 19 May 1953.

4. H.R.H. Prince Henry, D of Gloucester (1928). Born 31 Mar 1900, married (1935) Lady A. Montagu-Douglas-Scott, daughter of 7th D of Buccleuch, died 10 Jun 1974. Children: (i) H.R.H. Prince William, born 18 Dec 1941, died 28 Aug 1972. (ii) H.R.H. Prince Richard, born 26 Aug 1944, married (1972) Birgit Van Deurs. Child: Alexander, Earl of Ulster, born 28 Oct 1974.

5. H.R.H. Prince George, D of Kent (1934). Born 20 Dec 1902, married (1934) H.R.H. Princess Marina of Greece and Denmark, killed on active

service 25 Aug 1942.   Children: (i) H.R.H. Prince Edward, D of Kent,
born 9 Oct 1935, married (1961) Katherine, daughter of Sir W. Worsley.
Children: George, E of St Andrews, born 26 Jun 1962; Lady Helen
Windsor, born 28 April 1964; Lord Nicholas Windsor, born 25 Jul 1970.
(ii) Princess Alexandra, born 25 Dec 1936, married (1963) Hon. Angus
Ogilvy.   Children: James Ogilvy, born 29 Feb 1964, Marina Ogilvy, born
31 Jul 1966.   (iii) H.R.H. Prince Michael, born 4 July 1942.
6. H.R.H. Prince John.   Born 12 Jul 1905, died 18 Jan 1919.

Children of George VI
1. **H.M. Queen Elizabeth II.**   Born 21 Apr 1926, married to Philip, D of
Edinburgh on 20 Nov 1947, succeeded to the throne 6 Feb 1952, crowned
at Westminster Abbey 2 Jun 1953.   Children: (i) H.R.H. Prince Charles,
Prince of Wales (26 Jun 1958), D of Cornwall, born 14 Nov 1948.   (ii)
H.R.H. Princess Anne, born 15 Aug 1950, married Mark Phillips 14 Nov
1973.   (iii) Prince Andrew, born 19 Feb 1960.   (iv) Prince Edward, born
10 Mar 1964.
2. H.R.H. Princess Margaret.   Born 21 Aug 1930, married on 6 May 1960 to
Antony Armstrong-Jones (created E of Snowdon, 1961).   Children:
(i) David, Vt Linley, born 3 Nov 1961.   (ii) Lady Sarah Armstrong-Jones,
born 1 May 1964.

Private Secretaries to the Sovereign

1895–1901	Sir A. Bigge (Ld Stamfordham)	1936–43	Sir A. Hardinge
1901–13	Sir F. Knollys (Ld) (Vt)[1]	1943–52	Sir A. Lascelles
1910–31	Ld Stamfordham[1]	1953–72	Sir M. Adeane
1931–36	Sir C. Wigram (Ld)	1972–	Sir M. Charteris

[1] Ld Stamfordham and Ld Knollys were joint private secretaries 1910–13 to King George V.

Lord Chamberlains

1898	E of Hopetoun	1922	E of Cromer
1900	5th E of Clarendon	1938	6th E of Clarendon
1905	Vt Althorp (Earl Spencer)	1952	E of Scarbrough
1912	Ld Sandhurst (Vt)	1961	Ld Cobbold
1921	D of Atholl	1971	Ld Maclean

Civil List of the Crown

The annuities payable to the Sovereign and Members of the Royal Family
are known as the Civil List which is granted by Parliament upon the recommendation of a Select Committee.

Year	Privy Purse	Total
1900	£60,000	£385,000
1901	£110,000	£470,000
1931[a]	£97,000	£420,000
1938	£110,000	£410,000
1952	£60,000	£475,000
1972	[b]	£980,000
1975		£1,400,000

[a] By Command of the King the Civil List was reduced by £50,000 p.a. as from 1 Oct, 1931, in view of the national economic situation.

[b] In 1972 the Privy Purse, as a separate head, was abolished.

SOURCES.—*Imperial Calendar*; *Whitaker's Almanack*; *Dictionary of National Biography*; *Who Was Who*; *Who's Who*.

XVI
THE BRITISH ISLES

Scotland

UNDER the *Act of Union, 1707*, Scotland preserved her independent legal system, under which developed her system of education and local government which have never been assimilated to those of England and Wales. Her established (Presbyterian) Church was also secured by the 1707 Act. When the post of Secretary for Scotland was re-created (becoming Secretary of State for Scotland in 1926), the Lord Advocate was the principal Officer of State for Scotland, assisted by the Solicitor-General for Scotland. In 1900 there were Scottish Boards for local government, fisheries, in 1912 agriculture, and in 1919 health, while the Scotch Education Department (renamed Scottish in 1918) dated from 1872. In practice, even after the creation of the Scottish Secretary, the Boards had a statutory life independent of any Minister. The Boards were recognised as an anachronism by the Reports of the Royal Commission on the Civil Service in 1914,[1] and the Haldane Committee on the Machinery of Government in 1918.[2] Both reports suggested that there was inadequate ministerial responsibility for the activities of these Boards. In 1928 the Boards of Agriculture and Health and the Prison Commission for Scotland were abolished and their duties were assigned to statutory departments under the responsibility of the Secretary of State for Scotland. As the result of a general review of the Scottish administration by the Gilmour Committee,[3] the functions of the Departments of Agriculture, Education, Health, Prisons, and the Fisheries Board were vested directly in the Secretary of State for Scotland, by the *Reorganisation of Offices (Scotland) Act, 1939*, which also gave the Secretary of State the freedom 'to make such arrangements as he thinks fit to discharge the business of his office'. During and after the Second World War some additional administrative responsibilities were allocated to the Scottish Office. Following the Royal Commission Report on Scottish Affairs[4] published in 1954, there were further transfers to Scottish Departments of functions such as the responsibility for roads. Most 'United Kingdom' Departments (i.e. those whose responsibilities embrace Scotland) in the field of home affairs have regional offices in Scotland. The Home Office, though not counted as a United Kingdom Department, has certain responsibilities for what happens in Scotland, e.g. over dangerous drugs and aliens, as do the Ministries of Agriculture, Fisheries and Food and Departments of Education and Science. Several reorganisations have taken place since 1934, and in 1973 the Scottish Office Departments were the Department of Agriculture and Fisheries for

[1] Cd. 7338/1914.　　[2] Cd. 9320/1981　　[3] Cmd. 5563/1936-37　　[4] Cmd. 9212/1953-54.

Scotland, the Scottish Development Department, the Scottish Economic Planning Department, the Scottish Education Department and the Scottish Home and Health Department. The headquarters of the five Scottish Departments are in Edinburgh, with a liaison office in Whitehall. Scottish Ministers divide their time between their Edinburgh headquarters and Whitehall, especially while Parliament is sitting. The Secretary of State, the Scottish Law officers and the Parliamentary Under-Secretaries have usually been members of the House of Commons, but since the appointment of the first Minister of State to the Scottish Office in 1951 either this appointment or that of one or two Parliamentary Under-Secretaries has been held by members of the House of Lords. Scotland has its separate system of law courts and its bar, its own established church, and its own Heraldic authority, Lord Lyon King-at-Arms. A Scottish Grand Committee was established by the House of Commons in 1894. In 1957 and 1962 it was supplemented by two Scottish Standing Committees. In 1969 a Select Committee on Scottish Affairs was established, although it went into abeyance temporarily in 1972–3.

SOURCES.—Sir D. Milne, *The Scottish Office* (1957); H. J. Hanham, *Scottish Nationalism* (1969); J. Kellas, *The Scottish Political System* (1973); *A Handbook of Scottish Administration* (H.M.S.O., 1967); *Report of Commission on the Constitution* (Cmnd. 5460–1/1973).

Wales

The only significant devolution of administrative responsibility from Westminster to Wales has taken place since 1950, and this to a much more limited extent than in Scotland. In 1907 a Welsh Department of the Board of Education (now part of the Ministry of Education) was established. A Welsh Board of Health was set up in 1919, but was only to exercise such powers in Wales as the Minister thought fit. A Welsh Office in the Ministry of Housing and Local Government was also established. In 1951 a Minister for Welsh Affairs was appointed, holding the office jointly with the Home Office from 1951 to 1957. From 1957 to 1964 the Minister for Welsh Affairs was also the Minister of Housing and Local Government. A second parliamentary secretary was appointed at the Home Office from 1951 to 1957 to be responsible for Welsh Affairs; in 1957 a Minister of State for Welsh Affairs was appointed and in 1964 a Welsh Office was established with a Secretary of State for Wales. Since 1964 in many detailed ways powers have been devolved from Whitehall to the Welsh Office in Cardiff. In 1960 a Welsh Grand Committee analogous to the Scottish Grand Committee was appointed to consider all Bills and other parliamentary business relating exclusively to Wales.

Welsh national or separatist feeling has, however, expressed itself in forces other than the movement for home rule or devolution. The most important aspects of this have been the campaigns on such matters as the Church, education, land and temperance reform. The 1881 Welsh Sunday Closing Act and the 1889 Intermediate Education (Wales) Act were the beginning of separate legislation for Wales. In the twentieth century the most conspicuous milestone here was the act to disestablish the Church of England in Wales which finally came into force in 1920 after being suspended during World War I.

SOURCES.—D. Williams, *History of Modern Wales* (1950); K. O. Morgan, *Wales in British Politics, 1868–1972* (2nd ed. 1970); I. Gowan, Government in Wales in the 20th Century, in J. A. Andrews (ed.), *Welsh Studies in Public Law* 1970; A. Butt-Philip, *The Welsh Question* (1974); B. Jones (ed.), *Anatomy of Wales* (1972); *Report of Commission on the Constitution* (Cmnd 5460–1/1973).

Ireland 1900–1922

From 1900 to 1921 the Lord-Lieutenant of Ireland was responsible for the administration of Irish affairs, with an office in Dublin. His Chief Secretary was a member of the House of Commons, and assisted him in carrying on the parliamentary business of the department, for which he was the responsible minister. At the same time there were several departments in Dublin, working under the presidency of the Chief Secretary: the Department of Agriculture and Technical Instruction, the Irish Congested Districts Board, and the Local Government Board for Ireland. There were three boards of education commissioners, all of whom were appointed by the Lord-Lieutenant or the Government, and there was the Irish Land Commission. The Irish Public Works Board was controlled by the Treasury in London, and not by the Irish Government. There was scarcely any further devolution of administrative authority to Ireland between 1900 and 1922.

The Irish Office remained in existence until 1924 after the partition of Ireland, though the posts of Chief Secretary and Lord-Lieutenant lapsed in 1922, with the recognition of the Irish Free State. The functions previously exercised by the Irish Office became the responsibility of the Home Office (for Northern Ireland) and the Colonial Office handled relations with the Free State (in 1937 renamed Eire). When Ireland became a republic in 1949, the Commonwealth Relations Office continued to be the department responsible for relations with her. In 1966 this responsibility was transferred to the Commonwealth Affairs Office (since 1968 the Foreign and Commonwealth Office).

Lord-Lieutenant of Ireland 1900-22		Chief Secretary for Ireland 1900-22	
1895	Ld Cadogan	1900	G. Balfour
8 Aug 02	E of Dudley	7 Nov 00	G. Wyndham
3 Feb 06	E of Aberdeen	12 Mar 05	W. Long
19 Feb 15	Ld Wimborne	10 Dec 05	J. Bryce
12 May 18	Vt French	23 Jan 07	A. Birrell
2 May 21	Vt FitzAlan	31 Jul 16	(Sir) H. Duke
(*Office in cabinet only June 95–8 Aug* 02 *and* 28 *Oct* 19– 2 *Apr* 21)		5 May 18	E. Shortt
		10 Jan 19	I. Macpherson
		2 Apr 20	Sir H. Greenwood
		(*Irish Office wound up* 1922)	

Northern Ireland, 1922–1972

The Northern Ireland Parliament was created by the *Government of Ireland Act*, 1920. The powers of the Crown were exercised by the Governor, appointed by the Crown. Provision was made in the Act for the continued representation of Northern Ireland constituencies in the House of Commons of the United Kingdom. The constitutional position of Northern Ireland was thus unique in that it was part of the United Kingdom and sent representatives to the United Kingdom Parliament but was subject in most internal matters to the jurisdiction of a Parliament and Government of its own. The Government of Ireland Act conferred on that Parliament extensive powers for the regulation of the affairs of Northern Ireland, but excluded a number of specified matters from its jurisdiction. In respect of these excluded matters executive power remained with the United Kingdom Government, and only the United Kingdom Parliament could legislate. Consequently Northern Ireland was subject to two jurisdictions, and although most of Northern Ireland's public services were administered by Ministers who were members of the Northern Ireland Government, there were some public services, such as, for example, the Post Office services, the Customs and Excise service, and the Inland Revenue service, for which Ministers of the United Kingdom Government were responsible.

In respect of all matters on which the Northern Ireland Parliament was empowered to make laws, executive powers were exercisable by the Government of Northern Ireland. At the head of this Government was the Governor appointed by the Crown who formally summoned, prorogued and dissolved the Parliament, appointed the members of the Privy Council, and appointed Ministers to administer such Government departments as the Northern Ireland Parliament might establish. The departments were the Prime Minister's Department, the Ministry of Finance, the Ministry of Home Affairs, the Ministry of Development, the Ministry of Education, the Ministry of Agriculture, the Ministry of Commerce, and the Ministry of Health and Social Services. The Ministers in charge of these eight departments (together with the Minister in the Senate, the Minister of State in the Ministry of Development, and the Minister who was Leader of the House) formed an Executive Committee of the Privy Council which aided and advised the Governor in the exercise of his executive powers.

The Parliament of Northern Ireland consisted of a Senate and a House of Commons. The House of Commons had 52 members, Proportional Representation was used in the elections of 1921 and 1925 but after 1929, except for 4 members for Queen's University, Belfast, they were chosen directly by single-member constituencies. In 1969 the University constituency was abolished and four new territorial seats were created. The Senate had 26 members, 24 being elected by the House of Commons by proportional representation, and two being *ex officio*, the Lord Mayor of Belfast and the Mayor of Londonderry. The main differences between the Northern Ireland law relating to elections to the Northern Ireland Parliament and the United Kingdom law relating to elections to the United Kingdom Parliament were that, after 1950, Northern Ireland law retained the University seats (until 1963) and the 'business premises' qualification for a vote (until 1968), and required qualified electors either to have been born in Northern Ireland or to have been resident in the UK for seven years and to possess the requisite residence, business premises or service qualification. The Parliament of Northern Ireland could legislate on all matters except certain fields that were permanently excepted by the 1920 Act, such as the succession to the Crown, making of peace or war, the armed forces of the Crown, the making of treaties, honours, naturalisation and aliens, and certain functions that were reserved such as postal and telegraph services, the Supreme Court, and the important forms of taxation. It was also prohibited from making laws which would interfere with religious freedom or might discriminate against any religious body, and until 1961, from taking property without compensation. All United Kingdom bills applied to Northern Ireland unless there was express provision to the contrary. In general, legislation at Stormont followed very closely legislation in Westminster. The revenue of the Government of Northern Ireland was derived partly from taxes imposed by the United Kingdom Parliament (known as 'reserved' taxes) and partly from taxes imposed by the Northern Ireland Parliament (known as 'transferred taxes'). The powers of the Northern Ireland Parliament were similar to those of the United Kingdom Parliament as regards the appropriation of revenue. The Treasury was responsible for financial relations with Northern Ireland, and other departments were concerned with trade, commerce, and employment, but the Home Office retained the major responsibility for Northern Ireland.

Governors of Northern Ireland 1922–73		Prime Ministers of Northern Ireland 1921–72	
11 Dec 22	D of Abercorn	7 Jun 21	Sir J. Craig
7 Sep 45	Earl Granville		(1927 Vt Craigavon)
1 Dec 52	Ld Wakehurst	26 Nov 40	J. Andrews
1 Dec 64	Ld Erskine	6 May 43	Sir B. Brooke
2 Dec 68	Ld Grey		(1952 Vt Brooke-
(office abolished 19 Jul 73)			borough)
		25 Mar 63	T. O'Neill
		1 May 69	J. Chichester-Clark
		23 Mar 71	B. Faulkner
		(office suspended 30 Mar 72)	

General Elections of Northern Ireland, 1921–69

Date	Unionist	Ind. Unionist	Lib.	Lab.	Nat.	Sinn Fein Republican Abstentionist	Irish Lab. Rep. Lab. Soc. Rep. Ind. Lab.	Ind. & Other
24 May 21	40	..	..	..	6	6	..	..
28 Apr 25	32	4	..	3	10	2	..	1
22 May 29	37	3	..	1	11	..	..	..
30 Nov 33	36	2	..	2	9	2	..	1
9 Feb 38	39	3	..	1	8	..	1	..
14 Jun 45	33	2	..	2	9	..	3	3
10 Feb 49	37	2	..	..	9	..	2	2
22 Oct 53	38	1	..	..	7	2	3	1
20 Mar 58	37	..	..	4	8	..	2	1
31 May 62	34	..	1	4	9	..	3	1
25 Nov 65	36	..	1	2	9	..	2	2
24 Feb 69	36	3	..	2	6	..	2	3

Northern Ireland 1972—

After sectarian troubles and terrorist activities which from 1969 onwards cost several hundred lives and led to the sending of substantial British military forces, the British Government on 30 Mar 72 passed the *Northern Ireland (Temporary Provisions) Act.* This Act suspended Stormont and transferred all the functions of the Government and Parliament of Northern Ireland to a new Secretary of State for Northern Ireland, acting by Order-in-Council, for one year, (extended in March 1973 for a further twelve months). From Mar 1972 to Dec 1973 the Secretary of State was William Whitelaw. He was succeeded by F. Pym until Mar 1974 when M. Rees took over.

On 8 Mar 73 on a 58·7% poll, the electors of Northern Ireland voted, 591,820 for the province to remain part of the U.K. and 6,463 for it to be joined with the Republic of Ireland, Eire. Following a White Paper (Cmnd. 5259 published on 2 Mar 73) the *Northern Ireland Constitution Act 1973* was passed; this abolished the office of Governor and the Northern Ireland Privy Council; vested the executive power in the Crown, exercisable by the Secretary of State; provided for a complex system of power-sharing in a new Assembly (to be elected by proportional representation from multi-member constituencies) with an Executive to be appointed by the Secretary of State after consulting with the parties, and also authorised any department in Northern Ireland 'to consult' or 'enter into agreements with any authority of the Republic of Ireland in respect of any transferred matter'. Local elections were held on 30 May 1973 for 26 district councils (using proportional representation) in place of the old local government bodies. On June 28, 1973 the 78-member Assembly was elected; its composition was 22 Ulster Unionist (B. Faulkner) 13 other Unionist (12 anti-White Paper) 15 Loyalist Coalition (7 Vanguard (W. Craig) 8 Democratic Unionist (I. Paisley)), 3 Alliance (O. Napier) 1 Northern Ireland Labour Party (D. Bleakley) and 19 Social Democratic and Labour Party (G. Fitt).

The election was followed by prolonged negotiations over the formation of a Northern Ireland Executive, which was finally agreed in December. The Executive which took over on 1 January 1974 consisted of 6 Ulster Unionists accepting the Leadership of B. Faulkner, the Chief Executive, 4 Soc D.L.P. members under G. Fitt, the Deputy Chief Executive, and 1 Alliance Party member. Opposition to the Sunningdale agreement of December 1973 (which provided, among other things, for the establishment of a Council of Ireland) led to Mr Faulkner's repudiation by the Unionist Party. In May 1974 a strike of Protestant workers forced the ending of the Northern Ireland Executive and the temporary return to direct rule from Westminster.

SOURCES.—N. Mansergh, *The Government of Northern Ireland* (1936); T. Wilson (ed.), *Ulster under Home Rule* (1955); Sir F. Newsam, *The Home Office* (1954) pp. 167–70; R. J. Lawrence, *The Government of Northern Ireland* (1965); M. Wallace, *Northern Ireland: 50 Years of Self-Government* (1971); F. S. L. Lyons, *Ireland since the Famine* (1971); R. Rose, *Governing without Consensus: An Irish Perspective* (1971); I. Budge and C. O'Leary, *Belfast: Approach to Crisis; A Study of Belfast Politics 1613–1970* (1973). A. Maltby, *The Government of Northern Ireland, 1922–72: a Catalogue and Breviate of Parliamentary Papers* (1974).

The Channel Islands

The Channel Islands which were originally part of the Duchy of Normandy have been associated with England since 1066.   They have their own legislative assemblies, systems of local administration, fiscal systems, and courts of law.   The Islanders have general responsibility for the regulation of their local affairs subject to the prerogative of the Crown over appointment to the chief posts in the local administrations and the necessity of Royal Assent to legislative measures passed by the insular assemblies.   Most of the laws by which they are governed emanate from their representative assemblies and although they cannot be regarded as local authorities most of their public services are provided by these assemblies in the same way as local government services are provided and administered in Great Britain.

The Channel Islands are divided into 2 Bailiwicks, one comprising Jersey and the other, Alderney, Sark, and Guernsey with its dependants, Herm and Jethou.   Each Bailiwick has a Lieutenant Governor appointed by the Crown for a period of 5 years, through whom all official communications between the U.K. Government and the Islands pass, and in whom certain executive functions are vested.   A Bailiff also appointed by the Crown presides over the local legislatures, the States, and over the sittings of the Royal Court.   Since 1948 all members of the States who have the right to vote are elected directly or indirectly by the electorate.   The Islands have their own Courts of Law, but there remains leave to appeal to the Judicial Committee of the Privy Council.

The Island Assemblies may initiate legislation but they must then petition the Sovereign in Council to give these measures force of law.   Acts of the UK Parliament do not apply to the Channel Islands unless by express provision or necessary application.   As a general rule Parliament refrains from legislating on matters with which these assemblies can deal unless for some special reason a U.K. act must be preferred to local legislation.

The public revenues of the Islands are raised by duties on imported goods, by income taxes and other taxes.   Proposals made by the States for raising revenue require authorisation by Order in Council but responsibility for determining how the revenue shall be spent is, in practice, left to the States. Immunity from taxation for Crown purposes has been a privilege of the Islanders since the time of Edward VI.

SOURCE.—*Report of Commission on the Constitution* (Cmnd. 5460–1/1973).

The Isle of Man

This island was successively under the rule of Norway, of Scotland, of the Stanley family and of the Dukes of Atholl before it became a Crown Colony in 1765.   Since 1886 the internal affairs of the island have been regulated by the Tynwald, which has evolved from the Lord of Man's Council composed of his chief officials and other persons of importance and the House of Keys.   The latter comprises 24 representatives elected by all over the age of 21 who have resided in the island for 6 months.   The consent

of both the Legislative Council and the Keys is requisite for any Act of
Tynwald except when in three successive sessions of a Parliament the Keys
pass the same Bill, or a very similar one, which is twice rejected by the Council.
In that case the Bill is deemed to have been passed by the Council. All
legislation by Tynwald depends for its validity on confirmation by Orders
made by the Queen in Council.

Most of the public services are provided by Tynwald and administered
by Boards of Tynwald, but the Lieutenant Governor is the executive authority
for certain services, including the police and the administration of justice.
He is also responsible under insular legislation for initiating proposals for the
raising and disbursement of the public revenue. By the Isle of Man Act
of 1958 the Treasury's control over the Island's finances was removed
enabling the Tynwald to regulate its own finances and Customs, although
under the Act, the Island continues to make an annual contribution to the
Exchequer for defence and common services. There is a statutory body of
members of Tynwald known as the Executive Council with whom the
Lieutenant Governor confers before making proposals for the raising or
expenditure of money, and all such proposals subsequently require the
assent of Tynwald.

SOURCE.—*Report of Commission on the Constitution* (Cmnd. 5460-1/1973).

XVII
THE COMMONWEALTH

Main Territories under British Rule since 1900

Commonwealth Status 1 Jan 1975		Original entry into British rule and Status in 1900	Changes of Status
—	Aden	Colony (1839) and adjacent Protectorate	Acceded to South Arabian Federation 1963. Became People's Republic of South Yemen 1967
Ass. State	Antigua	Colony (1663)	*See* Leeward Isles
—	Ascension	Admiralty administered territory (1815)	Became dependency of Colony of St Helena 1922
Member	Australia	First settled 1788 6 self-governing colonies (1855 and later)	Federal government formed 1901. Dominion status recognised 1907
Member	Bahamas	First settled 1646 Colony (1783)	Independence granted 1973
Member	Bangladesh	—	Became East Pakistan 1947. Broke away from Pakistan 1971. Commonwealth Member 1972
Member	Barbados	Settled 1627 Colony (1662)	Part of West Indies Federation 1958–62; Independence granted 1966
—	Basutoland	Protectorate (1871) Colony (1884)	Independence granted 1966. Now Lesotho
—	Bechuanaland	Protectorate (1885)	Independence granted 1966. Now Botswana
Colony	Belize	(see British Honduras)	
Colony	Bermuda	First settled 1609 Colony (1684)	
Member	Botswana	—	Formerly Bechuanaland Protectorate. Independence granted 1966 as Republic
—	British Guiana	Ceded Colony (1814)	Independence granted 1966. Now Guyana
—	British Honduras	First settled 1638 Colony (separated from Jamaica 1884)	Changed name to Belize 1973
Dependency	British Indian Ocean Territory	Dependencies of Mauritius or Seychelles	The Chagos Archipelago and Aldabra, Farquhar and Desroches Islands were formed into a single British Dependency in 1965
—	British North Borneo	Protectorate (1888)	Administered by Chartered Company 1882–1946. Became part of North Borneo Colony 1946. Entered Malaysian Federation as Sabah 1963
Protected State	British Solomon Islands	Protectorate (1893)	
—	British Somaliland	Protectorate (1887)	Independence granted 1960 when it became part of Somalia, a Republic outside the Commonwealth
—	British Togoland	—	Administered by Britain under League of Nations mandate 1922–46 and U.N. Trusteeship 1946–57. Merged with Ghana 1957
Protectorate	Brunei	Protectorate (1888)	
—	Burma	Indian Province (1852)	Separated from India 1937. Independence granted in 1948 when it became a Republic outside the Commonwealth

357

Commonwealth Status 1 Jan 1975	Original entry into British rule and Status in 1900		Changes of Status
—	Cameroons (British)	—	Administered as part of Nigeria under League of Nations mandate 1922. Northern Cameroons incorporated in Nigeria 1961. Southern Cameroons joined Cameroun Republic, outside the Commonwealth
Member	Canada	Ceded Colonies from 1714 onwards. Self-governing Federation (1867)	Dominion status recognised 1907
—	Cape of Good Hope	Ceded Colony (1814)	Dominion status recognised 1907. Province of Union of South Africa
Colony	Cayman, Turks, and Caicos Islands	Ceded (1670) Dependencies of Jamaica (1848)	Separate dependencies under Colonial Office following Jamaican Independence 1962
Member	Ceylon	Ceded Colony (1802)	Independence granted 1948. Became Republic and changed name to Sri Lanka 1972
—	Christmas Island	Annexed (1888)	Part of Straits Settlements 1900 by incorporation with Singapore. Separate Colony Jan 1958. Transferred to Australia Oct 1958
—	Cocos-Keeling Islands	Annexed (1857)	Part of Straits Settlement 1903. Incorporated in Singapore Colony 1946. Transferred to Australia 1958
Protectorate	Cook Islands	Protectorate (1888)	Annexed 1900. Administered by New Zealand since 1901
Member	Cyprus	British administered territory (1878)	Annexed by Britain 1914. Colony 1925. Independence granted as Republic 1960
Ass. State	Dominica	Colony (1763)	See Leeward Isles
—	East African Protectorate	Protectorate (1895)	Became a Colony and protectorate of Kenya 1920. See Kenya
—	Egypt	Occupied by British since 1882	British Protectorate 1914–22
—	Eire	Part of U.K. (1801)	Part of Ireland. Independence granted as Irish Free State 1922 with Dominion status. Took name of Eire 1937. Independent Republic outside the Commonwealth 1949
Colony	Falkland Islands	Colony (1833)	
Member	Fiji	Colony (1874)	Independence granted 1970
Member	Gambia	Settlement began 1618. Colony (1843) and adjacent Protectorate (1888)	Independence granted 1965. Republic 1970
Member	Ghana	—	Formerly Gold Coast. Independence granted 1957. Republic 1960
Colony	Gibraltar	Ceded Colony (1713)	
Colony	Gilbert and Ellice Islands	Protectorate (1892)	Colony 1915
—	Gold Coast	Settlement began 1750. Colony (1821 and 1874)	Independence granted 1957. Now Ghana
Member	Grenada	Ceded Colony (1763)	Part of Leeward Isles 1871–1974. Independence granted 1974
Member	Guyana	—	Formerly British Guiana. Independence granted 1966. Republic 1970
Colony	Hong Kong	Ceded Colony (1843)	
Member	India	Settlement began 1601. Indian Empire (1876)	Independence granted 1947. Republic 1950

Commonwealth Status 1 Jan 1975		Original entry into British rule and Status in 1900	Changes of Status
—	Iraq	—	Administered by Britain under League of Nations Mandate 1932–32
—	Ireland	Union with Great Britain (1801)	Independence granted to 26 counties 1921. Known as Eire since 1937. Final severance 1949
Member	Jamaica	Colony (seized 1655 and ceded 1670)	Part of West Indies Federation 1958–62. Independence granted 1962
Member	Kenya	—	Formerly East African Protectorate. Colony and Protectorate of Kenya (1920). Independence granted 1963. Republic 1964
—	Labuan	Colony (1848) governed by North Borneo Company (1890)	Administered by Straits Settlement 1907. Became separate Straits Settlement 1912. Part of North Borneo (1946) now Sabah (1963)
—	Lagos	Colony (1861)	Amalgamated with protectorate of Southern Nigeria 1906
Ass. State and Colony	Leeward Isles	Colonies federated (1871)	Federated Colony dissolved 1956. (Antigua, Montserrat, St Kitts–Nevis and until 1940 Dominica and Virgin Is.) Part of West Indies Federation (except for Virgin Is.) 1958–62. Attained Associated Statehood 1967 (except for Virgin Is.)
Member	Lesotho	—	Formerly Basutoland Colony. Independence granted 1966 with indigenous monarch
Member	Malawi	—	Formerly Nyasaland. Part of Federation of Rhodesia and Nyasaland 1953–63. Independence granted 1964. Republic 1966
—	Malay States	9 Protectorates, 4 of which were federated	
—	Malaya	—	Formerly Malay States (federated and unfederated) and Straits Settlements. Independence granted in 1957 as elective monarchy. Merged in Malaysia Federation 1963
Member	Malaysia	—	Formed in 1963 by a federation of Malaya, Singapore, Sabah (North Borneo), and Sarawak; Singapore seceded in 1965. An indigenous elective monarchy
—	Maldive Islands	Protectorate (1887)	Independence granted 1965
Member	Malta	Ceded Colony (1814)	Independence granted 1964. Republic 1974
Member	Mauritius	Ceded Colony (1814)	Independence granted 1968
Ass. State	Montserrat	First settled (1642) as Colony	See Leeward Isles
—	Natal	Colony (1843)	Province of South Africa 1910
Member	Nauru	—	Administered by Australia under League of Nations mandate 1920–47 and under U.N. Trusteeship 1947–68. Independant Republic 1968
—	New Guinea	—	Administered by Australia under League of Nations mandate 1921–46 and under U.N. Trusteeship since 1946. United with Papua 1946 as Papua-New Guinea.
Condominium	New Hebrides	—	Administered as Anglo-French condominium since 1960
Member	New Zealand	Colony (1840)	Dominion status recognised 1907
—	Newfoundland	Settlement began 1623. Self-governing Colony (1855)	Dominion status recognised 1907. Under U.K. Commission of government 1933–1949. Acceded to Canada 1949

Commonwealth Status 1 Jan 1975		Original entry into British rule and Status in 1900	Changes of Status
Member	Nigeria	Protectorates (1900)	Colony of Lagos joined Southern Nigeria 1906. Protectorates of Northern and Southern Nigeria joined 1914. Independence granted 1960. Republic 1963
—	Norfolk Island	Settled 1788. Under New South Wales (1896)	Became dependency of Australian Government 1914
—	North Borneo	—	Colony created in 1946 mainly from British North Borneo. Entered Malaysian federation as Sabah 1963
—	Northern Rhodesia	Chartered Company territory (1889)	Administered by British South Africa Company. Became Protectorate 1924. Part of Federation of Rhodesia and Nyasaland 1953–63. Independence granted 1964. Now Zambia
—	Nyasaland	Protectorate (1891)	Part of Federation of Rhodesia and Nyasaland 1953–63. Independence granted 1964. Now Malawi
—	Orange Free State	—	Colony 1902. Province of Union of South Africa 1910
—	Pakistan	—	Part of Indian Empire. Independence granted 1947. Republic 1950. Left Commonwealth 1972
—	Palestine	—	Administered by Britain under League of Nations mandate 1922–48. Achieved Independence as State of Israel 1948
—	Papua	Protectorate (1884) Colony (1888)	Administered by Australia since 1906 United with New Guinea 1946
Member	Papua-New Guinea	—	Papua and New Guinea were united under Australian Trusteeship 1946. Independence granted 1975
Colony	Pitcairn	Settled 1790 Colony (1898)	
Colony	Rhodesia	—	Formerly Southern Rhodesia. Part of Federation of Rhodesia and Nyasaland 1953–63. Resumed status as a self-governing colony with name of Rhodesia 1964. Unilateral declaration of 'independence' 1965
—	Rhodesia and Nyasaland	—	Federation of Northern Rhodesia, Nyasaland, and Southern Rhodesia established in 1953 and dissolved in 1963
—	Sabah	—	Formerly North Borneo. Part of Malaysian Federation since 1963
Ass. State	St Christopher (St Kitts) and Nevis	Colony (1625)	See Leeward Isles
Colony	St Helena	Administered by E. India Co. 1673 Colony (1833)	
Ass. State	St Lucia	Ceded Colony (1814)	See Windward Isles
Ass. State	St Vincent	Ceded Colony (1763)	See Windward Isles
—	Sarawak	Protectorate (1888)	Ceded to Britain in 1946 as Colony. Part of Malaysian Federation since 1963
Colony	Seychelles	Dependency of Mauritius (1810)	Separate Colony 1903
Member	Sierra Leone	Colony (1808) and adjacent Protectorate (1896)	Independence granted 1961. Republic 1971
Member	Singapore	Under Indian government 1824 Became Independent Colony (1946)	Separate Colony 1946. Part of Malaysian Federation 1963–65. Seceded to form Republic 1965

Commonwealth Status 1 Jan 1975		Original entry into British rule and Status in 1900	Changes of Status
—	Straits Settlements (Singapore, Penang, Malacca)	Colonies (1867)	Part of Straits Settlements. Malacca, Labuan added 1912. Labuan and Penang joined Malay States 1948. Singapore joined Malaysian Federation 1963
Member	Sri Lanka	—	Formerly Ceylon. Independence granted 1948. Became Republic and changed name 1972
—	South Africa, Union of	—	Formed 1910 from the Colonies of Cape of Good Hope, Natal, Orange Free State, and Transvaal. Dominion status 1910. Became Republic 1961 and left the Commonwealth
—	South Arabia	—	Federation formed in 1959 from 6 states or sheikhdoms. A further 16 subsequently acceded together with (1963) the Colony of Aden. Became Republic of South Yemen 1967.
—	South-West Africa	—	Administered by South Africa under League of Nations mandate 1920–46 and under U.N. Trusteeship since 1946. Unilaterally incorporated in South Africa 1949
—	South Yemen	—	Formerly Aden Protectorate
—	Southern Rhodesia	Chartered Company (1889)	Administered by British South Africa Company. Self-governing Colony 1923. Part of Federation of Rhodesia and Nyasaland 1953–63. Now Rhodesia.
—	Sudan	Condominium with Egypt (1899)	Independence granted 1956 when it became Republic outside the Commonwealth
Member	Swaziland	—	British Protectorate 1903. Independence granted 1968. Indigenous Monarchy
—	Tanganyika	—	Administered by Britain under League of Nations mandate 1920–46 and under U.N. Trusteeship 1946–61. Independence granted 1961. Republic 1962. Merged with Zanzibar to form Tanzania 1964
Member	Tanzania	—	Formed by merging Tanganyika and Zanzibar 1964
Member	Tonga	Protectorate (1900)	Independence granted under indigenous monarchy 1970
—	Transjordan	—	Administered by Britain under League of Nations mandate 1922–28. Full independence recognised 1946
—	Transvaal	Annexed 1902	Responsible Government 1906. Province of Union of South Africa 1910
Member	Trinidad and Tobago	Ceded (1802 and 1814) Colony (combined 1889)	Part of West Indies Federation 1958–62. Independence granted 1962
—	Tristan da Cunha	British settlement (1815)	Dependency of Colony of St Helena 1938. (Evacuated 1961–63)
Member	Uganda	Protectorate (1894)	Independence granted 1962. Sovereign State 1963
Colony	Virgin Islands	Colonies (1666)	See Leeward Isles
—	West Indies Federation	—	Independence was granted in 1958 to a Federation of the colonies of Jamaica, Trinidad and Tobago, Barbados, the Leeward Isles (except for the Virgin Isles) and the Windward Isles. The Federation broke up in 1962 when Jamaica and Trinidad and Tobago became Independent. Some common institutions were continued by the other members of the Federation

Commonwealth Status 1 Jan 1975		Original entry into British rule and Status in 1900	Changes of Status
Member	Western Samoa	—	Administered by New Zealand under League of Nations mandate 1920–46 and under U.N. Trusteeship 1946–62. Independent Republic 1962. Full Commonwealth member 1970
Ass. States	Windward Isles	Colonies (1763 and 1814 federated in 1885)	The colonies Grenada, Dominica, St Lucia, and St Vincent. Part of West Indies Federation 1958–62. Attained Associated Statehood 1967
Member	Zambia	—	Formerly Northern Rhodesia. Part of Federation of Rhodesia and Nyasaland 1953–63. Independence granted as Republic 1964
—	Zanzibar	Protected State (1890)	Independence granted 1963. Republic 1964. Merged with Tanganyika as Tanzania 1964

Independent Self-Governing Members of the Commonwealth

United Kingdom
New Zealand[1] 1856
Canada[1] 1867
Australia[1] 1901
South Africa[1] 1909–61
Newfoundland[1] [2] 1907–33
Ireland (Eire) 1922–49
India[1] 1947 (Republic 1950)
Pakistan 1947–72 (Republic 1956)
Ceylon (Sri Lanka 1972) 1948 (Republic 1972)
Federation of Rhodesia and Nyasaland 1953–63[4]
Ghana 1957 (Republic 1960)
Malaya 1957 (Malaysia 1963) (Elective Monarchy)
West Indies Federation 1958–62[5]
Nigeria 1960 (Republic 1963)
Cyprus 1961 (Republic 1960)
Sierra Leone 1961 (Republic 1971)
Tanganyika (Tanzania 1965) 1961 (Republic 1962)
Jamaica 1962

Trinidad 1962
Uganda 1962 (Republic 1963)
Zanzibar 1963–64
Kenya 1963 (Republic 1964)
Zambia 1964 (Republic 1964)
Malta 1964 (Republic 1974)
Malawi 1964 (Republic 1966)
The Gambia 1965 (Republic 1970)
Singapore 1965 (Republic 1965)
Guyana 1966 (Republic 1970)
Botswana 1966 (Republic 1966)
Lesotho 1966 (Indigenous Monarchy)
Barbados 1966
Mauritius 1968
Swaziland 1968 (Indigenous Monarchy)
Nauru 1968 (Republic 1968)[6]
Fiji 1970
Tonga 1970 (Indigenous Monarchy)
Western Samoa 1970 (Indigenous Monarchy)
Bangladesh 1972 (Republic 1971)
Bahamas 1973
Grenada 1974

[1] These were recognised as having 'Dominion Status', in 1907.
[2] From 1933 to 1949 Newfoundland was governed by a U.K. Commission of Government. In 1949 Newfoundland joined the Canadian confederation as the tenth Province.
[3] Indian representatives were invited to attend Imperial Conferences and Prime Ministers' Meetings 1917–47.
[4] Although the Central African Federation, set up in 1953, and composed of N. Rhodesia, S. Rhodesia, and Nyasaland, was not a fully independent member of the Commonwealth, her Prime Ministers were invited to the Prime Ministers' Meetings 1955–62 and the Prime Minister of Rhodesia was invited 1962–1965.
[5] Barbados, Jamaica, Trinidad, Tobago, the Leeward and the Windward Islands all formed the West Indies Federation between 1958 and 1962.
[6] Special membership.

Commonwealth Prime Ministers' Meetings, 1900–
(Commonwealth Heads of Government Meetings 1971-)

(All have taken place in London unless otherwise stated)

30 Jun–11 Aug 02	Colonial Conference
15 Apr–9 May 07	Colonial Conference
23 May–20 Jun 11	Imperial Conference
Mar–May 17	Imperial War Conference
Jun–Aug 18	Imperial War Conference
1 Oct–8 Nov 23	Imperial Conference
19 Oct–23 Nov 26	Imperial Conference
1 Oct–14 Nov 30	Imperial Conference

14 May–15 Jun 37	Imperial Conference
1–16 May 44	Commonwealth Prime Ministers' Meeting
23 Apr–23 May 46	Commonwealth Prime Ministers' Meeting
11–22 Oct 48	Commonwealth Prime Ministers' Meeting
21–28 Apr 49	Commonwealth Prime Ministers' Meeting
4–12 Jan 51	Commonwealth Prime Ministers' Meeting
3–9 Jun 53	Commonwealth Prime Ministers' Meeting
31 Jan–8 Feb 55	Commonwealth Prime Ministers' Meeting
27 Jun–6 Jul 56	Commonwealth Prime Ministers' Meeting
26 Jun–5 Jul 57	Commonwealth Prime Ministers' Meeting
3–13 May 60	Commonwealth Prime Ministers' Meeting
8–17 Mar 61	Commonwealth Prime Ministers' Meeting
10–19 Sep 62	Commonwealth Prime Ministers' Meeting
8–13 Jul 64	Commonwealth Prime Ministers' Meeting
17–25 Jan 65	Commonwealth Prime Ministers' Meeting
6–15 Sep 66	Commonwealth Prime Ministers' Meeting
7–15 Jan 69	Commonwealth Prime Ministers' Meeting
14–22 Jan 71	Commonwealth Heads of Government Meeting (Singapore)
2–10 Aug 73	Commonwealth Heads of Government Meeting (Ottawa)
29 Apr–6 May 75	Commonwealth Heads of Government Meeting (Kingston, Jamaica)

Certain other meetings of comparable status have been held

20 Jun–5 Aug 21	Conference of Prime Ministers and London Representatives of the United Kingdom, the Dominions, and India	London
Jul–Aug 32	Imperial Economic Conference	Ottawa
4–13 Apr 45	British Commonwealth Meeting	London
27 Nov–11 Dec 52	Commonwealth Economic Conference	London
11–12 Jan 66	Commonwealth Prime Ministers' Meeting	Lagos

SOURCES.—*Commonwealth Relations Office List 1951*, pp. 56–58, and *C.R.O. List 1960*; *Annual Register 1900–*; *Keesing's Archives 1945–*.

Commonwealth Secretariat

As a result of the Commonwealth Prime Ministers' Meeting of Jul 1964 a Commonwealth Secretariat was established in London with its own civil servants seconded from Commonwealth Governments.

Secretary-General

Aug 65   A. Smith (Canada)

Viceroys and Governors-General

Australia 1901–

1 Jan 01	E of Hopetoun
9 Jan 03	Ld Tennyson
21 Jan 04	Ld Northcote
9 Sep 08	E of Dudley
31 Jun 11	Ld Denman
18 May 14	Sir R. Munro-Ferguson
6 Oct 20	Ld Forster
8 Oct 25	Ld Stonehaven
22 Jan 31	Sir I. Isaacs
23 Jan 36	Ld Gowrie
30 Jan 45	D of Gloucester
11 Mar 47	Sir W. McKell
8 May 53	Sir W. Slim
2 Feb 60	Vt Dunrossil
3 Aug 61	Vt de L'Isle
22 Sep 65	Ld Casey
30 Apr 69	Sir P. Hasluck

Bahamas 1973–

| 10 Jul 73 | Sir J. Paul |
| 1 Aug 73 | Sir M. Butler |

Barbados 1966–

| 30 Nov 66 | Sir J. Stow |
| 15 May 67 | Sir W. Scott |

Canada 1900

1898	E of Minto
10 Dec 04	Earl Grey
13 Oct 11	D of Connaught
11 Nov 16	D of Devonshire
11 Aug 21	Ld Byng
2 Oct 26	Vt Willingdon
4 Apr 31	E of Bessborough
2 Nov 35	Ld Tweedsmuir
21 Jun 40	E of Athlone
12 Apr 46	Vt Alexander
28 Feb 52	V. Massey
15 Sep 59	G. Vanier
4 Apr 67	R. Michener
14 Jan 74	J. Leger

Ceylon 1948–72

4 Feb 48	Sir H. Moore
6 Jul 49	Ld Soulbury
17 Jul 54	Sir O. Goonetilleke
2 Mar 62	W. Gopallawa
22 May 72	*Declared Republic (Sri Lanka)*

Fiji 1970–

| 10 Oct 70 | Sir R. Foster |
| 13 Jan 73 | Sir G. Cakobau |

The Gambia 1965–70

| 18 Feb 65 | Sir F. Singhateh |
| 24 Apr 70 | *Declared Republic* |

Ghana 1957–60

6 Mar 57 E of Listowel
1 Jul 60 Declared Republic

Grenada 1974–

7 Feb 74 L. de Gale

Guyana 1966–70

26 May 66 Sir R. Luyt
16 Dec 66 Sir D. Rose
23 Feb 70 Declared Republic

Viceroys of India 1900–47

1899 Ld Curzon
30 Apr 04 Ld Ampthill
(officiating)
13 Dec 04 Ld Curzon
18 Nov 05 E of Minto
23 Nov 10 Ld Hardinge of
Penshurst
4 Apr 16 Ld Chelmsford
2 Apr 21 E of Reading
10 Apr 25 E of Lytton
(officiating)
3 Apr 26 Ld Irwin
29 Jun 29 Vt Goschen
(officiating)
24 Oct 29 Ld Irwin
18 Apr 31 E of Willingdon
16 May 34 Sir G. Stanley
(officiating)
18 Apr 36 M of Linlithgow
25 Jun 38 Ld Brabourne
(officiating)
25 Oct 38 M of Linlithgow
20 Oct 43 Vt Wavell
24 Mar 47 Vt Mountbatten
(Earl)

Dominion of India— Governors–General 1947–50

15 Aug 47 Earl Mountbatten
21 Jun 48 Chakravarty Raja-
gopalachari
26 Jan 50 Declared Republic

Jamaica 1962–

6 Aug 62 Sir C. Campbell
27 Jun 73 F. Glasspole

Kenya 1963–64

12 Dec 63 M. Macdonald
12 Dec 64 Declared Republic

Malawi 1964–66

6 Jul 64 Sir G. Jones
6 Jul 66 Declared Republic

Malta 1964–

21 Sep 64 Sir M. Dorman
5 Jul 71 Sir A. Mamo
13 Dec 74 Declared Republic

Mauritius 1968–

1 Sep 68 Sir A. Williams
27 Dec 72 Sir R. Osman

New Zealand 1900

(*Governors*)

1897 E of Ranfurly
20 Jun 04 Ld Plunkett
22 Jun 10 Ld Islington
19 Dec 12 E of Liverpool

Governors-General

28 Jun 17 E of Liverpool
27 Sep 20 Earl Jellicoe
13 Dec 24 Sir C. Fergusson
18 Mar 30 Ld Bledisloe
12 Apr 35 Vt Galway
21 Feb 41 Ld Newall
16 Jun 46 Ld Freyberg
1 Dec 52 Sir C. Norrie (Ld)
3 Sep 57 Vt Cobham
9 Nov 62 Sir B. Fergusson
19 Oct 67 Sir A. Porritt
26 Sep 72 Sir D. Blundell

Nigeria 1960–63

1 Oct 60 N. Azikwe
1 Oct 63 Declared Republic

Dominion of Pakistan 1947–56

15 Aug 47 M. Jinnah
14 Sep 48 Khwaja Nazi-
muddin
19 Oct 51 Ghulam Moham-
med

6 Oct 55 Iskander Mirza
23 Mar 56 Declared Republic

Federation of Rhodesia and Nyasaland 1957–63

8 Oct 57 E of Dalhousie
*31 Dec 63 Federation
dissolved*

Sierra Leone 1961–71

27 Apr 61 Sir H. Lightfoot-
Boston
(*In Mar 67 the Consti-
tution was suspended*)
7 Apr 68 B. Tejan-Sie
(acting)
19 Apr 71 Declared Republic

South Africa 1910–61

31 May 10 Vt Gladstone
8 Sep 14 Vt Buxton
20 Nov 20 Prince Arthur of
Connaught
21 Jan 24 E of Athlone
26 Jan 31 E of Clarendon
5 Apr 37 Sir P. Duncan
1 Jan 46 G. van Zyl
1 Jan 51 E. Jansen
25 Nov 59 C. Swart

*The Union of South Africa
became an independent republic
outside the British Commonwealth on 31 May 61.*

Tanganyika 1961–62

9 Dec 61 Sir R. Turnbull
9 Dec 62 Declared Republic

Trinidad and Tobago 1962–

31 Aug 62 Sir S. Hochoy
31 Jan 73 Sir E. Clarke

Uganda 1962–63

9 Oct 62 Sir F. Crawford
9 Oct 63 Declared Republic

West Indies 1957–62

10 May 57 Ld Hailes
Feb 62 Federation dissolved

XVIII

INTERNATIONAL RELATIONS

Major Treaties and Documents subscribed to by Britain since 1900[1]

30 Jan 02	Anglo-Japanese Alliance	13 Apr 39	British Guarantee to Roumania and Greece
8 Apr 04	Anglo-French Entente		
31 Aug 07	Anglo-Russian Entente	12 May 39	British Guarantee to Turkey
18 Mar 15	Anglo-Russian Agreement over Constantinople		
25 Apr 15	Treaty of London (Italy)	25 Aug 39	Anglo-Polish Agreement of Mutual Assistance
May 16	Sykes-Picot Agreement (Middle East)	14 Aug 41	Atlantic Charter
31 Oct 17	Balfour Declaration (Palestine)	23 Feb 42	Anglo-American Mutual Aid Agreement (Lend-Lease 'Master Agreement')
28 Jun 19	Treaty of Versailles (Germany) and League of Nations Covenant[2]		
		26 May 42	Anglo-Soviet Treaty
10 Sep 19	Treaty of St Germain (Austria)	22 Jul 44	Bretton Woods Agreement (International Finance)
27 Nov 19	Treaty of Neuilly (Bulgaria)	11 Feb 45	Yalta Agreement
		26 Jun 45	United Nations Charter[3]
4 Jun 20	Treaty of Trianon (Hungary)	2 Aug 45	Potsdam Agreement
10 Aug 20	Treaty of Sèvres (Turkey)	6 Dec 45	Anglo-American Financial Agreement
6 Dec 21	Articles of Agreement for an Irish Peace	9 Feb 47	Peace Treaties with Italy, Hungary, Roumania, Bulgaria, and Finland
13 Dec 21	Washington Four Power Treaty (Pacific)		
6 Feb 22	Washington Nine Power Treaty (China)	17 Mar 48	Brussels Treaty Organisation
6 Feb 22	Washington Five Power Treaty (Naval)	16 Apr 48	Organisation for European Economic Co-operation
23 Aug 23	Treaty of Lausanne (Middle East and the Straits)	6 Jul 48	Economic Co-operation Agreement (Marshall Aid)
15 Oct 25	Locarno Pact	4 Apr 49	North Atlantic Treaty Organisation (Nato)
27 Aug 28	General Pact for the Renunciation of War (Briand-Kellogg)	5 May 49	Council of Europe
		4 Nov 50	Convention for the protection of Human Rights and Fundamental Freedoms
22 Apr 30	London Naval Treaty		
18 Jun 35	Anglo-German Naval Agreement	28 Nov 50	Colombo Plan (South and South-East Asia)
25 Mar 36	London Naval Treaty	8 Sep 51	Treaty of Peace with Japan
20 Jul 36	Montreux Agreement (Straits)	30 Dec 53	European Organisation for Nuclear Research established
7 Aug 36	Non-Intervention Agreement (Spain)		
26 Aug 36	Anglo-Egyptian Treaty	20 Jul 54	Geneva Conventions on Indo-China
29 Sep 38	Munich Agreement	8 Sep 54	South-East Asia Defence Treaty (Seato)
31 Mar 39	Franco-British Guarantee to Poland	3 Oct 54	London Nine Power Agreement (European security and integration)

[1] See also the section on the *Commonwealth* (pp. 357-64).

[2] The *International Labour Organisation* (I.L.O.) was created by the Treaty of Versailles, as a semi-autonomous organisation associated with the League of Nations. On 16 Dec 20 a statute was drawn up for the establishment of the *Permanent Court of International Justice* at the Hague. The Hague Court held its preliminary session on 30 Jan 22. It was dissolved by resolution of the League Assembly in Apr 1946.

[3] The Charter made provision for the continuance of the International Court of Justice at the Hague. The I.L.O. continued to function as one of the specialised agencies of the United Nations. (Among the other subsidiary organisations were F.A.O., U.N.E.S.C.O., W.H.O., I.M.F., etc. See *The Statesman's Year-Book, 1973-74*, pp. 10-23, for a brief summary of the organisations and their member countries.)

23 Oct 54 Western European Union (formerly Brussels Treaty Organisation)

21 Dec 54 European Coal and Steel Community (Britain made an agreement of association). Community formed on 18 Apr 51

4 Apr 55 Special agreement whereby Britain joined the Baghdad Pact (defence). (Pact signed 24 Feb 55)

15 May 55 Austrian State Treaty (occupation ended and declaration of neutrality)

29 Jul 57 International Atomic Energy Agency

4 Feb 59 European Atomic Energy Community (Euratom). Britain made an agreement of association. (Euratom formed 1 Jan 58)

21 Aug 59 Central Treaty Organisation (Cento). Formerly the the Baghdad Pact

20 Nov 59 European Free Trade Association

31 May 60 Antarctic Treaty

14 Dec 60 Organisation for Economic Co-operation and Development (formerly Organisation for European Economic Co-operation)

29 Mar 62 European Organisation for the Development and Construction of Space Vehicle Launchers

30 Sep 62 Convention on the High Seas

5 Aug 63 Test-ban Treaty

30 Aug 63 European Space Research Organisation

27 Jan 67 Outer Space Treaty

1 Jul 68 Nuclear Non-Proliferation Treaty

11 Feb 71 Treaty on prohibition of weapons of mass destruction on sea-bed

3 Sep 71 Quadripartite Agreement on Berlin

22 Jan 72 Treaty of Accession to European Economic Community and European Atomic Energy Community

League of Nations, 1919–1946

Britain was a founder member of the League of Nations. Between 1919 and 1922 the British Government conducted its relations with the League through its cabinet secretariat. After 1922 the Foreign Office was responsible for British representation at the League. A member of the Government was generally deputed to act as British representative at meetings of the League. No permanent national delegation stayed at Geneva. A. Eden was the only Minister appointed officially for League of Nations Affairs (7 Jun–22 Dec 35). Vt Cranborne was Parliamentary Under-Secretary at the Foreign Office with special responsibility for League of Nations Affairs from 6 Aug 35 until 20 Feb 38. The League was formally dissolved in 1946; although in practice it ceased to meet during the war.

United Nations, 1946–

Britain was one of the original signatories of the Charter of the United Nations. Since 1946 the British Government has had a permanent representative at the United Nations in New York. In addition, a Minister of State at the Foreign Office has usually been given special responsibility for United Nations affairs. From 1964 to 1970 the permanent representative was a Minister of State at the Foreign Office.

British Ambassadors to Leading Powers, 1900–

Austria-Hungary (–1914)

1896 Sir H. Rumbold
9 Sep 00 Sir F. Plunkett
7 May 05 Sir W. Goschen
1 Nov 08 Sir F. Cartwright
1 Nov 13 Sir M. de Bunsen

12 *Aug* 14 *War declared by G.B. on Austria-Hungary*

France

1896 Sir E. Monson
1 Jan 05 Sir F. Bertie (Ld)

19 Apr 18 E of Derby
27 Nov 20 Ld Hardinge of Penshurst
31 Dec 22 M of Crewe
30 Jul 28 Sir W. Tyrrell (Ld)

17 Apr 34	Sir G. Clerk	1 May 39	Sir P. Loraine	1 Mar 25	Sir R. Lindsay	
24 Apr 37	Sir E. Phipps	11 *Jun* 40	*War declared by*		*(Ambassador)*	
1 Nov 39	Sir R. Campbell		*Italy on G.B.*	12 Nov 26	Sir G. Clerk	
24 *Jun* 40	*Diplomatic mission*	5 Apr 44	Sir N. Charles	16 Dec 33	Sir P. Loraine	
	withdrawn		*(1944, High Com-*	25 Feb 39	Sir H. Knatch-	
23 Oct 44	A. Duff Cooper		*missioner; 1945,*		bull-Hugessen	
9 Jan 48	Sir O. Harvey		*Representative*	29 Sep 44	Sir M. Peterson	
13 Apr 54	Sir G. Jebb		*of H.M. Gov-*	10 May 46	Sir D. Kelly	
11 Apr 60	Sir P. Dixon		*ernment with the*	20 Apr 49	Sir N. Charles	
11 Feb 65	Sir P. Reilly		*personal rank of*	6 Dec 51	Sir K. Helm	
17 Sep 68	(Sir) C. Soames		*Ambassador)*	13 Jan 54	Sir J. Bowker	
13 Nov 72	Sir E. Tomkins	9 Oct 47	Sir V. Mallet	15 Nov 58	Sir B. Burrows	
		12 Nov 53	Sir A. Clarke	7 Mar 63	Sir W. Allen	
		19 Sep 62	Sir J. Ward	16 Mar 67	Sir R. Allen	

Germany

		17 Dec 66	Sir E. Shuck-	8 Feb 73	Sir H. Phillips
1895	Sir F. Lascelles		burgh		
1 Nov 08	Sir W. Goschen	16 Sep 69	Sir P. Hancock		

U.S.A.

4 *Aug* 14	*War declared by*			1893	Sir J. Pauncefote
	G.B. on Ger-		**Russia**		(Ld)
	many	1898	Sir C. Scott	4 Jun 02	(Sir) M. Herbert
10 Jan 20	Ld Kilmarnock	28 Apr 04	Sir C. Hardinge	23 Oct 03	Sir M. Durand
	(ch. d'aff.)		(Ld)	3 Feb 07	J. Bryce
29 Jun 20	Ld D'Abernon	10 Feb 06	Sir A. Nicolson	19 Apr 13	Sir A. Spring-
12 Oct 26	Sir R. Lindsay	23 Nov 10	Sir G. Buchanan		Rice
1 Aug 28	Sir H. Rumbold	1917	*Diplomatic mission*	1 Jan 18	E of Reading
2 Aug 33	Sir E. Phipps		*withdrawn*	25 Mar 20	Sir A. Geddes
29 Apr 37	Sir N. Henderson	1 Feb 24	Sir R. Hodgson	2 Feb 24	Sir E. Howard
3 *Sep* 39	*War declared by*		*(ch. d'aff.)*	11 Mar 30	Sir R. Lindsay
	G.B. on Ger-	.3 *Jun* 27	*Suspension of dip-*	29 Aug 39	M of Lothian
	many		*lomatic relations*	24 Jan 41	Vt Halifax (E of)
		7 Dec 29	Sir E. Ovey	23 May 46	Ld Inverchapel
	(Military Governors)	24 Oct 33	Vt Chilston	22 May 48	Sir O. Franks
1945	Sir B. Montgomery	19 Jan 39	Sir W. Seeds	31 Dec 52	Sir R. Makins
1946	Sir S. Douglas	12 Jun 40	Sir S. Cripps	2 Nov 56	Sir H. Caccia
1947	Sir B. Robertson	4 Feb 42	Sir A. Kerr	18 Oct 61	Sir W. Ormsby-
			(Ld Inverchapel)		Gore (Ld Har-
	(British High Commissioners)	17 May 46	Sir M. Peterson		lech)
1949	Sir B. Robertson	22 Jun 49	Sir D. Kelly	6 Apr 65	Sir P. Dean
1950	Sir I. Kirkpatrick	18 Oct 51	Sir A. Gascoigne	21 Feb 69	J. Freeman
1953	Sir. F. Hoyer Millar	1 Oct 53	Sir W. Hayter	4 Jan 71	E of Cromer
		19 Feb 57	Sir P. Reilly	3 Mar 74	Sir P. Rams-
	(Ambassadors to	29 Apr 60	Sir F. Roberts		botham
	West Germany)	27 Nov 62	Sir H. Trevelyan		
5 May 55	Sir F. Hoyer	27 Aug 65	Sir G. Harrison		**North Atlantic Council**
	Millar	3 Oct 68	Sir D. Wilson	1953	Sir C. Steel
7 Feb 57	Sir C. Steel	9 Sep 71	Sir J. Killick	1957	Sir F. Roberts
15 Feb 63	Sir F. Roberts	13 Nov 73	Sir T. Garvey	1960	Sir P. Mason
15 May 68	Sir R. Jackling			1963	Sir E. Shuckburgh
25 Jul 72	Sir N. Hender-		**Turkey**	1966	Sir B. Burrows
	son	1898	Sir N. O'Conor	1970	Sir E. Peck

Italy

		1 Apr 08	Sir G. Barclay		**The United Nations**
1898	Sir P. Currie (Ld)		*(Min. plen. ad. int.)*	1946	Sir A. Cadogan
17 Jan 03	Sir F. Bertie	1 Jul 08	Sir G. Lowther	1950	Sir G. Jebb
1 Jan 05	Sir E. Egerton	10 Oct 13	Sir L. Mallet	1954	Sir P. Dixon
1 Dec 08	Sir J. Rennell	5 *Nov* 14	*War declared by*	1960	Sir P. Dean
	Rodd		*G.B. on Turkey*	1964	Ld Caradon
21 Oct 19	Sir G. Buchanan	1 Nov 20	Sir H. Rumbold	1970	Sir C. Crowe
25 Nov 21	Sir R. Graham	2 Feb 24	(Sir) R. Lindsay	1973	Sir D. Maitland
26 Oct 33	Sir E. Drummond		*(H.M. Represen-*	1974	I. Richard
	(E of Perth)		*tative)*		

SOURCES.—*United Nations Yearbooks, 1946–. Foreign Office List 1953–66. Diplomatic Service List 1967–.*

Britain and Europe

A Chronology of Events

7 May 48   Churchill's speech at Hague Congress leads to formation of European Movement

5 May 49   Council of Europe established at Strasbourg

9 May 50   Schuman Plan launched leading to establishment of Coal and Steel Community
30 Aug 54   Final abandonment of Pleven Plan for European Defence Community
2 Jun 55   Messina meeting at which Economic Community negotiations begin (British observer withdraws Nov 55)
25 Mar 57   Treaty of Rome signed by the Six establishes E.E.C. and Euratom
20 Nov 59   EFTA established following failure to agree with E.E.C. on free-trade area
31 Jul 61   Conservative Government initiates negotiations to join E.E.C.
14 Jan 62   E.E.C. agrees Common Agricultural Policy
14 Jan 63   General de Gaulle vetoes British entry
2 May 67   Labour Government announces intention to apply following winter exploratory talks
27 Nov 67   General de Gaulle gives second veto
1 Dec 69   Hague E.E.C. summit agrees in principle to open negotiations for British entry
8 Jun 70   E.E.C. invites Britain to apply and negotiations start on 30 Jun.
7 Jul 71   White Paper (Cmnd 4715) sets out agreement reached on almost all major points
28 Oct 71   Parliament endorses (by 356 to 244) decision in principle to join on the terms negotiated
22 Jan 72   Treaty of Accession signed
17 Oct 72   Royal Assent to European Communities Act
1 Jan 73   Britain becomes member of E.E.C. and Euratom
1 Apr 74   'Renegotiation' of British membership opened at Brussels
11 Mar 75   'Renegotiation' concluded at Dublin meeting of E.E.C. Heads of Government.
9 Apr 75   Parliament endorses (by 396 to 170) 'renegotiation'

British Members of European Commission		*Cabinet Ministers with special EEC responsibilities*		
1 Jan 73	Sir C. Soames	19 Sep 1957–14 Oct 1959	R. Maudling
1 Jan 73	G. Thomson	27 Jul 1960–20 Oct 1963	E. Heath
		7 Jan 1967–29 Aug 1967	G. Thomson
		19 Jun 1970–25 Jul 1970	A. Barber
		28 Jul 1970– 5 Nov 1972	G. Rippon
		5 Nov 1972– 4 Mar 1974	J. Davies

British Ambassadors to the European Communities

17 Jul 60   Sir A. Tandy
18 Apr 63   Sir C. O'Neill
7 Apr 65   Sir J. Marjoribanks
30 May 71   *post vacant*
1 Jan 73   (Sir) M. Palliser

European Parliament. After 1 Jan 73 the European Parliament had 198 members. Britain was entitled to send 36, but in the absence of Labour representation sent only 22 in 1973–4. The first leader of the U.K. delegation was P. Kirk.

SOURCES.—Among the major works on international relations since 1900 are: A. J. P. Taylor, *Struggle for Mastery in Europe, 1848–1918* (1954); C. R. M. F. Cruttwell, *A History of the Great War, 1914–18* (1936); C. B. Falls, *The First World War* (1960); G. M. Gathorne-Hardy, *A Short History of International Affairs, 1920–39* (1950); E. H. Carr, *International Relations between the Two World Wars* (1947); E. H. Carr, *Twenty Years' Crisis* (1947); G. F. Hudson, *Far East in World Politics* (1939); W. M. Jordan, *Great Britain, France and the German Problem, 1919–39* (1943); F. S. Northedge, *British Foreign Policy: The Process of Readjustment, 1945–1961* (1962); A. J. P. Taylor, *Origins of the Second World War* (1961); J. W. Wheeler-Bennett, *Munich: Prologue to Tragedy* (1948); A. Wolfers, *Britain and France between the two Wars* (1940); Sir L. Woodward, *British Foreign Policy in the Second World War* (1962); W. McNeill, *America, Britain and Russia. Their Co-operation and Conflict 1941–46* (1953); F. S. Northedge, *The Troubled Giant, Britain among the Great Powers 1916–1939* (1967).

Among the main works on Britain and the international organisations are: F. P. Walters, *History of the League of Nations* (2 vols, 1951); G. L. Goodwin, *Britain and the United Nations* (1957); and A. H. Robertson, *European Institutions* (1966).

The Royal Institute of International Affairs has published the *Survey of International Affairs* annually since 1920. The main British documents of the period are edited by G. P. Gooch and H. Temperley, *British Documents on the Origin of the War* (11 vols, 1927–39), and edited by R. Butler and Sir E. L. Woodward (later J. P. T. Bury), *Documents on British Foreign Policy, 1919–39* (three series, still in course of publication).

Since 1915 the texts of major public documents have been printed in the *Annual Register*. For reference only, see *The Statesman's Year-Book*, and the *Year Book of International Organisations, 1951–*.

On Britain and Europe see: M. Camps, *Britain and the European Communities 1955–63* (1964); U. W. Kitzinger, *The Second Try* (1968); U. W. Kitzinger, *Diplomacy and Persuasion* (1973); C. Cosgrove, *A Reader's Guide to Britain and the European Communities* (1970).

XIX

ARMED FORCES

Service Chiefs

Royal Navy
Chief of Naval Staff

1899	Ld W. Kerr
1904	Sir J. Fisher (Ld)
1910	Sir A. Wilson
1911	Sir F. Bridgeman
1912	Prince Louis of Battenberg

First Sea Lord

1914	Ld Fisher
1915	Sir H. Jackson
1916	Sir J. Jellicoe
1917	Sir R. Wemyss
1919	Earl Beatty
1927	Sir C. Madden
1930	Sir F. Field
1933	Sir E. Chatfield (Ld)
1938	Sir R. Backhouse
1939	Sir D. Pound
1943	Sir A. Cunningham (Ld)
1946	Sir J. Cunningham
1948	Ld Fraser of North Cape
1951	Sir R. McGrigor
1955	Earl Mountbatten
1959	Sir C. Lambe
1960	Sir C. John
1964	Sir D. Luce
1966	Sir V. Begg
1968	Sir H. Le Fanu
1970	Sir P. Hill-Norton
1971	Sir M. Pollock
1974	Sir E. Ashmore

Army
Commander in Chief

1895	Vt Wolseley
1900	Ld Roberts (Earl)

Chief of Imperial General Staff

1904	Sir N. Lyttelton
1908	Sir W. Nicholson
1912	Sir J. French
1914	Sir C. Douglas
1914	Sir J. Wolfe-Murray
1915	Sir W. Robertson
1918	Sir H. Wilson
1922	E of Cavan
1926	Sir G. Milne
1933	Sir A. Montgomery Massingberd
1936	Sir C. Deverell
1937	Vt Gort
1939	Sir E. Ironside
1940	Sir J. Dill
1941	Sir A. Brooke (Ld Alanbrooke)
1946	Vt Montgomery
1948	Sir W. Slim
1952	Sir J. Harding
1955	Sir G. Templer
1958	Sir F. Festing
1963-4	Sir R. Hull

Chief of General Staff

1964	Sir R. Hull
1965	Sir J. Cassels
1968	Sir G. Baker

1971	Sir M. Carver
1973	Sir P. Hunt

Royal Air Force
Chief of Air Staff

1918	Sir H. Trenchard
1918	Sir F. Sykes
1919	Sir H. Trenchard
1930	Sir J. Salmond
1933	Sir G. Salmond
1933	Sir E. Ellington
1937	Sir C. Newall
1940	Sir C. Portal
1946	Sir A. Tedder (Ld)
1950	Sir J. Slessor
1953	Sir W. Dickson
1956	Sir D. Boyle
1960	Sir T. Pike
1964	Sir C. Elworthy
1968	Sir J. Grandy
1971	Sir D. Spotswood
1973	Sir A. Humphrey

Defence Staff
Chief of Defence Staff

1964	Earl Mountbatten
1965	Sir R. Hull
1967	Sir C. Elworthy
1971	Sir P. Hill-Norton
1973	Sir M. Carver

Defence Organisation

Committee of Imperial Defence, 1904–1946

The committee was first established in 1902 on a temporary basis to advise the Prime Minister, as a result of British experience in the Boer War of the need for planning and co-ordination of the Empire's defence forces. The C.I.D. was established permanently in 1904, as a small flexible advisory committee to the Prime Minister. Members were usually cabinet ministers concerned with defence, military leaders, and key civil servants. The Dominions also had representatives sitting on the committee occasionally. The Prime Minister was the chairman of the committee, which had no executive power, but exercised considerable influence. A secretariat was set up to assist the C.I.D., which was later adopted by the cabinet itself. During the first world war the C.I.D. was suspended. Its functions between 1914 and 1919 were taken over by the War Council (Nov 1914), the Dardanelles Committee (May 1915), the War Committee (Nov 1916), and finally the War Cabinet (Dec 1916–Nov 1919). The C.I.D. resumed plenary sessions in 1922. In the 'thirties the membership of the C.I.D. rose from about 11 to 18, and the committee became unwieldy. This led to the establishment of a Minister for the Co-ordination of Defence (1936–40), who was without a department, but worked through the Committee Secretariat. On the outbreak of the Second World War the C.I.D. was again suspended, and its responsibilities taken over by the War Cabinet. In 1946 the decision to make the suspension permanent was published in a White Paper on the C.I.D. (Cmd. 6923).

Secretaries to the C.I.D. 1904-1946

1904	G. Clarke	1912	(Sir) M. Hankey [1]
1907	Sir C. Ottley	1938	H. Ismay

Ministry of Defence. The C.I.D. was replaced by a cabinet defence committee, with executive power, and the Ministry of Defence was set up as a regular department on 1 Jan 47. It existed as an administrative body, responsible for liaison between the Service Ministries and co-ordination of defence policy until 31 Mar 64.

On 1 Apr 64 the complete reorganisation of the three Service Departments (Admiralty, War Office and Air Ministry) under the Secretary of State for Defence took place. A Defence Council was also established under the Secretary of State to exercise the powers of command and administrative control previously exercised by the separate Service councils, which became subordinate to it. Further reorganisation on 6 Jan 67 reduced the status of the administrative heads of the three Services from Ministers to Under-Secretaries of State, while creating two new posts: Minister of Defence (Administration) and Minister of Defence (Equipment). In June 1970 further reorganisation of these two posts later reduced them to that of a single Minister of State for Defence. The present membership of the Defence Council consists of the Secretary of State for Defence, the Minister of State for Defence, the three Service Under-Secretaries of State, the Chiefs of Defence, Naval, General and Air Staffs, the Chief of Personnel and Logistics, the Chief Scientific Adviser, the Chief Executive of the Procurement Executive and the Permanent Under-Secretary of State.

SOURCES.—F. A. Johnson, *Defence by Committee* (1960); D. N. Chester and F. M. G. Willson, *The Organisation of British Central Government* (1957); J. Ehrman, *Cabinet Government and War, 1890–1940* (1958). *Whitaker's Almanack 1965.*

[1] Sir M. Hankey (later Ld Hankey) became the Joint Secretary to the C.I.D. and the cabinet in 1916, and in 1923 he was also appointed Clerk to the Privy Council.

Total Forces Serving [a] (year ending 31 March)
(to nearest '000)

	1900	1910	1920	1930	1940 [b]	1950 [b]	1960	1970
Army	661	522	435	333	1,688	360	252	174
Royal Navy [d]	98	128	133	97	282	135	93	86
Royal Air Force	..	..	28	33	303	193	158	113
Total Forces	759 [c]	650	596	463	2,273 [e]	688	503	373

[a] Men locally enlisted abroad are excluded, except that the figures for the army include those whose documents are held in the U.K.
[b] Including Women's Auxiliaries. The figures for the war years include a number of casualties that had not been reported on the dates to which the figures relate. They also include men and women locally enlisted abroad.
[c] Including 278,000 non-regulars.
[d] Excluding the Royal Marine Police, except in 1940.
[e] The total strength of the Armed Forces reached its war-time peak in 1945 with 5,098,100 men and women serving.

Total Expenditure on Defence [a] (year ending 31 March)
(£ millions)

	1899–1900	1909–10	1919–20	1929–30	1939–40	1949–50	1959–60	1969–70
War Office	43·6	27·2	395·0	40·5	81·9	291·8	428·2	n.a.
Navy	26·0	35·8	156·5	55·8	69·4	186·8	364·6	n.a.
Air Force	..	..	52·5	16·8	66·6	201·6	485·1	n.a.
Defence Total [b]	69·8	63·0	604·0	113·1	626·4 [c]	740·7	1,475·7	2,266·0

[a] The figures refer to the Exchequer of the U.K. and include Northern Ireland only to the extent that services, taxes, etc., are reserved to the U.K. Parliament.
[b] The discrepancies between the service votes and the totals are due to the expenditures of the Ministries of Defence and Civil Aviation (1950 and 1960), and the Army Ordnance Factories.
[c] Including votes of credit of £408·5 m. Defence expenditure reached its war-time peak in 1944–5 at £5,125·0 m.

SOURCES.—*The Annual Abstract of Statistics, 1900–*; for a brief summary of the statistics. The *Army, Navy* and *Air Estimates* giving the full figures, are published annually as government white papers up to 31 Mar 64. From 1 Apr 64 figures are those given in Ministry of Defence Estimates.

Conscription

After a long controversy about conscription, H. Asquith announced the introduction of the first *Military Service Bill* on 5 Jan 16. Military service lapsed in 1919. It was first introduced in peace time on 26 Apr 39. The period of compulsory service was to have been six months, but war intervened. Conscription was extended to women from Dec 1941 until Jan 1947, but few women were called up after Nov 1944. The *National Service Act, 1947* provided for the continuation of military service after the war. The period of service was twelve months. It was increased to eighteen months in Dec 1948, and to two years in Sep 1950. A government white paper published on 5 Apr 57 [1] announced a progressive reduction in the national service intake. No men were to be called up after the end of 1960, so that by the end of 1962 there were no national servicemen left in the forces. (This was slightly modified by the *Army Reserves Bill*, introduced in 1962.)

[1] Cmnd. 124/1957

Rationing

The first national rationing scheme in this country came into operation on 31 Dec 17, with the rationing of sugar. This was followed in Jul 1918 by national schemes for meat, lard, bacon, ham, butter and margarine. The abolition of rationing began on 28 Jul 18 and was completed on 29 Nov 20. Butter and meat rations were most severely restricted in Apr–May 1918 and sugar in 1919. There was much controversy during the course of World War I over the form that rationing should take. National rationing was preceded by local schemes and even after Jul 1918 rationing was, in many cases, wider in extent locally than nationally. The characteristic feature of the World War I scheme was the tie to the retailer of each customer.

When World War II broke out in Sep 1939, prearranged plans for commodity control were at once put into effect. Rationing was introduced on 8 Jan 40 when bacon, butter, and sugar were put under control and extended during the following two years to meat, tea, margarine, lard, jam, marmalade, cheese, eggs, and milk. In Dec 1941 the 'points' system was introduced to ration such items as tinned meat and biscuits and from Jul 1942 sweets and chocolate were rationed under a system of 'personal points'. During the war animal feedstuffs, fertilisers, farm machinery, petrol, domestic coal, clothing and textiles were also rationed. Rationing was at its most stringent, however, in the immediate post-war years. In Jul 46, bread rationing, which in 1939 the Minister of Food had described as 'the last resort of a starving nation', was introduced for the first time ever and this was followed in Nov 1947 by the rationing of potatoes. In Dec 1947 the distribution of nearly all important foods was controlled with the exception of some fresh fruit and vegetables, fish and coffee; the bacon, butter, meat and fats rations were at their lowest ebbs and the basic petrol ration had been suspended altogether. The gradual abolition of rationing began in Apr 1948; it was not completed until the abolition of meat and butter rationing in Jul 1956, and of coal rationing in 1958.

During the Suez crisis of 1956, petrol rationing was re-introduced. It lasted from 17 Dec 56 to 14 May 57.

Principal Military Operations

Boer War, 1899–1902

Following the rejection by the British Government of the Boer ultimatum, the Transvaal and Orange Free State declared war on Britain in October 1899. Major operations against the Boers ended in the summer of 1900, but guerrilla warfare continued. Peace was finally concluded at Vereeniging on 31 May 02.

First World War, 1914–1918

Britain declared war on Germany on 4 Aug 14, when German troops invaded Belgium and on Austria-Hungary on 10 Aug 14. Turkey joined the Central Powers in Nov 1914, and Bulgaria in May 1915. On 30 Oct 18 an armistice was agreed between the Allied Powers and the Ottoman

Government. On 3 Nov 18 there was an armistice with Austria-Hungary, and on 11 Nov 18 with the German Government. The Treaty of Versailles was signed on 28 Jun 19.

Intervention in Russia, 1918–1919

British troops landed at Murmansk and Archangel in June and August of 1918. Troops also entered the Transcaucasus in August 1918. The withdrawal of troops from the Transcaucasus was completed by 5 Apr 19; and from Murmansk and Archangel by 28 Sep 19.

Second World War, 1939–1945

Britain declared war on Germany on 3 Sep 39, following the German invasion of Poland. On 10 Jun 40 Italy declared war on Britain. In 1941 Bulgaria, Finland, Hungary, and Roumania joined the Axis powers. Britain declared war on Japan on 8 Dec 41. The declaration of the defeat of Germany was made on 8 May 45. On 14 Aug 45 the Japanese surrendered and the war in the Far East was officially ended. (The first atom bomb was dropped by the Americans on Hiroshima on 6 Aug 45, and the second on Nagasaki on 9 Aug 45.)

Korean War, 1950–1953

Britain declared her support for the United States' action in Korea on 28 Jun 50, following the invasion of South Korea by North Korean troops, and the call for a cease fire by an emergency session of the United Nations Security Council. The intervention of Chinese troops fighting with the North Koreans was confirmed on 6 Nov 50. An armistice was signed between the United Nations and the Communist forces on 27 Jul 53.

Suez, 1956

Following the Egyptian nationalisation of the Suez Canal on 26 Jul 56, tension grew in the Middle East. The Israeli army attacked the Egyptians on 29 Oct 56 in the Sinai peninsula. The rejection of a British and French ultimatum by Egypt resulted in a combined British and French attack on Egypt on 1 Nov 56. Operations were halted at midnight on 6-7 Nov 56. On 26 Jan 61 full diplomatic relations were resumed between Britain and Egypt.

Northern Ireland, 1969–

On 14 Aug 69 the Government of Northern Ireland informed the U.K. Government that as a result of the severe rioting in Londonderry it had no alternative but to ask for the assistance of the troops at present stationed in Northern Ireland to prevent a breakdown in law and order. British troops moved into Londonderry that day, and into Belfast on 15 Aug 69. On 19 Aug 69 G.O.C. Northern Ireland assumed overall responsibility for security in the Province. The normal garrison of 2,500 troops in Northern Ireland had increased to 8,820 by Jul 70 and reached a peak of 21,500 in Aug 72. By mid-Feb 75 it had been reduced to 14,000.

British Costs and Casualties in the Major Wars

War	Total Engaged ('ooos)	Killed [b] ('ooos)	Percentage, Col. 3 to Col. 2	Cost (£m.)
1899–1902 Boer War	448	22	4·9	217
1914–18 World War I	9,669 [c]	947 [c]	9·8	3,810
1939–45 World War II	5,896 [d]	265 [d]	4·5	34,423

[a] These figures, particularly for World War I, are open to dispute.
[b] Including those dying of wounds, of disease, and while prisoners of war.
[c] Empire figures.   [d] Great Britain

British casualties in the Korean war were 749 killed.[1] Casualties in the Suez attack were 21 men killed.[2] In Northern Ireland between 1969 and 10 Feb 1975, 233 U.K. regular soldiers were killed, together with 46 members of the Ulster Defence Regiment. The total expenditure incurred on the Korean War by Britain was about £50 m.[3] The military expenditure incurred by the Suez operation was about £30 m.[4] Expenditure on the security forces in Northern Ireland between Aug 69 and Mar 74 was £84 m. (estimate for financial year 1973–4: £28 m.).

Major War Commanders

World War I

Allenby, E. 1st Vt (1919). 1861–1936
     Field-Marshal. C-in-C Egyptian Expeditionary Force 1917–19.

Beatty, D. 1st E (1919). 1871–1936
     Admiral of the Fleet. Commanded Grand Fleet 1916–19.

Fisher, J. 1st Ld (1909). 1841–1920
     Admiral of the Fleet. 1st Sea Lord 1914–15.

French, J. 1st E of Ypres. 1852–1925
     Field-Marshal. C-in-C British Expeditionary Force in France 1914–15. C-in-C Home Forces 1916.

Haig, J. 1st E (1919). 1861–1928
     Field-Marshal. Commanding 1st Army 1914–15. C-in-C Expeditionary Forces in France and Flanders 1915–19.

Hamilton, I. Sir (1915). 1853–1947
     General. C-in-C Mediterranean Expeditionary Force 1915.

Jellicoe, J. 1st E (1925). 1859–1935
     Admiral of the Fleet. Commanded Grand Fleet 1914–16.

Plumer, H. 1st Vt (1929). 1857–1932
     Field-Marshal. General Officer Commanding Italian Expeditionary Force 1917–18. 2nd Army British Expeditionary Force 1918–19.

Robertson, W. Sir. 1st Bt (1919). 1860–1933
     Field-Marshal. Chief of Imperial General Staff 1915–18. C-in-C Eastern Command 1918. Great Britain 1918–19. B.A.O.R. 1919–20.

[1] H.C. Deb., 1952–53, Vol. 518, Cols. *221-222*
[2] H.C. Deb., 1956–57, Vol. 561, Col *36.*
[3] H.C. Deb., 1952–53, Vol. 517, Col. *1218.*
[4] H.C. Deb., 1956–57, Vol. 575, Col. *51.*

Trenchard, H. 1st Vt (1936). 1873–1956
Marshal of the RAF. Assistant Commandant Central Flying School 1913–14. G.O.C. Royal Flying Corps in the Field 1915–17. Chief of Air Staff 1918–29.

Wilson, H. Sir. 1st Bt (1919). 1864–1922
Field-Marshal. Assistant Chief of General Staff to Ld French 1914. Commanded 1st Army Corps 1915–16. Eastern Command 1917. British Military Representative Versailles 1917.

World War II

Alexander, H. 1st E (1952). 1891–1969
Field-Marshal. C-in-C Middle East 1942–43. C-in-C North Africa 1943. C-in-C Allied Armies in Italy 1943–44. Supreme Allied Commander Mediterranean Theatre 1944–45.

Auchinleck, C. Sir. 1884–
Field-Marshal. C-in-C India 1941 and 1943–47. C-in-C Middle East 1941–42.

Brooke-Popham, H. Sir. 1878–1953
Air Chief Marshal. C-in-C Far East 1940–41.

Cunningham, A. 1st Vt of Hindhope (1946). 1883–1962.
Admiral of the Fleet. Ld Commissioner of the Admiralty and Deputy Chief of Naval Staff 1938–39. C-in-C Mediterranean 1939–42. Naval C-in-C Expeditionary Force North Africa 1942. C-in-C Mediterranean 1943. 1st Sea Ld and Chief of Naval Staff 1943–46.

Dill, J. Sir. 1881–1944
Field-Marshal. Commanded 1st Corps in France 1939–40. Chief of I.G.S. 1940. British Representative on Combined Chief of Staffs' Committee in U.S. 1941.

Douglas, W. 1st Ld (1948). 1893–1969
Marshal of the RAF. C-in-C Fighter Command 1940–43. Air Officer C-in-C Middle East 1943–44. Air Officer C-in-C Coastal Command 1944–45. Air C-in-C British Air Forces of Occupation in Germany 1945–46.

Dowding, H. 1st Ld (1943) 1882–1970
Air Chief Marshal. Air Officer C-in-C Fighter Command 1936–1940.

Fraser, B. 1st Ld (1946). 1888–
C-in-C Home Fleet 1943–44. C-in-C Eastern Fleet 1944–45.

Gort, J. 6th Vt Ireland (1902). 1st Vt UK (1945) 1886–1946
Field-Marshal. C-in-C British Expeditionary Force 1939–40. Commanded B.E.F. in withdrawal towards Dunkirk 1940.

Harris, A. Sir. 1st Bt (1953). 1893–
Marshal of the RAF. C-in-C Bomber Command 1942–45.

Ironside, W. 1st Ld (1941). 1880–1959
Field-Marshal. C.I.G.S. 1939–40. C-in-C Home Forces 1940.

Leigh-Mallory, T. Sir. 1892–1944
　　Air Chief Marshal. Air Officer C-in-C Fighter Command 1942.
　　Air C-in-C Allied Expeditionary Force 1943–44. Lost while flying to
　　take up appointment as Allied Air C-in-C South-East Asia.

Montgomery, B. 1st Vt of Alamein (1946). 1887–
　　Field-Marshal. Commander 8th Army 1942 in N. Africa, Sicily
　　and Italy. C-in-C British Group of Allied Armies N. France
　　1944. British Commander Allied Expeditionary Forces in Europe
　　1944–46.

Mountbatten, L. 1st E of Burma (1947). 1900–
　　Admiral of the Fleet. Chief of Combined Operations 1942–43.
　　Supreme Allied Command S.E. Asia 1943–46.

Percival, A. 1887–1966
　　Lieutenant-General. G.O.C. Malaya 1941–42.

Portal C. 1st Vt (1946) 1893–1971
　　Marshal of the RAF. Air Officer C-in-C Bomber Command 1940.
　　Chief of the Air Staff 1940–45.

Pound, D. Sir. 1877–1943
　　Admiral of the Fleet. C-in-C Mediterranean 1936–39.

Ramsay, B. Sir. 1883–1945
　　Admiral. Flag Officer commanding Dover 1939–42. Naval Com-
　　mander Eastern Task Force Mediterranean 1943.

Ritchie, N. Sir. 1897–
　　General. Commander of 8th Army, Libya, 1941.

Slim, W. 1st Vt (1960) 1891–1970
　　Field-Marshal. C-in-C Allied Land Forces S.E. Asia 1945–46.

Tedder, A. 1st Ld (1946). 1890–1967
　　Marshal of the RAF. Air Officer C-in-C Middle East 1941–43. Air
　　C-in-C Mediterranean Air Command 1943. Deputy Supreme Com-
　　mander under Gen. Eisenhower 1943–45.

Wavell, A. 1st E (1947). 1883–1950
　　Field-Marshal. Formed Middle East Command 1939. C-in-C India
　　1941. Supreme Commander S.W. Pacific 1941–43.

XX

THE PRESS[1]

National Daily Newspapers

(British Gazette), 5–13 May 1926
  Proprietors: His Majesty's Stationery Office. Printed at offices of *Morning Post*.
    Policy: Strong opposition to the general strike.
    Editor: W. Churchill.

(Daily Chronicle), 1869–1930
  Proprietors: E. Lloyd, 1871–1918. Frank Lloyd and family trading as United Newspapers Ltd. Lloyd family parted with their interest in 1918. Bought by D. Lloyd George and associates 1918. Sold to Sir T. Catto and Sir D. Yule, 1926. Bought by Inveresk Paper Co., 1928. Sold and incorporated with *Daily News* as the *News Chronicle*, 1930.
    Incorporated with *Daily News* as the *News Chronicle*, 1930.
    Policy: Liberal.
    Editors: W. Fisher, 1899. R. Donald, 1902. E. Perris, 1918–30.

(Daily Citizen), 1912–Jan 1915
  Proprietors: Labour Newspapers Ltd.
    Policy: Official Labour.
    Editor: F. Dilnot, 1912–15.

Daily Express, 1900
  Proprietors: A. Pearson, Daily Express (1900) Ltd. Acquired by London Express Newspaper Ltd., 1915. Ld Beaverbrook assumed control in 1916. In 1954 he relinquished it to Beaverbrook Newspaper Ltd. and transferred controlling shares to the Beaverbrook Foundations.
    Policy: Independent conservative.
    Editors: A. Pearson, 1900. R. Blumenfeld, 1902. B. Baxter, 1929. A. Christiansen, 1933. E. Pickering, 1957. R. Wood, 1962. R. Edwards, 1964. D. Marks, 1965. I. MacColl, 1971. A. Burnet, 1974.

(Daily Graphic), 1890–1926. 1946–52
  Proprietors: Founded by W. L. Thomas. Owned by H. Baines & Co. Amalgamated with *Daily Sketch* in 1926 (Kemsley Newspapers). Appeared as *Daily Sketch and Daily Graphic* 1926–46, as *Daily Graphic* 1946–52, then as *Daily Sketch*.

---

[1] The policies of national newspapers between 1900 and 1974 have inevitably fluctuated. 'Policy should here be taken only as a general indication of the nature of the paper. In very few cases have newspapers been the official organs of a political party.

Policy: Independent conservative.

Editors: H. Hall, 1891. H. White, 1907. W. Ackland, 1909. A. Hutchinson, 1912. A. Netting, 1917. H. Lawton, 1919. E. Tebbutt, 1923. H. Heywood, 1925–6. A. Thornton, 1946. N. Hamilton, 1947. H. Clapp, 1948–52 (see *Daily Sketch*).

(Daily Herald), 1912–1964

Proprietors: Daily Herald Printing and Publishing Society in association with Odhams Press Ltd. Formed Daily Herald (1929) Ltd. (Chairman: Ld Southwood). 49 per cent of shares held by T.U.C., 51 per cent by Odhams Press. 1960 new agreement between Odhams Press and T.U.C. 1961 Daily Mirror Newspapers, Ltd. take over Odham's Press. T.U.C. sign agreement for the paper to be published by the Mirror Group (International Publishing Corporation). 1964 T.U.C. sold their 49% holding to I.P.C. 1964, replaced by the *Sun*.

Policy: General support to Labour Movement, 1912–23, 1960–. Official Labour 1923–60.

Editors: R. Kenny, 1912. C. Lapworth, 1913. G. Lansbury, 1913. W. Ryan, 1922. H. Fyfe, 1923. W. Mellor, 1926. W. Stevenson, 1931. F. Williams, 1937. P. Cudlipp, 1940. S. Elliott, 1953. D. Machray, 1957. J. Beavan, 1960–64.
(Issued as a weekly paper during 1st World War, launched again as a daily in 1919.)

Daily Mail, 1896

Proprietors: A. Harmsworth (Ld Northcliffe), Associated Newspapers Ltd.

Policy: Independent. Right-wing Conservative.

Editors: T. Marlowe, 1899. W. Fish, 1926. O. Pulvermacher, 1929. W. McWhirter, 1930. W. Warden, 1931. A. Cranfield, 1935. R. Prew, 1939. S. Horniblow, 1944. F. Owen, 1947. G. Schofield, 1950. A. Wareham, 1955. W. Hardcastle, 1959. M. Randall, 1963. A. Brittenden, 1966. D. English, 1971.

Daily Mirror, 1903

Proprietors: A. Harmsworth, Sir H. Harmsworth (Ld Rothermere), 1914. Pictorial Newspaper (1910) Co. Daily Mirror Newspapers Ltd. 1961, bought by International Publishing Corporation (Chairman: C. King. H. Cudlipp, 1968). Control acquired by Reed International 1970 (Chairman: (Sir) D. Ryder, 1974 A. Jarratt).

Policy: Independent.

Editors: Mary Howarth, 1903. H. Fyfe, 1904. A. Kinealy, 1907. E. Flynn, 1915. A. Campbell, 1919. L. Brownlee, 1931. C. Thomas, 1934. S. Bolam, 1948. J. Nener, 1953. L. Howard, 1960. A. Miles, 1971. M. Christiansen, 1974.

(Daily News), 1846–1930

Proprietors: Daily News Ltd., 1901 (Chairman: G. Cadbury, 1901–11). Amalgamated with *Morning Leader*, as *Daily News and Leader*, 1912. Amalgamated with *Westminster Gazette*, 1928. Amalgamated with *Daily Chronicle*, 1930. Continued as *News Chronicle* (see below).

Policy: Liberal.

Editors: E. Cook, 1896. R. Lehmann, 1901. A. Gardiner, 1902. S. Hodgson, 1920–30.

(Daily Paper), 1904 (32 issues only)
    Proprietor: W. Stead.
      Policy: 'A paper for the abnormally scrupulous'.
      Editor: W. Stead.

(Daily Sketch), 1908–1971
    Proprietors: E. Hulton and Co. Ltd. Daily Mirror Newspapers Ltd., and
    Sunday Pictorial Newspapers (1920) Ltd. Bought by the Berry
    brothers, 1926, and merged with the *Daily Graphic*. Name
    changed to *Daily Graphic*, 1946–52. Subsidiary of Allied
    Newspapers Ltd. Kemsley Newspapers Ltd. Bought by Associ-
    ated Newspapers Ltd., 1952. Renamed *Daily Sketch*, 1953.
    Merged with *Daily Mail*, 1971.
    Policy: Independent Conservative
    Editors: J. Heddle, 1909. W. Robinson, 1914. H. Lane, 1919. H. Gates,
    1922. H. Lane, 1923. A. Curthoys, 1928. A. Sinclair, 1936.
    S. Carroll, 1939. L. Berry, 1942. A. Thornton and M. Watts,
    1943. A. Thornton, 1944. N. Hamilton, 1947. H. Clapp,
    1948. H. Gunn, 1953. C. Valdar, 1959. H. French, 1962.
    D. English, 1969–71.

Daily Telegraph, 1855
    Proprietors: Ld Burnham and family. Sold to Sir W. Berry (Ld Camrose), Sir
    G. Berry (Ld Kemsley) and Sir E. Iliffe (Ld) in 1928. Absorbed
    Morning Post, as *Daily Telegraph and Morning Post* in 1937. Ld
    Camrose acquired Ld Kemsley's and Ld Iliffe's interests in 1937.
    M. Berry (Ld Hartwell) succeeded him as Editor-in-Chief in 1968.
    Policy: Conservative.
    Editors: (Sir) J. le Sage, 1885. F. Miller, 1923. A. Watson, 1924.
    (Sir) C. Coote, 1950. M. Green, 1964. W. Deedes, 1974.

(Daily Worker), 1930–1966
    Proprietors: Daily Worker Cooperative Society Ltd. Descendant of the
    Sunday Worker, 1925–30. Publication suppressed 1941–42.
    Changed name to *Morning Star*, 1966.
    Policy: Communist.
    Editors: W. Rust, 1930. J. Shields, 1932. I. Cox, 1935. R. Palme Dutt,
    1936. W. Rust, 1939. J. Campbell, 1949. G. Matthews, 1959–
    1966.

(Financial News), 1884–1945
    Proprietors: Financial News Ltd, 1898 (H. Marks). Incorporated with the
    Financial Times in 1945.
    Policy: Finance, independent.
    Editors: H. Marks, 1884. Dr Ellis, 1916. H. O'Neill, 1921. W. Dorman
    and W. Lang, 1921. Sir L. Worthington-Evans, 1924. Sir E.
    Young, 1925. O. Hobson, 1929. M. Green, 1934. H. Parkin-
    son, 1938–45.

Financial Times, 1888
    Proprietors: Financial Times Ltd. Incorporated *Financier and Bullionist*.
    Incorporated the *Financial News* in 1945. Merged with West-
    minster Press Ltd. as Financial and Provincial Publishers, Ltd.
    1967.
    Policy: Finance, independent.
    Editors: W. Lawson. A. Murray, 1901. C. Palmer, 1909. D. Hunter,
    1924. A. Chisholm, 1938. A. Cole, 1940. H. Parkinson, 1945.
    (Sir) G. Newton, 1950. F. Fisher, 1973.

(Manchester) Guardian, 1821

Proprietors: The Manchester Guardian & Evening News Ltd. Renamed *Guardian,* 1959. The Scott Trust.

Policy: Independent liberal.

Editors: C. P. Scott, 1872. E. Scott, 1929. W. Crozier, 1932. A. Wadsworth, 1944. A. Hetherington, 1956. P. Preston 1945

(Majority), 1906 (10–14 Jul only)

Proprietors: Majority Ltd.

Policy: 'The organ of all who work for wage or salary'.

Morning Advertiser, 1794

Proprietors: Incorporated Society of Licensed Victuallers.

Policy: Defence of the interests of licensed trade.

Editors: F. Doney, 1894. H. Fyfe, 1902. G. Talbot, 1903. H. Byshe, 1913. A. Jackson, 1924. H. Bennett, 1927. F. Millman, 193?. E. Hopwood, 1947. D. Quick, 1954. L. Forse, 1956.

(Morning Herald), 1892–1900

Proprietors: Morning Newspaper Co. Became *London Morning* in 1898, and *Morning Herald* in 1899. Merged with *Daily Express* in 1900.

Policy: Independent.

Editor: D. Murray, 1892–1900.

(Morning Leader), 1892–1912

Proprietors: Colman family of Norwich. Merged with *Daily News,* as *Daily News and Leader* in 1912 (see *Daily News*).

Policy: Liberal.

Editor: E. Parke, 1892–1912.

(Morning Post), 1772–1937

Proprietors: Sir A. Borthwick (Ld Glenesk), 1876–1908. Lady Bathurst, 1908–24. Absorbed in *Daily Telegraph* in 1937 (Ld Camrose).

Policy: Conservative.

Editors: J. Dunn, 1897. S. Wilkinson, 1905. F. Ware, 1905. H. Gwynne, 1911–37.

(Morning Standard), 1857–1917

Proprietors: Bought from Johnston family by A. Pearson, 1904. Sold to D. Dalziel (Ld) in 1910. Ceased, 1917.

Policy: From 1904 supporter of tariff reform.

Editors: W. Mudford, 1874. G. Curtis, 1900. H. Gwynne, 1904. H. White, 1911–17.

Morning Star, 1966

Proprietors: Morning Star Co-operative Society. Successor to the *Daily Worker.*

Policy: Communist.

Editor: G. Matthews, 1966. T. Chater, 1974.

(New Daily), 1960–66

Proprietors: The British Newspaper Trust Ltd. Sponsored by the People's League for the Defence of Freedom, the Free Press Society, and the Anti-Socialist Front.

Policy: 'The only daily newspaper in Great Britain independent of combines and trade unions.'

Editor: E. Martell, 1960–66.

(News Chronicle), 1930–60

Proprietors: Amalgamation of *Daily News and Leader* and *Daily Chronicle* in 1930 (Cadbury family). Bought by Associated Newspapers Ltd. in 1960, and merged with *Daily Mail*.

Policy: Liberal.

Editors: T. Clarke, 1930. A. Vallance, 1933. G. Barry, 1936. R. Cruikshank, 1948. M. Curtis, 1954. N. Cursley, 1957.

(Recorder), 27 Oct 1953–17 May 1954

Proprietors: The Recorder Ltd. (Managing Director: E. Martell). A weekly suburban newspaper 1870–1939, continued as a weekly after 1954.

Policy: Independent. 'Keynote: pride in Britain and the British Empire.'

Editor: W. Brittain, 1953–4.

Sun, 1964

Proprietors: International Publishing Corporation (Chairman: C. King. H. Cudlipp, 1968). 1969 News International Ltd (R. Murdoch).

Policy: Labour. Independent since 1969.

Editors: S. Jacobson, 1964. R. Dinsdale, 1965. A. Lamb, 1969. B. Shrimsley, 1972.

The Times, 1785

Proprietors: Founded as the *Daily Universal Register*, became *The Times* in 1788. Owned by the Walter family, 1785–1908. Bought by Ld Northcliffe in 1908. Owned by J. Astor and J. Walter in 1922. 7 Aug 24, Times Association formed (comprising Lord Chief Justice, Warden of All Souls, Oxford, President of the Royal Society, President of the Institute of Chartered Accountants and Governor of the Bank of England). 21 Dec 66, Monopolies Commission approves common ownership of *The Times* and *The Sunday Times* by The Thomson Organisation. Times Newspapers Ltd. formed. President: G. Astor. Chairman: Sir W. Haley. 1967 K. Thomson.

Policy: Independent conservative.

Editors: G. Buckle, 1884. G. Dawson, 1912. H. Steed, 1919. G. Dawson, 1922. R. Barrington-Ward, 1941. W. Casey, 1948. Sir W. Haley, 1952. W. Rees-Mogg, 1967.

(Tribune), 1906–1908

Proprietors: F. Thomasson.

Policy: Liberal.

Editors: W. Hill and S. Pryor, 1906.

(Westminster Gazette), 1921–8 issued as a morning paper.
(See *Evening Papers*).

National Sunday Newspapers
(excluding all those not published in London)

((Illustrated) Sunday Herald), 1915–27

Proprietors: Sir E. Hulton. Renamed *Illustrated Sunday Herald*. Bought by Berry family in 1926 and renamed *Sunday Graphic* in 1927 (see below).

Policy: Independent conservative.

Editors: J. E. Williams. T. Hill, 1926–7.

(National News), 1917–18
Proprietors: Odhams Press Ltd.
  Policy: Independent.
  Editor: A. de Beck, 1917–18.

News of the World, 1843
Proprietors: News of the World Ltd. (Sir) G. Riddell (Ld), 1903–34. The Carr family 1934–69. 1969 News International Ltd. (R. Murdoch).
  Policy: Independent conservative.
  Editors: Sir E. Carr, 1891. D. Davies, 1941. R. Skelton, 1946. A. Waters, 1947. R. Cudlipp, 1953. S. Somerfield, 1959. C. Lear, 1970.

The Observer, 1791
Proprietors: F. Beer. Bought by Ld Northcliffe in 1905. Bought by W. Astor (Vt) in 1911.
  Policy: Conservative. Independent since 1942.
  Editors: F. Beer, 1894. A. Harrison, 1905. J. Garvin, 1908. I. Brown, 1942. D. Astor, 1948.

People, 1881 (since 1972 **Sunday People**)
Proprietors: W. Madge and Sir G. Armstrong. Sir W. Madge, 1914–22. M. L. Publishing Co. Ltd. The People Ltd. Odhams Press. 1961 amalgamated with International Publishing Corporation (Chairman: C. King. H. Cudlipp, 1968. A. Jarratt, 1972.
  Policy: Independent.
  Editors: J. Hatton. J. Sansome 1913. H. Swaffer 1924. H. Ainsworth 1925. S. Campbell, 1958. R. Edwards, 1966. G. Pinnington, 1972.

(Reynolds News), 1850–1967
Proprietors: Originally *Reynolds's Weekly Newspaper,* and later *Reynolds's Illustrated News.* Owned by J. Dicks and family since 1879. H. Dalziel (Ld) [1] appointed business manager in 1907. He became the sole proprietor in 1914. Bought by the National Co-operative Press Ltd. Incorporated the *Sunday Citizen.* 1962. Changed name to *Sunday Citizen and Reynolds News.*
  Policy: Support for the Labour and Co-operative movements.
  Editors: W. Thompson, 1894. H. Dalziel, 1907. J. Crawley, 1920. S. Elliott, 1929. (Sir) W. Richardson, 1941–67

(Sunday Citizen), 1962–67. (*See above, Reynolds News.*)

(Sunday Dispatch), 1801–1961
Proprietors: Sir G. Newnes. Originally the *Weekly Dispatch* until 1928. Bought by the Harmsworth family. Ld Northcliffe, Ld Rothermere from 1928. Associated Newspapers Ltd. Absorbed by the *Sunday Express* in 1961.
  Policy: Independent conservative.
  Editors: M. Cotton. H. Swaffer, 1915. B. Falk, 1919. H. Lane, 1933. W. Brittain, 1934. C. Brooks, 1936. C. Eade, 1938. H. Gunn, 1959–61.

---

[1] Ld Dalziel of Kirkcaldy, not to be confused with Ld Dalziel of Wooler, who was proprietor of the *Evening Standard* 1910–15.

Sunday Express, 1918
Proprietors: Sunday Express Ltd.   (Ld Beaverbrook; since 1954 Beaverbrook
            Newspapers Ltd.)
  Policy: Independent conservative.
 Editors: J. Douglas, 1920.   J. Gordon, 1928.   J. Junor, 1954.

(Sunday Graphic (and Sunday News)), 1915–60
Proprietors: Sir E. Hulton.   Originally called the *Sunday Herald*, renamed the
            Illustrated Sunday Herald.   Bought by the Berry family in
            1926, and renamed the *Sunday Graphic* in 1927.   Daily Graphic
            and Sunday Graphic Ltd., a subsidiary of Ld Kemsley's news-
            papers.   Incorporated the *Sunday News* in 1931.   Bought by
            R. Thomson in 1959.   Ceased publication in 1960.
  Policy: Independent.
 Editors: T. Hill, 1927.   A. Sinclair, 1931.   R. Simpson, 1935.   M. Watts,
            1947.   N. Hamilton, 1947.   I. Lang, 1948.   A. Josey, 1949.
            B. Horniblow, 1950.   P. Brownrigg, 1952.   M. Randell, 1953.
            G. McKenzie, 1953.   A. Hall, 1958.   R. Anderson, 1959.   A.
            Ewart, 1960.

(Sunday Illustrated), 1921–23
Proprietor: H. Bottomley.
  Policy: Independent.
  Editor: H. Bottomley.

(Sunday (Illustrated) News), 1842–1931
Proprietors: Originally *Lloyd's Sunday News*.   Sunday News Ltd.   United
            Newspapers Ltd (W. Harrison).   Merged with the *Sunday
            Graphic* in 1931.
  Policy: Independent liberal.
 Editors: T. Catling.   W. Robinson, 1919.   E. Perris, 1924.   E. Wallace,
            1929–31.

Sunday Mirror, 1963
Proprietors: International Publishing Corporation.
  Policy: Independent.
  Editor: M. Christiansen, 1963.   R. Edwards, 1972.

(Sunday Pictorial), 1915–1963
Proprietors: The Harmsworth family.   Taken over by Ld Rothermere in
            1922.   Sunday Pictorial Newspapers (1920) Ltd.   1961 absorbed
            by International Publishing Corporation (Cecil King).   1963.
            Became *Sunday Mirror* (*see above*).
  Policy: Independent.
 Editors: F. Sanderson, 1915.   W. McWhirter, 1921.   D. Grant, 1924.   W.
            McWhirter, 1928.   D. Grant, 1929.   H. Cudlipp, 1938.   R.
            Campbell, 1940.   H. Cudlipp, 1946.   P. Zec, 1949.   H. Cudlipp,
            1952.   C. Valdar, 1953.   L. Howard, 1959.   R. Payne, 1960.

((Sunday) Referee), 1877–1939
Proprietors: Printed by the Daily News Ltd.   Owned by I. Ostrer.   Incor-
            porated in the *Sunday Chronicle* in 1939 (which was published in
            Manchester and ceased independent publication in 1955).
  Policy: Conservative.
 Editors: R. Butler.   (Sir) R. Donald, 1922.   A. Laber, 1924.   M. Joulden,
            1933.

(Sunday Special), 1897–1904
Proprietor: H. Schmidt.

Sunday Telegraph, 1961
Proprietors: The Sunday Telegraph Ltd (M. Berry (Ld Hartwell)).
Policy: Independent conservative.
Editor: D. McLachlan, 1961. B. Roberts, 1966.

Sunday Times, 1822
Proprietors: Mrs. F. Beer. Bought by H. Schmidt. Amalgamated with the *Sunday Special* in 1904. Bought by the Berry family in 1915. Bought by R. Thomson in 1959. Thomson Allied Newspapers. 1967, Times Newspapers Ltd, formed to run *The Times* and *Sunday Times.*
Policy: Independent conservative.
Editors: L. Rees, 1901. W. Hadley, 1932. H. Hodson, 1950. C. D. Hamilton, 1961. H. Evans, 1967.

(Sunday Worker), 1925–30
Proprietors: The Communist Party through nominees. Published daily as the *Daily Worker* from 1930.
Policy: Communist.
Editors: W. Paul, 1925. W. Holmes, 1927.

London Evening Newspapers

(Evening Echo and Chronicle), 22 Mar–4 May 1915
Proprietor: E. Lloyd. Merged with *Star.*
Policy: Liberal

(Echo), 1868–1905
Proprietors: Consolidated Newspapers. F. Pethick-Lawrence in control, 1901–5.
Policy: Radical, progressive.
Editors: W. Crook, 1898. T. Meech, 1900. P. Alden, 1901. F. Pethick-Lawrence, 1901–5.

Evening News, 1881
Proprietors: A. Harmsworth (Evening News Ltd.), 1894. Associated Newspapers Ltd., 1905.
Policy: Conservative.
Editors: W. Evans, 1896. C. Beattie, 1922. F. Fitzhugh, 1924. G. Schofield, 1943. J. Marshall, 1950. R. Willis, 1954. J. Gold, 1967. D. Boddie, 1973.

Evening Standard, 1827
Proprietors: Bought by A. Pearson from Johnston family in 1904. Absorbed *St James's Gazette* in 1905. D. Dalziel (Ld),[1] 1910. Hulton and Co. 1915–23. Incorporated with *Pall Mall Gazette* and *Globe,* 1923. Bought by Ld Beaverbrook in 1923. Since 1954 controlled by Beaverbrook Newspapers Ltd.
Policy: Independent conservative.
Editors: S. Pryor, 1897. W. Woodward, 1906. J. Kilpatrick, 1912. D. Sutherland, 1914. A. Mann, 1916. D. Phillips, 1920. E. Thompson, 1923. G. Gilliat, 1928. P. Cudlipp, 1933.

---

[1] Ld Dalziel of Wooler, not to be confused with Ld Dalziel of Kirkcaldy who was proprietor of *Reynolds' News,* 1914–29.

R. Thompson, 1938. F. Owen, 1939. M. Foot, 1942. S. Elliott, 1943. H. Gunn, 1944. P. Elland, 1950. C. Wintour, 1959.

(Evening Times), 1910–11
Proprietors: London Evening Newspaper Co. (J. Morrison, Sir S. Scott, J. Cowley).
Policy: Conservative.
Editors: C. Watney, E. Wallace.

(Globe), 1803–1921
Proprietors: (Sir) G. Armstrong, 1871–1907. H. Harmsworth, 1907–11. W. Madge, 1912–14. Absorbed by *Pall Mall Gazette* in 1921, incorporated with *Evening Standard* in 1923.
Policy: Conservative.
Editors: Sir G. Armstrong, 1895. P. Ogle, 1907. J. Harrison, 1908 C. Palmer, 1912. W. Peacock, 1915–21.

(Pall Mall Gazette), 1865–1923
Proprietors: W. Astor (Ld), 1892. Sir H. Dalziel, 1917. Sir J. Leigh, 1923. Incorporated with *Evening Standard* in 1923.
Policy: Conservative.
Editors: Sir D. Straight, 1896. F. Higginbottom, 1909. J. Garvin, 1912. D. Sutherland, 1915–23.

(St James's Gazette), 1880–1905
Proprietors: E. Steinkopff, 1888. W. Dallas Ross. A. Pearson, 1903. Amalgamated with *Evening Standard* in 1905.
Policy: Conservative.
Editors: H. Chisholm, 1897. R. McNeill, 1900. G. Fiennes, 1903. S. Pryor, 1904–5.

(Star), 1887–1960
Proprietors: Star Newspaper Co. Owned by Daily News Ltd. Bought by Associated Newspapers Ltd, and incorporated in *Evening News*, 1960.
Policy: Liberal.
Editors: E. Parke, 1891. J. Douglas, 1908. W. Pope, 1920. E. Chattaway, 1930. R. Cruikshank, 1936. A. Cranfield, 1941. R. McCarthy, 1957–60.

(Sun), 1893–1906
Proprietors: T. P. O'Connor. H. Bottomley, 1900. Sir G. Armstrong and W. Madge, 1904–6.
Policy: Literary, non-political.
Editors: T. P. O'Connor. T. Dahle.

(Westminster Gazette), 1893–1928
Proprietors: Sir G. Newnes, 1893. Liberal Syndicate (Chairman: Sir A. Mond), 1908–15. A. Pearson, 1915–28. Last issue as evening paper 5 Nov 21. First issue as morning paper 7 Nov 21. Incorporated with *Daily News* in 1928.
Policy: Liberal.
Editors: J. Spender, 1896. J. Hobman, 1921–28.

Partisan Tendencies and Circulations of National Daily Newspapers in British General Elections, 1945–74

Newspaper	Circulation in thousands; Party support								
	1945	1950	1951	1955	1959	1964	1966	1970	Feb 1974
Daily Express	3,300 Con.	4,099 Con.	4,169 Con.	4,036 Con.	4,053 Con.	4,190 Con.	3,987 Con.	3,670 Con.	3,990 Con.
Daily Herald/Sun[a]	1,850 Lab.	2,030 Lab.	2,003 Lab.	1,759 Lab.	1,465 Lab.	1,300 ?* Lab.	1,274 Lab.	1,509 Lab.	2,966 Con.
Daily Mail	1,704 Con.	2,215 Con.	2,267 Con.	2,068 Con.	2,071 Con.	2,400 Con.	2,464 Con.	1,938 Con.	1,730 Con.
Daily Mirror	2,400 Lab.	4,603 Lab.	4,514 Lab.	4,725 Lab.	4,497 Lab.	5,085 Lab.	5,019 Lab.	4,850 Lab.	4,291 Lab.
Daily Sketch/ Daily Graphic[b]	896 Con.	777 Con.	794 Con.	950 Con.	1,156 Con.	847 Con.	844 Con.	839 Con.	—
Daily Telegraph	813 Con.	984 Con.	998 Con.	1,055 Con.	1,181 Con.	1,324 Con.	1,337 Con.	1,391 Con.	1,419 Con.
(Manchester) Guardian[c]	83 Lib.	141 Lib.	139 Lib./Con.	156 Lib./Con.	183 Lab./Lib.	278 Lab.	270 Lab./Lib.	297 Lab./Lib.	346 not clear
News Chronicle[d]	1,549 Lib.	1,525 Lib.	1,507 Lib.	1,253 Lib.	1,207 Lib.	—	—	—	—
The Times	204 Lab.	258 Con.	232 Con.	222 Con.	254 Con.	255 Con.	254 ?/Lib.	414 Con./Lib.	345 Con.

Total circulation	12,799	16,632	16,623	16,224	16,067	15,679	15,449	14,908	12,657
Total Conservative circulation	6,713 (52%)	8,333 (50%)	8,599† (52%)	8,487† (52%)	8,715 (54%)	9,016 (57%)	8,632 (56%)	8,252† (55%)	8,020 (64%)
Total Conservative vote	9,578 (40%)	12,503 (43%)	13,718 (48%)	13,312 (50%)	13,750 (49%)	12,001 (43%)	11,418 (43%)	13,145 (46%)	10,459 (36%)
Total Labour circulation	4,454 (35%)	6,633 (40%)	6,517 (39%)	6,484 (40%)	6,145† (38%)	6,663 (42%)	6,563† (43%)	6,656† (44%)	4,291 (34%)
Total Labour vote	11,633 (48%)	13,267 (46%)	13,949 (49%)	12,405 (46%)	12,216 (44%)	12,206 (44%)	13,065 (48%)	12,178 (43%)	11,458 (39%)
Total Liberal circulation	1,632 (13%)	1,666 (10%)	1,646† (10%)	1,409† (9%)	1,390† (9%)	—	524† (3%)	711† (5%)	—
Total Liberal vote	2,197 (9%)	2,622 (9%)	731 (2%)	722 (3%)	1,639 (6%)	3,093 (11%)	2,327 (8%)	2,117 (7%)	5,348 (18%)

a Name changed to *Sun* in 1964.
b Named *Daily Graphic*, 1946–52.
c 'Manchester' dropped from title in 1959.
d Ceased publication in 1960.
* Figure uncertain due to relaunching at that time.
† Includes paper(s) with divided support.

SOURCE of circulation figures: 1945, 1950: Nuffield election studies; thereafter, Audit Bureau of Circulation, excepting *Daily Telegraph* figures for 1951, 1955, 1959 (London Press Exchange).
The *Daily Worker*, the Communist daily paper, which changed its name to the *Morning Star* in 1966, is omitted: comparable circulation figures are not available. The number of Communist candidates at general elections was as often as not under fifty.
SOURCE.—C. Seymour-Ure, *The Political Impact of mass media* (1974).

National Newspapers Printing in more than one City

	London	Manchester	Glasgow
Daily Chronicle	1869–1930	1925–1930[1]	—
Daily Express	1900–	1927–	1928–1974
Daily Herald (Sun)	1912–	1930–1969	
Daily Mail	1896–	1900–	1946–1966[2]
Daily Mirror[3]	1903–	1955–	
Daily Sketch (Graphic)	1911–1971	1908–1953	—
Daily Telegraph	1855–	1940–	—
Daily News	1846–1930	{1921–1924	—
		{1929–1930	
News Chronicle	1930–1960	1930–1960	—
(Manchester) Guardian	1961–	1821–	
News of the World	1843–	1941–	—
Sunday Dispatch	1801–1961	1930–1961	
Sunday Express	1918–	1927–	1927–1974
Sunday Graphic	1915–1960[4]	1932–1952	—
(Sunday) People	1881–	1930–	—
Sunday Times	1822–	1940–1964	—
Sunday Chronicle	1939–1955	1885–1955	—

[1] The *Daily Chronicle* was printed in Leeds, not Manchester, 1925–1930.
[2] The *Scottish Daily Mail* was printed in Edinburgh, not Glasgow, 1946–66.
[3] The *Daily Mirror* was also printed in Belfast, 1966–1971.
[4] The Manchester printing of the *Sunday Graphic* was suspended from 1936–1950.

Circulations of National Newspapers, 1910–

National Daily Newspapers
(to nearest '000)

	1910	1930	1939	1951	1960	1965	1972
D. Express	400	1,603	2,486	4,193	4,130	3,981	3,341
D. Herald/Sun	..	750[b]	2,000	2,071	1,467	1,274	2,599
D. Mail	900	1,968	1,510	2,245	2,084	2,464	1,702
D. Mirror[h]	630	1,071	1,367[d]	4,567	4,545	4,957[i]	4,279
D. News	320	900	..	..	..	..	..
D. Sketch	750[a]	1,013	850[d]	777	1,152	844	..
D. Telegraph	230	222[c]	640[d]	976[e]	1,155[e]	1,351	1,434
D. Worker/							
M. Star	..	n.a.	100[d]	115	73[f]	..	..
Guardian	40	47	51	140	190	270	339
M. Leader	250	..	..	..	..	..	..
M. Post	n.a.	119	..	..	..	..	..
N. Chronicle[g]	800[a]	967	1,317	1,583	1,206	..	..
Times	45	187	213	254	255	258	340

Unless otherwise stated the figures are taken from *T. B. Browne's Advertiser's ABC*, 1910–40, and 1950–72 figures are from the Audit Bureau of Circulations, published in the *Newspaper Press Directory*.

[a] Circulation figure for 1915, *T. B. Browne*.
[b] P.E.P.: *Report on the British Press* (1938) gives 1082 for 1930.
[c] From the P.E.P. *Report*.
[d] From the P.E.P. *Report*. Figure for 1938.
[e] *Daily Telegraph* audited circulation figures.
[f] ABC circulation in 1956. Latest available figure.
[g] 1910 and 1930 figures are for *Daily Chronicles*.
[h] This does not include circulation of *Daily Record* (Glasgow), acquired by the *Daily Mirror* in 1955.
[i] For a period in 1964 the *Daily Mirror* became the only daily newspaper ever to top 5m. circulation.

National Sunday Newspapers
(to nearest '000)

	1900	1910	1930	1937	1951	1960	1965	1972
Lloyd's Weekly Newspaper	1,250	1,250	1,450 [b]	..	..	..	..	..
News of the World	400	1,500	3,250 [b]	3,850	8,407	6,664	6,176	5,995
Observer	60	n.a.	201	208	450	738	829	794
People	n.a.	n.a.	2,535	3,406	5,181	5,468	5,538	4,540
Reynolds News	2,000 [a]	2,000 [a]	420	426	712	329	236	..
Sunday Dispatch	n.a.	n.a.	1,197	741	2,631	1,520	..	..
Sunday Express	..	..	958	1,350	3,178	3,706	4,187	4,041
Sunday Graphic	..	..	1,100 [b]	651	1,121	890	..	..
Sunday Mirror	..	..	..	..	..	..	5,022	4,497
Sunday Pictorial	..	..	1,883	1,345	5,170	5,461	..	..
Sunday Referee	n.a.	n.a.	73	342	..	..	..	..
Sunday Telegraph	..	..	..	..	..	..	662	767
Sunday Times	n.a.	n.a.	153	270	529	1,001	1,290	1,456

Unless otherwise stated, the figures are taken from *T. B. Browne's Advertiser's ABC*, 1900–30; the figures for 1937 are from the *Report of the Royal Commission on the Press, 1947–49* (Cmd. 7700 and 7690/ 1949); 1951–72 are the Audit Bureau of Circulations' figures quoted in the *Newspaper Press Directory*.

[a] These figures should be treated with caution. They are from an advertisement in *T. B. Browne's Advertiser's ABC* for 1901 and 1911.
[b] From *Sell's World Press*.

London Evening Newspapers
(to nearest '000)

	1905	1910	1930	1939	1951	1960	1965	1972
E. News	300	300	667	822	1,752	1,153	1,238	854
E. Standard	n.a.	160	n.a.	390	862	586	680	494
Star	250	327	744	503	1,228	744	..	..

All circulation figures for evening newspapers exclude Sporting Editions. 1905–39 figures from *T. B. Browne's Advertiser's ABC*; 1951–65 figures are from the Audit Bureau of Circulations, published in the *Newspaper Press Directory*. Information on the circulations of other evening papers is not available.

Provincial Morning Daily Newspapers 1900–

Sporting newspapers and publications such as the *Hull Shipping Gazette* and the Hartlepool *Daily Shipping List* have been omitted. Bold type indicates newspapers still being published on 1 Jan 75.

BATH—*Bath Daily Argus* (1870). Merged with local evening paper, *Bath Daily Chronicle*, in Jan 1900.
BEDFORD—*Bedford Daily Circular* (1903). Merged with *Bedford Record* July 1939.
BIRMINGHAM—*Daily Argus* (1891). Merged with local evening paper, *Birmingham Evening Dispatch*, Jan 1902.
  Birmingham Daily Post (1857). Changed name to *Birmingham Post* May 1918. Became **Birmingham Post and Gazette** Nov. 1956.
  Birmingham Daily Gazette (1862). Merged with *Midland Express* and changed name to *Birmingham Gazette and Express* 1904. Merged with *Birmingham Post* Nov 1956.
BRADFORD—*Bradford Observer* (1834). Changed name to *Yorkshire Daily Observer* Nov 1901. Changed name to *Yorkshire Observer* Jan 1909. Merged with local evening paper, *The Telegraph and Argus*, Nov 1956.

BRIGHTON—*Morning Argus* (1896).   Ceased publication as morning paper May 1926.[1]
Sussex Daily News (1868).   Merged with *Evening Argus* Mar 1956.
BRISTOL—*Bristol Western Daily Press* (1858).   Changed name to **Western Daily Press** 1928.
Bristol Mercury (1790).   Changed name to *Bristol Daily Mercury* Dec 1901. Ceased publication Nov 1909.
Bristol Times and Mirror (1713).   Merged with *Western Daily Press* 1932.
CROYDON—*Surrey Morning Echo* (1908).   Ceased publication Jan 1910.
DARLINGTON—*North Star* (1881).   Merged with *Newcastle Daily Journal* 1926.
Northern Echo (1870).
EXETER—*Devon and Exeter Daily Gazette* (1772).   Merged with *Western Morning News* Mar 1932.
Western Times (1827).   Became weekly paper 1922.
HUDDERSFIELD—*Huddersfield Daily Chronicle* (1871).[2]   Ceased publication Dec 1915.
HULL—*Daily Mail* (1787).   Became an evening paper 1902.
Eastern Morning News (1864).   Ceased publication Nov 1929.
IPSWICH—**East Anglian Daily Times** (1874).
LEAMINGTON—*Leamington, Warwick, Kenilworth and District Morning News* (1896).   Originally *Leamington, Warwick, Kenilworth and District Daily Circular*.   Changed name and started morning publication in 1919.
LEEDS—*Leeds Mercury* (1718).   Changed name to *Leeds and Yorkshire Mercury* Oct 1901–Nov 1907.   Merged with *Yorkshire Post* Nov 1939.
Yorkshire Post (1754).
LEICESTER—*Leicester Daily Post* (1872).   Ceased publication Mar 1921.
LIVERPOOL—*Liverpool Courier* (1808).   Changed name to *Liverpool Daily Courier* Sep 1922.   Changed name to *Daily Courier* Oct 1922.   Ceased publication Dec 1929.
Liverpool Mercury (1811).   Merged with *Liverpool Daily Post* Nov 1904.
Liverpool Daily Post (1855).
Journal of Commerce (1861).
MANCHESTER—*Manchester Courier* (1825).   Ceased publication Jan 1916.
Daily Dispatch (1900).   Merged with *News Chronicle* Nov 1955.
(Manchester) Guardian (1821).   (*See under National Daily Newspapers.*)
Manchester Journal of Commerce.   Ceased publication 1911.
Telegraphic News.   Ceased publication 1901.
Daily Citizen (1912).   Ceased publication June 1915.
Daily Sketch (1909).   Ceased publication Apr 1911.
NEWCASTLE—*Illustrated Chronicle* (1910).   Ceased publication June 1925.
Newcastle Daily Chronicle (1858).   Merged with *North Mail* Mar 1923.
Newcastle Daily Journal (1832).   Became *Newcastle Journal and North Mail* Sep 1939.   Changed name to **Journal** Jul 1958.
North Mail (1901).   Incorporated *Newcastle Daily Chronicle* Mar 1923 and became *North Mail and Newcastle Daily Chronicle*.   Merged with *Newcastle Journal* in Sep 1939.
Newcastle Morning Mail (1898).   Changed name to *Morning Mail* Feb 1901. Ceased publication Aug 1901.
NORWICH—**Eastern Daily Press** (1870).
Norfolk Daily Standard (1885).   Became an evening paper in 1900.
NOTTINGHAM—*Nottingham Daily Express* (1860).   Changed name to *Nottingham Journal and Express* Apr 1918.   Changed named to *Nottingham Journal* 1921.   Merged with *Nottingham Guardian* Sep 1953 to become *Nottingham Guardian Journal*.   Ceased publication Jan 1973.
Nottingham Daily Guardian (1861).   Changed name to *Nottingham Guardian* Oct 1905.   Merged with *Nottingham Journal* Sep 1953.
OXFORD—*Oxford Morning Echo* (1860).   Ceased publication Jan 1900.
PLYMOUTH—*Western Daily Mercury* (1860).   Merged with *Western Morning News* Jan 1921.
Western Morning News (1860).
PORTSMOUTH—*Southern Daily Mail* (1884).   Ceased publication 1905.

---

[1] Localised editions of the *Argus* were published at Battle, Chichester, Eastbourne, East Grinstead, Hastings, Horsham, Hove, Lewes, Littlehampton, Rye, Tunbridge Wells, and Worthing. Those still publishing in 1926 were merged with the Brighton *Morning Argus* into the *Evening Argus*.
[2] Not published on Saturdays.

SHIELDS—*Shields Morning Mail* (1889). Ceased publication Feb 1901.
SHEFFIELD—*Yorkshire Early Bird* (1899). Became morning paper in 1929. Changed name to *Early Bird* Mar 1938. Merged with local evening paper, *Chronicle Midday*, May 1950.
Sheffield Daily Telegraph (1855). Changed name to *Sheffield Telegraph* Jun 1934; to *Sheffield Telegraph and Daily Independent* Oct 38–May 39; to *Telegraph and Independent* Jun–Jul 42; to *Sheffield Telegraph* Jul 42–Sep 65; to **Sheffield Morning Telegraph** Sep 65.
Sheffield and Rotherham Independent (1819). Changed name to *Sheffield Independent* Jan 1901. Changed name to *Sheffield Daily Independent* Feb 01–Oct 09. Changed name to *Daily Independent* June 1922. Amalgamated with *Sheffield Telegraph* Oct 1938.
YORK—*Yorkshire Herald* (1790). Became weekly 1936.
CARDIFF—*South Wales Daily News* (1872). Changed name to *South Wales News* Apr 1928. Merged with *Western Mail* Aug 1928.
Western Mail (1869).
Cardiff Journal of Commerce (1904). Changed name to *Cardiff and South Wales Journal of Commerce* July 1914. Changed name to *South Wales Journal of Commerce* June 1918. Ceased publication Apr 1935.
NEWPORT—*South Wales Daily News* (1872). Changed name to *South Wales News* 1928. Merged with *Western Mail* 1928.
SWANSEA—*Swansea Gazette*. Changed name to *Swansea Daily Shipping Register* 1900. Ceased publication 1918.
ABERDEEN—*Aberdeen Daily Journal* (1746). Merged with *Aberdeen Free Press* Nov 1922 and became **Aberdeen Press and Journal.**
Aberdeen Free Press (1853). Merged with *Aberdeen Daily Journal* Nov 1922.
GLASGOW—**Glasgow Herald** (1783).
North British Daily Mail (1847). Became *Glasgow Daily Mail* 1901. Merged with *Glasgow Record* 1901.
Daily Record (1895). Incorporated *Glasgow Daily Mail* 1901 and became *Daily Record and Daily Mail*. Changed name to *Daily Record and Mail* 1902. Changed name to **Daily Record** 1954.
Bulletin (1915). Became *Bulletin and Scots Pictorial* Jan 1924. Ceased publication July 1960.
DUNDEE—*Dundee Advertiser* (1861). Merged with *Courier and Argus* 1926 and became *Dundee Advertiser and Courier*.
Courier and Argus (1861). Merged with the daily edition of *Dundee Advertiser* 1926 and became *Dundee Advertiser and Courier*.
Dundee Advertiser and Courier (1926). Changed named to *Dundee Courier and Advertiser* 1926. Changed name to **Courier and Advertiser** 1926.
EDINBURGH—**Scotsman** (1817).
BELFAST—**Belfast News-letter** (1737).
Northern Whig (1824). Changed name to *Northern Whig and Belfast Post* June 1919. Ceased publication 1963.
Irish Daily Telegraph (1904). Merged with local evening paper, *Belfast Telegraph*, Apr 1952.
Irish News and Belfast Morning News (1881).

SOURCES.—*Willing's Press Guide 1900–*; the catalogue of the British Museum Newspaper Library at Colindale.

Main Political Weeklies

Economist, The 1843
Proprietors: The Economist Newspaper Limited. (Since 1928 50% of shares held by Financial Newspaper Proprietors Limited, later Financial News Ltd.)
Policy: Independent.
Editors: E. Johnstone, 1883. F. Hurst, 1907. H. Withers, 1916. W. Layton, 1922. G. Crowther, 1938. D. Tyerman, 1956. A. Burnet, 1965. A. Knight, 1974.

Nation, 1907
Proprietors: The *Nation.* 1931 Amalgamated with the *New Statesman.*
  Policy: Independent Radical.
  Editors: H. Massingham, 1907. H. Henderson, 1923. H. Wright, 1930–1931.

New Statesman, 1913
Proprietors: Statesman Publishing Company. 1931 Amalgamated with the *Nation,* The Statesman and Nation Publishing Company.
  Policy: Independent. Radical.
  Editors: C. Sharp, 1913.   K. Martin, 1931.   J. Freeman, 1961. P. Johnson, 1965. R. Crossman, 1970. A. Howard, 1973.

The Spectator, 1828
Proprietors: The Spectator Limited since 1898. J. St. L. Strachey, 1898. (Sir) E. Wrench, 1925. I. Gilmour, 1954. H. Creighton, 1967.
  Policy: Independent conservative.
  Editors: J. St. L. Strachey, 1897. (Sir) Evelyn Wrench, 1925. W. Harris, 1932. W. Taplin, 1953. I. Gilmour, 1954. B. Inglis, 1959. I. Hamilton, 1962. I. Macleod, 1963. N. Lawson, 1966. G. Gale, 1970. H. Creighton, 1973.

Time and Tide, 1920
Proprietors: Lady Rhondda 1920–1958. L. Skevington, 1958. T. Beaumont, 1960. W. Brittain, 1962.
  Policy: Independent.
  Editors: Lady Rhondda, 1920. A. Lejeune, 1957. L. Skevington, 1958. J. Thompson, 1960. W. Brittain, 1962.

Tribune, 1937
Proprietors: Tribune Publications, Ltd.
  Policy: Left-wing.
  Editors: W. Mellor, 1937. J. Hartshorn, 1938. R. Postgate, 1940. A. Bevan, 1942. J. Kimche, 1945. M. Foot, 1948. R. Edwards, 1952. M. Foot, 1956. R. Clements, 1959.

Newspaper Readership

(percentage of population over the age of 16)

	National Dailies	National Sundays
1939	67	82
1947	73	89
1961	85	93
1972	75	87

SOURCE.—*Abstract of Information,* IPA Research Dept. (1972 National Readership Survey).

The Press Council

The General Council of the Press was formed in 1953 under the chairmanship of W. (Ld) Astor. He was succeeded in 1955 by Sir L. Andrews, and in 1959 by G. Murray. In 1963 the Council was reorganised to bring in lay members and its title was changed to the Press Council. Ld Devlin became the first independent chairman. In 1969 he was succeeded by Ld Pearce. The objects of the Council were changed on the reorganisation and now include preserving the freedom of the Press; maintaining the highest professional and commercial standards in the Press; considering complaints about the conduct of the Press or the conduct of persons and organisations towards the press; watching for restrictions on the supply of information of public interest and importance; and reporting publicly on developments tending towards greater concentration or monopoly in the Press and publishing relevant statistical material.

SOURCES.—*The Cambridge Bibliography of English Literature*, Vol. III, pp. 797-8, lists all press directories, pp. 798-846 lists newspapers and magazines. *The History of the Times*, Pt II, pp. 1130-36 gives a chart of the Metropolitan morning and evening press from 1884–1947. There are several press directories which cover all or part of the period: *T. B. Browne's Advertiser's ABC, 1900–1932*; *Sell's Dictionary of the World's Press, 1900–1921* (including a *Who's Who* of notabilities of the British Press in 1914–21 editions); *Mitchell's Newspaper Press Directory* (became *Benn's* in 1946), 1900–61; *Willing's Press Guide, 1900–1961*. PEP: *Report on the British Press* (1938); *Report of the Royal Commission on the Press* (Cmd. 7700 of 1949, Minutes of Evidence, Cmd. 7317 of 1948); *Report of the Royal Commission on the Press* (Cmnd. 1811 of 1962); N. Kaldor and R. Silverman, *A Statistical Analysis of Advertising Expenditure and of the Revenue of the Press* (1948); A. P. Wadsworth, 'Newspaper Circulations' (in *Proceedings of the Manchester Statistical Society*, 1954). J. L. Hammond, *C. P. Scott of the Manchester Guardian* (1934); J. W. Robertson Scott, *The Life and Death of a Newspaper* (*The Pall Mall Gazette*) (1952); A. Gollin, *The Observer and J. L. Garvin* (1960); F. Williams, *Dangerous Estate* (1957); C. Seymour-Ure, *Politics, the Press and the Public* (1968). Press Council Annual Reports *The Press and the People*; H. P. Levy, *The Press Council* (1967). *Hulton Readership Surveys*, J. W. Hobson and Harry Henry, came out annually between 1947 and 1955. *National Readership Surveys* were first published in 1947 by the Institute of Practitioners in Advertising and again in 1954: they have appeared bi-annually since 1957 and were taken over in 1967 by the Joint Industry Committee for National Readership Surveys (JICNARS).

XXI
BROADCASTING AUTHORITIES

The British Broadcasting Corporation

The British Broadcasting Company Ltd. was formed by some 200 manufacturers and shareholders on 18 Oct 22, registered on 15 Dec 22, and
received its licence on 18 Jan 23. A system of paid licences for owners of
radio receivers was started in 1922. London, Manchester, Birmingham, and
Newcastle stations began to operate in November and December, 1922.
This was followed by the establishment of the *British Broadcasting Corporation* under royal charter (20 Dec 26), which came into operation on 1 Jan 27.
It was to be a public service body 'acting in the national interest' and financed
by licence fees paid by all owners of radio receivers. (A formal agreement with
the Postmaster General had been drawn up on 9 Nov 26.) Under the
royal charter the B.B.C. was granted a licence for ten years and was to be
directed by a board of governors nominated by the government. The charter
was renewed and modified 1 Jan 37, 1 Jan 47, 1 Jul 52, 30 Jul 64. On 12 Mar
73 it was announced that the current charter would be extended until 1981
(see Cmnd 5244/1973).

British Broadcasting Company, 1923–1926

Chairman: Ld Gainford

Managing Director: (Sir) J. Reith
(formerly **General Manager**)

Board members:

G. Isaacs (Marconi) [1]
B. Binyon (Radio Communication Co.)
A. McKinstry (Metropolitan Vickers)
J. Gray (British Thomson-Houston Co.)

Sir W. Noble (General Electric)
H. Pease (Western Electric)
W. Burnham (Burndept)
Sir W. Bull (M.P.).

British Broadcasting Corporation, 1927–

Board of Governors

Chairmen		Vice-Chairmen	
1 Jan 27	E of Clarendon	1 Jan 27	Ld Gainford
2 Jun 30	J. Whitley	1 Jan 33	R. Norman
28 Mar 35	Vt Bridgeman	25 Oct 35	H. Brown
3 Oct 35	R. Norman	8 Jun 37	C. Millis
19 Apr 39	Sir A. Powell	1 Jan 47	Marchioness of Reading
1 Jan 47	Ld Inman	7 Jan 51	Ld Tedder
9 Jun 47	Ld Simon	1 Jul 54	Sir P. Morris
1 Aug 52	Sir A. Cadogan	1 Jul 60	Sir J. Duff
1 Dec 57	Sir A. fforde	19 Sep 65	Ld Fulton
1 Feb 64	Sir J. Duff (*acting*)	11 Jun 66	R. Lusty
14 May 64	Ld Normanbrook	31 Jul 67	Ld Fulton
1 Sep 67	Ld Hill of Luton	1 Jan 68	R. Lusty
1 Jan 73	Sir M. Swann	15 Feb 68	Ld Fulton
		12 Nov 70–	
		31 Mar 75	Lady Plowden

[1] On the death of G. Isaacs, Marconi's were represented by F. Kellaway.

Governors

1927–31	Sir G. Nairne		
1927–32	M. Rendall		*Governors appointed to*
1927–32	Mrs P. Snowden (Vtess)		*represent national interests*
1932–36	H. Brown		*N. Ireland*
1933–35	Vt Bridgeman	1952–58	Sir H. Mulholland
1933–37	Mrs M. Hamilton	1958–62	J. McKee
1935–39	Lady Bridgeman	1962–67	Sir R. Pim
1935–39	H. Fisher	1968–73	Ld Dunleath
1937–39	Sir I. Fraser	1973–	W. O'Hara
1937–39	J. Mallon		
1938–39	Miss M. Fry		
1939–41[1]			*Scotland*
1941–46	Lady V. Bonham-Carter	1952–55	Ld Clydesmuir
1941–46	Sir I. Fraser	1955–56	T. Johnston
1941–46	J. Mallon	1956–60	E of Balfour
1941–46	A. Mann	1960–65	Sir D. Milne
1941–46	H. Nicolson	1965–71	Lady Baird
1946–49	Miss B. Ward	1971–	Lady Avonside
1946–49	G. Lloyd		
1946–49	Sir R. Peck		
1946–50	E. Whitfield		*Wales*
1946–50	Marchioness of Reading	1952–60	Ld Macdonald
1947–52	J. Adamson	1960–65	Mrs R. Jones
1950–54	Ld Tedder	1965–71	G. Williams
1950–52	Ld Clydesmuir[2]	1971–	G. Hughes
1951–52	F. Williams		
1950–56	Mrs Barbara Wootton		
1952–54	Sir P. Morris		
1951–55	I. Stedeford		
1952–56	Lady Rhys Williams		
1954–59	Ld Rochdale		
1955–60	Sir E. Benthall		
1956–61	Mrs T. Cazalet-Keir		
1956–62	Dame F. Hancock		
1959–60	Sir J. Duff		
	(*Vice-Chairman* 60–65)		
1960–62	E of Halsbury		
	(*Vice-Chairman* 66–67)		
1960–65	R. Lusty		*Directors-General*
1961–66	G. Cooke		
1962–68	Dame A Godwin	1 Jan 27	Sir J. Reith
1962–67	Sir A. Clarke	1 Oct 38	F. Ogilvie
1966–67	Ld Fulton	1 Jan 42	Sir C. Graves & R.
1966–68	J. Trower		Foot
1967–73	Sir R. Murray	24 Jun 43	R. Foot
1968–71[3]	Sir R. Bellenger	31 Mar 44	(Sir) W. Haley
1968–72[3]	P. Wilson	17 Jul 52	B. Nicholls (*acting*)
1968–73[3]	T. Jackson	1 Dec 52	Sir I. Jacob
1968–71	Sir L. Constantine (Ld)	31 Dec 59	(Sir) H. Greene
1968–73	Dame M. Green	1 Apr 68	(Sir) C. Curran
1969–71	Sir H. Greene		
1971–	(Sir) R. Allan (Ld)		
1972–	R. Fuller		
1972–	T. Morgan		
1972–	G. Howard		
1973–	V. Feather (Ld)		
1973–	Ld Greenhill		
1974–	Mrs S. Clarke		

[1] 5 Sep 39, the Board was reduced to 2 members (Chairman and Vice-Chairman) by Order in Council. The Board was reconstituted to its full strength of 7 members in 1941.
[2] 1 Aug 52, appointed Governor to represent Scottish interests.
[3] In 1967 the Board's strength was increased to 12 members.

SOURCE.—*B.B.C. Handbooks*, published annually since 1928.

B.B.C. Radio

The B.B.C. originally offered only a single service, known as the National Programme. Regional broadcasting, offering a choice of programme. In

1939 the existing pattern of broadcasting was replaced by a single Home Service; the Forces Programme, providing an alternative, began in 1940. In 1945 regional broadcasting was restored, and the Light Programme replaced the Forces Programme, while in 1946 the Third Programme, providing a second alternative, was introduced. Very high frequency (V.H.F.) broadcasting began in 1955. An additional network, Radio 1, began in 1967 when the existing services were renamed Radio 2 (formerly the Light Programme), Radio 3 (formerly the Third), and Radio 4 (formerly the Home Service). In 1967 local broadcasting was launched, at first with nine stations; by 1973, 20 stations were in operation.

B.B.C. Television

On 2 Nov 1936 the first scheduled public service television was started from Alexandra Palace. The service was suspended from September 1939 until June 1946. The first stations outside London, in the Midlands and the North, began transmitting in 1949 and 1951 respectively. By 1966, with more than 100 transmitting stations, B.B.C. Television was within the range of more than 99 per cent of the population of the United Kingdom on a 405-line standard. In April 1964 a second B.B.C. Channel was opened in the London area and by 1967 it was available to more than two-thirds of the population of the U.K. It was transmitted on 625 lines. In 1969 the first channel began to be transmitted on 625 lines as well as 405, and colour transmissions were started. By 1973, 92% of the U.K. population were within range of 625-line transmissions.

| | Licences ('000s) | | | | B.B.C. expenditure on revenue account £000s | |
	Total	Sound only	Sound and Television (Mono-chrome)	Colour Television		
1925	1,654	1,654	..	..	..	
1927	2,270	2,264	..	..	902	
1930	3,092	3,076	..	..	1,224	
1935	7,012	6,970	..	..	2,473	
1940	8,951	8,898	..	..	4,350	
1945	9,710	9,663	..	..	9,001	
					Home	External
1947	10,778	10,713	15	..	7,273	3,878
1950	12,219	11,819	344	..	9,579	4,471
1955	13,980	9,414	4,504	..	17,964	5,093
1960	15,005	4,480	10,470	..	30,560	6,408
1965	16,047	2,759	13,253	..	55,642	8,499
1970	18,184	2,279	15,609	273	81,134	10,565
1973	17,563	..	11,897	5,667	112,722	14,025

The difference between the total and other licences column is explained by the issue of free licences to the blind. The 1973 licence figures are for licences in force in Apr. 74.

The expenditure figures from 1940 onwards are for the year ending the following 31 Mar. The figures from 1947 onwards are for operational expenditure only.

Broadcast Receiving Licences and B.B.C. Expenditure

Broadcasting receiving licences were first issued for 10s. a year in 1922; the price for sound-only licences was raised to £1 in 1946 and to £1 5s. in

1965; it was abolished in 1971. Licences for television were introduced in 1946 when a combined radio and television licence cost £2; this was raised to £3 in 1954, to £4 in 1957, to £5 in 1965, to £6 in 1969, to £7 in 1971, and to £8 in 1975. Since 1968 owners of colour sets had to pay a supplementary £5, raised in 1975 to £10. In 1939–45 all licence revenue went to the government and the B.B.C. was financed by an annual grant-in-aid. The external services have continued to be financed in this way. From 1957 to 1963 a £1 excise duty was levied from the television licence fee.

Independent Broadcasting

The Independent Television Authority was set up by the Postmaster-General under section 1 (3) of the *Television Act, 1954*, on 4 Aug 1954 for a period of ten years. The Authority was to licence programme contracting companies and to regulate their output. The whole of the finance of Independent Television was to depend on advertising revenue though the Act specifically prohibited the 'sponsoring' of programmes by advertisers. The first Commercial programmes were transmitted on 22 Sep 1955. The *Television Act, 1964*, which came into effect on 31 Jul 1964 increased the I.T.A.'s power over programmes and advertising, enlarged the membership of the authority from 10 to 13 and extended its life for a further ten years.

The *Sound Broadcasting Act, 1972*, extended the functions of the Authority, from 12 July 72, to include the provision of local sound broadcasting services. The *Independent Broadcasting Authority Act, 1973*, consolidated the Television Act and the Sound Broadcasting Act and gave effect to the Government's intention to extend the 1964 and 1972 Acts to 1981 (see Cmnd 5244/ 1973).

Members of the Independent Television Authority 1954–1972 and Independent Broadcasting Authority 1972–

Chairman

31 Mar 55	Sir K. Clarke
8 Nov 57	Sir I. Kirkpatrick
6 Nov 62	Sir J. Carmichael (*acting*)
1 Jul 63	Ld Hill of Luton
1 Sep 67	Ld Aylestone
1 Apr 75	Lady Plowden

Deputy Chairman

4 Aug 54	Sir C. Colston
3 Jan 55	Sir R. Matthews
22 Jun 60	Sir J. Carmichael
29 Jul 64	Sir S. Caine
1 Jul 67	Sir R. Gould
29 Jun 72	C. Bland

Director-General

1 Oct 54	Sir R. Fraser
15 Oct 70	B. Young

National Members

N. Ireland

1955–60	A. Chichester
1960–65	Sir L. O'Brien
1965–71	D. Gilliland
1971–74	H. McMullan
1974–	W. Blease

Scotland

1955–58	T. Honeyman
1958–64	T. Talbot-Rice
1964–70	W. MacFarlane Grey
1970–	T. Carbery

Wales

1955–56	Ld Aberdare
1956–63	J. Alban Davies
1964–70	Sir B. Bowen-Thomas
1970–	T. Glyn Davies

Other Members

1955–56	Ld Layton
1955–56	Miss M. Popham
1955–57	Miss D. Powell
1955–58	G. Thorneycroft
1955–59	Sir H. Hinchliffe
1956–60	Miss D. Harris
1957–60	T. Summerson

1957–61	Dame F. Farrer	1964–69	Sir V. Tewson
1958–61	W. Beard	1965–70	Mrs M. Adams
1960–60	Sir J. Carmichael	1965–71	Lady Plummer
1960–64	Sir S. Caine	1966–73	Lady Sharp
1960–65	Mrs I. Graham-Bryce	1969–73	Sir F. Hayday
1960–64	A. Cropper	1969–74	S. Keynes
1961–64	Sir T. Williamson (Ld)	1969–74	J. Meek
1961–66	Dame A. Bryan	1970–	A. Page
1964–69	Lady Burton	1971–	Lady Macleod
1964–69	Sir P. Hamilton	1973–	W. Anderson
1964–69	H. Hunt	1973–	Mrs M. Warnock
1964–69	Sir O. Saunders	1974–	J. Ring

SOURCE.—*Independant Television Authority Report and Accounts 1954–72; Independent Broadcasting Authorities Report Accounts 1972.*

Programme Contracting Companies

The following programme companies have been under contract to the Authority.

They are listed together with their original date of appointment and their major controlling interests. In 1964 all were re-appointed to provide programmes until July 1968. On 11 June 1967 new contractors were announced to operate from 30 July 1968 to 29 July 1974.[1] In 1972 the Authority made plain its intention to renew the existing contracts with the programme companies for two years from 31 July 1974, subject to satisfactory performance and subject to review of rentals and areas.

A.B.C. Television. 1956–68 (Weekends North and Midlands). Chairman, 1956: Sir P. Warter. A wholly owned subsidiary of Associated British Picture Corporation (see Thames Television).

Anglia Television. 1958 (East Anglia). Chairman, 1958: Marquess Townshend of Raynam. Significant minority interests held by the (*Manchester*) *Guardian* and Romulus and Remus Films.

A.T.V. Network. (1955–1966 Associated TeleVision) 1955. (1955–68 Midlands, Monday to Friday; London, Saturday and Sunday; 1968– Midlands, all week). Chairman, 1955: P. Littler, 1960: Sir R. Renwick (Ld). Originally Associated Broadcasting Development Co., then renamed Associated Broadcasting Co. Now wholly controlled by Associated Television Ltd., in which substantial shareholdings are in the hands of the *Daily Mirror* and IPC group, Beaverbrook Newspapers (since 1965) and (formerly) Moss Empires.

Border Television. 1961 (Carlisle). Chairman: J. Burgess. Shares widely held.

Channel Television. 1962 (Channel Islands). Chairman, 1962: Senator G. Troy, 1963: Senator W. Krichefski, 1971: E. Collas. Controlling interest (formerly) held by a subsidiary of A.B.P.C. (see A.B.C. Television).

Grampian Television. 1960 (Aberdeen). Chairman, 1960: Sir A. King, 1968: I. Tennant. Shares widely held.

---

[1] Most of the existing contractors were reappointed for the new contract period commencing 30 Jul 68, although Harlech Television replaced T.W.W., and Rediffusion and A.B.C. Television came together to form Thames Television. The 7-day companies were appointed to serve the Midlands, Lancashire and Yorkshire, while the new London Weekend Television took over Saturday and Sunday in London.

Granada Television. 1955 (North Monday to Friday); 1968 (Lancashire all week). Chairman, 1955: S. Bernstein Ltd, 1971: C. Bernstein. A wholly owned subsidiary of the Granada group.

Harlech Television. 1968 (Wales and West of England). Chairman, 1968: Ld Harlech. Shares widely held.

London Weekend Television. 1968 (London Friday 7 p.m. to Sunday). Chairman, 1968: A. Crawley, 1971: J. Freeman. Significant minority interests held by Bowater Paper Corporation, I.T.C. Pension Trust, Lombard Banking, G.E.C., Pearl Assurance, the *Daily Telegraph* and the *Observer*.

Rediffusion Television (Associated Rediffusion 1955–64). 1955–68 (London Monday to Friday). Chairman, 1955: (Sir) J. Wills. Majority interests held by British Electric Traction and Rediffusion (see Thames Television).

Scottish Television. 1956 (Central Scotland). Chairman, 1957: R. Thomson (Ld), 1969: J. Coltart. Controlling interests held by The Thomson Organisation Ltd until 1968, when I.T.A. required it to divest itself of much of its holdings.

Southern Television. 1958 (South of England). Chairman, 1958: (Sir) J. Davis. Main shareholders, the Rank Organisation, the Amalgamated Press, and Associated Newspapers. The Amalgamated Press holding passed to the *Daily Mirror* group when the latter acquired the Amalgamated Press in Nov 1958. The *Television Act, 1954*, requirement of 'adequate competition' forced the *Daily Mirror* holding to be sold to Associated Newspapers, the Rank Organisation and D. C. Thomson Ltd.

Thames Television. 1968 (London Monday to Friday 7 p.m.). Chairman, 1968: Sir P. Warter, 1969: Ld Shawcross. Shares broadly divided between A.B.P.C. and Rediffusion, with controlling share held by A.B.P.C.

T.W.W. 1958–68 (Wales and the West of England). Chairman, 1958: E of Derby. Main shareholders *News of the World, Liverpool Daily Post,* E of Derby and J. Hylton (after 1965 his executors).

Tyne-Tees Television. 1956 (North-East). Chairman, 1956: Sir R. Pease, 1963: E. Fairburn, 1968: G. Daysh, 1972: Sir G. Cox. Significant shareholdings formerly held by the *Daily News* Ltd., Black Brothers, William Baird & Co.; in 1968 by Mercantile Investment Trust.

Ulster Television. 1959 (Northern Ireland). Chairman, 1959: E of Antrim. Shares widely held.

Wales (West and North) Television. 1962–4. Chairman, 1962: H. Hayden Williams, 1963 (*acting*): C. Traherne. Shares widely held. In 1964 this company was absorbed by T.W.W.

Westward Television. 1960 (South-West). Chairman: P. Cadbury. Shares widely held.

Yorkshire Television. 1968 (Yorkshire). Chairman, 1968: Sir R. Graham. Significant minority interests held by Telefusion and *Yorkshire Post.*

Independent Television News Ltd. 1955, Editor and chief executive: A. Crawley, 1955. (Sir) G. Cox, 1956. Managing director: D. Edwards, 1968–71. Editor: N. Ryan, 1968. This is an independent non-profit making company, to provide a common news service for all the contracting companies. The appointment of the managing director and the editor must have the approval of the I.T.A. (now the I.B.A.).

Programme Contracting Companies, Radio

The first five companies to be offered local radio contracts under the *Second Broadcasting Act, 1972,* were annnounced in June 1973. These London stations began transmissions in Oct 1973. By Jan 1975 the following stations were broadcasting:

London Broadcasting Company (London News Station). Chairman: Sir C. Trinder.

Capital Radio (London General Station). Chairman: R. Attenborough.

Birmingham Broadcasting. Chairman: A Parkinson.

Greater Manchester Independent Radio (Piccadilly Radio). Chairman: N. Pearson.

Radio Clyde. Chairman: F. Chapman.

Swansea Sound. Chairman: J. Allison.

Metropolitan Broadcasting Company (Tyneside/Wearside). Chairman: Sir J. Hunter.

Radio City (Sound of Merseyside) Ltd. (Liverpool). Chairman: T. Smith.

Stations had also been approved for Edinburgh, Plymouth, Nottingham, Teesside, Bradford, Portsmouth, Wolverhampton, Ipswich, Reading and Belfast.

SOURCES.—*Sykes Committee Report on Broadcasting,* Cmd. 1951/1923; *Crawford Committee Report on Broadcasting,* Cmd. 2599/1926; *Selsdon Committee Report on Television,* Cmd. 4793/1934–35; *Ullswater Committee Report on Broadcasting,* Cmd 5091/1935–36; *Hankey Committee Report on Television* Non-Parliamentary Papers, 1945; *Government Statement on Broadcasting Policy,* Cmd. 6852/1945–46; *Beveridge Committee Report on Broadcasting,* Cmd. 8116 and 8117/1950–51; *Government Memoranda on the Report of the Broadcasting Committee, 1949,* Cmd. 8291/1950–51, and Cmd. 8550/1951–52; *Government Memorandum on Television Policy,* Cmd. 9005/1953–54; G.P.O., *1st and 2nd Reports of the Television Advisory Committee,* 1952 (1953) and 1953 (1954); *Report from the Select Committee on Broadcasting (Anticipation of Debates)* H.M.S.O. 1966; *Pilkington Committee on Broadcasting,* Cmnd. 1753/1962; *Government Memoranda on Broadcasting,* Cmnd. 1770 & 1893/1962; *Firt Report from the Committee on Broadcasting etc. of the Proceedings of Parliament* (H.M.S.O., 1966); *Government Statement on Broadcasting,* Cmnd. 3169/1966.
Annual Reports and Accounts of the B.B.C. 1927–, Annual Reports and Accounts of the I.T.A. (I.B.A.) 1954–; B.B.C. Handbook 1927–.
Sir G. Beadle, *Television: a Critical Review* (1963); A. Briggs, *The History of Broadcasting in the United Kingdom,* Vol. I: *The Birth of Broadcasting* (1961); Vol. II: *The Golden Age of Radio* (1965); *The War of Words* (1970); E. G. Wedell, *Broadcasting and Public Policy* (1968); R. H. Coase, *British Broadcasting: a Study in Monopoly* (1950); B. Paulu, *British Broadcasting* (1956); B. Paulu, *British Broadcasting in Transition* (1961); Ld Reith, *Into the Wind* (1949); Ld Simon of Wythenshawe, *The B.B.C. from Within* (1953); H. H. Wilson, *Pressure Groups: the Campaign for Commercial Television* (1961); M. Gorham, *Broadcasting Sound and Television since 1900* (1952); S. Hood, *A Survey of Television* (1967); J. Scupham, *Broadcasting and the Community* (1967).

XXII

RELIGION

Church Membership Statistics

EXTREME caution should be observed in making use of church membership statistics, as no entirely reliable sources exist giving information about membership or attendance. The last reasonably authoritative figures of religious affiliations in Britain were taken from the 1851 census, though even then there was no compulsion to answer the questions on religion. Since then no census has included questions on religious affiliation. Strictly comparable figures are impossible to obtain for church membership and church attendance between 1900 and 1975. The definition of membership varies greatly from one denomination to another, as does the minimum age for reception into the church. At one extreme, the Roman Catholic Church officially records the Roman Catholic population of all ages, regardless of church attendance. Nonconformist churches with adult baptism, and in the case of the Methodists a probationary period before baptism, are the most exclusive. These statistics give no indication how frequently 'members' of the churches attended services. Moreover even within the denominations different figures are quoted at different times and in different sources. E.g. Church of England membership can be variously defined by figures for baptised membership, those for Easter communicants, and the Electoral Roll. In a report prepared by Gallup Poll for A.B.C. Television (University of London Press, 1964), *TV and Religion*, it was stated that in the three television areas of London, Midlands, and the North only 1 in 17 of those aged 16 and over, i.e., 6% say that they have no religious affiliation, yet the total of all the religious statistics available do not add up to anything like 94% of the population. A further problem is the definition of church-going. J. K. Lawton in an article in the British Council of Churches bulletin, *The Church in the World*, said that if church attendance was to be judged by the criteria of twice a month churchgoing the figure was 15%, if the criteria was one attendance in three months it rose to 40%. A Gallup survey done for the magazine *Sunday* (May 1966) suggested that about 10 million people go to church most Sundays or at least once a month. No precise information is available on the effect of religious broadcasting on attendance at church services. Some studies of church attendance and religious affiliations that have attempted to fill out these necessarily very inadequate figures are: *Religious Broadcasts and the Public*, by the B.B.C. Audience Research Department (1955); 'How Many in the Pew?' in *The Economist* of 30 Aug 58; *Puzzled People*, by Mass Observation (1948);

A Survey of Social Conditions in England and Wales, chapter 18, by A. M. Carr-Saunders, D. C. Jones, and C. M. Moser (1958); R. F. Neuss, *Facts and Figures about the Church of England No. 3* (1966); and Gallup Poll figures for church membership and attendance.

More general works on religion in Britain in the twentieth century are: R. B. Braithwaite, *The State of Religious Belief* (1927); E. O. James, *History of Christianity in England* (1949); R. Lloyd, *The Church of England in the Twentieth Century* (2 vols, 1948–50); G. Spinks (ed.), *Religion in Britain since 1900* (1952); R. F. Wearmouth, *The Social and Political Influence of Methodism in the Twentieth Century* (1957); J. Highet, *The Scottish Churches* (1960). Maps on the strength of religion in Britain are given in *The Reader's Digest Atlas of Britain* (1965). The most convenient summary of facts and statistics is to be found in R. Currie and A. Gilbert's chapter in A. H. Halsey (ed.), *Social Trends in Britain since 1900* (1972).

THE CHURCH OF ENGLAND

Principal degrees of membership for the Provinces of Canterbury and York.

(Totals for 43 dioceses) [a]

Year	Home population of the two provinces ('000s)	Estimated baptised membership		Estimated confirmed membership		Membership of parochial electoral rolls	
		('000s) [d]	Per 1,000 home pop.	('000s) [d]	Per 1,000 pop. aged 13 and over [e]	('000s)	Per 1,000 pop. of appropriate age
1901	30,673 [b]	n.a.		n.a.		n.a.	
1911	33,807 [b]	n.a.		n.a.		n.a.	
1921	35,390 [b]	22,000	622	8,100	301	3,537 [f]	140
1931	37,511 [b]	23,800	634	9,000	302	3,686	145
1941	39,173 [c]	24,900	636	9,200	294	3,423 [g]	120
1951	41,330 [b]	25,800	624	9,400	284	2,923 [h]	95
1960	43,296	27,323	631	9,792	281	2,862	89
1970	46,429	27,736	597	9,514	254	2,559	73

[a] In 1910 there were 15,864 parochial churches; in 1966 there were 17,755.
[b] Enumerated in the Registrar General's censuses of ecclesiastical areas.
[c] Estimates based on the Registrar General's annual estimates of population at 30th June.
[d] Calculated by the Statistical Unit of the Central Board of Finance of the Church of England by reference to the age composition of the home population, born and resident in the two provinces, and to the respective rates of infant baptisms at Anglican fonts per 1,000 live births; and to the respective rate of Anglican confirmations per 1,000 males and females living at age 15 years. (It is not possible to include in these estimates baptised and confirmed Anglicans who were born abroad but are now resident in the two provinces.)
[e] In the Church of England very few boys and girls are confirmed before the age of 13 years.
[f g h] Figures for 1924, 1940, and 1953, respectively.
[i] 1957 was the first year that persons of 17 years and over were included in the electoral rolls. In previous years the minimum age was 18 years.

SOURCES.—*Facts and Figures about the Church of England*, Nos. 1–3. Edited by R. F. Neuss, Published by the Church Information Office (1966). The Statistical Unit, Central Board of Finance of the Church of England.

Archbishops and leading Bishops of the five principal Dioceses in the Church of England [1]

(These are the only Sees automatically represented in the House of Lords)

Archbishops of Canterbury

1896	F. Temple (*Frederick Cantuar:*)
1903	R. Davidson (*Randall Cantuar:*)
1928	C. Lang (*Cosmo Cantuar:*)
1942	W. Temple (*William Cantuar:*)
1945	G. Fisher (*Geoffrey Cantuar:*)
1961	A. Ramsey (*Michael Cantuar:*)
1974	F. Coggan (*Donald Cantuar:*)

Archbishops of York

1891	W. Maclagan (*Willem Ebor:*)
1909	C. Lang (*Cosmo Ebor:*)
1929	W. Temple (*William Ebor:*)
1942	C. Garbett (*Cyril Ebor:*)
1956	A. Ramsey (*Michael Ebor:*)
1961	F. Coggan (*Donald Ebor:*)
1974	S. Blanch (*Stuart Ebor:*)

Bishops of London

1897	M. Creighton (*Mandell Londin:*)
1901	A. Winnington-Ingram (*A. F. London:*)
1939	G. Fisher (*Geoffrey Londin:*)
1945	J. Wand (*William Londin:*)
1956	H. Campbell (*Henry Londin:*)
1961	R. Stopford (*Robert Londin:*)
1973	G. Ellison (*Gerald Londin:*)

Bishops of Durham

1890	B. Westcott (*B. F. Dunelm:*)
1901	H. Moule (*Handley Dunelm:*)
1920	H. Henson (*Herbert Dunelm:*)
1939	A. Williams (*Alwyn Dunelm:*)
1952	A. Ramsey (*Michael Dunelm:*)
1956	M. Harland (*Maurice Dunelm:*)
1966	I. Ramsey (*Ian Dunelm:*)
1973	J. Habgood (*John Dunelem:*)

Bishops of Winchester

1895	R. Davidson (*Randall Winton:*)
1903	H. Ryle (*Herbert E. Winton:*)
1911	E. Talbot (*Steuart Edward Winton:*)
1924	F. Woods (*Theodore Winton:*)
1932	C. Garbett (*Cyril Winton:*)
1942	M. Haigh (*Mervyn Winton:*)
1952	A. Williams (*Alwyn Winton:*)
1961	S. Allison (*Falkner Winton:*)
1974	J. Taylor (*John Winton:*)

[1] Names in brackets are those used as signature.

THE CHURCH IN WALES

The Church in Wales was disestablished from 31 March 1920

Year	Parochial Easter Day Communicants Estimated No. ('ooos)	No. of Churches
1920	160	1,755
1930	167	1,774
1940	175	1,766
1950	n.a.	n.a.
1960	183	1,783
1968	154	1,700

SOURCE.—Information from the Secretary, the Representative Body of the Church in Wales.

EPISCOPAL CHURCH IN SCOTLAND

Year	Communicants ('ooos)	No. of Church Buildings
1900	46	354
1910	52	404
1920	57	416
1930	60	415
1940	62	404
1950	57	397
1960	57	369
1965	55	358
1673	46	341

SOURCES.—*The Year Book for the Episcopal Church in Scotland*; *Whitaker's Almanack* (figures for 1910 and 1920); *The Statesman's Year-Book* (figures for 1930 and 1940).

BAPTIST UNION
British Isles [a]

Year	Members ('ooos)	No. of Places of Worship [b]
1900	366	2,579
1910	419	2,889
1920	405	2,866
1930	406	2,965
1940	382	3,044
1950	338	3,110
1960	318	3,053
1965	295	3,048
1971	264	2,994

[a] These are statistics actually received from the churches; no estimates are made for churches omitting to return figures.
[b] England and Wales only.

SOURCE.—*The Baptist Handbook, 1900–* .

CONGREGATIONAL UNION
United Kingdom [a]

Year	Members ('ooos)	No. of Places of Worship
1900	436	4,607 [b]
1910	494	4,721
1920	n.a.	n.a.
1930	490	3,556
1939	459	3,435
1950	387	3,173
1959	212	2,984
1965	198	2,799
1971	165	2,266

On 5 Oct 72 the Congregational Union merged with the Presbyterian Church in England to form the United Reformed Church.

[a] 1900 and 1910 figures for British Isles.
[b] Figure for 1901.

SOURCE.—*The Congregational Year Book, 1900–1972.*

PRESBYTERIAN CHURCH
England

Year	Members ('ooos)
1900	76
1911	87
1922	84
1930	84
1940	82
1950	82
1960	71
1965	70
1971	57

On 5 Oct 1972 the Presbyterian Church in England merged with the Congregational Union to form the United Reformed Church.

SOURCES.—1900 and 1911, *The Official Handbook of the Presbyterian Church of England*; 1922–72, *The Statesman's Year-Book.*

UNITED REFORMED CHURCH

	Members	Church buildings
1973	1,912,136	2,139

METHODIST CHURCH [a]
Great Britain and Ireland

Year	Members and Probationers ('000s)	Churches, etc.
1900	520	9,037
1910	544	n.a.
1920	512	9,013
1930	548	9,070
1940	823	n.a.
1950	776	n.a.
1959	729	n.a.
1965	690	n.a.
1971	605	9,162

[a] Up to 1930 these figures are for the Wesleyan Methodist Church. The Methodist Church was formed in 1932 by a union of the Wesleyan, Primitive, and United Methodist Churches. The United Methodists were themselves formed by a union of three separate bodies in 1905.

SOURCE.—*The Minutes of the Methodist Conference, 1900–* , W. S. F. Pickering, *Anglo-Methodist Relations* (1961) gives figures (for England only) for all bodies (1906–1957).

THE CHURCH OF SCOTLAND [a]
(Presbyterian)

Year	Total Communicants on Rolls ('000s)	No. of Places of Worship
1901	1164	n.a.
1911	1220	1,703
1921	1278	1,704
1931	1281	2,795
1941	1269	2,507
1951	1273	2,348
1959	1307	2,242
1966	1234	2,166
1971	1134	2,088

[a] In 1929 the United Free Church of Scotland rejoined the Church of Scotland.

SOURCE.—*The Church of Scotland Year Book.*

THE ROMAN CATHOLIC CHURCH
Great Britain

Year	Estimated Catholic Population ('000s) [a]	Catholic Baptisms ('000s)	No. of Public Churches and Chapels [f]
1900	5415	n.a.	1,536
1910	5515	n.a.	1,773
1920	5704	n.a.	1,408
1930	6024 [b]	66	1,564
1940	3444 [c]	70	1,802
1950	3884 [c]	87	1,971
1960	4818	112 [d]	3,204
1971	5447	105 [e]	3,668

[a] These figures include England and Wales, Scotland, Ireland, 1900–30, and N. Ireland, 1940–.
[b] This figure is made up of the English estimate for 1930, the Scottish estimate for 1926, and the Irish estimate for 1911.
[c] The figures for 1940 and 1950 include the N. Irish Catholic population taken from the 1937 census.
[d] Figure for 1959.   [e] Up to 7 years.
[f] England and Wales.

SOURCE.—Census reports quoted in *The Statesman's Year-Book*, 1900–.

Roman Catholic Archbishops of Westminster

1892 H. Vaughan (Cardinal, 1893)   1943 B. Griffin (Cardinal, 1946)
1903 F. Bourne (Cardinal, 1911)   1956 W. Godfrey (Cardinal, 1958)
1935 A. Hinsley (Cardinal, 1937)   1963 J. Heenan (Cardinal, 1965)

SOURCE.—*The Catholic Directory*, 1900–.

THE JEWISH COMMUNITY [a]
Great Britain

Year	Estimated No. of Jews ('000s)	Approx. No. of Synagogues
1900	160	80 [d]
1910	243	200 [d]
1920	287	200 [d]
1929 [b]	297	300 [e]
1940	385 [c]	200 [e]
1950	450	240 [e]
1960	450	240 [e]
1972	450	240 [e]

[a] Statistics for 1900 for G.B. and Ireland, 1910 for the British Isles, 1920 for U.K., 1929 for G.B., 1940–60 for G.B. and N. Ireland.
[b] No Jewish statistics available, 1930–34.   [c] Including about 35,000 refugees.
[d] From *Whitaker's Almanack*.   [e] From *The Statesman's Year-Book*.

SOURCE.—*The Jewish Year Book*, 1900–.

Other Denominations

Data on the smaller denominations is of very uneven quality. No evidence seems available about the adherents of the Sikh, Muslim or Hindu religions and for some faiths the only statistic available is the number of churches or congregations rather than the number of adherents. However, some recent figures are worth recording.

Welsh Independents .... 92,990 (1968) [a]
Plymouth Brethren .... 80,000 (1971) [b]
Assemblies of God .... 65,972 (1966) [a]
Jehovah's Witnesses .... 55,876 (1969) [a]
Salvation Army .... 51,075 (1972) [b]
Elim Four Square Gospel Alliance 44,800 (1967) [a]
Society of Friends .... 29,909 (1968) [b]
Seventh-Day Adventists .... 12,145 (1971) [b]
Mormons .... 11,400 (1966) [a]

The Unitarians claimed 272 places of worship in 1972[b] and the Christian Scientists had 304 branches.[b]

SOURCE.—[a] A. H. Halsey (ed.), *Social Trends in Britain since 1900* (1973).
 [b] *Whitaker's Almanack* (1973).

NORTHERN IRELAND
Religious Affiliations
(to nearest '000)

Year	Roman Catholic	Presbyterian	Protestant Episcopalian	Methodist	Others
1911	430	395	327	46	52
1937	428	391	345	55	60
1951	471	410	353	67	69
1961	498	413	345	72	98
1971	478	406	334	71	88

SOURCE.—*Census.*

Marriages by Manner of Solemnisation
England and Wales

	1901	1911	1919	1934	1952	1962	1967
No. of marriages ('000s)	259	275	369	342	349	348	386
	Percentage						
Church of England	66·6	61·1	59·7	53·5	49·6	47·4	44·9
Roman Catholic	4·1	4·4	5·2	6·5	9·4	12·3	11·2
Jewish	0·7	0·7	0·5	0·7	0·5	0·4	0·4
Baptist			1·9	1·8	1·5	1·7	1·4
Congregationalist	12·8	13·0	2·3	2·1	2·0	1·9	1·7
Methodist			5·6	5·3	4·8	4·9	4·5
Other Religion			1·6	1·8	1·6	1·8	1·7
Religious Marriage	84·2	79·1	76·9	71·6	69·4	70·4	65·9
Secular Marriage	15·8	20·9	23·1	28·4	30·6	29·6	34·1
	100	100	100	100	100	100	100

SOURCE.—*Annual Reports of the Registrar-General.*

XXIII

INTEREST GROUPS

1. Interest Group Activities

The Scope of Interest Group Activities. Governmental consultation with organised groups of 'affected interests' and other appropriate persons has been normal constitutional practice in the twentieth century. Indeed, statutes often make such consultations mandatory in certain executive actions such as promulgating administrative regulations. Both in these formal consultations and in the informal discussions between groups and the government there are a variety of procedures and participants. The extent and methods of interest group activity are surveyed in the following works, S. E. Finer, *Anonymous Empire* (1958; 2nd ed. 1966), J. D. Stewart, *British Pressure Groups* (1958), and A. Potter, *Organized Groups in British National Politics* (1961). All of these general works contain useful bibliographies of interest group studies.

Group Strategies. It is impossible here to list all of the methods for group access to the government. Nevertheless, some studies of group relations with particular political institutions are worth noting.

Legislative Strategy: H. H. Wilson, *Pressure Group: The Campaign For Commercial Television* (1961).

Executive Strategy: H. Eckstein, *Pressure Group Politics: The Case of The British Medical Association* (1960).

Political Party Relations: M. Harrison, *Trade Unions and the Labour Party Since 1945* (1960).

Participation in Government Committees: P.E.P., *Advisory Committees In British Government* (1960).

Judicial Relations: R. B. Stevens and B. S. Yamey, *The Restrictive Practices Court. A Study of the Judicial Process and Economic Policy* (1965).

Public Opinion Campaigns: H. H. Wilson, 'Techniques of Pressure', *Public Opinion Quarterly* (1951).

See also R. J. Lieber, *British Politics and European Unity* (1970) and U. W. Kitzinger, *Diplomacy and Persuasion* (1973).

2. Types of Organised Interests

Trade Unions. The main association representing workers is the Trades Union Congress (founded in 1868).

Business. The most important organisation representing business interests is the Confederation of British Industry. The C.B.I. was formed in 1965 by a merger of the Federation of British Industries (1916), the National

Association of British Manufacturers (1915), and the British Employers' Confederation (1919). In addition to this powerful confederation most industries are also represented by their own specialised associations, many of which are affiliated with the C.B.I. It is estimated that there are now about 2,500 trade associations of which about 1,000 represent manufacturing industry. The variety of these associations, their structure and activities are discussed by Political and Economic Planning in *Industrial Trade Associations* (1957). Also important in representing industrial interests as well as commercial interests is the Association of British Chambers of Commerce (1860), the history of which is presented in A. R. Ilersic and P. F. B. Liddle, *Parliament of Commerce* (1960). There are numerous associations representing trading enterprises. The most important federation of these is the National Chamber of Trade (1897). Both the Chambers of Commerce and the Chambers of Trade are organised on the basis of affiliated local chambers representing area interests rather than commodity interests. The multitude of specialised commodity associations of merchants is discussed in H. Levy, *Retail Trade Associations*, (1942).

Finance, Insurance, and Property. The largest association representing property owners is the National Federation of Property Owners and Ratepayers (1888). This and other property organisations are discussed by the Property Council in *The Property Developer* (1964). The relations between developers and insurance organisations is explored by B. P. Whitehouse in *Partners in Property* (1964). Another important financial interest is the Building Societies Association (1869) which has extensive dealings with the Treasury. Its development is outlined in S. J. Price, *Building Societies* (1958). Little has been written about the political activities of other financial institutions, but see P. Ferris, *The City* (1965).

The Professions. Professional organisations commonly have the dual purpose of not only representing the interests of the profession in public affairs but also administering the qualifications for entrance into the profession. Examples would be the Royal Institute of British Architects (1834) and the Royal Institution of Chartered Surveyors (1868). However, there are also some associations organised to advance knowledge in the profession and to represent its interests. Outstanding examples of non-qualifying associations are the British Medical Association (1832) and the National Union of Teachers (1870). The organisation and development of the main professions are discussed in A. M. Carr-Saunders and P. A. Wilson, *The Professions* (1933) and in G. Millerson, *The Qualifying Associations* (1964). In addition to these general works there are also numerous studies of particular professions which, in passing, discuss organisational relations with the government. Amongst these are A. Tropp, *The School Teachers* (1957) and B. Abel-Smith, *A History of the Nursing Profession* (1960).

Agriculture. The main organisation representing farmers is the National Farmers Union (1908). Also important are the Country Landowners Association (1907) representing large landowners and the National Union of Agricultural Workers (1920) representing farm labourers. These three main groups and some of the numerous specialised commodity associations are discussed in P. J. O. Self and H. Storing, *The State and the Farmer* (1962).

Causes and Voluntary Services. There are a large number of groups representing causes or offering voluntary services. These may seek to influence public policy by direct contact with Parliament and the Ministries or indirectly through the publication of information and research or appeals to public opinion. Many of these organisations and their work are described in *Voluntary Social Services* (National Council of Social Services, 1966). Some notable examples of these causes and their respective groups are as follows:

Amenities: Council for the Protection of Rural England (1926).

Animals: Royal Society for the Prevention of Cruelty to Animals (1824).

Children: National Society for the Prevention of Cruelty to Children (1884). Child Poverty Action Group (1965).

Community: National Council of Social Service (1919).

The Elderly: National Old People's Welfare Council (1940). (Name changed to Age Concern (1971).)

Family: National Citizens Advice Bureaux Council (1939).

Health: Royal National Institute for the Blind (1868).

Housing: Shelter (1966).

International Relations: League of Nations Union (1919–45). United Nations Association (1945). Campaign for Nuclear Disarmament (1958).

Pacifism: Peace Pledge Union (1934).

Pornography: The National Viewers and Listeners Council (1964).

Prisoners: Howard League for Penal Reform (1886).

Race Relations: Runnymede Trust (1968).

Religious: Lord's Day Observance Society (1831).

Temperance: United Kingdom Alliance (1853).

The pressure-group activities of some 'cause' groups have been studied in considerable detail. Examples are J. B. Christoph, *Capital Punishment and British Politics* (1962) and G. Wootton, *The Politics of Influence: British Ex-Servicemen, Cabinet Decisions and Cultural Change*, 1917–1957 (1963).

Local Authorities. The interests of the local authorities have been represented by two main kinds of groups. First, there are the associations of each tier of local authorities. Most powerful amongst these have been the Association of Municipal Corporations (1873–1974) and the County Councils Association (1889–1974). They were replaced in 1974 by the Association of Metropolitan Authorities and the Association of County Councils; a new District Council Association was also formed. In addition, there are associations representing each of the professions in local government services. Examples would be the Institution of Municipal Engineers (1873) and the Institute of Municipal Treasurers and Accountants (1885). All kinds of municipal employees are also represented by the National and Local Government Officers Association (1905), which is described by J. H. Warren, the General Secretary of N.A.L.G.O., in *Local Government Service* (1952). The best guide to local authority Organisations is the *Municipal Yearbook*.

XXIV

BIBLIOGRAPHICAL NOTE

THIS book does not attempt to provide an extensive bibliography of works on British politics since 1900. That would demand a separate volume and much of its contents would duplicate bibliographies already available. The main sources of factual data used in compiling this book are listed separately in the appropriate sections. There are, however, some works of reference of such major importance and reliability that it seems useful to collect them together as a help or reminder to those involved in research.

Many of the standard and most useful sources for reference are Stationery Office publications. Summaries, guides, and short-cuts to these publications are provided in the Stationery Office: *Catalogue of Government Publications* (annually), the *Sectional Lists of Government Publications*, published by the Stationery Office for individual departments, the *List of Cabinet Papers 1880–1914* (PRO handbook), the *General Index to Parliamentary Papers, 1900–1949* (H.M.S.O.), the three volumes by P. and G. Ford, *Breviate of Parliamentary Papers* (1900–16, 1917–39, 1940–54), and C. Hughes, *The British Statute Book* (1957).

For reference to day-to-day political events the *Official Index to the 'Times'* is the most complete guide, though before 1906 *Palmer's Index to the 'Times'* is difficult to use successfully and is by no means complete. *Keesing's Contemporary Archives* since 1931 give a concise summary of news reported in the national Press, though they were not published in their present fuller form until 1937. Brief chronologies of the year's major events (including some very minor ones) are printed in the *Annual Register* (since 1954 the *Annual Register of World Events*), which also covers them in greater detail in the main text of the book. Still briefer summaries of the year's events are to be found in *Whitaker's Almanack*.

For biographical details of leading figures in British politics since 1900 the main sources are the *Dictionary of National Biography* (1901–11, 1912–21, 1922–30, 1931–40, 1941–50, 1951–60), the *Concise Dictionary of National Biography, 1901–50*, *Who Was Who* (1897–1916, 1916–28, 1929–40, 1941–50, 1951–60, 1961–70) and *Who's Who*, for those still alive. As supplements to these, for lesser-known figures in the Labour and Co-operative movement see also the *Labour Who's Who*, 1924 and 1927 (The Labour Publishing Company) the *Herald Book of Labour Members* (1923, with a supplement in 1924) and *The Dictionary of Labour Biography*. Appointments are recorded in many official sources. The major annual publications are: the *Imperial Calendar and Civil Service List*, *H.M. Ministers and Heads of Public Departments* (published since 1946, from four to six times a year), and the *London Gazette*, where appointments are announced officially, which appears about once a fortnight. Official appointments are also recorded in the annual *Lists of the Foreign Office*, the

Colonial Office, and the *Commonwealth Relations Office*, the *Army*, *Navy* and *Air Force Lists*, the *Law Lists*, and the *Annual Estimate* of the civil, revenue, and service departments. There are three handbooks on Parliament, giving the names of M.P.s, details of procedure and officials: *Dod's Parliamentary Companion* (annually), *Vacher's Parliamentary Companion* (published from four to six times a year) and F. W. S. Craig's *The Political Companion* (published quarterly since 1968). Extremely valuable sources of reference for the House of Commons are the books *House of Commons* published by the *Pall Mall Gazette* in 1906, 1910 and 1911, and since 1885 by the *Times* after each General Election (1922–4 excepted). Other sources of biographical information are *Debrett's* and *Burke's Peerage*, *Burke's* new *Extinct Peerages (1972)* and *Burke's Dictionary of the Landed Gentry*, the *Directory of Directors*, the *Authors' and Writers' Who's Who*, and other directories devoted to the members of particular professions.

The annual almanacks are also an extremely useful source of information. Amongst these the most notable are: the *Constitutional Year Book* (published until 1939), *Whitaker's Almanack*, *The Statesman's Year-Book*, the *Yearbook of International Organisations*, the *United Nations Yearbook*, and *Britain: An Official Handbook* (published by the Central Office of Information). Another valuable source is *Committees, Councils and Boards* (2nd ed. 1973).

The major sources for British statistics are already quoted in notes to the tables throughout the book. The most readily available is the *Annual Abstract of Statistics* (H.M.S.O.). This appears both annually, and in a form covering a ten-year period, since 1945. The *Censuses of Population, Industry* and *Production* though infrequent provide the firmest figures. Much of the information in annual publications is only estimated. The reports of the major revenue departments: the *Commissioners for Customs and Excise*, the *Commissioners for Inland Revenue*, and the *Registrars-General for England and Wales* and for *Scotland* are major sources of statistical information — as are the reports of the other Government Departments, and especially the *Ministry of Labour Dept. of Employment (and Productivity)* with its monthly *Gazette* (until 1917 this was the *Board of Trade Labour Gazette*), and *Annual Abstract of Labour Statistics*. Other major sources of information are *The London and Cambridge Economic Service* published about three times a year in the '*Times' Review of Industry* and the *Abstract of British Historical Statistics* by B. R. Mitchell and P. Deane (1962). Much statistical information is presented in A. H. Halsey (ed.), *Trends in British Society since 1900* (1972).

A useful guide to works on British politics is the subject index of the British Museum Library. Bibliographical references can be checked through the *Cumulative Book Index*. For information on many aspects of British politics the *Encyclopaedia Britannica* or *Chambers's Encyclopaedia* may give a lead. Weekly journals, especially the *Economist*, may provide much additional information. Apart from *The Times*, the national dailies are not indexed, which makes reference a slow process. But newspaper libraries generally have their own index system and may be of much help.

The learned journals with most material on British politics are *The Political Quarterly* (1930–), *Parliamentary Affairs* (1947–), *Political Studies* (1953–), and the *British Journal of Political Science* (1971–). *The Table* (the Journal of the Commonwealth Parliamentary Association, 1931), *Government and Opposition* (1965–) and the *Journal of Contemporary History* (1966–) also contain much that is relevant.

No attempt is being made in the book to provide a bibliography for this century. An extensive bibliography is already available for much of the period by C. L. Mowat in his book *Britain between the Wars* (1955) and in his article, 'Some Recent Books on the British Labour Movement', *Journal of Modern History*, xvii, No. 4, Dec 1945. He also published *British History since 1926: A Select Bibliography* (The Historical Association, 1960). Another critical bibliography is supplied by A. J. P. Taylor, *English History 1914–45* (1966). See also R. M. Punnett, *British Government and Politics* (1971). Other bibliographies include J. Palmer, *Government and Parliament in Britain: a bibliography* (1964, The Hansard Society), E. J. Hobsbawm, 'Twentieth Century British Politics', *Past and Present*, No. 11, Apr 1957 and H. R. Winkler, 'Some Recent Writings on Twentieth Century Britain', *Journal of Modern History*, xxxii, No. 1, Mar 1960. See also 'Bibliography of British Labour History' in the *Journal of Modern History*, Vol. 41 No. 3, Sep 1969, compiled by William H. Maehl Jr.

INDEX

This index lists all major items in the book, but it is not exhaustive; it does not include individual names of people or places, the names of publications, of Bills or Acts of Parliament, or separate entries in bibliographies. References to important items are grouped together, with sub-headings, in the order in which they appear for the first time in the book. The Index of Ministers on pp. 83–121 supplements this index, and should be used for finding details of Ministries on pp. 1–58.